THE ROUGH GUIDE TO

Panama

This second edition updated by

Sara Humphreys

with additional contributions by

Raffa Calvo

D0018291

ROUGH GUIDES

roughguides.com

Contents

Introduction to

Panama

Encompassing cloud-forested highlands, glorious palm-fringed islands, vibrant indigenous cultures and Central America's most ebullient capital city, Panama offers a surprisingly varied landscape for such a small country. This slender, serpentine nation has a unique history: from the loot-laden mule trains of the Spanish Camino Real to the scything open of the rainforest by the world's most famous canal, Panama has long proved valuable as a shortcut between the Atlantic and Pacific oceans. Constituting a biological crossroads, too, the isthmus boasts an even greater density of plant biodiversity than Amazonia.

Panama's compact size means the vast majority of its sights are easily accessible. From the comfort of your hotel in the capital, you can head out in the morning to tramp in the footsteps of the conquistadors through spectacular, primate-packed rainforest, yet be swinging your hips to a salsa beat or dining on damask by candlelight in downtown Panama City the same evening. The ancient and modern, artificial and natural are irresistibly juxtaposed: vast computerized Panamax container ships transiting the canal slice through primeval rainforests teeming with fluorescent frogs and elusive wild cats, only half an hour by dugout from where Emberá villagers practise subsistence agriculture. Visiting the country's fringes and little-visited interior, you can explore archipelagos and untracked jungle, basing yourself in small towns, friendly villages and remote eco-lodges, and from Volcán Barú – Panama's highest peak – you can witness the unique and breathtaking sight of the sun rising over both Atlantic and Pacific oceans.

Despite these attractions, Panama has often been overlooked as a tourist destination, overshadowed by its neighbour Costa Rica, and mistakenly viewed at times as a US annexe – thanks to the US occupation of the former Canal Zone and the dollarized economy. Add to that Panama's not entirely undeserved reputation for money-laundering and the current trend of attracting North American retirees, and it's no wonder that

ABOVE STREET ART, PORTOBELO **OPPOSITE** COLONIAL ARCHITECTURE, PANAMA CITY tourists have initially been slow to appreciate the country's multifaceted identity and outstanding natural beauty.

Yet the US is only one of many **cultural influences** – which derive from Spain and other parts of Europe, West Africa, the West Indies, China, India and the Middle East – fused with the fascinating heritage of the eight indigenous peoples that survived the Spanish conquest.

Panama's complexities and contradictions confront you at every turn, which can intrigue and frustrate in equal measure. The Panamanian government has actively started to promote **tourism**, yet there's often very little information on offer. The colourful traditional attire of Panama's indigenous populations is unashamedly used as photo fodder, but the people themselves are frequently ignored by their government. Many inhabit the tropical rainforests of Panama's national parks, which remain desperately underfunded and are threatened by government-sanctioned projects.

Indeed, it's hard to visit Panama and not be both amazed and perturbed by the pace of change in this small, young nation, as skyscrapers increasingly fill Panama City's skyline and motorways push deeper into the Darién. The world's grandest canal celebrated its centenary in 2014, to much media hype, and the country increasingly features on backpackers' itineraries. Outside the big attractions, though, it's easy enough to get off the beaten track. Make the effort to seek out the country's lesser-visited corners – far-flung island or deepest jungle – and you'll discover a remarkably authentic slice of undeveloped Latin America.

CARIBBEAN SEA

Guabito
Changuinola
Bocas Town
Almirante
Archipiélago de
Bocas del Toro

San Miguel
de la Borda

PARQUE
INTERNACIONAL
LA AMISTAD

Golfo de
los Mosquitos

Coclé del
Norte

Lago
Gatún

Río
Sereno
Cerro
Punta

COSTA RICA

Boquete

Chiriquí
Grande

Volcán

Volcán
Barú

El Copé

El Valle

Paso Canoas

David

Santa Fé

Penonomé

Antón

Aguadulce

Puerto
Armuelles

San Félix

INTERAMERICANA

Santiago

Chitré

Boca
Chica

Las Lajas

Golfo de
Chiriquí

Soná

Mariato

Las
Tablas

Punta
Burica

Santa
Catalina

Isla
Cébaco

Península
de Azuero

Tonosí

Isla de
Cañas

Isla Coiba

Punta
Mariato

N

0   50
kilometres

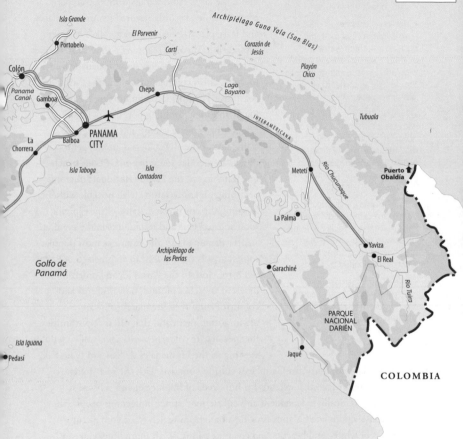

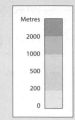

Metres

2000
1000
500
200
0

Isla Grande

Portobelo

El Porvenir

Archipiélago Guna Yala (San Blas)

Cartí

Corazón de
Jesús

Colón

Panama
Canal

Gamboa

Chepo

Lago
Bayano

Playón
Chico

Tubuala

La
Chorrera

Balboa

PANAMA
CITY

INTERAMERICANA

Isla Taboga

*Isla
Contadora*

Meretí

Río Chucunaque

Puerto
Obaldía

La Palma

Golfo de
Panamá

*Archipiélago de
las Perlas*

Yaviza

El Real

Garachiné

Río Tuira

PARQUE
NACIONAL
DARIÉN

Isla Iguana

Pedasí

Jaqué

COLOMBIA

PACIFIC OCEAN

Where to go

The vast majority of visitors fly in to cosmopolitan **Panama City**, where countless brash skyscrapers stare across the bay at the rocky peninsula of **Casco Viejo**, the city's rapidly transforming colonial centre, whose elegantly restored mansions, palaces and leafy plazas demand at least a day's leisurely exploration. If you're planning a short visit, it's easy to base yourself in the city and make daily forays to the Spanish **colonial forts** along the Caribbean coast near Portobelo, the monumental **Panama Canal** and the crumbling port city of **Colón**. Should the frenetic energy and interminable traffic din of the city's clogged arteries get too much, a quiet day lounging on a **Pacific beach**, birdwatching in the **Parque Nacional Soberanía** or fishing on **Lago Gatún** are all possible without forgoing the epicurean delights of the capital's sophisticated bars and restaurants in the evening.

After Panama City, the country's most popular tourist area is the Caribbean archipelago of **Bocas del Toro**, close to the Costa Rican border. Its deserted stretches of sand, powerful surf and colourful coral reefs are matched by an oft-forgotten mainland that offers opportunities for spectacular wilderness hiking as well as wildlife viewing in the Humedales de San San Pond Sak. Bocas's bohemian vibe and Afro-Caribbean culture contrasts with the vast stretch of **Guna Yala**, an archipelago that extends for hundreds of kilometres and is home to Panama's most politically independent and culturally distinct indigenous people, the Guna. Its densely populated islands provide a base from which to explore picture-postcard cays of white-sand beaches and coconut palms. With more time, you can explore the less accessible aquatic wonderlands of the Pacific coast, with world-class scuba diving and sport fishing in the mangrove-rich protected marine parks of the **Golfo de Chiriquí** and **Coiba**, the penal colony turned wildlife reserve, generally reached from the laidback surfing hotspot of **Santa Catalina**.

From there it's a short hop east to the rolling pastureland and quaint villages of the **Azuero Peninsula**, a region that revels in its colonial heritage. Once neglected by visitors, its festivals, including the country's most ardent Carnaval, overflow with enthusiastic accordion and violin playing, colourful costumes, masks, rodeos and lashings of seco – Panama's potent national tipple – and provide ample opportunities to interact with the outgoing locals.

CLOCKWISE FROM TOP THE CHIRIQUÍ HIGHLANDS; A NGÄBE FAMILY; SHOE-SHINE STALL

The dorsal mountain range dividing Panama's two coasts rises dramatically from the Pacific coastal plains that constitute the country's agricultural heartlands, with the most impressive peaks located in the spectacular **national parks** of Chiriquí's **Western Highlands**, surrounding the alpine towns of **Boquete** and the less touristed **Cerro Punta**. Here it's hard to resist the allure of verdant cloud forests filled with orchids, quetzals and hummingbirds, precision rows of shade-grown coffee plantations and fast-flowing rivers, perfect for whitewater rafting or kayaking. Further east, the **Cordillera Central** hosts other parks and rainforested peaks laced with waterfalls above the small communities of **El Copé**, **Santa Fé** and **El Valle**, all of which offer rewarding hiking, birdwatching and horseriding.

Few visitors venture east of Panama City to the **Darién** jungle, which has gained almost mythical status, as much for FARC guerrillas and drug-traffickers as for its spectacular scenery and wildlife. Requiring patience, money and more than a smattering of Spanish, the rewards are ample: sinuous river journeys by dugout, great canopies of cathedral-like rainforests sheltering some of Panama's most spectacular fauna, and remote indigenous communities, keen to share their skills and culture with visitors.

ARTS AND CRAFTS IN PANAMA

It may not have the sprawling markets of Mexico or Guatemala, but Panama's arts and crafts are thriving. From appliqué textiles to coiled basketry, woodcarving to mask-making, the range of materials reflects the country's multi-ethnic make-up. Here's our pick of the top five crafts:

Basketry and woodcarving Head for the Darién to pick up some exquisite Emberá basketry in villages such as Mogué and La Chunga, or smooth cocobolo and tagua carvings of animals in Wounaan communities like Puerto Lara. See p.286, p.289 & p.279.

Straw hats Panama's hats may not be true Panama hats – they are made in Ecuador – but some finely woven specimens are available: consider buying a *sombrero pintao* in La Pintada, or an *ocueño* in Ocu. See p.143 & p.161.

Devil masks Although made for festivals around the country, the most famous mask-makers hail from La Villa de los Santos and Chitré, their workshops stuffed full of terrifying salivating dragon or gargoyle-like monsters in kaleidoscopic colours. See p.157.

Molas Guna women's distinctive multicoloured, embroidered *molas* are transformed into everything from cushion covers to Christmas stockings using traditional geometric designs or modern-day icons such as Batman. Widely available everywhere in Guna Yala, you'll just as easily trip over them on the street corners of Panama City. See p.85.

Beaded necklaces Though once fashioned out of dyed pebbles, shells and bone worn by Ngäbe and Buglé warriors, these modern-day colourful *nguñunkua* (*chaquira* in Spanish) still make beautiful adornments. You'll find them sold in stalls along the Interamericana near Tolé. See p.205.

OPPOSITE FROM TOP HARPY EAGLE; FESTIVAL DE LA MEJORANA; VIEW FROM CERRO ANCÓN

Author picks

To research this guide, Rough Guides authors spent countless hours squatting in dugout canoes, tramping though rainforest and fending off sandflies as they travelled from the cocktail bars of Bocas to the Emberá villages deep in the Darién. Aside from the major sights, here are some personal picks.

Top boat trip The Humedales de San San Pond Sak are at their best at sunrise, as the mist clears, and you glide through the wetlands on the look out for herons and hawks, sloths and snakes, and the extraordinary-looking manatee. **See p.240**

Memorable jungle experience After a dawn hike through the Darién rainforest, and a lengthy stakeout of a nest, the sight of a majestic adult harpy eagle swooping down to feed its chick is truly special. **See p.286**

Most exhilarating flight Peering out of your eight-seater twin-prop over Guna Yala will leave you gasping at the countless tiny specks of white sand dotted with coconut palms that dazzle in translucent turquoise shallows. **See p.251**

Most panoramic view The vistas from the summit of Cerro Ancón take your breath away: on one side the city with its shimmering skyscrapers dwarfing the colonial architecture of Casco Viejo, on the other a procession of vast ships passing through the Panama Canal. **See p.69**

Challenging hike It's hard to beat the four-day trek across the cordillera from Boquete to Bocas, hiking through cloud forest, traversing rivers and sleeping in Ngäbe villages, with the reward of a soak in the Caribbean at the end. **See p.187**

Most enjoyable fiesta While the extreme hedonism of Carnaval grabs the headlines, tiny Guararé's Festival de la Mejorana is a more mellow but joyous affair, including heavy doses of *pindín* – upbeat folk music featuring accordion-playing – and competitions in traditional skills. **See p.165**

Best ice cream The sweltering heat of Panama City is best alleviated by a cone from Granclement: choose from mouthwatering sorbets and unusually flavoured *helados*, such as Earl Grey tea and vanilla and walnut. **See p.79**

> Our author recommendations don't end here. We've flagged up our favourite places – a perfectly sited hotel, an atmospheric café, a special restaurant – throughout the guide, highlighted with the ★ symbol.

When to go

Squeezed between between seven and nine degrees north of the equator, Panama is located firmly within the **tropics**, with a climate to match: relentlessly hot and humid in the lowlands, cooling off fractionally to give balmy nights, whereas in the highlands, temperatures vary significantly with altitude, and can be chilly at night.

Most travellers visit during the shorter **dry season** (*verano*, "summer"), which runs from late December to the end of April, and with good reason. Azure skies predominate, at least on the drier Pacific plains, sheltered by Panama's mountainous spine. The firmer going underfoot makes it easier to travel on unpaved roads and explore the rainforests, and the reduced rainwater run-off ensures clearer waters to swim in. The dry season also includes the lively holiday periods of Christmas, New Year, Carnaval and Holy Week, when flights and hotels in popular tourist spots are at a premium.

You'll avoid the crowds and the mark-ups in the **rainy season** (*invierno*, "winter"), which stretches from May to December. Although the mountainous and rainforested regions in Panama are best avoided during the wettest months, since peaks are constantly swathed in cloud and tracks are boggy, if you stick to the lowland areas on the Pacific coast, the downpours, while frequent and intense, rarely last more than a few hours at a time, leaving plenty of sunny, dry periods to enjoy. In particular, the otherwise parched Azuero Peninsula offers much more picturesque scenery during its understated rainy season.

By contrast, the **Caribbean coast** receives almost twice as much rain as the Pacific, with virtually no recognizable dry season. Regional variations impact here too: the Trade Winds (at their strongest Dec to mid-Feb) make the water choppy and outer islands inaccessible in Bocas del Toro and Kuna Yala, while Bocas enjoys two relatively dry spells around March and October.

AVERAGE DAILY TEMPERATURES AND RAINFALL

	Jan	Feb	Mar	Apr	May	Jun	Jul	Aug	Sep	Oct	Nov	Dec
PANAMA CITY												
Max/min (°C)	30/22	31/22	32/23	32/23	31/24	30/23	30/23	31/23	30/23	30/23	30/23	30/23
Max/min (°F)	86/71	87/71	89/73	89/73	87/75	86/73	86/73	87/73	86/73	86/73	86/73	86/73
Rainfall (mm)	33	18	13	74	201	203	178	198	198	262	254	137
BOQUETE												
Max/min (°C)	25/13	27/13	28/14	29/14	28/15	27/14	27/14	27/14	27/14	28/14	27/14	27/13
Max/min (°F)	77/55	80/56	82/58	84/59	82/59	80/58	81/58	81/58	80/57	83/57	81/56	82/56
Rainfall (mm)	2.5	38	81	231	472	432	467	660	546	925	376	121
BOCAS DEL TORO												
Max/min (°C)	31/20	31/20	31/21	31/21	32/22	32/22	32/22	32/22	32/22	32/22	32/22	31/21
Max/min (°F)	88/68	88/68	88/70	88/70	90/72	90/72	90/72	90/72	90/72	90/72	90/72	88/70
Rainfall (mm)	204	235	188	323	273	287	387	346	254	219	390	485

16

things not to miss

It's not possible to see everything Panama has to offer in one trip – and we don't suggest you try. What follows, in no particular order, is a selective taste of the country's highlights: remote islands, great coffee, colonial architecture and unique wildlife. Each one has a page reference to take you straight into the guide, where you can find out more. Coloured numbers refer to chapters in the Guide section.

1

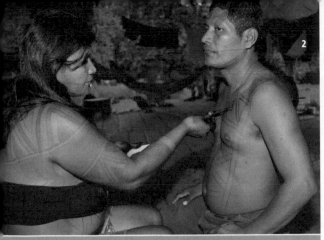

1 ARCHIPIÉLAGO DE LAS PERLAS

Page 121
Choose from a myriad of idyllic tropical islands ringed with white-sand beaches and azure waters.

2 STAY IN AN EMBERÁ VILLAGE

Page 284
Experience traditional village life with the Emberá in the Darién and learn the medicinal secrets of the rainforest.

3 BIRDWATCHING

Page 42
Get close to the country's 978 bird species – including dazzling hummingbirds, the resplendent quetzal and the blue-crowned motmot.

4 COLONIAL ARCHITECTURE

Pages 110, 148 & 57
From ruined Caribbean fortresses to Baroque Pacific churches, Panama possesses some fine conquest-era buildings, including the gleaming spires of the Catedral Metropolitana in Panama City.

5 CASCO VIEJO
Page 56

Seek out hidden gems in the colonial churches, leafy plazas and narrow streets of Panama City's colonial city centre.

6 SANTA FÉ
Page 208

A fresh climate, abundant orchids and picturesque waterfalls make this village an appealing retreat.

7 PANAMA CANAL
Page 95

The twentieth century's greatest engineering feat is best experienced first-hand with a transit through the locks.

8 ISLAND LIFE IN GUNA YALA
Page 245

Stay in a simple cane-and-thatch *cabaña* amid swaying coconut palms, dipping into the warm Caribbean waters to cool off, on one of many postage-stamp-sized islands in the archipelago.

9 OUTDOOR SPORTS
Page 187

There are plenty of ways to soak up the spectacular scenery of Chiriquí's Western Highlands, from a pulse-quickening swing on a canopy ride, to a more serene paddle in a kayak

10 DIVING AND SNORKELLING
Pages 226 & 211

There's some great snorkelling to be done off the coral reefs of Bocas del Toro, while the aquatic paradise off Isla Coiba provides world-class diving.

11 COFFEE IN BOQUETE
Page 187

Learn to detect floral, caramel, citrus and spice aromas in some of the world's finest gourmet coffee estates.

12 CHILLING IN BOCAS
Page 230

Laidback bars, party hostels, mellow lodges and Caribbean cuisine make Bocas a fine spot to let your hair down.

13 HEAD INTO THE DARIÉN
Pages 282–289

Glide upriver into one of the world's last wilderness areas, past vast buttress roots, tangled vines and the soaring forest canopy.

14 GUNA CULTURE
Page 264

Learn about the rich cultural traditions of the island-dwelling Guna.

15 FESTIVALS
Page 36

Panama's diverse heritage has resulted in a fascinating array of festivals from Carnaval's wildest party in Las Tablas to the vibrant, rebellious celebration of Afro-colonial culture in the Caribbean's annual *congos*.

16 HIKING
Page 40

The combination of magnificent views, picturesque waterfalls and lush forest makes hiking in central and western Panama a constant delight.

11

12

13

Itineraries

The following itineraries combine some of the most popular and the less well-known attractions, covering the length and breadth of the isthmus, from idyllic Caribbean beaches to steaming rainforest, taking in colonial forts, gourmet coffee farms, surf breaks and mountain retreats.

THE GRAND TOUR

You could just about manage this itinerary in three weeks and indeed it's possible to visit several sites as day-trips from Panama City, but for a richer experience take it at a more leisurely pace.

❶ **Panama City** Stroll round Casco Viejo and visit the canal museum before dining in the open air or heading for the capital's rooftop bars and lively clubs. **See p.59**

❷ **The canal** Whether you're watching giant container ships squeeze through the locks or transiting on a boat, the beauty and engineering brilliance of the world's most famous shortcut is awe-inspiring. **See p.95**

❸ **Colonial forts** While the Spanish forts at Portobelo boast more cannons, San Lorenzo's atmospheric location, towering above the Río Chagres, is hard to beat. **See p.110**

❹ **Santa Fé** Refreshing waterfalls, gorgeous views and an abundance of flowers make this friendly mountain village in Veraguas an ideal place to unwind. **See p.208**

❺ **Boquete** At the foot of Volcán Barú, Panama's highest peak, Boquete is the centre of both gourmet coffee production and adventure activities. **See p.184**

❻ **Bocas del Toro** Bohemian Bocas, traditionally associated with diving, surfing, and snorkelling by day, and drinking and partying by night, has

an ever-expanding menu of appealing day-trips. **See p.225**

❼ **Guna Yala** One of the largest semi-autonomous areas in the world, the Comarca Guna Yala offers visitors near-deserted tropical beaches and culturally rich island-villages, as well as mangroves and rainforest on the mainland. **See p.245**

❽ **Lago Bayano** Popular with Panamanians, but less well known to foreign tourists, this reservoir hosts a splendid network of limestone caves. **See p.277**

❾ **Parque Nacional Darién** The one place to stay is the remote bunkhouse at Rancho Frío, where you can immerse yourself in the sights, sounds and smells of the rainforest. **See p.282**

SAND, SEA AND SURF

Possessing lengthy coastlines bordering the Atlantic and Pacific, and almost 1500 islands, Panama has plenty of beaches to laze on or surf off as well as boasting some impressive marine life.

❶ **Playa Bluff, Isla Colón** This 5km expanse of deserted sand hosts a consistent beach break and is perfect to stroll or ride along on horseback. At night, in season, you can watch turtles lay their eggs. **See p.223**

❷ **Parque Marino Golfo de Chiriquí** Explore coastal mangroves and secluded coves by

ABOVE FROM LEFT PANAMA CANAL; SCHOOL OF FISH, ISLA COIBA

kayak, looking out for green iguanas sunning themselves on the rocks. **See p.203**

❸ **Isla Coiba** Providing opportunities to swim with rays, whales and sharks, Coiba is a diver's paradise, though it provides some great snorkelling too. **See p.214**

❹ **Santa Catalina** Panama's top surfing spot has a world-class break, but also a good beach for novices and a mellow après-surf scene. **See p.211**

❺ **The Azuero Peninsula** The southern end of the Azuero is fringed with endless stretches of sand and prized surfing spots that you can sometimes have all to yourself. **See p.151**

❻ **Archipiélago de las Perlas** The soft sugary sand of Playa Cacique is Isla Contadora's standout beach, but take a catamaran cruise to some of the archipelago's deserted cays and islands. **See p.121**

❼ **Western Guna Yala** This end of the *comarca* hosts the country's greatest concentration of picture-postcard white-sand beaches, with the sunken wreck at Isla Perro providing the most popular snorkelling. **See p.257**

TRADITIONAL CULTURE

Combining village homestays with festival-going will give you greater insight into Panama's diverse indigenous and colonial cultural heritage.

❶ **Festival de los Congos, Portobelo** Instituted by *cimarrones* – escaped African slaves – in colonial times, this ebullient festival makes mockery of the Spanish court with its outlandish costumes, ferocious devils and Congo drums. **See p.115**

❷ **Isla Tigre** Still carrying out community-based practices and home to the Guna dance, Isla Tigre is best visited during the annual October fair or the February re-enactment of the Guna revolution. **See p.262**

❸ **La Marea** Learn the skills of Emberá basketry and sleep in a hammock in an open-sided *bujía* – wooden house on stilts – allowing the sounds of the Darién jungle to lull you to sleep in this welcoming community. **See p.285**

❹ **Corpus Christi, La Villa de Los Santos** This ultimate fusion of indigenous and colonial Catholic culture is a riot of colourful costumes, mythical characters and religious ceremony. **See p.163**

❺ **Soloy** A handful of families in this dispersed community offer homestays, providing insight into Ngäbe culture and the chance to explore the surrounding mountain scenery. **See p.205**

❻ **Traditional chocolate making** Visit the Ngäbe communities of Río Oeste Arriba or Silico Creek to learn about artisanal chocolate making and get to taste some of the product. **See p.227**

❼ **Naso communities, Río Teribe** Get shown round Seiyik, seat of central America's last remaining monarch, and learn how to construct and pilot a traditional bamboo raft. **See p.241**

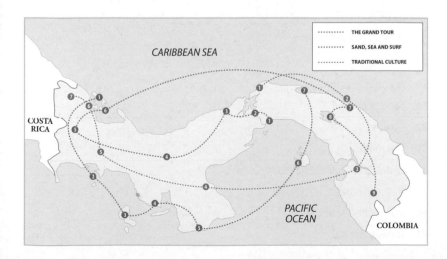

DIABLOS ROJOS, PANAMA CITY

Basics

Getting there

The vast majority of visitors to Panama arrive by air, landing at Tocumen International Airport in Panama City. Seats are generally more expensive and more heavily subscribed during the dry season (late Dec to April), especially the peak holiday periods of Christmas, Easter and Carnaval (in Feb or March) when many Panamanians living in the US return home. Though flights are easily booked through the internet it is still sometimes cheaper to make arrangements via a travel agent, bearing in mind the crucial distinction between Panama City in Central America (airport code PTY) and the one in Florida (airport code PFN).

Panama's reliable national carrier, Copa Airlines, often offers the best rates and has an efficient online booking service. It flies to several US cities and to numerous destinations in Latin America and the Caribbean. All **ticket prices** given below include the relevant taxes.

Visitors travelling down from **Central America** may choose to make the longer but cheaper bus journey through Costa Rica, generally along the Pan-American Highway via the Pacific border crossing at Paso Canoas, though there are a couple of other border posts at Río Sereno in the Western Highlands and at Guabito on the Caribbean (or Atlantic) coast in Bocas del Toro.

Alternatives to flying from **South America** are a great deal more complicated, involving a number of boat and bus journeys on the Caribbean side, and are only for the adventurous. Cruise ship visitors will dock at the cruise ship terminals in either Colón, at the Caribbean end of the Panama Canal, or on the Calzada de Amador in Panama City, on the Pacific side. Sailing boats carrying backpackers from Cartagena usually unload passengers in El Porvenir, in Guna Yala, or in Puerto Lindo or Portobelo, further west along the coast in Colón Province. Other yacht arrivals will probably call in at the Balboa Yacht Club on the Calzada de Amador or at the Shelter Bay Marina west of Colón.

Flights from the US and Canada

Given the historical links between the **US** and Panama it's no surprise that there are numerous direct flights; Delta, United and American Airlines, alongside Copa and Avianca, fly daily to Panama City from various US cities, including New York, Washington, Los Angeles, Orlando and Miami, with the last the main portal, offering several daily connections.

Bargains are thin on the ground, though Copa often has special return **fares** for as little as US$275 return for the three-hour trip from Miami. More typically, return fares range from US$400 (low season) to US$600 (high season), costing more for the five-hour flight from New York or Washington (US$550–800) and the six-hour one from Los Angeles (US$550–900). It is often slightly cheaper to fly to San José, Costa Rica, and take one of the daily buses (US$82 return) down to Panama (see p.24).

Since David airport, in western Panama, was upgraded a few years ago there has been talk about direct flights from the US – keep checking the websites.

There are no direct flights from **Canada**; connections have to be made in the US, making it at least a nine hour journey, with prices typically CAN$800–1100. Slightly cheaper direct charter flights can sometimes be purchased in high season through Transat (Ⓦtransat.com) from Calgary, Montreal and Toronto or through Sunwing (Ⓦsunwing.ca) from Montreal and Toronto.

Flights from the UK and Ireland

The dearth of direct flights from Europe in part explains the relatively low number of European visitors compared to the number of tourists from North America. There are currently no direct flights from the **UK** or **Ireland**, with KLM operating daily flights to Panama City from Amsterdam and Air France making the trip five times a week (£700–900 from UK & Ireland) from Paris for similar prices. Iberia operates frequent, but more expensive departures from several Spanish cities. The cheapest route from

---

A BETTER KIND OF TRAVEL

At Rough Guides we are passionately committed to travel. We believe it helps us understand the world we live in and the people we share it with – and of course tourism is vital to many developing economies. But the scale of modern tourism has also damaged some places irreparably, and climate change is accelerated by most forms of transport, especially flying. All Rough Guides' flights are carbon-offset, and every year we donate money to a variety of environmental charities.

the UK or Ireland is often via the US with a US carrier (see p.23), which may save you over £100, though the lengthier flying time and the extra hassle of clearing US immigration generally makes the KLM or Air France routes via Amsterdam or Paris a more appealing option.

Flights from Australia, New Zealand and South Africa

From Australia, New Zealand and South Africa it is a long, expensive haul to Panama, with no direct flights. Most routes from **Australasia** (Aus$3500–4000) travel via the US, generally passing through Los Angeles, though flights via Santiago or Buenos Aires are also possible with the journey time (26hr-plus) much the same. From **South Africa** (30hr-plus), travel can be via London, South America or the US (ZAR$17,000–21,000).

Flights from Central and South America

Various countries in **Latin America** have direct connections with Panama City, generally either through Avianca or, more usually, through Copa, which connects with over forty destinations across Latin America and the Caribbean. In Costa Rica, award-winning Nature Air operates daily flights from San José to Bocas del Toro (US$241 one way, including carbon offsetting), while Panama's domestic carrier Air Panama makes three trips a week from San José (US$423) to Panama City via David. Flights from Colombia are around US$450–600 return.

By bus from Central America

It is possible to travel overland to Panama City (with drop-offs at David and Santiago en route) along the **Pan-American Highway** all the way from Tapachula, Mexico, with Ticabus (@ticabus.com; US$200 one way). Ticabus operates a series of comfortable long-distance air-conditioned buses with the obligatory diet of Hollywood movies that pick up (and drop off) passengers at the major cities in Central America en route, though you will have to spend a couple of nights in hotels on the way, which increases the cost. Transportes Galgos (@transgalgosinter.com.gt) will also get you to Guatemala City from Tapachula (US$30 one way), from where you can transfer to Ticabus. Agencia Tracopa (@tracopacr.com; US$21 one way) operates a daily service from San José to David.

By boat from Colombia

The only break in the 50,000-odd km of the Pan-American Highway is an 87km stretch of swamp and mountainous jungle between Carepa on the Colombian border and Yaviza in Panama in what is known as the Darién Gap (see p.42 & p.280). Up until the early 1990s, thrashing your way through here **overland** was a famous challenge for adventurers. However, it is now forbidden as it is extremely dangerous due to the presence of drug-traffickers, Colombian paramilitaries and smugglers, with the threat of death or kidnapping adding to the usual jungle hazards. A (somewhat) safer alternative for those wanting to save money on air fares is to travel by **boat** along the Caribbean coast, though if you are out of luck with the weather, timings and bookings, the overall saving is likely to be negligible. Still, an adventure of sorts is guaranteed. This route requires a reasonable command of Spanish or travelling with someone who has one. A multi-day sailing trip from Cartagena or Sapzurro in Colombia, to the western end of Guna Yala province, is another possibility (see box opposite).

To make the coastal journey from Colombia, it is first necessary to get to **Turbo**, a small city in the Antioquia Department on the Pan-American Highway (accessible by regular buses from Medellín, which are safe during the day), and take the regular morning launch (8–9am) across to Capurganá (2hr 30min; US$29), a burgeoning low-key Caribbean resort unreachable by road but within striking distance by sea of Puerto Obaldía (1hr; around US$15), a small military outpost across the border in Panama, at the eastern end of Guna Yala. Note that in high season there is usually more than one departure a day from Turbo. Since there is no regular crossing to Puerto Obaldía, departure times and charges from **Capurganá** depend on numbers, though the place is pleasant enough to hang out in for a few days while you're waiting for fellow travellers to roll up. Note also that both sea crossings can be exceedingly rough (especially between Nov and Feb) and are not for the faint-hearted; the boats are small and the waves loom large, though life jackets are provided. A large plastic bag to cover your luggage is a must, as well as some waterproof protection for yourself.

Morning flights to and from **Puerto Obaldía** (1hr; US$111) are operated by Air Panama (daily except Sat), though timings can vary. If you are

SAILING TO PANAMA

An increasingly popular passage from or to Colombia involves a four- to five-day **sailing trip** from Cartagena or Sapzurro (close to the Colombia–Panama border), taking in some of the more remote tropical islands of Guna Yala en route to Cartí (from where it's another US$40 to reach Panama City (see p.251)), Portobelo or Puerto Lindo (see p.113 & p.118). Typically backpacker rates are US$480–600 per person from Cartagena (US$450–500 from Sapzurro), including food and non-alcoholic beverages, though some require you to help around the ship, be it crewing or cooking. In addition to being cheaper, the Sapzurro route has the advantage of avoiding the roughest seas by hugging the coast, thereby affording more time to explore Guna Yala. Be prepared to hang around at your departure point for a few days since preparations can take some time. Horror stories abound of drunken captains and poorly maintained boats, so do your homework; hostel recommendations of particular captains can be helpful but should be viewed critically since hostels usually receive commission for supplying passengers. You're best getting the lowdown from other travellers who have made the trip. Travelling between November and February can be dangerous with rough seas, so much so that some captains do not make the crossing during that period.

feeling adventurous and are prepared to hang around in Puerto Obaldía, you can get a ride on one of the speedboats bound for Cartí, at the western end of Guna Yala but it is as expensive as flying (see p.267). Before leaving Colombia, get an exit stamp from **immigration** at Capurganá (daily 9am–5pm) and an entry stamp for Panama on arrival in Puerto Obaldía (daily 8am–4pm). Military police will meet the boat and escort you to the relevant authorities. Your belongings will be thoroughly searched for drugs and you are likely to be required to show proof of onward travel and possibly a yellow fever vaccination certificate (see p.33) and sufficient funds (a credit card will do) to cover your stay. A serious grilling and further searches await you at customs and immigration at Albrook Airport in Panama City.

AIRLINES

Aer Lingus W aerlingus.com
Air Canada W aircanada.com
Air France W airfrance.com
Air New Zealand W airnz.co.nz
Air Panama W airpanama.com
American Airlines W aa.com
Avianca W avianca.com
British Airways W ba.com
Copa Airlines W copaair.com
Delta W delta.com
Iberia W iberia.com
KLM (Royal Dutch Airlines) W klm.com
Nature Air W natureair.com
Qantas Airways W qantas.com
South African Airways W flysaa.com
United Airlines W united.com

AGENTS AND OPERATORS

Aventouras US toll free ☎ 800 930 2846, W aventouras.com.
Specialists in eco- and community-based tourism in Latin America, with an emphasis on cross-cultural interaction.
Journey Latin America UK ☎ 020 8622 8469,
W journeylatinamerica.co.uk. Long-established UK-based tour operator offering tailor-made itineraries and tours; includes trips combining Panama with Peru and other countries, as well as a Panama highlights package and even a family holiday.
North South Travel UK ☎ 01245 608291, W northsouthtravel .co.uk. Friendly, competitive travel agency, offering discounted fares worldwide. Profits are used to support projects in the developing world, especially the promotion of sustainable tourism.
STA Travel UK ☎ 0871 230 0040, US ☎ 800 781 4040, Australia ☎ 134 782, New Zealand ☎ 0800 474 400, South Africa ☎ 0861 781 781; W statravel.com. Worldwide specialists in independent travel; also student IDs, travel insurance, car rental and more. Good discounts for students and under-26s.
Travel CUTS Canada ☎ 800 667 2887, W travelcuts.com. Canadian youth and student travel firm offering discount flights and several trips combing Panama with Costa Rica and other countries in Central America.
Tucan Travel UK ☎ 020 8896 1600, W tucantravel.com.
Award-winning small travel operator offering Panama in combination with Costa Rica and other Central American destinations on some of their adventure overland tours.

Getting around

Panama has a fairly comprehensive and very efficient bus network, used by the majority of the population, which will get you around most of the mainland, though the level of comfort varies enormously. Along the western section of the Inter-americana – the Panamanian section of

the Pan-American Highway – luxury vehicles with reclinable seats, air conditioning, nonstop videos and on-board toilets speed along for several hours for a handful of dollars, while at the other end of the scale chivas – converted pick-up trucks packed like the proverbial sardine can – grind their way up twisting mountain roads to remote villages for not a lot less.

There are many good paved **roads** in central and western Panama, even to small villages up in the mountains, and dirt roads are also generally well graded, though in the rainy season they can soon become a quagmire. East of Panama City there are few roads of any description.

For the longer trips from Panama City – over the Cordillera Central to Bocas, deep into Darién or to the more distant islands of Guna Yala – an **internal flight** on one of Panama's two domestic airlines will save a lot of time. Indeed with only one road – sometimes impassable in the rainy season – into Guna Yala, climbing aboard a plane is sometimes the only way into the archipelago. And to hop from island to island in Guna Yala or ease upriver to visit Emberá villages in the Darién, the main mode of transport is a motorized **dugout** or *cayuco*.

While Panama City has a comprehensive **bus** system, it can be interminably slow on some routes, so taking a **taxi** is often easier and is inexpensive. In the other towns and cities, most places of interest are within easy walking distance though a taxi – rarely costing more than a couple of dollars – can save you from melting in the heat.

By bus

The vast brick building fronted by battalions of buses just down the road from Albrook Airport on the edge of Panama City is the Gran Terminal de Transportes de Panamá, the highly efficient hub of the **national bus system**. Most of the capital's local transport and all international and regional buses leave from here (see p.73).

The main centres, such as Santiago, Chitré and David, also have large efficient **bus terminals** on the outskirts of town complete with toilet, left-luggage and restaurant facilities; from there regional connections and local buses – usually a mixture of battered Toyota minivans with extra fold-down aisle seating and the more comfortable Coasters – head out into the countryside in centrifugal fashion. In the smaller settlements, minibuses or *chivas* hang out in the plaza or main street waiting for an adequate number of passengers. Generally, the more rural the location, the more laissez-faire the bus timetable and the more likely it is that passengers will be picked up anywhere along the route.

Along most regional bus routes from Panama City, transport runs from 5.30–6am until 9–10pm, whereas the first buses heading into the capital from the provinces may leave from 1–4am to ensure passengers arrive for the start of the commercial day. Local transport in the provinces usually peters out around 6.30–7pm, while in the capital buses run along popular routes until around midnight. The timetables for many routes can now be consulted online at ⓦthebusschedule.com/pa, which is kept reasonably up to date.

The Interamericana is punctuated with official and unofficial (generally at a major intersection) bus stops, where you can flag down transport, but on Friday and Sunday afternoons and at either end of a holiday period when buses are jam-packed you can be left stranded for hours.

Ticket prices range from 30¢ for any bus in the Panama City metropolitan area to around $5 for a two-hour ride in moderate comfort, or $15 for a relaxing seven-hour recline all the way to David. There are set prices for every route, often posted on the bus window, and tourists are rarely overcharged – if in doubt ask a local on the bus what the fare is in advance. **Luggage** generally goes for free, either on the roof or in the luggage compartment, although surfboards sometimes incur extra charges. Security is not usually an issue.

FINDING YOUR WAY

Panama is not without its frustrations: **streets** often have several names, rarely marked on a signpost; **telephone numbers** change frequently, especially for mobile phones and even for government offices; and **websites** are often not updated, or domain names left to lapse – all of which makes contacting people difficult. Moreover, the **pace of change** in Panama at the moment is phenomenal: new places to stay are mushrooming; bars, discos and restaurants, especially in Panama City and tourist areas, regularly open, close, move or change name, often lasting the summer partying and tourist season, but failing to make it through winter. This guide will help you navigate this dynamic country, but it's always worth checking details on the ground.

Booking ahead for busy holiday periods and international journeys is a must, though it is only possible for international and some long-haul domestic routes and entails going in person to the travel company ticket office, usually located in the bus terminal, in Panama City, David or Changuinola, to purchase the ticket in cash.

By plane

Flying within Panama is a convenient and safe experience though you might have your heart in your mouth landing in the more flimsy twin-props at some of the more remote airstrips of Guna Yala and Darién. Panama has one **domestic airline** that serves the major urban areas, several locations along the largely inaccessible Comarca de Guna Yala and a handful of destinations in the Darién, which are also hard to reach by road, especially in the rainy season. It operates out of Marcos A. Gelabert Airport (☎238 2700), more commonly known as **Albrook Airport** after the former US air-force base it occupies, which lies 3km northwest of the city centre. All internal flights depart from or arrive here.

Propeller planes seating forty to fifty passengers generally ply the urban routes, while smaller puddle hoppers operate in the Darién and Guna Yala to suit the shorter runways – sometimes only as long as the island they're on. **Air Panama** (☎316 9000, ✆airpanama.com) serves around twenty destinations, including San José, Costa Rica, via a connecting flight from David. Prices remain constant irrespective of the season, with the maximum domestic fare one way currently around $158 (including taxes), but with many much cheaper. Luggage allowances are 12kg plus 2.3kg carry-on but full-size surfboards incur an extra charge of $20.

Compared with the long-distance buses, plane **timetables** are fairly sketchily adhered to, especially in Guna Yala and Darién. Flights to David, Bocas and Guna Yala book up quickly in advance of a holiday weekend.

By car

Away from the traffic hell that is Panama City, **driving** in Panama is generally fairly straightforward, with very good, well-signposted roads connecting the main urban centres, though it can be a different story in some of the more remote or mountainous areas.

The **Interamericana** (also called the Carretera Panamericana), Panama's main thoroughfare – part of the Pan-American Highway that travels almost 48,000km from Alaska to Chile – runs 486km from the Costa Rican border at Paso Canoas in the west, skirting several major cities, crossing the canal and bludgeoning its way through the capital before continuing another 282km and grinding to an abrupt halt in Yaviza in the eastern Darién.

Traffic for the Azuero Peninsula peels off onto the **Carretera Nacional** at Divisa, 34km east of Santiago, and branches off north across the Cordillera Central at Chiriquí for the sinuous journey across the continental divide down to the islands of Bocas del Toro on western Panama's only transisthmian route. Though an excellent paved road, it is sometimes blocked by landslides during the wettest months of the rainy season.

The only other routes across the isthmus lie east of the canal. The frequently log-jammed **Transístmica** links the capital with the country's second city of Colón; the faster **Autopista Panamá–Colón**, a toll road aimed at improving commercial traffic runs parallel. An hour east of Panama City, beyond Chepo, a roller coaster of a potholed road heads north from the Interamericana 30km over the mountains to Cartí, providing the only road link with Guna Yala, accessible most of the year; though it's paved, 4WD is advised. The final stretch of the Interamericana, from Panama City to **Yaviza**, is almost completely paved – only a short section of dirt just after Metetí, which becomes a quagmire in heavy rains, remains. Expect an increasing number of police checkpoints as you near the Costa Rican border, where you'll generally be waved on fairly nonchalantly, or along the road to Yaviza, where the bureaucratic rigmarole can take some time.

Despite Panama's decent road network, **driving at night** is best avoided because there's little illumination outside the urban centres, and drink driving, one of the main causes of accidents nationally, is common. Though there is a legal limit of 86 milligrams, it is rarely adhered to or enforced.

If you are involved in a car accident, Panamanian law requires that you should not move the vehicles but should wait near them until the traffic police (Transito) arrive; a statement from them is required to file any insurance claim. The **speed limits** are 40kph in urban areas, 60kph on secondary roads and 100kph on primary roads unless otherwise indicated but the speed limits are neither widely advertised nor followed. Two of the most dangerous roads are the Interamericana, which copious buses and heavy trucks thunder along, and the route across the Cordillera Central to Bocas del Toro, when bad weather can make the hairpin bends even more scary. Outside the hair-raising free-for-all of Panama City (see p.75), urban driving is not too threatening.

Hitching is possible, though with all the obvious attendant risks on the main thoroughfares, where it is unlikely anyone will stop. In the rural areas, where there is no or at best infrequent bus service, it is quite usual to thumb a lift on the back of a private pick-up, though you should offer to pay at least the equivalent of a bus fare.

Car rental

Renting a car enables you to cover more terrain in a shorter time, affords greater flexibility and makes it easier to explore some of the out-of-the-way spots though if you're staying in Panama City and the canal area it's much more convenient to use buses and taxis. Rental costs vary greatly among providers, so shop around and note that rates fluctuate according to season and demand. Virtually all rental vehicles have air conditioning. A manual economy car is the cheapest option (approximately $35–40/day, $200–250/week, including taxes and basic insurance cover). For a 4WD, which is probably only necessary if you want to get off the beaten track and into the national parks, bank on paying almost double that. Fuel is just over $4 a gallon and petrol stations (often 24hr) are liberally sprinkled along the main roads.

You'll find all the usual international car rental firms in Panama. The larger firms have their head offices at Tocumen International Airport, with many running a downtown office and sometimes branches at Albrook and David airports. Some operators have offices in other major cities and tourist towns.

Rates are sometimes cheaper if booked online in advance and fluctuate according to the season. The minimum age for most car rental companies is 25 but 23 will suffice for some firms provided a credit card is produced as security. A driving licence – international or from your country of origin – as well as a passport will need to be shown.

By taxi

A convenient and relatively cheap way to whizz round the capital – traffic permitting (see p.75), taxis are widely available in most of Panama's urban centres, ostensibly charging fixed rates according to zones (which are rarely adhered to) or generally agreed prices for particular routes. This means that most trips within the capital should not exceed $4; in other cities and towns it should not exceed a couple of dollars. A small surcharge is added for more than two passengers and prices are higher at night. While most Panamanian taxi drivers are very honest and adhere to standard rates, in Panama City and tourist areas like Boquete, the chances of a driver taking advantage of the uninformed increases so you should make local enquiries about likely charges and then agree on a price before getting into a cab.

Taxis, generally in the form of a 4WD twin cab, are also a practical way of reaching more rural locations that are poorly served by public transport. Official cabs should be yellow with their licence number on the door, though in the country you are more likely to come across unofficial drivers whose service is generally just as reliable. Taxi drivers can also be hired as tourist guides though most will only guide in Spanish – ask your accommodation for a recommended driver. There is no set hourly charge, but around $15 an hour is the going rate in Panama City, though petrol costs also need to be factored in.

By boat

Panama boasts over 1500 islands and it's almost inevitable you'll require water transport at some stage on your trip, be it smooth sightseeing in a canal transit or a bumpy water-taxi ride in Bocas. Fairly robust ferries equipped with life jackets and radio transmitters leave Panama City for Isla Taboga, and the Archipiélago de las Perlas, according to regular timetables, whereas in the remoter regions of eastern Guna Yala you could be seated on a plank in a leaking motorized dugout bailing out with a yoghurt carton, having spent a couple of hours asking round for a ride. Frequent water-taxis serve Bocas from Almirante for fixed fares ($6), whereas any trip to the Pacific island of Coiba may mean getting a group of interested people together and negotiating a deal with a fisherman.

Travelling by motorized dugout or occasionally, if you're lucky, in a slightly more comfy skiff (panga), is the norm among the communities of Guna Yala and Darién. If a boat is already heading the way you want to travel the fare will be cheaper. Otherwise, private boat rental (which needs to cover fuel and the boat operator's time and often their assistant) can be expensive; awareness of the going price for diesel will help your ability to haggle, as will knowledge of the amount of fuel necessary to cover the distance given the size of the engine. Note that the seaworthiness of vessels varies enormously and many are overloaded and lack life jackets even when heading for long trips on potentially hazardous waters. Every few months a boat somewhere sinks or capsizes and people drown. Make sure you check out your transport before committing to a journey.

By bike

Away from the Interamericana and Panama City, **cycling** is pleasant – with wonderful views and quiet roads – and growing in popularity both as recreation and a means of transport, though you won't find cycle lanes or cycle routes. Mountain bike **rental** is on the increase in tourist areas such as El Valle, Boquete, Bocas and Santa Fé, though the quality of the machine on offer is extremely variable, as are the rates ($3–5/hr, $10–15/day). In Panama City a couple of rental places are on the Calzada de Amador, which actually possesses a cycle path, as does the recently inaugurated Cinta Costera. Exodus, the UK adventure holiday specialist (Ⓦexodus.co.uk), offers cycling holidays in Panama.

Accommodation

From secluded mountain eco-lodges to thatched cane cabañas on a deserted island, from partying backpackers' hostels to smart boutique hotels, Panama offers a wide range of accommodation. Panama City inevitably has the greatest variety, though prices are generally a lot higher than in the rest of the country. In touristy areas such as Bocas and Boquete prices are creeping up and more lodgings now exist at the higher end of the market, though there is very little outside Panama City that could truly be described as luxury. Nevertheless, the number of comfortable lodges (often foreign-owned) and B&Bs is increasing. In Guna Yala you could just as likely be sleeping in a hammock, while in the Darién you might be snoozing on the raised wooden floor of a traditional Emberá dwelling.

The names given to accommodation in Panama are equally varied. **Posada** and **lodge** usually indicate a fair degree of comfort in pleasant natural surroundings, whereas places prefaced with **hospedaje**, **pensión** or **residencial** are generally much simpler small family-owned lodgings. The word **cabaña** may conjure up an image of a simple thatched hut in an idyllic natural setting, but can just as easily mean a dark, windowless cement cell in an unremarkable location. **Hostal** usually signifies a place with dorms for backpackers but occasionally is merely a synonym for a family-run hotel. **Hotel** too can cover a mixed bag from a plush international five-star high-rise to a dilapidated shack, and also includes the famous by-the-hour push-button motel, often referred to as **un push**, which rents out rooms short term for sexual liaisons. In no way unique to Panama, they are scattered all over the country, most visibly along the Interamericana, with such enticing names as "*Sueño Lindo*" (Sweet Dreams) or "*Las Mil y Una Noches*" (Thousand and One Nights). As for the much-abused prefix "eco", it may simply denote pleasant natural surroundings, and is no guarantee of sustainable environmental practices or social responsibility. Neither name nor price is much of an indication of what you'll get for your money though a private bathroom is often squeezed into even fairly rudimentary and minuscule lodgings. In the lowlands, even the cheapest establishments usually have air conditioning, though not necessarily hot water; in the highlands air conditioning and fans are unnecessary and usually absent though hot water is almost always available. **Wi-fi** is widely available, except in Guna Yala and the Darién, and almost always free. As in most other Latin American countries, toilet paper should not be put down the **toilet**, but into the adjacent wastebasket, because it can clog the system in all but the most modern top-end hotels; if in doubt, enquire at reception.

Hostels

Panama's **hostel** scene is expanding as the country attracts increasing numbers of backpackers. Currently there are about two dozen in the country – mainly in Panama City, Bocas, Boquete and David – which struggle to meet the growing demand, and advance booking is often necessary to be sure of a bed, where bookings are allowed. A dorm bunk usually costs around $12–15, occasionally including coffee or a light breakfast, and increasingly with air conditioning in lowland areas, while some establishments also offer private rooms at $25–35. Most have common areas, shared kitchens, free wi-fi or internet access and bags of useful information about the surrounding area.

Camping

There is virtually no organized **camping** in Panama, though a few lodgings allow tents if asked and there are now a few places that will provide tents to rent in summer (Dec–April). In rural communities you can almost always find someone willing to allow you to camp on their land for a small fee. Alternatively, there are kilometres of empty beaches to pitch a tent on, although you should always seek local advice since they are not universally safe. Touristy areas such as Santa Clara and Isla Bastimentos have periodically reported thefts and muggings while at night on a completely uninhabited island in Guna Yala you run the risk of encountering the odd drug smuggler. The **national parks** (see pp.37–40) seem more set up for camping since they have set fees (usually $5/person a night), but rarely offer facilities beyond those shared with the park wardens at the park entrance. Most of the parks and protected areas also offer dormitory accommodation (usually $15/person) and use of the kitchen.

Homestays

Homestays, a good budget accommodation option, often help the local economy more directly while providing an opportunity to engage in cross-cultural interaction. They may also be the only way of finding a room during major fiestas in a town that is short of formal lodgings. In indigenous communities, such as in Guna Yala and Darién, a homestay is frequently the norm when overnighting in a village, which you will need to arrange with the chief or tourist coordinator on arrival.

Pricing and taxes

Most mid-range and high-end accommodation operates a dual **pricing system**: high-season rates (mid-Dec to end of April) generally coincide with the dry season, whereas the rest of the year counts as low season, when it's possible to find significant discounts, especially for online bookings. On top of high-season rates, some establishments in Panama City and the major holiday destinations hike their prices even higher for Carnaval, Easter (Semana Santa), Christmas and New Year. Some lodgings in places that are primarily weekend retreats, such as Isla Grande and El Valle, charge more Friday to Sunday, occasionally demanding a two- or three-night minimum stay.

Places with more than nine rooms are subject to a ten-percent **tourist tax** (though even smaller lodgings sometimes charge), which is not always included in the advertised rate but has been factored into our prices. For each listing we give the cheapest rate for a double room (one double bed) in high season (outside the extra price hikes for public holidays) with a private bathroom – where available; we indicate if only shared bathrooms are available. Note too that in mid-range hotels a double room often means a room with two double beds and you might have to specify one double

bed (*una cama doble*, or *una cama matrimonial*) if you want to keep costs down. Room costs are usually based on two people sharing, but many rooms have an extra single bed, which a third person can have for an extra $10–15. Children under 12 are often admitted free.

Food and drink

Given Panama's clichéd status as the "melting pot of the Americas", it's no surprise Panamanian cuisine is infused with numerous culinary influences, notably Afro-Antillean, indigenous, Spanish, Chinese and American. Cosmopolitan Panama City offers the greatest variations in terms of gastronomy and price (see pp.79–82), from a $3–4 plate of noodles and chicken in the public market to ornate fusion cuisine served on damask tablecloths. You can take your pick from Italian, Japanese, Lebanese, Brazilian, American – and thankfully not just McDonald's and KFC – Swiss or Indian fare. In the capital, Panamanian food rarely features on the menus of the mid- to high-end restaurants, outside a few tourist-orientated venues, but in markets, hole-in-the-wall restaurants and out in the interior, it's much easier to find local culinary specialities – often heavy on starch and frequently fried.

Outside the capital and the major tourist destinations of Boquete and Bocas, there is less variation and dining is often more informal and a lot cheaper; travellers on a tight budget can easily find simple well-cooked food in *fondas* (basic restaurants), which offer *comida corriente* – also known as the the *menu del día* – (meal of the day) for very little. **Vegetarians** will be challenged since, as elsewhere in Central America, even the veggie staple of beans and rice can be cooked in pork fat. Your best bet is to head for a Chinese restaurant, present in most towns, or one of the proliferating pizzerias, or stock up with the fresh fruit and vegetables that abound in many local markets.

Breakfast

Panama's filling **desayuno típico** (traditional breakfast), aimed at sustaining workers for a hard day's labour in the fields, offers a chance to boost cholesterol levels. Panama's deep-fried favourites

TRADITIONAL DISHES

PANAMANIAN MAINS

Unless you are vegetarian, you should not leave Panama without sampling the country's **national dish**, *sancocho* – a tasty soup. Variations on the theme are served in many parts of Latin America and even within Panama the meal is prepared in numerous ways; essentially it's a hearty chicken-based soup with large chunks of yuca and other filling root vegetables, or maybe even plantain and sweetcorn, flavoured with cilantro – a herb similar to coriander but more pungent – exemplifying the Caribbean culinary influence. Other Panamanian variations of ubiquitous **Latin dishes** include the unappetizing-sounding *ropa vieja* ("old clothes" – spicy shredded beef over rice), *ceviche* (white fish, shrimp or octopus marinated in lime juice with chopped onion and garlic plus hot pepper and fresh coriander) and *mondongo* (a slow-cooked tripe and chorizo-based stew with plenty of root vegetables, laced with garlic and coriander or cilantro), the latter a traditional dish for celebration (*mondongada*) with family and labourers after the installation of the roof on a new house.

COASTAL CUISINE

With so much coastline, it's no wonder seafood is a Panamanian staple in both the Pacific and Caribbean lowlands. In the latter, the Afro-Antillean influence is dominant – typical dishes include rice cooked in coconut milk and seafood prepared with spices and judicious amounts of lime. *Corvina* (sea bass) is the most widely eaten fish, but you can also find snapper, grouper, dorado, shrimp, langoustines, crab and lobster, though you should refuse the last four if offered them during the closed season (Dec 1 to April 15 in the Pearl Islands, March 1 to June 30 along the Caribbean coast) unless you know they have come from a freezer. Locally farmed trout is a speciality of the Chiriquí Highlands.

GREENS AND SPICES

While starch and carbohydrates abound in most traditional foods, **greenery** is scarce. Don't be surprised if the salad accompaniment is merely a lettuce leaf supporting a slice of tomato and a couple of onion rings. Green vegetables are also conspicuous by their absence in many restaurants outside the capital, though they can often be found in local markets. Spices are generally used sparingly, but if you require more kick there's usually some *salsa picante* lurking on a table to take the roof of your mouth off.

include tortillas (thick cornmeal cakes), *carimañolas* (mashed boiled yuca – cassava or manioc – stuffed with ground beef) and *hojaldres* (discs of sweetened leavened dough, which at best are delightfully crispy and tasty but at worst are chewy and dripping in grease). Costa Rica's national dish, *gallo pinto* (literally "speckled rooster"), is another popular way to kick-start the day, a moist rice, beans and onions mix often accompanied with a dollop of *natilla* – a local sour cream that is also lavished on strawberries in the Chiriquí Highlands – and fried or scrambled eggs.

If such a heavy plateful is more than you can stomach first thing in the morning, head for a **panadería** (bakery) for a pastry and a shot of coffee, or pick up some fresh fruit at the local market. In the more expensive hotels in Panama City and in European or North American-owned establishments outside the capital, you can also expect combinations of cereals, fruit, yoghurt and toast.

Lunch and dinner

While it's possible to grab a light **lunch** – a flaky *empanada* (pasty) with a beef-, pork- or chicken-based filling or an *emparedado* (sandwich) – in urban areas, for most Panamanians lunch is the main meal of the day. In the *fondas* and cheaper restaurants ordering an *almuerzo* or *menu del día* (lunch of the day) will get you a filling plate of chicken with rice, plus beans or lentils, or maybe fish and plantain down on the coast, for $3–4. Some places throw in a soup starter and dessert to give you a three-course set meal at very little extra cost. Set-meal *cenas* (dinner of the day) are also available early evening in some places. Otherwise, **evening eating** is generally more low-key except when dining out for a special occasion.

Predominantly self-service *cafeterías* – the Panamanian equivalent of American diners – keep going from around 6 or 7am until 11pm or midnight in the urban centres. Out in the countryside, local restaurants and *fondas* may also open for all three meals but shut up shop shortly after nightfall, depending on demand. Lunch in formal dining establishments is usually served from noon until 3pm, dinner from 6 or 7pm until around 10pm, with the midday meal usually offering better value for money. Mid-range and high-end restaurants often add the seven-percent sales tax (ITBMS) on top of the advertised fare, and some even add an obligatory ten-percent **service charge**, which is not always included on the menu price list. Where we give meal prices we have factored in these extra charges.

Street food and snacks

Street food, though not widespread, can range from chunks of fresh pineapple or watermelon to plantain crisps (*platanitos*) deep-fried on the spot. Small **roadside grills** often serve *carne en palito* (meat on a little stick) – fairly miniscule kebabs comprising slivers of (occasionally spicy) marinated beef, which take the edge off your appetite. During the day, you'll also see men pushing carts laden with fluorescent liquids and blocks of ice around the main squares, peddling **raspados** – paper cones filled with shavings of ice, drizzled over with a sickly flavoured liquid, made still sweeter by a slurp of condensed milk and much loved by kids.

Drink

Aside from Panama's tasty tap water, there's a wide range of beverages to sample, from lethal paint-stripper home-brews to delicious fruit concoctions served in a variety of manners, not to mention beer and rum, which are consumed in vast quantities during Panama's many festivals.

Alcoholic beverages

Beer is the most popular alcoholic drink; Panama's four main labels – Soberana, Panamá, Balboa and Atlas – are all fairly inoffensive lagers, with Balboa slightly more full-bodied and the current favourite. Though none will set the pulses of beer aficionados racing, when ice-cold they definitely hit the spot, costing a dollar swigged out of a bottle in a local *cantina*, and up to $5 served on a serviette in a frosted glass in a plush nightclub. Imported beers such as Heineken and Budweiser, and even Guinness, are widely available in Panama City and tourist towns but are more expensive.

The national tipple, the transparent, throat-singeing **seco** (a rough sugar cane spirit), is significantly more potent (35 percent) and more commonly consumed by men in the interior, particularly during fiestas, as is rum. A lethal home-brew favoured by *campesinos* is *vino de palma*, made from fermented palm sap, as is *guarapo*, sugar cane juice distilled to knockout strength. **Wine** – usually Chilean or Californian – is becoming increasingly available at reasonable rates in Panama City and in tourist areas such as Bocas and Boquete.

Non-alcoholic beverages

Away from the alcohol, there is a wide range of **fruit-based drinks**, which in most parts of the country (see opposite) you can enjoy with ice, safe in the knowledge that the water is drinkable. Mango, pineapple, soursop, passion fruit, tamarind and a host of other fruits can be savoured in a range of forms: as a *jugo natural* (pure fruit juice), a *licuado* (a fresh fruit, water and sugar shake), a *batido* (a milk shake) or a *chicha* (a sweet maize-based fruit concoction) – not to be confused with its alcoholic cousin, generally dubbed *chicha fuerte* – a potent fermented maize brew made in bulk for special celebrations, particularly among indigenous and *campesino* communities.

The similar-sounding *chicheme*, a surprisingly tasty Panamanian speciality of ground maize, milk, vanilla and cinnamon, most revered in La Chorrera, should be sampled at some stage. So should *pipa* – fresh juice sipped through a straw straight from the coconut – and Panamanian **coffee**. Outside the country, Panama's reputation as the world leader in producing gourmet coffee is a secret known only to connoisseurs; you can sample the most prized beans in Boquete and Panama City, though elsewhere you're more likely to be sipping the more mundane but perfectly satisfying Café Duran, which will be strong and is sometimes offered with condensed milk. While black **tea** is widely available in cities and tourist areas, tea lovers will usually have to content themselves with herbal varieties elsewhere – chamomile (*manzanilla*) or cinnamon (*canela*) are the most common offerings.

Iced **tap water** is generally served on arrival in restaurants, except where water quality is poor – Bocas, the Darién and Guna Yala – in which case you'll need to order mineral water.

Health

In the construction eras of the transisthmus railroad and canal, Panama was synonymous with disease, in particular yellow fever, malaria and cholera. Thankfully, times have changed,

and most of Panama poses little threat to your health: yellow fever has been eradicated; malaria only persists in a few isolated areas; tap water is safe to drink in most of the country, and sophisticated medical care is widely available in the main population centres. Your most likely medical ailment will be travellers' diarrhoea from a change of diet and climate, or sunburn from overdoing it on the beach.

That said, you should ensure that your basic **inoculations** are up to date and consult a travel medical centre professional to help you decide what other precautions to take. If you intend only to explore the canal area and chill on the beach, you'll probably need little more than sun block and insect repellent, but if you're bent on venturing into the Darién jungle, all kinds of insect- and water-borne hazards need to be considered. **Medical insurance** is essential – see p.35 & p.44.

Inoculations

Most inoculations that involve multiple jabs need six to eight weeks to complete. There are no compulsory vaccinations to visit Panama but in addition to ensuring that your **routine injections** are current (tetanus, diphtheria and polio, and MMR), hepatitis A and typhoid are generally recommended, though you can also have a combined hepatitis A and B jab, advisable for long-term travellers. **Yellow fever** is nearly always flagged up as a hazard on health websites in relation to Panama, although the last documented case was in 1974. Nevertheless, there is still deemed to be a very slight risk of the disease in the Darién and remoter parts of Guna Yala. Moreover, since November 2008 the Panamanian government has required travellers entering the country from countries where yellow fever is listed as endemic, such as Colombia and Brazil, to carry proof of vaccination at least ten days prior to entry – ironic given that Panama is also on the list – though this requirement is rarely enforced.

Rabies is another potential hazard, more from vampire bats in cattle-ranching areas than from feral dogs, and one that should only really be considered by travellers expecting to spend time in the remoter rural areas.

General precautions

A major plus is that **tap water** in most of Panama is safe to drink, which means the usual travel worries about avoiding ice in drinks and salads washed in ordinary water can be dispensed with. The exceptions are in Guna Yala, much of the Darién and the remoter parts of Bocas. On the main tourist islands of Guna Yala and Bocas bottled water, though expensive, is widely available, but it is less easily obtained in the Darién. That said, since disposing of non-organic waste such as plastic bottles is a particularly acute environmental issue in these areas, try to bring a water filter or use water purification tablets as much as possible. These are usually available in Panama City (see p.41) but it's a better bet to bring them with you. While vile-tasting chlorine or iodine tablets are still effective and widely available, most companies now produce tablets to neutralize the unpleasant aftertaste. Seek advice on the relative merits of chlorine versus iodine; the latter, for example, though considered more effective against giardia parasites, is generally not recommended for pregnant women. Campers with their own stove can of course boil water to sterilize it.

Since food safety is related to water safety and to food storage, exercise common sense when eating **salads** or **unpeeled fruit** in the few areas in Panama where the water is not potable. **Street food**, though frequently very tasty, is another potential minefield, particularly at fiestas when mounds of chicken and rice stand around in the hot sun for hours. Make sure the food is well cooked in front of you and, if the stall has been dishing up food all day, that any raw meat or fish has been stored in a cooler box with ice before cooking – and avoid anything swimming in mayonnaise.

Intestinal problems

Travellers' **diarrhoea** (TD) lasting a few days is the most common ailment encountered, as likely to be due to the change in diet and climate as to contaminated food or water-carrying bacteria, viruses or parasites. If afflicted by the runs, the best cure is to rest and rehydrate, drinking plenty of clean water with rehydration salts. Sachets of Dioralyte or Electolade are worth keeping in your first-aid kit, though equivalents are easily purchased in pharmacies in the major urban centres. Diarrhoea remedies such as Imodium and Lomotil should only be used in emergencies, such as when embarking on a long-distance plane journey or a jungle trek, since stopping the flow is not actually healthy. If symptoms persist, especially if there is blood in the stool or vomiting occurs, consult a doctor, who will probably prescribe a course of antibiotics.

Sunburn and dehydration

Skin cancer is on the increase, largely because of overexposure to UV radiation – indeed it is the most prevalent form of cancer in the US. In the fierce tropical sun of Panama, a high-factor sun cream (SPF 15 or higher with both UVA & UVB protection), a sun-hat and sunglasses are an absolute must. Up to forty percent of the sun's rays can be reflected back up from water or sand, even if you're sitting in the shade; nor is an overcast day free from damaging UV light. When travelling in a dugout – a likely scenario if exploring the Darién or Guna Yala – you could be faced with hours without any protection. Serious sunburn, sunstroke and heatstroke are therefore all very real health hazards and far more likely than catching a tropical disease. Keeping up your fluid intake to avoid dehydration is just as essential.

Malaria

There is low risk of **malaria** in more remote areas of the Caribbean lowlands in Bocas and Veraguas, and a slightly higher risk east of the canal, in the Darién and in more isolated areas of Guna Yala. Transmitted by a parasite in the saliva of an infected anopheles mosquito (active from dusk to dawn), its symptoms – fever, chills, headaches and muscle pains – are easily confused with flu.

It is most effectively combated through **prevention** – wearing long loose sleeves and trousers for protection, dousing yourself in repellent and sleeping under a mosquito net or in screened rooms. Most effective chemical insect repellents contain DEET, with the 25–35 percent varieties considered adequate for most needs. However, a few recent studies have started to raise questions about DEET's possible neurological side effects as well as damage to the environment. Whatever the medical opinions on the subject, you have to wonder about a solution that will melt your pen if it gets too close. Recently, more organic, non-chemical products, based on oils such as eucalyptus, citronella, cedar or verbena, are appearing on the market. They are generally more expensive but give less fierce protection, which wears off much more quickly. They can be effective enough when used with other preventive measures, although if you are in a malarial area you might want to stick to DEET. Mosquito coils are widely available across Panama, even in small villages; if seeking a natural alternative, candles can help deter the insects. In neither case should they be used in enclosed indoor environments.

A range of anti-malarial tablets are on the market, all of which should be purchased prior to arriving in Panama and started in advance of visiting the malarial area, though a public medical centre (*centro de salud*) in a malarial area should stock a supply for post-exposure treatment. West of the canal, chloroquine is the drug of choice, generally taken once a week a fortnight in advance of entering a malarial area and for four weeks afterwards. East of the canal, where mosquitoes are chloroquine-resistant, mefloquine (also known as Larium) is often prescribed, though it can have particularly severe side effects. Malarone is a less controversial alternative but is currently the most expensive anti-malarial drug on the market. It is taken daily only two days before entering an infected area, to be continued for a week after leaving. Whatever you choose, it is important to finish the course of anti-malarials because of the time lag between bite and infection. If you become ill with flu-like symptoms after returning home, consult a doctor and inform them you've been to a malarial risk area.

Other bites and stings

Taking steps to avoid being bitten by **insects** is of paramount importance (see above). In addition to malaria, mosquitoes can transmit dengue fever, which induces flu-like symptoms similar to malaria but with more extreme aches and has been on the increase in Central America and the Caribbean in recent years. Sandflies (*chitras*) are a more likely pest for travellers, proliferating during the rainy season, and not only at the beach; almost invisible, you will become aware of them only when they bite. Sandfly bites itch more and for longer than mosquito bites – calamine lotion or antihistamine cream will usually reduce the aggravation. In forested rural areas in various parts of Panama bites from an infected sand fly can cause cutaneous leishmaniasis, whose symptoms can remain dormant for up to six months before sores and swellings break out on the skin. Though there is no vaccine, the disease is treatable through a series of jabs.

An overfamiliarity with Indiana Jones films can lead to the misconception that the greatest danger in the rainforest is a **snake bite**. While Panama has its share of venomous snakes – bushmaster, fer-de-lance and coral for starters – you are unlikely to see one, let alone get bitten. Nevertheless, donning long trousers and closed shoes or (even better) boots reduces the risk, as does avoiding walking in the forest at night. Should a snake manage to get its fangs into you, immobilize the affected area, apply a light-pressure bandage (not tourniquet) above and below the bite and seek immediate medical attention. Even a local medical centre should have some anti-venom.

There's a whole host of **other beasts** on land that may bite or sting, but only when threatened: scorpions – more commonly seen at night – and some spiders, for example; while in the sea jellyfish, sting rays and fire coral can all be painful. If you are prone to allergic reactions to bites and stings, make sure you carry some antihistamine tablets, which can reduce swelling and itchiness, as well as antihistamine cream or calamine lotion to cool and ease the pain.

Medical resources for travellers

There are a number of useful **online resources**, though their information may not be sufficiently nuanced (see p.35) for your needs. The websites listed generally note travel medical centres, where you can get jabs, and give general advice on the most common ailments and diseases that you might encounter. Travel medical centre professionals generally have access to more detailed and specific health information; you are strongly advised to consult them as well as carrying out your own research.

US AND CANADA

Centers for Disease Control and Prevention (CDC) ☎ 800 232 6348 (24hr health helpline), Ⓦ cdc.gov/travel. Official US government travel health site that's laden with info.
Public Health Agency of Canada Ⓦ phac-aspc.gc.ca. Distributes free pamphlets on travel health and provides a comprehensive list of travel clinics in the country.
Travellers' Medical and Vaccination Centre Ⓦ tmvc.com. List of travel health centres in Canada and vaccination costs plus brief travel health tips.

UK AND IRELAND

Fitfortravel Ⓦ fitfortravel.nhs.uk. Excellent NHS (Scotland) public access site with country-specific advice, the latest health bulletins and information on immunizations.
Hospital for Tropical Diseases Travel Clinic ☎ 020 7388 9600 (Travel Clinic), ☎ 020 7950 7799 (24hr Travellers Healthline Advisory Service – see website for additional country-specific information), Ⓦ thehtd.org.
MASTA (Medical Advisory Service for Travellers Abroad) ☎ 0870 606 2782, Ⓦ masta-travel-health.com. List of affiliated travel clinics where you can get vaccinations and detailed country-specific health briefs.
National Travel Health Network and Centre Ⓦ nathnac.org. Excellent website for health professionals and the travelling public

providing factsheets on various travel health risks and a free database of country-specific health info.
STA Travel UK Ⓦ statravel.co.uk/travel-clinic.htm. List of STA travel clinics in England and vaccination prices; full-time students with student card can get a ten-percent discount.
Tropical Medical Bureau ☎ 1850 487 674, Ⓦ tmb.ie. List of travel clinics in Ireland and country-specific info from US consular service.

AUSTRALIA, NEW ZEALAND AND SOUTH AFRICA

Travellers' Medical and Vaccination Centre Ⓦ traveldoctor .com.au. User-friendly site listing travel clinics in Australia, New Zealand and South Africa plus accessible factsheets on travel health and postings of health alerts worldwide.

Accessing medical care

Both state and private **medical care** is very good in Panama, particularly in Panama City; many doctors work in the public sector hospitals in the morning and run private clinics in the afternoon. The main problem the public sector faces is a lack of resources, particularly in the more remote rural villages, so most Panamanians who can afford private health care as well as almost all expats will head for a private clinic, where service is likely to be more immediate. The average cost of a consultation with a private doctor starts at $50, provided no X-rays or laboratory tests need doing, whereas a government-run doctor at the local clinic will see you for $5.

While **travel insurance** may cover costs, it will only do so after you file a claim on your return; you still need to be able to access sufficient funds to cover the bills at the time. Many doctors in the main cities have trained in the US at some stage and so speak good English. The US Embassy has a list of bilingual doctors in Panama City on its website (Ⓦ panama.usembassy.gov/medical2010.html).

There is now thirty-day free medical cover for foreign tourists entering via Tocumen International Airport. You are likely to be handed a brochure on arrival and a list of participating clinics and hospitals can be found on the tourist office website (Ⓦ visit panama.com/component/k2/item/4703.html).

The media

Aside from one government TV channel and one radio station, the media in Panama is privately owned. The five national daily Spanish-language news-papers – and three Chinese-language

papers – are widely available from street vendors in urban areas, and in supermarkets countrywide, while it's hard to escape TV in Panama – screens adorn most eating and drinking establishments, even upmarket restaurants, and are standard in most hotels.

Newspapers

The most respected **paper** is *La Prensa* (Ⓦprensa .com), which also produces informative supplements with in-depth writing and interesting features on tourism, history and culture. *La Estrella de Panamá* (Ⓦlaestrella.com.pa) and *Panamá América* (Ⓦpa-digital.com.pa) also count as "quality press", with *El Siglo* (Ⓦelsiglo.com) and *La Crítica* (Ⓦcritica.com.pa), the popular tabloid options.

Given the large US expat population, there is no shortage of **English-language news**. Aside from the imported *Miami Herald International Edition* and *USA Today*, there is the online *The Panama News* (Ⓦthepanamanews.com), which has the mantra "writing for thinking people not cattle". It pulls no punches and frequently contains features that border on the slanderous but, picking through them with healthy scepticism, you will gain some valuable insights into the dirty side of politics and business.

Liberally sprinkled round hotel lobbies and restaurants around the country, the free bilingual weekly *The Visitor/El Visitante* (Ⓦthevisitorpanama .com) offers a bland summary of Panamanian news, some features and a decent listings section of events in the main tourist zones of Panama City, Bocas and Boquete. The latter two expat enclaves also produce free monthly papers in English: *The Bocas Breeze* (Ⓦthebocasbreeze .com) and *The Bajareque* (Ⓦelbajareque.net); primarily run by and for expats, they contain some useful listings.

TV and radio

On evenings in a bar or cafeteria you're likely to catch an unremittingly awful soap opera (*telenovela*) on one of Panama's six terrestrial **television** channels. Many middle-class Panamanians have access to cable TV with channels in Spanish and English.

Check out Ⓦcoolpanama.com for a list of **radio stations**, frequencies and their musical preferences.

Festivals and public holidays

Panama is awash with festivals and public holidays. Alongside the numerous commemorations of historical events, there are copious Catholic celebrations – including each town's patron saint bash, agricultural fairs and cultural extravaganzas that reflect the country's ethnic diversity. Whatever the differences in the details, they all demand the ability to survive several days and nights of music, dancing and processions, fuelled on mountains of street food and gallons of booze. Head and shoulders above the rest stands Carnaval, a five-day marathon of hedonism at its most outlandish in the tiny Azuero town of Las Tablas (see box, p.167). See below and the relevant sections of the book for details of the major festivals.

A festivals calendar

JANUARY

Feria de las Flores y del Café Mid-Jan. Ten-day celebration in Boquete to mark the coffee harvest with carpets of flowers, food and craft stalls, the daytime family entertainment followed by night-time discos.

FEBRUARY

Revolución Dule Feb 25. Celebrates the Kuna Revolution of 1925, their Independence Day, with colourful reenactments of battles against the Panamanian authorities held across the *comarca*.

Carnaval Four days of wild partying and processions running till dawn on Ash Wednesday. Celebrated countrywide, but especially in Las Tablas and Panama City, with an aquatic parade on the Saturday in Penonomé.

MARCH

Semana Santa or Holy Week March–April. Celebrated everywhere, but most colourfully on the Azuero Peninsula.

Festival de los Diablos y Congos Vibrant biennial weekend event in Portobelo, showcasing Afro-colonial culture and resistance to the Spanish conquest in a mass of costumes, dances and devils (2011, 2013).

APRIL

Feria de las Orquídeas Five days in early April in Boquete. Over a thousand orchids, craft stalls and a programme of cultural events.

Feria Internacional de Azuero Ten days in La Villa de Los Santos. Major agricultural fair with stalls, presentations and competitions reflecting the area's colonial and cattle-farming traditions.

JUNE

Festival de Corpus Christi Late May/early June. Celebrated across the country but most spectacularly in La Villa de Los Santos with processions and dramatic devil dances.

JULY

Fiestas Patronales de la Virgen del Carmen July 16, Isla Taboga. The virgin gets to circumnavigate the island in a procession of decorated boats.

Fiestas Patronales de la Santa Librada July 20–22, Las Tablas. A mix of religious and folkloric parades incorporating the Festival de la Pollera, which showcases Panama's gorgeous national dress.

AUGUST

Festival del Manito Ocueño Thurs–Sun, dates vary. In Ocú, Azuero Peninsula. Lively folk festival featuring a mock duel and peasant wedding.

OCTOBER

Feria de Isla Tigre Mid-Oct, Isla Tigre (Digir Dupu), Guna Yala. Multi-day festivity of Guna culture.

Festival de la Mejorana Five days in mid-Oct, Guararé, Azuero Peninsula. Panama's premier folk festival, involving music, dancing and parades.

Festival del Cristo Negro Oct 21, Portobelo. The most revered pilgrimage in the country, attracting thousands bedecked in purple robes.

NOVEMBER

Primer Grito de la Independencia Nov 10, La Villa de los Santos. The "First Cry of Independence", celebrated as part of "El Mes de la Patria". Patriotic flag-waving parades and marching bands, attended by the president.

Public holidays

Panama has several national **public holidays** (see below), during which most government offices, businesses and shops close. When the public holidays fall on or near a weekend the government often grants a last-minute *puente* (bridge), usually a Monday or a Friday, making a long weekend and prompting a mass exodus from the city to the beach or the countryside, with a scramble for plane tickets and accommodation. ⓦ qppstudio.net/publicholidays.htm is a good source of up-to-date information. Note that services shut down in Panama City on August 15 to celebrate the foundation of Panamá La Vieja, while other towns and cities have their own multi-day festivities during which most services close down.

Over many public holidays, as well as during national elections, *ley seca* (literally **dry law**) is enacted, which means that, theoretically, alcohol can't be purchased or consumed during that period.

NATIONAL PUBLIC HOLIDAYS

Jan 1 Año Nuevo. New Year's Day.

Jan 9 Día de los Mártires. Martyrs' Day, in remembrance of those killed by US troops in the 1964 flag riots.

Feb Carnaval. Four days up to and including Ash Wednesday.

March–April Viernes Santo (Good Friday).

May 1 Día del Trabajo. Labour Day.

Nov 3 Separación de Panamá de Colombia. Anniversary of the 1903 Separation from Colombia and primary Independence Day.

Nov 4 Día de la Bandera. Flag Day.

Nov 5 Día de Colón. Celebrating the city's Separation from Colombia.

Nov 10 Primer Grito de la Independencia. "First Cry of Independence", marking the unilateral declaration of independence from Spain in La Villa de Los Santos.

Nov 28 4 Independencia de Panamá de España. Independence from Spain – 1821.

Dec 8 Día de la Madre. Mother's Day.

Dec 25 Día de Navidad. Christmas Day.

National parks

Almost a quarter of Panama's land lies within the boundaries of its fourteen national parks – add in reserves, refuges and other protected areas, and the figure is over a third. Under siege on all sides from urban development, pollution and deforestation (see p.309), these nevertheless constitute one of Panama's major attractions: you can trek through pristine rainforest, explore Spanish colonial forts, haul yourself up volcanic peaks or swim with sharks and manta rays. Some, such as the legendary Darién, Central America's largest wilderness, and Cerro Hoya, at the tip of the Azuero Peninsula, are particularly inaccessible and involve a lot of planning, perseverance and often money to reach; others, such as Camino de Cruces and Soberanía, are a stone's throw from Panama City, making an easy day-trip and providing a great opportunity to flush out some of Panama's dazzling birdlife.

Panama's ecosystems are astonishingly diverse – little surprise given that the country stands at the crossroads of two oceans and two continents, a vital link in the biological corridor between North and South America. Since the country is so slender, many of the parks offer a hugely varied **topography**: several straddle the continental divide, ranging from lofty moss-covered cloud forest pierced by rugged peaks to humid lowland rainforest; others protect dense swathes of mangrove, harbouring caimans, crocodiles and crustaceans while protecting vital mud flats for thousands of migratory birds. The three **marine parks** offer coral reefs, turquoise waters and islands encircled with sugar-sand beaches and coated in tropical forest that supports everything from fluorescent poison-dart frogs to primordial iguanas. Ruined colonial fortresses, a crumbling Devil's Island penitentiary and a rare tract of dry tropical forest also lie within national park boundaries.

Planning your trip

Which parks and reserves you decide to visit will depend on your interests and several practical

concerns – transport, the time and money at your disposal, accommodation and the time of year. The map (see below) gives a brief overview of the activities various parks offer; further details are in the relevant chapters. ⓦanam.gob.pa/index.php (click on "Parques Nacionales") has information in Spanish on the various national parks.

Eco-tourism is being championed as a viable way forward for local indigenous communities to make a living while protecting the environment, although concrete government support for projects is lacking. A handful of Emberá villages in the Chagres and Darién parks in particular have established links with local operators (listed in the relevant chapters – see p.75 for some Panama City-based companies) to receive tour groups and a few

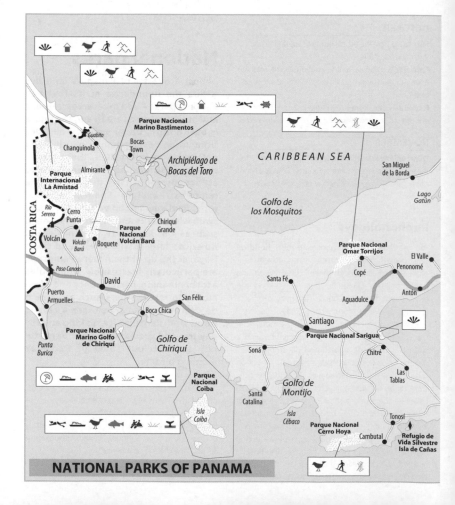

NATIONAL PARKS OF PANAMA

have even established their own websites – though they're not always up to date – to encourage more independent travellers. While it is far less hassle to go with a tour operator, it is usually cheaper to organize your own visit, with the additional benefit of knowing that your money is going to the community rather than the agency.

Visiting the parks

The national parks are managed by the National Department for the Environment, the **Autoridad Nacional del Ambiente** (see Ⓦ anam.gob.pa). Dealing with tourists is in theory the job of Panama's national tourist agency, the ATP, but ANAM staff in the regional and local offices, as well as the *guardaparques* (park wardens) are often very helpful and likely to be of more direct use.

ANAM offices are generally open Monday to Friday from 8.30am to 3.30pm. If you need a permit, to book accommodation, or to hire a guide, it's best to drop by the regional or larger town offices to sort matters out in advance. If this is not possible, you can usually organize something on the spot – indeed, in theory, there should be a full-time resident warden at each national park entrance although in practice, it is not always the case.

If you decide to organize your visit by telephoning one of the ANAM offices, ask to talk to someone in *Áreas Protegidas*, and note that most ANAM employees only speak Spanish. With tourism very much a fledgling business in Panama, it may

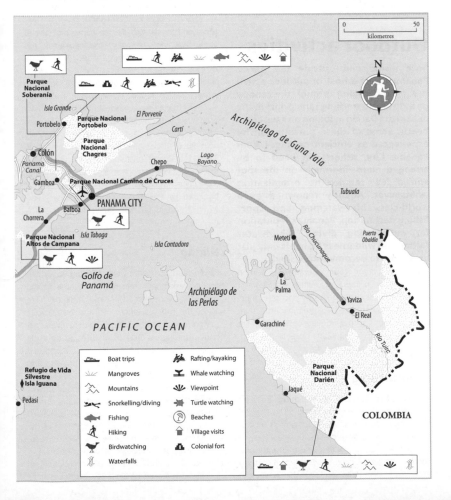

be some time before there is an integrated approach and anything like standardized **facilities** across the national parks. In most places, you will need to ask the park warden, and possibly hire them as a guide since maps and trail signs are conspicuously absent.

Given the general lack of infrastructure and information and the dilapidated state of some facilities, the park fees in some locations can seem excessive – though they are substantially less for nationals and residents. Most places charge $5–10 per person to visit ($20 for Coiba), plus $5 per person to camp and around $15 for a bed for the night. Charges for the smaller reserves are generally around $5. However, these minor niggles are substantially outweighed by the outstanding beauty of the parks themselves, which you can often have all to yourself.

Outdoor activities

Both inside and outside the parks, Panama offers a host of outdoor activities, from swinging through the canopy on a zip line to tracking tapir prints in the mud of the Darién or lolling on a deserted beach. Some of these pursuits can be experienced as efficient packages from Panama City; others will need to be arranged more informally on the spot and a few require no organization whatsoever. Already renowned as a world-class birdwatching and sport fishing destination, Panama's reputation for outstanding diving, whitewater rafting and wilderness hiking is only just beginning to become established.

Several excellent **tour operators**, providing knowledgeable bilingual or multilingual naturalist guides work out of Panama City and offer tours around the country (see p.75) though for the more distant locations, such as Boquete or Coiba, you are better off looking for operators closer to the destination; they are listed in the relevant chapters.

Birdwatching

Panama offers first-class **birdwatching**, Boasting over 960 species of bird, including 55 varieties of hummingbirds and spectacular show birds such as the emerald and ruby resplendent quetzal (easy to see in the Chiriquí Highlands), the country also contains the world's largest concentration of harpy eagles (most likely to be spotted in the Darién or in

Amistad). Though Panama acts as a magnet for serious twitchers laden with tripods, checklists and hefty avian tomes (see p.313), it might persuade even those who have viewed birdwatching as a dull pastime, involving hours of trying to identify one indistinguishable brown bird from another, to think again. It's hard not to be impressed by the dazzling flashes of parrots and macaws in flight or the ludicrous painted bills of toucans swooping across the treetops.

Since many of these glamorous birds spend much of their time tantalizingly high up in the canopy, it is worth splashing out on at least a small pair of binoculars, which will significantly enhance your birdwatching experience. So too will engaging a **guide**. Alongside the big-name tour operators in the capital (see p.75) there are small-scale specialists, such as Birding Panama (Ⓦbirdingpanama.com) and Birding in Panama (Ⓦbirdinginpanama.com), as well as numerous local residents scattered across the country, whose contact details are given in the relevant chapters. Daily rates for a professional bilingual naturalist guide contracted in the capital can range from $80–120, partly depending on how far you travel, but if you want something less expensive or just want someone to be able to point out some of the more obvious species, engaging someone locally from one of the villages for a few hours can cost as little as $15. A good way to start off is to attend one of the regular birdwatching-for-beginners walks ($5) in the Parque Natural Metropolitano in Panama City; organized by the Panama Audubon Society and advertised on its website (Ⓦpanamaaudubon.org), they are open to all.

Hiking

Panama also affords a myriad of **hiking** opportunities. Vast wilderness areas such as La Amistad and the Darién are ideal for adventurous multi-day hikes across the isthmus, often involving bivouacking, staying in indigenous villages, fording rivers and wading through metres of mud. Aside from the Panama City operators, guides can be engaged locally in places such as Santa Fé, Boquete and Cerro Punta, at far less cost, though you'll need some Spanish. If you fancy a more modest outing, parks in the canal basin offer a range of trails from a gentle circular route to a reasonably strenuous rainforest tramp, following in the footsteps of the conquistadors. Note you'll need warm clothes for the chilly nights in the peaks of western Panama.

Basic hiking and camping gear can often be purchased at any of the Do It Best hardware shops in the main cities though the best selection (albeit still fairly limited) can be found at Outdoor Adventure in Albrook Mall (☎ 303 6120) and Multicentro (☎ 302 0157) in Panama City. Do It Best in Albrook Mall usually stocks water filters and water purification tablets.

Rafting and kayaking

The fast-flowing rivers that tumble down from the highlands of western and central Panama, carving their way through dramatic scenery, have put Panama on the map for **whitewater rafting** and **kayaking**. The top destination is the Río Chiriquí Viejo, which runs parallel with the Costa Rican border. Though the descent is shorter and slightly less wild since its damming for a hydroelectric project, it's still an impressive run, with Category II to IV rapids. The rivers are at their wildest during the heavy rains (May–Nov), but you'll manage to find enough water flowing somewhere to raft and kayak year-round. Boquete operators (see p.187) are best placed to organize Chiriquí destinations, while companies in the capital head for rivers in the Chagres basin or in neighbouring Coclé Province.

Sea kayaking is gradually growing in popularity, offering a great way to explore rocky coastlines and mangroves, and access remote beaches among the islands of Guna Yala (see box, p.252), or round Coiba (see p.211) and Boca Chica (see p.204) in Chiriquí.

Diving

Diving in the **Pacific** can be truly spectacular, particularly in the Golfo de Chiriquí and the Archipiélago de las Perlas. Pick the right time of year (see p.308) and you're likely to spot manta rays, moray eels, sharks, schools of dolphins and migrating humpback and sperm whales – some scuba operators offer whale-watching tours. Large pelagic fish such as marlin, sailfish, amberjack, dorado and tuna also abound, which reel in sport fishing enthusiasts too. The jewel in this marine crown is Isla Coiba; located on the edge of the second-largest reef on the Pacific side of the Americas, it offers world-class diving.

Among the coral reefs of Bocas and Portobelo on the **Caribbean** side, diving can also be enjoyable, if not as spectacular as at some other Caribbean destinations. Visibility can vary enormously, especially after heavy rain. However, the rainbow-coloured soft corals of Cayo Crawl off Isla Bastimentos make for breathtaking snorkelling and there are plenty of other fun spots to explore.

Reputable local **dive shops** operate out of Bocas, Portobelo, Santa Catalina, Isla Contadora and Pedasí, on the Azuero Peninsula, while Scuba Panama (☎ 261 3841, Ⓦ scubapanama.com), the country's oldest outfit, organizes expeditions from Panama City.

Sport fishing

Panama means "abundance of fish" according to one reading of the indigenous language Cueva, and the country offers some phenomenal **fishing**. The Bahía de Piñas on the Pacific coast of the Darién, location of the exclusive *Tropic Star Lodge* (Ⓦ tropicstarlodge.com), is widely considered to be the world's top saltwater fishing destination, with the Golfo de Chiriquí, and Coiba in particular, a close second and the Islas Perlas not far behind.

Foreign-owned **fishing lodges** are mushrooming along the Pacific coast, most of which offer multi-day package deals that cover accommodation, meals and fishing excursions costing up to several thousand dollars. Recommended outfits include: Panama Big Game Fishing (Ⓦ panamabiggamefishing.com), Coiba Adventure Sportfishing (Ⓦ coibaadventure .com) and Pesca Panama (Ⓦ pescapanama.com).

Surfing

The Pacific coast offers some top-drawer **surfing**; in the internationally renowned breaks round Santa Catalina, the waves can reach 4m or more during March and April, with the high season continuing until August (though a good ride on 2m breakers is guaranteed year-round). There is also some fine surfing to be had round Playa Venao and neighbouring beaches on the southern coastline of the Azuero Peninsula. Bocas offers varied breaks, plus welcoming bars and a decent après surf scene, while local surfers confined to Panama City tend to dash to the nearby Pacific beaches of Coclé for a weekend escape.

Other activities

Those who prefer an adrenaline rush in the air rather than on the water or up in the hills should head for the Boquete Tree Trek (see p.188), which can justifiably be considered the Tarzan of all **canopy adventures**, boasting a dozen zip lines, though more modest versions exist in El Valle (see p.138) and near Portobelo (see p.117). Similar adrenaline surges are guaranteed **kitesurfing** at Punta Chame on the Pacific coast (see p.132).

If all that sounds too energetic there are plenty of ways to enjoy the outdoors without too much physical exertion; pass by any small fishing village and you can usually find a **boatman** willing to take you for a chug round the mangroves, drop you off for a laze on a deserted beach or even throw a line for a spot of fishing. Similarly relaxing is a plod along an empty beach or through the rainforest on **horseback**, which offers the chance to soak up the scenery without frightening away the wildlife – though don't necessarily expect a safety helmet, or a saddle that fails to remind you what you've been doing for the next week.

Mountain bikers in search of company might consider contacting Boa Panama (**W**boapanama .com for English-speaking and Spanish-speaking contacts), an association of recreational off-road cycling enthusiasts, which organizes weekend outings.

Spectator sports

While football is popular in Panama, the sport that arouses the greatest passions is **baseball**. With a highly ranked national team, and a number of successful major league baseball stars to its credit, baseball is Panama's national sport. An inexpensive and captivating evening's entertainment awaits if you attend one of the fiercely contested national league matches that take place in the dry season – check **W**fedebeis.com for fixtures – particularly in the more intimate stadiums in the interior. Under the floodlights, a raucous spirit prevails, with people partying in the stands and screaming to the accompaniment of brass bands and drums, with plenty of tasty street food on hand.

Close behind comes **boxing**, which has produced more Panamanian world champions than any other sport. Of these, two stand out: "Panama Al Brown", a bantamweight from Colón, who became the first Latin American world champion in 1929, and Roberto Durán, after whom the stadium outside Panama City was named.

Less illustrious, though still given passionate support when the occasion demands, the national **football** team won its first international trophy in 2009, triumphing in the Central American championships. Generally, though, the team can do with all the help it can muster so if you fancy going to cheer them on check out **W**panamafutbol.com, although the professional league matches played out in the low-key stadiums in the interior, at Santiago or David, may provide greater entertainment.

Another sport in which Panama enjoys a rich heritage is **horse racing**, which is easily accessible in Panama City (see p.85).

Travel essentials

Costs

Costs are higher than in Central American countries such as Guatemala and Nicaragua, and have risen to Costa Rican levels in some areas. Staying in hostel dorms, eating in inexpensive local restaurants and using public transport you can easily survive on $30–40 a day, less if camping, with anything from $40–90 on top for a day's guided excursion – snorkelling, surfing, fishing, horseriding or kayaking, for instance.

Staying in more comfortable accommodation and eating in more touristy restaurants can mean a daily food and lodgings budget of $90 with excursions and maybe car rental ($35–40/day) on top, though a lot depends on whether you stay in Panama City and the canal area, where prices are significantly higher, or make for the interior.

High-end accommodation – only really available in Panama City and at a handful of resorts across the rest of the country – will set you back over $250 a night, with a three-course meal (without drinks) in one of the city's top restaurants averaging $40. For advice on tipping, see p.47.

Crime and personal safety

The presence of FARC guerrillas and cocaine smugglers in the Darién jungle has helped promote the popular misconception that Panama is a dangerous country to visit. In fact it is much safer than most other Central American states, with only a few areas to avoid or take special care.

The eastern strip of the **Darién** and **Guna Yala** that borders Colombia tops the danger list as a no-go area; it contains the fabled Darién Gap, which has long held a fascination for travellers seeking adventure by hacking through jungle to the border. While this was difficult but feasible, it is now very dangerous and prohibited; since the 1990s several travellers attempting the overland route have been kidnapped or killed. There are still ways of visiting the Darién safely both in an organized group and as an independent traveller, and for crossing to Colombia on the Caribbean side by boat (see p.24), all of which can provide excitement without putting your life in acute danger.

The second major trouble spot is **Colón**, where extreme caution needs to be exercised even during daylight hours (see p.106). **Panama City** also has several areas to avoid, generally poor neighbourhoods with inadequate housing and high unemployment rates. As with many cities worldwide, **violent crime** is on the increase, but ninety percent of this is estimated to be drug-related, often among rival gangs; petty crime too is on the rise in some areas, especially where there are significant economic disparities between the general population and those who are making decent money from tourism, such as in Bocas. That said, by far the vast majority of visitors enjoy their time in Panama without incident, with the main issues being theft of money and/or passport and the odd traffic accident. The usual common-sense guidelines apply.

The police

If you are a **victim of crime**, report to the *Policía de Turismo* (Tourist Police) in Panama City (see p.86) or the main police station in other towns. Even though your possessions are unlikely to be recovered, a police report (*denuncia*) will be required to make an insurance claim. At the police station, you will probably need to present your ID, which by law you should always carry with you, though it is acceptable to carry a photocopy of your passport details provided it also includes a copy of the entry date stamp on the same page.

Culture and etiquette

No society is homogenous but Panama is particularly diverse, and customs vary widely. Overall, though, people are very courteous – driving in Panama City aside – and quite formal; **greetings** are customary before any exchange, such as asking for information, and the "usted" form of address is preferred to the "tu" form, which is reserved for close friends, although this is beginning to change among younger people or those who have spent significant periods of time out of the country. This formality is also reflected in **clothing**, particularly by the urban middle classes, who like to dress up to go out. Dress is also important on the beach; no nude sunbathing is permitted in Panama, except on one beach on Isla Contadora (see p.123), and beachwear should stay on the beach – cover your body in town.

Suitably modest attire (covered shoulders) is appreciated in churches. When visiting **indigenous communities**, cultural sensitivity is important as regards dress, alcohol and photography (see p.261).

Drugs

Drugs are widely available in Panama, **marijuana** and **cocaine** in particular, and you're quite likely to be offered something at some stage. However, possession of either is illegal and makes those caught liable for a prison sentence. While the police might – and only might – turn a blind eye to a joint being smoked discreetly on a deserted beach, being caught with some weed trying to cross a border can have serious consequences. Possession of cocaine is punished very heavily, in part because Panama is a known transit point for drugs heading from Colombia to the US.

Electricity

The **voltage** in Panama is 110 volts and sockets take flat two- and occasionally three-pronged plugs. **Power cuts** and subsequent surges occur fairly frequently so if travelling with a laptop you may want to bring a surge protector. In many remote parts of the country, such as some islands of Guna Yala and in much of the Darién, in national parks or in isolated villages, there is limited or no electricity at night so a torch is essential.

Entry requirements

Requirements for Panama can be confusing; they change frequently and updates can take a while to filter through to all immigration officials. Check for the latest regulations at a Panamanian consulate in advance of your trip and don't forget that if you are transiting via the US, you will need a transit visa, or a visa waiver application to be made online in advance of travel (see ⓦusimmigrationsupport .org), as well as a machine-readable passport. The Panamanian immigration authorities' website is also worth checking (ⓦmigracion.gob.pa).

At the time of going to press, citizens of **most European countries**, including the UK and Ireland, the US, Canada, Australia, New Zealand and South Africa do not need a visa and can get their passport stamped for ninety days on arrival provided they can produce a passport valid for at least six months after departure, an onward (or return) bus or plane ticket and proof of funds (usually $500 or a credit card).

If you are arriving from one of the WHO-listed yellow fever countries you may be asked to produce your vaccination certificate (see p.33).

As regards tourist visa **extensions**, there is disagreement even among immigration offices and officials as to whether you are now allowed a ninety-day tourist visa extension (*prórroga de turista* or *extensión de visa*). We suggest you make enquiries at immigration in Panama in advance of your visa expiry; if the answer is no, you can always pop over to Costa Rica for a couple of days before returning.

EMBASSIES AND CONSULATES ABROAD

Australia C/- RSM Bird Cameron, Level 12, 60 Castlereagh St, Sydney, NSW 2001 ☎ 02 9150 8409, ✉ panaconsul.sydney @bigpond.com.au.

Canada 130 Albert St, Suite 300, K1P 5G4, Ottawa ☎ 613 236 7177, ⓦ embassyofpanama.ca.

New Zealand 300 Queen St, Auckland Central ☎ 09 379 8550, ✉ gthwaite@iprolink.co.nz.

South Africa Kloof Ave, Waterkloof, Pretoria ☎ 012 346 0703, ✉ ambassador@panamaembassy.co.za.

UK Panama House, 40 Hertford St, London W1J 7SH ☎ 020 7493 4646, ⓦ panamaconsul.co.uk.

US 2862 McGill Terrace, NW Washington, DC 20008 ☎ 202 387 5601, ⓦ embassyofpanama.org.

Gay and lesbian travellers

Homosexuality was only decriminalized in Panama in 2008, which is illustrative of the country's prevailing social conservatism but also of the fact that things are beginning to change. The Asociación de Hombres y Mujeres Nuevos de Panamá (AHMN; ⓦ facebook.com/AHMNP) is active in campaigning for LGBT rights and low-key Gay Pride marches have been held since 2005. The LGBT scene is discreet in Panama; the clutch of nightclubs is not widely advertised (see ⓦ farraurbana .com). However, on the Panama pages of LGBT travel websites (see for example ⓦ purpleroofs .com/centralamerica/panama.html, ⓦ gayjourney .com/hotels/panama.htm and ⓦ globalgayz.com) the number of openly "gay-friendly" accommodation listings, though small, is gradually increasing. In general, hotels in Panama City and North American- and European-run establishments are likely to be more tolerant.

Insurance

It would be unwise to head for Panama without **insurance** that covers theft, loss, illness, injury and flight cancellation. Before you take out a new policy, make sure that you aren't already covered: some all-risks home insurance policies may cover your possessions while abroad, and many private medical schemes also apply when overseas. In Canada, provincial health plans usually provide some cover for medical treatment when out of the country. Some student insurance packages also include vacation travel. When shopping around for a policy, bear in mind that what are termed **dangerous sports**, which usually include the likes of scuba diving and whitewater rafting, sometimes require an additional premium to be paid. Should you have to seek medical attention, keep all receipts, and if you lose something valuable, get a police report (*denuncia*). Whatever the situation you will still need to access sufficient funds to cover such emergencies (hence the usefulness of a credit card) while on your trip, and apply for reimbursement on your return home.

Internet

Cyber cafés come and go but there are always a sufficient number to make internet access easy, even in small towns, where the local library usually has a couple of PCs. Rates are generally $1–2 an hour and note that the "@" sign is usually achieved by pressing ALT, "6" and "4" keys simultaneously. Almost all hostels and most hotels now offer free wi-fi where internet connectivity is available.

Language

Spanish is the official language of Panama and the first language of over two million of the population, though a recorded thirteen other first languages are spoken across the country. The

---

ROUGH GUIDES TRAVEL INSURANCE

Rough Guides has teamed up with WorldNomads.com to offer great **travel insurance** deals. Policies are available to residents of over 150 countries, with cover for a wide range of **adventure sports**, 24hr emergency assistance, high levels of medical and evacuation cover and a stream of **travel safety information**. Roughguides.com users can take advantage of their policies online 24/7, from anywhere in the world – even if you're already travelling. And since plans often change when you're on the road, you can extend your policy and even claim online. Roughguides.com users who buy travel insurance with WorldNomads.com can also leave a positive footprint and donate to a community development project. For more information, go to ⓦ **roughguides.com/travel-insurance**.

latter are mainly indigenous but include Panamanian Creole English, preferred by around 100,000 Afro-Antillean Panamanians, primarily resident in Bocas, Colón and Panama City, and Cantonese or Hakka, spoken by around 60,000 Chinese-Panamanians. While many urban middle-class Panamanians speak **English**, some of whom are bilingual, the "everybody-speaks-English" myth is easily dispelled. Official estimates reckon around fourteen percent of the population can communicate in English but in small towns and rural areas you'll find many speak virtually no English and in a number of the remote indigenous communities some villagers, especially women, do not even speak Spanish. Your travel experience in the country will be greatly enhanced by learning at least the basics of Spanish before you arrive. The Contexts section of this guide is a useful starting point (see p.314).

Learning Spanish in Panama

A good way of getting to grips with Spanish is to attend a **language school**. This also gives you an entrance into Panamanian life, especially if you take up the cultural immersion or homestay options and become involved in the volunteering projects on offer. Most schools run an extra-curricular programme, which almost inevitably includes salsa classes and excursions, while some courses specialize in language learning combined with activities such as scuba diving or surfing.

Group, small group (2–4) and one-to-one tuition is usually available; group classes, the cheapest option, generally comprise four hours of lessons per day at rates of around $200–250 per week, not including board and lodging. Make sure the institution is registered, that staff are qualified and that the teaching methodology is not just "chalk and talk" before committing any money. ⓦgoabroad.com/language-study -abroad contains a list of recommended schools, but some of the more established ones are listed below.

LANGUAGE SCHOOLS

Habla Ya Panama Plaza Los Establos, Boquete 20–22 ⓣ 720 1294; also in Bocas Town on Av "G" Norte ⓣ 757 7352, ⓦ hablayapanama.com.

Spanish by the River Entrada a Palmira, Alto Boquete ⓣ 720 3456, ⓦ spanishatlocations.com.

Spanish by the Sea Calle 4a, behind *Hotel Bahía*, Bocas del Toro, Isla Colón ⓣ 757 9518, ⓦ spanishatlocations.com.

Spanish Panama Edif Americana, 1a, Vía Argentina, Panama City ⓣ 213 3121, ⓦ spanishpanama.com.

Laundry

Most mid-range and top-end hotels offer a **laundry** service, while aparthotels (see p.76) and some hostels have their own washing machines for guest use. Otherwise you have the choice of a *lavamático* (not as easy to locate in Panama City as in the provinces), an old-fashioned launderette, where you bundle your clothes into a machine, and then a dryer, paying no more than $3–5 for a load, including detergent and conditioner. The more ubiquitous *lavanderías*, which more closely resemble dry cleaners, usually cost slightly more, especially if you want clothes ironed.

Living and working in Panama

If you're setting up your own business or are a foreign retiree who can fulfil the basic requirements, securing a **residential visa** is easy. Otherwise, residential and work permits are not easily come by unless you have specialist skills and – in theory at least – the recruiting company is unable to employ a Panamanian.

It's possible to arrange **voluntary work**, which can be carried out on a tourist visa, in advance. Try one of the various reputable international agencies, such as Volunteer Abroad (ⓦgoabroad.com /volunteer–abroad), or directly through the websites of Panamanian organizations; alternatively you may be able to show up on the spot. Key areas include conservation or social development projects, usually in poor, marginalized communities. Before you plunge into volunteering, do your homework to ensure that the programme is both bona fide and sustainable and that you are sufficiently skilled and experienced for the job. If training is provided, ensure that there is adequate time devoted to it – often a problem if organizations are hard-stretched.

Volunteering in projects, particularly with marginalized or vulnerable groups, is fraught with ethical dilemmas, which usually have no easy or "right" solution and can have unexpected negative side effects. While a couple of weeks on a turtle monitoring project may be fine, it's rarely a good idea to drop into a social development project for such a short time since a constant rotation of volunteers can be unsettling for individuals and communities, especially for vulnerable groups such as orphaned children.

That said, there are several well-established **programmes** in Panama. In Bocas del Toro, turtle conservation projects abound (see p.236) and various other long-standing social operations include: SOS Children's Villages (Asociación Aldeas Infantiles SOS de Panamá, Ⓦ sos-childrensvillages .org), which work with orphaned children; Fundación Pro Niños de Darién (Ⓦ darien.org.pa), an NGO operating in over a hundred communities in the Darién, aiming to improve child nutrition through health education and the development of sustainable agricultural practices; and Nutrehogar (Ⓦ nutrehogar.org), which also focuses on child health. Various language schools (see p.45) also have volunteer programmes.

Mail

It is reliable, but if speed is of the essence the standard Panamanian **postal service** is probably not for you; a postcard from Panama can take five to ten days to reach North America or Europe (45¢ stamp) and a couple of weeks or longer to meander to Europe (both 45¢ stamp), Australasia or South Africa (60¢ stamp). While post offices (*correos*) are relatively elusive in Panama City (see p.86), they are more visible in the provinces; they are marked on our maps. Opening hours (generally Mon–Fri 8am–5pm; Sat 8am–noon) vary. For a speedier delivery, send your letter or parcel express from the post office, though this service is not valid for Europe. Alternatively, use one of the more expensive private mailing or courier services widely available such as Fedex (Ⓦ fedex.com/pa/) or Mail Boxes Etc. (Ⓦ mbe.com).

Post offices also offer an *entrega general* (**poste restante**) service, keeping letters for up to a month. Passport ID needs to be shown when claiming post and you can't collect on behalf of another person. The sender should address items as follows: receiver's name, *Entrega General*, name of town, name of province, Republica de Panamá. If you are receiving post in Panama City then the postal zone also needs to be specified – enquire at the branch in question.

Maps

Both country and city **maps** of Panama are increasing in number and quality though there's still some way to go. There are also some rudimentary trail maps for the parks in the former Canal Zone, usually available from the park offices. International Travel Maps (1:300,000; available online at Ⓦ itmb .com and Ⓦ amazon.com; $13) – updated in 2012 – and National Geographic (Ⓦ nationalgeographic .com) both produce good maps of Panama. In **Panama** itself, large-scale maps are available at the Instituto Geográfico Nacional Tommy Guardia (Mon–Fri 8.30am–4pm) on Avenida Simón Bolívar,

opposite the entrance to the university in Panama City, though some are several years out of date and would really only be of use if you were planning some wilderness hiking.

Money

Panama adopted **US dollars** (referred to as *dólares* or *balboas*) as its currency in 1904, shortly after separation from Colombia. Apart from a seven-day print flurry in 1941, producing what is known as the "seven-day-dollar" (now a collector's item), the country has always used US paper currency, though it mints its own coinage: 1, 5, 10, 25 and 50 centavo pieces, and a dollar coin, which are used alongside US coins. Both $100 and $50 notes are often difficult to spend, so try to have $10 or $20 as the largest denominations you carry.

Cards

With over a thousand **ATMs** across the country, the most convenient way to access your money is by drawing some out on a credit card (you'll need your PIN number). Most home banks charge a fee for credit-card withdrawal – check before departure – and all ATMs in Panama levy $3 per transaction. Visa and MasterCard are the most widely accepted **credit cards** across the country, both at ATMs (recognizable by the red *Sistema Clave* sign outside) and to pay for services such as plane tickets, tourist hotels, restaurants, goods in shops and car rental. **Debit cards** such as Maestro and Cirrus are valid in many ATMs though they sometimes do not actually work in practice. Banistmo, which took over HSBC in Panama, is the best bank to seek out if you wish to withdraw cash against your credit card.

Most establishments in Bocas del Toro, Guna Yala and the Darién only accept cash and denominations of $20 and below are preferred because of problems with counterfeit $50 and $100 notes. Note also that heading into a major holiday weekend, ATMs may run out of money, especially if there is only one machine in town.

You should inform your bank at home that you are travelling to Panama before your departure so that they don't block your credit card.

Note that there is only one ATM in the whole of Guna Yala (in Narganá), one in the archipelago of Bocas del Toro (in Bocas Town, Isla Colón), and only two in the Darién (in Metetí and La Palma).

Banks, travellers' cheques and transfers

Most **banks** are open from 8am to 3pm Monday to Friday, and from 9am to noon on Saturday, though busier branches in the capital have extended hours; almost all branches have ATMs, as do many large supermarkets.

It is difficult to change foreign currency in Panama – change any cash into US dollars as soon as you can. In Panama City there are branches of the Banco Nacional de Panamá at the airport and on Vía España in the El Cangrejo district, or you could try Panacambios, a *casa de cambio* also on Vía España. Foreign banks will generally change their own currencies.

Travellers' cheques are best used as a back-up, if at all, since they are rarely accepted outside banks and even some branches of Panama's three major banks – Banco Nacional, Banistmo and Banco General – refuse to handle them. American Express cheques in dollars are your best bet. Be sure to keep the purchase agreement and a record of the cheques' serial numbers safe and separate from the cheques themselves. In the event of loss, contact the issuing company immediately – they should be able to replace the cheques within 24 hours.

Money transfers can easily be carried out through Western Union (Ⓦ westernunion.com), which has over one hundred offices sprinkled round the isthmus, with a concentration in Panama City.

Bargaining and tipping

Bargaining for goods is not the norm in Panama. If you're buying several items from a single stall in a craft market you can usually negotiate a slight discount (*descuento*), but it's rarely the lengthy social ritual it can be in some countries. Bear in mind too that while $40 for an intricate *mola* or $70 for a Panama hat may seem like a lot, they are likely to have taken several weeks to make.

Tipping is not universally expected and should be reserved for good service. While ten percent is customary in mid-range (or above) restaurants, it should not be automatic. In local *fondas* you might round up a $2.80 lunch to $3. Porters in hotels are usually tipped $0.50–1 per bag; the going rate at Tocumen airport is $1 per bag. In hotels you might consider leaving a tip of $1–2 per day for the person who has cleaned your room, but it's not *de rigueur*. It's not usual to tip taxi drivers or guides on organized tours. If, however, you hire the services of an ANAM park warden (*guardaparque*) to take you on a guided hike, you should ask what the going rate is; if there isn't one, $15 should be adequate for a full-day outing.

Overtipping is not helpful; it sets a precedent which other travellers may not be able to live up to, and can upset the micro-economy, particularly in small villages.

Opening hours

Opening hours vary but generally businesses are open Monday to Saturday from 8–9am to 5–6pm. Government office hours are Monday to Friday 8.30am–3.30pm. Shops usually open their doors Monday to Saturday from 9am to 6pm, though places selling souvenirs and crafts to tourists may open on Sundays too and Chinese-Panamanian supermarkets often open early (6.30–7am) until late (10pm–midnight); some of the larger outlets of the major supermarket chains, eg Super 99, Extra and El Rey, operate 24 hours.

Churches rarely have official opening hours and are all free to visit; most are open from around 8am until early evening, with the odd one closing for lunch.

Phones

Telephone boxes are found even in the smallest of villages, where the lone phone box – assuming it works – may be the community's only means of communication with the outside world. Easy to use, with instructions in English as well as Spanish, some phones accept both coins (5, 10 and 25 centavos) and cards; others only accept pre-paid phonecards (generally $3, $5, $10) purchasable at shops, Cable and Wireless offices and local pharmacies. Note that some cards can only be used for either international or local calls but not both. Seven-digit phone numbers denote **landlines** – the first three digits comprise the area code, whereas eight-digit numbers are for **mobile phones**.

Making a call

To make a call **to Panama** you need to dial the international prefix (generally 00), followed by 507 – the country code for Panama – followed by the number. Phoning out **from Panama** you need to prefix the country code (UK – 44; Ireland – 353; US & Canada – 1; Australia – 61; New Zealand – 64; South Africa – 27) with 00. Local calls to landlines anywhere in Panama cost a pittance and are usually free from a hotel room. International calls are also relatively

> ### USEFUL PHONE NUMBERS
> **Police**, including Transit Police ☎104
> **Ambulance**: Red Cross ☎455; Seguro Social ☎107 – both are free
> **Directory enquiries** ☎102
> **International operator** ☎106

cheap provided you do not use a hotel phone. Some internet cafés (and Cable & Wireless offices) also have phone booths and offer decent rates for international calls as well as a degree of comfort, quiet and privacy. Off-peak time for international calls is between 6pm and 6am and weekends.

Mobile phones

Mobile phones have mushroomed in Panama, which now has as many different numbers – almost three and a half million – as it does people. Mobiles have transformed the lives of some indigenous communities that live far from the main population centres, and can be very useful for travellers too, especially in the more remote areas when wanting to confirm transport or a reservation from a dugout in the Darién. Crucially, though, **coverage** varies among the four service providers of Mas Móvil (from Cable & Wireless), Digicel, Movistar and Clarocom in particular regions: especially in the Darién and Guna Yala, where your need is likely to be greatest. Enquire before you purchase. If you have an unlocked mobile phone on an 850 GSM (the setting for much of the Americas), you can easily purchase a SIM card on arrival from numerous corner shops in Panama City, or even online before you depart. Once the initial credit has expired, pre-paid airtime cards are available at shops around the country. Incoming calls are all free in Panama. Alternatively, you might consider renting a mobile or satellite phone; the executive business hotels can usually procure one for you.

Photography

The dazzling sunlight of any tropical country, especially in the dry season, can make it difficult to take decent **photographs**. The best times for the light are just after dawn and late afternoon to dusk, but since the sun rises and sets quickly it doesn't give you much time. If you need to purchase any photographic equipment, such as camera batteries or memory cards, Panafoto in Panama City (see ⓦ panafoto.com) is really your only bet.

People are fascinating subjects, but be sensitive. If you want to photograph one or more people, rather than a market scene with people in it, you should ask their permission. In indigenous villages in particular, ask the village chief or the head of the tourist committee what the protocol is – some villages do not permit photography. Tour groups to a village may be encouraged to snap away but you should still ask for permission from the individuals concerned. In Guna Yala, in particular, each island has its own regulations (see p.261).

Senior travellers

Given that Panama is one of the world's top **retirement** destinations, especially for North Americans, Panamanians are well used to meeting older foreign travellers. Though senior Panamanian and resident foreign retirees are eligible for incredible **discounts** on everything from flights to cinema tickets, visitors generally are not.

Time

Panama is four hours behind Greenwich Mean Time throughout the year, the same as Eastern Standard Time in the US, though note time changes for daylight-saving hours. Panama is one hour ahead of Costa Rica. If in doubt, consult ⓦ timeanddate.com.

Toilets

Public toilets are thin on the ground in Panama. You will generally find them in airports and bus terminals, which require payment of a few cents to an attendant, who in return will hand you an inadequate few sheets of paper – always travel with an emergency toilet roll. Other options are fast-food joints and cafeterias, and petrol stations. Most places outside top-end or very modern hotels with their own septic system require you to throw used toilet paper into an adjacent basket – alas sometimes missing altogether from the most rudimentary establishments. In Guna Yala and parts of Bocas, a toilet cistern is no guarantee of a water treatment system; everything may still flush straight out to sea.

Tourist information

The official **tourist agency** is the Autoridad de Turismo Panamá (ATP; ⓦ atp.gob.pa); it has a slowly improving website (in English too) at ⓦ visit panama.com. The recent tourist boom has caused a number of swanky new air-conditioned tourist offices to be built in many of the major towns and resort areas though unfortunately most are not yet geared up to assisting passing tourists; nor is the website much help. You may be lucky enough to get a map and, if you have a specific question, the employee will probably do their best to help you, but do not expect lists of local accommodation or tourist attractions, nor assume the person will speak English. **Reception staff** at a good hostel or hotel are a far better bet for reliable information.

The Visitor/El Visitante (ⓦ thevisitorpanama.com), a free, weekly tourist promotion **magazine** in English and Spanish, omnipresent in hotels and touristy restaurants throughout the country, lists attractions and upcoming events. See p.82 and p.226 for other sources. Panama's **national parks** and other protected areas, which encompass many of Panama's natural wonders, are administered by the National Environment Agency, ANAM (Ⓦanam.gob .pa; see p.39).

Travellers with disabilities

Organized tourism is in its infancy in Panama and awareness of the needs and rights of **people with disabilities** is a fairly recent phenomenon – they were only granted equal rights by law in 1999. As a result, Panama isn't really geared up to accommodate travellers with disabilities. That said, Tocumen International Airport has disabled access and many mid-range and luxury hotels in Panama City have facilities for people with disabilities, although as elsewhere in the world "disabled facilities" tends to be synonymous with "wheelchair access" rather than spanning the spectrum of special needs. The three resorts mentioned in "Travelling with children" (see below) also advertise "disabled access" and most cruise ships that take in Panama tend to be suitably equipped. Eco-Adventure International (Ⓦeaiadventure.com) runs several tours to Panama for travellers with disabilities and senior travellers, though unlike Costa Rica the country does not yet feature as a destination on the dozens of other disability specialist travel websites (see Ⓦdisabled travelers.com, Ⓦwheeltheworld.net or Ⓦflying -with-disability.org), which are nonetheless worth consulting for general travel advice and useful links on flying and travel agents.

Travelling with children

Latin cultures are very family-oriented and Panama is no exception. While there is no pre-packaged entertainment for **children** such as theme parks, there's plenty for kids to enjoy, including boat trips, snorkelling, horseriding, exploring the canal and walking in the rainforest. Many **hotels** have extra beds or pull-outs in rooms for children and under-12s are often free, with older kids admitted at discount rates. The large resort hotels – the *Decameron* at Farallón on the Pacific coast, the *Hotel Meliá* on Lago Gatún and the *Gamboa Rainforest Resort* – have special activities laid on and child-minding services. Small B&Bs and eco-lodges whose staff are concerned that kids may spoil the tranquillity sometimes do not permit children or have a minimum age of 12 or 14.

Habla Ya Language Centre (Ⓦhablayapanama .com) in Boquete offers family and children's **Spanish courses**, while various tour operators in the UK and North America (check out Ⓦwildland .com in the US, Ⓦfamilytours.co.uk in the UK, and Ⓦaudleytravel.com for both the US and UK) now include **family-oriented itineraries** in Panama. Travelling to Guna Yala and to the Darién, which can be challenging enough for adults, would be hard work with kids in tow unless you stay at the few high-end establishments. Sticking to Panama City and the canal area, the Pacific beach resorts, El Valle, Bocas and Boquete would be much easier and more enjoyable all round, especially if you're on a modest budget.

Women travellers

It is perfectly safe for women to travel alone in Panama. In **urban areas**, you might get the odd cat-call or hiss and going alone to a bar in Panama City or a rural *cantina* the hassle is likely to be greater. In more **rural areas**, you may get some surprised looks and, depending on your age, questions about your presumed husband and children. In general you are likely to be treated with courtesy. As regards safety at night – in Panama City and Colón primarily but in other urban centres too – the same common-sense precautions apply as in cities in any country you're travelling in and whether female or male.

Panama City

1

Panama City

Proudly positioned in the crook of land overlooking the Pacific, the soaring skyline of Panama City surveys the ocean before it, much as Vasco Nuñez de Balboa did when he chanced upon the body of water after a bloody journey south across the isthmus almost five hundred years ago. From its inception, the city has been situated on one of the world's great crossroads, and it has thrived on trade, attracting migrants from all over the world to a cosmopolitan melting pot bubbling with energy and ambition. Panama has long been considered a bridge between two continents and nowhere is this divided identity more apparent than in the capital, where glitzy skyscrapers, laser-lit nightclubs and chic restaurants more reminiscent of Miami than Latin America are juxtaposed with colonial churches, clamouring street vendors and chaotic traffic. Though it is the undisputed political, economic and social centre of Panama and home to 1.3 million – just over a third of the country's population – the city has very little in common with the rest of the country, which is often vaguely referred to as "el interior".

On the southwest end of the bay stands the old city centre of **Casco Viejo**, a jumble of immaculately restored colonial buildings, crumbling ruins and run-down housing on a rocky promontory, while a few kilometres to the northeast rise the shimmering skyscrapers of **El Cangrejo** and **Marbella**, the modern banking and commercial district, and the penthouse apartments of **Punta Paitilla** and **Punta Pacífica**. Further east, amid sprawling suburbs whose tentacles extend 30km along the coast, stand the ruins of **Panamá Viejo**, the first European city to be founded on the Pacific coast of the Americas, while west of the city centre the former US Canal Zone town of **Balboa**, with its clipped lawns and restrained utilitarian architecture, retains a distinctly North American character despite having been turned over to full Panamanian control in 1999. In the background, the Panamanian flag proudly flies on the summit of **Cerro Ancón**, a surprising oasis of greenery on what was once a major US military base.

For the vast majority of visitors to Panama, the capital provides their first point of contact. Many spend their entire stay here, since it makes a good base from which to explore many of the country's attractions while enjoying the material comforts of sophisticated city living – the canal, a handful of national parks and the Caribbean coast as far as Portobelo can all be visited on **day-trips**. Other visitors, keen to leave behind the frenzied construction and thronging streets and escape into the country's outstanding wilderness areas, still linger a couple of days to savour the colonial architecture of Casco Viejo and the vitality of the modern city, including its many bars and restaurants.

While it is easy to tire of Panama City's irrepressible energy, oppressive heat and relentless traffic, it's as simple to escape to nearby places of real tranquillity: the **Amador Causeway**, a breezy breakwater offering fabulous views of the canal and the city skyline;

Walking up Cerro Ancón p.69
Panamá Viejo's treasure trail p.71
Major domestic bus routes p.73

Diablos Rojos p.74
Las chivas parranderas p.82
Sports and leisure in Panama City p.85

PARQUE SANTA ANA

Highlights

❶ Casco Viejo Perched on a rocky promontory, the evocative colonial centre has ancient churches, leafy plazas and grand buildings. **See p.56**

❷ Amador Causeway The perfect afternoon promenade, soaking up the views while marvelling at the architecture of Frank Gehry's biodiversity museum, before a sundowner on Isla Flamenco. **See p.67**

❸ Cerro Ancón Vantage point offering an unparalleled panorama of the city's towering skyscrapers and imposing canal. **See p.68**

❹ Parque Natural Metropolitano This patch of tropical rainforest within the city limits

provides the perfect spot to hone your birdwatching skills. **See p.70**

❺ Panamá Viejo The crumbling remains of the original Panama City, set in mud flats and mangroves on the outer limits of the metropolis. **See p.70**

❻ Nightlife From cocktails on the rooftops of skyscrapers to cheap beer in low-key indie bars, from salsa techno or reggaeton in outdoor discos to upmarket dining in the colonial centre, Panama City has it all. **See p.82**

❼ Isla Taboga The perfect day-trip from the bustle of the city, offering a lovely boat trip across the mouth of the canal, a laidback fishing village and pleasant scenic walks. **See p.86**

HIGHLIGHTS ARE MARKED ON THE MAP ON P.54

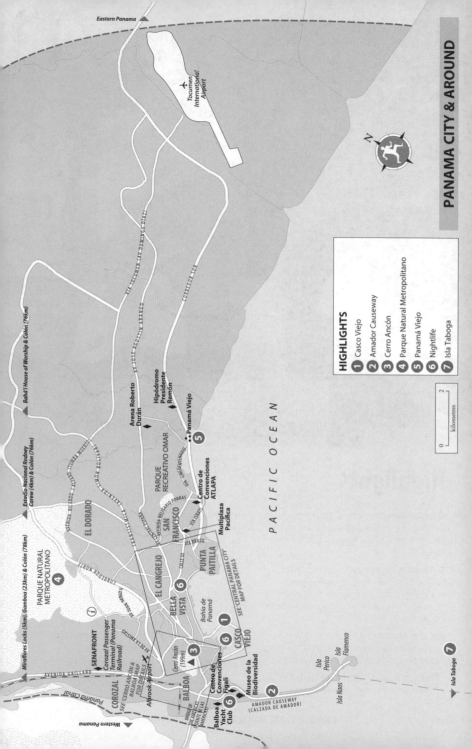

PANAMA CITY & AROUND

HIGHLIGHTS

1. Casco Viejo
2. Amador Causeway
3. Cerro Ancón
4. Parque Natural Metropolitano
5. Panamá Viejo
6. Nightlife
7. Isla Taboga

0   2
kilometres

Eastern Panama

Tocumen International Airport

Western Panama

Miraflores Locks (5km), Gamboa (23km) & Colón (78km)

Panamá Canal

AVENIDA GAILLARD

Bahá'í House of Worship & Colón (76km)

Estadio Nacional Rodney Carew (4km) & Colón (76km)

PARQUE NATURAL METROPOLITANO

Arena Roberto Durán

Hipódromo Presidente Remón

Panamá Viejo

Parque Recreativo Omar

Centro de Convenciones ATLAPA

PACIFIC OCEAN

EL DORADO

CORREDOR NORTE

SAN FRANCISCO

EL CANGREJO

BELLA VISTA

PUNTA PAITILLA

Multiplaza Pacífica

VIA BRASIL

Bahía de Panamá

SEE 'CENTRAL PANAMA CITY MAP' FOR DETAILS

SENAFRONT

Corozal Passenger Terminal (Panama Railroad)

COROZAL

SEE 'CERRO ANCÓN & BALBOA MAP' FOR DETAILS

Albrook Airport

Cerro Ancón (199m)

BALBOA

Centro de Convenciones Figali

Museo de la Biodiversidad

Balboa Yacht Club

BRIDGE OF THE AMERICAS (PUENTE DE LAS AMÉRICAS)

CASCO VIEJO

AMADOR CAUSEWAY (CALZADA DE AMADOR)

Isla Naos

Isla Perico

Isla Flamenco

Isla Taboga

Isla Taboga, the sleepy "Island of Flowers" an hour's boat ride off the coast; or the **Parque Natural Metropolitano**, the only natural tropical rainforest within the limits of a Latin American capital.

Brief history

Founded by the conquistador Pedro Arias de Ávila, better known as **Pedrarias**, in 1519, Panama City quickly flourished as the base for further Spanish conquest along the Pacific coast, and later as the pivotal transit point for plundered treasure from South America and traded goods from the east bound for Spain. By the mid-seventeenth century Panama City had a population of around five thousand, its customs house, cathedral and convents comprising some of the grandest constructions in the New World. The city's opulence invited numerous attacks by the **pirates** then ravaging the Spanish Main, and in 1671 the Welsh buccaneer **Henry Morgan** sacked the city (see p.294), which was engulfed in flames. Known as **Panamá Viejo**, the ruins of Pedrarias's settlement still stand amid the sprawling suburbs of the modern city, and have been partially restored in recent years as a tourist attraction (see pp.70–72).

Two years after Morgan's assault, the settlement was relocated on a rocky peninsula jutting out into the bay 8km to the southwest, a more defendable and salubrious site than its swampy predecessor. Named **Panamá Nuevo**, the new city developed in the area known today as **Casco Viejo**.

The gold rush and the railroad

Once the Spanish had rerouted their treasure fleet around Cape Horn in 1746, Panama City's commercial importance slowly began to decline, only substantially picking up again in the mid-nineteenth century due to the isthmus's popularity as a transit point in the **California Gold Rush** and the completion of the **Panama Railroad** in 1855. The railroad, and subsequently the French and US canal construction efforts, brought immense prosperity and a wealth of new cultural influences that transformed the city and its inhabitants, who by 1920 totalled almost sixty thousand.

The canal

The **canal**, completed in 1914, confirmed Panama City's importance as a global trading centre; yet it immediately became a straightjacket for the capital, as the outbreak of World War I, two weeks prior to the waterway's official inauguration, opened the floodgates to large-scale **US military occupation** of the Panama Canal Zone, the 8km strip of land either side of the waterway under US jurisdiction. During World War II, defence installations proliferated and the predominantly US population topped one hundred thousand. Though other migrants continued to pour in, the lives of the city's population were regulated by the US military in the adjacent Canal Zone, who controlled everything from refuse collection and water supply to construction permits, and whose affluence and spending power inevitably shaped commercial development. No surprise then that Panama City found itself at the forefront of increasing nationalist sentiment that periodically erupted into violence, most notably in the flag riots of 1964 (see p.299). Only after the handover of the canal had been assured, in the canal treaty of 1977, could the capital, and the country, start to plan its own path.

Modern times

The introduction of banking secrecy laws in the 1970s led to the rapid expansion of the financial services sector, including an influx of **narco-dollars**. Despite the tightening of banking regulations, El Cangrejo remains a hive of intrigue and some of the luxury high-rise apartments there and in Punta Paitilla stand empty, the astronomical rents paid by their fictitious occupants providing a useful means of laundering money. With the handover of the last US bases to Panamanian control at the end of 1999, huge amounts of real estate were made available, enabling the city to expand further, though

1

its spread inland is still checked by the backdrop of hills that form the protected
Panama Canal Basin.

Casco Viejo

Most of Panama City's historical monuments and tourist attractions are concentrated
in the colonial city centre of **San Felipe** – more commonly called **Casco Viejo**
(sometimes Casco Antiguo) these days – which makes it the best place to start your
tour of the capital. For centuries the heart of Panama City's social and political life,
and still home to the presidential palace, Casco Viejo, after decades of neglect, was
declared a UNESCO World Heritage Site in 1997 and is gradually being restored to
its former glory. Now upmarket restaurants and cafés sit alongside chic offices and
apartments in renovated colonial buildings, but the poor families talking on the
doorsteps of crumbling, scarcely habitable houses are just as much part of the
neighbourhood. Ongoing restoration projects are making it a much more pleasant
place to visit and the increased police presence – including the highly visible tourist
police, often on bicycles – ensures greater safety. Note that caution should still be
exercised when walking around at night; stick to the well-lit streets.

Avenida Central

The best way to see Casco Viejo is on foot – you can reach it from the rest of the city
by taxi or by taking any bus to Plaza Cinco de Mayo, then walking up **Avenida Central**,

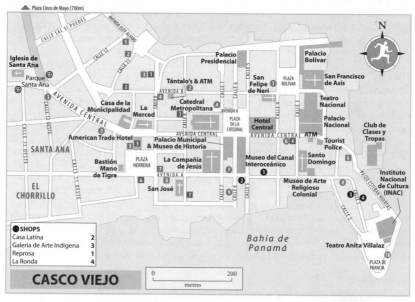

■ ACCOMMODATION		● CAFÉS & RESTAURANTS				■ BARS & CLUBS			
American Trade Hotel	5	Las Bóvedas	10	Diablo Rosso	9	Danilo's Jazz Club	5	Onplog	2
Las Clementinas	2	Café Coca-Cola	3	The Fish Market	5	Espacio	4	Platea	6
Los Cuatro Tulipanes	4	Caffè Per Due	8	Granclement	6	Habana Panamá	1	Relic	3
Hospedaje Casco Viejo	7	Casa Sucre	2	René Café	4	Mojitos (sin Mojitos)	7	Villa Agustina	8
Luna's Castle	1	Casablanca	1	Super Gourmet	7				
Magnolia Inn	3								
Panamericana	6								

past Parque Santa Ana and the famous *Café Coca Cola*, as it narrows into a cobbled street, passing through the now invisible city walls into the historic centre. The rows of lottery ticket sellers – who number over ten thousand across the country – doing a brisk trade on the left-hand pavement provide an obvious clue to the function of the striking blue-and-white-striped Art Deco building – one of two homes of the national lottery (the other lies on Avenida Perú). A stone's throw further along on the left is the gleaming white and cream Neoclassical **Casa de la Municipalidad**, seat of the city's government.

Iglesia de la Merced
C 10 at Av Central

Next door to the Casa de la Municipalidad stands the crumbling Baroque facade of the city's oldest church, **Iglesia de la Merced**, which in 1680 was reconstructed on its present site using the original stones from Panamá Viejo. The facade is the best-preserved section of the church, which gives way inside to some poorly conceived twentieth-century restoration work, though the gilded wooden altar retains some appeal.

Plaza de la Catedral
Craft market daily 8am–6pm; flea market first non-bank-holiday Sunday of the month 10am–5pm

Midway down Avenida Central the street opens out into the old quarter's most impressive square, **Plaza de la Catedral**, also known as Plaza Mayor and Plaza de la Independencia since the proclamations of independence from Spain and separation from Colombia were made here, in which the *Grand Hotel*, on the east side of the plaza and under restoration, played a starring role. Numerous busts of the nation's founding fathers are scattered beneath the shady trees surrounding the striking central gazebo, with the Republic's first president, Manuel Amador Guerrero, taking pride of place. In the seventeenth and eighteenth centuries, the space was used for bullfights and theatrical presentations, becoming a park at the end of the nineteenth century, now frequented by elderly residents reading the paper and occasional street vendors.

A daily **craft market**, Artesanías Maggy, is tucked away in the southwestern corner of the square, and a small **flea market** is held in the plaza once a month, with stalls selling arts, crafts and bric-a-brac. In the summer months the square often hosts free evening concerts.

La Catedral
Plaza de la Catedral • No fixed opening hours • Free

Flanked by white towers sparkling with inlaid mother-of-pearl, the hybrid Neoclassical and Baroque olive and cream sandstone facade of the **Catedral Metropolitana** dominates the square. It was built between 1688 and 1796 using some of the stone brought from the ruins of Panamá Viejo (see pp.70–72). Three of its bells were also recovered from its ruined predecessor, and reputedly owe their distinctive tone to a gold ring thrown by Queen Isabella I of Spain into the molten metal from which they were cast. The cathedral's interior is tatty in places, though the large altarpiece carved from seven types of Italian marble is suitably imposing. To its right lies a trapdoor marking the entrance to tunnels – not open to visitors – designed as escape routes, connecting the cathedral to the churches of La Merced and San José.

Museo de Historia de Panamá
Palacio Municipal, Plaza de la Catedral • Mon–Fri 8.30am–3.30pm • $1 • ☎ 228 6231

Southeast of the cathedral is the **Palacio Municipal**, a splendid example of Neoclassical architecture. Originally constructed in 1910 on the site of the former city hall, its

1

ground floor houses the **Museo de Historia de Panamá**, which offers a cursory introduction to Panamanian history, focusing on symbols of independence such as the national flag, the national anthem and the coat of arms, alongside an eclectic mixture of maps and artefacts, with explanations in Spanish. Despite some recent interactive additions, it will probably only appeal to history buffs. The languorous nude reclining in the entrance hall represents Panama bathing in the waters of the two oceans.

Museo del Canal Interoceánico

Plaza de la Catedral • Mon–Fri 9am–5pm • $2; audioguides in English or Spanish $3 extra • ☎ 211 1649, ⓦ museodelcanal.com

Housed in a three-storey French colonial building, complete with mansard roof and shutters, the excellent **Museo del Canal Interoceánico** offers a comprehensive account of both the French and US endeavours to build a canal across the isthmus, and of the protracted handover of the canal to Panama's control (see p.294, p.297 & p.300).

The highly polished marble entrance hall bears witness to the museum's former life as the city's grandest hotel. The bulk of the exhibition lies on the **second floor**, expounding the history of the transisthmian route, from the first Spanish attempt to find a passage to Asia to the contemporary management of the canal. Although the museum is rather text-heavy (in Spanish – the most conspicuous sign in English asks visitors to refrain from sitting on an original Panama Railroad waiting-room bench), there are plenty of photographs, video montages and maps offering striking comparisons between the different working conditions of the French and US canal eras which bring to life the enormity of the achievements.

The **third floor** displays cover the apartheid living conditions of gold and silver roll employees (see p.298), more information and artefacts from the US canal drama and a barrage of press reports on the deteriorating Panamanian–US relations that eventually led to the handover of the canal. The museum has wheelchair access and a small **shop** selling modern and original canal memorabilia. Take a sweater as the air conditioning is fierce.

Palacio Presidencial

Between C 6 and C 5 • To arrange a free guided tour, a letter in Spanish suggesting possible dates needs to be emailed or hand-delivered to the Oficina de Guías (Mon–Fri 8.30am–3.30pm; ☎ 527 9740, ask for Sra Griselda Bernal, ✉ gbernal@presidencia.gob.pa), round the back of the yellow building on the waterfront by C 4; visits (Tues, Thurs & Fri mornings) last about an hour – bring your passport • Free

Originally built in 1673 for an unscrupulous colonial judge, who embezzled state funds to furnish his opulent mansion, the **Palacio Presidencial** later served as a customs house, teacher training college and even a prison before being rebuilt in 1922 as the presidential residence in grandiose neo-Moorish style under the orders of President Belisario Porras. It is commonly known as the "Palacio de las Garzas" after the white egrets given to Porras by his poet friend Ricardo Miró, and they have lived freely around the patio fountain ever since. The pair of elegant blue cranes that also stalk the patio were donated by the South African government. The streets around the palace are closed to traffic and pedestrians but the presidential guards allow visitors access via Calle 5 to view the exterior of the building during the day.

It is also possible to go on a free **guided tour** of the palace, which is well worth the hassle even though it only covers a few rooms and requires organizing several days in advance (see above). After admiring the marble floor and mother-of-pearl encrusted columns of the Moorish vestibule, the tour moves up to the first floor and the long *Salón Amarillo* (Yellow Hall), used for official ceremonies. From the presidential throne to the gilt mirrors and heavy drapes, the room is replete with shades of gold, amber and mustard, while striking murals by Roberto Lewis offer a selective romp through Panama's history. In the adjoining *Comedor del Palacio* (Dining Room), where state banquets are held, Lewis's distinctive murals are even more prominent, depicting idyllic country scenes. At the far end of the dining room a door leads off to the *Salón del Cabinete* (Cabinet Room), which contains portraits of all Panama's presidents. In addition to these main rooms, the tour allows you a peek at some of the splendidly tiled Moorish-themed anterooms.

Plaza Bolívar and around

A block back from the waterfront on Avenida B, elegant **Plaza Bolívar**, dotted with manicured trees, provides the perfect spot for a glass of wine or a meal at its pavement café-restaurants, though at lunchtime the peace is periodically interrupted by the cries of primary-school children spilling out of class seeking out snow-cones (*raspados*) from the waiting vendors. On the eastern side, next to the Palacio Bolívar (see below), the seventeenth-century **Iglesia y Convento de San Francisco de Asís**, with its imposing bell tower, is finally being restored after being closed for several years.

Monument to Simón Bolívar

Rebuilt after a fire in 1756, the plaza was dedicated in 1883 to **Simón Bolívar**, whose central **statue**, crowned by a condor, dominates the space. The monument was erected in 1926 to commemorate one hundred years since the Amphyctionic Congress, the first **Panamerican gathering**, organized by Bolívar, aimed at unifying the newly independent Latin American countries in their relations with Spain. Although "El Libertador" (The Liberator) failed to attend the congress, and his dreams of unity ultimately foundered, it was considered a historic event.

Palacio Bolívar and the Salón Bolívar

East side of Plaza Bolívar • Mon–Fri 8.30am–3.30pm • Free

The **Palacio Bolívar**, whose impressive peach and white facade extends along the eastern edge of the square, is well worth a peek inside.

Having served as part of a convent, military barracks and a school at various times, the building now houses the Ministry of Foreign Affairs, among other government offices. It has also been beautifully restored, providing the courtyard – the **Plaza de los Libertadores** – with a magnificent translucent roof allowing in lots of natural light. From a raised platform at the far side a bronze bust of the visionary Liberator looks on. To the right as you enter is the **Salón Bolívar**, formerly the chapter house of a Franciscan monastery where the Amphyctionic Congress took place, and now a small museum. It contains a replica of the Liberator's gold ceremonial sword, encrusted with over a thousand diamonds, and the congress's original documents.

Iglesia San Felipe de Neri

Corner of Plaza Bolívar, at Av "B" and C 4 • Daily 7am–7pm • Free

After being closed for a number of years, first for restoration and then on account of a dispute within the diocese, the airy vaults of **Iglesia San Felipe de Neri** are finally open to the public. Built in 1688 it was one of the earliest churches; it has served as a shrine to the cathedral and then, much later, as a children's home and orphanage.

Teatro Nacional

Eastern end of Av "B" • Mon–Fri 9.30am–5pm • $1 • ☎ 262 3525

The handsome **Teatro Nacional** was one of the first grand national buildings to be commissioned by the newly independent state; it was built on the site of a former convent and designed by Italian architect Genaro Ruggieri. The magnificent Italianate Neoclassical edifice opened its doors to the public in 1908 to initial success but the global depression of the 1930s brought a slump in the venue's fortunes, and it became a cinema for a while before falling into neglect. Extensively restored in the early 1970s,

1

the theatre reopened in 1974 with a performance by Margot Fonteyn, the British ballerina and long-term Panama resident, whose bronze bust adorns the foyer, alongside that of Roberto Lewis, whose allegorical frescoes depicting the birth of the nation can be seen on the vaulted ceiling. The building was renovated again in the early 2000s, and it's well worth paying the $1 entry to poke around the splendid Baroque interior, though finding the building open can be a challenge. One of the best ways to enjoy the theatre's splendour is obviously to attend one of the occasional productions, which are sometimes free (see p.84).

The ramparts

Two hundred metres southeast of the Teatro Nacional, steps lead up to **Paseo Esteban Huertas**, a delightful, breezy, bougainvillea-covered promenade that runs some 400m along the top of what were the ramparts. The walkway along the defensive sea wall is a favourite haunt of smooching couples – earning it the nickname Paseo de los Inamorados – and Guna traders displaying their handicrafts to passing tourists. At the far end, before descending the steps into the Plaza de Francia, you get fine views across the bay. Peek over the wall here and you can glimpse the windows of the dungeons where prisoners were allegedly left at low tide to drown when the high tide flooded the cells.

Plaza de Francia

The **Plaza de Francia**, at the southeastern tip of Casco Viejo, is an irregularly shaped space bounded by the sea wall and the renovated arches of **Las Bóvedas** (vaults), Spanish dungeons that also functioned as storehouses, prison cells and barracks for the fort that occupied the plaza until the early twentieth century. They now contain a chic restaurant of the same name (see p.79). Formerly the Plaza de Armas, the city's main square, the space is dominated by a substantial monument dedicated to the thousands of workers who died during the disastrous French attempt to build the canal (see p.294). The central **obelisk** (with a secret door leading to a maintenance staircase behind one of the frieze panels) is topped by a proud Gallic cockerel and ringed by busts of the key figures involved, including Ferdinand de Lesseps, the French diplomat who first conceived of the canal yet whose ignorance and vanity were central to the project's ultimate failure. Behind, vast marble tablets chronologically outline the bare bones of the dream to build a transisthmian waterway.

The Neoclassical **French Embassy** overlooks the square from the north, fronted by a huge statue of former Panamanian president Pablo Arosemena. The large gleaming white building to the east is home to the **Instituto Nacional de Cultura** (INAC, the National Institute of Culture), the body responsible for maintaining the country's museums. It was spruced up for the James Bond film *Quantum of Solace*, in which it featured as a Bolivian hotel. Adjacent is the intimate Teatro Anita Villalaz (see p.84).

Iglesia y Convento de Santo Domingo

Av "A" at C 3 · Closed for restoration at the time of writing

At the ruined **Iglesia y Convento de Santo Domingo**, restoration work is continuing apace. Completed in 1678, it is most famous for the **Arco Chato** (flat arch) over its main entrance. Only 10.6m high, but spanning some 15m with no keystone or external support, it was reputedly cited as evidence of Panama's seismic stability when the US Senate was debating where to build a interoceanic canal. Ironically, the arch inexplicably collapsed just after the centenary celebrations for Panama's independence in 2003, but has subsequently been restored to its former glory.

Museo de Arte Religioso Colonial

Av "A" at C 3 • Mon–Fri 9.30am–3.30pm • Free

The single room of the **Museo de Arte Religioso Colonial** has a small collection of religious paintings, silverwork and sculpture from the colonial era. The detailed information panels will really only appeal to colonial history buffs who can read Spanish.

Iglesia de San José

Av "A" at C 8 • Mon–Fri 9am–noon & 2–5pm, Sat 9am–noon

The **Iglesia de San José**, built in 1673 but subsequently remodelled, is exceptional only as home to the legendary Baroque **Altar de Oro** (Golden Altar), which illuminates the otherwise gloomy interior. A carved mahogany extravaganza gilded with 22-carat gold leaf, it was one of the few treasures to survive Henry Morgan's ransacking of Panamá Viejo in 1671 thanks, apparently, to having been painted or covered in mud to disguise its true value. Legend has it that on being asked by Morgan where the gold was, the priest pleaded poverty to explain its absence, even persuading the buccaneer to make a donation to the church.

Plaza Herrera

At the western limit of Casco Viejo is **Plaza Herrera**, a pleasant square lined with elegant nineteenth-century houses. This was originally the Plaza de Triunfo, where bullfights were held until the mid-nineteenth century, but was renamed in 1887 in honour of General Tomás Herrera, whose equestrian statue stands in its centre. Herrera – after whom the Azuero Peninsula province is named – was the military leader of Panama's first short-lived independence attempt in 1840. Just off Plaza Herrera to the west stands **Bastión Mano de Tigre** (Tiger Hand Bastion), a crumbling and indistinct pile of masonry that is the last remaining section of the city's original defensive walls on the landward side. To the north a gleaming white facade announces the recently restored *American Trade Hotel* (see p.76), which dates back to 1917.

In contrast, tucked away at the western end of the square is a striking wooden residential building, named **La Boyacá** after a nineteenth-century gunboat, its front carved like the prow of a ship. Beyond, Avenida A heads into the poor barrio and no-go area of **El Chorrillo**, which was devastated during the US invasion, leaving hundreds dead and thousands homeless. It has since been rebuilt, but the coloured concrete tenements that replaced the old wooden slum housing are already run-down. Despite a substantial increase in police presence, drug gangs continue to run riot at night and the place is dangerous even during the day.

Parque Santa Ana

Parque Santa Ana, the social hub of the impoverished neighbourhood of Santa Ana, marks the transition between the old colonial centre of Casco Viejo and the more commercial modern city. As the centre of activity outside the city walls in the early nineteenth century it hosted colourful markets and bullfights; now it offers some respite from the swirling traffic, and is often populated by many of the locality's older residents, discussing the latest news. The pedestrianized section of Avenida Central starts on the park's northeastern side, where a row of shoe-shine booths provides another social focus.

Central Panama City

In contrast to the relative calm of the city's historical centre and ancient remains, the **modern city** streets of **central Panama City** reverberate with traffic noise and pavements

1

CENTRAL PANAMA CITY

Albrook Bus Terminal & Metro (1.5km) and Albrook Airport (2km) P.N. Metropolitano (1.5km)

Edificio de la Administración del Canal (300m)

CERRO ANCÓN

Corte Suprema de Justicia

Smithsonian Tropical Research Institute Earl S Tupper Centre

Cerro Ancón (199m)

Hospital

Museo de Arte Contemporáneo

Palacio Legislativo

Museo Afro-Antillano

Museo de Ciencias Naturales

Basilica Don Bosco

Archivos Nacionales

PLAZA PORRAS

AVENIDA PERÚ (1 SUR)

AVENIDA CUBA (2 SUR)

Marañon

AV DE LOS MÁRTIRES

PLAZA CINCO DE MAYO

5 de Mayo

Museo Antropológico Reina Torres de Arauz

AVENIDA JUSTO AROSEMENA (AV 3 SUR)

AVENIDA MÉXICO (4 SUR)

CALIDONIA

AV 5 SUR

AVENIDA BALBOA

Hospital Santo Tomás

Balboa Monument

EL CHORILLO

Mercado de Mariscos

Parque Santa Ana

SANTA ANA

CASCO VIEJO

SEE 'CASCO VIEJO' MAP

CALLE CURUNDÚ

AV 3 NORTE LUIS F. CLEMENT

AV 2 NORTE (J.F. DE LA ROSA)

AV 1 NORTE

VIA SIMÓN BOLIVAR

VIA ESPAÑA

LA

● CAFÉS & RESTAURANTS			
Athens Pizza	15	Niko's Café	12
Beirut	20	NY Bagel Café	2
Café Boulevard Balboa	24	Palacio Lung Fung	1
Café Suzette	3	La Papa	18
Caffè Pomodoro	5	Petit Paris	28
Churrería Manolo	4	Pita–Pan Kosher	29
Habibi's	23	La Posta	21
Loving Hut	6	Restaurante Jimmy	14
Machu Picchu	9	Restaurante de Mariscos	26
Manolo's	10	Rincón Habanero	8
The Market	25	Rincón El Tableño	17
Masala	13	Siete Mares	11
Mercado Público	27	Las Tinajas	19
Napoli	16	El Trapiche	7
Nelson's Café	22		

are packed with people squeezing in and out of the patchwork of shops, banks, hotels and restaurants or threading their way through street vendors, hawkers and other shoppers. Wedge-shaped central Panama City arguably stretches 3km round the Bahía de Panama, from Avenida Central and Plaza Cinco de Mayo – home to the central government buildings – to Punta Paitilla, encompassing the older residential and commercial districts of Calidonia and La Exposición, fanning out to include Bella Vista and the newer, plusher financial districts of Marbella and El Cangrejo.

Avenida Central

The pedestrianized stretch of **Avenida Central**, from Parque Santa Ana north as far as Plaza Cinco de Mayo, is one of the oldest and most colourful shopping districts. Blasts

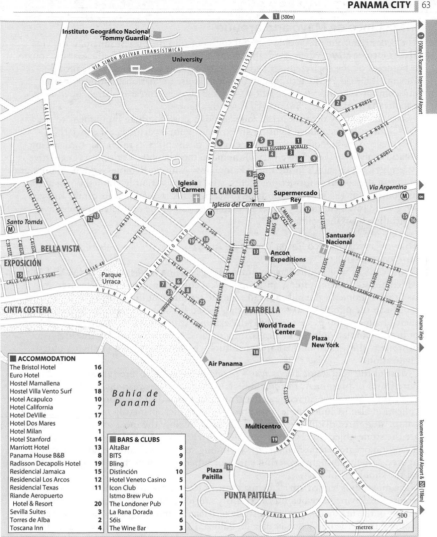

ACCOMMODATION	
The Bristol Hotel	16
Euro Hotel	6
Hostel Mamallena	5
Hostel Villa Vento Surf	18
Hotel Acapulco	10
Hotel California	7
Hotel DeVille	17
Hotel Dos Mares	9
Hotel Milan	1
Hotel Stanford	14
Marriott Hotel	13
Panama House B&B	8
Radisson Decapolis Hotel	19
Residencial Jamaica	15
Residencial Los Arcos	12
Residencial Texas	11
Riande Aeropuerto Hotel & Resort	20
Sevilla Suites	3
Torres de Alba	2
Toscana Inn	4

BARS & CLUBS	
AltaBar	8
BITS	9
Bling	9
Distinción	10
Hotel Veneto Casino	5
Icon Club	1
Istmo Brew Pub	4
The Londoner Pub	7
La Rana Dorada	2
Séis	6
The Wine Bar	3

of air conditioning and loud music pour out from the huge, predominantly Hindu-owned superstores that line the avenue selling cheap clothing, electronics and household goods, while on the street itself hawkers flog pirate DVDs and cheap sunglasses and vendors quench the thirst of shoppers with fruit or sugar cane juice. Nowhere is the enormous cultural diversity of the city more evident, a constant kaleidoscope of Hindus in saris, Kuna women in their traditional costumes, bearded Muslims in robes and skullcaps, *interioranos* in sombreros, Chinese, Afro-Antillanos and Latinos. In the evening, in the pedestrianized area round Cinco de Mayo, extra food stalls pop up selling kebabs and sausages and as the night wears on, prostitutes tout for custom. Exercise caution when walking round the streets either side of Avenida Central and north of the Parque Santa Ana, and avoid wandering around the side streets at night.

1

Plaza Cinco de Mayo and around

The pedestrian zone of Avenida Central spills out into the busiest square in the city, **Plaza Cinco de Mayo**, where the traffic mayhem takes over again. To the east the square is bordered by the neglected Neoclassical building that was originally the proud Panama Railroad Pacific terminal and is set to house the national anthropological museum for a second time (see below). Tucked away at its rear is a large, open-air **handicrafts market** (see p.84), which is worth a browse.

Over the road, by the pedestrian zone, stands a small fountain monument to the six volunteer firemen killed fighting an exploded gunpowder magazine in 1914. Diagonally opposite, on the northwestern side of the plaza, is the rather uninspiring **Palacio Legislativo** (Legislative Palace), home to the Asamblea Legislativa (Legislative Assembly), which stands in the raised Parque José Antonio Remón Cantera, in honour of one of the country's former presidents, who was mysteriously gunned down at the hippodrome in 1955. Peer behind the towering black monolith at its centre and you are greeted by an enormous, rather unflattering head of the murdered president, protruding from the granite.

Museo Antropológico Reina Torres de Araúz

Plaza Cinco de Mayo • ☎ 501 4151

At the time of writing the **Museo Antropológico Reina Torres de Araúz** (MARTA), which houses Panama's finest anthropological collection, had been relocated to its original home in the old railroad's Pacific terminus building and is due to reopen to the public in 2014, after being closed for several years. Despite a major theft of almost 300 pieces in 2003, the exhibits still contain an impressive array of **pre-Columbian gold**, some beautifully painted **ceramics** and a fascinating array of stone sculptures from the **Barriles culture** – believed to be the country's oldest civilization.

Most of the gold items are *huacas* – precious objects recovered from the burial sites of prominent *caciques* (chiefs). These include weapons, tools and some very intricately carved jewellery, often in fantastical zoomorphic designs. The collection also includes some well-preserved ceramics, primarily for ceremonial use, comprising three distinctive regional designs. Possibly the most intriguing exhibits are the stone objects recovered from Sitio Barriles, west of Volcán (see p.194), including ornate ceremonial *metates* (grinding stones) and curious large carved figures, some seemingly depicting chiefs or other prominent men being carried on the shoulders of slaves.

The museum is named after Panama's foremost anthropologist, Reina Torres de Araúz; the driving force behind the country's regional and national museums, and author of the first major published study of Panama's indigenous peoples, she was awarded the Orden de Vasco Nuñez de Balboa, Panama's greatest national honour.

Museo de Arte Contemporáneo

Between Av de los Mártires and C San Blas • Tues–Sun 9am–5pm; Thurs late opening until 8pm • $5 • ☎ 262 8012, ⓦ macpanama.org

The privately owned **Museo de Arte Contemporáneo** houses a permanent collection by Panamanian artists in a range of media and periodically hosts interesting exhibitions. Photos of all the works can be seen on the website.

Smithsonian Tropical Research Institute (STRI)

Av Roosevelt • Mon–Fri 9am–5pm • Free • ☎ 212 8000, ⓦ stri.si.edu

The Smithsonian Tropical Research Institute's **Earl S. Tupper Research and Conference Centre** is set in leafy grounds and hosts an impressive bookshop (see p.85), a research library and a very pleasant, modestly priced cafeteria. Visits to Isla Barro Colorado (see p.102) can be arranged at the bookshop.

Calidonia and La Exposición

Beyond Plaza Cinco de Mayo, Avenida Central continues north, the city's main thoroughfare and still a busy shopping street as it runs through **CALIDONIA** and **LA EXPOSICIÓN**. These twin barrios are sandwiched between Avenida Central, which soon metamorphoses into Vía España, and Avenida Balboa, which runs along the bay. Consisting of a dense grid of streets, where the sound of construction work is never far away, they are crammed with cheap hotels, though a sprinkling of parks and museums provide welcome relief. This older section of the modern city dates back to the boom construction eras of the Panama Railroad and Canal in the mid- and late nineteenth century (see p.294 & p.297), when predominantly West Indian immigrants poured into the city, with a further influx forced out of the canal areas once the Zone was created.

Museo Afro-Antillano
Av Justo Arosemena (also known as Av 3 Sur), on the corner with C 24 • Tues–Sun 9am–4pm • $1 • ⑩ samaap.org

Housed in an unmarked wooden former church, the **Museo Afro-Antillano** is dedicated to preserving the history and culture of Panama's large West Indian population. The Church of the Christian Mission, as it was then, constituted the social centre of the barrio of El Marañon, a thriving Afro-Antillean community dating back to the construction of the railroad (see p.294). As property prices escalated in the 1970s and developers moved in with bulldozers, residents were forced out to the city suburbs. The community has maintained a precarious toehold in the centre of the city through this small but worthwhile museum, which highlights the pivotal role that Afro-Antilleans played in the construction of the railroad and the canal. The exhibits, featuring photographs, tools and period furniture, with texts in English, provide a sharp reminder of the harsh working and living conditions of black, "silver roll" canal workers, which contrasted acutely with the privileges of white American "gold roll" employees, in the days of the Canal Zone. The museum is also involved in organizing the annual **Afro-Antillean Fair** that takes place over Carnaval at the Centro de Convenciones ATLAPA (see p.84).

Museo de Ciencias Naturales
Av Cuba, between C 29 and C 30 • Tues–Sat 9am–3.30pm • $1

Two blocks east of Avenida Central, the **Museo de Ciencias Naturales** offers a basic introduction to Panama's geology and ecology. For those who are not turned off by taxidermy and the musty smell of formaldehyde, the museum's modest collection may prove diverting, not least specimens of Panama's fauna that you are unlikely to see in the wild, such as the harpy eagle and jaguar.

Plaza Belisario Porras

On Avenida Perú, between calles 33 and 34, the formal gardens of the **Plaza Belisario Porras** honour the three-time president and founding father of the same name. In the vast monument to the former leader, Porras cuts a dashing figure, overlooked by splendidly restored government buildings and the balustraded Spanish Embassy. With your back to the monument, looking up Calle Ecuador to Avenida Central, you can spy the rose window of the neo-Romanesque **Basílica de Don Bosco** (daily 6am–6pm), built in the 1950s. As well as being pleasantly airy with some lovely stained glass, the place is a glittering blue mass of modern mosaics, crafted in Italy and then brought to Panama for the centennial celebrations.

Bella Vista, Marbella and El Cangrejo

The neighbouring areas of Bella Vista, Marbella and El Cangrejo form the financial and commercial core of Panama City – what is often nebulously referred to as the Área

1

Bancaria. The once leafy barrio of **BELLA VISTA**, either side of Calle 50, brimmed with colonial mansions dating back to the 1930s has all but been taken over by modern high-rise buildings. To the north on Vía España stands the incongruous twentieth-century neo-Gothic wedding cake of the **Iglesia del Carmen**. Particularly impressive when illuminated at night, the stained-glass windows up the aisles depict tropical flowers, while those higher up in the nave relate tales from the Old and New Testaments. The neo-Byzantine mosaic altarpiece also grabs your attention.

The church marks the beginning of **EL CANGREJO**, home to many of Panama City's classier hotels and restaurants, as well as upmarket stores and shopping centres. Here, and in the adjacent areas of Bella Vista and **MARBELLA**, much of the city's nightlife is concentrated. These areas are all fairly safe after dark.

Avenida Balboa and the Cinta Costera

The sweeping arc of **Avenida Balboa** that connected the city's historic heartland, Casco Viejo, to its symbols of industrial progress, the skyscrapers of Punta Paitilla, has been irrevocably altered by the recent addition of the **Cinta Costera**. This multimillion-dollar undertaking aimed to ease the traffic congestion by constructing a parallel four-lane highway between the two areas on a vast tract of reclaimed land, alongside a promenade complete with trees, benches and leisure facilities for city residents to enjoy. The jury is still out on the project, which appears to have provided more concrete than anything else.

Mercado de Mariscos
Mon–Sat 6am–6pm; closed first Mon of the month for fumigation

At the southern end of the Cinta Costera stands the distinctive blue-roofed **Mercado de Mariscos**. A fabulous place to wander around, it sells all shapes and sizes of seafood, some waving their antennae at you from tanks. Tuck into an enormous *ceviche* for $3, or choose a fish to fry yourself or take upstairs to *Restaurante de Mariscos* (see p.80), where for a few dollars they'll cook it for you.

Monumento a Vasco Núñez de Balboa and around

The boulevard's main attraction, midway along, is the magnificent **Monumento a Vasco Núñez de Balboa**. Erected in 1913, it shows the sixteenth-century explorer atop a globe, sword in one hand and flag in the other; once looking out in perpetual triumph on the southern ocean he "discovered", he now seems a tad lost in the traffic. Set back across Avenida Balboa is the grand Neoclassical facade of **Hospital Santo Tomás**, the largest public medical facility in the country.

Parque Urracá

A further 800m along the embankment from the Balboa monument, the pleasant **Parque Urracá** is named after the indigenous chief who famously defeated the Spaniards and later escaped from captivity (see p.293). Hemmed in by high-rises, this welcome green space comes alive in the late afternoons at weekends as locals congregate to play football and socialize.

Punta Paitilla, Punta Pacífica and San Francisco

Jutting out into the sea at the northeastern end of the bay, the artificial peninsula of **Punta Paitilla**, packed with over fifty shimmering skyscrapers, constitutes one of Panama City's most emblematic views. Built around 1970, the forty-storey high-rises containing luxury apartments, many of which lie empty due to absent or fictitious owners, became one of the most exclusive residential areas and – with a synagogue and various kosher food stores and restaurants in the vicinity – a major Jewish

1

neighbourhood. There are no specific sights but the area is pleasant enough to wander through if only to experience the eerily deserted streets squeezed between precarious-looking tower blocks, where your only human encounter is likely to be with an aproned domestic servant out on an errand.

Round the headland, the more recently built skyscrapers of **Punta Pacífica** – many still under construction – house yet more opulent ocean-view residences, with the sail-shaped Trump Tower easily the most distinctive. Both exclusive enclaves form part of the broader district of **San Francisco**, which is also gradually falling prey to the city's skyscraper addiction. The area's two main landmarks are the **Centro de Convenciones ATLAPA**, the city's main convention centre (see p.84) and Parque Recreativo Omar Torrijos (see box, p.85), generally shortened to **Parque Omar**, the city's largest green space, after the Parque Metropolitano.

Former Canal Zone

Established in 1903 to protect the canal, the **former Canal Zone** ran the length of the waterway extending approximately 8km either side of it, though excluding Panama City and Colón. Under US military control until 1977, it was jointly administered by the US and Panamanian authorities until the eventual handover in 1999 (see p.300). Though now gradually being swallowed up by Panama City's urban sprawl, **Balboa** – what was effectively the administrative capital of the "Zone" – still retains some of its pleasant leafy landscaping and original architecture, most notably the palatial **Canal Administration Building** and exclusive residential enclave of Quarry Heights. Above, **Cerro Ancón** affords splendid views of the city and canal, including south to the **Amador Causeway**, which marks the Pacific entrance to the canal, and north to the forested **Parque Natural Metropolitano.**

Amador Causeway

Away from the deafening traffic, accompanying pollution and stultifying heat of downtown Panama City, the refreshing breezes of the **Amador Causeway** (Calzada de Amador) – the canal's Pacific breakwater – have made it an attractive weekend recreational area for middle-class Panamanians as well as a draw for tourists. Reinvigorated as a trendy spot to dance the night away, the causeway is also a pleasant venue to wine and dine while enjoying close-ups of transiting ships or more distant views of the Paitilla skyline. More practically, it is the departure point for **ferries** to Taboga and the Archipiélago de las Perlas as well as for canal tours (see p.88, p.123 & p.95). Consisting of three interconnecting islands – Islas Naos, Perico and Flamenco – the 3km causeway first came into existence in 1913, to help prevent crosscurrents from silting up the entry to the canal. The causeway's strategic location, protruding out into the bay, also resulted in Isla Flamenco becoming the site for a US military base. The island now hosts the command centre for the Autoridad del Canal de Panamá (ACP), which controls all traffic transiting the canal.

The best way to explore the area is on foot or by **bike** – at the northern end of the causeway, you can rent bikes (see p.75), which can provide a fun way to get around since a cycleway runs along most of its length.

The causeway

Leaving Balboa, the wedge-shaped area of Amador marks the unofficial entrance to the causeway, where you can't fail to notice the monstrous Vegas-style **Centro de Convenciones Figali**, the preferred venue for international rock concerts. A few hundred metres later, at the tip of the Amador wedge, where the road funnels into

1

the causeway proper, lies the most talked-about construction project of recent years, the **Museo de la Biodiversidad**, which is due to open some time in 2014 (☎830 6700, ⓦbiomuseopanama.com).

Isla Naos

Moving down the causeway, along the palm-lined cycleway and jogging path, the first island you encounter is **Isla Naos**, location of a marine research centre for the Smithsonian Tropical Research Institute (STRI), which maintains a small reserve on the adjoining peninsula, Punta Culebra. The **Punta Culebra Nature Centre** (Jan–March daily 10am–6pm; April–Dec Tues–Fri 1–5pm, Sat & Sun 10am–6pm; $2; ⓦstri.si.edu) is probably only worth popping into if you are travelling with young children. Set in a rare patch of tropical dry forest, the reserve offers a small visitor's centre, a couple of pools containing marine life and a short trail through the forest, where you should keep an eye out for green iguanas and two-toed sloths. Next to the reserve entrance is the departure point for the ferry to Taboga (see p.88).

Isla Perico and Isla Flamenco

The road then moves on to **Isla Perico** and then **Isla Flamenco**, which features a cruise terminal and a flash marina sheltering sleek yachts and motorboats, surrounded by pricey bars and restaurants – a real tourist trap for unwary cruise ship visitors, though its wonderful views make the island a choice spot for a sundowner (see p.81).

Cerro Ancón

You can get a taxi to the summit for $10–12 from any central area, including waiting time

Visible from most of the surrounding area, the huge Panamanian flag fluttering in the breeze on the summit of **CERRO ANCÓN** (199m) is one of the city's most distinctive landmarks, affording sweeping **vistas** of both the city and the canal. What's more, the

WALKING UP CERRO ANCÓN

Although you can get a taxi to the summit of Cerro Ancón, it's well worth **walking** up in the early morning or late afternoon, when you're likely to encounter keel-billed toucans croaking from the treetops and a host of other wildlife. To get there on foot, cross Avenida de los Mártires, behind the Palacio Legislativo on Plaza Cinco de Mayo, and cut through to the road that winds through the old Gorgas Hospital and Supreme Court (see map opposite). Skirting round the northern side of the hill, the road divides: to the right, it drops down to the Canal Administration Building, while ahead it climbs to **Quarry Heights**, the former US military command centre, which is now an exclusive leafy residential area (renamed Altos de Ancón) and is worth a short detour for its unique Zonian wooden architecture.

From the Quarry Heights security gate, it's a twenty- to thirty-minute hike to the **summit**; take first left, then immediate right. A few hundred metres later you'll pass a police checkpoint and gate, which is only open to traffic between 7am and 6pm, though you can slip through on foot at any hour. The views from the top are spectacular, encompassing the old and new cities and, on the other side, the canal.

hill is topped with a protected area of secondary **forest** harbouring white-tailed deer, agoutis, sloths, Geoffroy's tamarin and white-faced capuchin monkeys.

By the mirador overlooking the city, just below the flagpole, the seated serene bronze figure is of poet **Amelia Denis de Icaza**, who is remembered for "*Al Cerro Ancón*"; written in 1900, it served as a nationalist rallying cry.

Steps down the eastern side of hill, by the main gate, lead down to the theme-park-style **Mi Pueblito** (Tues–Sun 9am–9pm; free), a set of four rather tacky replica villages, recreating various traditional architectural styles while flogging overpriced crafts. The main incentive is the café-restaurant on the pseudo-Spanish colonial square, whose fresh fruit juices aid recovery from any physical exertion on the hill.

Edificio de la Administración del Canal de Panamá

Western slope of Cerro Ancón • No hours; tell the security guard that you want to see the "murales"

The stately **Edificio de la Administración del Canal de Panamá** (Canal Administration Building), which dominates the hill's western slope, houses four arresting **murals** that celebrate the Herculean achievement of building the canal. Decorating an elegant domed marble rotunda, just inside the main entrance, they were painted by New York artist William Van Ingen, known for his work in the Library of Congress in Washington DC, and they graphically convey the enormous scale and complexity of the labour. A series of evocative lithographs adorn the outer walls of the rotunda.

Balboa

West of Cerro Ancón lies the district of **BALBOA**, whose centre, **El Prado**, is a palm-lined grassy rectangle measured to match the length and width of a lock chamber that cuts through the district, extending from the Goethals Monument at the foot of the administration steps to Stevens Circle at the far end. When George Goethals took over as chief engineer of the canal in 1907, he surveyed all that his predecessor, John Stevens, had achieved and prophetically wrote to his son, "Mr Stevens has done an amount of work for which he will never get any credit, or if he gets any, will not get enough". Nowhere is this more evident than in the monuments to their labours: while **Stevens Circle** consists of a small and rather neglected memorial down the far end of the Prado, the cream marble **Goethals Monument** monolith stands tall at the foot of the canal authority's seat of power, with water cascading over three stepped marble platforms – symbolizing the three sets of locks – into a pool below.

1

Centro de Capacitación Ascanio Arosemena
Edif 704 • Mon–Fri 7.15am–4.15pm • Free • ☎ 272 1111

Diagonally across from the Goethals Monument stands the former Balboa High School, site of the dramatic "flag riots" (see p.299) of 1964 that culminated in the deaths of 21 Panamanians, whose names are honoured in a memorial near the back of the building. Today, the old school is home to the **Centro de Capacitación Ascanio Arosemena**, which trains canal employees and contains an excellent collection of **photographs** of the canal construction and other **memorabilia**, including rusting tools, porcelain from the *Tivoli Hotel* – the grandest hotel of the Canal Zone era – and Goethals' hat rack. If your Spanish is not up to the canal museum in Casco Viejo then this exhibition, with bilingual labelling, will give you a good enough flavour. To reach the displays, enter the former school gates, taking the first right turn through a building, across a courtyard and into a second building.

Teatro Balboa and beyond
A stroll down the Prado takes you to Avenida Arnulfo Arias Madrid, across which stands the faded Art Deco **Teatro Balboa** (see p.84), worth peeking inside for its splendid mosaic floors. Turning left along the main road, you hit the main intersection with Calle la Boca, where you cannot fail to notice the vainglorious bronze **monument** to former president Arnulfo Arias Madrid (see p.299), standing on the end of what looks like a giant seesaw with citizens imploring his help crawling towards him.

Parque Natural Metropolitano
Main entrance and park office are 200m along Av Juan Pablo II after the junction with Av Ascanio Villalaz • Daily 6am–5pm; office hours Mon–Fri 8am–5pm, Sat 8am–1pm • $4; 2hr guided tours $50/group of 1–5 people • ☎ 232 5552, ⓦ parquemetropolitano.org

Though it's not quite far enough from the city centre to escape the hum of traffic, the **Parque Natural Metropolitano** nevertheless offers real tranquillity. A hilly patch of semi-deciduous tropical forest, the park offers some excellent **birdwatching** and glimpses of the city and canal area from three lookouts and five short but well-marked **trails**. Arriving early in the morning enhances your chances of seeing sloths entwined round branches, agoutis or koatis snuffling in the undergrowth and colourful and abundant birdlife, including golden-collared mannakins, slaty-tailed trogons and red-lored Amazon parrots. With 24 hours' notice, you can arrange for a guided **tour** in English or Spanish; birdwatching tours are also held periodically (see p.40).

Park trails
The most interesting meander is the 1.7km **Camino del Mono Tití**, named after the Geoffroy's tamarin monkeys that can occasionally be sighted when making the moderate climb to the viewpoint. From the main park entrance, you'll need to walk 1km along the **Sendero El Roble**, so called because of the pink-flowering oak trees along the path. To make a circular route, walk the Mono Tití trail one way, returning via the steeper but shorter **Sendero La Cienaguita** ("little marsh" – only visible in the rainy season). You can pick up a free **map** at the main entrance, but it's hard to get lost since the park is only about two square kilometres and the trails are well signed.

Panamá Viejo

Vía Cincuentenario • Museum Tues–Sun 8am–5pm; Plaza Mayor and bell tower Tues–Sun 8.30am–6.30pm • $3 museum, $4 ruins, $6 combined ticket; tickets are sold at the museum and at the entrance to the Plaza Mayor • ☎ 224 2155, ⓦ panamaviejo.org • Metrobuses from the front of Albrook bus terminal run about every 30min, passing along the Cinta Costera, and stop outside the museum (30min); to catch the return bus, wait on the corner of the road heading back into the city close to the pedestrian crossing near the bell tower

You'll need some imagination to reconstruct the neglected ruins of Panamá La Vieja, or

PANAMÁ VIEJO, as it's more often called, once the premier colonial city on the isthmus (see box below). This is especially so since a new road has just been built through the site. Yet while there's no comparison with the magnificent Mayan sites elsewhere in Central America, the view from the bell tower alone makes a half-day visit worthwhile.

Museo del Sitio de Panamá la Vieja

It's worth visiting the **Museo del Sitio de Panamá la Vieja** first, as it will help orientate you. The two-storey block contains some interesting exhibits with information predominantly given in Spanish though with some summaries in English. The top floor displays items discovered during archeological excavations, described in greater detail on the ground floor. There are some exquisitely preserved **pre-Columbian artefacts** – though labels are often frustratingly absent – together with pottery, coins and utensils from colonial times, and a useful interactive **scale model** of the city in 1671.

The convents

Once outside the museum, backtrack 100m to peer over at the **Puente del Matadero** ("Bridge of the Slaughterhouse"), named after the neighbouring abattoir, which marked the western limit of the old city. Returning east along the shoreline, continue along the gravel path a few hundred metres past extensive mud flats being probed by hundreds of migrating waders. Passing the scarcely visible or recognizable Iglesia y Convento de la Merced – which survived Morgan's assault and was relocated to Casco Viejo – and the Iglesia y Convento de San Francisco, cross the road at the speed ramp, turning east down Calle de la Empedrada. To the left stands the well-preserved **Iglesia del Convento de la Concepción**, the city's only convent for women, built in 1597. Peer over the nearby wall and you'll find the impressive remains of the convent's seventeenth-century reservoir. The tour continues past the skeletal remnants of the Jesuit Iglesia y Convento de la Compañía de Jesús before reaching the Cincuentenario.

The Plaza Mayor

Once across the road, you are drawn to the vast open space of the **Plaza Mayor**, overlooked by the imposing cathedral **bell tower**, one of Panama's most distinctive

---

PANAMÁ VIEJO'S TREASURE TRAIL

If you've buffed up on your history while touring Casco Viejo, you'll probably already be familiar with the tale of **Nuestra Señora de la Asunción de Panamá**, to give Panamá Viejo its full name. The original site of the Pacific settlement was established in 1519 by the infamous Pedro Arias de Ávila. Despite the surprisingly swampy location, Panama City prospered; by the early seventeenth century, it boasted an impressive cathedral, seven convents, numerous churches, a hospital, two hundred warehouses and around five thousand houses, driven by the city's commercial importance as the Pacific terminal of the Spanish Crown's **treasure trail**, sending silks and spices from the East and plundered silver and gold from Peru to Europe via the isthmus. This trade route necessitated the construction of a huge customs house, a treasury and a mint located in the most heavily fortified area of the Casas Reales (Royal Houses), the symbol of the Spanish Crown's might, originally separated from the rest of the city by a moat and wooden palisade.

Following the Welsh pirate Henry Morgan's sacking of the city in 1671 (see p.294), the place was razed to the ground. Little more than a pile of rubble now remains of these once impressive buildings, a result of some of the original stones being quarried for construction of the new city, coupled with modern governments' neglect, although the Iglesia del Convento de la Concepción and the cathedral bell tower have been restored.

1

landmarks. The view from the top allows you to appreciate the city's former grandeur. The plaza constituted the social hub of the city, hosting events ranging from political rallies to bullfights, and it was surrounded by the most prestigious buildings, including to the east the *Cabildo* (City Hall) and the cathedral – **La Catedral de la Nuestra Señora de la Asunción**. The stone edifice that replaced the original wooden structure was completed between 1619 and 1629. The magnificently restored belfry now has a modern staircase, which is worth climbing for the views. Sporadic free guided tours are conducted in English and Spanish but depend on numbers, available staff and the weather. Enquire at the small information booth near the tower, or at the museum.

Leaving the cathedral by the vestibule, you can just make out the remains of the **Casa Alarcón**; formerly the domicile of the bishop, this nobleman's home dating back to the 1640s is the largest known and best preserved private house on the site. Beyond lies the crumbling Dominican Iglesia y Convento de Santo Domingo.

The northern remains

A few hundred metres north along the Cincuentenario, little remains of the **Iglesia de San José**, which survived the fire of 1671 and contained the splendid golden altar that now sits in the church of the same name in Casco Viejo (see p.61). At the old northern city limit, a couple of hundred metres beyond, Panamá Viejo's famous **Puente del Rey** (King's Bridge) still spans the Río Gallinero, where it marked the gateway to the Camino Real, the conquistadors' mule trail across the isthmus. If you explore that far, exercise caution, since the surrounding Río Abajo neighbourhood is an impoverished barrio and tourist muggings are not unknown.

Bahá'í House of Worship

Apartado 143, Zona 15 • Daily 9am–6pm; Sunday service is at 10am (30min) • Free • ☎ 231 1191 • Take any Transístimica bus bound for San Isidro or Milla Ocho; get off at Supermercado Rey at Milla Ocho, from where a short taxi ride will cost a few dollars

In the foothills of the Cordillera Central, your eye is caught by the alien-looking hilltop dome that is the **Bahá'í House of Worship**, which offers splendid vistas across the eastern suburbs to the Pacific. The Bahá'í faith developed in nineteenth-century Persia, and this is one of seven churches around the world, with the eighth being constructed in Chile. Interested visitors can attend the Sunday service or wander through the delightful flower-filled gardens.

ARRIVAL AND DEPARTURE — PANAMA CITY

Panama City is the country's transport hub for both international and national traffic, with an international and a domestic airport, a port, a cruise ship terminal and a gigantic bus terminal. When it comes to moving on, most people use the country's efficient and extensive **bus system** to travel around though internal **flights** are plentiful, reasonably priced and simple to arrange. They're particularly useful for reaching Guna Yala, Bocas del Toro and remote areas of the Darién. **Car rental** is also easy though fairly pricey (see p.28), but worth it if you're heading off the beaten track.

BY PLANE

TOCUMEN INTERNATIONAL AIRPORT

The entry point for most visitors to Panama is Tocumen international airport (Aeropuerto Internacional de Tocumen ☎ 238 2703), located about 24km northeast of Panama City. **Facilities** The airport has a couple of helpful tourist information desks, a bank, ATMs, a left luggage office, and a Cable and Wireless office upstairs providing internet and international phone facilities.

Taxis into town Most passengers take a private or *colectivo* taxi into the city. There are two official taxi service

providers, one of which maintains a desk in the entrance hall displaying the official rates, which you should consult if in doubt. At the time of writing rates were $28 including toll fees on the Corredor Sur expressway, for one or two people to central Panama City ($11/person for three or more passengers), and $33 for the Amador Causeway and Cerro Ancón.

Buses into town Unless you have been to Panama before and have a Metrobus card (see p.74), you can't travel into the city by bus since the cards are currently not sold at the airport. If you do have a card, you can catch a bus into the city centre from a bus stop across the main road outside the terminal. Metrobuses destined for Albrook bus terminal pass every 20–40min (6am–midnight; 45min–1hr, longer in rush hour). Make sure you take one labelled "Corredor" that takes the faster toll road. If you arrive after dark, you should take a taxi since hanging round the bus stop can be risky.

Getting to the airport Metrobuses displaying "Tocumen Corredor" leave from the front of Albrook bus terminal (every 20–40min 6am–midnight; 45min–1hr), picking up passengers at the new Cinco de Mayo–Marañon metro station, and at stops along the Cinta Costera. Passengers alight at a bus stop 200m from the terminal entrance.

ALBROOK AIRPORT

Domestic flights from the country's one domestic carrier Air Panama touch down at low-key Albrook airport (officially Aeropuerto International Marcos A. Gelabert; ☎ 238 2700). Several car rental firms have offices here; there's also an ATM and a tourist desk.

Taxis into town Albrook is only 3km northwest of the city centre, and taxis to most places in the city from here should not top $3–4, although the more luxurious cabs waiting immediately outside the terminal will charge you double the fare of a taxi flagged down on the road, which is easy to do during the day.

AIRLINES

The country's domestic airline, Air Panama (☎ 316 9000, ⓦ flyairpanama.com), conveniently flies out of Albrook airport, and serves 19 destinations including San José, Costa Rica, via a connecting flight from David. While in theory Air Panama accepts online credit-card bookings, the website rarely works. Nor is credit-card payment over the phone accepted. You need to purchase a ticket in person at Albrook airport (daily 5am–6pm) or at their office on Av Balboa (Mon–Fri 8am–6pm, Sat 8am–1pm; see map, pp.62–63).

BY BUS

All regional buses arrive at the upper level of Albrook bus terminal (officially El Gran Terminal Nacional de

MAJOR DOMESTIC BUS ROUTES

Destination	Frequency	Duration	Cost
Aguadulce	Every 25min, daily 4.15am–9pm	3hr	$6.35
Antón	Every 20min, daily 5.20am–8pm	2hr	$4.60
Bayano (via Chepo)	Every 40min, daily 5.30am–5.45pm	2hr	$3.60
Chame	Every 15min, daily 5.30am–9pm	1hr 20min	$2.85
Changuinola (via Almirante)	Daily 8am & 8pm	10hr	$29
Chitré	Roughly every 50min, daily 6am–11pm	3hr 30min	$9.05
Colón	Express bus approximately every 30min, 4.40am–10pm	1hr 15min	$3.15
	regular bus every 20–30min 3.40am–1am	2hr	$2.15
El Copé	Every 30min 6am–6.30pm	3hr	$6.50
David	Two companies each run hourly buses, daily 6am–8.30pm. Both have express services at 10am & 11pm express	7hr	$15.25 $20.60
Gamboa	Daily 5am, 5.45am, 6.30am (6am on weekends), 8am, 10am, noon, 2pm, 4.30pm, 6.30pm, 9pm; Mon–Fri also 1 & 3pm	45min	$1.25
Meteti	Daily every 40min 3.15am–4.40pm	5–6hr	$9
Ocú	Hourly 7am–5pm	4hr	$9
Penonomé	Every 20min, daily 4.50am–10.45pm	2hr	$5.50
San Carlos	Every 30–40min, daily 6am–8.30pm	1hr 30min	$3.25
Santiago	Two companies run 37 buses between them, daily 1am, 3am & hourly 6am–midnight	4hr	$9
Soná	Every 2hr, daily 6.45am–5.30pm	5hr	$9.70
Las Tablas	Hourly, daily 6am–7pm	4hr	$8
El Valle (de Antón)	Every 25–30min, daily 7am–7pm	2hr	$4.25
Villa de Los Santos	Hourly, daily 6am–11pm	3hr 30min	$9.05
Yaviza	Daily every 40min 3.15–11.30am; thereafter, take the bus to Meteti, and transfer to a local bus to Yaviza.	6–7hr	$14

1

Transportes, more commonly referred to as "El Terminal"), the national bus terminal 3km northwest of the city centre, close to Albrook Airport.

Getting into town Local buses (including the new Metrobuses) into the city leave from the ground level at the front of the terminal. Taxis also stop here and should take you to your lodgings for no more than $3–4 for one or two passengers if you're heading for a central area such as Casco Viejo or El Cangrejo, though they may try to charge more if you arrive late at night or don't seem to know what you're doing. The new Metro's line's end terminus is also here, which can take you to Plaza Cinco de Mayo – which gives walking access to Casco Viejo – or along to El Cangrejo.

Getting to the bus terminal To get to the bus terminal from the city centre, take a bus bound for Albrook on Vía España, along the Cinta Costera/Av Balboa, or at the side of the Palacio Legislativo off Plaza Cinco de Mayo. Alternatively, take the Metro from El Cangrejo or Plaza Cinco de Mayo.

Onward travel by bus To catch a bus out of town, tickets must first be purchased from the appropriate ticket office inside the terminal, before passing through a turnstile (a 10¢ coin is needed or a swipe card – Rapi pass – purchased for $1 at a kiosk in the bus terminal) to a numbered departure bay at the back. For several major destinations, there is more than one company operating transport, some offering both express and cheaper stopping buses, though companies charge the same price for the same service.

Travelling to Costa Rica Ticabus (☎ 314 6385, ⓦ ticabus.com), with an office at the terminal, runs overnight and daytime buses (daily 11am & 11.55pm; 15–16hr; $55 & $41) to San José, Costa Rica. Advance booking is advisable. Alternatively, take a Padafront (☎ 314 6264) or Panachif (☎ 314 6885) bus to Paso Canoas (see p.203) at the border (9 regular buses daily, two express at 10.30pm & 11.45pm; $16.90, $20.55 for the overnight express), via David, and transfer to Costa Rican transport.

GETTING AROUND

Panama City's vast urban sprawl continues to expand outwards and upwards at an alarming rate, and navigating your way around can at first seem a daunting prospect. But as with most large cities, places of interest to tourists are concentrated in a few areas easily accessible by **bus** or **taxi**, or, in the case of Casco Viejo, **on foot**. Avoid travelling at **rush hour** (7.30–9am and 4.30–6.30pm), when traffic grinds to a halt in horn-honking mayhem. The new **Metro** so far only has one line, but it provides a quick way of travelling between El Cangrejo and Albrook bus terminal.

BY BUS

Tickets and hours Travelling by bus is the cheapest way to get about, costing a mere 25¢, no matter where you travel within the metropolitan boundary. There are two types of public buses. Best known, but being phased out, are the chicken buses, known in Panama as *diablos rojos*, or red devils (see box below). Though they operate fixed routes, there are no fixed timetables; destinations are painted on the windscreen. Newer, a/c Metrobuses (ⓦ mibus.com.pa) operate the same hours and also cost $0.25, though this will rise to $0.75 once they have completely replaced the *diablos rojos*. You need a pre-paid card (*tarjeta*), which you swipe on entry and exit, to ride the Metrobus. Cards are available at supermarkets (such as

El Rey on Vía España and El Machetazo on Av Central) as well as at the Albrook bus terminal and from a kiosk on Plaza Cinco de Mayo. The initial card costs $2 and then you need to buy credit. Buses circulate every few minutes on the busiest routes – from 5.30/6am until 11pm/midnight, but less frequently on Sundays.

Bus stops and destinations Metrobuses only stop at designated stops, which are less numerous than the stops for *diablos rojos*. Some drivers of *diablos rojos* will also pick up and drop off at other places as the whim takes them. See ⓦ mibus.com.pa for Metrobus routes. The city's main arteries and bus routes run vaguely southwest to northeast along Av Balboa and the Cinta Costera, Av Central (which becomes Av España) and Av Justo Arosemena (Av 3 Sur).

DIABLOS ROJOS

Whether as a cramped passenger or a terrified pedestrian, you're unlikely to leave Panama City without having a life-threatening encounter with a **diablo rojo** (red devil), one of the multicoloured converted old US school buses. Named for the devil-may-care attitude of many of the drivers, these anachronistic, fume-belching beasts are both safety hazards and cultural icons. The most exotic designs are air-brushed on and mix the religious and the profane: Jesus might jostle for position with pop singers in a psychedelic collage of fantasy landscapes, cartoon characters and Gothic monsters. Inside, feather boas, tassels and rosaries decorate the windscreen.

Arguably more is spent on the artwork than on maintenance, and many preventable **accidents** – some fatal – and breakdowns are caused by negligent owners or wild drivers. Add to that cramped seating, lack of ventilation and deafening music and it's easy to see why Panamanians are glad to see these buses gradually being taken off the roads.

1

Getting to Casco Viejo No buses go into Panama City's historical centre, Casco Viejo; you'll need to ask for a bus that passes Plaza Cinco de Mayo, then walk up the pedestrianized section of Av Central.

BY METRO

Metro route Panama City's new Metro system – Central America's first – currently has only one line with 15 almost completed stations, though a second line is planned. It runs from the Albrook bus terminal via Plaza Cinco de Mayo and then northwards towards El Cangrejo and beyond, as far as the districts of Los Andes and San Isidro.

Fares You will need to purchase a rechargeable Metro card (*tarjeta*; $2) at one of the stations and then pay for each journey; at the time of writing fares had yet to be determined.

BY TAXI

Taxis are plentiful – around 28,000 in the city at the last count – and relatively cheap.

Fares Taxis are supposed to follow an overcomplicated zonal pricing schedule (see ⓦ transito.gob.pa) set by the transport authorities, but in practice the price is often down to supply and demand, your negotiating skills in Spanish and whether they want to take you. For most destinations in the city you shouldn't pay more than $3–4 during normal working hours, the exception being to Panamá Viejo or the Amador Causeway, where prices are often inflated (usually to a minimum of $5) because the driver is concerned about finding a passenger for the return trip. If you're unsure, ask around for the current rates beforehand and agree a price before

getting into a cab. Note that the more comfortable a/c tourist taxis hovering outside the mid- to high-end hotels, recognizable by the SET licence plates, charge much higher rates.

Tours by taxi Taxi drivers often serve as chauffeurs and unofficial city tour guides; you may be charged anything between $15–25/hr, in part depending how far you want to travel.

BY CAR

Though rental cars are readily available from both airports and along Vía España near El Cangrejo, it's not worthwhile until you're ready to leave the city since buses and taxis are cheap and plentiful. Besides, the free-for-all attitude of many drivers makes driving a stressful experience.

BY BICYCLE

You would need to have a death wish to cycle in most of Panama City. The exceptions are along the new Cinta Costera round the bay, and the Amador Causeway, where the existence of a cycleway and the general lack of traffic and fumes make for a pleasant ride.

Bike rental and repairs On the Amador Causeway by *Las Pencas*, Bicicletas Moses (daily 8am–6.30pm, shorter hours in winter; ☎ 211 3671) rents bikes by the hour ($3.50/hr), plus tandems and fun pedal buggies for two or four (up to $18/hr). Rates vary according to demand so check in advance. You will need to present your passport. Bicicletas Rali (☎ 223 8054, ⓦ bicicletasrali.com), in Extreme Planet, next to Multicentro on Av Balboa, sells bikes and spare parts and does repairs.

INFORMATION

Tourist information The main tourist office of the Autoridad de Turismo Panamá (ATP) in Panama City is behind the ATLAPA Convention Centre in San Francisco on Vía Israel (Mon–Fri 8.30am–4.30pm; ☎ 526 7102) but it's not worth dragging yourself over there since you're unlikely to get more than the odd glossy brochure

or map, if you're lucky. Much better sources of information are the hostels and some of the more upmarket hotels and tour operators.

Maps Free city maps of variable quality abound, generally with the advertising hotels, restaurants and tourist services marked.

TOUR OPERATORS

Advantage Tours ☎ 232 6944, ⓦ advantagepanama .com. Specializes in birding tours, with a couple of great and affordable locations for multi-day excursions in the Darién. They also offer reasonably priced day-trips to an Emberá village and to Fuerte San Lorenzo, via Gatún Locks.

Ancon Expeditions ☎ 269 9415, ⓦ anconexpeditions .com. Very professional and expensive outfit, offering top notch bilingual naturalist guiding services for single-day excursions and multi-day adventures: birdwatching across Panama, trekking in the Darién or traversing the isthmus along the Camino Real. The unique experiences offered in the private reserve of Punta Patiño in the Darién and the

birding expertise are likely to be worth the extra outlay, but the inflated rates for a Panama Canal transit or Emberá village tour are harder to justify.

Aventuras Panamá No 32, C 63 Oeste ☎ 260 0044, ⓦ aventuraspanama.com. Adventure is the name of the game here, in particular kayaking and whitewater rafting down a variety of rivers within a couple of hours of Panama City in Panama and Coclé provinces.

Barefoot Panama ☎ 6780 3010, ⓦ barefootpanama .com. Well-regarded US-run organization specializing in customized adventure and eco-tours to cater for all tastes, both single and multi-day itineraries.

1

Ecocircuitos Albrook Plaza, 2nd Floor, No 31 ☎314 0068, ⓦ ecocircuitos.com. Actively involved in promoting sustainable tourism and supporting several community-based projects, this outfit offers a wide range of day- and multi-day excursions including sea kayaking, jungle trekking and yoga retreats.

Emberá Tours ☎250 1165 or ☎6519 7121, ⓦ emberatourspanama.com. Run by Garceth Cunampio, an English-speaking Emberá guide who organizes excursions to villages up the Chagres, as well as birdwatching trips to the Darién.

Expediciones Tropicales ☎317 1279, ⓦ xtrop .com. Focusing on river and sea kayaking in the canal area and in Guna Yala, the company has a high number of indigenous staff and works closely with indigenous communities.

My Friend Mario ☎253 6500, ⓦ myfriendmario.com. Popular local outfit from La Chorrera offering inexpensive day-trips for budget travellers – the Emberá village tour is particularly good value.

Panama Exotic Adventures ☎314 3013, ⓦ panama exoticadventures.com. French-run organization (with Spanish and English also spoken), specializing in multi-day adventure trips to the Darién (and Guna Yala).

Panamá Orgánica ☎6079 6825, ⓦ panamaorganica .com. Small outfit offering customized budget tours to hard-to-access areas such as the Darién and Guna Yala, working with local communities and independent operators. Can also help arrange transport to Colombia and day-trips from Panama City.

Sendero Panamá ☎6429 8163, ⓦ senderopanama .com. Run by certified bilingual naturalist guides, at the more expensive end of the market, this company offers a range of acclaimed day-trip and multi-day adventures.

Whale Watching Panama ☎6758 7600, ⓦ whale watchingpanama.com. Offers pricey day-trips from Panama City in small boats round Taboga (from $125) and the Islas Perlas ($200) to spot humpback whales in the migration season (July–Oct). Sightings in the latter are almost guaranteed.

ACCOMMODATION

There are **accommodation** options to suit all tastes and all budgets in Panama City, but beds are in short supply so it's a good idea to book ahead. If you're thinking of coming for Carnaval or any other busy holiday period, an advance **reservation** is an absolute must. Some mid-range hotels offer special business rates (open to all) or reductions for internet bookings. Note that hotels located on a major bus route, such as Vía España or Avenida Perú, can get **noisy** from around 5.30–6.00am, when the traffic starts up and the horn honking begins, until late at night, so ask for a room at the back on one of the higher floors. As for **facilities**, hot water is standard in **hotels** (though not necessarily in hostels) and most have a/c and cable TV, with many now offering wi-fi or other internet connections. If you're thinking of staying for a week or more, or are with a family, you might consider an **aparthotel**, which can be better value. These have kitchen/lounge/dining facilities but offer hotel services, such as cleaning, laundry and breakfast. Long-term rentals and corporate rates are often negotiable. Check out ⓦ airbnb.com or ⓦ panamacasa.com for smart modern **apartment rentals** (from around $600/week, $1700/month) in the banking district and its environs.

CASCO VIEJO

Most budget travellers opt for the backpacker hostels in Casco Viejo, the old colonial centre, where there are also some very comfortable choices. The restoration of many of the area's historic buildings and absence of buses make it a pleasant retreat from the congestion and the pollution of the rest of the city. Lively bars and restaurants have also made it a popular nightlife destination, though most places are relatively pricey.

★**American Trade Hotel** Plaza Herrera ☎211 2000, ⓦ acehotel.com/panama; map p.56. Overlooking one of the most elegant plazas, a gleaming white facade proudly announces Casco Viejo's first fully restored grand hotel. White and wood predominate in light airy rooms, many of which have their own balustraded balcony. Every detail has been considered, from plush bathrobes to fully stocked minibars as modern comforts are carefully blended into the historical structure. Substantial discounts for advance booking online. **$249**

Las Clementinas C 11 & Av "B" ☎228 7613,

ⓦ lasclementinas.com; map p.56. Half a dozen beautifully decorated suites, with hand-painted tiles, wooden floors and a blend of antique and stylish modern furnishings. All have lofty ceilings, fully equipped kitchens and access to a fabulous rooftop terrace. Service is top-notch. **$310**

★**Los Cuatro Tulipanes** Casa las Monjas, Av Central between C 3 & C 4 ☎211 0877, ⓦ loscuatrotulipanes .com; map p.56. Offering bohemian chic in Casco Viejo, this is a range of sumptuous apartments in beautifully restored colonial houses, with traditional hotel services if required. Weekly rates ($950) and substantial discounts in low season. Three-night minimum stay. **$190**

Hospedaje Casco Viejo C 8 and Av "A" ☎211 2127, ⓦ hospedajecascoviejo.com; map p.56. Clean, relaxed and surprisingly spacious hostel with numerous private rooms in a quiet street by the Iglesia de San José. The bathrooms have seen better days but you can't complain for the price. Small shared kitchen and interior patio plus free wi-fi and basic breakfast. Rooms with shared or private bathroom. Dorms **$11**, doubles **$25**

1

Luna's Castle C 9 Este between Av "B" & Av Alfaro ☎ 262 1540, ⓦ lunascastlehostel.com; map p.56. Great backpacker party venue set in a rambling property with a balcony overlooking a square, and both private rooms and dorms (fan or a/c $2 extra). Run by experienced owners, it offers free internet, shared kitchen, solar hot water, laundry, balconies, ping pong, a cine-centre, free pancake breakfasts and an on-site bar; just don't expect much sleep. Dorms $15, doubles $32

Magnolia Inn C 8 and Boquete, behind the cathedral ☎ 202 0872, ⓦ magnoliapanama.com; map p.56. Lovingly restored, two floors of this colonial mansion are part boutique hotel, part luxury hostel. The deluxe six-bed dorm in particular offers excellent value, boasting a/c, mattresses and private reading lights, plus use of a beautifully furnished, comfortable dining and lounge area to relax in. The handful of private rooms at various prices offers affordable luxury. Dorm $15, doubles $80

★**Panamericana** Plaza Herrera ☎ 202 0851, ⓦ panamericanahostel.com; map p.56. Beautifully restored colonial mansion enlivened by artistic touches in fluorescent paint, with shared balconies and a great rooftop terrace-bar offering panoramic views of Casco Viejo. Large, airy rooms with high ceilings and excellent beds, plus spacious hot showers and a comfy TV lounge and decent-sized kitchen downstairs make this a top choice. The only downside is that some rooms by the stairs can be noisy. Dorms $13, doubles $35

CALIDONIA AND LA EXPOSICIÓN

Between Casco Viejo and the banking district of El Cangrejo lie the areas of Calidonia and La Exposición, which offer a wide selection of unexceptional but affordable modern hotels and *pensiónes*. Note that the streets off the main arteries are not very safe at night and some of the hotels offer rooms by the hour, while places to eat are few and far between, though generally quite cheap.

Hostel Mamallena Primera Calle Perejil off Vía España ☎ 6676 6163, ⓦ mamallena.com; map pp.62–63. Popular backpacker place for chilling in a hammock on the communal balcony or in the courtyard garden, or lounging in front of the TV. Dorms have a/c with quality mattresses while private rooms (also with a/c) have shared bathrooms. The friendly, helpful staff have bags of info and deals on trips and there are plenty of trimmings – free wi-fi and PCs with Skype, complimentary tea, coffee and all-day pancake breakfast, cheap airport transfer, washing machine. Only the location could be improved. Dorms $13, doubles $33

Hotel Acapulco C 30 between Av Cuba & Av Perú ☎ 225 3832, ⓔ hotelacapulco@hotmail.com; map pp.62–63. A travellers' favourite for its solid value and friendly service. Some of the well-maintained, functional rooms have small balconies; other pluses include late check-out and on-site restaurant. $39

Hotel Dos Mares Av Perú at C 30 ☎ 227 6150, ⓦ hotel-dosmares.com; map pp.62–63. New and slightly more upmarket than many of its surrounding competitors, with bar-restaurant and fabulous rooftop pool and terrace – hosting Saturday-night barbecues – affording spectacular views of the bay. The comfortable modern rooms have spotless small bathrooms, fridge and safe, and there's internet access in the foyer. Good value. Breakfast included. $51

Hotel Stanford Panama Plaza Cinco de Mayo ☎ 262 4930; map pp.62–63. Fantastic location overlooking the busy plaza offering recently refurbished en-suite rooms, each with fridge, safe and desk, at affordable rates. Go for a room with a view across the bay but away from the bar and casino and the rooftop terrace, which often throbs to the beat of weekend parties. $46

Residencial Jamaica Av Cuba at C 38 Este ☎ 225 9870; map pp.62–63. Hidden behind a nicely trimmed hedge, *Jamaica* offers a good deal for the price – so is often full. Rooms are bright and clean. $25

Residencial Texas C 31 between Av Perú and Cuba, beside the national lottery ☎ 225 1467, ⓔ hoteltexas @mixmail.com; map pp.62–63. Friendly, secure place offering good-value rooms with spotless tiled bathrooms, decent hot showers and good mattresses, though the furniture is tired. $38

BELLA VISTA, MARBELLA AND EL CANGREJO

The safer and somewhat quieter districts of Bella Vista, Marbella and El Cangrejo, the hub of the city's nightlife and commercial activity, have the densest concentration of accommodation. Though prices are generally higher in these areas – apart from the hostels – you're within striking distance of most restaurants, bars, clubs, shops and casinos, and it's fairly safe to stroll around at night.

The Bristol Hotel Av Aquilino de la Guardia at C 50 ☎ 264 0000, ⓦ thebristol.com; map pp.62–63. From the moment you glide across its gleaming marble foyer, this boutique hotel exudes exclusivity. The rooms are elegant and sumptuously furnished, while vast marble bathrooms, 24hr butler service, spa services and an award-winning restaurant mean the only thing lacking is a pool. $208

Euro Hotel Vía España 33 by Colegio Javier ☎ 263 0802, ⓦ eurohotelpanama.com; map pp.62–63. No-frills hotel with clean, compact rooms piped with ambient music, which thankfully can be switched off. Swimming pool, plus free wi-fi. $60

Hostel Villa Vento Surf C 47 at C Margarita A. de Vallarino ☎ 397 6001; map pp.62–63. Modern hostel in the heart of the banking district but within reach of restaurants and nightlife. There's one en-suite fan-ventilated room and some small dorms with a/c but comfortable bunks. Guests have use of a kitchen, a lounge area, where surf videos

1

are *de rigueur* and which opens out onto the pool and BBQ patio – the hostel's main draw. Dorms $15, double $35

Hotel California Vía España at C 43 Este ☎ 263 7736, ⓦ hotelcaliforniapanama.net; map pp.62–63. Not the most convenient location but this is a very popular hotel, offering good-value rooms (single, double and triple), free wi-fi and a rooftop jacuzzi. $44

★**Hotel DeVille** C Beatríz M. Cabal at C 50 ☎ 206 3100, ⓦ devillehotel.com.pa; map pp.62–63. Plum in the heart of the financial district, this boutique hotel provides the best value for those seeking top-class accommodation with a more personalized service than the international luxury hotels can offer. Elegant, spacious rooms possess dark wooden furniture and opulent marble bathrooms. The strikingly designed on-site restaurant serves excellent French fusion cuisine. $99

★**Hotel Milan** C Eusebio A. Morales 31 ☎ 263 7723, ⓦ hotelmilan.com.pa; map pp.62–63. Sought-after hotel in a great location, so book well in advance. The place boasts sixty expansive tiled rooms and suites (some with jacuzzi) with direct-dial phones. Good value if you take advantage of the 15 percent cash discount. Discounted: $66

Marriott Hotel C 52 and Ricardo Arias ☎ 210 9100, ⓦ marriothotels.com; map pp.62–63. A Marriott that truly merits its 5-star rating, comprising excellent rooms and service with full business amenities, pool and casino – located plum in the middle of the business district. $208

Radisson Decapolis Hotel Av Balboa, Multicentro ☎ 215 5000, ⓦ radisson.com/panamacitypan; map pp.62–63. Brash or stylish (depending on your viewpoint) thirty-floor glass-and-steel edifice leading into the Multicentro Mall and Majestic Casino, offering big, tastefully designed rooms with all the frills – go for one on an upper floor with an ocean view. On-site restaurant (excellent breakfast buffet), sushi bar and pool. Big discounts for advance booking. $120

Residencial Los Arcos Av Justo Arosemena at C 44 ☎ 225 0569, ⓔ losarcospanama@gmail.com; map pp.62–63. Compact place on the edge of Bella Vista with well-maintained rooms. The big plus is showers with proper showerheads – a rarity in this price bracket. $44

Sevilla Suites C Eusebio A. Morales opposite Rincón Suizo ☎ 213 0016, ⓦ sevillasuites.com; map pp.62–63. Smart aparthotel aimed at the business market in a convenient location. Offers nicely furnished suites with kitchenettes, living/dining area and wi-fi at daily and weekly rates ($473). Enjoy the complimentary breakfast on the patio after a few lengths in the rooftop pool or a session in the mini-gym. $99

Torres de Alba C Eusebio A. Morales at Vía Veneto ☎ 300 7130, ⓦ torresdealba.com.pa; map pp.62–63. Expansive, well-furnished suites boasting lots of natural light, decent-sized kitchens (including washing machine) and all the usual mod cons. The gym and rather small pool are too close to

street traffic to provide much relaxation. Great location but opt for a higher floor to escape the noise. $109

★**Toscana Inn** C "D" at C Eusebio A. Morales ☎ 265 001, ⓦ toscanainnhotel.com; map pp.62–63. Top mid-range hotel in an excellent location, with warmly decorated en-suite rooms containing all modern amenities, enhanced by efficient, friendly service. Includes a good buffet breakfast. $109

FORMER CANAL ZONE

There are an increasing number of lodgings scattered round the former Canal Zone, an area that includes the Amador Causeway, Balboa and Cerro Ancón, stretching to Albrook, Clayton and Miraflores Locks. These often offer greater tranquillity and, in some cases, superb views, though they are some distance from the main watering holes, which will mean spending more on taxi fares.

Albrook Inn C Las Magnolias 14, Albrook ☎ 315 1789, ⓦ albrookinn.com; map p.68. Convenient for early domestic flights from Albrook Airport and fine if you've your own transport, this otherwise out-of-the-way hotel is located in a tranquil residential suburb. Rates for comfortable motel-style rooms and suites include a buffet breakfast served in verdant surroundings. A small pool with jacuzzi provides another treat. $73

The Balboa Inn Las Cruces, 2311a, Balboa ☎ 314 1520, ⓦ thebalboainn.com; map p.68. Conveniently situated in the quiet residential area of Balboa, yet close to bus and taxi routes, this B&B offers simple but nicely furnished rooms with excellent beds and plenty of natural light. The delightful garden breakfast terrace allows you to enjoy your full American breakfast while birdwatching. $72

Country Inn & Suites Amador Causeway ☎ 211 4500, ⓦ panamacanalcountry.com; map p.68. A standard motel in a stunning location, right by the canal entrance. Pay the extra $15 to watch the ships from your balcony – otherwise you may get a view of the car park. The large, bright rooms are equipped with all conveniences. There's an onsite *TGI Friday's* and a couple of pools. Breakfast included. $73

★**La Estancia B&B** C Amelia Denis de Icaza, Quarry Heights, Cerro Ancón ☎ 314 1581, ⓦ bedand breakfastpanama.com; map p.68. The capital's best accommodation for nature lovers, halfway up Cerro Ancón, surrounded by trees, with agoutis and toucans nearby. The helpful owners oversee simple (not all en suite and none have TV), comfortable and light rooms, and can arrange tours and transfers. You'll need a taxi to reach a restaurant but order a takeaway, grab some wine from the honesty bar and chill on the balcony. $94

★**Hostal Amador Familiar** Av Amador, round the corner from Tamburelli's, Ancón ☎ 314 1251, ⓦ hostalamadorfamiliar.com; map p.68. Maroon three-storey Canal Zone building with a laidback atmosphere, attracting a mix of Panamanians and foreigners. There are basic compact en-suite rooms (with fan or a/c), free wi-fi, laundry service and cheap airport transfers, plus a pleasant outdoor open-sided kitchen-cum-social area, where you prepare your complimentary DIY breakfast. Dorms $15, doubles $33

OTHER AREAS
Panama House B&B (formerly Casa del Carmen)
C Primera El Carmen 32 ☎ 263 4366, ⓦ panamahousebb .com; map pp.62–63. Attracts a wide age range with their

restful patio and garden, and free services including breakfast, internet, shared kitchen, laundry, hot water and barbecue area. Strongly recommended and usually full, so book ahead. Dorms US$17, doubles US$50

Riande Aeropuerto Hotel & Resort Av Tocumen ☎ 291 9012, ⓦ hotelesriande.com/aeropuerto; map pp.62–63. Not a place to base a stay in Panama City, but this motel-like joint does the job if you've an early flight out of Tocumen (or a late arrival) as it's a couple of minutes away and offers a free airport transfer. $113

EATING

Panama City's cosmopolitan nature is reflected in its **restaurants**: anything from US fast food to Greek, Italian, Chinese, Japanese and French cuisine can easily be found in addition to traditional Panamanian dishes and excellent seafood. Bookings are advisable at weekends, if there's live music or a show, and during holiday periods. The most celebrated areas to eat out in are **Bella Vista** and **El Cangrejo** – along and around Vía España, Vía Argentina, Vía Veneto and Calle Uruguay – and **Casco Viejo**, with a handful of restaurants sprinkled along the **Amador Causeway**. Cheap hot and cold **takeaway** meals are available from the Rey supermarket (open 24hr) on Vía España, while the **food courts** in the city's numerous shopping malls (see p.84) are popular at weekends.

CASCO VIEJO
Casco Viejo is a destination for the city's smart set, jamming the streets in the evenings with their 4WDs as they head for the chic venues in converted colonial houses, though there are a few open-air restaurants, where you can soak up the historic surroundings, and the odd inexpensive hole-in-the wall joint, where you can get a meal for under three dollars.
Las Bóvedas Plaza de Francia ☎ 228 8058, ⓦ restaurantelasbovedas.com; map p.56. Soak up the history as well as the fine wine in the dimly lit caverns of these former dungeons. The French-inspired cuisine is both mouthwatering and tastefully presented, but it plays second fiddle to the intimate ambience. Mains $20–45. Live jazz after 9pm on Fri & Sat. Mon–Sat 5.30pm–midnight.
Café Coca-Cola Plaza Santa Ana, C 12 at Av Central ☎ 228 7687; map p.56. The self-proclaimed "oldest café in Panama" and something of an institution among the city's older residents, who gather to drink coffee, read the paper and discuss the news. Filling Panamanian staples (*ceviche*, chicken with rice, soups) for about $3, and generously portioned breakfasts cooked to order. Good coffee. Daily 7am–11pm.
Casa Sucre Av "B" and C 8 ☎ 393 6130, ⓦ casasucre coffeehouse.com; map p.56. Laidback artsy café decked with eclectic antiques and a similarly eclectic spread of coffee-table books, from Chinese World Heritage Sites to Mayan architecture. Serves gourmet coffees, deli sandwiches, breakfasts and its signature dish, a filling soup served in a bread bowl ($8). Free wi-fi. Mon–Wed 8am–6pm, Thurs–Sat 8am–8pm, Sun 9am–6pm.
Caffè Per Due Av "A" at C 3 ☎ 228 0547; map p.56. Italian-owned and operated, this little gem serves scrumptious oven-crisped pizzas ($7–11) and salads ($6–8) and is a popular spot for afternoon coffee and cake. Tues–Sun 8.30am–10pm.

Casablanca Plaza Bolívar at C 4 ☎ 212 0040; map p.56. A delightful outdoor setting (with a/c inside if you prefer) plays host to well-prepared, wide-ranging dishes from burgers, kebabs and salads ($9–15) to more substantial seafood, meat or poultry mains. Kick-start dinner with a mojito before trying ribs in passion fruit sauce. The atmosphere is great though the quality can vary when it's really busy. Daily noon until late.
★**Diablo Rosso** Av "A" at C 7 ☎ 228 4833, ⓦ diablorosso.com; map p.56. Eclectic mix of design boutique and funky art café, serving inventive salads, dips and delicious cakes. "*Cena cine*", involving food and a film, takes place on Tues nights. Tues–Sat 9am–7pm.
The Fish Market Av Central at C 10 ☎ 6721 6445; map p.56. New addition to the Bohemian scene offering a changing menu of high-quality gourmet seafood served in plastic bowls out of a trailer truck for around $10–12. Enjoy the food in an open-air courtyard, accompanied by music at weekends. Wed–Sat 6–11.30pm.
★**Granclement** Av Central at C 4 ☎ 223 6277, ⓦ granclement.com; map p.56. A fabulous indulgence after tramping the streets of Casco Viejo, this French-style artisanal ice-cream parlour offers flavours you wouldn't dream of – basil, lavender, Earl Grey tea – as well as chocolate every which way and an array of mouthwatering sorbets, though at a price. Daily noon–8.30pm.
★**René Café** Plaza Catedral at C 7 ☎ 262 3487; map p.56. Provided a 4WD isn't parked out front, the outdoor tables provide a splendid vantage point for admiring the cathedral while savouring a good-value three-course set-menu lunch ($10) washed down with a glass of wine. The five- to seven-course tapas-style dinner is a pricier $25 and better enjoyed in the intimate Provençal ambience inside. Mon–Sat 10am–3pm & 6–10pm.

1

Super Gourmet Av "A" at C 6 ☎212 3487, ⓦsupergourmetcascoviejo.com; map p.56. Upmarket café serving delicious deli sandwiches and excellent light lunches for $6–9. Set yourself up for the day with a full breakfast (from around $5). Mon–Sat 8am–5pm, Sun 10am–4pm.

CALIDONIA AND LA EXPOSICIÓN

Reflecting their working-class populations, most dining options in these neighbourhoods are inexpensive and particularly busy at lunchtimes, serving up traditional Panamanian fare.

Café Boulevard Balboa Av Balboa at C 31 Este ☎225 0914; map pp.62–63. An a/c oasis of civilization in the dust, noise and endless construction work outside, livened up by a smart lunchtime business crowd. Specializing in toasted sandwiches ($5–8), the lengthy menu also includes more filling Panamanian dishes and a good-value three-course *menú del día* for around $8. Mon–Sat 6.30am–1am.

Mercado Publico Av "B" and Av Balboa; map pp.62–63. A dozen *fondas* serving heaps of tasty hot food for under $3 with communal seating. Mon–Sat 4am–3pm.

Nelson's Café Av Central at C 18 Este; map pp.62–63. Offers an appetizing plateful of *comida típica* for under $3, usually with a generous amount of vegetables. Daily 6am–11pm.

Restaurante de Mariscos Av Balboa, above the Mercado de Mariscos; map pp.62–63. Best for lunch so you can enjoy the hustle and bustle of the stalls below, where you can buy your seafood – the restaurant will cook it for a few dollars. Or opt for something from their own menu (from around $8). Daily 11am–6pm.

Rincón El Tableño Av Cuba at C 31 Este; map pp.62–63. Popular cafeteria whose huge customer turnover ensures the *comida típica* is hot and fresh. Try the *tamales* or the house speciality, *chicheme chorrerano*, downed with a fresh juice. Panamanian breakfasts go for under $3 and lunch for under $5. Daily 6am–4pm.

BELLA VISTA, MARBELLA AND EL CANGREJO

From the converted colonial mansions of Bella Vista to the neon lights of El Cangrejo, this area offers by far the greatest variety of dining and drinking venues, mainly at the mid to high end of the price scale.

Athens Pizza C 57 Este at Vía España ☎223 1464; map pp.62–63. Tasty filling meals from around $7. Greek dishes, including salads, abound, and the pizza is great comfort food – all served on covered tables surrounded by images of Greece. Mon & Wed–Sun 11am–11pm.

Beirut C 49a Este at Av Justo Arosemena, opposite the Marriott ☎214 3815; map pp.62–63. A grotto-like ceiling, faux vines, murals and mosaics provide the setting for appetizers from $6 a dish and good-value, large combo platters, with mains from around $12. Hookah rental and occasional belly-dancing at weekends are additional attractions. Daily noon–11pm.

Café Suzette Vía Argentina opposite Churrería Manolo's ☎393 2257; map pp.62–63. This delightful Venezuelan-run café-restaurant is a great lunch spot, serving delicious sweet and savoury crêpes – try the smoked turkey and brie – for under $8. Free wi-fi. Daily 8am–9pm.

★**Caffè Pomodoro** Vía Veneto at C Eusebio A. Morales in ApartHotel Las Vegas ☎269 5836; map pp.62–63. Extremely popular Italian place offering pasta and pizzas ($5–10) plus more sophisticated Italian fare such as clams in white wine ($20). The tropical garden, decorated with fairy lights, is buzzing in the evening. Daily 7am–midnight.

Churrería Manolo Vía Argentina 12 ☎264 3965, ⓦchurrerianmanolo.com; map pp.62–63. Café specializing in sweet cigar-shaped churro pastries for just over a dollar, as well as serving coffees, sandwiches and more substantial mains ($9–12). Daily 7am–1am.

Habibi's C Uruguay at C 48 ☎264 3647; map pp.62–63. Buzzing corner terrace that's a well-established gathering spot for groups heading off to party. Prices alas have been shooting up with the place's popularity – $3.50 for a local beer. Stick to the tasty Middle Eastern dishes; meze start at just $13 for one, up to $45 for six. Belly-dancing Fri & Sat. Daily noon–late.

Loving Hut C Manuel Espinosa Batista, Edif Cali ☎240 5621, ⓦlovinghut.com/pa; map pp.62–63. Part of a global veggie and vegan chain, this no-nonsense cafeteria dishes up delicious, inexpensive food. You can "pick and mix" a healthy plateful for under $5. Mon–Sat 10.30am–8.30pm.

Machu Picchu C Eusebio A. Morales 18, at C "D" ☎264 8501; map pp.62–63. The original Peruvian restaurant in Panama, decorated with pictures of its namesake and Andean weavings, and specializing in seafood. The room is plain and the atmosphere low-key but the moderately priced cuisine is decent and the pisco sours slip down a treat. Mon–Sat noon–10.30pm, Sun noon–9pm.

Manolo's Vía Veneto at C "D"; map pp.62–63. A city institution with a popular corner terrace (or a/c dining), which is a great spot for a drink while people-watching. There's a good variety of light bites and more substantial mains on the menu but the food is no more than average and prices are creeping up. Daily 6am–2am.

The Market C 48 and C Uruguay ☎264 9401, ⓦmarketpanama.com; map pp.62–63. The place to come to tuck into a juicy Aberdeen Angus steak or a deli burger in a cheerily decorated venue with walls bedecked with wine bottles. Save space for some key lime pie or cheesecake. There's weekend brunch too. Daily noon–2.30pm & 7–10.30pm.

Masala Av Justo Arosemena between C 44 Este and C 45 Este ☎225 0105; map pp.62–63. Cosy little restaurant with Indian trimmings and wooden tables or comfortable

1

floor cushions. Mains are around $20 but the *thali* taster platters, which could easily feed two, offer good value. Mon–Sat noon–3pm & 6–10pm.

Napoli C 57 Este at Vía España ☎263 8800; map pp.62–63. Generally considered to dish up the best pizza in the city, this favourite of middle-class Panamanians is jammed with families at weekends. The thin-crust pizzas are excellent (10″ from $7) and the pasta dishes fine, but the atmosphere is boring. Tues–Sun 11am–midnight.

Niko's Café C 51 Este at Vía España ☎223 0111, ⓦnikoscafe.com; map pp.62–63. The unpromising frontage masks another city institution. This no-frills cafeteria is the original of an expanding empire (other outlets in Albrook bus terminal, El Dorado Mall and C 50). You can take out or eat in various good-value hot dishes – seafood, meat and a variety of generic pasta options plus sides for around $5–6. Daily 24hr.

★**NY Bagel Café** Cabeza de Einstein, C Arturo Motta at Vía Argentina ☎390 6051, ⓦnewyorkbagelcafe.com; map pp.62–63. A popular hangout for travellers, expats and local business folk, serving a wide variety of their namesake plus fruit smoothies, good coffee and more. Most items are under $5; free wi-fi. Mon–Fri 7am–8pm, Sat 8am–8pm, Sun 8am–3pm.

La Papa C 51 Este at Av Federico Boyd ☎265 5800, ⓦlapapa.net; map pp.62–63. There's a vast and varied menu at this very popular Colombian restaurant. Portions are large, the quality is good but the dishes are quite pricey (mains around $20). Take your pick from substantial salads, wraps, kebabs, steaks and paellas, plus Colombian specialities such as *arepas* and *ajaico* – a hearty chicken and potato soup served with capers, cream and avocado. Daily 11.30am–3.30pm & 6.30–10.30pm.

Petit Paris C 53 Este opposite Felipe Motta ☎391 8778, ⓦpetitparispanama.com; map pp.62–63. A genuine French-run patisserie-boulangerie-bistro serving beautifully prepared food at Paris prices. Forget the delicious bread and quiches and indulge in the exquisitely crafted cakes and chocolates ($4–6), to be enjoyed with great coffee or a hot chocolate. Free wi-fi and live music Wed evenings. Mon–Sat 7am–11pm, Sun 7am–8pm.

★**La Posta** C 49 at C Uruguay ☎269 1076, ⓦlapostapanama.com; map pp.62–63. The Fifties' Havana ambience of this beautifully restored mansion set in lush tropical gardens makes this a favourite of Panama's elite. The tiled floors, wooden ceiling fans and Cuban music all enhance your appreciation of the gourmet cuisine. Prices are not as exorbitant as they might be (mains from around $22) and you can get a bottle of wine for under $25. Mon–Sat noon–3pm, 7–11pm.

★**Restaurante Jimmy** C Manuel M. Icaza at Vía España ☎223 1525, ⓦparilladajimmy.com; map pp.62–63. Extremely popular 24hr restaurant-cafeteria in the heart of El Cangrejo, with a wide choice of

Panamanian and Greek food, plenty of light bites and fresh, strong coffee. A second, larger, open-air version serving succulent barbecued fare sits opposite the ATLAPA Convention Centre on Calle Cincuentenario (daily 11.30am–11.30pm). Daily 24hr.

Rincón Habanero Vía Argentina, opposite El Trapiche ☎213 2560; map pp.62–63. Sample a slice of Cuba in this dark wood-panelled restaurant, from the rum (make sure to have a mojito) to the cigars and even on the plasma screen. The handful of cosy tables are always packed with people enjoying reasonably priced food ($7–12) featuring copious black beans, accompanied by hot salsa tunes. Mon–Sat 11am–11pm.

Siete Mares C Guatemala at Vía Argentina ☎264 0144; map pp.62–63. Holding the reputation for the best seafood in Panama City, this place generally delivers. Mains from around $17 include corvina with crab in Pernod, and jumbo shrimps in passion fruit sauce, to be savoured in sleek surroundings, from the glass waterfall at the entrance to the piano-bar accompaniment (Mon–Sat from 8pm). Daily 11.30am–11pm.

Las Tinajas C 51 at Av Federico Boyd ☎263 7890, ⓦtinajaspanama.com; map pp.62–63. This delightful colonial mansion in Bella Vista is a favourite destination of tour groups, who flock here to experience authentic Panamanian food and a traditional dance show involving swishing *polleras* and devil dances. Grab a table early to ensure a decent view of the tiny stage. Shows are Tues–Sat at 9pm for $5 provided you spend at least $12 on food and drink. Try the *surtido de mariscos*, a platter of seafood appetizers. Mon–Sat 11.30am–11pm.

El Trapiche Vía Argentina between C Guatemala & Av 2B Norte ☎269 4353; map pp.62–63. Frequently billed as the place to go to try traditional food, such as *mondongo* (tripe) and *tamal de olla* (local tamale without the leaf wrapping), though it attracts Panamanians too. Prices are moderate (mains $8–13) and there's a lively atmosphere on the terrace, but the food quality is variable. Daily 7am–11pm.

FORMER CANAL ZONE

The Amador Causeway provides a cool, breezy setting with fabulous views across the bay. The downside is that a taxi there and back (there are few and infrequent buses) will add another $10–15 to your bill.

Asterios Vía Amador ☎314 1998; map p.68. Fast food it may be but it's healthier than most – grilled chicken, wraps and salads – and fairly inexpensive. The best option in a neighbourhood lacking in restaurants. Daily 10.30am–10pm.

★**Kayuco** Isla Flamenco, Amador Causeway ☎314 1998; map p.68. With outdoor tables overlooking the marina, this is by far the liveliest place in the area to enjoy a few sundowners with friends accompanied by some

1

sizzling grilled seafood (from snacks at $5 to a mixed grill for two for around $12). Daily noon–late.

Mi Ranchito Amador Causeway, near the Punta Culebra Nature Centre ☎ 228 4909, ⓦ restaurante miranchito.com; map p.68. This restaurant's pleasant open-air tables are extremely popular with locals for enjoying cocktails, seafood and sunset city views. Mains from $9. Daily noon–late.

OTHER AREAS

Palacio Lung Fung Transístmica and C 62 Oeste ☎ 260 4011; map pp.62–63. Some way from the action, in Los Angeles, but every taxi driver knows this vast oriental palace, whose thousand-seater upstairs ballroom with its glittering chandeliers is packed at weekends with Panamanians enjoying the dim sum breakfast (until 11.30am). The food is average but the social experience makes it well worth the trip. Daily 7am–11pm.

Pita-Pan Kosher Bal Harbour, Punta Paitilla ☎ 264 2786; map pp.62–63. An illuminated 3-D mural of Jerusalem welcomes you to this casual cafeteria popular with Jewish families, serving moderately priced appetizing dishes, with lots of veggie options – hummus, babaganush and falafel, alongside the ubiquitous pasta and pizza and even kosher sushi. Mon–Thurs 7am–3pm, Fri 7am–5pm, Sun 9am–9pm.

NIGHTLIFE AND ENTERTAINMENT

There's plenty to keep you entertained in Panama City: from a hip-swinging salsa session to an evening at the opera; from a flutter at the roulette table to an evening of jazz in Casco Viejo; from a booze cruise up the canal to a folk-dancing performance. Panama City arguably has the best **clubbing** in Central America, although many places feel like imitations of Miami. In addition, there are plenty of **bars**, casinos and cinemas, plus **venues** putting on rock concerts, as well as a smattering of more highbrow culture to keep you busy in the evenings.

ESSENTIALS

Clubs Nightclubs are known as *discotecas* – ask for the former and you'll end up at a strip joint. Places open, close and reinvent themselves at an alarming rate: the current hotspots in terms of *discotecas* and bars are located in and around Casco Viejo, Calle Uruguay in Bella Vista, spreading out towards El Cangrejo and Marbella, blasting everything from techno to reggae and reggaeton to salsa. Most *discotecas* are open Tuesday to Saturday, and get going around midnight. Entry will generally set you back $10–20 and may include an open bar up until a certain time and the usual "Ladies' Night" enticements. Local beers cost around $4, with imports, spirits and cocktails $5–6. If you're in a group, buying a bottle of spirits between you (which can sometimes get the entry charge waived) or a *cubetazo* (bucket of beer) will help keep costs down. In the smarter bars and clubs you'll need to dress up – no shorts or sandals.

Casinos and bowling Several large casinos are conveniently located near or in the high-end hotels. The larger ones, such as the Majestic (in Multicentro by the *Radisson Decapolis Hotel*) and the *Hotel Veneto Casino*, often have live music at weekends. There's also a great state-of-the-art bowling alley, Extreme Planet, with vast sports screens, a bar and comfort food.

What's on To find out what's on, pick up a copy of *La Prensa* (or check online at ⓦ prensa.com), or the free weekly *The Visitor/El Visitante* (ⓦ thevisitorpanama.com). ⓦ thepanamadigest.com and ⓦ quehacerhoypanama .com also have events listings, while ⓦ conciertospanama .org has up-to-date information on classical concerts, ⓦ teatrodepanama.com lists theatre performances, ⓦ operapanama.com informs you about the occasional opera production, and ⓦ panamarock.com has gig listings.

NIGHTLIFE
CASCO VIEJO

Danilo's Jazz Club American Trade Hotel, Plaza Herrera, Casco Viejo ☎ 211 2000; map p.56. Backed by

---

LAS CHIVAS PARRANDERAS

Increasing in popularity with locals and tourists, *chivas parranderas* – **party buses** – are generally remodelled *diablos rojos*, some of which flaunt the added danger of being open-sided, with only a few ropes to prevent rum-soaked revellers from flying out as the bus lurches round the corner on its city tour. Your $25–30 fee will cover a guide, a band or DJ and unlimited rum and seco. **Tours** (usually Fri & Sat 8pm–midnight) need a minimum number to run, so put your name down in advance. A number of companies now operate variations on the theme – from a fire engine to a limo – though not all are licensed. Increasingly, VIP *chivas* are being offered, complete with air conditioning, plasma screens and even dry ice. More established companies include Chiva Parrandera (☎ 225 8500), Chiva Fiestas (☎ 221 0399, ⓦ chivafiesta.com) and Rumbabus Panama (☎ 229 7066, ⓦ rumbabuspanama.com).

internationally acclaimed Panamanian jazz great Danilo Pérez (to whose foundation some of the proceeds go), this new 50-seater club is an exciting recent addition to the Casco Viejo scene and is set to be a major venue for the annual international jazz festival in January, also organized by Pérez (⊛panamajazzfestival.com). Bar menu available. Cover charge. Wed–Sat 7pm–1am, Sun 3–10pm.

Espacio Av "B" and C 9; map p.56. Unlikely open-air venue in a crumbling shell of a building, but it pulls in the crowds at summer weekends. Simply a bar, a DJ and his sound gear, churning out electronica. Cover charge for events. Thurs–Sat 9pm until late.

Habana Panamá C Eloy Alfaro at C 12 ☎211 0152, ⊛habanapanama.com; map p.56. Lavish evocation of the golden era of 1930s Havana, playing son, salsa and jazz. Live charanga orchestra or salsa band, plus food and bar. Fri & Sat from 9pm.

Mojitos (sin Mojitos) Plaza Herrera, no phone, ⊛mojitossinmojitos.com; map p.56. This small, intimate cellar-like bar, buzzing with expats, locals and travellers, is a must for a night out in Casco Viejo, offering cheap drinks (though no mojitos!) and tasty home-made meat and veggie burgers. Tues–Sat 6pm–late.

Onplug C 11 at C Eloy Alfaro ⊛facebook.com/onplog; map p.56. Funky Bohemian cultural space owned by Panamanian musician Cienfue, aimed at encouraging and promoting new artists. The distinctive decor features umbrellas hanging from the ceiling and a host of recycled materials. Tues–Sat 7pm until late.

★Platea C 1 opposite Club de Clases y Tropas; map p.56. Sophisticated, atmospheric bar in a restored colonial property, where staff in Panama hats mix cocktails for an older clientele. Great live music: Latin jazz on Thurs, salsa on Fri and classic rock on Sat. Mon–Sat 6pm–2am.

Relic Luna's Castle, C 9 Este between Av "B" & Av Alfaro ⊛relicbar.com; map p.56. Funky plant-filled basement courtyard with subdued lighting and driftwood-hewn tables, accompanied by a mix of indie, hip-hop and rock. Inevitably populated with travellers from the adjoining hostel but the inexpensive drinks and vibrant scene attract some Panamanians too. Occasional live art events. Tues–Sat from 8pm.

Villa Agustina Av "A", between Plaza Herrera & C 8 ⊛lavillaagustina.com; map p.56. Trendy outdoor party venue set in a painted and plant-filled courtyard illuminated by pretty lights. It's a hot spot in the dry summer months – less so in the rainy season – popular with backpackers and locals, with cheap booze and occasional big-name DJ events blasting out *música varieda*, heavily laced with electronica. Cover charge for events. Thurs–Sun 6pm until late.

BELLA VISTA, MARBELLA AND EL CANGREJO

AltaBar C 47 at C Uruguay ☎390 2582, ⊛altabar panama.com; map pp.62–63. Current hotspot just off Calle Uruguay, which also has an upstairs terrace bar-restaurant with sports screens and bar. The dancefloor (Wed–Sat), bar and stage are downstairs surrounded by fluorescent white seating, all behind ornate black-and-gold doors. Live acts occasionally perform, though big-name DJs tend to hold sway. Tuesday is often men's gaming night, Thursday's Ladies' Night. Entry $10–15. Tues–Sat 5pm until late.

BITS Hard Rock Hotel, Av Balboa by Multicentro ☎380 1111, ⊛hrhpanamamegapolis.com; map pp.62–63. *The Bar in the Sky* (BITS) is just that: Latin America's highest rooftop bar on the 62nd floor, with indoor and outdoor seating offering 360-degree views of the glittering city lights from behind a glass surround. Mon & Tues 7pm–2am, Wed–Sun 7pm–4am.

Bling Hard Rock Hotel, Av Balboa by Multicentro ☎380 1111, ⊛hrhpanamamegapolis.com; map pp.62–63. A Vegas-style laser-light disco with VIP tables, hot DJs and dancers. The usual features apply: 2-for-1 drinks, ladies' nights (women usually have free entry before 11pm), and cover charges (from $10) for DJs or live music. Mon & Tues 7pm–2am, Wed–Sun 7pm–4am.

Hotel Veneto Casino Vía Veneto at C Eusebio A. Morales ☎340 8686, ⊛venetopanama.com; map pp.62–63. Dull by day, but a festive atmosphere by night, especially at weekends, drawing a mixed crowd of casual and smart dressers who come to socialize, eat, listen to live music and watch sports on the myriad screens as much as to gamble. Daily 24hr.

Istmo Brew Pub C Eusebio A. Morales at Vía Veneto; map pp.62–63. If you're craving something other than the standard *cerveza* try this half open-air, half dungeon-like bar – all the beer is brewed on site (from $4) in beautiful copper kegs. The pool table and football matches on TV also bring in the punters. Daily 4.30pm–late.

The Londoner Pub C Uruguay between C 47 at C 48 ☎214 4883, ⊛londonerpub.web.fc2.com; map pp.62–63. Leather-backed seats, walls plastered in rugby shirts and photos of London do a fair job of persuading you you're in England's capital. There's even English beer and cider on tap and some pricey fish 'n' chips on the menu. The pool tables are occupied by British expats and young Panamanian males. Mon–Sat from 5pm.

La Rana Dorada Vía Argentina at Einstein's Head ☎269 2989, ⊛laranadorada.com; map pp.62–63. Brasserie-bar popular with young expat and middle-class Panamanians, serving beer, cocktails and food. The home-brewed beer and the trendy location attract crowds that spill out onto the street. Its sibling bar in Casco Viejo (Av Eloy Alfaro at C 11; ☎212 2680) is equally popular. Daily noon–late.

1

S6is C Uruguay between C 48 and C 49 ⊕264 5237; map pp.62–63. A mainstay of the party scene, popular with various age groups, this small cocktail lounge with DJ can get packed at weekends. It's pronounced "seis". Thurs–Sat 8pm–4am.

The Wine Bar C Eusebio A. Morales in ApartHotel Las Vegas ⊕265 4701; map pp.62–63. Long-standing favourite that provides a convivial setting amid faux vines, bottles galore and murals of rustic scenes, marred only by the over-vigorous a/c. Choose from over two hundred bottles,or just enjoy a glass while chilling to mellow live music (Mon–Fri after 9pm; Sat & Sun after 7.30pm). The food is secondary (and ordinary) but you can also order off the menu of the adjacent *Caffé Pomodoro* (see p.80). Daily 5pm–late.

OTHER AREAS

Distinción Plaza Paitilla Mall, Vía Israel ⊕215 6081, ⊛distincionpanama.com; map pp.62–63. The most central gay venue with resident DJs and occasional events; electronica presides on Saturdays. Open bar until midnight. Cover charge $7–10. Fri and Sat 10pm–3am.

Icon Club Av Juan Pablo II at Tumba Muerto ⊕6230 0378, ⊛facebook.com/pages/icon-club-panama; map pp.62–63. Currently the biggest gay club, featuring laser lights, foam parties, dancing boys and drag acts. Cover charge for events (up to $10). Thurs–Sun 9pm–3am.

Zona de la Rumba Amador Causeway, before Centro de Convenciones Figali; map pp.62–63. A constantly revolving strip mall of discos, bars and restaurants to suit every mood, from house to hip-hop, salsa to rock; you'll either love it or loathe it. Tues–Sat 9pm until late.

CINEMAS

There are several **cinemas** in the capital – mostly multiplexes in shopping malls showcasing the latest Hollywood offerings, generally in English with subtitles (*subtitulada*; see ⊛cinespanama.com), though less mainstream fare can sometimes be found at Cinépolis.

Cinemark Albrook Mall ⊕314 6001. Vast thirteen-screen complex.

Cinépolis Multiplaza Pacífica Vía Israel ⊕302 6262, ⊛cinepolis.com.pa. State-of-the art multiplex with 3-D and VIP screens that also puts on occasional arthouse features advertised under *El Otro Enfoque*.

Multicentro Upstairs at Multicentro ⊕208 2507. With VIP and 3-D screens as well as 10 standard screens, you can grab a bite to eat at the food court first.

THEATRES AND CONCERT VENUES

Centro de Convenciones ATLAPA Vía Israel, San Francisco ⊕526 7200, ⊛atlapa.gob.pa. The centre has two auditoriums: Teatro Anayansi, seating almost three thousand, hosts pop, jazz, classical, ballet, circus acts and even ice-skating, with plays and beauty pageants in the smaller Teatro La Huaca.

Centro de Convenciones Figali Amador Causeway ⊕314 1414, ⊛figaliconventioncenter.com. The venue of choice for international rock artists.

Teatro Anita Villalaz Plaza de Francía, Casco Viejo ⊕211 4017. Once part of the Supreme Court, this intimate 250-seater hosts a range of cultural activities, from poetry readings to reggae nights.

Teatro Balboa Av Arnulfo Arias Madrid, Balboa ⊕228 0327. Spacious Art Deco theatre, staging all kinds of events, including concerts by the resident National Symphony Orchestra.

Teatro En Círculo Av 6C Norte, El Carmen ⊕261 5375. One of the premier venues for plays.

Teatro Nacional Av "B" between C 3 & C 4, Casco Viejo ⊕262 3525. Savour one of the occasional classical concerts, ballets or operas in the sumptuous Rococo interior of the capital's premier artistic venue.

Teatro La Quadra C "D", El Cangrejo ⊕214 3695. Small theatre putting on experimental and avant-garde theatrical productions, with a strong social development focus.

Theatre Guild of Ancón At the foot of Cerro Ancón, by the police station ⊛anconguild.com. Community theatre established to entertain Zonians that still puts on English-speaking productions.

SHOPPING AND MARKETS

Despite the hype about duty-free **shopping** in Panama City, there's actually very little around and though the streets are bulging with malls and shops, you are unlikely to be overly impressed by either the selection or the prices – indigenous **crafts** and other **souvenirs** aside. The **Albrook Mall**, a two-storey kilometre of retail therapy with discount stores jostling for attention amid more upmarket boutiques, is the number one shopping venue, due in part to its proximity to the bus terminal and the vast food court you can raid when you begin to flag. **Multicentro** (Av Balboa, Punta Paitilla) and **Multiplaza** (Vía Israel, Punta Pacífica) both have dozens of more upmarket boutiques. **Vía España** in El Cangrejo is another shopping area, containing an eclectic mix of bargain stores, would-be chic boutiques and tourist-oriented shops, while **Avenida Central**, a much older commercial area, is the place to browse if you're on a tighter budget and want a feel for the day-to-day transactions of the average city-dweller.

ARTS AND CRAFTS

Some of the best quality *molas*, basketry and woodcarvings are stocked in shops dotted round Casco Viejo, though the prices are higher. Vía Veneto is another area replete with souvenir shops. If a *mola* is on the shopping list, you'll probably get a better price from the Guna craftspeople who spread out their wares on the pavements along Vía Veneto, or in the plazas of Casco Viejo, and who can often organize you a trip to Guna Yala too. In the city's several craft markets the stalls are generally run by members of the community who made the crafts, with more money usually trickling down to the artisans.

Casa Latina Av "A" at C 5 ☎ 228 9828; map p.56. Very pricey offerings but of exquisite quality: the absolute very best of Panamanian handicrafts as well as a range of beautiful Peruvian alpaca knitwear. Daily 10am–7pm.

Centro de Artesenías Amador Causeway south of the **Centro de Convenciones Figali** ☎ 6674 3071; map p.54. Offers some of the better crafts available in the markets: hammocks, *molas* made into place mats, glasses cases and the like, basketry and earrings. Mon–Sat 9am–6pm, Sun 9am–5pm.

Galería de Arte Indígena C 1, Casco Viejo ☎ 228 9557; map p.56. The best selection of Wounaan and Emberá basketry in the capital at suitably elevated prices, alongside high quality *tagua* and *cocobolo* carvings. Daily 9am–8pm.

Mercado de Artesenías Maggy Plaza de la Catedral, Casco Viejo; map p.54. A dozen stalls squeezed into the corner of the plaza selling a range of decent crafts alongside the usual tourist tat at prices that are not far off those in the fancier, more formal shops. Daily 8am–6pm.

Mercado de Buhonería y Artesanías Av 4 at Av "B", behind the old Pacific railroad terminus just off Cinco de Mayo; map pp.62–63. Numerous stalls that attract few shoppers, including a couple selling a good range of hats and hammocks. Mon–Sat 9am–6pm.

Reprosa Av "A" at C 4, Casco Viejo ☎ 228 4913, ⓦ reprosa.com; map p.56. Beautifully crafted gold and silver reproduction pre-Columbian and Spanish colonial jewellery. Also at Av Samuel Lewis on the corner with C 54, Obarrio (☎ 269 0457). Daily 9am–6pm.

La Ronda C 1, Casco Viejo ☎ 211 1001; map p.56. Excellent selection of arts and crafts at Casco Viejo prices. Daily 9am–7pm.

BOOKS

Exedra Books Vía España at Av Brasil ☎ 264 4252, ⓦ exedrabooks.com. The largest bookshop in Panama City, with selections in Spanish and English. Also has a coffee shop and hosts occasional talks and events. Mon–Sat 9.30am–9.30pm, Sun 11am–8.30am.

Gran Morrison Vía España, next to El Rey supermarket ☎ 202 0029. This small department store has a reasonable selection of books in English on Panama. Mon–Sat 9am–6pm, Sun 9.30am–6pm.

STRI Earl Tupper Research Centre Av Roosevelt ☎ 2212 8029, ⓦ stri.si.edu; map pp.62–63. The Smithsonian bookshop stocks an excellent selection on wildlife, ecology and environmental issues in both Spanish and English. Mon–Fri 10am–4.30pm.

DIRECTORY

Embassies and consulates Australia (Honorary Consul), Importadora Ricamar, C 16, Río Abajo (☎ 305 5001); Canada, C 53 Este, Torres de las Americas, Tower A, Piso 11, Punta Pacífica (☎ 264 9731, ⓦ canadainternational.gc.ca/panama); Colombia, Condominio Posada del Rey, Planta Baja, Vía Italia, Punta Paitilla (☎ 392 5586, ⓦ panama.embajada.gov.co); Costa Rica, Av Samuel Lewis, Plaza Omega by the Santuario Nacional (☎ 264 2980, ⓦ embajadacostaricaenpanama .com); Ireland, Torre Delta, 14th floor, Vía España (☎ 264 6633, ⓔ irishconspma@online.ie); South Africa, C 50 at C 69, Edif Plaza Guadalupe, Oficina 404, San Francisco (☎ 226 2559, ⓔ cralaw@cwpanama.net); UK, C 53, Torre MMG, Marbella

---

SPORTS AND LEISURE IN PANAMA CITY

There are not too many opportunities to watch or participate in sport in the capital but catching a **baseball** game at the Estadio Nacional Rod Carew (about 8km northeast from the city centre on Vía Ricardo J Alfaro, off the Corredor Norte) is a real treat worth the taxi fare (see p.42).

Horseracing has a rich tradition in Panama, and takes place 10km east of Panama City en route to the airport at the Hipódromo Presidente Remón (races Thurs 5.30pm, Sat & Sun 2pm; ☎ 217 6060, ⓦ hipodromo.com). Panama's recent resurgence as a global **boxing** powerhouse has encouraged an increased number of bouts in the capital city, above all in the slick new Arena Roberto Durán, named after Panama's former megastar. Watch the press for details.

For those who want to participate in sport rather than spectate, the leafy **Parque Recreativo Omar Torrijos** (on Av Porras, San Francisco) is a prime destination, with public facilities for tennis, basketball, baseball and football plus a jogging route as well as plenty of space to picnic. Best of all it has a lovely, clean outdoor **swimming pool** (Tues–Sun; $2), though avoid the weekend crowds.

Of course most visitors to Panama come for the **hiking**, **birdwatching**, **surfing**, **fishing**, **diving** or **snorkelling**, some of which can be done as a day-trip from the capital, either independently or on a tour (see p.75).

1

(☎269 0866, ⓦgov.uk/world/panama); US, Av Demetrio Basilio Lakas, Clayton (☎207 7000, ⓦpanama.usembassy .gov).

Health Excellent medical care is available in the city in both the public and private sector, with many US-trained and English-speaking staff. Recommended public hospitals include Hospital Santo Tomás, C 34 Este at Av Balboa (☎227 4122, emergencies ☎507 5600), and Hospital Santa Fé, Vía Simón Bolívar at Av Frangipani (☎227 4733, ⓦhsantafe.com). Recommended private medical care is available at Clínica Hospital San Fernando, Vía España, Las Sabanas, next to *McDonald's* (☎305 6300, ⓦhospitalsanfernando.com); and Centro Medico Paitilla, Av Balboa at C 53 (☎265 8800, ⓦcentromedicopaitilla .com). The Centro de Medicina Natural on C 42 Este at Av Mejico, Edif Guadalupe (☎225 0867) offers natural and traditional methods of treatment. If you need to see a dentist, try Clínica Dental Fábregas (☎399 4251) in Hospital Punta Pacífica or the Eisenmann Dental Clinic (☎269 2750), C 53 at Av Samuel Lewis. Staff in both speak English.

Immigration The immigration office (*Migracíon*) is at Av Ricardo J. Alfaro, Tumba Muerto (Mon–Fri 8.30am–3.30pm; ☎507 1800, ⓦmigracion.gob.pa).

Internet Many public places are free wi-fi hotspots, provided you register your laptop. Most hotels and hostels also offer free wi-fi, at least in the foyer. They also often have a PC or laptop for guest use. Internet cafés are also fairly widespread, noticeably along Vía Veneto in El Cangrejo and Parque Santa Ana, close to Casco Viejo. Rates are usually $1/hr.

Money exchange If you need to change currency, head for Panacambios (Mon–Sat 9am–6pm; ☎223 1800) on the ground floor of the Edif Plaza Regency on Vía España.

Pharmacies Farmacias Arrocha is the largest chain, often open 24hr with a huge branch on Vía España, in front of the *Hotel El Panamá*. The large 24hr supermarkets also have pharmacy counters.

Police Policía de Turismo, Vía España opposite the *Riande Hotel Continental* (☎269 8011) and Av Central at C 3, Casco Viejo (☎511 9261).

Post office The main post office (see p.46) is opposite the Basílica Don Bosco, on Av Central, between C Ecuador & C 34 Este. Other convenient branches are on in the Plaza Concordia (below the *Hotel El Panamá*), El Cangrejo, Calidonia and in Balboa at the end of the Prado on Av Arnulfo Arias Madrid.

Telephones The main Cable & Wireless office (Mon–Fri 8am–6pm, Sat 8am–4pm) is on Vía España, next to the National Bank and Plaza Concordia, and has comfortable facilities to make international phone calls, as do some internet cafés. Phone boxes are dotted around the city (see p.47).

Isla Taboga

Twenty kilometres off the coast and about an hour away by boat, the lush hills of **Isla Taboga** have provided one of the most popular weekend escapes for Panama City residents since the capital's sixteenth-century foundation. These days most visitors are day-trippers, who spend their time lounging on the beach, bathing in the shallow waters and strolling the traffic-free streets of the fishing village of **San Pedro**, where most of the island's thousand-odd inhabitants live. Other popular diversions include a **boat trip** round the island, which allows close-ups of pelicans thrusting fish down the gullets of squawking chicks in the nesting months of January to June. There is also reasonable **snorkelling** on the far side of Taboga and Isla El Morro and round a wreck off Isla Urabá, though currents can be strong.

Much of the island, together with neighbouring Isla Urabá, comprises a wildlife refuge for a large colony of brown **pelicans** – check with ANAM (see p.39) if you want to visit. Elsewhere, hibiscus, bougainvillea and sweet-smelling jasmine are in evidence, hence Taboga's affectionate nickname the "Island of Flowers". The island is also famous for its succulent pineapples, though they are now a rarity. The vibe on Taboga is gradually changing due to increasing numbers of resident expats; that said, for the most part the island holds onto its relaxed atmosphere. Packed on summer weekends and holidays, at other times the place can feel gloriously deserted.

Brief history

Taboga's present-day tranquillity belies a turbulent past. The Spanish arrived in 1515, and wasted no time in enslaving and removing the native Cueva Indians before populating the island with freed slaves from elsewhere and constructing a fort on the adjoining **Isla El Morro** – its cannons are sprinkled round the island. Taboga's excellent

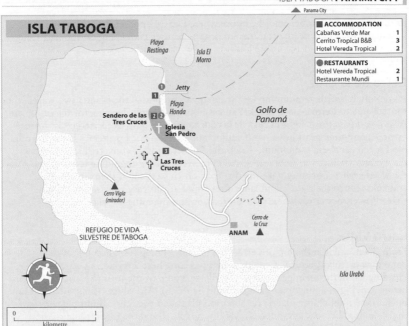

natural harbour has crucially shaped the island's history, forming the base for Francisco Pizarro's expeditions against the Incas, as well as for pirates such as Morgan and Drake. After an English steamship company established its headquarters on Isla El Morro, Taboga became a buzzing port for supplies and repairs and, though the island's maritime importance has dwindled, many contemporary Taboganos still live off the sea, either through small-scale fishing or unloading tuna from fishing boats to larger trans-shippers.

The beaches

Approaching Isla Taboga's floating pier, you are greeted by the sight of the whitewashed buildings and red rooftops of San Pedro, strung out to the left behind **Playa Honda**, a shingly strip dotted with small fishing boats. Turning right after leaving the pier takes you to Taboga's better beach, **Playa Restinga**, a golden crescent, half of which forms a sand bar reaching to Isla El Morro, which is submerged at high tide. Its appeal is somewhat diminished by the piles of overgrown rubble from the demolished *Hotel Taboga* at the back. Even so, crowds of Panamanians happily swim off both beaches, but it is worth considering that much of the island's sewage flows into the bay, and after heavy rains rubbish can wash up on the shore.

San Pedro

Heading back towards **San Pedro**, along the jasmine-scented Calle Abajo, a steep path to the right leads up to the **plaza**, the social hub of the island – where villagers of all ages gather to watch or play football or volleyball, dance or simply hang out. At one end, steps lead up to the gleaming white stucco walls of the **Iglesia San Pedro**, built in 1550 and reputedly the second oldest church in the western hemisphere. Leaving the square via Calle Arriba at the opposite end, and turning left, you come across a shrine

1

to the Virgen del Carmen and the house where Pizarro apparently lived, while a brightly tiled plaque nearby commemorates the painter Paul Gaugin, who had a short stint working on the canal before heading off for the South Seas.

Cerro de la Cruz

It's definitely worth summoning up the energy to do one of the island's two walks. The shorter hike to **Cerro de la Cruz** takes an easy thirty minutes. Leaving town along Calle Abajo, you pass the delightful **casa de la concha** on the right, decorated by its former owner, a one-time pearl fisher, with scallop and pearl shells. Further on is the site of an old French canal-era **sanitorium**, which the Americans later converted into a rest and recuperation centre for "gold roll" canal employees before upgrading it to a hotel. After the weed-strewn **cemetery**, take the dirt road down to the left, then a path up an embankment to the right 100m later, after which it's an easy walk to the gigantic sixteenth-century cross, where you can soak up the sweeping sea view.

Cerro Vigía

From the mirador at the top of **Cerro Vigía** (370m), Taboga's highest point, the panorama is truly spectacular, making the hour-long hike a rewarding experience. Heading along the main path out of the village, you pass the turn to Cerro de la Cruz, before arriving at a junction. Straight ahead lie the ANAM offices (signposted but not open to the public), the island's desalination plant and the refuse dump; to the right, the widening dirt road meanders slowly up the hill. The more direct route to the summit, up the **Sendero de las Tres Cruces**, presents a more challenging but shorter climb through lush forest, not least because of poor signposting. After heavy rain, the path becomes a mudslide, but the rewards are almost-guaranteed sightings of green and black poison-dart frogs and tarantulas. The route is indicated from the plaza, by the phone box; after the housing ends, turn sharp right and keep to the right of the stream until, ten minutes into the forest, the route bears left across a stream, which the path crisscrosses several times before arriving, forty-five minutes later, at three well-tended crosses – the burial sites of a trio of buccaneers who foolishly tangled with some Taboganos. Bearing left again, the trail soon emerges from the undergrowth onto the dirt road to the summit.

ARRIVAL AND DEPARTURE ISLA TABOGA

By boat Two companies run boats to the island. Most people travel on the *Calypso Queen* (☎ 314 1730) as it is one of the highlights of a visit, giving passengers close-ups of the ships waiting to transit the canal and a chance to glimpse dolphins and even migrating whales (July–Oct). There are daily departures from La Playita on the Amador Causeway, near the entrance to the Punta Culebra Nature Centre (high season: Mon–Fri 8.30am returning at 4.30pm, Sat, Sun & public holidays 8am, 10.30am & 4pm, returning 9am, 3pm & 5pm; 50min; $14 return). On weekends and public holidays in particular you'll need to get there an hour beforehand to be sure of a seat, or even purchase a ticket a day in advance. In the rainy season, there are often fewer departures, so ring to confirm times. A newer company, National Tours Ferry (☎314 0571), runs a speedboat from the Balboa Yacht Club (daily 9am & 3pm, returning 9am & 4pm; 30min; $16).

INFORMATION AND ACTIVITIES

Money Make sure you take sufficient cash with you as there is no ATM on Taboga.
Tourist information The English-language website ⓦ taboga.panamanow.com is a useful resource.
Boat trips A couple of hours in a *panga* should cost around $60. Enquire by the jetty.

Whale watching Whale Watching Panama (☎6758 7600, ⓦ whalewatchingpanama.com) offers pricey day-trips from Panama City round Taboga (from $125) to spot humpback whales in the migration season (July–Oct).

ACCOMMODATION AND EATING

Some locals rent out **rooms** informally in their houses for $20–40, often meeting the morning ferry to seek out guests; otherwise enquire at *Restaurante Mundi* by the jetty. **Eating** options on the island are restricted and service is slow, so if you join the summer weekend crowds it's probably worth bringing a picnic.

★**Cabañas Verde Mar** Opposite the jetty ☎ 6410 9641, ✉ verdemartaboga@gmail.com. Five simple self-catering cabins spread around shady tropical gardens, each with two bedrooms (with a/c, and accommodating up to four) and balcony complete with hammock. $30/person

Cerrito Tropical B&B Up the hill from the village centre ☎ 6489 0074, ⓦ cerritotropicalpanama.com. The friendly B&B offers both plain rooms equipped with a/c, fan, private bathroom and shared balcony, and one- to three-bedroom apartments with kitchenettes and private balconies ($143–299). $104

Hotel Vereda Tropical Above the main path ☎ 250 2154, ⓦ hotelveredatropical.com. This Spanish colonial hacienda-style place is the most comfortable of the island's limited and overpriced accommodation options; rooms are tastefully decorated with rustic tiling, although only some overlook the ocean. Its terrace provides lovely views to accompany excellent food – try the house *corvina* in coconut and passion fruit sauce ($14) – but prices are high and service is hit-and-miss. Daily 7.30–10.30am, 12.30–3.30pm & 6.30–9pm. $72

Restaurante Mundi By the jetty. Comprising a few tables on a small deck over the water, this informal restaurant serves up tasty seafood dishes with rice or *patacones* (from $8), even delivering to the beach if required. Daily 7am–9pm.

The Panama Canal and central isthmus

The Panama Canal and central isthmus

Running 80km across the isthmus between the Pacific and Atlantic oceans, straddling the provinces of Panama and Colón, the Panama Canal remains a colossus among engineering achievements, a truly awe-inspiring sight and justifiably the country's prime tourist attraction. What's more, it can easily be explored on an excursion from Panama City, with the Centro de Visitantes de Miraflores offering the best location from which to view the action. Though the corridor that flanks this vital thoroughfare is home to almost two-thirds of Panama's population, for much of its length the waterway cleaves through pristine rainforest, large tracts of which are protected within national parks.

Parque Nacional Soberanía is one of the most accessible tropical rainforest preserves in Latin America, while **Isla Barro Colorado** is home to the world-renowned Smithsonian Institute. Both support an exceptional degree of biodiversity and offer easy day-trips from the capital. The quiet town of **Gamboa** is the embarkation point for excursions to the island and for most tours offering partial transits of the canal; it is also the starting point for rainforest hikes and birdwatching outings along the famous Camino del Oleoducto (Pipeline Road). Three of the area's national parks – Soberanía, the smaller adjacent **Parque Nacional Camino de Cruces** and the larger, less accessible **Parque Nacional Chagres** – also offer the opportunity to walk along the remnants of the historic, partially cobbled Camino de Cruces and the Camino Real, which mule trains carved across the forested spine of the isthmus in colonial times to transport Spain's plundered treasures from Panama City to the Caribbean coast.

The canal reaches the Atlantic at **Colón**, Panama's second city, synonymous with poverty and crime in the minds of many Panamanians, yet compelling and rich in history, with a strong Afro-Antillean and Afro-Colonial heritage. Either side of Colón stretch kilometres of Caribbean coastline peppered with small communities, more or less untainted by tourist development, as well as the country's most impressive colonial ruins. To the west, along the **Costa Abajo**, the formidable remains of the colonial **Fuerte San Lorenzo** still guard the mouth of the Río Chagres amid untouched tropical rainforest; to the northeast lies the **Costa Arriba**, an isolated region of rich coral reefs and laidback fishing villages, much of which is nominally protected by the **Parque Nacional Portobelo**, set around the ruins and beautiful natural harbour of the old Spanish port of **Portobelo**.

At the Pacific end of the canal, some two hours by boat from Panama City, lies the **Archipiélago de las Perlas**. A former hideout of privateers and pirates and a long-standing weekend refuge for the capital's social elite, the archipelago's translucent waters and powdered beaches offer a pricey slice of tranquillity.

PORTOBELO

Highlights

❶ Canal transit Experience the great, iconic waterway on a boat and marvel at the tropical scenery. **See p.95**

❷ Miraflores Locks Get a close look at the precision manoeuvring of gargantuan container vessels as they squeeze through the lock chambers. **See p.96**

❸ Hiking Follow in the footsteps of the conquistadors along the old booty trails of the Camino de Cruces or Camino Real through tangled, lush rainforest. **See p.97** & **p.99**

❹ Birdwatching in Soberanía Over 500 bird species have been recorded here: grab your

binoculars and scan the canopy at dawn. **See p.98**

❺ Stay in an Emberá village Overnight in traditional thatched homes, sharing Emberá culture and learning about the surrounding rainforest. **See p.104**

❻ Spanish colonial forts Step back in time at the desolate, evocative ruins of Fuerte San Lorenzo, or the well-preserved forts of Portobelo. **See p.110** & **p.113**

❼ Archipiélago de las Perlas Picturesque islands offering near-deserted beaches and fine snorkelling and diving. **See p.121**

HIGHLIGHTS ARE MARKED ON THE MAP ON P.94

THE PANAMA CANAL AND CENTRAL ISTHMUS

HIGHLIGHTS

1 Canal transit
2 Miraflores Locks
3 Hiking
4 Birdwatching in Soberanía
5 Stay in an Emberá village
6 Spanish colonial forts
7 Archipiélago de las Perlas

N

CARIBBEAN SEA

PACIFIC OCEAN

GUNA YALA

PANAMÁ

PANAMA CITY

COLÓN

COCLÉ

NUEVO TONOSI

Darién

DARIÉN HIGHWAY (INTERAMERICANA)

Chepo

San Miguel
Archipiélago de las Perlas
Isla Contadora
Isla Pedro González
Isla San José

0   10
kilometres

Archipiélago de las Perlas (see inset)

Tocumen International Airport

PARQUE NACIONAL CHAGRES
Cerro Hope
Cerro Jefe (1007m)
Río Pequení
Río Chagres
PN Chagres Office
Cerro Azul
PARQUE NACIONAL CAMINO DE CRUCES
Lago Alajuela
PN Chagres Main Office
Chilibre
Río Boquerón
Nuevo Vigía
3 PN Soberanía Office
Canopy Tower Ecolodge
Parajso
Gaillard Cut
1
Pedro Miguel Locks
2 Miraflores Locks
Arraiján
Balboa
Western Panama

Cuango
Miramar
Nombre de Dios
La Guaira
Isla Grande
Puerto Lindo
Nuevo Tonosí
Portobelo
6
PARQUE NACIONAL PORTOBELO
Cerro Brujo (979m)
Río Nombre de Dios
Río Piedra
Costa Arriba
María Chiquita
Boquerón
Río Gatún
Sabanitas

TRANSISTMICA HIGHWAY (TRANSISTMICA)
AUTOPISTA PANAMÁ-COLÓN
Gamboa Rainforest Resort
Gatún
Parque Municipal Summit
Rainforest Discovery Centre
4
Panama Canal Railway
PARQUE NACIONAL SOBERANÍA
Isla Barro Colorado
Lago Gatún
Panama Canal

Colón
Cristóbal
Centro de Observación de la Ampliación del Canal
Gatún Locks
Río Chagres
Achiote
Gatún Dam
Piña
6 Fuerte San Lorenzo
Isla Galeta

Escobal
Cuipo
Río Lagarto
Costa Abajo
Boca del Río Indio
Río Indio
Miguel de la Borda

0   25
kilometres

The Panama Canal

The **PANAMA CANAL** is the country's most recognizable landmark, crucial to its economy and inextricably entwined with its historical and cultural development. Arguably the world's most important waterway, it sees around fourteen thousand vessels and over three hundred million tons of cargo pass through its locks every year – a figure that may double once the canal's ambitious expansion plan has been realized in 2015. A gargantuan feat of engineering, the construction of the Panama Canal, completed in 1914, set the standards for twentieth-century engineering. At $352 million it was the most expensive project ever undertaken, with the world's largest earthen dam creating the world's largest artificial lake. The most enormous locks ever built contained the greatest amount of concrete ever used – just over three million cubic metres, the equivalent of sixty Empire State Buildings – and possessed the largest ever swing doors. Yet it is the combination of the scale and ingenuity of the achievement with its ruggedly beautiful tropical setting that makes the canal so special.

There are several ways to appreciate what the canal has to offer, all of them within easy striking distance of the capital. Most people take a trip to **Miraflores Locks** – a convenient fifteen-minute bus ride out of Panama City – which has a well-situated visitor centre with a museum and viewing platform, offering a fine view of ships as they

TRANSITING THE CANAL

To fully appreciate the canal, you need to see it up close. Things may not be quite as you'd expect – the gargantuan Panamax vessels (the largest on the canal) are manoeuvred with surprising delicacy, while the banks of this vast commercial enterprise are lined with jungle and spotted with unspoilt islands. In a **partial transit** from Gamboa to the tip of the Amador Causeway (or vice versa) you get to experience the excitement of passing under the impressive Bridge of the Americas, through the narrow Gaillard Cut and being raised and lowered in the lock chambers of both Miraflores and Pedro Miguel Locks. The **full transit** takes in the most breathtaking scenery, crossing Lago Gatún and weaving among tiny forested islands. You'll glide past a silent stream of giant ships before passing through the enormous Gatún Locks and terminating in Colón, from where it can be up to a two-hour bus journey back to Panama City.

Although completing a full transit might hold a certain cachet, the advertised 8–9 hours can often be a lot longer if you get caught up in one of the frequent log jams in Gatún Locks. A partial transit provides enough excitement and interest for most people and if you take a northbound trip, docking around 1pm in Gamboa, you can skip the bus transfer to enjoy a drink at the *Gamboa Rainforest Resort* before getting the public bus back to the city, with the added bonus of avoiding the inflated taxi fare from the causeway at the other end.

The cheapest way to see the canal is to try and get a job as a **line-handler** – a person who helps keep the boat positioned in the locks; it's a requirement for all transiting cruising vessels to have four line-handlers. If you're interested, check out ⓦpanlinehandler.com.

INFORMATION AND TOURS

The two companies listed below offer similar trips, charging $175 for the full transit and $135 for the partial, which includes a transfer between the relevant marina on the Amador Causeway and the boat, bilingual guided commentary, soft drinks, meals and snacks. In the tourist season (Dec–April) there are frequent transits; out of season there are fewer, with a full crossing often only once a month. Various tour operators also offer canal transits, though they all use the boats listed below – you're essentially just paying to be picked up from your accommodation.

Canal and Bay Tours ☎209 2009, ⓦcanal andbaytours.com. Two larger craft are used for full transits, while the partial transit often employs the smaller *Isla Morada*, a 1912 wooden vessel said to have been previously owned by Al Capone. All tours leave from La Playita, Isla Naos, at 8am.

Panama Canal Tours ☎226 8917, ⓦpmatours .net. The company caters predominantly to foreign tourists. Southbound partial transits leave from Flamenco Marina at 9.30am (starting with a bus ride to Gamboa); northbound partial transits and full transits leave at 7.30am.

pass through. Facilities at the canal's other viewing platform, across the isthmus at the equally impressive three-chamber **Gatún Locks**, are not as developed and take longer to reach, though you can get even closer to the action (see p.110). Different perspectives again are offered by fishing or boating trips on **Lago Gatún**, and by speeding across the isthmus and alongside the canal by **train**. But by far the best way to get your head around the technical brilliance, natural beauty and sheer magnitude of the feat is to travel along the canal ("transit") on a boat.

2

The Panama Canal Railway Company

Corozal Passenger Terminal, Building T376, Corozal West • Mon–Fri departs 7.15am (1hr), returning from Colón at 5.15pm; reservations are advisable and it's worth getting there early (6.30am) to secure your vantage point • $25 one way • ☎ 317 6070, ⓦ panarail.com • A taxi costs around $6 from the city centre to the terminal

The Corozal Passenger Terminal of the **Panama Canal Railway Company** is the departure point for the scenic transisthmian train journey. The original Panama Railroad, built in the 1850s during the California Gold Rush (see box, p.108), transported over $700 million in gold before the completion of the Union Pacific Railroad across the US in 1869 made it obsolete, forcing it into bankruptcy. Following a short revival during the canal's construction, the railway fell into disrepair until 1998 when the government agreed to privatize it. Though the railway company predominantly ferries freight to and from the Atlantic and Pacific container ports, it offers a commuter passenger service to Colón that is very popular with tourists. A supremely comfortable way to enjoy the canal, it serves up old-world elegance in wood-panelled, carpeted carriages with large windows. In fine weather, make sure you also get out onto the open viewing deck.

Miraflores Locks

A mere fifteen minutes from downtown Panama City along the Avenida Omar Torrijos are the **Miraflores Locks (Esclusas de Miraflores)**, where the four-storey **Centro de Visitantes de Miraflores** provides a prime location for observing the canal in action. Marking the Pacific entrance to the waterway, the locks raise or lower vessels 16.5m

---

THE BIG DITCH

Erroneously nicknamed **The Big Ditch**, the 77km canal eschews straight lines as it weaves its way from the Pacific to the Caribbean or Atlantic entrance, which is actually 42km to the west, on account of Panama's eel-like shape. British politician and historian James Bryce dubbed the waterway "the greatest liberty Man has ever taken with nature", though ironically it has resulted in a symbiotic relationship between the two: the canal's constant thirst for water to feed the locks is highly dependent on the preservation of the adjacent national parks to protect the water catchment area.

The vast **lock chambers** measure 304.8m by 33.53m, affording colossal Panamax vessels a mere 0.6m of leeway either side, yet they function in much the same way as they did when they were first used. Once the gates are closed, these vast vessels are kept aligned by cables attached to pairs of electric locomotives known as mules (*mulas*). The huge tunnel-like culverts then kick in with phenomenal efficiency, taking only eight minutes to fill the giant chamber with the equivalent of 43 Olympic swimming pools.

Tolls for ships are calculated depending on type of vessel, and size and type of cargo. The average toll for the largest vessels is $126,000 for the 8–10-hour transit but the costs don't stop there, since up to three tugboats are also required for the more difficult stages of the operation at a cost of up to $13,000 per boat, not to mention the obligatory canal pilot. Once the canal expansion programme is complete (see box, p.302), these costs are set to rocket. It is no wonder then that annual profits are well in excess of $1 billion. Yet for all the sums, the canal still represents a major saving in time and money for ships that would otherwise have to travel 15,000km round the treacherous seas of Cape Horn.

between sea level and the artificial Lago Miraflores in two stages, a process best appreciated from the visitor centre's observation deck.

Centro de Visitantes Miraflores

Daily 9am–5pm, including holidays • $8 museum and viewing decks, $5 lower viewing deck only • ☎ 276 8617, ⓦ pancanal.com • Take any Gamboa or Paraíso bus from the Albrook terminal (see p.73) to the Miraflores stop, or it's $8–10 by taxi

The **Centro de Visitantes Miraflores** houses an informative introductory museum on the canal's history and workings as well as an **observation deck** only metres from the locks. Optimum viewing times for vessels transiting are before 11am, when ships are usually entering the canal from the Pacific, and after 3pm, when they are exiting.

The **museum**, which serves to promote the Autoridad del Canal de Panamá (ACP) as much as to inform you about the canal, squeezes both the French and US construction efforts into the ground-floor exhibition – for more in-depth coverage go to the canal museum in Casco Viejo (see p.58). Against a vast montage of historical photos and a soundtrack of blasting dynamite, the bare bones of the enterprise are covered through impressive scale models and bilingual texts. Sound effects continue on the first floor as the focus shifts to the biodiversity of the canal's catchment area, while on the floor above, the spotlight turns to engineering; highlights include a virtual high-speed transit of the canal, complete with illuminated 3-D topographic map, and the chance to experience life inside a lock culvert (thankfully without the water). The centre also houses a couple of thinly stocked cafés, a restaurant and a gift shop.

ACCOMMODATION AND EATING   THE PANAMA CANAL

Holiday Inn Ciudad de Saber (City of Knowledge), Clayton ☎ 317 4000, ⓦ hinnpanama.com. Bang opposite the Miraflores Locks, so you can watch the canal action night and day, though you'll need an upper-floor room. The well-appointed, spacious rooms have giant plasma-screen TVs, crisp white sheets, sparkling bathrooms and the usual business amenities. But you are a long way from the city so taxi fares will hit the wallet hard. Breakfast included. **$120**

Restaurante Miraflores Miraflores Visitor Centre, Miraflores Locks ☎ 232 3120. Average and overpriced buffet fare ($31 for lunch, $34 for dinner) play second fiddle to the location, so reserving a balcony table well in advance is a must. You'll see more canal action if you opt for the evening floodlit experience. It's not cheap, but it's a once-in-a-lifetime experience. Daily noon–11pm.

The road to Gamboa

Once beyond the Miraflores and Pedro Miguel Locks, the road to Gamboa (Carretera Gaillard) skirts the emerald rainforest of the contiguous **Parque Nacional Camino de Cruces** and **Parque Nacional Soberanía**, both of which have trails to suit hikers, bird lovers and anyone interested in the Spanish conquest. It then ascends to the continental divide at the **Parque Municipal Summit**, before swooping down to the bridge across the Río Chagres, which marks the entrance to the somnolent canal-era town of Gamboa. Unfortunately buses to Gamboa, though regular, are infrequent, so that visiting several sites in one day is tricky unless you have your own transport.

Parque Nacional Camino de Cruces

The park entrance is 2km up the Carretera Chivo Chivo, a right turn a couple of bends after the Miraflores Locks • Daily 8.30am–4.30pm • $5 • ☎ 500 0839 • Any Paraíso or Gamboa bus from Albrook's bus terminal (see p.73) will drop you off at the bottom of the Carretera Chivo Chivo, which requires a high clearance vehicle, or 4WD in the rainy season

Despite bearing the name of the conquistadors' famous trade route across the isthmus (named after the now-submerged settlement of Cruces), the **Parque Nacional Camino de Cruces** is often overlooked as a tourist destination. Yet, while it is hard to escape the sound of nearby traffic in places, the reserve is a prime location for spotting sloths and provides important traces of colonial times.

There are four **trails** on offer: the **Sendero Capricornio** provides an easy 1km circular stroll from the park office through some of the park's mainly dry semi-deciduous forest. But it's worth expending slightly more energy on the **Sendero Mirador** (3.2km total), which offers a moderate hike up to a breezy wooden watchtower, affording an impressive panoramic view of the canal and distant city skyscrapers. The remaining two trails, the **Ruinas de Cardenas** and **Camino de Cruces**, are both still in need of clearance work, though you don't need to venture far along the latter before you'll come across some of the original cobblestones.

Camping is permitted near the park office, though there are no facilities beyond a bathroom and running water.

Pedro Miguel Locks and the Gaillard Cut

Just over three kilometres beyond Miraflores lie the smaller **Pedro Miguel Locks**, which are closed to the public. The canal then narrows into the infamous **Gaillard Cut**, where over two-thirds of all canal excavation occurred. Its 13km stretch posed the most persistent technical headache for engineers, and severe landslides continued long after the eventual opening of the canal. On the left, a little beyond Paraíso, the canal's former dredging headquarters, rows of small white crosses mark the **French Cemetery**, which sits on the continental divide, a poignant reminder of the doomed French attempt to build a canal in the 1880s. The road then climbs, passing a turn-off to the elegant, cable-stayed **Centennial Bridge**, opened in 2004 to celebrate Panama's hundred years of independence. After 3km of dense rainforest the road forks: to the right it cuts through the Parque Nacional Soberanía to the Transístmica and the new motorway, which both link Panama City with Colón, while to the left it continues to Gamboa.

Parque Nacional Soberanía

The park office is 15km northwest of Panama City on the road to Gamboa where the road forks • Park office daily 8.30am–4.30pm, though there is always a warden on site • $5 • ☎ 232 4192

Providing the most accessible substantial body of tropical rainforest from Panama City, a mere thirty-minute drive away, the **PARQUE NACIONAL SOBERANÍA** is one of the country's most visited national parks and well worth exploring. Stretching north and west from the **park office**, which lies 15km northwest of Panama City, it hugs the canal and encircles Gamboa, covering over 190 square kilometres. The park encompasses a stretch of the majestic **Río Chagres**, the canal's lifeblood, which you can explore by boat, and several well-maintained trails either side of the town, including a stretch of the historic Camino de Cruces and a world-renowned birding hotspot, the Camino del Oleoducto.

The trails

You can pick up a **map** and pay your fee at the office or at the entry barrier to the Camino de Oleoducto, if there is someone there when you arrive. There are three substantial trails within the park, although they're not particularly close to each other

---

WILDLIFE IN THE PARQUE NACIONAL SOBERANÍA

With 525 recorded bird species, 105 mammals, 79 reptiles and 55 amphibians, the chances of spotting **wildlife** in the Parque Nacional Soberanía are high. White-tailed deer, agoutis, coatis, pacas, howler monkeys and Geoffroy's tamarins are fairly commonplace, but you'll need a good guide to locate the rarer, more elusive nocturnal kinkajous or silky anteaters. Following an extensive breeding programme, several harpy eagles have been released into the park in recent years so there is a slim chance of catching sight of these endangered birds (see box, p.286). Other birds to look out for include crested eagles, red-lored Amazons, great jacamars and trogons – the park's symbol.

or the park office, arguably making the area best enjoyed with a car, parking at the various trailheads, or on a tour (see p.75).

Although most of Soberanía's trails are easy and safe enough to do on your own, you're strongly advised to hike the Camino de Cruces with a **guide** as the trail is overgrown and difficult to follow in places and the occasional robbery has been known. Several Panama City tour operators do the trip, as well as offering excursions to the Camino de Oleoducto (see p.75), which would solve the transport difficulties, or you can hire a ranger from the park office as a guide – a much cheaper option, though they are unlikely to speak English.

Camino del Oleoducto

By far the most tramped trail is the unpromising-sounding **Camino del Oleoducto** (Pipeline Road), so named because it was originally built to service an oil pipeline constructed across the isthmus by the US in World War II in case transportation via the canal became impossible. The pipeline was never used but the 17.5km dirt-road service track, which lies a kilometre beyond Gamboa, draws birding enthusiasts from around the world. Though visually unremarkable since it is no wilderness trail, the likely wildlife sightings more than compensate. Even if you can't tell a white-whiskered puffbird from a band-tailed barbthroat, you cannot fail to be impressed by the array of brightly coloured birds, and you'll see a great deal more if you go with a good guide (see p.42 & p.75).

Camino de Cruces and the Sendero de la Plantación

A 10km section of the isthmus-crossing **Camino de Cruces** traverses the park's dense vegetation from the borders of the Parque Nacional Camino de Cruces (see p.97) – to access the trailhead, head 6km up the road that forks right at the park office. The trail ends up at the shores of the Río Chagres, site of the barely distinguishable remains of the Ruinas de Venta de Cruces, which served as a resting post for weary, booty-laden mules and conquistadors. However, you don't have to venture that far to get a flavour of the history – a ten-minute hike along the path will bring you to a restored section of the original sixteenth-century paving stones.

If you decide to walk the whole trail, you can avoid returning along the same route (in an exhausting eight-hour trek) by hopping across the Chagres to the *Gamboa Rainforest Resort* (see p.101) and reviving yourself with a drink, before catching one of the regular buses back. You would need to organize a boat to meet you in advance; the park wardens can arrange this for a couple of dollars. Alternatively, hike half of the Camino de Cruces, breaking off down the 5km **Sendero de la Plantación (Plantation Trail)**, the gravelly remnants of a paved thoroughfare that once led to the largest private agricultural venture in the old Canal Zone, harvesting rubber, coffee and cocoa, which you can still occasionally spot growing wild amid the rainforest. It eventually disgorges you onto the road to Gamboa, where you can flag down one of the regular Gamboa–Panama City buses.

Canopy Tower Ecolodge

Semaphore Hill • Day visits $120/person • ☎ 264 5720, ⓦ canopytower.com • It's a steep 1km to the lodge from the drive entrance on the main road to Gamboa

For serious nature lovers who can't afford the overnight rates (see p.100), it's still worth considering a day-trip to the **Canopy Tower Ecolodge**. These are actually partial day-trips, which have to be organized in advance, and include one meal, the park fee and a guided walk, where you're likely to spot manakins, antbirds, tinamous, sloths, coatis and agoutis, as well as an abundance of butterflies and insects. You also get time on the truly special canopy-level **observation deck**, which is equipped with a telescope and even sun loungers, allowing you to indulge in some spectacular armchair birdwatching.

2

Rainforest Discovery Centre

2km along the Camino de Oleoducto from central Gamboa • Daily 6am–4pm • Peak hours (6–10am) $30, other hours $20; 20 percent discount for advance booking • ☎ 314 1141 in Panama City, ☎ 6450 4850 visitor centre, ⓦ pipelineroad.org

The **Rainforest Discovery Centre**, on the park boundary, boasts an impressive canopy observation tower with multi-level viewing platforms, a series of short trails and an interpretive centre, whose main draw is the **observation deck**, where bird feeders attract scores of hummingbirds. The drawback is the hefty entrance fee, especially if you arrive during prime birding time (6–10am) though it's definitely worth the outlay if you're keen on birds or you make a day of it, taking a picnic. Profits go towards environmental education, research and conservation projects.

ARRIVAL AND DEPARTURE   PARQUE NACIONAL SOBERANÍA

By bus Gamboa-bound buses from Panama City's Albrook terminal can drop you off at the park office, several kilometres away from the main trails, and 2.5km further along the road, at the entrance to the Sendero de la Plantación – also the turn-off for the *Canopy Tower Ecolodge* (see p.99). For the Camino del Oleoducto, alight at the park in Gamboa, walk 1km along the road parallel to the railway and canal, then follow the signs up a dirt road to the right to the entrance barrier.

By car There are car parks at the trailheads.

By taxi A taxi from central Panama city will cost around $20–30 depending on where in the park you want to go.

ACCOMMODATION

ANAM refuge Visitors can lodge at the basic ANAM refuge at the end of the Camino del Oleoducto (cold water and basic cooking facilities only) but you will need to carry your own food. $5/person

Camping You can arrange to camp along the Sendero de la Plantación or the Camino del Oleoducto (no facilities but near running water). $5/person

Canopy Tower Semaphore Hill, Parque Nacional Soberanía ☎ 264 5720, ⓦ canopytower.com. US radar tower converted into a four-storey, twelve-room ecolodge with a genuine commitment to conservation. Simple, functional single rooms with shared bathroom are offered alongside more comfortable en-suite doubles and suites; all have screens, fans and hot water. Guests get a free guided walk each day, with excursions catering primarily for birders. Rates (multi-day packages offer good deals) include full board, with decent meals served from the wonderfully panoramic dining lounge. $352

Parque Municipal Summit

On the road to Gamboa • Daily 9am–4pm • $5 • ☎ 232 4850, ⓦ parquesummit.org • Take any Gamboa bus, getting off at the stop right outside the park gates

The once down-at-heel **Parque Municipal Summit** (formerly Summit Botanical Gardens and Zoo) is undergoing an ambitious overhaul. Though some of the animal cages are still depressingly small, Summit merits a visit in order to see fauna that you are unlikely to spot in the wild. In the early rainy season you may see colonies of oropendolas and caciques, while hummingbirds and toucans are more common year-round. The gardens' star attractions are some of Panama's most endangered and elusive residents – a jaguar, a tapir, and a forlorn harpy eagle that is soon to get a mate.

Summit is also a popular picnic spot so be aware that during weekends and school holidays your ears are more likely to be greeted by reggaeton than birdsong.

Gamboa

Surrounded by the luxuriant vegetation of the Parque Nacional Soberanía and bordered by the impressive Río Chagres and Lago Gatún, into which the river spills, you would expect **GAMBOA** to be a thriving tourist destination. Yet despite being the portal to a variety of attractions on and off the water, the sleepy former Canal Zone town has yet to be revitalized by the tourist traffic, partly since most visitors tend to make day-trips out from Panama City. For nature lovers and birding enthusiasts in particular, Gamboa provides access to the legendary Camino del Oleoducto and the adjacent Rainforest Discovery

Centre. It is also the departure point for excursions to the scientific research station on Isla Barro Colorado (see p.102), for boats offering Pacific-bound partial canal transits, fishing trips or wildlife viewing on Lago Gatún (see p.102), and for cultural excursions to indigenous Emberá communities upriver. The town is easily accessed by bus and though some activities need organizing in advance, others can be arranged on the spot.

The most noticeable activity in town takes place on weekdays on the lake shore, where the canal dredging division is located. Otherwise, there's little to do in the town except soak up the tranquil yesteryear feel, taking in the attractive (and often empty) canal-era architecture, indulging in a little birdwatching around the wooded fringes, or strolling along the Chagres, looking out for iguanas and turtles sunning themselves along the riverbanks, and marvelling at the constant procession of container ships. Alternatively the *Gamboa Rainforest Resort* (@gamboaresort.com) hosts a range of activities.

Brief history

Isolated Gamboa – its only road access via an old single-track bridge shared with the Panama Railroad – has never been a major scene of activity. Built in 1911 as a settlement for around seven hundred "silver roll" employees and families (see p.298), its population did not increase significantly until the canal's dredging division relocated there from Paraíso in 1936. By 1942, Gamboa's residents exceeded 3,800, much more than the current population, and the community could boast a cinema and golf course. But once the Panama Canal Authority started to transfer operations to Panama City following the 1977 treaties, services began to close and the town dwindled, although the golf course has recently been upgraded (@summitgolfpanama.com).

ARRIVAL AND DEPARTURE   GAMBOA

By bus Gamboa is a 50min bus ride from Panama City. Buses make regular daily departures (5am, 5.45am, 6.30am – 6am on weekends – 8am, 10am, noon, 2pm, 4.30pm, 6.30pm, 9pm; Mon–Fri also 1pm & 3pm) from the very far end of the Albrook terminal (by *Niko's Café*). After crossing the bridge into Gamboa, the bus circles the tree-filled park, where you alight for the Sendero del Oleoducto or Rainforest Discovery Centre, before it heads up towards the *Gamboa Rainforest Resort*, where it turns, taking the same route back. Catch it back to Panama City outside the entrance to the dredging division, at the park corner.

By taxi A taxi from Panama City costs around $35 (30min).

ACCOMMODATION AND EATING

During the week, inexpensive meals are available from the **fondas** opposite the canal's dredging division, which close after feeding lunch to the workers. Otherwise there is a hard-to-locate – so ask – small **shop** at the back of some houses on the way to the Sendero del Oleoducto, or bring a **picnic**.

Canopy B&B 114a Jadwin Ave ☎883 5929, @canopytower.com. This beautifully restored two-storey canal-era house provides five tastefully decorated airy rooms with a/c, fan, wi-fi and private bathrooms. Also with comfortable common areas and reductions on day-passes to the Canopy Tower (see p.99). A set dinner can be pre-ordered for $24/person. **$154**

Gamboa Rainforest Resort ☎314 5000, @gamboaresort.com. The best bet for a bite to eat, though you'll be paying elevated tourist prices, and the quality of food and service is variable. A lunchtime buffet is available at the main *Corotú* restaurant, while snacks and cocktails are served at the *Monkey Bar* terrace, a splendid breezy spot with fabulous views across the Chagres, and the riverside *Los Lagartos* offers superlative opportunities for wildlife viewing. Corotú: daily 6.30am–10.30pm; Monkey Bar: Tues–Sun 11.30am–5pm.

Ivan's Bed & Breakfast 111 Jadwin Ave, Gamboa ☎314 9436, @gamboaecotours.com. Tucked away in a delightful old wooden canal house, this friendly establishment run by Gladys and Ivan Ortíz is aimed primarily at birdwatchers, comprising four simply furnished but comfortable en-suite rooms with fans and hot water. Continental breakfast is included, with other meals provided on request. Ivan leads local birding tours and can help organize other excursions. Breakfast included. **$100**

Mateo's Bed & Breakfast C Humberto Zárate 131a ☎6690 9664, @gamboabedandbreakfast.com. You'll get a warm welcome in these simple fan-ventilated cabins with large windows and two single beds (cold water only). Surrounded by tropical vegetation and a well-tended garden, there is plenty of space to indulge in armchair or hammock birdwatching. Excellent value, with breakfast included. Use of kitchen or other meals on request. **$35**

Lago Gatún

Following the damming of the Río Chagres in 1910, the waters took three years to rise, culminating in the formation of **LAGO GATÚN**, the largest artificial lake in the world at the time, covering 425 square kilometres – roughly the size of Barbados. The lake now provides 33km of the waterway's total 77km length, with the ships following the original course of the Río Chagres, where the lake is at its deepest, and collects and releases the 43 million gallons of water necessary for each vessel to transit the canal.

The undulating topography ensured that this impressive body of water developed into a place of great beauty, with dozens of peninsulas and tree-topped islands, and a myriad of inlets easing their tentacles into the lush rainforest, all of which are best explored by boat. Favourite destinations are **Isla Barro Colorado** (see p.102) and the archipelago of **Isla Tigre** and **Islas Brujas**. You can't land on the seventeen or so islands, but with a good pair of binoculars you can usually observe from your boat the islands' monkeys cavorting in the trees. Several tour operators include the islands on their wildlife viewing trips (see p.75) though some, unfortunately, can't resist the urge to feed the monkeys.

Other **wildlife** to look out for, which can easily be spotted while on a fishing trip, includes crocodiles and caimans slithering in the muddy shallows, as well as sloths and snakes entwined round branches. The lake is famous for its prolific peacock bass, and fishermen hanging out at the public dock, before the bridge, will happily take you out for a few hours **angling** for around $70 for the boat.

Isla Barro Colorado

Tours Tues, Wed & Fri 7.15am–4.10pm • $70 including boat transfer from Gamboa and lunch • Book through the STRI (☎ 212 8951, ⓦ stri.org) or in person at the STRI's Earl S. Tupper Building (see p.64), or via a tour operator (see p.75) • Tours depart from the Smithsonian Tropical Research Institute (STRI) jetty, 1km beyond Gamboa

Home to the most studied patch of tropical forest in the New World is **Isla Barro Colorado** (BCI), whose name derives from the dominant reddish clay (*barro colorado*). Administered by the Smithsonian Tropical Research Institute (STRI), it draws scientists from all over the world to pore over the sixteen square kilometres of flora and fauna, but can also be visited on a day-long **tour**, which makes for a diverting outing.

After a short **talk**, you set out on a **guided walk**, during which you'll learn about some of the island's 1300-plus plant species and 110-odd species of mammal, over half of which are bats. A favourite route leads to the "Big Tree", an enormous 500-year-old kapok with a 25m diameter, laden with epiphytes. Although the small island is home to both ocelots and pumas, you're unlikely to see more than their prints in the mud. Much more visible are the vast colonies of leafcutter ants, estimated to chew fifteen percent of all leaves produced in the forest to feed the fungus they eat in their subterranean nests. After **lunch** in the cafeteria, you can watch for wildlife in the immediate vicinity of the research station, where you're likely to see howler monkeys, but you are not allowed back in the forest unaccompanied.

Parque Nacional Chagres

The park headquarters (daily 8.30am–4.30pm) are at Campo Chagres, a small headland jutting into Lago Alajuela; there's also a park office at the end of main road in Cerro Azul • $5

North of Panama City, encompassing large tracts of the Provinces of Colón and Panama, the vast, sprawling rainforested wilderness of **Parque Nacional Chagres** stretches from the northern rain-soaked mountains overlooking the Caribbean to the park's highest peak, Cerro Jefe (1007m), in the south. The tropical vegetation harbours large but elusive populations of tapirs, endemic salamanders and an abundance of birdlife, including harpy eagles and the rare Tacarcuna bush tanager, and is laced with waterfalls and rivers rich in fish as well as otters, caimans and crocodiles. Hikers are also drawn to the area, particularly by the prospect of following in the steps of the conquistadors along the **Camino Real**, which slices across the western edge of the reserve.

At the heart of the park, the powerful **Río Chagres** and its tributaries – home to several Emberá and Wounaan villages that welcome visitors – carve their way through rugged terrain spilling into the scenic elongated **Lago Alajuela** at the park's southwest corner. A reservoir, Lago Alajuela was built to help regulate the water level in Lago Gatún further downriver.

Supplying forty percent of the water necessary for the canal to function and providing all the water for domestic and industrial consumption – as well as electricity through **hydroelectric power** – in Panama City and Colón, the Río Chagres is of vital importance to the country. In order to protect the river and its catchment area, the national park was formed in 1985, its 1296 square kilometres making it one of the country's largest reserves.

2

Río Chagres and around

Most tourist activities rely on the area's main artery, the **Río Chagres**, be it **whitewater rafting** the cascading torrents of the upper river or more leisurely **kayaking** along the slower, lower stretches, both of which are generally organized as day-trips from Panama City (see p.75). One of the best ways to explore the park is by visiting one of the numerous **Emberá** communities, sprinkled along the banks of the Chagres and its tributaries (see box, p.104). The Emberá, together with the closely related Wounaan, have been relocating from the Darién since the late 1960s. Since their traditional means of livelihood – semi-nomadic subsistence agriculture and hunting – are now largely denied to them thanks to the restrictions of living within a national park, they are being encouraged to make a living from tourism.

As with the neighbouring parks of Camino de Cruces and Soberanía, Parque Nacional Chagres also includes important traces of the country's colonial past, containing a lengthy portion of the **Camino Real**, one of the conquistador mule routes across the isthmus, which skirts the eastern shores of Lago Alajuela. There is currently no clearly marked route but several tour companies offer day or multi-day guided hikes along this historic trail (see p.75).

Cerro Azul

On the southern edge of Parque Nacional Chagres, 40km northeast of Panama City, the area known as **Cerro Azul** is one of two entry points to the park – the other being at Lago Alajuela (see p.105). Though designating both a mountain peak and a nearby village, Cerro Azul generally refers to the mountainous area around both. It is very popular with more affluent Panamanians – and increasingly with foreign retirees – many of whom have second homes peppered along the fringes of the park boundary, attracted by the accessible fresh mountain air and great views (when the mists clear). It's not as wild as the Darién or Amistad, but for birdwatchers and nature lovers with limited time, Cerro Azul makes for a convenient break from Panama City, with a couple of comfortable accommodation options within reach of the forest. You can easily get within striking distance of the park with an ordinary vehicle, since the roads are asphalt as far as the gated residential area of Altos de Cerro Azul, or by bus.

Cerro Jefe

The main draw is the park's highest point, **Cerro Jefe**, an important location for endemic mosses, orchids, ferns and bromeliads, with an impressive mirador and two short, rather overgrown birdwatching trails near the summit. To get there from the park office the route is less interesting, between open fields for about 3km before

2

VISITING AN EMBERÁ COMMUNITY

At only a couple of hours' travel away from Panama City and Colón, the **Emberá village tour** is an established favourite with cruise ships and tour operators (see p.75). Publicity brochures glibly talk about the Emberá "living much as their ancestors did centuries ago" although you don't need to look further than the use of outboard motors, mobile phones and Spanish – not to mention the jeans and T-shirts often donned once the tourists have evaporated – to see that the Emberá are undergoing radical change. Staying **overnight**, or preferably for several nights, affords a better opportunity to interact with villagers and venture deeper into the forest. That said, the day-tours can still offer visitors a fascinating partial snapshot of traditional Emberá life and culture, and there are obvious benefits to communities: income that will afford them greater self-determination, renewed cultural pride and a revival of ancestral skills and traditions.

THE TOUR ITINERARY

Although villages vary in setting and character, excursions are similar. **Prices** ($85–150, not necessarily including the $5 park entry fee) and tour group sizes vary; though even travelling in a small party is no guarantee you won't be cheek by jowl with other tourists once in the village, especially during the cruise ship season (Oct–April). Morning pick-up (8am–8.30am) is followed by an hour's bus journey to Lago Alajuela, where life-jacketed tourists fan out towards different villages in motorized dugouts. The **boat trip** (30–60min depending on the village location and river water levels) is itself a highlight, gliding through vine-laden forest with raptors wheeling overhead and metallic kingfishers flashing past. At the **villages**, traditional wood and thatch buildings sit on stilts, and you'll be greeted by enthusiastic kids and women, who form a dazzling collage of fluorescent sarong-like skirts (*uhua*) and multicoloured bead-and-silver-coin necklaces, their hair often adorned with hibiscus flowers.

    Activities generally include a village tour, a talk about the traditional Emberá way of life (see p.275) and a demonstration of basketry or woodcarving as well as a short walk into the rainforest with one of the village elders to learn about medicinal plants. A simple lunch precedes traditional dances accompanied by drums, bamboo flutes and maracas, after which tourists can get their bodies painted with jagua dye, frolic with the kids in the river and peruse the finely made crafts on display. Unlike the Guna, the Emberá are fairly comfortable being photographed and general shots of the village (though not inside homes) and dances are allowed, though permission should be sought from individuals. Most tours pile back into the dugouts at 2.30–3pm for the return trip.

VISITING INDEPENDENTLY

It is possible and cheaper to visit **independently** – several of the communities have their own website with mobile phone contact numbers (listed below). They generally charge from $70/ person (1–2 people, less for larger groups) for the day, which is approximately what they receive per tourist from the tour operators. But you'll still need to ring in advance to ensure a boat ride, and reaching Puerto de Corotú, the departure point for most villages on Lago Alajuela, is time-consuming on public transport (2hr 30min) and will probably also require some travel by taxi. To reach Corotú, take any bus signed "Transístmica" from the front of Albrook bus terminal. Change at San Miguelito onto a bus bound for La Chibima. After the bus stop, turn into the first road on your right, where you can find a taxi to take you to the port (around $10). For a less touristy scene, visit an Emberá community in the Darién (see p.284), where with far fewer, and smaller tour groups, it's easier to learn about village life without disrupting it.

CONTACTS

Comunidad Drua ☎6709 1233 (Ivan), ⓦtrail2 .com/embera. Tours cost $90/person, for two people.

Comunidad Emberá Quera ☎6703 9475, ⓦemberapanama.com. On Río Gatún. $70/person for two people, or from $115/person overnight, including all transport, meals and activities.

Comunidad Pararará Puru ☎6758 7600, ⓦembera villagetours.com. $175/person for 2 people, or $120

for at least five people. More expensive than most as can offer bilingual guiding.

Comunidad Tusipono Emberá ☎6539 7918 (Antonio Tócamo), ⓦemberatusipono09.blogspot .com. Only does day tours.

Emberá Errebachi Tulio ☎275 3076, ⓔtuliotours @gmail.com. On Río Piedra, Colón, also visited by Panama Outdoor Adventures (see box, p.117). $25/person.

plunging into elfin forest, where the road forks. From there it's another 1.5km through cloud forest up to the antenna-covered Cerro Jefe, beyond which the **mirador** offers a splendid panorama along the Pacific coast and across the unending canopy of Chagres, even as far as the Caribbean on a clear day.

The trails
Beyond the mirador on Cerro Jefe, two paths head off down the steep hill, eventually petering out: the narrow and frequently boggy **Sendero Vistamares** and the **Sendero Xenoris**, 1.5km further along on the left. Both offer the chance to see speckled antshrikes, crested guans, yellow-eared toucanets and crimson-bellied woodpeckers. If you really want to explore, **Sendero Guayaral** is a tough but rewarding tramp from the park office at Cerro Azul to a refuge at Cerro Brewster (9km each way), which can be made easier by hiring horses to take your gear; arrange a guide in advance with the office in charge of the park at the ANAM Headquarters in Albrook in Panama City.

ARRIVAL AND GETTING AROUND   **PARQUE NACIONAL CHAGRES**

Despite its proximity to Panama City, the reserve's vastness and the lack of tourist development make **access** difficult, especially if you're reliant on public transport. So most tourists visit with a tour operator (see p.75), generally bound for the western end, round **Lago Alajuela**, around 35km north of the capital by road. There, several jetties serve as departure points for kayaking, fishing or rafting excursions, or for visiting an Emberá village or hiking along the Camino Real. Other than die-hard birdwatchers, few tourists head for the **Cerro Azul** entrance.

LAGO ALAJUELA

By bus Take a Colón bus from Albrook bus terminal, getting off at Mini Super Mario along the Transístmica, and walk the remaining 3km.

By boat The jetties at Madden Dam, Nuevo Vigia and Victoriano Lorenzo, further round the lake from the Park HQ, are the embarkation points for visits upriver to Emberá communities (see box opposite).

By car The headquarters at Campo Chagres are about a 40min drive from Panama City, possible in an ordinary car.

CERRO AZUL ·

By bus Take any transport bound for 24 de Diciembre or Chepo from Albrook terminal, getting off at La Doña Super 99 (just before Xtra); cross the road to the bus terminal at the back of the shopping centre, where minibuses wind up to Cerro Azul (every 30–45min, 6am–6pm).

By car Head east along the Corredor Sur from Panama City; 6km past the airport turn-off, you enter the nondescript town of 24 de Diciembre, where Cerro Azul is signposted off to the left, just before Supermercado Xtra. The park office is at the end of the main road.

ACCOMMODATION

ANAM camping at Lago Alajuela and Cerro Azul offer camping space with bathrooms, cold-water showers and shared kitchen facilities with the wardens but you'll need to bring all your food. Both prefer advance notice; contact the central office in Panama City (☎ 500 0877). $5/person

Ginger House Altos de Cerro Azul ☎ 297 7037, ⓦ gingerhouse-panama.com. Well-appointed guesthouse providing home comforts set in lovely gardens offering three spacious, spotless rooms (private or shared bathroom) plus communal lounge, patio and hammock areas, affording wonderful views. Full board. $152

Colón

Situated at the Atlantic entrance to the Panama Canal, with a population of around 42,000, **COLÓN** makes it into few holiday brochures; for most Panamanians its name is a byword for poverty, violence and urban decay. Yet vestiges of its former grandeur remain, worth exploring by taxi (for safety reasons) for an hour before heading out to several tourist destinations of note which lie within striking distance. Moreover, the people of Colón, mostly descendants of West Indians who came here to build the canal, are as warm and friendly as anywhere in the country and just as fond of partying. Sadly, most visitors come here solely to shop at the **Colón Free Zone**, a walled enclave on the edge of the city, where goods from all over the world can be bought at very low prices.

Brief history

As work began on the construction of the Panama Railroad in 1850, the settlement now known as Colón began to mushroom on a low-lying lump of coral known as **Isla Manzanillo**. Surrounded by mosquito- and sandfly-infested mangrove swamps and lacking a source of fresh water, the location was so unfavourable that the workers initially lived on a brig anchored in the bay rather than on the island itself. American historian H.H. Bancroft, on his arrival in 1851, summed up the general view: "The very ground on which one trod was pregnant with disease, and death was distilled in every breath of air". Yet the Americans in charge of the railway bewilderingly insisted on establishing the **Atlantic terminal** here, and in 1852 unilaterally named the place **Aspinwall** after one of the railway's owners. This upset the New Grenadan (present-day Colombia and Panama) authorities, who insisted that it be called Colón, after Cristobál Colón (aka Christopher Columbus), leading to a long-running dispute that the Colombians finally won by ingeniously instructing the postal services not to deliver letters from the US if addressed to Aspinwall.

The railway brought many immigrants and a degree of prosperity to the town despite the constant threat of yellow fever, malaria and cholera. Since then, wealth – via canal construction, a spell as a fashionable cruise ship destination in the 1950s and the success of the Free Zone, founded in 1949 – has come and gone, and Panama's main port predominantly remains a slum city. In the face of extreme poverty and soaring unemployment levels, it is little surprise that many have turned to crime, particularly drug and arms trafficking, as a way to survive.

The city centre

At the entrance to Colón, opposite the train station, is the **Aspinwall monument**, a rather dull column honouring the American founders of the city and owners of the Panama Railroad. A left turn takes you past the bus terminal, behind which lies the port enclave of **Cristóbal**, then north up dilapidated **Avenida del Frente**. Running along the waterfront of Bahía Limón, it was once the city's main commercial road but is now in disrepair. Just off Avenida del Frente on Calle 6 is the boxing **Arena Teófilo Panama Al Brown**, named in honour of one of the city's most famous sons – he was the first Latin American world boxing champion in the 1930s and one of the greatest boxers of all time.

At the northernmost end of Avenida del Frente, overlooking the Caribbean, stands the still-impressive **New Washington Hotel** (☎ 441 7133). Initially constructed in wood around 1870 to house railway engineers, the current stone edifice dates from 1913. It's worth stopping to have a peek at the spectacular entrance hall, with its chandeliers and ornate double marble staircase – poignant reminders of Colón's former splendour. To the right of the hotel as you face the sea is the unassuming dark-stone Episcopalian **Christ Church by the Sea** (under restoration at the time of writing), the first Protestant church in Central America, built in the mid-1860s for the railroad workers.

Four blocks east along the seafront, a statue of Christ the Redeemer, arms outstretched, faces down Avenida Central, the city's main street, which is lined with monuments. The **Catedral de la Inmaculada Concepción de María**, built between 1929

SAFETY IN COLÓN

Although sometimes exaggerated, Colón's reputation throughout the rest of the country for **violent crime** is not undeserved, and if you come here you should exercise extreme caution – mugging, even on the main streets in broad daylight, does happen, with the preferred method a knife discreetly pointed at some point of your anatomy until you hand over the goods, which you should do without fuss. Don't carry anything you can't afford to lose, try and stay in sight of the police on the main streets, and consider renting a taxi (recommended by your hotel) to take you around, both as a guide and for protection.

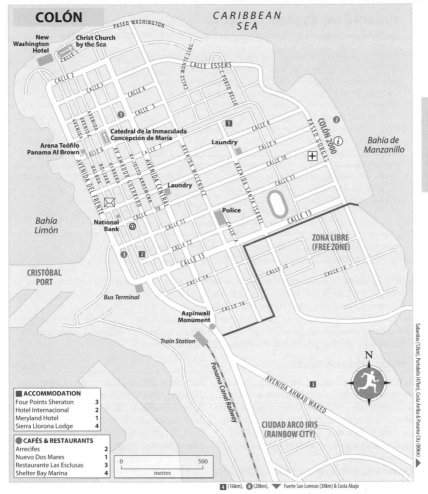

and 1934 with high, neo-Gothic arches and some attractive stained-glass windows can be found three blocks west of Avenida Central on Calle 5.

Along the waterfront of the Bahía de Manzanillo, on the eastern side of the city, **Colón 2000** comprises a collection of shops and restaurants primarily catering to cruise ship passengers. The Super 99 has an inexpensive café and an ATM.

Zona Libre de Colón

Tourists are allowed in on presentation of a passport at the gate but to purchase anything proof of passage out of the country will need to be shown • ⑳ colonfreezone.com

The southeast corner of Colón is occupied by the **Zona Libre**, a citadel covering more than a square kilometre. This is the second-largest **duty-free** zone in the world, after Hong Kong. With an annual turnover of more than $16 billion and a contribution to the economy of around $1.3 billion, the Zona provides eight percent of Panama's GDP and is experiencing substantial growth. The Zona Libre is basically a forbidden city for

2

BUILDING THE PANAMA RAILROAD

So often overshadowed by the building of the Panama Canal, the **Panama Railroad** was the world's first transcontinental railway and a phenomenal engineering feat in its own right. Anticipating the gold rush, wealthy American businessman William Aspinwall constructed a 76km track linking the Atlantic and Pacific Oceans to facilitate trade between New York and the East Coast and rapidly developing California. At an incredible total cost of almost $8 million (six times the original estimate), it became the most expensive track per mile in the world, though the hefty first-class transit fee, $25 in gold, also made it one of the most profitable.

The **human costs** were brutal. During the five years of construction an estimated 6000–10,000 workers died, though appallingly records were only kept of the white employees, who constituted a fraction of the workforce. The high death toll enabled the railroad to sustain a grisly sideline in pickling bodies in barrels to sell to hospitals worldwide. Although most of the labourers came from the Caribbean, others migrated from as far as India, Malaysia and Ireland. Despite the constant influx, work occasionally stalled since at any one time only a third of the men, who spent long days up to their waists in swamp, attacked by mosquitoes and disease, were fit enough to wield a shovel.

Little sign of the appalling human cost remained when the inaugural transit was made in 1855 amid much pomp and champagne. As one of the passengers wrote, "It affords the observant traveller an opportunity of an easy enjoyment and acquaintance with intertropical nature unsurpassed in any part of the world". The same is still true today.

Colón residents unless they work there – indeed many workers are bussed over from Panama City, which is a source of much friction locally.

Inside the Zona, the contrast with the rest of Colón could not be greater – immaculate superstores line clean, well-paved streets and the only smell is of money and expensive perfume. Most of the trade is in bulk orders; it's debatable how much of a saving you make if you're just shopping for the odd item.

ARRIVAL AND DEPARTURE   COLÓN

By train The most comfortable way to reach Colón is on the fabulous Panama Canal Railway train, which costs $25 one way (see p.96) to the Atlantic terminus, from where it's a short taxi ride ($1–2) or 10min walk to the bus terminal. If you walk, keep to the left-hand side of the road, hugging the fence, otherwise you are likely to get mugged.

By bus Buses arrive from and leave for Panama City every 20min between 4am and 10pm, though it's worth paying a little extra for the half-hourly express coaches (1hr 30min). The bus terminal (on the corner of Av del Frente and C 13) is one of the safer areas of the city during the day but you should still try to arrive in daylight.

Other destinations include Achiote (see p.112), Escobal (see p.112), La Guaira, for Isla Grande (see p.119) and Portobelo (see pp.113–118).

GETTING AROUND AND INFORMATION

By taxi Though the city centre is compact, you are strongly advised not to wander around but to use licensed yellow taxis or the fancier, pricier tourist taxis (white with a yellow band) wherever possible. Consult your hotel about hiring a reliable driver to do your sightseeing; hourly rates (approximately $15) depend on where you go and the number of passengers.

By car Budget (☎ 441 7161) and Hertz (☎ 441 3272) both have car rental offices in Colón 2000.

Tourist information The tourist office is in Colón 2000 (Mon–Fri 8.30am–3.30pm; ☎ 500 0877).

ACCOMMODATION

Colón's budget options are in areas best avoided but there are sufficient business **hotels**, some quite affordable. It's worth splashing out on a place that has armed security and a restaurant, so you won't have to go out at night.

IN COLÓN

★ **Four Points Sheraton** Millennium Plaza, Av Ahmad Waked, Corredor Zona Libre ☎ 447 1000, ⓦ fourpoints .com. Colón's top hotel offers fifteen storeys of stylishly furnished rooms with all the usual luxuries and bright, floor-to-ceiling windows that afford splendid panoramas of the city. $105

Hotel Internacional Av Bolívar at C 12 ☎ 445 2930. A good deal located on one of the safest streets in the city (all things being relative), within a stone's throw of the bus terminal. Rooms are basic but comfortable, with cable TV and clean bathrooms. There's wi-fi throughout, a couple of PCs, a (sporadically open) rooftop bar and a reasonable restaurant (closed Sun). $41

Meryland Hotel C 7, opposite Parque Sucre ☎441 7055, ⓦhotelmeryland.com. Behind the fancy pseudo-colonial facade lies a somewhat overpriced business hotel. The area is quiet and leafy, and the beds are really comfy, but the en-suite rooms (cable TV and a/c) are tired and functional. Facilities include an on-site restaurant (daily 6am–midnight), internet access and laundry service. $61

OUTSIDE THE CITY

Sierra Llorona Lodge Santa Rita Arriba, 25km from Colón on the western tip of Chagres National Park ☎6574 0083, ⓦsierrallorona.com. This private lodge with landscaped grounds is set in lush forest. Popular with birdwatchers and a treat for all nature-lovers, the lodge offers superb panoramic views, and consists of seven simple, comfortable and breezy en-suite rooms and family suites (no TV, phone or a/c). Meals can be provided on request, and knowledgeable guides can be hired for hikes or birdwatching. Day-passes are available too ($5/person). Accessible by 4WD, bus plus 4.5km uphill hike, or pre-arranged pick-up. Breakfast included. $90

EATING AND DRINKING

For safety reasons you're often best off eating in or near your hotel, especially in the evening. If you do decide to go out, take a taxi for all but the shortest journeys.

IN COLÓN

Arrecifes C 3 Paseo Gorgas, behind Colon 2000 ☎441 9308. Nice terrace overlooking the sea slightly away from the cruise ship crowds, and with a/c tables too. Offers a superior *menú del día* for $6 and plenty of seafood dishes. Mon–Sat 11.30am–10pm, Sun 11.30am–8pm.

Nuevo Dos Mares C 5, between Av Central and Arosemena ☎445 4558. Specializing in Caribbean cuisine, this restaurant offers a wide range of tasty fish and seafood dishes (from $9), served with coconut rice, fried yuca or *patacones*. Take a taxi there and organize a pick-up time. Mon–Sat noon–7.30pm.

Restaurante Las Esclusas C 11 & Av Balboa ☎445 0904. Security guard and CCTV make this first-floor venue a

reliable evening dining option outside your hotel. Despite an atmosphere on a par with a motorway service station, the service is professional and the food decent; alongside appetizing seafood mains ($9–12) there's a variety of salads, sandwiches, chicken and pork dishes. Daily 9am–9.30pm.

OUTSIDE THE CITY

Shelter Bay Marina Fort Sherman ☎433 0471, ⓦshelterbaymarina.com. Lovely bayside setting for sipping a cocktail or enjoying a leisurely lunch on your way back from San Lorenzo (see p.110). The food's nothing fancy – soups and salads (around $5), gourmet sandwiches and burgers ($7–9) and a few flame-grilled options ($11–14) – but the location provides adequate compensation. Daily 7.30am–9.30pm.

Around Colón

Southwest of Colón, a road runs through to the enormous **Gatún Locks**, where you can get up close to gigantic container ships being raised and lowered between sea level and Lago Gatún. Once across the canal, the road divides: to the right it meanders 22km through dense forest to the evocative ruins of the colonial **Fuerte San Lorenzo**, standing guard at the mouth of the Río Chagres; to the left, it rises above the shoreline of Lago Gatún, offering splendid views across the water and its sprinkling of tree-topped islands before undulating through agricultural land to the rarely visited coastal communities of the **Costa Abajo**. Those interested in marine ecology should consider heading to the coast northeast of the city to visit **Isla Galeta**, where the Smithsonian has a research centre.

Isla Galeta marine research and education centre

Isla Galeta • Tues–Sun 9am–3pm • $5; groups of under 10 people need to pay the guide's fee ($20) • ☎212 8191, ⓦstri.si.edu • No public transport, but a taxi from Colón including wait time will cost around $20, or it's easily accessible by car (see the website for directions)

About 12km northeast of Colón lies **Isla Galeta**, which is actually a headland and home to the Smithsonian's **marine research and education centre**. A far lesser known attraction than Isla Barro Colorado, the centre is more on the scale of Punta Culebra (see p.68), its main attraction a modest boardwalk through the **mangroves**, where crabs and tree snakes can be spotted. There's also an **interpretive centre** and a handful of exhibits, including touch pools and the 15m skeleton of a Bride's whale. Given the high cost of a taxi here, it's only worthwhile if you have your own transport.

Gatún Locks and around

Eight kilometres southwest of Colón, accessible by bus or taxi, are the truly impressive **Gatún Locks**. Comprising three sets of double lock chambers, they stretch for 3km, if you include the approach walls, which made them the greatest concrete structure in the world until the Hoover Dam's completion in 1930. The dam is to your left a couple of kilometres further along the road after crossing the bridge below the locks – an experience which affords a rare close-up of the tremendous studded steel plate breastplates of the lock's mitre gates.

Gatún Dam

Despite being the longest in the world when it was built, at 2.3km, and a brilliant technical achievement, the earthen **Gatún Dam** is not as visually impressive as it should be, though the curved concrete **spillway** at its centre can be an awe-inspiring sight when the floodgates are opened following heavy rains.

Gatún Visitors Pavilion

Gatún Locks • Daily 8am–4pm • $5 • ☎ 443 8878

The poorly signposted **Gatún Visitors Pavilion** receives far fewer visitors here than at Miraflores, though the viewing platform is breathtakingly close to the action, allowing you to marvel at the magnitude of the operation. Unlike at Miraflores there is no commentary but the centre does possess a small gift shop.

Centro de Observación de la Ampliación del Canal

Lago Gatún, on the eastern side of the new locks • Daily 8am–4pm • $15 • ☎ 276 8325

The new **Centro de Observación de la Ampliación del Canal** (Canal Expansion Observation Centre) overlooks the construction of the three new longer and wider locks and sliding lock gates. Although you're further from the action than at Miraflores or even at Gatún Locks, the elevated position on the side of a hill affords a panoramic view of both the locks and Lago Gatún, which you don't get at the other sites. For the steep entry fee, you also get two short videos (in English or Spanish) and access to a very short interpretive trail through the rainforest. There's also a snack bar, a tourist-priced restaurant, and lots of shade and seating for picnics.

ARRIVAL AND DEPARTURE   GATÚN LOCKS AND AROUND

By bus Catch any Costa Abajo bus from Colón (see p.108). For the locks, get off just before the traffic lights at the swing-bridge across the canal and walk up the road on the left. For the dam, take the first left after the locks. For the Centro de Observación de la Ampliación del Canal, get off just after crossing the railway line about 2km before the locks, and walk 3km up a gravel road.

By taxi A taxi from Colón will take you to the locks and back for around $15–20 including wait time, more if you want to include the new observation centre.

Fuerte San Lorenzo

Mouth of the Río Chagres, 13km northwest of Gatún Locks • Daily 8am–4pm • $5

Perched high on a rocky promontory, standing guard over the mouth of the Río Chagres, the well-preserved ruins of **Fuerte San Lorenzo** bear witness to its importance during Spanish colonial times. Its spectacular location, commanding views of both the brooding river and the glistening Caribbean, coupled with its isolation and forest surroundings make it a far more evocative place than the more accessible and more visited Portobelo. Along with the forts at Portobelo, the place was declared a World Heritage Site in 1980 and is now a popular destination on the cruise ship circuit, but if you get there early (or visit during the rainy season) you can often have the place to yourself.

The fort is set within the 120-square-kilometre **Área Protegida San Lorenzo**, amid a swathe of secondary forest and swampland, which provide excellent **birdwatching**. Though the only developed trail lies close to the village of Achiote (see p.112), a wander down any of the tracks off the road to the fort with your binoculars is likely to be productive. Some areas are still out of bounds on account of unexploded mines that the US military left behind after deciding it was too expensive to clear – there are warning signs about the dangers but they are not everywhere, so stick to the paths.

2

Brief history

Construction of the original sea-level earth-and-wood fort began in 1595 to protect loot-laden Spanish boats sailing down the Chagres to Portobelo from attack by foreign vessels. Though Francis Drake failed to take the place in 1596, it fell to one of **Henry Morgan**'s privateers in 1670, enabling Morgan and his band to pass unhindered up the river and destroy Panama City. The fort was rebuilt in coral stone in the 1680s in its present cliff-top location, where it was eventually ruined in 1740 by the British. Although San Lorenzo was rebuilt and further strengthened the fortifications were never really tested again, though they were used as part of the US military defences in World War II – note the still visible anti-aircraft platform next to the tower.

Exploring the fort

As you cross over the **drawbridge** (not the original one) and through the smart squat stone-and-brick **guardhouse**, the main entrance to the fort, you come out onto the **esplanade**, which offers the best view of the fort and served to collect rainwater that was channelled off into a **water tank** over the parapet in front of you. The vast grassy area below is the **parade ground**, containing the ruined troops' and officers' quarters. Taking the ramp down, follow the wall along to the ruins of the **powder magazine** and the **tower** built into the side of the hill, now scarcely more than a deep hole filled with litter. Though the adjacent wall parapets and cannons have now gone, the view is as it always was, and it's easy to picture watchmen anxiously gazing out towards the horizon for enemy ships. Before climbing back up towards the guardhouse, peer inside some of the many remarkably preserved **vaults** underneath the esplanade, used to store equipment and food and, much later, prisoners. Crossing the drawbridge once more you'll find yourself on the **exterior platform**, with the one surviving sentry box to the left. Here the parapet is still intact, as are the nine **cannons** pointing out towards the putative enemy.

ARRIVAL AND DEPARTURE	FUERTE SAN LORENZO
By tour With no public transport to San Lorenzo, your best bet is to go on a tour – several operators (see p.75) run day-trips from Panama City combining San Lorenzo with a visit to Gatún Locks (approximately $210/person). **By taxi** A taxi (including waiting time at the fort) from Colón will cost around $40–45. **By car** Renting a car would allow you to stop off at Gatún Locks on the way, enjoy a bite to eat at the *Shelter Bay Marina* (see p.109), or explore more of the protected area. Once over	the canal, take the well-signposted road straight ahead towards Fort Sherman, the former US military base. After crossing the remains of excavations made for the French canal, the road continues for 12km, reaching a checkpoint at the entry to the former fort, where you may need to show ID. The road to San Lorenzo bends off to the left, continuing for another 10km along a tarred road to the fort. You'll come across the park office after a couple of kilometres, where there may be someone to relieve you of your park fee.

The Costa Abajo

The area to the west of the canal is known as the **Costa Abajo**, which includes a number of inland communities sandwiched between Lago Gatún and the Caribbean coast as well as a handful of coastal villages. A hinterland in tourist terms, the area will really only appeal to avid birdwatchers and those who want to get off the beaten track.

2

Two villages here earn a trickle of visitors. **Escobal**, attractively situated on Lago Gatún, is a pleasant spot to engage in a little kayaking, fishing or horseriding while **Achiote**, further inland, is a prime location for birdwatching. The other settlements strung out along the wild, windswept coastline rarely see tourists.

Escobal

The road to **Escobal** (and Cuipo beyond) periodically offers glimpses of sparkling Lago Gatún and its many wooded islands through the trees and prolific elephant grass. After about 10km the road divides: to the right it heads back up towards the coast via Achiote; ahead it continues to the sprawling lakeside fishing village of Escobal, which enjoys an ethnically diverse population, primarily populated by descendants of canal labourers and communities displaced by the damming of the Río Chagres. It's an attractive spot to relax and engage a boatman to explore some of the tiny islands and secret inlets on the vast reservoir, or go horseriding or hiking in the forest.

ARRIVAL AND DEPARTURE   ESCOBAL

By bus Daily buses marked "Costa Abajo Cuipo" pass through Escobal (6.30am, 8am, then every 40min until noon & hourly until 7–8pm; 45min–1hr).

ACCOMMODATION AND EATING

Restaurante Doña Nelly Main road by main bus stop ☎ 434 6029. Simple local restaurant with outside seating dishing up decent fried chicken or fish with the customary portions of rice or *patacones* and beans. Daily 7am–8pm.
Sra Raquel de Tuñon's Down the last road on the left when leaving the village ☎ 6638 4912. If you have a tent, head for this lovely camping spot down by the lakeside, where you can enquire about a boatman to take you out on the lake. New, inexpensive wood-and-thatch *cabañas* were under construction at the time of writing. Camping $12/tent

Achiote

Located in a flat-bottomed valley just outside the Área Protegida San Lorenzo, the hamlet of **Achiote** provides a good base for exploring the area. Strung along the main road backing onto a flower-filled and forested hillside and surrounded by bucolic countryside, its five hundred inhabitants primarily survive on livestock rearing and subsistence agriculture, with coffee the main crop. It is also home to a community-based eco-tourism project, which focuses on **birdwatching** and **hiking** as well as offering a tour of a local coffee farm.

The 435 recorded bird species are spread across the Área Protegida San Lorenzo, which encompasses tracts of mangrove, cativo and palm swamps and vast swathes of other secondary forest types, including some deciduous growth.

Sendero El Trogón

$5 combined entry to the trail and the Área Protegida San Lorenzo

The main birdwatching trail is the **Sendero El Trogón**, which lies 4km before Achiote, within the park boundary, and was so named on account of the three types of trogon that frequent the area. Although a pleasant walk, the birding is often easier (and free) along the more open areas of the main road. If you're willing to dodge the occasional speeding bus or truck, you'll get a chance to see brilliant chestnut-mandibled and keel-billed toucans, blue-headed parrots and beautiful blue cotingas.

ARRIVAL AND TOURS   ACHIOTE

By bus From Colón, take the bus bound for Miguel de la Borda (daily 6.30am–7pm, approximately every 45min; 45min–1hr to Achiote; 2hr 30min to Miguel de la Borda) or, more commonly, Río Indio, also confusingly marked "Costa Abajo". The last bus back to Colón passes through Achiote from Miguel de la Borda at 4–4.30pm.

Tours To visit the reserve, you need to arrange a guide for hiking or birdwatching (approximately $25/2hr) with local eco-tourism group Los Rapaces (☎ 6122 0559), though they can be hard to reach. They can also organize homestays and a visit to the local coffee farm ($2) in the harvesting season (Dec–Jan).

ACCOMMODATION AND EATING

La Cascá Main road, towards the far end of the village. This inexpensive community restaurant serves up tasty, filling fare, though it's often be a case of eating whatever's in the pot that day. Daily 7am–7pm.

Centro El Tucán Main road at the village entrance

☎ 6019 8753. The centre has two basic dormitories (fans and mosquito screens) with shared cold-water showers, plus an on-site kitchen. Mobile coverage is intermittent here so if you fail to make contact in advance you can usually find someone to let you in, provided you arrive before nightfall. Dorms **$10**

Piña to Miguel de la Borda

There are regular buses from Colón to Miguel de la Borda, passing through Piña (6.30am–6pm, every 45min; 2hr 30min); boats to Coclé del Norte cost around $12/person

Beyond Achiote the road rises, twists and turns through pleasantly undulating pastures before reaching the coast at the village of **Piña**. Here bracing winds and waves batter the rugged coastline while treacherous currents throw up driftwood and fishing debris on the black-streaked beaches. The coastal road meanders a further 40km through a string of settlements to the village and river of **Miguel de la Borda**. Here, the truly adventurous can negotiate passage by boat to the small community of **Coclé del Norte**, which maintains links with the rest of the country via motorized dugout up the river of the same name to Coclecito, followed by a *colectivo* to Penonomé (see pp.140–143). The boats leave infrequently and hardly at all when the seas are rough (Nov–Feb).

There are currently no places to stay along this stretch of coast though you can probably find a very basic bunk or hammock for the night, or pay to pitch a tent, with a little Spanish and perseverance.

Portobelo

In colonial times the scenically situated town of **PORTOBELO** was the most important settlement on the isthmus after Panama City, since all the plunder from South America passed through here en route for Spain. The ruined fortresses, remnants of the conquistadors' attempts to safeguard the treasure from the envious grasp of pirates and privateers, constitute the town's primary tourist sites. Indeed, a soldier's-eye view across the turquoise bay from the forts' rusting Spanish cannons is one of the most popular postcard views in Panama, conveying the impression of a remote military outpost surrounded by dense vegetation. It therefore comes as a shock to most visitors to find the forts smack in the middle of an economically deprived modern town, with dilapidated houses propped up against the historical ruins and kids playing football in what was once a parade ground. The town itself is mostly squeezed along a thin strip of land between the main road and the bay, which spills into the Caribbean, and is easily walkable. A half-day provides ample time to explore the colonial relics, leaving you the afternoon to enjoy a nearby beach or arrange a boat trip round the bay.

Portobelo gets busy for two famous **festivals** (see box, p.115): the Festival del Nazareño in October and the hugely enjoyable Afro-colonial Festival de Congos y Diablos, which takes place every two years in March, with smaller annual celebrations taking place along the coast in the weeks leading up to Carnaval.

Note there is no bank or ATM in Portobelo or in any of the villages further along the coast. The last ATM is at the supermarket in Sabanitas (see p.116).

Brief history

It is said that Christopher Columbus, believing himself to be on the verge of death after days on a storm-tossed sea, spotted a beautiful sheltered bay surrounded by forested hills and gratefully exclaimed, "Che porto bello". While the name stuck, the strategic importance of the natural harbour was not truly appreciated until 1585, when it became clear that Nombre de Dios – then the principal Spanish port on the Panama's Caribbean coast – was too exposed and should be relocated to Portobelo. As if to reinforce the point, Sir Francis Drake destroyed Nombre de Dios in 1595 before dying of dysentery – his coffin supposedly lies at the bottom of the ocean at the entrance to the bay, near an islet which bears his name.

In 1597 San Felipe de Portobelo was officially founded, prompting further fortification and providing a new target for spoil-hungry pirates and privateers, including notorious buccaneer Henry Morgan, who pounced at night in 1668, and squeezed one hundred thousand pesos from the Spanish authorities in exchange for not levelling the place. British naval commander Sir Edward Vernon, attacking seventy years later, made no such concession and destroyed the two fortresses. Though new forts were built in the mid-eighteenth century – those still visible today – they were smaller, since Portobelo's commercial importance was already waning as the Spanish had rerouted their ships round Cape Horn. When the Spanish garrison finally abandoned the town in 1821, its 150 years of strategic significance came to an end.

Fuerte Santiago and around

Main road • Open access • Free

Fuerte Santiago is the first fort you encounter before entering the town proper from the west, built in the mid-eighteenth century following the destruction of the original fortifications by the British. The main entrance takes you through a vestibule protected by gun ports to the grassy **parade grounds**, where the ruined walls of the officers' quarters, barracks, kitchen and artillery emplacement are visible to your left. More impressive are the lower and upper **batteries**, their cannons pointing out across the bay.

Mirador El Perú

If you've time, it's worth crossing over the road from Fuerte Santiago for the steep five-minute climb to the **Mirador El Perú**. The mirador is on the site of a watchtower of the former **Fortaleza Santiago de la Gloria**, whose scarcely visible overgrown ruins are now bisected by the main road below.

Fuerte San Fernando

Across the bay from Fuerte Santiago • Open access • Free • Take a water-taxi ($3) from the jetty by Fuerte Santiago

Across the bay from Fuerte Santiago you can make out what little remains of **Fuerte San Fernando** peeking through dense foliage. As with the other forts, many of the original stones were plundered for construction of the canal. Though smaller than its sibling fort, the scenic spot gives a different perspective on the town.

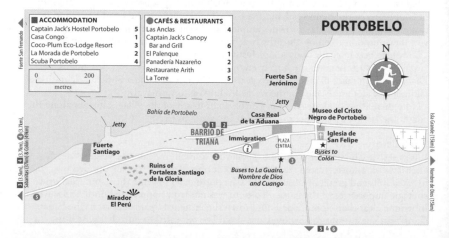

THE FESTIVALS OF PORTOBELO

Two very different **festivals** bring this otherwise lethargic town to life, causing traffic to grind to a halt well before the first fort, and streets to heave with people, as you find yourself knee-deep in discarded polystyrene containers, beer cans and chicken bones.

EL FESTIVAL DEL NAZAREÑO

In mid-October, Portobelo bursts into a frenzy of religious fervour and wild partying at the Festival del Nazareño – more commonly dubbed the **Festival del Cristo Negro** (Black Christ Festival) after Panama's most revered religious icon, a striking, dark-skinned Christ with a penetrating gaze and bearing the cross, which resides in the Iglesia de San Felipe. The effigy's iconic status was cemented in 1821 when it apparently spared the townsfolk from an epidemic that was sweeping the isthmus.

Though the main **procession** occurs on October 21, the build-up begins days before as up to forty thousand pilgrims, including general party-goers and a small number of criminals wanting to atone for their crimes, march on town. Thousands walk the 35km from Sabanitas and a handful hoof it from further afield, some crawling the last stretch on their hands and knees, a few in ankle-length purple robes, urged on by faithful companions wafting incense, rocking miniature shrines in front of their eyes, or even pouring hot wax on their backs. To compound the suffering, the pilgrims are frequently overdosing on carbon monoxide from the festival traffic, which weaves in and out of the bodies struggling along the scorching asphalt. Shelters, food stalls and medical posts are set up along the route while the town itself is jam-packed with makeshift casinos, stalls selling religious paraphernalia and food outlets dishing out chicken and rice.

At 8pm an ever-changing cohort of robed men begin to parade the icon, bedecked in a claret robe, round the packed town in a rhythmical swaying, to the accompaniment of brass and drum, followed by the penitents. Once the candlelit litter has been returned to the church around midnight, the pilgrims discard their robes at the entrance as an explosion of fireworks marks the start of a hedonistic feast of drinking, gambling and dancing that continues through the night. "El Naza", as the statue is affectionately known by devotees, gets another celebratory town outing on the Wednesday of Holy Week, this time clothed in purple, though the festivities are not quite as grand.

CONGOS AND DEVILS

At weekends leading up to Carnaval, **Congo** societies along the Costa Arriba erupt in colourful explosions of traditional song, dance and satirical play-acting that originated in the sixteenth century among outlawed communities of escaped slaves, known as *cimarrones*. Congregating in mock palaces – a parody of the Spanish court – each with its king (*Juan de Dios*) and queen (*Mecé*) togged out in extravagant costumes and ludicrously large crowns, they communicate in their own dialect. The men sport painted faces, conical hats and outlandish tattered clothes, worn inside-out and decorated with everything from empty beer cans to teddy bears; the women wear multicoloured *polleras*, their hair garlanded with flowers, and dance to beating drums and choral chants. In the many comic rituals, "prisoners", including the odd unsuspecting tourist, are taken and released for ransom – a few coins or an offer of a beer will usually do. The celebrations reach their climax on Ash Wednesday with the Festival de los Diablos. The ferocious scarlet-and-black devils (representing the evil spirits of the Spanish colonials), who have been previously running amok in frightening masks, brandishing whips, are captured by a posse of angels, who drag them off to be baptized.

In an attempt to preserve this waning culture, and aware of its potential to generate tourist income, the Portobelo authorities support a biennial Festival de los Diablos y Congos in March, which is well worth seeing.

Casa Real de la Aduana

Plaza Central • Daily 8am–4pm • $5

The small **Plaza Central** in the town centre is dominated by the two-storey coral stone and brick **Casa Real de la Aduana**, built in 1638 to replace an earlier wooden structure. A third of the world's gold, alongside copious other treasures, passed through this customs house for over a century; there was only one entrance and one exit to reduce fraud and theft and to ensure the Crown got its full royal cut of the spoils. Destroyed in an earthquake in 1882, it underwent a $1 million restoration in 1997 and now houses a small, diverting two-room **museum** containing models of the original forts, costumes and other exhibits including the obligatory pile of cannon balls. However, it's debatable whether it merits the hefty entrance fee.

Fuerte San Jerónimo

Behind the Casa Real de la Aduana • Open access • Free

Down by the waterside and hemmed in by housing lies **Fuerte San Jerónimo**, the town's largest and most impressive ruin. The former **parade ground** stretches along the eighteen gun emplacements of the lower battery, with nearly all the original rusting cannons intact. It's worth walking along to the high battery, where you can still see the rainwater reservoir, storage rooms for gunpowder and the latrines, and get a soldier's-eye view of the entrance of the bay.

Iglesia de San Felipe

Main road • 6am–6pm • Free

One of the town's major landmarks, and focus of the annual Festival del Nazareño (see box, p.115), is the **Iglesia de San Felipe**, which overlooks a bare square. Although its construction started in 1606, the church was only completed in 1814, making it the conquistadors' last religious building in Panama, with the bell tower added in 1945. Inside you'll find white walls and a large carved gilt mahogany altarpiece, though the focus of attention inevitably is on the object of so much devotion, the so-called **Cristo Negro**, a dark-skinned, lifelike statue of Jesus bearing the cross that peers out from behind a glass casement.

Museo del Cristo Negro de Portobelo

Iglesia de San Juan de Dios, behind the Iglesia de San Felipe • Closed at the time of writing

Behind the Iglesia de San Felipe lies the Iglesia de San Juan de Dios, containing the **Museo del Cristo Negro de Portobelo**. Although it hosts a splendid collection of the luxurious velvet robes donated by wealthy devotees for the Christ to wear, it was closed in 2012 due to lack of funding. At the time of writing, it was uncertain when it would reopen.

ARRIVAL AND INFORMATION   PORTOBELO

Most people visit Portobelo as a day-trip from Panama City (1hr 30min on public transport each way), though there are an increasing number of places to stay.

By bus Take any Colón-bound express bus, getting off at the El Rey supermarket at the Sabanitas junction (the last chance to get money from an ATM), where you can hop on a Portobelo bus (leaving Colón every 30min 6am–9pm, 6.30pm on Sun; 1hr 10min). Buses take about 20min to cover the 12km to Sabanitas and a further 50min for the remaining 35km to Portobelo. At busy festival or holiday times, it's worth going into Colón itself to make sure of a seat. All buses from Colón labelled "Costa Arriba" also stop in Portobelo. Return buses to Colón leave from the square in front of the Iglesia de San Felipe every 30min; the last bus is at 6pm.

Tourist information The tourist office (Mon–Fri 8.30am–4.30pm; ☎ 448 2200) is in a beautifully restored old merchant's house at the corner where the road forks coming into town, though information is limited.

ACCOMMODATION

Portobelo's **accommodation** options have improved immensely recently though if you're hitting town for a festival, you will still need to make a **reservation** well in advance. There's nowhere safe to camp around the town itself but you could pitch a tent on one of the beaches if you get a boat out there.

2

Captain Jack's Hostel Portobelo Casa 3c la Guinea, 2min uphill from town ☎448 2009, ⓦhostelportobelo .com. Though with a lovely veranda, overall this place is rather cramped with four stuffy fan-ventilated dorms (though good mattresses), usually packed with travellers arriving from, or waiting for, a boat to Colombia. It also hosts a surprisingly pricey, though good, restaurant. Dorms **$13**

Casa Congo Waterfront west of the Aduana ☎202 0111, ⓔinfo.casacongo@gmail.com. Four light, warm en-suite rooms filled with local Congo art, plus a/c and fan and a mini-fridge. It's worth splashing out the extra $10 for a room with a private balcony overlooking the bay. **$80**

Coco-Plum Eco-Lodge Resort Main road, 2.5km before town ☎448 2102, ⓦcocoplum-panama.com. Quite a nice spot to stay but overpriced, this cheerful lodge has a dozen funkily furnished though dark en-suite rooms decorated with conch shells and marine-themed murals

(a/c & TV) set in a plant-filled garden. There's a hammock-strewn jetty, a thatched balcony bar with pool table and an on-site scuba outfit (see box below). **$60**

La Morada de Portobelo Waterfront west of the Aduana ☎6528 0679. Striking Congo-themed murals invite you to this welcoming spot. Three flats (two for 6 people, one for 4), with a shared grassy lawn by the water's edge. **$200**

Scuba Portobelo Main road, 2.5km before town ☎261 3841, ⓦscubapanama.com. Although catering for divers, anyone can stay here. Five light, en-suite a/c rooms and shared balcony with hammocks afford superlative sea views. Spread around pleasant grounds, six slightly older, rather faded cabins with similar amenities accommodate up to four, plus there's dormitory with a/c available at weekends. A low-key restaurant serves a few filling staples but there are good restaurants within walking distance. Dorms **$17**, doubles **$53**, cabins **$64**

EATING AND DRINKING

Las Anclas Coco-Plum Eco-Lodge ☎448 2102. Don't let the fun fishy decor distract you from the tasty squid, lobster, crab and the like – try the mixed seafood in coconut milk (US$11), plus daily specials prepared by the Colombian chef. Daily 8am–8pm.

Captain Jack's Canopy Bar and Grill Captain Jack's Hostel Portobelo ☎448 2009, ⓦcaptainjackvoyages .com. Tuck into Thai chicken curry, pasta or seafood mains (from US$12) on the cool veranda, which offers nice views of the church and bay. Breakfasts under $5. Mon & Wed–Sun 11am–11pm.

El Palenque Casa Congo, west of the Aduana ☎202 0111. A cheerfully painted Congo-themed interior and an excellent terrace right by the water's edge, offering a small but varied menu, from wraps ($7) to more substantial seafood dishes ($12). Part of the Fundación Bahía de Portobelo's (ⓦfundacionbp.org/es) programme aimed at the area's social, cultural and economic development. Wed–Sun noon–8pm.

Panadería Nazareño On the main street before the main square ☎6957 7088. This bargain bakery is open all day and sells juices for under $2, tasty sandwiches

---

ACTIVITIES AROUND PORTOBELO

Given the numerous reefs and scuttled ships in the waters round Portobelo, it is no surprise that it's one of the country's top **diving** and **snorkelling** destinations – though you won't get the diversity and quantity of fish that you can find in the Pacific. Popular dive spots include a B-45 plane wreck by Drake's Island, where some still hold out hope of uncovering the privateer's sunken lead coffin amid the encrusted coral; the varied marine flora and fauna of the Three Sister Islands; and the labyrinth of canyons off Isla Grande. The town's two main scuba companies are located on the main road on the left shortly before Portobelo; both are PADI-certified with good reputations. Two Oceans Divers (☎6678 8018, ⓦ2oceansdivers.com) operates out of *Coco-Plum Eco-Lodge*, whereas Scuba Portobelo (☎448 2147, or ☎261 4064 in Panama City, ⓦscubapanama.com), a little further out, has its own lodgings.

For kayaking in the mangroves or hiking or birdwatching in the rainforest, contact Jason (English- and Spanish-speaking) of Portobelo Adventures (☎6954 7847, ⓔportobeloadventures @yahoo.com; or ask at *Coco-Plum*), who charges around $40/person for around six-hour excursions. You can also contract boatmen hanging round the main **jetty** by Fuerte Santiago. A drop-off and pick-up at **Playa Blanca**, Portobelo's prettiest beach, reachable only by boat, usually coasts around $40–45.

Twenty kilometres before Portobelo, and 4km up a dirt track along the picturesque Río Piedra valley, **Panama Outdoor Adventures** (ⓦpanamaoutdooradventures.com) hosts a **Canopy Tour** ($45). Other activities include **river tubing** ($15) and **horseriding**, which can include a visit to an **Emberá village** just across the river ($50) or a whole day in the saddle ($85; lunch extra). You can hike in from the road or arrange a pick-up or transport from Panama City, but should contact them at least a day in advance.

from $3, cheap pizzas and a delicious variety of fresh bread. Tues–Sun 7am–9pm.

Restaurante Arith Main road, before the church. Thatched and open-sided with wooden beams draped with fishing nets, this busy place serves breakfasts and lunches of inexpensive solid staples, including fantastic *patacones*. Daily 8am–7pm.

La Torre Main road 2km before Portobelo ☎448 2039. A breezy upstairs open-sided restaurant preparing good, reasonably priced seafood – try the *cambombia en salsa de coco* ($11) or *almejitas al jingebre* ($9). Daily 8am–6pm.

Parque Nacional de Portobelo

Bordering the Parque Nacional Chagres, the **Parque Nacional de Portobelo** covers 360 square kilometres of varied landscape around Portobelo. From Cerro Bruja (979m), the carpet of rainforest sweeps down to a 70km wriggle of coastline, taking in coral reefs, mangroves – home to crab-eating raccoons – and golden beaches, where four species of turtle come to lay their eggs. There are also significant populations of green iguana. Deforestation was already a major concern before the area was declared a park in 1976, but continued surreptitious tree-felling is putting even greater strain on the park's scarcely protected and highly fragmented natural resources. As yet, no trails or accommodation have been developed.

Puerto Lindo

The nicest place to hang out on the peninsula is **Puerto Lindo**, a small fishing village en route to Isla Grande, its clutch of simple dwellings strung out along a sheltered, palm-fringed bay, where fishing vessels and yachts bob nonchalantly in the natural harbour. It's become a popular transit point for travellers heading to or from Colombia by sailboat (see box, p.25). The consequent increase in backpacker traffic has meant that – as well as a shop selling basic supplies and a reasonable **restaurant** and bar – there's some inexpensive **accommodation**, offering meals, tours and a fine spot for simply relaxing.

ARRIVAL AND DEPARTURE   PARQUE NACIONAL DE PORTOBELO

By bus The La Guaira bus from Colón (see p.108) passes through Puerto Lindo.

ACCOMMODATION AND EATING

NUEVO TONOSÍ

Don Quijote Main road ☎448 2170. A large roadside restaurant at Nuevo Tonosí (between Portobelo and Puerto Lindo), serving up delicious, moderately priced French–Italian cuisine, including home-made pasta, tasty thin-crust pizzas and an assortment of *parilladas* and Panamanian favourites. Fri–Sun & public holidays 8am–9pm.

PUERTO LINDO

Bambu Guest House ☎448 2247, ☎6710 0168, ⓦ panamaguesthouse.com. Dutch-run establishment nestled in a luscious garden overlooking the bay with three stylishly furnished en-suite rooms and a communal dining balcony, affording great ocean views. Yacht tours (see ⓦ oceantrips.com) or rainforest walks with a local guide can be arranged. $5 extra for a sumptuous breakfast. $70

Casa X Water's edge by the yacht club. Informal restaurant serving delicious, freshly prepared seafood with a side of salad, *patacones* or rice ($8), to be washed down with a glass of wine. Daily noon–8pm.

Hostal Wunderbar On the left, main road, just after the turn-off to Cacique ☎448 2426, ⓦ hostelwunderbar .com. A range of dorm beds and doubles (some with a/c) in a large, Guna-style house and a less appealing modern concrete building. There's a kitchen, and a basic grocery, restaurant and bar nearby. The pool table and traditional *cayucos* (dugout canoes) for rent are nice touches, but the ongoing construction work detracts from the ambience. Dorms $11, doubles $35

★**El Perezoso** 2–3km before Puerto Lindo, on the right ☎6962 6060, ⓦ perezosopanama.com. The open-sided garden restaurant of this Italian-run establishment, with an Italian and Panamanian menu, is a delight, as is the food. Best to get in touch if you're intending to dine, since it closes early if business is slack. There are also two rustic wooden A-frame cabins (for 4–6 people) with fans and mosquito nets, which are nothing special but are inexpensive. Camping $5/person, cabins $30

Isla Grande

Isla Grande's popularity as a weekend getaway for Panamanian urbanites has often led to hyperbolic descriptions of its beaches and overall beauty. In truth, it doesn't measure up to the stunning islands of Guna Yala or Bocas del Toro, but if you're in the area and want a quick shot of Caribbean vibe, a dose of fresh air and a splash in the sea before tucking into some Creole cuisine, then Isla Grande will do very nicely.

As there is no ATM on the island you'll need to bring cash, although most of the accommodation options take credit cards.

2

The main village

At just 3km long and under a kilometre wide, with only a couple of paths and no roads, it's easy to orient yourself on the island. Most of its four hundred residents of predominantly Afro-Antillean descent live off fishing and tourism and reside in the **main village**, which is strung out along a coastal footpath running the length of the island. The village jetty, by *Cabañas Jackson*, constitutes the hub of "downtown" Isla Grande, where most accommodation options, bars and restaurants are located and the reggae vibe is at its most pronounced. At weekends in the dry season and peak holiday times, when the island bulges with up to a thousand fun-loving Panamanians, the place is throbbing, often with music blaring from portable stereos (despite the island's attempts to ban them) and the one decent stretch of sand at La Punta, on the southwestern tip, is inevitably packed. Apart from a thimble-sized public beach, most of the sand, grass and the shade lies within the confines of the *Hotel Isla Grande*; a $4 pass allows you use the facilities that include showers, toilets, sun loungers, picnic tables and a volleyball court.

The rest of the island

Behind the village, a steep flight of concrete steps pushes through the dense foliage across the island to a decent snorkelling beach (of a now defunct resort). If you don't fancy the climb, hop in a water-taxi. On the island's highest point stands the 85m **lighthouse** built by the French in 1894; though in poor condition, it affords superb panoramic views from the top.

ARRIVAL AND DEPARTURE   ISLA GRANDE

Access to the island is generally from the fishing village of **La Guaira**. Alternatively, boat transport from Puerto Lindo costs $5 one way.

TO LA GUAIRA
By bus Six buses make the journey to La Guaira from Colón (approximately every 2hr, 9.30am–5pm; 1hr 40min) via Sabanitas and Portobelo. The last bus back to Colón is usually at 1pm (4pm on Sun), though check with the bus driver that these times still hold.
By car Cars an be left by La Guaira dock for free, or in the more secure partially fenced area nearby ($3/day). Either

way, don't leave valuables in the vehicle.

FROM LA GUAIRA TO ISLA GRANDE
By water-taxi At La Guaira a water-taxi ($3) takes you 200m across the water to the main jetty by *Cabañas Jackson*, which is the unofficial information point – for a little extra you can be taken directly to lodgings further afield.

ACCOMMODATION

There's a reasonable range of basic **accommodation** on the island, none of it particularly cheap, though midweek in low season you can bargain for better rates.

Cabañas Jackson By the main jetty ☎448 2311. Cheap, cheerily painted cement rooms (fans, cold water and private bathrooms) with tiled floors and so-so

mattresses, accommodating couples or families, with an adjacent shop selling basic provisions. **$30**
★**Hotel Sister Moon** Northeastern tip of the island

WATERSPORTS ON ISLA GRANDE

A popular **boat excursion** leads you through a mangrove "tunnel of love" to the best local white-sand beach and **snorkelling** destination, **Isla Mamey**. A half-day trip (about $75) can be arranged through your hotel or directly with one of the men hanging out at the main jetty. Isla Mamey plus a tour round the island will set you back $95. **Surfers** should head for Playa Grande on the mainland towards Nombre de Dios.

---

236 8489, ⓦhotelsistermoon.com. Scattered over the breezy hillside overlooking the island's only surf break, thatched cabins on stilts (with fans and mosquito screens) comprise the island's nicest accommodation – make sure you get a full sea view. Next to the cosy restaurant is a small pool and sun deck providing an excellent view of the waves. Breakfast included for dorms, but not for rooms. Dorms $25, doubles $69

Villa Ensueño East of the main jetty by the monument of the crucifixion 448 2964, info@villaensueno.com. Very popular, comprising sixteen clean, brightly painted en-suite rooms (firm beds, a/c 6pm–9am, mosquito screens) and shared porches looking onto a garden. This gets noisy and lacks privacy at weekends as picnic tables in the grounds are rented out to day-trippers. Boat trips can be arranged at the hotel and full-board packages are on offer. $55

EATING

The island's **restaurants** predominantly serve fresh seafood almost straight from the boats, often accompanied by coconut rice or plantain. The opening hours below are for the dry season; you'll be lucky to get anyone to serve you a meal midweek during the rainy season.

El Bucanero Close to La Punta. Relaxed beach bar-restaurant, where you can sit with your toes in the sand at a couple of tables with umbrellas, or under a makeshift awning, or up at the bar. Fairly inexpensive seafood dishes ($7–9) are served. Daily 11am–8/9pm.

El Nido del Postre Between the main jetty and La Punta 448 2061. Certainly the plushest place on the island, with tablecloths, table decorations, and a dining

area bedecked in artificial lilac flowers. The food is good too, if overpriced, with seafood dishes the main fare (mains around $20). Daily 8am–8pm.

Restaurante Villa Ensueño Villa Ensueno 448 2964. Built out over the water next to the island's Cristo Negro – a large stone crucifix – this is one of the best places to dine, offering inexpensive delights including *fufú* (fish soup in coconut milk; $6) and lobster. Daily 11am–9pm.

The eastern Costa Arriba to Cuango

For most people the Costa Arriba stops at Portobelo; very few venture much further along the windswept coastline, though bearing right at the fork after Nuevo Tonosí takes you through a string of surfing beaches and sparsely populated villages – Viento Frío, Palenque and Miramar – before terminating at Cuango.

Nombre de Dios

The most compelling of the coastal settlements, **Nombre de Dios** is famed as the Atlantic terminus for the Camino Real, where in colonial times treasure was transferred from exhausted mules to ships bound for Spain. The village derived its name from the apocryphal words of its founder, Diego de Nicuesa, who, desperate to land his starving crew, espied the spot and cried out, "Paremos aquí en el nombre de Dios!" Sadly no trace remains of the town's famous historical past, largely thanks to Sir Francis Drake, who razed the place to the ground in 1595, thus persuading the Spanish to move their operation to Portobelo.

Nevertheless Nombre de Dios is a scenic place to stroll through, situated on the palm-fringed Río Fato, and with a pleasant five-minute meander up to a **mirador** established by a local environmental group offering a view of the village and the turquoise sea beyond. **Playa Damas** is the best local beach, a short hop by boat.

Miramar and around

There's little reason to stop off in **Viento Frío** and **Palenque** but at the forlorn port of **Miramar**, the next village along – and the only place you can get petrol – a small beachside hotel and a couple of restaurants offer succour to those who get stranded here for a couple of days waiting for a boat to Guna Yala. At the end of the tarred road lies **Cuango**, with a tangible end-of-the-road feel, though the vast new Decameron resort being built the other side of the river may change all that.

ARRIVAL AND DEPARTURE

By bus Buses to Cuango from Colón (daily 9am, 11am, 1pm, 3pm & 4.30pm; 2hr 30min) are marked "Costa Arriba–Cuango"; the last return bus departs at 2–3pm. They all stop at Nombre de Dios, Viento Frío, Palenque and Miramar en route. Nine more buses (6am–5.45pm) run from Colón to Nombre de Dios.

ALONG THE COSTA ARRIBA TO CUANGO

Boats to El Porvenir In Miramar, you can negotiate passage to El Porvenir in Kuna Yala but you'd be well advised to find out in advance about possible departures – ring *Bohío Miramar* (see below) – since they are irregular and rare in the storm season (Dec–Feb).

ACCOMMODATION AND EATING

NOMBRE DE DIOS

Casita Rio Indio 5min along the Nombre de Dios road from Portobelo after the fork to La Guaira ⓦ panama -casitarioindio.chez-alice.fr. Set well back from the road in verdant surroundings by a stream is a simple wooden *cabaña* with two very rustic rooms at bargain rates. The friendly French owners can provide inexpensive breakfast and dinner but you'll need to venture out to the kiosk down the road, or bring supplies, for lunch. Activities such as horseriding ($20) or night outings to look for caimans can be organized. Ask the Nombre de Dios bus to drop you off, or catch a taxi ($10) from Portobelo. $\overline{\underline{\$12}}$

MIRAMAR AND AROUND

Bohío Miramar On the beach ☎ 6549 3556. If you need to overnight in the village, this place right overlooking the sea offers four small, spotless rooms with good beds, a/c, TV and an adjoining restaurant. $\overline{\underline{\$40}}$

Coral Lodge Near the community of Santa Isabel, close to the border with Guna Yala ☎ 838 9988, ⓦ corallodge.com. At the far eastern tip of the province lies this luxury eco-resort comprising seven bungalows set over water, which can be accessed by boat from Miramar. $\overline{\underline{\$335}}$

Archipiélago de las Perlas

Set in coral-rich crystalline waters in the Golfo de Panamá only a twenty-minute flight southeast of Panama City, the 220 islands and islets that comprise the **Archipiélago de las Perlas** (Pearl Islands) were named by Vasco Nuñez de Balboa in 1513 after their once prolific black-lipped pearl oysters. Sprinkled over an area of around 1700 square kilometres, only a handful of islands are inhabited and many remain under-explored, though various controversial development projects are threatening to change that.

Currently, the attractive **Isla Contadora** is the only island with a developed tourist infrastructure though **Isla Saboga**, with its golden beaches, holds plenty of appeal. With time to explore, you could also visit the vast **Isla del Rey**, which supports only a rudimentary hotel in its main settlement, San Miguel. On the other hand, if you're not on a budget, then consider the wonderful coral and sand of **Isla San José**, only accessible via the exclusive *Hacienda del Mar* (ⓦ haciendadelmar.net). Air Panama has flights to both and Sea Las Perlas (ⓦ sealasperlas.com) provides a ferry service to Isla del Rey.

In addition to the lure of countless deserted sugar-sand **beaches** and **reefs** teeming with multicoloured fish, a visit to the archipelago between June and October can be rewarded with sightings of humpback **whales** that come to breed. As elsewhere in Panama, high season coincides with the dry season but since the archipelago receives far less rainfall than the mainland and prices are lower and beaches less crowded, it's worth considering a visit at other times.

2

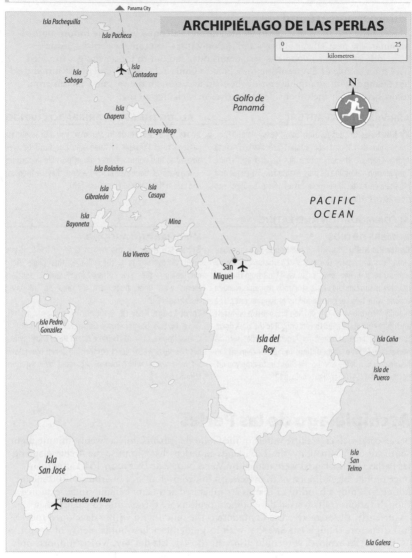

Isla Contadora

Home to the main public airstrip, **Isla Contadora** is by far the most developed and most popular destination in the archipelago. It derives its name from the counting house the conquistadors established on the island to tot up their riches from the pearl trade before shipping them off to Europe. As well as possessing its own fine selection of lovely soft-sand beaches, Contadora provides a sound base for snorkelling trips to the corals and crystalline waters of neighbouring islands, visits to sea-bird colonies and whale-watching. Away from the shoreline, the wooded areas provide shelter and food for a surprising array of wildlife – deer, agoutis and iguanas can all be spotted here.

Only a handful of families are permanently resident, while workers from nearby Isla Saboga commute daily to service the 180 luxury villas, which remain empty for much of the year. **Inland**, the centre of the island is occupied by a football pitch, which comes alive in late afternoon. South of the pitch there's a small whitewashed church, while the road up the eastern side of the pitch passes one of the island's two **ponds**, on the left, which are magnets for thirsty wildlife such as magnificent frigatebirds that skim the surface scooping up water at dusk. However, it's the beaches and views that constitute Contadora's main attractions.

The beaches

Playa Larga, on the island's eastern side, provides the longest stretch of sand and the most sheltered swimming in the warmest water; an abandoned ferry is the only eyesore. Moving south round the headland, **Playa de las Suecas** ("Swedish Women's Beach"), Panama's only public nudist beach, is suitably secluded and also offers the island's best snorkelling round the headland towards Playa Larga, where sharks, stingrays and turtles can often be seen. Another few minutes' stroll, skirting the end of the runway, brings you to the island's loveliest swathe of soft, sugary sand, **Playa Cacique**. Backed by lush vegetation, it looks across turquoise waters to nearby Isla Chapera.

On the northern side of the island the charming sheltered cove of **Playa Ejecutiva** stands out, backed by manicured grass dotted with shady trees. Further east, at the northern end of the airstrip, *The Point Hotel* surveys **Playa Galeón**, where the ferries arrive and depart, and fishermen can take you to Isla Saboga or further afield.

ARRIVAL AND GETTING AROUND   ISLA CONTADORA

By boat There are currently two ferries operating from Panama City. The cheaper ferry run by Sea Las Perlas (☎391 1424, ⓦsealasperlas.com) leaves the Balboa Yacht Club on the Amador Causeway (daily 7.30am, returning 3pm from Playa Galeón; 2hr; $45 one way; $90 return). Tickets are sold online and at their offices in the Albrook Mall (8am–7pm) and at the *The Point Hotel* on Isla Contadora. The more expensive and luxurious Ferry Las Perlas leaves from the Trump Tower, Punta Pacífica (daily 8am, returning from Playa Galeón at 3.40pm; 1hr 50min; $57 one way; $95 return).

Tickets are sold online (ⓦferrylasperlas.com), or phone ☎6200 0080.
By plane Air Panama currently makes one daily flight from Albrook Airport, two on Fridays (20min; $73 one way), and has an office on Contadora by the airstrip (daily 8am–noon & 2–6pm; ☎250 4009).
By golf cart Most hotels and the dive operator Coral Dreams do a thriving trade in golf cart and ATV rental. Prices vary (starting from $35/hr or $75/24hr) so shop around.
By taxi Golf cart taxis can also take you to your destination for around $5.

SLAVES, PIRATES AND PEARLS

Little is known about the **indigenous population** of the archipelago, which was wiped out in the sixteenth century after news of the abundance of **pearls** reached the conquistadors' greedy ears. Needing labour to harvest them, the Spanish brought over African slaves, the ancestors of most of the current population. Over the next few centuries, the maze of islands provided hideouts for pirates plundering Spanish galleons en route from Peru, often with the help of local bands of *cimarrones* (escaped slaves).

The end of Spanish rule did not spell the end of the pearl trade, which thrived until the oyster beds became diseased in the 1930s. Though they have recovered to an extent – pearl fishers still operate from Isla Casaya – there's little chance of a new pearl rivalling the archipelago's most famous find, the pear-shaped Peregrina ("pilgrim"). Plucked in the sixteenth century, it belonged to Spanish and English royalty before ending up with Hollywood legend **Elizabeth Taylor**.

Tourism in the islands took off in the 1970s when businessman and diplomat Gabriel Lewis Galindo bought the island for a bargain $30,000. By constructing roads and selling off plots to other wealthy Panamanians, he established Panama's first resort island.

2

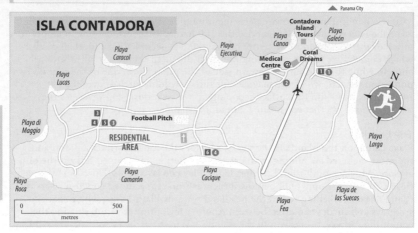

■ ACCOMMODATION				
Contadora Inn B&B	4	Hotel Perla Real	5	
Gerald's	1	The Shoppette	2	
Hibiscus House	3	Villa Romantica	6	

● CAFÉS & RESTAURANTS				
Casa Tortuga	3	Gerald's	1	
La Fonda de Clarita	2	Restaurante Romántica	4	

ACCOMMODATION

There's no such thing as budget **accommodation** on Contadora and most lodgings are overpriced for what they offer. All places listed below have a/c. Off-season midweek rates drop considerably and are often negotiable. **Camping** is frowned upon, though you can easily arrange transport to camp on one of the nearby, uninhabited islands.

★**Contadora Inn B&B** Paseo Urraca ☎6699 4614, ⓦcontadoraislandinn.com. Gorgeous two-house B&B offering excellent service with nine beautifully appointed en-suite rooms. In each of the two houses, guests share a spacious kitchen and lounge area, books and games, opening out onto a large balcony backed by luscious forest, with a cooler hammock-strewn *rancho* below. $95

Gerald's Above the airstrip ☎250 4159. Ten well-appointed, comfortable, cool tiled rooms with flat-screen TV, fridge and spacious bathroom. The real treat is the rooftop sun deck with plunge pool and sea views. Breakfast with tasty home-made bread included. $112

Hibiscus House Paseo Urraca ☎6781 1638, ⓦcontadoravacationrental.com. Five light, modern rooms, several with French windows opening onto the back patio, which in turn looks out over tropical forest. There's also a comfortable, shared living-dining and kitchen area, which you can use to cook your own food. The owner, a

pilot, can fly you to and from the island in his own plane, and golf cart rental is cheap. Breakfast included. $110

Hotel Perla Real Paseo Urraca ☎6982 0962, ⓦperlareal.com. Lovely modern rooms set incongruously round a Spanish colonial-style courtyard with fountain (only running in the rainy season!), strangely juxtaposed with a jacuzzi. Two suites with kitchenette are available. Doubles $110, suites $155

The Shoppette Main square ☎6542 0791. Above the shop and *fonda* are eight new, featureless en-suite tiled rooms with good mattresses and cable TV. The main advantage is that they are relatively cheap. $75

Villa Romantica Playa Cacique ☎250 4067, ⓦvilla-romantica.com. Superbly located on the bluff overlooking the beach, though the quirky decorations – seemingly straight out of Vegas – may not be to everyone's taste. Beds are large and comfy and rooms have cable TV but you'll want a sea view to justify the price. $105

EATING AND DRINKING

As with accommodation, **eating** options are limited and supply problems from the capital can mean some dishes are not always available – though the vast stocks of Möet and Chandon in the village shop on the main square look unlikely to run out.

Casa Tortuga Paseo Urraca ☎6253 6000. Genuine Italian restaurant in family environment (which may mean sharing a table with other guests). Pricey but tasty set three-course menus cost around $30, with wine on top.

Reservations are a must. Wed–Sun 6–10pm.

La Fonda de Clarita Behind the main square. Formerly *Sagitario's*, this is the better of the two cheap local *fondas*, offering a handful of tables and a good place to chat to locals. The *menú del día*, usually involving chicken or fish with abundant rice and lentils, is tasty and good value at under $5. Daily 7am–2pm & 6–9pm.

★ **Gerald's** Above the airstrip ☎ 250 4159. Tiled *rancho* with comfortable wooden furniture providing a congenial ambience to enjoy the best cuisine on the island. Specialities are seafood and meat dishes (mains from $13),

accompanied by moderately priced wine served in elegant lead crystal glasses. Daily noon–3pm & 6–10pm.

Restaurante Romántica Playa Cacique ☎ 250 4067. The food's usually decent enough, but the delightful breezy cliff-top setting is the real draw. Everything is grilled, with seafood, including lobster and crayfish, the house speciality ($12–45). Daily 7am–3pm & 6–10pm.

Isla Saboga

Just across from Contadora lies the slightly larger **Isla Saboga**, whose four hundred inhabitants populate the main village, **Puerto Nuevo**, perched on the hilltop above the main pink-shell beach, spilling off a central paved path. Many villagers commute to Contadora to work; others fish and ferry tourists in their boats or carry out subsistence agriculture. The island's eighteenth-century hilltop **church** – one of the few traces of Spanish occupation left in the archipelago – is worth a quick peek inside before you head across to the delightful **Playa Encanto** (idyllic before the ferry disgorges the tourists at 10am), where the multi-million-dollar development started in this area has yet to secure its stranglehold.

At low tide, it's an exciting two-hour scramble south over rocks and across coves to the soft salt-and-pepper expanse of the island's premier beach, **Playa Larga**, from where you can hike down a dirt road back to the village in under half an hour.

ARRIVAL AND DEPARTURE   ISLA SABOGA

By boat A 10min boat ride from Isla Contadora's Playa Galeón costs $10 for a single passenger, less for more people.

ACCOMMODATION AND EATING

Beach Club Saboga Playa Encanto ☎ 399 6535. Catering mainly to wealthy day-trippers and weekenders from Panama City, this raised-deck *rancho* at the back of the beach offers a small bar menu ($5–30), pricey cocktails

and superlative sea views. Daily 10am–5pm.

Señora Mare's Village centre ☎ 6641 0452. The warm Señora Mare offers a handful of clean, simple double and single rooms with ceiling fan. **$25**

ACTIVITIES ON ISLA CONTADORA

Most organized **activities** on Contadora involve getting on or in water, which your hotel can usually arrange for you. Although there's reasonable **snorkelling** off some of Contadora's beaches, there is more to see a little further afield. The PADI certified Coral Dreams (☎ 6536 1776, ☒ coral-dreams.com), down by the airport, offers half-day snorkelling ($50 including equipment and soft drinks) and **diving** for both beginners and certified divers. Tourists can be packed rather sardine-like in the boat in the busy summer months, so check on numbers in advance. The snorkelling excursion usually takes in the islands of **Chapera, Mogo Mogo** and the sandy cay of **Boyarena**, which lie in a cluster south of Contadora and were locations for several series of the US reality TV show *Survivor*.

A newer operator, Contadora Island Tours (☎ 6758 7600, ☒ contadoraislandtours.com; tours $50–150), operates out of *The Point Hotel*, and offers a more varied tour diet accompanied by naturalist guides: kayaking, fishing, catamaran cruises, glass-bottomed boat excursions, snorkelling trips and **birdwatching** – the islands of Pacheca and Pachequilla, about 3km northwest of Contadora, are important sea-bird nesting sites.

Whale Watching Panama (☎ 6758 7600, ☒ whalewatchingpanama.com) offers **whale-watching** day-trips from Contadora ($150) and from Panama City ($200/person for a minimum of six people) in small boats round the archipelago to spot humpback whales in the migration season (July–Oct). Sightings are almost guaranteed.

Alternatively, arrange to be dropped at one of the nearby islands, with a tent (or sheet sleeping bag and mosquito net) and some supplies, and ask to be picked up a day or two later. On a clear night the stars are truly scintillating.

Central Panama

PANAMA'S HATS

Central Panama

It was on the Caribbean coast of central Panama, at the foot of the steep rainforested slopes that straddle the provinces of Colón and Veraguas, that Christopher Columbus tried – and failed – to settle in 1502, though not before his reports of gold had reached the ears of the Spanish Crown. The isolated black communities sprinkled along the coastline today are descended from the African slaves who were brought over to work in the gold mines that the conquistadors eventually established. Across the continental divide, the Pacific coastal plains of Coclé and Veraguas were some of the first areas to be settled by the colonizing Spanish, who drove the indigenous population up into the forested mountainous spine of the Cordillera Central, where, several hundred years later, their descendants, the Ngäbe and Buglé, still live and fight – this time against the Panamanian government and international hydroelectric and mining companies.

Lower down, the gentler, denuded Pacific slopes are predominantly populated by peasant farmers, claiming varying mixtures of indigenous, African and Hispanic ancestry, and the land is taken up with arable and cattle farming. For this reason, central Panama is often ignored by tourists as they speed along the Interamericana, heading for the loftier peaks of Chiriquí or the golden beaches of Bocas. Yet there are good reasons to linger along the way. Accessible **beaches** are strung out along the Pacific coast, only an hour's drive from the capital, luring surf- and beach-loving urbanites in equal measure, but it is the mountains that hold most appeal, offering a splendid array of hiking and birdwatching opportunities. The volcanic tors of **Parque Nacional Altos de Campana** afford sweeping vistas of the coastline, while the scenic crater town of **El Valle** boasts outdoor activities and a lively craft market. Further west, **Parque Nacional Omar Torrijos** offers peaks shrouded in mist and a chance to explore the little-visited rainforested Caribbean slopes. Back down in the plains, the towns of **Aguadulce** and **Penomené** have their own, low-key appeal, and provide access to some of the country's most important historical sites, such as the old colonial church at **Natá**, which contains wonderful wooden carvings, and the pre-Columbian remains of **El Caño**, an important ancient ceremonial and burial site.

The road to El Valle

All buses heading west out of Panama City cross the **Bridge of the Americas**, suspended 1600m above the mouth of the canal, where the **Interamericana** starts its journey to the Costa Rican border almost 500km away. After grinding through the urban sprawl of **La Chorrera**, 40km to the southwest, the road crests at Loma Campana, where you've scarcely time to gasp at the views across the sparkling Golfo de Panamá and the brooding peaks of the Cordillera Central – assuming you dare risk taking your eye

La Rana Dorada – Panama's threatened golden frog p.136
La India Dormida p.137
Hiking around El Valle p.139
Festival del Toro Guapo p.143
Panama's hat – the Sombrero Pintado p.144
La Cascada Las Yayas p.145
Los Cucuás de San Miguel Centro p.146

Highlights

❶ Parque Nacional Altos de Campana
Spectacular views greet hikers in this rugged landscape, only an hour from Panama City.
See p.130

❷ Playa Santa Clara A couple of vibey bars and casual restaurants make this the mellowest stretch of beach in the area. **See p.132**

❸ El Valle Lovely crater town filled with flowers and fruit trees, its surroundings home to horseriding, hiking, zip lines and fabled golden frogs. **See p.134**

❹ Natá One of the oldest churches in the Americas, with a dazzling white exterior and intricate wooden carvings adorning the interior.
See p.148

❺ El Salado Tuck into some succulent jumbo shrimps at one of the casual seafood restaurants at El Salado. **See p.149**

❻ Parque Nacional Omar Torrijos Hire a local guide to scale the rainforested peaks of this little-explored park or get the binoculars out for some birdwatching. **See p.168**

HIGHLIGHTS ARE MARKED ON THE MAP ON P.130

off the hair-raising traffic – before it swoops down like a roller coaster onto a narrow alluvial plain hemmed in between the mountains and the Pacific.

Just before the descent, a road off to the right winds up to the country's oldest **national park**, which provides some enjoyable hiking and birdwatching. Once down on the flatland, a string of entrances to various **beaches** peel off the Interamericana, providing the nearest decent stretches of sand to Panama City, with spots to appeal to all kinds of beach-lovers, most reachable by bus. Shortly after crossing over the border from the Province of Panama into Coclé, a road heads north into the mountains and the delightful weekend resort of **El Valle**.

Parque Nacional Altos de Campana

The park entrance is 3km uphill from the ANAM office, on the right-hand side, after a sign declaring "No Estoy" • Daily 8am–4pm • $5

Established in 1966 as part of the protection for the canal basin, the **PARQUE NACIONAL ALTOS DE CAMPANA** is Panama's oldest national park, and at only 55km from the capital, just off the Interamericana, one of the most accessible. It's often overlooked by tourists, visited only at weekends by fleeing urbanites in search of cool fresh air and exercise, or by enthusiastic birdwatchers. But the stellar views from the park's summits – the highest, Cerro Campana, tops 1000m – make Altos de Campana a worthwhile hiking day-trip, and its dramatic and singular landscape of craggy tors and lava fields hosts a surprising range of species.

Although the denuded lower western and southern slopes have suffered from deforestation, elsewhere peaks are cloaked in pre-montane and tropical forest. Of the

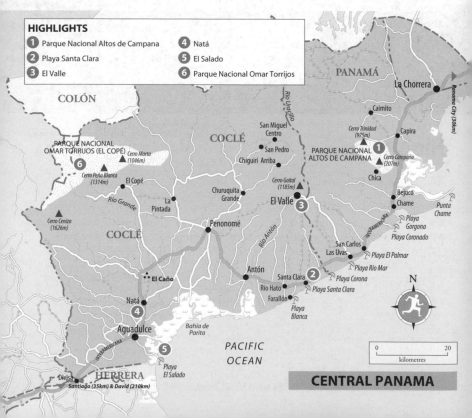

HIGHLIGHTS
1. Parque Nacional Altos de Campana
2. Playa Santa Clara
3. El Valle
4. Natá
5. El Salado
6. Parque Nacional Omar Torrijos

CENTRAL PANAMA

park's 39 **mammal** species, the black-eared opossum is the most numerous though it'll be tucked up in its den during the day. More likely sightings include two- and three-toed sloths, coatis and Geoffroy's tamarin monkeys. Colourful **birds** also abound, including the striking orange-bellied trogon, rufous motmot and collared aracari. Above all, though, the fifty square kilometres of park is renowned for its 62 **amphibian** and 86 **reptile** species, including the near-extinct golden frog (see p.136) in the area's western fringes.

If you've time after exploring the park, head for the village of **Chicá**, a few kilometres along the road at the end of the bus route. It makes a pleasant postscript, with bougainvillea-filled gardens and several *fondas* serving traditional **food**.

The trails

The park's network of five interconnecting **trails** is concentrated in the southeastern section. Easily accessible and relatively well demarcated, most are shady strolls, with one a moderately strenuous hike through scenic forest.

3

Sendero Panama

The flattish **Sendero Panamá** (1.5km) is the main trail and leads to the other trails, first to the moderately strenuous Sendero La Cruz, then *senderos* **Rana Dorada** and **Zamora** – both are barely a few hundred metres long. The slightly longer **Sendero Podocarpus**, a little further along, is, however, worth a detour (see below). The trail eventually peters out and you can either return the way you came, or turn right to descend what becomes a disintegrating asphalt road down to the main road, where you can flag down a bus, or walk back down to the park entrance.

Sendero La Cruz

About 800m along the Sendero Panamá, the **Sendero La Cruz** climbs steeply to the right, through trees dripping with epiphytes. Twenty minutes later the path forks: to the left it climbs to the 1000m domed peak of **Cerro Campana**, the park's highest point, while to the right it descends and then climbs again for another forty minutes, culminating in a giant boulder topped with an enormous cross. Unless you're a proficient rock-climber, follow the trail under the boulder for an easier clamber to the other side. Although at 860m **Cerro La Cruz** is lower, it affords the better panorama, taking in the meandering Río Chame and the distant blocks of the Pacific beach resorts, the rugged ridge of the Cordillera Central disappearing into the distance.

Sendero Podocarpus

The **Sendero Podocarpus** (600m), a loop trail off the Sendero Panamá, takes you through some of Panama's only native conifers of the same name, ending up in the park's campsite at *Refugio Los Pinos*. To return to the Sendero Panamá, turn left at the T-junction below the campsite, then left again once you reach the main path to return the way you came, or right at the second junction to reach the main road.

ARRIVAL AND INFORMATION   PARQUE NACIONAL ALTOS DE CAMPANA

By bus Take any San Carlos, Capira or Chame bus from the Albrook Bus Terminal to the town of Capira, about 50km west of Panama City. Ask to be dropped off on the Interamericana a few hundred metres after the Shell garage at *Restaurante Lily's*, where minibuses bound for the mountain village of Chicá, via the park, depart (hourly, 7am–8pm, returning on the hour; 40min).

By car The park is signposted off the Interamericana to the right 5km beyond Capira. You can leave the car at the park entrance. Follow the path up beside the large house, where a sign marks the trailhead.

ANAM office The ANAM park office (☎ 254 2848), where you may get a map, is on the left-hand side of the road, after a winding 4km ascent from the Interamericana turn-off. Unfortunately, it's over 3km further up the mountainside to the park itself and the trailhead, though you may be able to persuade the bus to wait while you sort out the formalities.

ACCOMMODATION AND EATING

★**Quesos Chela** Interamericana ☎ 223 7835. If you've time, stock up with supplies en route to the park in Capira at Quesos Chela, one of Panama's gastronomic gems, producing fresh yoghurts, croissants, empanadas and a variety of European breads, as well as its renowned

cheeses. Daily 8am–8pm.

Refugio Los Pinos In the park (see p.130). A pleasant camping spot surrounded by pine trees, about a 30min hike from the trailhead. There's a latrine and space to make a fire but no water or electricity. $\overline{5}5$/person

The Pacific beaches

Once the Interamericana hits the coastal plain at the western edge of Panama Province, roads start to branch off the main artery like blood vessels, feeding the various **beaches** along the Pacific coast, with locations to suit surfers, swimmers and sunbathers and sand ranging from charcoal grey through tan to pale cream.

Punta Chame

Travelling west along the Interamericana, the first exit travels the length of a 12km sandy spit to the low-key fishing village of **Punta Chame**, where the vast flat beach, strong winds and choppy waters have transformed this otherwise deserted swathe of sand into Panama's centre of **kitesurfing** during the season (Nov–May; ⓦkitesurfing panama.com, ⓦhokogi.com). Beware the stingrays at low tide. At the mouth of the more sheltered Bay of Chame sits Isla Taborcillo, dubbed Isla de John Wayne, which was purchased by the iconic actor after shooting *Río Bravo* in Panama and has now been converted into a family resort complete with swinging saloon doors, sheriff's office and swaggering gunslinging tough guys.

Playa Gorgona to Playa Río Mar

Two popular getaways signposted off the Interamericana are playas **Gorgona** and **Coronado**, once the most fashionable weekend destinations for middle-class residents of Panama City, with beachfront properties overlooking the marbled charcoal sand. There are two surfing magnets in the neighbourhood – at Playa Malibu in Gorgona and at Punta Teta (predictably dubbed "Tits" by surfing gringos), 3km down a dirt road not long after the Coronado exit. The only substantial settlement in the area, 12km on from El Rey, just off the Interamericana, is **San Carlos**, worth noting mainly as a place to buy provisions and catch a bus. The other surfing hotspots in the area lie down two asphalt roads a few kilometres west of San Carlos at **Playa El Palmar** and **Playa Río Mar**. Playa El Mar hosts one of Panama's longest-established surf schools, which specializes in courses for beginners (ⓦpanamasurfschool.com). Non-surfers should continue a further 20km to hit the best beaches on this stretch of coast.

Playa Santa Clara

Thirty kilometres east of Penonomé, **Playa Santa Clara** is probably the loveliest beach in the area, a seemingly endless belt of pale sand lapped by calm waters with pleasantly informal bars and restaurants – though large concrete developments are beginning to encroach here, and quad bikes and jet skis roar about the place at weekends.

Farallón

A few kilometres further along the coast from Playa Santa Clara, at the equally impressive beige swathe of **Farallón** (slowly being rebranded as Playa Blanca), things are even busier, and the local fishing village is becoming increasingly hemmed in among greedy resorts, condominium complexes and gated retirement communities. Most accommodation can fix up some gentle **horseriding** along the beach or a **boat trip** with one of the local fishermen.

ARRIVAL AND DEPARTURE

BY BUS
Buses generally only drop off passengers at the "entrada" (exit) on the Interamericana, from where a 10min stroll or a sweaty 8km hike – depending on the destination – will get you to the beach though sometimes taxis are available. The following directions are from Panama City.

For Punta Chame Take a Chame-bound bus (every 15min, 5.30am–9pm) as far as Bejuco (70min) and transfer to the hourly(ish) pick-up trucks or taxis (around $20) for the remainder of the journey.

For Gorgona Take a San Carlos bus (every 30–40min, 6am–8.30pm) alighting at the Gorgona exit, 8km further west of the Punta Chame junction; the beach is within walking distance.

For Coronado take a San Carlos bus – at the Coronado exit minibuses (50¢) and taxis ($4–5) will shuttle you to the

THE PACIFIC BEACHES
sand. The highly visible El Rey supermarket, which contains an ATM and is next to a petrol station, marks the turn-off.

For Playa El Palmar and Playa Río Mar Take an Antón bus (every 20min, 5.20am–8pm); you will probably need to hike the 2km down the road from the Interamericana stop to the beach.

For Santa Clara To get to Santa Clara, 13km west of Corona, take an Antón bus; taxis are likely to be hanging round the turn-off from the highway, or you can arrange a pick-up in advance.

For Farallón (Playa Blanca) To get to Farallón, 3km west of the Santa Clara exit, take an Antón-bound bus and get off at the turn-off. You can walk the 2km or get a taxi.

For El Valle Regular buses also run from San Carlos to El Valle (every 30min, 6am–6pm; 20min).

3

ACCOMMODATION

The **accommodation** is as varied as the sand along this stretch of coastline; you can take your pick from a thousand-room all-inclusive resort to a tent on the beach. Our list below runs from the surf-happy eastern stretch, where Playa Coronado offers the best options, westwards towards Santa Clara, which boasts a mega-resort and plenty of popular hammock and tent spots.

THE EASTERN BEACHES
Coronado Golf & Beach Resort Av Punta Preita, Playa Coronado ☎ 264 3164, ⓦ coronadohotelpanama.com. A sprawling, hacienda-style place 1km off the beach in extensive, landscaped grounds. There's plenty to entertain guests: an eighteen-hole golf course, Olympic pool, tennis courts, stables and chocolate massage at the spa, and that's before they've even thought about the sea. Very busy at weekends. Breakfast included. $153

★ **Hostal Casa Amarilla** Punta Chame ☎ 6032 7743, ⓦ hostalcasaamarilla.com. Charming guesthouse set in lush grounds offering a range of accommodation options, all beautifully decorated and immaculately maintained, from simple wooden cabins in the grounds to larger, more comfortable lodgings in the main house – all reasonably priced. Delicious, moderately priced French cuisine tops off the experience (breakfast $8, lunch and dinner around $15). Cabins $35, doubles $77

Hotel Punta Chame Villas Punta Chame ☎ 240 5590, ⓦ hotelpuntachamevillas.com. Packed with windsurfers during the season (Dec–April), this fifteen-room hotel offers spacious well-equipped rooms, each with private balcony or patio, a nice pool and a good restaurant serving delicious fresh seafood (mains from $9). $151

El Littoral Av Punta Prieta, Playa Coronado ☎ 240 1474, ⓦ litoralpanama.com. Classy health centre-cum B&B offering yoga, Pilates, acupuncture and massage, and with a swimming pool and comfy common areas. $105

Nitro City Punta Chame ☎ 202 6875, ⓦ nitrocitypanam .com. In contrast to the tranquillity of the village's other lodgings, this family-friendly but pricey place is all about action and adrenaline, on land or in the sea, indoors or out: free activities include volleyball, table tennis, table football and air hockey, with rental and lessons available for the more energetic options: motorcross, mountain biking, wakeboarding, kitesurfing, jet skiing, SUP – the list is endless. Slick rooms, their walls plastered with advertisements. Midweek discounts and day-passes available ($30). $215

PLAYA SANTA CLARA AND FARALLÓN
Restaurante y Balneario Playa Santa Clara Playa Santa Clara ☎ 993 2123. A rare opportunity for organized camping on the beach, including security and showers. For $10 you can bag a simple *rancho* during the day, complete with hammocks for lolling in, and use of showers and bathrooms. There's a simple on-site seafood restaurant, and day-trippers can use the showers for $3. $5/person

★ **Las Sirenas** Playa Santa Clara ☎ 993 3235, ⓦ lasirenas.com. Tranquil, fully equipped one- or two-bedroom cottages (sleeping 4 or 6) located either over the hilltop in bougainvillea or plum on the beach. Add to each a large patio, hammock and BBQ, and you have the nicest lodgings in the area. $182

★ **Togo B&B** C La Venta. Thoughtfully designed and exquisitely appointed rooms (one with kitchenette) in an airy house set within a verdant, tree-filled garden. Living space is shared with the owners though there are plenty of hammocks and shady patio spots for privacy. Breakfast is included and meals can be ordered. $127

★**Villa Botero Panamá B&B** Playa Santa Clara, C Aviación at C Arroyo ☎ 993 2708, ⓦ villaboterobb.com. A short hop from the beach, this charming B&B offers a couple of beautifully furnished rooms in a colonial-style tiled-roof cottage with all mod cons – wi-fi, flat-screen cable TV, fridge – overlooking a pool and surrounding garden with use of a shared kitchen. Full breakfast included. **$125**

EATING AND DRINKING

The large resorts take care of the catering and evening entertainment for their guests. Otherwise there is a sprinkling of local bars and *fondas* amid a handful of restaurants aimed exclusively at tourists and expats, where prices are high. Hours given are for high season. In the rainy season, opening hours depend a lot on the weather and some places may shut down completely for a few weeks.

THE EASTERN BEACHES

★**Los Camisones** La Ermita, km 104 off the Interamericana to the right between San Carlos and Santa Clara ☎ 993 3622, ⓦ loscamisones.com. Its reputation for serving the best seafood in the country (including paella) has pushed the prices up in recent years, though this Spanish-Panamanian restaurant rarely disappoints. A changing menu dependent on available fresh produce is enjoyed in a relaxed large *rancho* set in a pleasant garden. Most mains $16–25. Mon–Thurs 9.30am–9pm, Fri–Sun 9.30am–11pm.

Restaurante El Parque Centre of San Carlos. Reliable, inexpensive local place (with a/c) selling platefuls of Panamanian and Chinese regulars for under $5, and the *menu del día* for even less. Daily 8am–10pm.

PLAYA SANTA CLARA AND FARÁLLON

La Fogata C Central Arriba, Farallón (Playa Blanca) ☎ 908 3975, ⓦ lafogatapanama.com. Cosy *rancho* in a garden setting, specializing in Caribbean-Panamanian cooking, so plenty of coconut rice. Try the signature "Sexy lobster special", a veritable seafood orgy of prawn cocktail, lobster, jumbo shrimps, dessert and coffee for $35. Daily noon–3pm, 6–10pm.

★**Pipa's Beach Bar** Farallón (Playa Blanca) ☎ 6252 8430, ⓦ pipasbeach.com. At the end of the sandy road, past the landmark *Decameron* hotel, this informal bar-restaurant is smack on the sand. The excellent lobster and trimmings will set you back a hefty $30 but you can tuck into other fresh seafood dishes for just over $10. Also rents out *ranchos*, sun loungers and umbrellas. High season: daily 10am–6pm, and dinner by reservation; low season closed Tues.

Restaurante y Balneario Playa Santa Clara ☎ 993 2123. Beach *rancho* with wooden picnic tables selling moderately priced fish and seafood (from around $7) and cheap chilled beer. Great for soaking up the sunsets. Mon–Fri 9am–6pm, Sat & Sun 9am–7pm, in the dry season.

Santa Clara Beach Bar and Grill By Las Veraneras, Santa Clara ☎ 6602 1048, ⓦ santaclarabeachbar.com. Simple open-sided restaurant, with the sea views the main draw. Linger over a late breakfast at the weekend, or tuck into lunch at other times: breaded shrimps, fish, burgers or fried chicken served with yuca, chips, *patacones* or rice – most for around $10. Hammock-strung *bohíos* on the sand are for rent too. Mon–Fri 11am–6pm, Sat & Sun 9am–6pm.

Xoko Interamericana, entrance to Santa Clara ☎ 908 8090. It won't win any architectural awards and the highway location is hardly conducive to intimate dining, but the cuisine of this highly acclaimed Spanish restaurant more than compensates. Specializing in tapas, paella and other seafood dishes, they also do a mean portion of *papas bravas*. You shouldn't be in a hurry to be served though. Mon–Thurs & Sun noon–9pm, Fri & Sat noon–10.30pm.

El Valle

About a 100km southwest of Panama City, just beyond San Carlos, a windy road ascends 600m into the cordillera – Panama's mountainous spine – to **EL VALLE**, a small town of around seven thousand inhabitants nestled in the crater of a now-extinct volcano. Undulating hills rise to the south and west, ascending to more dramatic, forested peaks to the north, often shrouded in mist. The picturesque location, cool climate and relative proximity to the capital (90min by car) have made El Valle the holiday-home location of choice for Panama City's elite – a fact which becomes immediately obvious after a quick peek at the immaculately kept gardens and luxury residences down the aptly named Calle de los Millonarios (Millionaires' Road). Quiet during the week, the place comes alive at weekends and on public holidays as a stream of 4WDs arrives from the city and the otherwise still roads resound with the sound of clopping hooves or revving quad bikes.

The huge explosion that blew the top off the volcano three million years ago left a vast caldera that over time filled with rainwater. When the crater-lake drained, it left

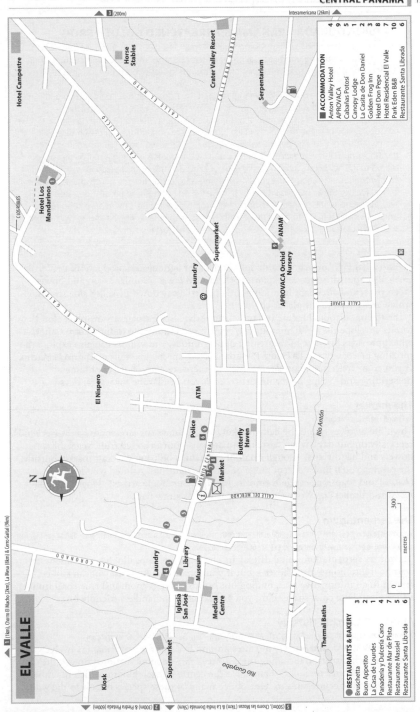

EL VALLE

3

N

▲ **1** (1km), Chorro El Macho (2km), La Mesa (8km) & Cerro Gaital (9m) ▲

▲ **3** (200m)   Interamericana (26km) ▲

CALLE ANA DORADA

Hotel Campestre

Horse Stables

Crater Valley Resort

Serpentarium

CALLE EL HATO

CALLE EL CICLO

Hotel Los Mandarinos

LOS ROBLES

CALLE EL GAITAL

Laundry

@

Supermarket

ANAM

APROVACA Orchid Nursery

9

CALLE EL VALLE

CALLE ESPAVE

El Nispero

ATM

Police

6 6

Butterfly Haven

AVENIDA CENTRAL

7 8

Market

Río Antón

10

Laundry

4 3

Library

Museum

2

4

5

1

CALLE DEL MERCADO

CALLE CORONADO

Iglesia San José

Medical Centre

Supermarket

Kiosk

Thermal Baths

CALLE LOS MILLONARIOS

Río Guaydabo

0   metres   300

▲ **5** (500m), Chorro las Mozas (1km) & La India Dormida (5km) ▲   **2** (300m) & Piedra Pintada (600m) ▲

■ ACCOMMODATION

Anton Valley Hotel	4
APROVACA	9
Cabañas Potosi	5
Canopy Lodge	1
La Casita de Don Daniel	2
Golden Frog Inn	3
Hotel Don Pepe	8
Hotel Residencial El Valle	7
Park Eden B&B	10
Restaurante Santa Librada	6

● RESTAURANTS & BAKERY

Bruschetta	3
Buon Appetito	2
La Casa de Lourdes	1
Panadería y Dulcería Cano	4
Restaurante Mar de Plata	5
Restaurante Massiel	6
Restaurante Santa Librada	6

LA RANA DORADA – PANAMA'S THREATENED GOLDEN FROG

Decorating everything from pre-Columbian talismans to tacky T-shirts and lottery tickets, Panama's **golden frog** (*rana dorada*) is one of the country's most enduring cultural icons, associated above all with El Valle since the surrounding cloud forest provides its only known habitat.

In ancient times the Guaymí (or Ngäbe) revered the frog, carving ceramic and golden likenesses for jewellery and *huacas* – precious objects buried with chiefs and other prominent citizens – of this symbol of fertility and prosperity. Indeed legend had it that possessing one of these "true toads" in life would ensure good fortune in the afterlife as it would transform into a golden *huaca*. Even today it is believed that a glimpse of this tiny dazzling amphibian in the wild will bring good luck, though a sighting is highly improbable thanks to the deadly chytrid fungus, which decimated amphibian populations worldwide and wrought devastation in the area in 2006. The waterborne fungus, which attacks the skin and suffocates the animal, was thought to have wiped out the wild population – you can see captive frogs at El Nispero (see opposite). Promisingly, though, there have been recent isolated sightings in the forest of these emblematic amphibians, which together with some successful breeding in captivity give hope for their eventual recovery in the wild.

---

behind a flat layer of rich volcanic soil. Perfect for agricultural production, the fertile earth also nourishes the vast expanses of trimmed lawn, abundant fruit and flower-laden trees, and attendant hummingbirds tucked away down El Valle's side streets, which are central to the place's charm.

The town's surroundings are instantly impressive. Spectacular stream-filled cloud forests envelope the elevated mountain reserve of **Monumento Natural Cerro Gaital**, which provides first-rate birdwatching opportunities, and visitors can also explore the puzzling petroglyphs of **La Piedra Pintada** and the spectacular falls of **Chorro El Macho**. If you enjoy fresh mountain air, meanwhile, there are enough decent hiking, horseriding and cycling opportunities to keep you in El Valle for several days.

The market
Av Central • Daily 7am–6pm

Town life revolves round the daily **market**, which draws the largest crowds at weekends, especially on Sundays, when farmers and artisans pour in to sell fruit, vegetables, flowers and handicrafts. Though small, it's Panama's best-known craft market outside the capital; you'll find a decent range of ceramic figurines, painted wooden trays (*bateas*) and soapstone carvings (mostly by Ngäbe or Buglé artists) alongside Guna *molas* and Emberá or Wounaan basketry as well as straw hats.

The serpentarium
Signposted to the right (2 blocks) from Av Central at the town entrance, after the petrol station • Daily 8am–5pm – though you may have to ask around to get someone to open up • $3 • ☎ 983 6680 or ☎ 6569 2676

The town's **serpentarium** could display its charges more appealingly – specimens are crammed into home-made boxes – but if your Spanish is up to it, you can still be treated to an informative tour, finding out how to tell a (venomous) true coral from a (harmless) false coral snake. Plus, you get a chance to handle a friendly boa.

APROVACA Orchid Nursery
Signposted to the left on the way into town, next to ANAM • Daily 9am–4pm • $2 • ☎ 983 6472, Ⓦ aprovaca.org

The **APROVACA Orchid Nursery** nurtures around five hundred of Panama's twelve hundred orchid species, including the country's rare endemic national flower, the delicate *flor del espíritu santo* – named for the centre of each bloom, which resembles a white dove. The centre aims to reintroduce many of these species back into the wild.

El Nispero

1km off Av Central, by the ATM • Daily 7am–5pm (EVACC closed on Tues) • $5 • ☎ 983 6142 • To get there, turn up between the police station and the ATM and follow the rocky unmade road for about 1km

For many, El Valle is synonymous with golden frogs (see box opposite) and your best chance of glimpsing the diminutive amphibians is at the local zoo, **El Nispero**, where they form the proud centrepiece of the impressive new Centro de Conservación de Anfibios de El Valle (EVACC for short). Sixteen other threatened native species of frog, toad and salamander have also been collected for study and breeding in captivity, with a view to releasing them back into the wild once the fungus is no longer a threat. The rest of the zoo – which started life as a plant nursery and still functions as such – crams 55 species of bird, alongside ocelot, margay, capybara, several types of monkey and even Manuel Noriega's tapirs, adopted after the US invasion, into inadequate cages.

The Butterfly Haven

Left off Av Central, opposite the ATM (1.5 blocks) • 9am–4pm; closed Tues, and all Oct & Nov • $4 • ☎ 6062 3131, ⓦ butterflyhaven.com

A new addition to the El Valle tourist scene, **The Butterfly Haven** has a butterfly house with around 250 live butterflies flitting around as well as a nursery you can visit and learn all about the life cycle of lepidoptera. There's also a garden café and gift shop.

The museum

Av Central, next to the church • Sun 10am–2pm, but ask around for access on other days • 50¢

On the south side of the main street, west of the market, protrude the whitewashed twin towers of the small **Iglesia de San José**, behind which is a modest one-room **museum**. Many of the displays – lumps of volcanic rock, household objects and contemporary crafts – are forgettable, but there are some striking polychromatic pre-Columbian ceramics and interesting carved faces.

The thermal baths

End of C del Macho • Daily 8am–5pm • $3 • ☎ 6621 3846

The low-key **thermal baths** (*pozos termales*) by Río Anton allegedly have medicinal powers. The weekends are hectic, but the warm cement pool can be a pleasant experience midweek – take your swimming costume. There are also a couple of pots of exfoliating, mineral-rich mud on hand, which are fun to slather all over your body before rinsing off and taking to the pool.

Chorro El Macho

Road to Cerro Gaital, 2km from the town centre • Daily 8am–5pm • $4 • Cross the bridge over the Río Guayabo at the west end of Av Central, then take the right-hand fork. Alternatively, from the market take the bus to La Mesa, which passes the entrance

One of El Valle's most popular excursions is to **Chorro El Macho**, a picturesque 35m **waterfall** set in a private ecological reserve. A short circular path leads to a viewing

---

LA INDIA DORMIDA

The undulating hilltop at the western end of El Valle, known as **La India Dormida**, is believed to be the slumbering silhouette of Flor del Aire, beautiful daughter of Urracá, the indigenous chief famed for his fierce resistance to Spanish colonization. The story goes that while battles were raging, Flor fell in love with one of the conquistadors, unaware that she was admired by Yaraví, the tribe's most courageous warrior. Failing to get Flor's attention, Yaraví took the drastic measure of hurling himself off a mountain in front of the whole village. Understandably distraught, Flor renounced her love for the Spaniard and wandered off into the forested hills, where she eventually died of grief. Her body, it is said, is immortalized in the shape of a mountain. With a great deal of imagination and a little prompting from a local resident, you can usually make out her recumbent form, denuded of trees except for the distinct forested section to the right-hand side, which more clearly resembles the tresses of her hair.

platform at the base of the falls, where lizards bask on the rocks and hummingbirds dart through the foliage. Though you can't take the plunge here, near the entrance there is delightful natural swimming pool in the river, or you might prefer a guided nature walk with a bilingual guide.

The Canopy Adventure

Chorro El Macho • Daily 8am–3.30pm • Five platforms $54 • ☎ 983 6547

The **Canopy Adventure**, accessed via the park entrance, adds adrenaline to the delightful flora and fauna and its five cables – one taking you across the face of the falls – forms one of El Valle's major attractions. If you're heading for Chiriquí you might want to save your cash to do the more impressive Boquete Tree Trek (see p.188). But here the adventure has the potential to combine thrills with a guided (uphill) hike through the rainforest (around 30min).

Chorro Las Mozas and La Piedra Pintada

The left fork from the bridge over Río Guayabo leads to the **Chorro Las Mozas** falls; fifteen minutes' walk from town, it's a popular place for the local youth to splash around, especially at weekends.

In contrast, a fifteen-minute walk along the central prong of the fork leads to a massive petroglyph known as **La Piedra Pintada** ($1.50 entry), where there's no shortage of kids offering to guide you to the giant rock face and attempt to explain the mysterious pre-Columbian carved spirals and anthropomorphic and zoomorphic figures. You can continue up the path that follows the stream, which becomes more of a scramble as it forges through the forest, passing three pretty waterfalls. Ten minutes after the third one, to the right, stands the smaller petroglyph of **Piedra El Sapo**, named after the toad-like shape of one of its hieroglyphs, before the path continues up to the mythical ridge of La India Dormida (see box, p.137).

ARRIVAL AND GETTING AROUND — EL VALLE

By bus Buses pull in across from the covered market on Av Central (also known as Av or C Principal), which acts as the town's unofficial bus terminal, among them regular services to and from Panama City (every 30min 7.30am–6.30pm; 2hr). To travel west from El Valle, take a San Carlos minibus (every 30min 6.30am–6pm; 20min) and get off at the "entrada" at Las Uvas, on the Interamericana; here you have to flag down a westbound bus coming from Panama City. The large ones to Santiago or David are almost always full and so rarely stop; your best bet is to get a smaller bus to Penonomé and change, though on Friday afternoons or at the start of a public holiday you could be in for a long wait for any bus to have space.

By bicycle Though most places can be reached on foot, cycling is convenient and bikes can be rented at *Hotel Don Pepe* ($2/hr, $10/day) or at several other lodgings in the town.

By taxi Taxi rides should not cost more than a couple of dollars to most places though finding one available is about as easy as locating one of El Valle's fabled golden frogs.

By local minibus During the day, occasional blue minibuses circulate the village and will drop you off wherever you want, while half-hourly yellow school buses shuttle back and forth from Capirita, at the eastern end of the village, to La Pintada to the west. Minibuses also head up the mountain to La Mesa (every 30min 7am–4pm), the access point for Cerro Gaital.

INFORMATION

Tourist information There's a small tourist kiosk (daily 8.30am–4.30pm; ☎ 983 6474) next to the market, which may have a map, although the owners of Artesanías Don Pepe, below *Hotel Don Pepe*, or the adjacent David's Place sell better maps of the area and are also excellent sources of local information. A couple of town websites are kept relatively up to date: ⓦ el-valle-panama.com and ⓦ antonvalley.com.

ANAM office The ANAM office (Mon–Fri 8.30am–3.30pm) is signposted to the right off Av Central on the way into town.

ACTIVITIES AND GUIDES

Birdwatching Enthusiastic birdwatchers can join one of the tours offered by the *Canopy Lodge* (see opposite) from $75/person.

Panama Explorers Club Crater Valley Resort, C Ranita de Oro and C Caiprita, at the eastern end of town ☎ 983 6942, ⓦ pexclub.com. Organizes a range of

HIKING AROUND EL VALLE

Though not as lofty as the peaks of Chiriquí, the mountains encircling El Valle still offer a wealth of **hiking** opportunities. For most hikes you'll need a **guide**, since trails are not well marked and if the mist descends it's easy to lose your way, though on a clear day you can manage **La India Dormida** (see box, p.137) without being accompanied. There are several routes up the legendary hill, the most direct being to follow the path up past the Piedra Pintada, hugging the stream until you reach the top. A better circular route heads out past the baseball stadium, bearing left at the next fork. When the road ends, a path off to the right brings you out on the lower part of what is presumed to be Flor's body (see box, p.137). Walking north along the deforested ridge, you can enjoy the splendid views across the crater before taking the path down from the "head" that eventually passes the refreshing waterfalls and natural swimming pools near La Piedra Pintada, where you can cool off.

A more challenging hike scales the area's highest peak, the forbidding forest-clad **Cerro Gaital** (1185m), for which you'll need a permit from ANAM ($5) either from the office in town, by the orchid nursery, or the one at the northern entrance to the reserve near La Mesa, which is often unstaffed. The most direct route involves a steep climb from a path behind *Hotel Los Mandarinos*, for which you'd need a guide. Alternatively, you can labour 7–8km up the road to La Mesa (or take the bus), bearing right at the fork after the village and arriving, a few hundred metres later, at the entrance of the **Monumento Natural Cerro Gaital**. The orchid-rich reserve is as a haven for **birdwatchers** as well as hikers, harbouring a rainbow of hummingbirds, honeycreepers, toucanets, tanagers and trogons, as well as the elusive black guan. A 2.5km loop trail, Sendero El Convento, winds through cloud forest, circling the summit, with a turn-off to a mirador, which on a clear day affords stellar views down to the coast.

3

outdoor activities in the area, including abseiling (rappelling), kayaking, mountain biking and hiking.

Stables (no name) C El Hato, just before Hotel Campestre ☎6646 5813. This long-established stable offers horseriding ($12/hr); it's worth paying a few extra dollars for a guide (Spanish-speaking) to accompany you. A popular route, lasting around 4hr, takes you round Cerro Gaital: $48/person (for 1–2 people; cheaper rates for larger groups) including guide.

GUIDES

Note that many of the hotels also have their own local guides whom they regularly call on.

Mario Bernal ☎231 3811 or ☎6693 8213, ✉mariobernalg@hotmail.com. An internationally renowned naturalist from El Valle, who is in great demand. English and Spanish spoken.

Mario Urriola ☎6569 2676, ✉info@panamabird guide.com. A professional biologist and enthusiastic ornithologist, who also runs the serpentarium. English and Spanish spoken.

Rodolfo Méndez Contact Hotel Don Pepe or ☎660 75174. For Spanish speakers seeking less specialized expertise, Rodolfo, better known as "El Chacal", has a good general knowledge of the area.

ACCOMMODATION

Most of El Valle's accommodation can be found within walking distance of Avenida Central. Prices can be higher than elsewhere in the interior and are often higher at weekends than during the week. Holiday weekends are busy, when a minimum two- or three-night booking may be required.

Anton Valley Hotel West end of Av Central ☎9836 6097, ⓦantonvalleyhotel.com. Comfortable, tastefully furnished rooms sharing a couple of pleasant patios with games and books to entertain. Has a small pool and offers bike rental, wi-fi, massage and various other extras. $20 midweek reductions. $82

★**APROVACA** Signposted to the left on the way into town, next to ANAM ☎983 6472, ⓦaprovaca.org. Excellent value and a quiet place to stay – either in the comfortable dorm, with en-suite bathroom and a small kitchen, patio area and laundry facilities, or in the spotless

en-suite room. Rates include wi-fi and entry to the orchid nursery. Dorms $12, double $30

Cabañas Potosí On the road to Chorro las Mozas, 1km west of town ☎983 6181, ⓦelvalepotosi.com. A welcoming place with four simply furnished, clean concrete cabins (with double and single bed) with shared patios facing La India Dormida. The cockerels in the flower-filled grounds, where you can also camp, should ensure an early start. Camping $10/person (own tent $5/person), cabins $54

★**Canopy Lodge** On the road to Chorro El Macho ☎264 5720, ⓦcanopylodge.com. Though not actually in the canopy (unlike its Gamboa cousin; see p.99), this lodge overlooking the Río Guayabo is superbly situated in a private nature reserve. It's aimed at birding enthusiasts, but the fine surroundings, tasteful furnishings and comfortable common areas make it a fine spot for anyone to unwind. Minimum three-night stay preferred; prices include meals and one birding tour. **$254**/person

La Casita de Don Daniel At the foot of La India Dormida, La Pintada ☎ 6615 5511, ✉ lacasitade dondaniel@hotmail.com. Friendly, family environment with three inexpensive double rooms and a riverside campsite, where you can rent a tent ($20) or pitch your own, with use of bathrooms and communal kitchen. Best to contact in advance as it's not always open. Camping **$10**/tent, doubles **$40**

★**Golden Frog Inn (Villa Rana Dorada)** C Las Veraneras ☎ 983 6117, ⊕ goldenfroginn.com. Satisfying views across the crater valley floor from this superior hillside inn, a 20min walk from the town centre. A handful of rooms and suites, some with private verandas and fully equipped kitchens, are set in a nicely landscaped garden with a decent-sized pool, a shared kitchen and hammock deck for enjoying the daily happy hour. Doubles **$70**, suites **$135**

Hotel Don Pepe Av Central, by the market ☎ 983 6835, ✉ hoteldonpepe@hotmail.com. Centrally located block with clean, comfy en-suite rooms with the customary amenities (hot water, fan and cable TV) and an upstairs deck with hammocks and chairs. There's a restaurant and craft shop downstairs and wi-fi access. **$49**

Hotel Residencial El Valle Av Central, by the market ☎ 983 6536, ⊕ hotelresidencialelvalle.com. The unpromising motel-like exterior belies light, comfy and clean en-suite rooms with sizeable windows, cable TV and wi-fi. A great open-sided hammock deck provides views across to the hills. Other benefits include bike rental and use of communal kitchen and laundry. A good deal. **$55**

Park Eden B&B C Espavé ☎ 983 6167, ⊕ parkeden .com. The frilly furnishings may not be to everyone's taste, but the comforts provided (microwave, cable TV, coffee maker, fridge) and fabulous tree-filled grounds together with friendly service make this a good B&B. Packages available. **$121**

Restaurante Santa Librada Av Central ☎ 986 6376. The best budget option, located at the back of a restaurant and opening onto a small garden. The handful of basic, clean rooms have cold-water showers; some are brighter than others and mattress quality is variable. **$20**

EATING AND DRINKING

Bruschetta Anton Valley Hotel, west end of Av Central ☎ 983 5118. The lively but cosy atmosphere here, together with the moderate prices (salads $6–8; seafood dishes from $9), makes this a popular place. The menu features Panamanian dishes, some international favourites and pseudo-Italian bruschettas. Since there's only a sprinkling of the sought-after patio tables, it's worth booking ahead at weekends. Service can be slow. Daily 7–9.30am & 11am–11pm.

★**Buon Appetito** Behind *Panadería y Dulcería Cano*. Tiny Italian-run pizzeria tucked away behind the bakery, producing fresh, home-made pasta dishes and tasty, moderately priced (under $9) thin-crust pizzas cooked in a wood-fired oven. There are only four tables, so be sure to reserve a spot – especially in the evening. Also does takeaway. Thurs & Fri 6–9pm, Sat & Sun noon–9pm.

La Casa de Lourdes C El Ciclo, tucked behind Hotel Los Mandarinos ☎ 983 6450, ⊕ lacasadelourdes.info. Lovers of fine dining should make the pilgrimage to the spectacular Tuscan-style villa-restaurant of celebrity chef Lourdes Fábrega de Ward, where inventive gourmet Panamanian cuisine (such as *corvina* in cashew fruit) is

served on the elegant poolside terrace. Mains from around $20. Reservations a must at weekends. Daily noon–3pm & 7–8.30pm.

Panadería y Dulcería Cano Av Central ☎ 983 6420. Just the place to stock up with some sticky buns, cakes and bread to keep you going on a hike. Daily 7.30am–8pm.

Restaurante Mar de Plata Av Central below Hotel Don Pepe ☎ 983 6201. This great, cheerful café-restaurant is a favourite lunchtime stop for Panamanian families. Tasty traditional mains from $7, including top-quality *patacones* with a few Peruvian additions – try the fried *ceviche* – to wash down with delicious home-made juices and *batidos*. Daily 7am–10pm.

Restaurante Massiel Av Central. Friendly, efficient place serving *comida típica* and fast food – chicken with rice is under $5 and hamburger combos go for much the same. It's also good for breakfast. Daily 7am–8pm.

★**Restaurante Santa Librada** Av Central ☎ 983 6376. The best and most popular inexpensive option in town serving Panamanian favourites for under $7 plus the more unusual *corvina al curry* and several chargrilled dishes. Daily 7am–9pm.

Penonomé and eastern Coclé

The capital of the province of Coclé, **PENONOMÉ** was founded by Spanish colonizers in 1581 and briefly served as capital of the isthmus after the destruction of Panamá

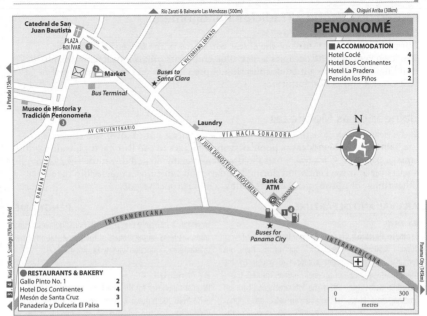

Viejo. Standing at the geographical centre of Panama (a plaque marks the fact), this bustling market town remains important both as a transit point and for the surrounding fertile land, which is used for fruit, vegetables, rice and maize as well as for pig, poultry and cattle farming. The seventeen thousand inhabitants are predominantly *mestizo*, while some have Arab and Chinese origins. Fittingly for a town that served as a *reducción de Indios* – a place where conquered indigenous groups were forcibly resettled – Penonomé was named after Nomé, a local chieftain cruelly betrayed and executed.

Though a provincial capital and major agricultural centre, Penonomé is a surprisingly small town, with a very rural feel, containing a couple of modest sights and a pretty river all within walking distance. Its aquatic celebrations for Carnaval are a real crowd-puller (see p.142), and it makes a decent base for visiting other places of interest nearby, notably the tranquil village of **La Pintada**, famed for its finely woven **sombreros** and the scenic mountains to the north, including **Chiguirí Arriba**, with its hiking trails and spectacular views and the vibrant Cucuá community of San Miguel Centro. Topping the mist-swathed peaks to the northwest, **Parque Nacional Omar Torrijos** is a treat for birdwatchers and hikers.

Plaza Bolívar and around

The town's main drag, Avenida J.D. Arosemena (also known as Vía Central), runs a few hundred metres from the Interamericana to the pleasant **Plaza Bolívar** (also known as Plaza 8 de Diciembre). Featuring a statue of Simón Bolívar, the square is flanked by government buildings and the **Catedral de San Juan Bautista**, where the early morning or evening light projects dancing rainbows of colours through the new stained-glass windows. To the east of the cathedral, a small *plazuela* features monuments to Penonomé's glitterati including a bust of **Victoriano Lorenzo**, a local nationalist hero who was eventually tricked into capture and executed by firing squad (see p.296).

Museo de Historia y Tradición Penonomeña

C San Antonio • Tues–Sun 9am–4pm, • $1 • ☏ 997 8490

Located in quiet San Antonio, the oldest part of town, the **Museo de Historia y Tradición Penonomeña** occupies a tiled blue-and-white *quincha* (wattle and daub) building and contains a modest collection of pre-Columbian ceramics, colonial religious art and period furniture.

Balneario Las Mendozas

If the heat gets too much, a five-minute walk northeast out of town will take you to the **Balneario Las Mendozas**, a popular swimming area in the Río Zaratí, location of the aquatic parade at Carnaval, when the floats are literally floated down the river. Though a party place at weekends and during holidays, you can enjoy a quieter dip here at other times, or upstream at **Las Tres Peñas**, a more attractive pool.

ARRIVAL AND DEPARTURE   PENONOMÉ

BY BUS

From/to Panama City Buses from Panama City (every 20min, 4.50am–10.45pm; 2hr) pull in at the "bus terminal", which comprises a couple of streets by the market, just southeast of the main square. Through buses also drop passengers off at the Interamericana turn-off (*entrada*) into town, where you can catch other long-distance buses. From the junction it's a 10min walk to the bus station. Transport leaves for Panama City from the south side of the Interamericana opposite the *Hotel Dos Continentes* at similar intervals.

Westbound buses The large buses to Santiago, Chitré and Las Tablas pull in for a pit stop at the *Restaurante Universal*, just east of the *Hotel y Suites Guacamaya*; David

buses rarely stop since they're usually full. Other westbound transport picks up passengers at the petrol station at the Interamericana junction with Av J.D. Arosemena.

BY MINIBUS

Regular minibuses for the beachside resort of Santa Clara leave from 200m down J.D. Arosemena at the junction of C Victoriano Lorenzo, whereas all other minibuses can be located round the marketplace.

Destinations Aguadulce (hourly 5am–7/8pm; 1hr); Chiguirí Arriba (6am, 9am then every 60–90min until 6.30pm; 1hr 15min); El Copé (every 20min, 6am–7pm; 1hr); La Pintada (every 10min 6am–8pm; 20min); San Miguel Centro (infrequently; 1hr 30min).

ACCOMMODATION

All the accommodation listings given here lie on the Interamericana and are suitably motel-like, with midweek reductions. Cheaper, very basic lodgings can be found round the plaza in town.

Hotel Coclé Interamericana, Iguana Mall west of Av J.D. Arosemena ☏ 908 5039, ⓦ hotelcocle.com. Bland, new business hotel currently offering the highest level of comfort in town: modern rooms with large beds, room service, safe, large flat-screen TV and laundry service. Plus there's a business centre, gym, pool and bar-restaurant. $85

Hotel Dos Continentes Interamericana, at the junction with Av J.D. Arosemena ☏ 997 9326, ⓦ hoteldoscontinentes.net. Long-standing labyrinth of

rather faded en-suite rooms with decent beds and noisy a/c units, offering reasonable value nevertheless. $33

Hotel La Pradera Interamericana, several hundred metres west of Av J.D. Arosemena ☏ 991 0106, ⓔ hotelpradera@cwpanama.net. Decent modern amenities plus an on-site bar-restaurant and small pool. $55

Pensión Los Piños Intermaericana 200m east of Av J.D. Arosemena ☏ 997 9518. Easily missable, squat building offering eleven cheap basic rooms with bathroom and fan (extra for a/c & TV). $25

EATING AND DRINKING

Inexpensive places serving traditional food are dotted along the main street and around the market, with more varied cuisine served in the hotel restaurants.

Gallo Pinto No. 1 C Nicanor Rosas. One of several in this local chain with *comida típica* for $3–4 in all its outlets, though you can't beat this one for people-watching, on the corner overlooking the market. Daily 6am–8pm.

Hotel Dos Continentes Interamericana, at the junction with Av J.D. Arosemena ☏ 997 9325. The glass-fronted restaurant is justifiably popular, serving a good range of international dishes and Panamanian staples.

FESTIVAL DEL TORO GUAPO

The small agricultural town of **Antón**, just off the Interamericana almost midway between Farallón and the provincial capital, Penonomé, really only registers on the tourist radar once a year, during the festival of **Toro Guapo** ("Fierce Bull") in mid-October, when the pleasant colonial square and whitewashed church are transformed by hordes of visitors.

The fun-filled five-day extravaganza takes its name and much of its action from the cattle farming that has defined the area for centuries and is well worth sampling. Alongside the usual array of folkloric dancing, colourful street parades, beauty pageants and progressively more drunken revelry are **toros** – men who cavort around the streets, charging at all and sundry. They dress in fantastical costumes draped over wooden or bamboo frames, topped with a bull's head adorned with ribbons and mirrors.

Many of the surrounding villages produce such a beast, with the creativity of the costume and acrobatic skills of the wearer a source of local pride, to be displayed during the parade on the final morning. After being blessed in the church, the bulls are led round the town as they playfully harass the *pollera*-swishing dancers, accompanied by bands of drummers. Listen out among the beats for the distinctive chime of the *almirez* – a bell-shaped bronze mortar of Afro-colonial origin that pharmacists once used to grind their medicinal herbs, and is now a musical instrument unique to Antón.

Other festival highlights include **water fights** (*mojaderas*), competitions testing traditional **rural skills**, such as carrying firewood, peeling coconuts and milking a cow, and dancing by extravagantly dressed **diablos limpios** ("clean devils" – see p.163). Strangest of all is the **cutarras**, when a poor cow is wrestled to the ground by several farmers, often the worse for wear, who then struggle to fix sandals (*cutarras*) over the hooves, recalling an old trick of cattle rustlers attempting to hide the telltale hoof prints.

ARRIVAL AND ACCOMMODATION

By bus Antón is well served by bus from Panama City (every 20min, 5.20am–8pm; 2hr), especially as additional buses are laid on during the festival.

Hotel Rivera Interamericana ☎987 2245, ⓦhotelrivera–panama.com. A/c rooms with cable TV, wi-fi and even a pond-sized pool. **$39**

Breakfasts are excellent. Daily 6.30am–10pm.

Mesón de Santa Cruz Paseo Andaluz, off C Damian Cortes ☎908 5311. Delightful restaurant in a converted church, with spacious courtyard, where religious motifs still prevail in the artwork and decoration. Specializing in Panamanian, Chifa (Chinese-Peruvian) and Spanish dishes, there's plenty of choice and the quality is good. Don't miss the sangria either. Mains from $10. Daily 11am–10pm.

El Paisa Av J.D. Arosemena. Bakery with a couple of stand-up tables inside and some outdoor seating. Good for a cup of coffee or a fruit juice and a sticky bun. Daily 6am–9.30pm.

La Pintada

Aficionados of Panama's hats – as opposed to Panama hats, which are made in Ecuador – should consider making a detour out to the village of **La Pintada**, 15km northwest of Penonomé in the foothills of the cordillera, which is famed for its high-quality palm-woven *sombrero pintado* or "*pintao*" (see box, p.144). It is a major and expanding business in the village and surrounding area, involving several thousand individuals. The **Mercado de Artesanías La Pintada** (daily 9am–4pm), which displays the crafts of around a hundred local families, sells a wide range of hats in addition to decorated gourds, soapstone carvings, pots and various knick-knacks, though finding the place open can be tricky, especially in the rainy season. Not so with master hat-maker Señor Quirós, next door, who lives at the back of his shop, **Artesanías Reinaldo Quirós** (daily 8.30am–7.30pm), and also has a good collection. Both locations are on the left-hand side of the football pitch and are easy to spot.

Another place of potential interest is the local **cigar factory**, Cigarros Joyas de Panamá (Mon–Sat 7am–5pm; ☎692 2582), now garnering an international reputation for its hand-rolled organic Cuban-seed tobacco cigars. Just drop by and witness the dexterity

3

PANAMA'S HAT – THE SOMBRERO PINTADO

Though not as famous nor as sought after as its Ecuadorian cousins, Panama's own straw hats are growing in reputation. Ubiquitous in rural Panama, worn by men and women, both as everyday work attire and a luxury accessory, they vary in style according to province and function. But while the hats have their origins in indigenous societies, Coclé's **sombrero pintado** or *pintao* ("painted hat"), which takes its name from the black and white design, has become the most popular and emblematic.

Quality (and therefore price) is principally determined by the number of **rings** (*vueltas*), but takes into consideration the consistency and fineness of the weave. A coarse seven-ring weave takes a week to make and costs around $10–20 whereas a 22-ring *fino* usually requires four to six weeks and can sell for up to $500. The cost may seem high, but immense and skilled labour is involved. Once cut, the fibres are stripped from the leaves and cooked to be made pliable before being dried and bleached in the sun. For a high-quality *sombrero pintado*, the finest fibres are culled from bellota alongside coarser junco fibres, naturally dyed by being boiled with chisná leaves and buried in earth for several days, to form the distinctive black rings, while fine threads of sisal (*pita*) are used to stitch everything together.

---

with which some workers roll up to six hundred cigars a day. Single or boxed cigars can be bought on the spot.

ARRIVAL AND DEPARTURE   LA PINTADA

By minibus Minibuses leave Penonomé for La Pintada every 10min (6am–8pm; 20min) from behind the market.

Return buses run to a similar timetable.

ACCOMMODATION AND EATING

La Pintada Inn 4km north of La Pintada ☎ 6539 6118 for Spanish, ☎ 6519 7848 for English, ⊛ lapintadainn .com. If you'd like a base up in the hills, head for this new eight-room B&B in a lovely location beyond La Pintada and reachable by bus. It has a pleasant woodland walk down to a river, where you can bathe, and also offers hiking and horseriding. With advance notice you can order dinner

($12.50) to enjoy in the lovely *bohío*. **$50**

Restaurante La Casa Vieja Main square ☎ 983 0597. A new addition to the few inexpensive local restaurants dotted round the village, this more upmarket steakhouse serves a decent pepper steak among other meat and poultry dishes. Mains around $14–16. Mon–Thurs & Sun noon–8pm, Fri & Sat noon–10pm.

Chiguirí Arriba and Churuquita Grande

From the market area in Penonomé, *chivas* head off through the surrounding cultivated fields to villages scattered in the folds of the cool, forested mountains that rise to the north. **Chiguirí Arriba**, 30km to the northeast, makes an easy day-trip, with plenty of good hiking trails, spectacular views across forested limestone hummocks and a 30m waterfall, **Cascada Távida**, set within a private reserve of the same name nearby ($5 entry). Local kids will happily guide you there for a small tip. More adventurous trips across the mountains to El Valle, or over to the Caribbean rainforests can be organized though there's no reason – with a little Spanish, a local guide and the right supplies and equipment – why you can't do this independently.

If you're in the area in late January, it is worth dropping by the village of **Churruquita Grande** for the citrus-filled **Festival de la Naranja** to marvel at the elaborate and inventively crafted wood and thatch displays overflowing with local produce, vying for the prize of best stall.

ARRIVAL AND DEPARTURE   CHIGUIRÍ ARRIBA AND CHURUQUITA GRANDE

By bus Buses leave Penonomé by the market (6am, 9am then every 60–90min until 6.30pm; 75min) for Chiguirí Arriba, via Churuquita Grande.

By car An ordinary saloon car is fine as far as Chiguirí Arriba, but 4WD is needed to reach Villa Távida from the main road (15min drive). Otherwise, it's a 1hr walk.

ACCOMMODATION

Villa Távida Chiguirí Arriba 28km northeast of Penonomé on the Chiguirí Arriba road ☎ 6485 0505, ⓦ posadalavieja.com. Set in the Reserva Privada Távida this delightful *cabaña* with two rooms is all that remains of the former eco-resort *La Posada del Cerro La Vieja*, which has now closed. Each room, with double bed, double sofa bed and cable TV, can accommodate up to four people. There are cooking facilities, an outdoor dining area and a thatched hammock-filled *bohío* from which to admire the views. **$198**

Parque Nacional Omar Torrijos

The park entrance is 4km beyond Barrigón, which is 3km northwest of Penonomé • Daily 6am–5pm • $5

A difficult place to get to, this little-visited, 250-square-kilometre protected carpet of lush forest astride the continental divide is well worth the effort. The national park's mouthful of a full name, **Parque Nacional General de División Omar Torrijos Herrera**, was given on its formation in 1986 in remembrance of Panama's flamboyant populist leader, whose plane mysteriously crashed into one of the area's highest peaks, Cerro Martha, in 1981. These days it is more usually referred to as "Parque Omar Torrijos" or "El Copé" after the nearby village. Averaging twenty degrees Celsius in the cloud-forested peaks of the Cordillera Central, the canopy cascades down to the more moist vegetation of the Caribbean side, where temperatures average 25°C and the area receives an incredible 4m of rainfall.

There's some fine **wildlife**: tapirs, peccaries and all five of Panama's species of large cat roam the undergrowth, while red-fronted parrotlets, orange-bellied trogons and the extraordinary bare-necked umbrella bird draw birdlovers. You're more likely to hear than see the three-wattled bellbird, which has one of the loudest birdcalls in the world – a bizarre metallic "dong" that carries almost a kilometre.

Around the visitor centre

A few hundred metres beyond the park entrance, an informative **visitor centre**, with a rear balcony offering splendid views, marks the start of a couple of fairly short, well-kept circular routes (2km and 4km) and an interpretive loop, aimed at enhancing visitors' appreciation of the abundant and diverse flora.

Cerro Peña Blanca

Hikers should consider aiming for **Cerro Peña Blanca** (1314m), which occasionally peeks out from the mist to the west of the park entrance. The moderately strenuous four-hour trail ascends west from Barrigón and on a rare clear day you are rewarded at the summit with spectacular views of both oceans.

La Rica

The other popular route heads over the continental divide from the park entrance down to the community of **La Rica**, a good four-hour hike away. A guide is essential for both these excursions. Set in verdant surroundings laced with waterfalls and natural swimming pools and within reach of giant guayacán, cuipo and cedar trees, La Rica is the perfect spot to appreciate the park's natural beauty, though getting there can be a very muddy affair for much of the year.

LA CASCADA LAS YAYAS

A worthwhile diversion on the way to the national park entrance from Barrigón is **La Cascada Las Yayas** (daily 8am–6pm; $2; ☎ 6809 6372). A shady 300m trail offers several viewpoints from which to appreciate the series of three falls, the highest of which is 25m. The falls, inevitably, are at their most impressive in the rainy season though in the dry season there's the pleasure of taking a dip in the pool at the base of the main cascade. The surrounding rainforest is excellent for spotting hummingbirds and amphibians, especially in the late afternoon.

3

ARRIVAL AND INFORMATION

By bus First, take a bus to the mountain village of El Copé. There are direct buses from Panama City (hourly, 6am–6.30pm; 3hr), while minibuses from Penonomé are even more frequent (every 20min, 6am–7pm; 1hr). Buses from Aguadulce run every 45min–1hr (6am–6pm; 1hr). Occasional minibuses (7am–5pm) make the journey to the even smaller village of Barrigón, after which only a 4WD can crawl the remaining steep 4km to the park entrance; on foot the hike will take well over an hour. For the return, the last bus back to Penonomé from El Copé is at 7pm, slightly earlier for Aguadulce. Buses

PARQUE NACIONAL OMAR TORRIJOS

heading west along the Interamericana will pick up/drop off passengers at the junction.
By 4WD taxi To arrange 4WD transport in advance, contact Faustino Ortega (☎ 983 9265). Costs are approximately $15 from El Copé to the park entrance, $6 to the park from Barrigón.
ANAM office At the park entrance. The office has no phone; for information contact the regional ANAM office in Penonomé (☎ 997 7538) and ask to talk to Hellington Ríos in Áreas Protegidas.

ACCOMMODATION

★ **Albergue Navas** Barrigón ☎ 983 9130. Anna and Santos Navas are warm, long-standing hosts providing three simple cinder-block rooms with shared outside toilet and shower; meals, made with fresh produce from their *finca*, are served in the family kitchen. Santos and his son are wonderfully knowledgeable guides, whose services can also be hired by non-guests ($12/group), though you'll need some Spanish. The family also owns a rustic cabin at La Rica, within the park. Meals are included. **$35**/person
ANAM Park entrance; contact Hellington Ríos at ☎ 997 7538 in the ANAM regional office, Penonomé. A spacious solar-powered self-catering cabin near the entrance affords sweeping vistas, though conditions

are often misty, and comprises a large lounge, a dormitory with four bunks and a kitchen equipped with a stove, fridge and basic utensils. Bring a sleeping bag as it's chilly at night. The park wardens are usually willing to be hired as guides. Camping is possible but there is no electricity and it is likely to be very wet. Dorms **$15**, camping **$5**/person
La Mica Just outside El Copé ☎ 6549 7321 (Macedonia), 🖳 lamica.org. A biological station offering basic cabin or dormitory facilities and guided nature hikes of the area ($15/day for a small group). They can also help arrange homestays in the scenically located community of Santa Marta on the park border. Meals are $5 each. Dorms or cabins **$10**/person

---

LOS CUCUÁS DE SAN MIGUEL CENTRO

San Miguel Centro, 35km northeast of Penonomé, is home to the **Cucuá** community, who are famed for their devil dance conducted in elaborate, cream-coloured, pyjama-like costumes made from cucuá bark, painted with geometric shapes using natural dyes and topped with a fanciful deer mask complete with real antlers and a peccary's jawbone. As with other devil dances, it was originally associated with Corpus Christi celebrations; at one time in danger of dying out it is now regularly performed at folk festivals across Panama and is the central attraction of the annual **Festival de los Cucuás**, which takes place in March in San Miguel Centro. The bark "material" used for the costumes is beaten against a tree until smooth, then washed in soap and hot water before being laid out to dry. Such has been the demand for the costumes in recent years (they can sell for around $500) that the cucuá tree has become endangered, prompting a recent reforestation programme.

Descended from the Guaymi, like the Ngäbe and Buglé, and originally from Veraguas, the Cucuás fled the Spanish colonizers centuries ago to settle in the mountains of Coclé. These days they live primarily from coffee cultivation and the sale of *artesanías*; the latter, along with the devil dance, forms a major part of a community-based eco-tourism project aimed at preserving and promoting Cucuá culture.

ARRIVAL AND ACCOMMODATION

By bus *Chivas* for San Miguel Centro (1hr 30min) leave infrequently from Penonomé bus terminal.
San Miguel Centro homestays Simple homestay lodging is offered by the eco-community project for a

modest fee; extra is charged for a performance by the dance troupe. To organize a visit, ask around the *mercado de artesanías* in Penonomé, where members of the Cucuá community are often selling their crafts.

Aguadulce and western Coclé

Travelling west along the Interamericana, across the flatlands of Coclé, the terrain becomes duller and drier as you pass endless fields of sugar cane and cattle and enter the crescent known as the Arco Seco (Dry Arc), which sweeps round the Bahía de Parita west of the Pacific beaches to the eastern section of the Azuero Peninsula. Plum in the middle of what transforms into an unpleasant dust bowl in the dry season stands the important agro-industrial town of **AGUADULCE**, synonymous with sugar, salt and – more recently – shrimps. Though the town itself is unremarkable, at the right time of year you can observe its agricultural processes first-hand, while avid birdwatchers head for the saltpans of **Playa El Salado** to the southeast. East of Aguadulce lie two of Panama's major historical attractions, the intriguing pre-Columbian site of the **Parque Arqueológico El Caño** and the splendid colonial church of **Natá**.

Brief history

Salt had been harvested in the area by the indigenous population long before a boat-load of colonizers landed in the mid-nineteenth century, naming the place Aguadulce ("freshwater") – apparently amazed at the purity of the water they'd drawn from a local well given its proximity to the sea. The town's coastal location allowed it to develop into a major port during the twentieth century but with the access channel constantly silting up and competition from road transport along the Interamericana, the port scarcely functions these days.

The town centre

As usual, life centres on the main square, **Plaza 19 de Octubre**, where the **Iglesia de San Juan Bautista** exhibits a mishmash of styles, the original altar frescoes having disappeared beneath an expensive pile of red brick – the current altarpiece. Look out for the incongruous German grandfather clock inside.

El Museo de la Sal y el Azúcar

Plaza 19 de Octubre • Tues–Sat 8.30am–3.30pm • Free • ☎ 997 4280

Across the park, the charming two-storey nineteenth-century building that was once the post office now houses the Museo Regional Stella Sierra (named after a local poet, whose work is on display), much better known by its previous title, **El Museo de la Sal y el Azúcar**. Currently temporary exhibitions are shown on the ground floor with the permanent display squeezed into a room on the first floor, though this is set to change. There's a modest assortment of pre-Columbian relics, photos and instruments from the early days of the salt and sugar industries, plus some weaponry and uniforms from the civil war, during which two major battles were fought in the town. Space is also devoted to the town's two most famous citizens – the aforementioned poet, Stella Sierra, and Rodolfo Chiari, one of Panama's former presidents.

ARRIVAL AND DEPARTURE   **AGUADULCE**

By bus Buses from Panama City (every 25min, 4.15am–9pm; 3hr) halt at two bus stops on the Interamericana for Aguadulce; the western one by the *Hotel Interamericana* is the main one; return buses to Panama City (similar timetable) leave from the nearby junction with Av Rafael Estévez, which leads into the town centre. If you don't fancy walking to downtown Aguadulce, regular minibuses costing a few *centavos* run along the road while taxis only charge $1.

Destinations Chitré (every 20min, 4am–6pm; 1hr); El Copé (every 45min, 6am–6pm; 1hr); Penonomé (hourly, 5am–7pm; 1hr). All leave from the main square. Buses for Santiago (every 20min, 5.30am–6.30pm; 1hr) leave from Av Rafael Estévez, 300m from the Interamericana, though they also pick up from the main square. Buses to David (from Panama City) stop on the Interamericana, across the road from the *Hotel Interamericana*, if they have spare seats.

ACCOMMODATION AND EATING

Fonda la Fula Av Rodolfo Chiari, towards the Interamericana. This place has the best reputation for traditional food; a basic affair with long aluminium tables under a corrugated iron roof, it is famous for its *sancocho*. Thurs–Sun 6am–late.

Hotel Carisabel Calle Vía El Puerto ☎997 3800, ⓦ hotelcarisabel.com. Pleasant, compact rooms with more furniture and better paintwork than the *Interamericano*, and with the same amenities, including a fishpond-size pool and a bar-restaurant offering decent food. $̲4̲4̲

Hotel Interamericano Interamericana ☎997 4363. Bland but functional en-suite rooms (hot water, cable TV, a/c & fan), though the main attraction is the excellent large swimming pool, which transforms into a local party place at weekends, so select your room carefully. The on-site restaurant has a vast menu to suit most palates (mains $6–10) and lunchtime family meal deals. $̲4̲4̲

Hotel Sarita Behind Super Carnes on Av Alejandro T. Escobar ☎997 4437. For the budget traveller, this long-standing central hotel offers good-value accommodation, where you can choose between a basic double with fan, cold water and local TV, or, for $15 extra, one with a/c, hot water and cable TV. $̲1̲5̲

Panadería y Restaurante La Espiga Main square ☎997 4333. Bright and airy cafeteria-style place, serving decent food from sandwiches, through burgers and salads, to traditional Panamanian mains ($6–9); it is particularly popular at weekends when locals come to socialize over breakfast (including great fresh juices) and enjoy the paper. Daily 6.30am–10.30pm.

Parque Arqueológico El Caño

18km north of Aguadulce, just off the Interamericana • Tues–Sat 8am–3.30pm; closed Sun & public holidays • $1 • ☎ 228 6231 (not working while the museum's closed for restoration) • Buses between Aguadulce and Penonomé can drop you on the Interamericana at the entrance to the village, from where it's a further 3km walk to the site – a taxi from Natá ($7) might be easier (see below)

The **Parque Arqueológico El Caño** is one of Panama's most significant pre-Columbian archeological sites, which narrowly escaped bulldozing in the 1970s. Sadly, a combination of plunder, vandalism and neglect means there is relatively little for the lay visitor to appreciate, while the park's floodplain location makes it a mosquito-infested quagmire in the rainy season. Even so, the well-preserved skeletons are quite impressive and worth a look if you're in the area and not pressed for time.

An important ceremonial site from 500 to about 1200 AD, El Caño later became a cemetery, and was still in use as such after the conquest. One of the most fascinating finds was over a hundred basalt statues that formed what was described as the "Temple of the Thousand Idols", which were illegally decapitated by an American Indiana Jones-style adventurer in the early twentieth century, and the best of their zoomorphic and anthropomorphic heads are now scattered in museums in the US, with a few in Panama City's anthropological museum. Only the **stone pedestals** remain. There are also **funeral mounds**, two of which have been excavated, displaying fairly complete skeletons. One, presumed to be a chief's burial mound, has thrown up a number of gold and emerald items, which are currently being examined by archeologists so not yet on display. A small **museum** displays ceramics and lesser stone statues though was closed for restoration at the time of writing.

Natá

It's hard to picture **NATÁ**, a quiet backwater 7km south of the El Caño turn-off (11km north of Aguadulce), as the major Spanish settlement it once was, until you arrive at the plaza to be confronted with the expansive dazzling white Baroque facade of the **Basílica Menor Santiago Apostól**. Possibly the oldest church in the Americas still in use, and recently fully restored to its former glory, the church bears testament to the town's historical importance.

Founded in 1522 by Gaspar de Espinosa (whose bust surveys the church from the square) and named after the local indigenous chief, the town supposedly gained its subsequent full name, **Santiago de Natá de los Caballeros**, from a hundred knights (*caballeros*) – hand-picked by King Charles V of Spain – who were sent to subjugate the local population and spread the Catholic word. The surrounding fertile plains made

Natá a perfect base for confronting the main indigenous resistance forces under Cacique Urracá, who relentlessly attacked the site (see p.293), and for providing supplies to the now long-abandoned gold mines on the Caribbean coast.

Basílica Menor Santiago Apostól

Plaza 19 de Octubre • Daily 8am–6pm • Free

Apart from the splendid bell tower, the church's main attractions are the ornately **carved wooden altars** framed by exquisite columns laden with vines, flowers and angels, which adorn an otherwise simple wooden interior. Though the least elaborate, the main altar importantly contains images of the patron saint, Santiago el Menor (James the Lesser), and the co-patron, San Juan de Díos, who are removed from their niches and paraded round the town on their saint days of July 25 and March 8, respectively.

ARRIVAL AND DEPARTURE	NATÁ
By bus Regional buses westbound to Aguadulce or eastbound to Penonomé drop and pick up passengers at the entrance to Natá on the Interamericana (every	15–20min), a 10min walk from the village. Local shuttles between Aguadulce and Penonomé may even enter for a quick sweep of the plaza.

Playa El Salado

Driving southeast out of Aguadulce, a newly tarred road showcases the town's other two major industries as it navigates 8km between mud and salt flats and shrimp farms to the mangrove-lined coast at **Playa El Salado**. In the dry season, salt is heaped like snow by the evaporation pools while September and October are the best months to catch flocks of migrating waders; among the numerous sandpipers and plovers, look out for striking black-necked stilts probing the mud for crustaceans and lovely roseate spoonbills filtering the tidal pools.

At weekends, many Aguadulceños head this way to escape the heat of the town and lounge on the pleasant beach, or loll about in **Las Piscinas**, shallow stone baths built on the flats, offering views of the bay, that catch the salt water as the tide moves out to provide a warm pool, though a sharp exit is necessary once the tide turns. The biggest attraction for many, though, is the jumbo shrimps, for which the fishing village is famous, and which you can sample at one of the restaurants dotted along the road.

ARRIVAL AND DEPARTURE	PLAYA EL SALADO
By minibus The only scheduled bus departure leaves Aguadulce's main square at 7am (15min) with the return bus leaving Playa el Salado at 8am. Other intermittent	departures depend on demand and at weekends the bus sometimes doesn't run at all. **By taxi** Taxis here from Aguadulce charge $6–7.

EATING AND DRINKING	
Restaurante Johnny y Los Mauditos (formerly Johnny Tapia) Just after the village mirador, on the main road ☎ 6774 5386. This unpromising concrete block with a tin roof, overlooking mangroves, is justifiably famed for its jumbo shrimps – a plateful will set you back a mere $8.50, or you can go the whole hog and share a vast seafood platter for $40. Mon & Thurs–Sun 11am–10pm.	**Restaurante Reina del Mar** Main road, almost at the end of the village ☎ 997 2960. Boasting a pleasant view across the scrub, this friendly restaurant dishes up moderately priced, freshly prepared seafood, including Ngäbe clams, shrimps, *ceviche* and fish. Mon–Thurs noon–10pm, Fri–Sun 11am–10pm.

The Azuero Peninsula

CORPUS CHRISTI, LA VILLA DE LOS SANTOS

The Azuero Peninsula

Mention the Azuero Peninsula, the box-shaped land mass that protrudes into the Pacific, and clichéd images abound of smiling women dancing in *polleras*, cowboys lassoing cattle and quaint village squares with whitewashed colonial churches. Yet the peninsula often delivers on such images: peasant farmers stride off to the fields at the crack of dawn, *sombrero* on head and machete slung across shoulder; some hamlets still contain adobe houses adorned with bougainvillea, topped with terracotta tiles; and small villages celebrate their saint day with bands of accordionists and fiddlers playing foot-tapping folk melodies. That said, the pace of development is increasing: trucks rattle along tarred rather than dirt roads; towns often now include unprepossessing cement-block mini-supers with zinc roofs; and vast tracts of land are being gobbled up by mushrooming real estate agents and mining companies, looking to force rapid and irrevocable social change on communities. For the moment, though, cattle farming and agriculture still prevail in the interior while coastal communities continue to derive their livelihood from fishing.

The peninsula, which covers a substantial 7616 square kilometres, is sometimes referred to as Eastern and Western Azuero, with no connecting road across the dividing mountainous spine that runs down the western flank. The former comprises the vast bulk of the terrain and the small provinces of Herrera and Los Santos, clustered around their respective provincial capitals of **Chitré** and **Las Tablas**, which make good bases for exploring the region. The Western Azuero, on the other hand, is an oft-forgotten sliver of Veraguas Province that trickles down the western seaboard, dotted with small ranching and fishing communities and ending in one of Panama's least explored wilderness areas, the **Parque Nacional Cerro Hoya**, which nourishes sparkling waterfalls and is home to several endemic species of animals and plants. That and the little-visited **Reserva Forestal El Montuoso** contrast acutely with the rest of the peninsula, which more than anywhere else in the country has been stripped of forest due to excessive logging and slash-and-burn agriculture. The desert-like **Parque Nacional de Sarigua**, at the heart of the **Arco Seco** (Dry Arc) – Panama's driest, hottest region that curves around the eastern shore of the Azuero – is a compelling reminder of the consequences of such practices. For a visitor, this means choosing your time to visit carefully; when fed by the rains, the verdant rolling pastures punctuated by villages ablaze with flowers and fruit trees make up a picturesque landscape, but when the clouds dry up, they lose much of their natural beauty, becoming parched and dusty as temperatures soar.

Panama's Spanish colonial heritage is also at its most visible and vibrant in the Azuero, from cattle ranching and bullfighting through Baroque churches to elaborate costumes – the best examples of which are crafted on the peninsula – and distinctive

MAGNIFICENT FRIGATEBIRD, ISLA IGUANA

Highlights

❶ Azueran artesanía Catch the artisans at work in village workshops, where they craft exquisite ceramics, devil masks and straw hats, as well as embroidered *polleras* and *montunos*. **See p.157**

❷ Festivals Try out the major fiestas: the glitz of Carnaval at Las Tablas; devil dances for Corpus Christi in La Villa; and the nation's biggest folkloric jamboree, the Festival de la Mejorana, in Guararé. **See p.163, p.165 & p.167**

❸ Isla Iguana A wildlife retreat of black and green iguanas, chest-puffing frigatebirds and shoals of rainbow-coloured fish. **See p.171**

❹ Playa Venao A lovely swathe of beach best appreciated by surfing the waves or horseriding along the sands. **See p.172**

❺ Isla de Cañas Camp out among the turtles that arrive in their thousands to nest along glorious sand each year. **See p.174**

❻ The Western Azuero Explore the undulating hillsides and rugged coastline of the peninsula's western flank, whose near-deserted beaches offer the most spectacular sunsets. **See p.176**

HIGHLIGHTS ARE MARKED ON THE MAP ON P.154

music that enliven the numerous religious festivals. This has led to the region being fondly dubbed the *cuña* (cradle) of national culture and traditions by many Panamanians – a statement which takes little account of the cultural affinities or contributions of the country's non-*mestizo* populations and conveniently ignores the existence of much earlier cultures. Vestiges of pre-Columbian communities, the most ancient of which was an eleven-thousand-year-old fishing village at Sarigua – currently the oldest known settlement on the isthmus – provide evidence both of an earlier history and of the conquistadors' brutal efficacy in wiping it out, still notable today when you notice the absence of indigenous communities in the region.

The Azuero's greatest appeal lies in its many **festivals** (see p.155), but there's more to the peninsula than partying: for the nature lover, **Isla Iguana** and **Isla de Cañas** offer very different but fascinating wildlife experiences, the former a major nesting site for the chest-puffing frigatebirds, boasting coral beaches and rich snorkelling, while the latter affords a rare opportunity to witness the mass breeding of olive ridley **turtles**. The peninsula's eastern seaboard hosts various important **wetlands** teeming with birdlife. Deserted **beaches** fringe the coastline – broad tan, chocolate and black stretches of sand welcome top-notch **surfing** waves while world-class **sport fishing** takes place off the legendary "Tuna Coast", with many enthusiasts using understated **Pedasí** as a base. In contrast, the more undulating, and slightly greener western flank of the peninsula offers a chance to get off the beaten track and explore a more rugged coastline.

THE AZUERO PENINSULA

HIGHLIGHTS

1. Azueran artesanía
2. Festivals
3. Isla Iguana
4. Playa Venao
5. Isla de Cañas
6. The Western Azuero

Chitré and around

CHITRÉ is the main urban centre in the Azuero Peninsula, and it makes an ideal base for exploring the surrounding area and for attending the region's numerous festivals. A laidback commercial town with an attractive colonial centre, Chitré was founded in 1848, though indications are that conquistadors had been there since the mid-1500s. For the provincial capital of Herrera Province, life centres on the bustling streets around Calle Manuel María Correa, where you'll also find the interesting regional **museum**, and the well-manicured **Parque Unión**, flanked by the splendid **cathedral**, notable for its impressive yet restrained wooden interior. The compact colonial quarter of Chitré can easily be explored in a couple of hours, leaving time to peruse the crafts in the suburb of **La Arena**, noted for its ceramics.

Bird-lovers will also be drawn to the nearby mud flats of **Playa Agallito** and the wetlands of **Cenegón del Mangle** and **La Ciénega de las Macanas**, which attract prolific birdlife, particularly migratory waders. Of more general interest is the attractive village of **Parita**, possessing a delightful church, and, further afield, the surreal desert-like **Parque Nacional de Sarigua**. Some of these locations are not easily accessible without your own transport, especially in the rainy season.

Catedral de San Juan Bautista

Parque Unión • Daily 6am–8pm • Free

The most obvious place to start a tour of Chitré is the imposing **Catedral de San Juan Bautista**. Constructed between 1896 and 1910, it underwent a major restoration in the late 1980s, which took the unusual step of exposing some of the exterior stone walls, to provide a striking contrast with the snow-white facade and bell towers. The restrained polished wooden interior also makes a refreshing change from the ornate decor in many Catholic churches, especially the gilded mahogany altar, which is complemented by bright stained-glass windows.

Parque Unión and around

To the side of the cathedral are the immaculate formal gardens of the **Parque Unión**. The neatly clipped flowerbeds and swaying palm trees around a stately bandstand provide the backdrop for the mixing of modernity and tradition: young suited executives hold forth on their mobile phones while elderly *campesinos* in *montunos* and *sombreros de junco* – the traditional embroidered shirts and workday straw hats – discuss the local news. Stroll two blocks east to **Parque Centenario**, a more low-key affair, surrounded by squat red-tiled houses with wrought-iron grillwork.

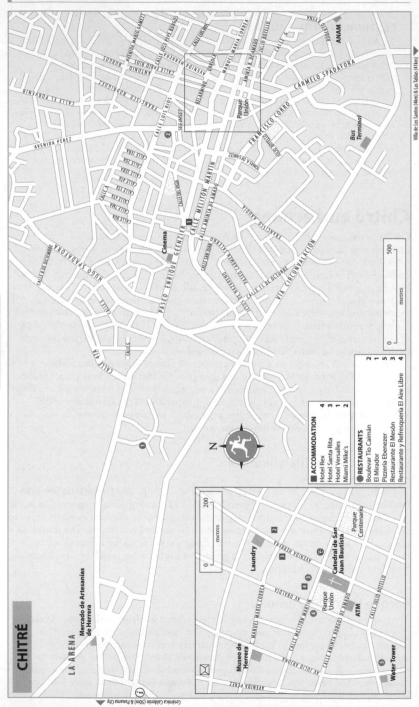

CHITRÉ

LA ARENA

Mercado de Artesanías
de Herrera

Museo de Herrera

Laundry

Catedral de San
Juan Bautista

Parque
Centenario

Parque
Unión

ATM

Water Tower

Cerámica Calderón (50m) & Panamá City

ACCOMMODATION

Hotel Rex	4
Hotel Santa Rita	3
Hotel Versalles	1
Miami Mike's	2

RESTAURANTS

Boulevar Tío Caimán	2
El Mirador	1
Pizzería Ebenezer	5
Restaurante El Mesón	3
Restaurante y Refresquería El Aire Libre	4

Bus Terminal

Parque Unión

ANAM

Cinema

Villa de Los Santos (4km) & Las Tablas (41km)

Museo de Herrera

Parque Bandera, C Manuel María Correa • Mon–Sat 8am–4pm, Sun 9am–noon • $1

Housed in an elegant converted colonial mansion and former post office, the **Museo de Herrera** is probably the best museum outside Panama City, though is nevertheless quite modest (explanations only in Spanish). Downstairs focuses on the pre-Columbian era: a couple of fine ceremonial **metates** stand out, as well as the impressive collection of **ceramics**. A reproduction **burial chamber** shows a life-size model *cacique* decked out in his gold arm and leg bands, while copies of gold **huacas** from the anthropological museum in Panama City line the walls. Upstairs, fast forward several hundred years to the colonial and post-colonial periods, with displays of **traditional musical instruments** and **costumes**, which inevitably include elaborate *polleras* and devil outfits, and various **tools** from rural life, some of which are still used today. Don't miss the pouch made from a bull's scrotum used to carry staples for mending fences. The museum also offers **cultural tours** of the area, but only in Spanish.

ARRIVAL AND DEPARTURE CHITRÉ

By bus Chitré's bus terminal (❶ 996 6426) is 1km south of the town centre on the bypass, Vía Circunvalación, with frequent minibus shuttles to the main plaza, where you can catch the return bus to the bus terminal. Taxis from the bus terminal cost around $2 to most places in town. Getting to Chitré from Panama City involves taking one of the regular large buses from Albrook bus terminal (hourly, 6am–11pm; 3hr 30min). Destinations Aquadulce (every 20min, 4am–6pm; 1hr); La Arena (every 10–15min, 6am–9pm); La Villa de los

Santos (every 10–15min, 6am–9pm; 15min); Las Minas (every 30min, 6am–6pm; 45min); Las Tablas (every 10–15min, 6am–9pm; 40min – change for Pedasí and Tonosí); Macaracas (every 30–45min, 6am–6pm; 1hr); Ocú (every 30min, 6.30am–7pm; 1hr); Panama City (1.30am, 2.45am, then hourly, 4am–6pm; 3hr 30min); Pesé (every 15–20min, 6.30am–6.30pm; 30min); Playa Agallito (every 30min, 6am–6pm); Santiago (every 30min, 5am–6.30pm; 1hr 10min – change for David).

GETTING AROUND AND INFORMATION

By car It might be worth renting a car (4WD in the rainy season) for a couple of days, especially to get to the less accessible protected areas or to explore further inland. There are several of the international rental companies in town.

ANAM office The ANAM office is near Vía Circunvalación (Mon–Fri 8.30am–3.30pm; ❶ 996 7675); contact it for permission to visit La Reserva Forestal El Montuoso (see p.162) or the Parque Nacional de Sarigua (see p.159).

ACCOMMODATION

Hotel Rex Parque Unión, C Melitón Martín ❶ 996 4310, ✉ hotelrex@hotmail.com. You're paying more for the prime location on the plaza so it's worth splashing out for the French windows and a view over the park. Slightly faded furnishings but pleasant wooden panelling and comfy beds make it a reasonable option for the unfussy. Takes credit cards. **$55**

★**Hotel Santa Rita** C Manuel María Correa, at Av Herrera ❶ 996 4610. Good value in a prime location, this ageing but well-maintained hotel has dark, simple en-suite rooms (fan or a/c, cable TV, good bed and hot water) off long corridors at modest prices. There's a $10 discount on weekdays. **$33**

MASK-MAKERS

Ghoulish **devil masks**, which form the centrepiece of Corpus Christi celebrations (see p.163) across the country and feature in other festivals throughout the year, make great souvenirs. They are made predominantly from papier-mâché coated onto a greased clay or earthen mould; their horns, wooden teeth and eyes – usually ping-pong balls or marbles – are added later. Though you'd be hard put to squeeze a full-size headpiece into your hand luggage, increasingly smaller versions are being made for the tourist trade. They're available in various craft centres and agricultural fairs, and you can also visit some of the mask-makers in their workshops. Expect to pay $10–12 for a small mask and from $50 for a large one. One renowned artisan is **José González** (❶ 996 2314); his workshop in the outskirts of Chitré is tough to find but ring and he'll pick you up, or enquire at the Museo de Hererra (see above). Another, specializing in *diablos sucios* (see box, p.163), is **Dário López** (❶ 974 2933), whose hard-to-miss workshop is on the Carretera Nacional, just north of Parita, beyond the petrol station.

Hotel Versalles Paseo Enrique Geenzier ☎ 996 4422, ⓦ hotelversalles.com. Don't delude yourself with visions of Parisian splendour, though rooms in this functional motel-like business hotel on the main approach road are comfortable and well equipped (a/c, phone, wi-fi, satellite TV, room service and hot water), if lacking in character. Small pool and bar-restaurant. **$64**

Miami Mike's Av Herrera, at C Manuel María Correa ☎ 6603 9711, ⓦ miamimikeshostel.com. Cheerily decorated, small-scale, fan-ventilated hostel offering little more than a bunk, a kitchen-cum-living area and a fantastic rooftop view but run by an affable American, at rock-bottom rates. Dorms **$10**

EATING AND DRINKING

Boulevar Tío Caimán Plaza San Pedro ☎ 996 8040. Enjoy some succulent seafood dishes on a breezy tiled patio by the public swimming pool. Mains start from around $9 including some slightly more inventive dishes such as *corvina* with grapes and cashew nuts and you can even buy wine by the glass. Mon–Sat 8am–11pm, Sun noon–10pm.

El Mirador Up the hill off the Carretera Nacional between Chitré and La Arena ☎ 974 4647. Atmospheric open-air hilltop spot (well signposted) to enjoy a cheap beer while admiring the sunset or the twinkling night lights of Chitré. Specializes in whole fish and seafood (mains from $6). Mon 4–10pm, Tues–Fri 10am–10pm, Sat 1–10pm, Sun noon–9pm.

Pizzería Ebenezer C Aminta Burgos de Amado, near Parque Unión ☎ 996 8831. Reputedly the town's best pizzas (mid-sized from $6), with a wide selection of toppings. Greek specialities, tacos, burritos and other comfort food available. Mon–Sat 10am–10pm, Sun 4–10pm.

★ **Restaurante El Mesón** Downstairs at the Hotel Rex ☎ 996 2408. Eschew the a/c dining room for the much nicer open-air café overlooking the park. Breakfasts under $5, while lunch and dinner mains start at around $9, and include well-prepared snacks (toasted sandwiches, burritos), the usual Panamanian and international regulars and Spanish specialities like paella, chorizo and tongue. Free wi-fi. Daily 6am–11pm.

Restaurante y Refresquería El Aire Libre Parque Unión, Av Obaldía ☎ 996 3639. Pleasant open-sided restaurant overlooking the park; packed at breakfast and lunch, offering a cheap *menú del día* – the customary plateful of rice, beans and chicken or fish. Daily 6am–10pm.

La Arena

The only reason travellers stop off at **La Arena**, a suburb-like village 5km west of Chitré, is to peruse the **ceramics**, for which it is famous. Get off the bus (from the bus terminal or the centre of town) or abandon your taxi along the Carretera Nacional once you see roadside displays of pottery.

ARRIVAL AND SHOPPING   LA ARENA

By bus Regular buses from Chitré's terminal (every 15min, 6am–9pm) pass through town.

By taxi A taxi from the town centre or bus station will cost around $3.

Cerámica Calderón Just off the main road ☎ 974 4946. This is one of the best-known places to shop for ceramics in La Arena; while here, you can witness the pots being moulded and fired in giant kilns on the premises. Daily 7am–4pm.

Parita

Parita is a few hundred metres off the Carretera Nacional; take any bus bound for Santiago or Aguadulce from Chitré (approx every 30min, 6am–8pm)

Founded in 1556, **PARITA** is one of the oldest, best-preserved and most picturesque villages on the peninsula. The village is just 11km northwest of Chitré, and easily reachable by public transport: arrive shortly after sunrise or just before dusk to catch the best light for photographs. Take in the sparkling white eighteenth-century **Iglesia Santo Domingo de Guzmán**, with its attractive clay-tiled roof. Peek inside and you'll see some ornately carved wooden altarpieces and a similarly elaborate pulpit. Surrounding the plaza, terraces of pastel-coloured traditional adobe (*quincha*) cottages with tiled roofs take you back in time, though a line of telegraph poles remind you that the village was not totally bypassed by the twentieth century. Party time in Parita occurs in the days leading up to August 8, the celebration of the village's foundation.

Playa Agallito

Buses between Chitré and Playa Aqallito, via Av Herrera, run every 30min (6am–6pm; 15–20min); a taxi should cost $4–5

Despite the continued clearing of mangroves to make way for shrimp farms, the silty mud and salt flats of **Playa Agallito** still provide sustenance for thousands of **shore birds** and **waders**, many migratory, who return to the same spot to feed each year. This avian feast is the main reason to come here, as it's one of the country's top spots for catching sight of the splendid roseate spoonbill as well as American oystercatchers and wood storks, amid a potpourri of terns, egrets, herons and sandpipers. The best time to visit – bring the binoculars – is at high tide when birds feed close to shore.

Parque Nacional de Sarigua

The park entrance is located off the Carretera Nacional just north of Parita • Daily 8am–4pm • $5

A little further up the coast from Playa Agallito, **PARQUE NACIONAL DE SARIGUA** comprises a desert-like wasteland, covered with a layer of surreal bronze-coloured dust. Birdlife is restricted to a coastal sliver of threatened mangrove. This eighty-square-kilometre protected reserve stretches out into the Bahía de Parita and is squeezed between Río Santa María and Río Parita on land. Behind the mangroves, vast salt flats and tracts of dry forest lie bleak saline-streaked gullies dotted with cactus, acacia and snowy blobs of wild cotton. Less a tourist attraction, as it is often heralded, than a cautionary tale, Sarigua is testament to the devastating consequences of a century of slash-and-burn agriculture and overgrazing, which has made it by far the hottest and driest area in the country.

The silver lining to this sad tale of environmental degradation is that the resulting erosion has helped uncover important **archeological remains**, including evidence of an eleven-thousand-year-old fishing village, the oldest known settlement on the isthmus, and more recent traces (between fifteen hundred and five thousand years ago) of an ancient farming community. When walking around the park it's easy to stumble on shards of ancient ceramics or discarded shells, just as the sparse vegetation makes it easier to spot boas curled around parched branches, armadillos digging in the undergrowth or lizards and iguanas sunning themselves. The landscape is best appreciated from the top of the rickety **mirador** by the **ranger station**, from where you can also make out distant shrimp farms. Rangers offer **guided walks** for a tip, but note that the park is rather undeveloped, with only one very short **trail** so far.

ARRIVAL AND DEPARTURE	PARQUE NACIONAL DE SARIGUA
By bus and taxi To reach Sarigua either take a bus to Parita and a taxi ($3) from there, or take a taxi from Chitré ($10).	**By car** The turn-off is well signposted off the Carretera Nacional north of Parita; note that 4WD is necessary in the rainy season.

Refugio de Vida Silvestre Cenegón del Mangle

The park entrance is located at the mouth of the Río Santa María off the Carretera Nacional east of París • Daily 8am–4pm • $5

At the mouth of the Río Santa María, with around eight square kilometres of mangrove rich in wildlife, the **Refugio de Vida Silvestre Cenegón del Mangle** is known for its heronries packed with grey and tri-coloured herons and great white and cattle egrets, though numbers have been decreasing in recent years. There is a 500m boardwalk through the mangroves to better view the birds, especially during the nesting season (June–Sept). In the dry season, there's little reason to visit.

ARRIVAL AND DEPARTURE	REFUGIO DE VIDA SILVESTRE
By car It's a 45min ride from Chitré: 7km northwest of Parita on the highway, turn right at a bus shelter and petrol station to París – a far cry from its namesake in Europe, and	actually named after a local indigenous chief. At the fork by the village church, bear right and then right again at an unmarked crossroads a few hundred metres later. The tarred

road soon peters into dirt, which continues another 4km before signs to the reserve re-emerge, which you follow to the park office. 4WD is necessary in the rainy season.

By taxi To get here by taxi (4WD in the rainy season) will cost around $25 from Chitré or $15 from Parita.

La Ciénaga de las Macanas

4km east of El Rincón, which is 32km northwest of Chitré • Daily 8.30am–3.30pm • $3

The region's largest freshwater wetland area **is La Ciénaga de las Macanas**, a shallow lake with swampy surroundings and patches of dry forest set on Río Santa María's floodplains. It attracts an abundance of resident and migratory birdlife visible from the **observation tower** near the water's edge. Here in addition to waders and ducks you might be surprised to see Brahman cattle chomping through the greenery; they help regulate the invasive water hyacinth and since the marsh-cum-lake is a multi-use site, limited farming and fishing is allowed, though conservationists are keen to reduce the number of grazing livestock.

Amenities are better here than at nearby Cenegón del Mangle: beside the tower are toilets, picnic tables, a short interpretive path and a jetty protruding over the water, with a couple of boats tethered. If you fancy **boating** on the water to get closer to wildlife or throw a fishing line, contact one of the eco-tourism groups in the nearby village of **El Rincón** (de Santa María).

ARRIVAL AND TOURS	LA CIÉNAGA DE LAS MACANAS
By bus Take a bus to El Rincón from Chitré; from here it is around 4km to the marsh (right at the church, then right at the fork).	**Boat trips and guides** Contact the local environmental organization GEMA (☎976 1040; or Hector Escudero ☎6021 4919), which offers guiding services (in Spanish) and boat trips, and can arrange transport for you.

The central peninsula

The best way to get a feel for rural life in the Azuero, which in some places has remained much the same for over a century, is to head west of the Carretera Nacional into the **agricultural heartland** of the peninsula. Here you pass rolling hills of pastureland sprinkled with giant hardwoods, fields of sugar cane and flower-filled towns and villages, where the unhurried pace of life is infectious. There is precious little accommodation in these places, but the main population centres are well connected by public transport on decent roads and two or three can easily be combined into a day-trip. To experience life in the more remote villages, pack a sleeping bag or tent and clamber aboard one of the infrequent *chivas* from the plaza of one of the larger centres and improvise once you reach the end of the road – literally. The hospitality of most people on the peninsula is such that you're bound to find somewhere to spend the night for a few dollars, with a bar and a hole-in-the-wall *fonda* nearby to sustain you.

Pesé

One of the prettiest towns within reach of Chitré, lying 24km southeast and surrounded by a carpet of sugar cane, **PESÉ** is known for its Good Friday re-enactment of the Passion of Christ, and its liquor; the ironic juxtaposition of faith and booze is evident the moment you set eyes on the church, which looks disapprovingly across the road at the Varela Hermanos **distillery**, producer of Panama's national knockout (35 percent) tipple, seco. What Spanish émigré and founder José Varela started up as a sugar mill and refinery in 1908, became a distillery in 1936 and the business has never looked back, now supplying ninety percent of Panama's spirits. As you can find out for yourself on a tour of the place (☎917 0300, ⌨varelahermanos.com; Jan–April), the factory produces a million cases of spirit a year, much of which ends up down the throats of revellers at the Azuero's many celebrations, such as the annual **Festival de la Caña de Azúcar** held in Pesé to mark the end of the harvest.

ARRIVAL AND EATING   PESÉ

By bus Buses leave Chitré bus terminal for Pesé every 15–20min (6.30am–6.30pm; 30min).

Restaurante Marithel C José Varela Blanco, 50m from the church ☎ 6648 9901. This friendly restaurant with a shady patio draped with foliage and hibiscus flowers serves a decent beef stew and the like for around $2.50. Daily 7am–3pm.

Ocú

Twenty kilometres west of Pesé, the larger village of **OCÚ** makes up for the lack of quaint charm by attracting visitors for its **festivals** (see box below) and **hat-making**. Above all it is renowned for the distinctive white sombrero Ocueño, with a thin black trim, which is still produced in the village's home-based **workshops**. Try **Artesanías Ocueña** (daily 9am–4pm; ☎ 6458 4529) a women's cooperative in the centre of town, on Plaza Sebastian Ocú, which also produces fine *polleras*, *montunos* and other embroidery items.

ARRIVAL AND DEPARTURE   OCÚ

By bus Buses leave Chitré bus terminal for Ocú every 20min (6.30am–6.30pm; 1hr) with the last bus back to Chitré at 7pm. Buses from Santiago terminal also run to Ocú every 20min (6am–6pm; 1hr) with the last return bus at 6pm.

ACCOMMODATION AND EATING

Residencial Ocú 50m down off the main square by the church ☎ 974 1374, ⓦ residencialocu.com. A dozen simple en-suite rooms with cold-water showers are set round a nice shady patio with rocking chairs and hammocks. Rooms are spotless and offer a/c, local TV and beds possessing decent mattresses. $28

El Punto Ocueño Main plaza opposite the church. Busy cafeteria dishing up an inexpensive *menu del día* or *cena* for $2.50 or you can have a plate of roast chicken or chow mein for around $3. Mon–Fri 6am–6pm, Sat & Sun 6am–noon.

Las Minas, Los Pozos and Macaracas

Though Pesé and Ocú are the more common day-trip destinations in the central peninsula, it is a pleasant drive, by bus or car, to cover the further 30km through **Las Minas** and **Los Pozos**, before either returning to Chitré or continuing southeast to **Macaracas**. There's nothing particular to see or do in any of these places, except chill out and watch rural life unfold. The party most likely to attract outsiders occurs in Macaracas. The **Fiesta de los Reyes Magos** (Three Wise Men) features a two-hour dramatization of the Adoration of the Magi, which has taken place in the church plaza every January 6 for almost two hundred years.

> ### OCÚ'S FESTIVALS
>
> The **Festival del Manito** (Aug 16–20) is Ocú's premier event to attend. Apart from the usual parades, there are two stand-out elements: the **tamarind duel** (*duelo del tamarindo*) and the **peasant wedding** (*matrimonio campesino*). The latter is self-explanatory but a wonderful sight: following a mock church wedding, the bride, decked out in an all-white *pollera*, is paraded on horseback through the streets while the groom holds an umbrella above her head to protect her from the sun (or rain). In contrast, testosterone-fuelled duels from bygone days, when men fought to the death over women, family honour, or simply from overdoing the liquor, are re-enacted every year with swords and sabres on a platform in the centre of the plaza. The town's other five-day extravaganza, **La Feria de San Sebastián** (Jan 16–20), is an agricultural fair honouring the patron saint.

4

By bus Buses leave Chitré for Las Minas every 30min (6am–6pm; 1hr); for Los Pozos every 25min (6am–7.25pm; 45min); for Macaracas every 2hr (6am–6pm; 40min).

Reserva Forestal El Montuoso

The park entrance is located at Tres Puntas, 4km before the village of Chepo • Daily 8am–4pm • $5

Up the valley from Las Minas, the seriously denuded peaks of the optimistically named **RESERVA FORESTAL EL MONTUOSO** pale in comparison with the richly forested mountain ranges in Chiriquí, Bocas or the Darién, so if you're heading for one of those locations, El Montuoso can easily be skipped. But if you're lingering in the Azuero and aching to get into the hills, this is the best place to come, until the rugged wilderness of Parque Nacional Cerro Hoya (see p.175) becomes more accessible.

The 120-square-kilometre reserve, dubbed the "*pulmón*" ("lung") of Herrera, was created in 1977 to safeguard the five rivers that rise in the mountainous region – some of the Azuero's major water sources – and to protect the rapidly vanishing tracts of forest being eaten away by illegal farming and timber extraction. In response, several reforestation projects have been initiated. Though only twenty percent of the reserve is now forested, what remains is concentrated around the reserve's highest point, Cerro Alto Higo (953m). Steep-sided mountains cleaved by river-eroded ravines harbour plenty of wildlife to interest the visitor, such as red brocket and white-tailed deer, howler monkeys, white-faced capuchins and collared peccaries. This is also one of the easiest places to spot the endemic brown-backed dove while other specialities include violet sabrewings and blue-throated goldentails – both hummingbirds – and the ever-acrobatic orange-collared manakin.

Exploring the reserve

The park office is set in a lovely orchard, where a short, pretty **trail** crisscrosses the nascent Río La Villa up to a cascading pool. The main trail, **Sendero Alto Higo**, leads up the mountain of the same name, heading off to the left after Chepo, at a place known as the Caras Pintadas (Painted Faces), an imaginative reference to the petroglyph near the start of the path, where rare sundews are in evidence in winter. A moderately strenuous hike of just over an hour brings you out at a peak by a radio mast, which offers a tantalizing restricted view – thanks to some unfortunately located trees – towards the Golfo de Montijo.

By bus Buses run from Chitré bus terminal to Las Minas (every 30min, 6am–6pm; 1hr), though the remaining 11km to the reserve requires a 4WD taxi in the rainy season, or a ride in the sporadic *chiva* bound for Chepo.

ANAM bunkhouse The park bunkhouse, a 5min walk from the road at Tres Puntas, has two comfortable dormitories and use of a shared kitchen and a camping area. You'll need to stock up with food before you reach the limited shopping options of Las Minas and note that alcohol is prohibited at this particular park. Dorms $\overline{$15}$, camping $\overline{$5}$/person

The road to Las Tablas

Just south of Chitré, the Carretera Nacional crosses the Río La Villa, the peninsula's longest river, which marks the provincial boundary between Herrera and Los Santos, and continues southeast, running parallel to the coast, a few kilometres inland. After skirting the diminutive yet historically important town of **La Villa de Los Santos**, whose small museum and impressive church interior merit a detour, the road bypasses tiny **Guararé**, host to the country's largest folkloric festival, before arriving in the provincial capital, **Las Tablas**, about halfway down the peninsula.

La Villa de Los Santos

LA VILLA DE LOS SANTOS is famous for the vibrant costume-clad celebrations of Corpus Christi, an historic rebellion against Spanish colonial rule, and the **Feria Internacional de Azuero**, the peninsula's annual five-day agricultural jamboree in April. If you arrive outside party time, though, it's easy to be disappointed. "Los Santos", or "La Villa" as the town is usually called, is much smaller and quieter than neighbouring Chitré, and not as spruced up or as vibrant as La Tablas.

You'll need little more than an hour to check out La Villa's two main attractions, the church and museum, both on the **central plaza**, aptly named after the great Latin American liberator **Simón Bolívar** to whom the town's influential citizens addressed a letter on November 10, 1821, asking to join his revolutionary movement against Spain, in what was called the *Primer Grito de la Independencia* (**First Cry for Independence**). This unilateral declaration started the domino effect that led to national independence from Spain eighteen days later and is celebrated annually with the customary flag-waving parades of marching bands, traditional folk costumes, speeches and fireworks.

Museo de la Nacionalidad

North side of Parque Simón Bolívar • Tues–Sat 8.30am–3.30pm, closed for lunch • Free • ☎ 966 8192

The room in which the letter to Simón Bolívar was penned, complete with original furniture, forms part of the beautifully restored **Museo de la Nacionalidad**.

FESTIVAL DE CORPUS CHRISTI

By far the most fascinating and famous of La Villa's celebrations is the **Festival de Corpus Christi**, a heady mix of **Christian** and **pagan** imagery in an exciting narrative of dance, drama and dialogue. It features a cast of larger-than-life characters and dancers decked out in extravagant costumes, interwoven with a series of religious ceremonies. Corpus Christi became an important tool in Spanish colonization across Latin America, as the invaders attempted to woo the indigenous population to the Christian faith by incorporating elements of their traditions and rituals into the ecclesiastical ceremonies. Though there is plenty of local variation, the basic good-versus-evil plot is the same.

The action starts on the Saturday before Corpus Christi when church bells at noon bring hordes of *diablos sucios* (dirty devils) rampaging onto the streets. Clad in crimson-and-black-striped jumpsuits, wearing ferocious devil masks with flame-coloured headdresses and letting off fireworks at will, they terrify all and sundry to the beat of drums and whistles. Fast forward to Wednesday, several masses later, when at 11.30am on the Eve of Corpus Christi, the Diabla or Diablesa (though as with all roles, performed by a man) also races around the town announcing the arrival of her husband, the Diablo Mayor, who convenes with three other devils in the central plaza. Joking and knocking back the booze, they carve up the globe in a bid for world domination. Before dawn on Corpus Christi, Santeños roam around town, on foot and on horseback, in search of the Torito Santeño – a man in a bull's costume – who is causing havoc, but is eventually rounded up in the **Danza del Torito** as the party proceeds through the streets to a large communal breakfast. The centrepiece of the drama unfolds mid-morning before the church, on a magnificent carpet of petals, as the Archangel Michael and the *diablos limpios* (clean devils), distinguishable from the bad guys by their white sleeves and a rainbow of handkerchiefs attached to the waist, vanquish the villains in the Danza del Gran Diablo or Diablitos Limpios before allowing them in to the service. All the dance troupes – including an assortment of dwarves, roosters, vultures, Mexican conquistadors and escaped African slaves – attend the mass, which then relocates outside as Holy Communion is offered to the townsfolk before the serious partying begins.

Further merrymaking takes place a week later culminating in Saturday's **Día del Turismo**, which provides a highlights show on stage in the plaza, and Sunday's Día de la Mujer, offering Santeñas, whom tradition has prohibited from participating thus far, the chance to dust off their *polleras* and join in the fun.

4

Making the most of the town's historical status, much of the museum – which was formerly a school and a prison (though not at the same time) – overflows with details (in Spanish) of various leading characters in the independence movement. The museum building probably holds greater appeal for the casual visitor than most of the exhibits, though the restored traditional kitchen out at the back is of modest interest.

Iglesia San Atanasio
Northeastern side of Parque Simón Bolívar • Free

The central attraction in the main plaza is the gleaming white **Iglesia San Atanasio** whose interior is even more impressive, containing a series of magnificent carved altars – a profusion of spiralling columns adorned with vine leaves, winged cherubs and flowers, all dripping with gold. Most splendid of all is the main altar, framed by an even more opulent archway that predates the completion of the church. Though the first stones were laid some time between 1556 and 1559, the edifice was not completed until two hundred years later in 1782. Note also the painted wooden tracery above the nave and the life-size entombed Christ figure in the glass sepulchre, which is paraded around the streets on Good Friday in a candlelit procession. The church is also the focal point for the town's famous **Festival de Corpus Christi** (see box, p.163). Although it is celebrated throughout Panama, the festivities in La Villa stand head and shoulders above the rest.

Parque Rufina Alfaro
Av 10 de Noviembre, three blocks southeast of Parque Simón Bolívar

At the southeastern end of town, **Parque Rufina Alfaro** celebrates the local heroine of the independence movement, **Rufina Alfaro**. A monument to the plucky Santeña has her seemingly emerging from a swamp, and her wide girth and substantial bosom caused upset at the statue's unveiling since from all accounts she was a diminutive maid. That said, her actual existence is in doubt although her alleged heroics have passed into national mythology. So the story goes, she exploited the local Spanish commander's affections and secured crucial intelligence for the independence movement about when to attack the army barracks before heading the march there that cemented the bloodless coup.

ARRIVAL AND DEPARTURE   LA VILLA DE LOS SANTOS

By bus Local buses shuttle between Chitré and La Villa (every 10–15min, 6am–9pm; 15min) and can drop you off at Parque Simón Bolívar. Direct buses leave Panama City for

La Villa (hourly, 6am–11pm; 3hr 30min); for the return to Panama City, or other major destinations, board a Chitré-bound minibus and change there.

ACCOMMODATION AND EATING

Hotel La Villa A few hundred metres off the Carretera Nacional ☎ 966 9321, ⓦ hotellavillapanama.com. The better of the town's two hotels, though service can be indifferent and you'll either love or hate the folkloric-themed decor, is a pleasant low-key place with good-value rooms (a/c, hot water, cable TV and firm beds), ranging from single rooms to suites, in a garden setting with a pool and moderately priced restaurant. $45

Hotel Restaurante Kevin Just south of the bus

terminal ☎ 966 8276, ⓔ hotelranchokevin@yahoo .com. Motel comprising compact, clean, functional rooms with the standard amenities set round a grassy area. Set back from the main road. Filling *comida criolla* is served at the restaurant. $32

Zapatos los Cuates Main road, close to the fairgrounds. This gringo-run Mexican joint under a breezy *rancho* sells tacos, burritos and the like for under $6 and is a good place for a drink. Tues–Sun 3pm–midnight.

Guararé

The somnolent town of **GUARARÉ**, 6km north of La Tablas, springs to life once a year, as enthusiastic crowds arrive in droves to enjoy the famous Festival de la Mejorana (see box opposite). That aside, Guararé's other claim to fame is as the birthplace of Panama's greatest sporting legend and one of the all-time greats of world boxing, **Roberto Durán**, better known as Manos de Piedra ("Hands of Stone").

Casa Museo Manuel Fernando Zárate

Five blocks north of the main square • Mon–Sat 8.30am–3.30pm, Sun 9am–noon • Free

The Festival de la Mejorana (see box below), first held in 1949, was the brainchild of a local teacher, Manuel Zárate, whose nostalgia for Panama while studying abroad made him realize the need to promote and preserve the country's cultural traditions. The **Casa Museo Manuel Fernando Zárate** chronicles Zárate's life and the festival's history. Walls are plastered with photos, including portraits of previous *reinas*, some antique *polleras* and menacing devil costumes.

ARRIVAL AND ACCOMMODATION

GUARARÉ

By bus Any Chitré–Las Tablas bus can drop you off on the Carretera Nacional at Guararé.

Hotel La Mejorana Main road ☎ 994 5794. Virtually the only place to stay in town though it's near impossible to

get a bed during the festival. Rooms are small but fairly comfortable with lots of highly varnished wooden furniture. $22

Las Tablas

Famed for hosting Panama's wildest Bacchanal during Carnaval, at any other time of year **LAS TABLAS** moves at a much more sedate pace. In comparison with neighbouring Chitré, the provincial capital of Las Tablas is a modest town, though it possesses a sprinkling of the necessary amenities to satisfy a passing tourist, as well as an attractive **church** and a small **museum**, dedicated to Belisario Porras, three-time president and Las Tablas's most famous citizen. Besides these, the only other building of note in town is the **Escuela Presidente Porras**, with a smart maroon-and-cream exterior, and a distinctive clock tower and majestic portal. Built in 1924, this immaculately kept state school possesses high ceilings, large windows and beautiful louvered shutters.

4

FESTIVAL DE LA MEJORANA

Panama's largest and best folk festival is the **Festival de la Mejorana** (ⓦfestivalnacional delamejorana.com), named after Panama's five-stringed guitar, the *mejoranera*. The five-day jamboree, which coincides with the *patronales* for the Virgen de la Mercedes on September 24, is for lovers of Hispanic traditions; there's not a techno-beat in earshot, and although the booze flows as at most Panamanian festivals, it's a less hedonistic affair than many. The plaza resounds with folk music day and night, and dancers and musicians from around the country converge on the otherwise empty main square to entertain and compete. Adults and children vie for medals in violin, accordion, or *mejoranera* playing, and drumming, singing or dancing. Even traditional work clothes and activities are judged. Bullfights are also on the agenda, usually dominated by seco-sodden guys staggering around a muddy field waving a filthy rag at a tired bull, cheered on by supporters – a far cry from the celebrity matadors of Spain. The festival highlight on Sunday morning is the **Gran Desfile de Carretas**, when superbly decorated ox-carts parade through the town, accompanied by *tunas* (African-inspired bands of call-and-response singers and drummers).

Inevitably all eyes are on the float carrying the **Reina del Festival de la Mejorana**, decked out in her *pollera de gala* finery, topped by a gold crown. It's an incredibly prestigious position, a national honour that lasts beyond the queen's year-long reign. What's more, families are prepared to shell out $15,000 for the privilege, and that's just for starters. Should there be more than one candidate at the October deadline, a run-off is held over three rounds (*escrutinios*) lasting several months, during which the candidates' families have to outdo each other in fundraising – a process that has the organizing committee rubbing its hands in glee since it means more cash for the festival coffers. The belle with the most financial backing at the end gets to wear the crown; her rivals have to settle with being princesses. The highest sum paid so far to secure festival glory is $70,000, some of which the queen gets to spend on her regalia – no cheap matter given that the elaborately embroidered *polleras de gala* cost several thousand dollars – and on other necessities such as dancing lessons and float decoration.

Most business in Las Tablas is conducted along the two main streets, Avenida 8 de Noviembre (also Av Carlos López) and Avenida Belisario Porras, which converge in the leafy **main plaza** – the vortex of the maelstrom that is Carnaval but at any other time a tranquil shady spot to enjoy a snow-cone or ice cream.

Brief history
Spanish nobles apparently founded the town in 1671; having fled Panamá Viejo after its sacking by pirate Henry Morgan, they were swept by fierce winds onto the shores of the Azuero. Here – so the story goes – among a pile of stones and bathed in light, an image of the **Virgen de Santa Librada** appeared before them as a statue, which they interpreted as a sign that their new settlement should be established on that very spot. Santa Librada, unsurprisingly, was adopted as the patron saint. The name Las Tablas is thought to have derived from the planks (*tablas*) salvaged from the ships and used to construct the initial houses.

Iglesia de Santa Librada
Parque Belisario Porras • Free

The **Iglesia de Santa Librada** overlooks Parque Belisario Porras with a figurine of the patron saint set at the facade's apex. The magnificent golden altar, which suffers from an overdose of pale-faced cherubs, illuminates the otherwise pedestrian interior though look out for the reliquary said to contain a segment of the saint's leg. Although

4

LAS TABLAS

▲ La Villa de Los Santos (37km) & Chitré (41km)

0 — 500
metres

● RESTAURANTS
Restaurante Hotel Piamonte — 2
Restaurante y Pizzería El Caserón — 1

■ ACCOMMODATION
Hospedaje Martha — 2
Hotel Don Jesús — 1
Hotel Piamonte — 3/4
Hotel Sol del Pacífico — 5

■ BARS
Billar Cincuentenario — 2
Jair Sports Bar — 1

VÍA CIRCUNVALACIÓN
CALLE SANTA LIBRADA
CALLE FRANCISCO GONZÁLEZ
AV CARLOS LÓPEZ
Bus Terminal
Police
CALLE EMILIO CASTRO
Banco Nacional de Panamá
AVENIDA 8 DE NOVIEMBRE
Buses to Playa Uverito
CALLE LOS SANTOS
CALLE 12 DE OCTUBRE
CALLE RAMÓN MORA
CALLE DEL ESTUDIANTE
Estadio Olmedo Solé
AVENIDA ROGELIO GAEZ
Iglesia Santa Librada
Buses to Cañas
Laundry
Cemetery
Museo Belisario Porras
Escuela Presidente Porras
AVENIDA BOLÍVAR
CALLE MOISÉS ESPINO
Buses to Chitré & Pedasí
CALLE AGUSTÍN BATISTA
CALLE 3 DE NOVIEMBRE
VÍA CIRCUNVALACIÓN
Buses to Tonosí
N

originally built in 1789, a lot of the church structure visible today dates from the late 1950s, having suffered an earthquake in 1802 and a major fire in 1958.

Museo Belisario Porras

Parque Belisario Porras • Tues–Sat 8.30am–3.30pm, Sun 8am–noon • $1 • ☎ 994 6326

Diagonally across the square from the church the neat, red-tiled **Museo Belisario Porras** celebrates the life of Panama's most illustrious president in the house of his birth. Ironically its most striking exhibit is the Napoleonic-size tomb intended to house Porras' remains, which lies empty as family members wrangle over whether the bones should be moved from the prestigious Cementerio Amador in Panama City, where they are currently interred. Walls in the single display room are plastered with faded photos, certificates and memorabilia. These only partly succeed in conveying (in Spanish) the extent of his many achievements (see p.296). On one famous occasion the statesman's bust, which stands outside the museum, was stolen and discarded in a latrine. On hearing the news, Porras wryly remarked: *"Mis enemigos, no pudiendo llegar hasta mí, mi han hecho descender hasta ellos"* ("Since my enemies cannot reach me, they have dragged me down to their level").

CARNAVAL AND OTHER FESTIVALS

CARNAVAL

For many people Las Tablas is synonymous with **Carnaval**, the nation's wildest party, which sees an estimated eighty thousand people squeeze into the narrow streets and central plaza for the five-day Bacchanal. Though scaffolding is erected and bodies cram every window and balcony ledge, it is still a crush, so it's not for the claustrophobic or faint-hearted. The festivities revolve around a Montagues-versus-Capulets-style feud renewed every year that divides the town down the middle in their loyal support for either **Calle Arriba** (Ⓦ carnavalescallearriba .com) or **Calle Abajo** (Ⓦ calleabajolastablas.com), during which swords are substituted for water pistols and the Calles shell out $500,000 each year to compete for the best music, supporters, fireworks, costumes, floats and queen.

The proceedings start on the Friday night in a blaze of fireworks with the coronation of the new queens, followed by dancing until dawn in a swirl of seco and sweat. Mornings kick-start around 10am with *culecos* or *mojaderos*, which essentially entail being doused by hosepipes from large water tankers as you dance in the street. The queens parade around the square enthroned on gigantic themed floats followed by percussion and brass *murga* bands, who work themselves up into a frenzy to inspire the *tunas* – the all-singing all-dancing support groups – to pump up the volume and outdo the opponents with insulting lyrics. The glam factor is ratcheted up a few notches at night, both on the streets and on the even more extravagant and glitzy floats, and general hedonism takes off until people flake out, often in cars or in the park, before starting all over again the next day. The good times are formally ended when a sardine is symbolically buried in the sand at dawn on Ash Wednesday to mark the start of Lent.

FESTIVAL DE SANTA LIBRADA

Commemorated annually from July 19 to 22 is the **Festival de Santa Librada**. Though there is no shortage of boozing and carousing, the event is less frenetic and a shade less hedonistic than Carnaval, though with all the usual attractions of traditional costumes, dancing and music, street food, bullfighting, fireworks and, of course, the religious devotions. They start on July 19 as the pilgrims file into town, bearing an effigy of the saint, who is dripping in gold jewellery given by devotees, but for tourists July 22 is the day to aim for since it incorporates the **Festival de la Pollera**, offering a chance to see streams of women decked out in Panama's glorious national dress sashaying through the streets.

FESTIVAL DE MIL POLLERAS

A more recently established dusting off of the *polleras* occurs at the end of the second week of January in the Festival de Mil Polleras when thousands of women from all over the country converge on the town to show off their regional variations of the national dress, accompanied by *tuna* bands.

4

ARRIVAL AND DEPARTURE
LAS TABLAS

By bus Transport from Panama City (hourly, 6am–7pm; 4hr) pulls in at the main bus terminal, from where it's an easy walk four blocks down Av 8 de Noviembre to the main square. The bus stop for services to and from Chitré and Pedasí is located outside Supercentro Praga on Av Belisario Porras, a few blocks from the plaza. The terminal for buses for Tonosí is three blocks south of the main square, and the bus for Cañas leaves half a block north of the square (see map, p.166).

Destinations Cañas (one bus daily, 1.30–2pm); Chitré (every 10–15min, 6am–9pm; 45min); Pedasí (every 30min, 6.30am–7.30pm; 40min); Tonosí (10 daily 8am–5.30pm; 1hr 20min).

ACCOMMODATION

Hospedaje Martha C Moisés Espino ☎ 994 1012. Ideal for budget travellers, offering small, clean a/c en-suite doubles plus cheaper options ($18) with fan and shared bathroom off a long corridor. **$25**

Hotel Don Jesús C Ramón Mora, four blocks north of the plaza ☎ 994 6593, ⓦ hoteldonjesus.com. The town's nicest lodgings in a converted family home with well-appointed rooms and good service. Guests share a comfortably furnished lounge-balcony area for breakfast (not included in the price) and chilling out. A pond-size pool and wi-fi are welcome extras and there's a restaurant. **$44**

Hotel Piamonte Av Belisario Porras ☎ 994 6372. Located on both sides of the road, offering cheaper accommodation on one side and slightly more expensive rooms with frillier bedspreads on the other. The larger, brighter, pricier rooms ($40) overlooking the street are the nicest. **$30**

Hotel Sol del Pacífico C Agustín Cano Castillero ☎ 994 1280. This fairly central three-storey modern block offers the best value for money in town, with clean, comfortable rooms with a/c and TV – though it's worth checking out several – and hot-water showers of varying temperatures. For an extra $20 you can get a larger, more modern and comfortable room. **$30**

EATING, DRINKING AND NIGHTLIFE

Evenings midweek are quiet unless there's a baseball match on at the Estadio Olmedo Solé (Jan–May; ⓦ fedebeis.com) – a highly entertaining party atmosphere to be savoured even if you don't know a home plate from a dinner plate.

Billar Cincuentenario Av 8 de Diciembre on Plaza Belisario Porras. With great views over the plaza from its first-floor balcony, this unpromising-sounding joint is a relaxing place to enjoy a chilled beer, with a video jukebox as well as pool tables for entertainment. Daily 10am–late.

Jair Sports Bar C Emilio Castro, along from the baseball stadium. A popular weekend hangout with disco, serving up American-style snacks – buffalo wings, nuggets, burgers – to help soak up the seco. Live music sometimes. Thurs–Sat 6pm–late.

Restaurante Hotel Piamonte Av Belisario Porras ☎ 994 6372. Nicely prepared Panamanian dishes at reasonable rates (mains from around $9), ensuring that the restaurant attracts more than just the hotel guests. Daily 7am–10pm.

★ **Restaurante y Pizzería El Caserón** C Moisés Espino & C Agustín Batista ☎ 994 6066. Top billing goes to this congenial open-sided joint with outdoor terrace. It serves up plenty of moderately priced seafood and *parrilladas* (mains $5–9) and cheap pizzas (from $4), and you can bring a beer to have with the meal. Daily 7am–11pm.

Playa El Uverito and Puerto Mensabé

Playa El Uverito, 10km from Las Tablas, is a favourite beach of Tableños for weekend partying and picnicking, though if you come midweek, you can have a scenic stretch of chocolate sand (ignoring the piles of rubbish on the way down to the beach, left over from said partying) all to yourself. Another kilometre further south, at the river mouth, **Puerto Mensabé** also has a pleasant **beach** and excellent casual restaurant; the fish could hardly be fresher since it's right next to where the fishermen land and fillet their catch.

ARRIVAL AND DEPARTURE
PLAYA EL UVERITO AND PUERTO MENSABÉ

By bus Services for Playa Uverito (6–7 daily, 7am–5pm) leave from beside the Banco Nacional de Panamá on C Ramón Mora in Las Tablas. Return buses leave Playa Uverito at similar intervals (6–7 daily, 6.20am–5.30pm).

By taxi A taxi from Las Tablas should cost around $6.

ACCOMMODATION AND EATING

There are a couple of very nice B&Bs at Playa El Uverito a short stroll away from several local restaurants that can cater for your lunchtime and evening meals.

B&B Posada del Mar Playa El Uverito ☎394 2049, ⓦposadamar.com. This lovely guesthouse, just back from the beach, makes an ideal getaway for a couple of nights' quiet self-indulgence, with the possibility of water-based activities if you want. There are four well-appointed en-suite rooms (a/c, fan, cable TV and wi-fi) and a spacious patio balcony overlooking the beach. **$99**

Hotel La Luna Playa El Uverito ☎6525 9410, ⓦhotel-laluna.com. Artistically designed, this boutique hotel comes with a lovely pool, vast tiled rooms, minimalist decor, floor-to-ceiling glass windows and sofas on the balcony to sink into and watch the waves (make sure you get an upstairs room). Though not on the beach, it is a stone's throw away and has a modest on-site restaurant open for breakfast and dinner, offering a small changing menu, with an Italian bias (main $8–9). **$88**

The southern coast

At the flat southeastern tip of the peninsula, the tiny, quaint colonial town of **Pedasí**, 40km down from Las Tablas, is becoming the centre of an unlikely development boom, attracting tourists and luxury real estate developers in equal measure though as yet, its character remains relatively intact. The nearby wildlife refuges of **Isla Iguana** and **Isla de Cañas** draw wildlife enthusiasts while the waves that batter the headland and southern coastline act as magnets for surfers. As the main road turns southwest, beyond Pedasí, skirting the golden arc of Playa Venao and mangrove-lined bay encircling Isla de Cañas, the farmland becomes hillier and more rugged, eventually arriving in **Tonosí**, the peninsula's last main town, nestled in a valley. Heading south from there, the road deteriorates before petering out at the remote coastal community of **Cambutal**, halfway along the coast. To the west, the Azuero's western massif looms, containing its highest peaks, which top 1500m and crown the little-explored **Parque Nacional Cerro Hoya**. With a dearth of public transport connections and poor roads, this corner of the peninsula sees few visitors.

Pedasí

Near the southeastern corner of the peninsula lies the town of **PEDASÍ**. A former small fishing village, it was catapulted into the national consciousness in 1999 when it became known as the birthplace of Panama's first female president, **Mireya Moscoso** (see p.300), a fact that immediately hits you on arrival: a vast billboard shows a photo of the woman herself, complete with presidential sash, with a bronze bust in the main square a further reminder, if you needed one. There's nothing to really see or do in Pedasí, once you've glanced around the plaza, but it is a tranquil place to hang out, and it provides a solid base for trips to Isla Iguana and Isla de Cañas, as well as being within easy reach of a string of great **surfing beaches**. Other **activities** that can be organized in town, depending on the time of year, include snorkelling, kayaking, horseriding and turtle watching.

ARRIVAL AND INFORMATION   PEDASÍ

By bus Minibuses from Las Tablas run approximately every 45min (6am–6.45pm; 45min). Those heading back to Las Tablas leave from beside the supermarket at similar intervals, with the last bus at 4pm. The elusive buses bound for Cañas (see p.175) stop outside The Bakery on the main road but timings are vague.

By plane There are three flights a week to and from Panama City, (Wed, Fri & Sun; 55min; $105 one way). The airport is 1.5km west of town.

Tourist information Pedasí's tourist office (Mon–Fri 8.30am–3.30pm; ☎995 2339) lies 50m off Av Central on the road to Playa Arenal – but don't hold your breath for any useful information.

TOURS AND ACTIVITIES

Tours Dive 'N' Fish (operating out of the Pedasí Sports Club, on Av Central on the way into town; ☎ 995 2894, ⓦ dive-n-fishpedasi.com) is Pedasí's only tour operator. It is PADI-certified, offering two-tank dives to Isla Iguana ($95) and Islas Frailes ($125). It also organizes snorkelling tours to Isla Iguana ($75) and horseriding in the hills ($75). In season whale-watching trips are on offer ($75) as well as trips to Isla de Cañas for nocturnal turtle-watching ($75). Most trips include a box lunch and need a minimum of two people. Several lodgings, such as *Casita Margarita*, *Dim's Hostal* and *Casa de Campo*, also offer outings to their guests at varying rates, while most accommodation will be able to provide you with the name of a reliable guide, boatman or taxi driver if you prefer to arrange something yourself.

Bike rental Baba House (one block east of Av Central, behind the supermarket) rents out bicycles ($8/day).

Horseriding Contact Javier for horseriding on the beach (☎ 6502 3902; $20/hr).

Surfing Shokogi (☎ 6701 5476, ⓦ shokogi.com) gives lessons in surfing, kiteboarding and SUP, sells gear and rents out equipment.

Naturalist guides Recommended (Spanish-speaking) local independent naturalist guides include Edison Cedeño (☎ 6660 9709), Mario Espino (☎ 6789 7272) and Victor Vera (☎ 6505 4357, ⓔ victorvera56@gmail.com); all do tours to Isla Iguana or can take you birdwatching elsewhere.

Las Tablas (40km) & Chitré (81km) ▲   Playa Arenal (3km) ▲

Police

PEDASÍ

Pedasí Sports Club
(Dive 'N' Fish)

Bank ATM

0   100
metres

N

ⓘ

Laundry

1

Supermarket

2

CALLE ESTUDIANTE

Buses to Las Tablas
& Taxis

AVENIDA CENTRAL

CALLE AGUSTÍN MOSCOSO

3
@
4

Library

CALLE LAS TABLAS

@   **3**

5

C. OFELIA RELUZ

CALLE LA POLICIA

6

(200m), **4** (1km), Playa El Toro (3km) & Playa La Garita (3km)

■ **ACCOMMODATION**
Casa de Campo	1
Casita Margarita	6
Dim's Hostal	2
Hostal Plaza Pedasí	3
Residencial Moscoso	5
La Rosa de los Vientos	4

● **RESTAURANTS AND BAKERY**
Dulcería Yely	4
Pasta y Vino	2
Restaurante Ejecutivo	3
Restaurante Tiesto	1

▼ Playa Venao (30km) & Cambutal (85km)

ACCOMMODATION

★**Casa de Campo** Av Central ☎ 995 2733, ⓦ casacampopedasi.com. Exquisitely designed, locally owned B&B comprising spacious, elegant rooms with tiled floors, plenty of wood and chic bathrooms, as well as comfortable outdoor areas (including one with TV) to retreat to, spread out among the landscaped, tree-filled compound. The large swimming pool is another huge plus. $110

Casita Margarita Av Central ☎ 995 2898, ⓦ pedasihotel.com. The priciest place in Pedasí, this American-owned five-room boutique B&B offers spotless well-appointed rooms nicely furnished in wood, with elegant shared living area and hammock-strung balcony. A vast buffet breakfast is included and trips can be organized. Reductions for five-night stays or longer. $119

★**Dim's Hostal** Av Central ☎ 995 2303, ⓔ mirely @iname.com. The attraction here is the wonderful hammock-filled *rancho* beneath two vast mango trees at the back of the glorified eight-room tree-house. Cosy and quirky, the rustic en-suite rooms nevertheless offer a/c, cable TV, hot water and wi-fi. Breakfast is included and the welcoming owner can arrange excursions for modest sums. $53

Hostal Plaza Pedasí On the main plaza ☎ 995 2408, ⓔ hostalplazapedasi@hotmail.com. A handful of simple, small whitewashed en-suite rooms and a small restaurant on the patio is in the making – a decent budget option. $40

Residencial Moscoso Av Central ☎ 995 2203. Ironically, given that it shares the name of the ex-president, it's the cheapest budget option in town, with minute rooms with reasonable beds and a choice of fan, a/c ($10 extra), TV and shared or private bathroom. $18

★**La Rosa de los Vientos** On the road to Playa El Toro ☎ 677 80627, ⓦ bedandbreakfastpedasi.com. Delightful, colonial-style architecture set in tropical grounds 1km outside Pedasí and within walking distance of the beach. Three crisp, bright rooms open out onto a shared porch. $65

EATING AND DRINKING

Dulcería Yely C Ofelia Reluz, just off the main road ☎ 995 2205. Dalila Vera's bakery is a national institution that has served delicious home-made cakes to locals, Hollywood film stars and presidents. Specialities include *queques* (coconut cakes made with local sugar cane honey and a touch of aniseed) and *flan casero*, to take out or enjoy there with a cup of *chicha* or *chicheme*. Daily 7am–9pm.

★**Pasta y Vino** Road to Playa El Toro, three blocks from the plaza ☎ 6695 2408. Authentic Italian home-made cooking in the owners' house – so with only a handful of tables (book ahead) – and a small, though changing, menu of lovingly prepared, inexpensive food. Tues–Sun 6–10pm.

Restaurante Ejecutivo C Las Tablas, on the plaza ☎ 995 2753. Solid Panamanian dining option with non-stop TV, inexpensive heaped platefuls of rice and noodles in various guises, plus seafood and meat options (from $6). A good variety of traditional fried breakfasts are on the menu for around $3. Daily 8am–11pm.

Restaurante Tiesto Main plaza ☎ 995 2812. No-nonsense place serving filling sandwiches, tacos and pizzas (and some less enticing sweet goodies) to eat in or take out. Tues–Sun 2–10pm.

Refugio de Vida Silvestre Isla Iguana

Admission to the park is $10, payable on the island • You will need to present your passport on arrival

Undoubtedly the best day-trip to make from Pedasí is to **Isla Iguana**, a tiny lump of basalt 4km offshore, which forms the centrepiece of the **REFUGIO DE VIDA SILVESTRE ISLA IGUANA**. The reserve was created in 1981 to protect one of the largest and oldest coral reefs in the Golfo de Panamá, home to over two hundred species of colourful fish though the coral is not in great condition, thanks in part to the US military; in the 1990s a large chunk of the reef was blown off when two large bombs – relics of US training during World War II – had to be detonated. Though covered mainly in dry scrub and grass, a grove of tall coconut palms and a sprinkling of other fruit trees hark back to the 1960s when Isla Iguana was last inhabited.

Bear in mind that you should avoid travelling to the island during major holiday periods. Despite repeated attempts by ANAM to control visitor numbers, fishermen desperate for extra income continue to bring boatloads of tourists, which can total six hundred in a day at peak times, inevitably putting huge pressures on the island's natural resources. In fact, Isla Iguana is a far better destination between May and December as the calmer conditions make for a smoother crossing and more rewarding snorkelling; the sea can be so rough between January and March that it's sometimes too dangerous to set out. In the migratory season (June–Dec, but especially Sept & Oct) **humpback whales** are visible, sometimes in the company of **dolphins**. The area's rich marine life makes it popular with **scuba divers** (see opposite).

4

Playa El Cirial

The rugged coastline of guano- and cactus-covered basalt is interrupted by two coral-sand beaches: the larger **Playa El Cirial**, where all boats pull up, accommodates the park office and a modest visitor's centre. Playa El Cirial's small crescent of silky sand backs a sheltered cove of translucent water barely covering coral formations inhabited by a rainbow of reef fish, making it a superb spot for **swimming** and **snorkelling**.

Playita del Faro

From Playa El Cirial, a 200m **path** across the island through iguana-favoured scrub takes you to **Playita del Faro**. Strong offshore currents mean swimming and snorkelling are sometimes prohibited here, but at low tide rock pools offer plenty to explore. The basalt outcrop to the left as you reach the beach provides a vantage point for one of the island's main attractions: Panama's largest colony of **magnificent frigatebirds**, estimated to be around five thousand. January to April offer the best chance of seeing males puffing out their extraordinary inflatable scarlet pouches, yet nesting goes on all year.

On a tour Dive 'N' Fish (see p.170) arranges snorkelling and diving trips to the island. Some Pedasí hotels and private guides also organize excursions here.

By taxi and boat Most Pedasí lodgings should be able to provide you with contact details of a fisherman with a boat at Playa Arenal – the nearest beach to the island, 3km from Pedasí – and a taxi driver to get there ($2.50 one way). There are no buses. Arrange a pick-up time with the taxi. An average price is $60–70 for a small boat for a half-day trip; the crossing can take upwards of 40min depending on conditions.

INFORMATION

Tourist information A useful website (in Spanish) for pre-trip information is ⓦislaiguana.com.
ANAM office The ANAM office in Pedasí (Mon–Fri 8.30am–3.30pm; no phone) can, in theory, provide further information about visiting the island though the office is often closed.
Money The last bank until Tonosí has an ATM and is on the main road into town.

ACCOMMODATION

Camping There are only rudimentary camping facilities in the form of a latrine and a *rancho* to pitch the tent under. Collected rainwater provides the only water for showering, and electricity is also lacking. You'll need to bring drinking water as well as food and a camping stove with you. $\overline{\underline{S10}}$/person

The surfing beaches

The southeastern tip of the Azuero Peninsula offers desolate beauty: kilometres of smooth dark sands punctuated by rocky outcrops and pounded by surf, with a few (foreign-owned) intimate lodgings spaced along the coast, ranging from an informal surf camp to one of the top boutique hotels in the country. Although not as renowned as Santa Catalina, these beaches – all within striking distance of Pedasí – offer excellent surfing, with some waves reaching 4m. Though the most consistent conditions are encountered between March and November, the coastline is surfable all year round.

The beaches around Pedasí

Playa El Toro and **Playa La Garita** are a walkable 3km or short taxi ride ($4–5) away from Pedasí; follow the road out of the main square until the fork, heading left to El Toro and right to La Garita. Three kilometres south of Pedasí at the village of El Limón, a road leads off 7km to the band of chocolate sand and rocks at **Playa de los Destiladeros** (bear right at the fork), which offers good surfing as well as fabulous views across the ocean.

ARRIVAL AND ACCOMMODATION   **THE BEACHES AROUND PEDASÍ**

By taxi A taxi from Pedasí to Playa de los Destiladeros will cost around $8.
Posada de los Destiladeros Playa de los Destiladeros ☏995 2771, ⓦpanamabambu.net. Offers value for money with its nine rustic bungalows (for 2–4 people) set in tropical grounds; sun decks overlooking the beach, a pool and comfortable communal areas ensure total relaxation. Can arrange horseriding, snorkelling, fishing trips and island excursions. Breakfast included. $\overline{\underline{S110}}$
Villa Camilla Playa de los Destiladeros ☏232 0171, ⓦvillacamillahotel.com. Perched on the hilltop a 10min walk from the beach, its terracotta exterior visible from the road, this exclusive and rather formal hotel also houses a gourmet restaurant open to non-guests for dinner (8am–10pm; closed Wed evening), and offers a range of activities and excursions. Midweek reductions. $\overline{\underline{S190}}$

Playa Venao and around

Thirty-five kilometres from Pedasí, at the small fishing village of **El Ciruelo**, are a couple of small B&Bs where you can laze in a hammock doing very little, canter along the sands or head out on a fishing trip. A little further along the road the protected **Bahía de Achiotines** harbours a mainland coral reef that attracts 150-odd species of fish, making it a pleasant spot to don mask and snorkel.

The imposing 3km swathe of charcoal-coloured sand that is **Playa Venao** (or Venado) is the region's best-known surfing spot, which provides waves suitable for beginners and more experienced practitioners alike. A glorious arc, its beauty is now being threatened by some ill-considered hotel developments on the beach itself. A few kilometres out from the bay, the guano-flecked rocky stacks of **Islas Frailes** are at times covered in thousands of nesting sooty terns and other passing sea birds though you'll need a good pair of binoculars to get a decent view from the boat since landing is impossible.

ARRIVAL AND DEPARTURE   PLAYA VENAO AND AROUND

By bus Buses from Las Tablas (see p.175) and Pedasí (see p.169) bound for Cañas pass through El Ciruelo and Playa Venao after 45min–1hr. Return buses from Cañas, 15min from Playa Venao, leave at 7am, 9am and 3pm. Note that these timetables are very approximate as buses frequently leave earlier or later than scheduled.

By taxi A taxi from Pedasí to Playa Venao costs around $24.

ACCOMMODATION AND EATING

A handful of pleasing lodgings exist in the vicinity of Playa Venao, where you can arrange horseriding and boats for fishing or visiting Isla de Cañas, Isla Iguana or Islas Frailes. Prices are often much higher for weekends.

EL CIRUELO

Casa de Estrella ☎6471 3090, ⓦcasadeestrella.com. Laidback and modestly furnished, with a great shared balcony overlooking the sea, TV/DVD, dining room and kitchen. There's also a gas barbecue grill to cook up your catch. $44

Sereia do Mar El Ciruelo ☎6523 8758, ⓦfacebook .com/pages/sereiadomar.com. Smart, tranquil B&B (four rooms with a/c, TV, DVD and fridge) with a lovely long balcony overlooking the sea plus a hammock-strewn *rancho* and use of the kitchen. Midweek rates are much lower. $88

PLAYA VENAO

La Choza 200m from the beach break; contact Hotel El Sitio ☎832 1010, ⓦminihostels.com/hostel/la-choza -de-playa-venao. Compact, comfortable fan-ventilated rooms, a breezy balcony and intimate garden-*rancho* kitchen facilities. Dorms $15, doubles $35

★Eco Venao ☎832 0530, ⓦecovenao.com. Superb hilltop overlooking the bay, 1km beyond the main beach. The lovingly restored wooden farmhouse offers eight bunks and a couple of simple private rooms with shared kitchen and bathrooms. Also, moderately priced cane-and-thatch *cabañas* and two stone bungalows are spread across the grounds. Campers share the lodge facilities, including the numerous hammocks and a volleyball court. Boat trips can be arranged, or you can explore the bay on horseback or in a kayak. There's a great on-site restaurant with a mellow vibe offering varied cuisine (mains from $9). Camping $7/person, dorms $12, doubles $33

Venao Cove West end of beach ☎6427 2129, ⓦplaya -venao-panama.com. Brightly painted hostel in a great setting, overlooking the beach with comfortable eight-bed dorms with shared facilities or more exclusive en-suite three-bed dorms ($10.50 extra) and two private rooms. Kitchen for use and bags of hammock room outdoors for lazing about. Dorms $12, doubles $45

Villa Marina East end of beach ☎263 6555, ⓦvillamarinapanama.com. Tucked away at the back of the sand, this spacious hacienda-style boutique hotel is set in lush grounds surrounded by tropical forest with a stone infinity pool overlooking the beach. Tastefully designed with all mod cons (a/c, cable TV and wi-fi) plus continental breakfast but rather overpriced even so. $165

Cambutal, Guánico Abajo and Tonosí

For most people Playa Venao is remote enough, though die-hard surfers may want to try the even more out-of-the-way spots around **Cambutal**, a small fishing village another 60km through undulating cattle country – spectacularly lush in the rainy season, desperately barren once the moisture has been sucked out of it – down a deteriorating road. Here the picturesque, charcoal Playa Cambutal and some of the surfing beaches further west get serious 3m waves while non-surfers can explore the caves, blowholes and crevices of this impressively rugged coastline.

Fifteen kilometres east, around Punto Morro, is the less publicized **Guánico Abajo**. There are some basic *cabañas*, good surf, mangroves to explore and the nearby **Playa Marinera**, cream-coloured sands hemmed in by cliffs, where over thirty thousand olive ridley turtles lay their eggs each year. To reach both places you first have to pass through **Tonosí**, which is little more than a glorified regional crossroads surrounded by hilly cattle ranches. but which has all the basic amenities around the main square, including an ATM, as well as the local ANAM office.

ARRIVAL AND INFORMATION

By bus From Tonosí's plaza a handful of *chivas* serve Cambutal (last departure 1pm), Guánico Abajo and surrounding villages. One bus a day goes from Las Tablas to Cambutal (via Tonosí)

By car In the dry season a high clearance saloon car can just make it down to Cambutal and Guánico Abajo, but once the rains start a 4WD is a must.

CAMBUTAL AND GUÁNICO ABAJO

ANAM office The ANAM office just off the main square in Tonosí (Mon–Fri 8.30am–3.30pm; ☎ 995 8180) can help with information on Isla de Cañas. The even smaller ANAM outpost (Mon–Fri 8.30am–3.30pm) should be able to provide information on accessing Parque Nacional Cerro Hoya.

Money The only bank (with ATM) in the area is on the main square in Tonosí.

ACCOMMODATION

CAMBUTAL

Hostal Kambutaleko ☎ 6677 0229, ⓦ hostal kambutaleko.com. Breezy hilltop hostel boasting simple fan-ventilated doubles with private bathroom and fridge (in some) plus a shared ocean-view terrace. No kitchen. **$45**

Hotel Playa Cambutal ☎ 832 0948, ⓦ hotelplaya cambutal.net. The new colonial-style hotel on the beach offers ten spacious ocean-view rooms. Fishing charters, kayaking, horseriding and hiking excursions can all be

arranged. Breakfast included. **$149**

TONOSÍ

Hotel Mi Valle Main square ☎ 995 8089, ⓦ hotelmivalle.com. New functional hotel overlooking the park in the centre of town offering 24 bland but clean en-suite rooms with the usual amenities (a/c, satellite TV, wi-fi), some of which have fridges. The on-site restaurant serves inexpensive Panamanian fare. **$30**

Refugio de Vida Silvestre Isla de Cañas

The $5 admission charge, payable to ANAM, is rarely collected

In the bay to the west of Playa Venao, nestled among the mangroves and a stone's throw from the swampy shoreline, lies the long sliver of land that is **ISLA DE CAÑAS**, a place synonymous with **turtles**, which arrive annually in their thousands, availing themselves of a glorious 14km band of sand to lay their eggs.

Turtles are not the only attraction, however. The reserve extends into a swampy tangle of mangroves both on the island's shore-side and along the mainland, providing roosting and nesting sites for water birds, which can be seen close up on a round-the-island **boat tour**, which also takes in a pre-Columbian archeological site (with little to see) and a strangely formed cave dubbed the "*casa de piedra*". You can also partake of a couple of hours' gentle **fishing** or a ride in a **horse and cart** around the island's beaches and cultivations – rice, maize, banana and cocoa are all grown alongside vast quantities of juicy watermelons, which should be sampled while you are there.

TURTLE-WATCHING AT ISLA DE CAÑAS

Five species of turtle nest on the island, the most numerous being the world's tiniest sea turtle, the olive ridley. Their extraordinary mass **nesting**, or *arribada* (arrival), when thousands storm the beach over several nights, is a sight to behold. Pacific green turtles also nest in large quantities alongside significantly smaller numbers of loggerhead, leatherback and hawksbill. Nesting primarily takes place between May and November, with September to November considered the peak months, though timing your visit to coincide with an **arribada** – generally several days either side of a full moon – is tricky. The island was designated a protected area in 1994 and many of the eight-hundred-strong population are involved in a cooperative protecting the turtles – for which they are permitted to harvest a percentage of the eggs for consumption and sale. Villagers also act as turtle-watching guides ($10), an offer worth taking up if only to increase the likelihood of more eggs hatching rather than being sold on the black market. Since female turtles are easily spooked by bright lights, it's better not to bring cameras, or torches, unless infrared; rely on the guide and let your eyes adjust to the light (see opposite).

ARRIVAL AND INFORMATION
ISLA DE CAÑAS

TO THE JETTY

By bus Take the bus from Las Tablas (1.30–2pm) or Pedasí (7am & noon) to Cañas village; you may be able to persuade the driver to drive the extra kilometres to the island dock (El Encerrao) for a few extra dollars. Otherwise, take a taxi from Cañas.

By car If you're driving, the turn-off to the jetty is 6km west of Cañas village, opposite *fonda* El Refugio; from there it's another 2km down a tarred road.

By taxi A taxi from Pedasí costs around $30.

TO THE ISLAND

By boat The island is only about 50m across the water, so shout across if you haven't arranged transport in advance, or ring ☎6716 4095 to call for transport; a boat will be sent over ($1) though ideally not at low tide as it means wading through swamp to meet it.

INFORMATION AND GUIDES

Advance bookings Isla Cañas Tours (☎6718 0032, ⓦfacebook.com/infoictours) is the village tourism cooperative. You can contact its president, Daniel Pérez, directly on that number (in Spanish), or via the tourist office in Pedasí (see p.169). The cooperative does all-inclusive packages to the island or can give information on getting there yourself. Emails are answered promptly.

Guides Trained community guides are assigned to visitors ($15) to lead the turtle watch. Fernando Dominguez (☎6716 4095) is a reliable local guide with a couple of boats who can take you to explore the mangroves and nearby river estuary, on the lookout for crocodiles, or doing artisanal fishing.

ACCOMMODATION

Village accommodation The village cooperative has very rudimentary cabins with fans or a/c for an extra $10; alternatively you can pitch a tent, or stay with a family.

There are also a couple of small inexpensive restaurants. Camping $̄5̄/person; cabins $̄2̄0̄

Parque Nacional Cerro Hoya

Park entry is $5, payable to ANAM, either in Santiago (see p.208) or Las Tablas (see map, p.166)

Tucked away in the southwest corner of the Azuero Peninsula, one of the country's most inaccessible parks, **PARQUE NACIONAL CERRO HOYA**, covers 325 square kilometres of the isthmus' most ancient volcanic rocks. Reaching the area requires an adventurous spirit since formal trails and accommodation are both lacking and transport is tricky. But the rewards are plenty: giant mahogany, cedar, cuipo and ceiba trees soar above carpets of moist **forest**, containing over thirty species of endemic plants, which rise up from the sea to lofty Cerros Hoya (1559m), Moya (1478m) and Soya (1326m). A few scarlet and great green **macaws** maintain a fragile foothold in the forests, as does the endemic Azuero **parakeet**; other critically endangered species include the **Azuero spider** and **howler monkeys** while substantial populations of **white-tailed deer** pick their way through the forest floor, shared with agoutis, collared peccaries and coatis. As the park's name suggests (*hoya* means river bed), the massif nourishes over ten major rivers, home to caimans and otters, and hundreds of streams that tumble down to the coast, leaving natural **swimming pools** and **waterfalls** in their wake. The protected area extends out into the sea, including precious mangroves and secluded coves enclosed by sheer cliffs, providing sheltered sands for hawksbill, olive ridley and even some leatherback turtles to lay their eggs.

Created in 1985, in a desperate attempt to stop the Azuero's haemorrhaging of forest though destructive agricultural practices, the national park and its protecting agencies are helping the population of about two thousand – scattered around 25 communities – to make a livelihood from sustainable agroforestry, eco-tourism, animal husbandry and fishing projects. The best time to visit is in **dry season** when the views are more spectacular, the mud less overwhelming and the hiking more pleasurable, though waterfalls and rivers – two of the major attractions – are inevitably less impressive.

ARRIVAL AND INFORMATION
PARQUE NACIONAL CERRO HOYA

FROM THE WEST

To Arenas and Flores Reaching the park is easier from the west, where a tarred road leaves the Interamericana just east of Santiago, skirting the coast over 100km down to the villages of Arenas and Flores. Both are served by infrequent buses from Santiago bus terminal.

From Arenas to the park boundary To reach the park proper necessitates travelling along a dirt road, and crossing two major rivers for the remaining 18km from Arenas to Restingue, a coastal hamlet at the park boundary. This is only possible in the dry season; once the rains start, the Río Varadero becomes impassable.

Information and guides Enquire at the Hostal Familiar Iguana Verde (☎6865 8908) in Malena (see below); the community turtle organization can arrange a local guide.

Organized tours You can explore the park with Tanager Tourism, run by the owners of *Hotel Heliconia* (see below).

FROM THE EAST

To El Cobachón To access Cerro Hoya from the east, take the dirt road west from Cambutal for 22km to the hamlet of El Cobachón, close to the park boundary. Whether on horseback, in a 4WD or on foot (which entails some shortcuts along the beach at low tide, so a tide timetable is a necessity), the road from Cambutal is still only accessible in the dry season since rivers need to be forded. Once there, Marcelino Rodríguez usually accepts campers at his place, while Daniel Saénz comes highly recommended as a guide, and can also arrange horses.

To Los Buzos Alternatively, take a boat from Cambutal or Los Buzos, which will be costly ($80), unless you get a lift with ANAM or catch a *colectivo* heading that way.

ANAM OFFICES

Whichever side you choose to tackle Cerro Hoya, you will need to consult with ANAM: in Las Tablas (☎994 7313) or Cambutal (no phone); or in Santiago (☎998 4271) from the Veraguas side.

The Western Azuero

The little explored coastline of the **Western Azuero** is very different in feel to the dry flat stretches of sand that line the eastern seaboard. Receiving much more rain, the countryside is greener and lusher, despite the cattle-ranching and occasional rice cultivation. As the sole access road threads its way further south across the increasingly undulating landscape it offers tantalizing glimpses of rocky coastline, hidden coves and foaming surf. Best of all, since the beaches face west, they witness glorious sunsets.

Settlements are few and far between in the Western Azuero: the first place of note, some 50km south of the turn-off from the Interamericana, is **MARIATO**, with a broad central boulevard dotted with *fondas*, whose main feature is a temple-like bank, with ATM. With a couple of small supermarkets and a petrol station, Mariato is a good place to stock up with essentials if you're travelling in your own vehicle or planning on self-catering. Eleven kilometres further south, the coastal village of **MALENA** is noteworthy for its turtle conservation project, which includes taking tourists on turtle watches in the season (July–Oct; ☎6685 8908, ⓦplayamalena.com), while the tiny hilltop hamlet of **TORIO**, another 4km south, is the unlikely centre of the area's nascent tourism scene, offering a couple of places to stay and eat. The increasingly roller-coaster road then bypasses the new surfing hotspot of **PLAYA MORILLO**, before arriving in Arenas and Flores, where the tarred road comes to a halt before the massif that is the Parque Nacional Cerro Hoya

ARRIVAL AND DEPARTURE   THE WESTERN AZUERO

By bus Infrequent buses run between Santiago and Mariato (approximately every 1hr–1hr 30min, 6am–6pm; 1hr), some of which continue to Torio.

ACCOMMODATION AND EATING

MARIATO

Hotel Heliconia Main road, Palmilla, 8km south of Mariato ☎6676 0220, ⓦhotelheliconiacom. Modern, nicely furnished, four-room B&B with a porch offering comfortable seating and surrounded by a lush tropical garden. The Dutch biologist owners are engaged in reforestation projects and eco-tourism under the name of Tanager Tourism.

The most popular trip is a three-day tour to Isla Coiba, but they can also arrange excursions to Cerro Hoya. $75
Restaurante Julio José Main road, on the left, just before Mariato. Cosy little covered roadside patio with a handful of wooden tables where you can tuck into a whole fish with *patacones* and a smidgen of salad for only $3.50. Mon & Wed–Sun 11am–6pm.

MALENA

Anna's place Main road. Anna, the current chair of the local turtle conservation group, rents out simple, fan-ventilated rooms in her house, across the road from the beach; she can also arrange for you to watch turtles nesting in the season. $20

TORIO

Cabañas Torio Main road, just before Torio ☎6939 1436, ⓦ torioresort.com. Hidden behind a rather forbidding concrete compound wall in vaguely landscaped grounds, this resort offers a handful of cramped, though clean, cabins, along with an open-air *rancho* restaurant. The place lacks atmosphere and is overpriced but there's little else around. $38

★ **White Spider Hostel** 100m east of the main road at the bakery ☎6644 8508, ⓔ whitespiderhammocks @yahoo.com. Run by a former Peace Corps volunteer, this small hostel can't be beaten for price, providing a small fan-ventilated dorm with comfortable bunks (no mosquito net), shared open-air bathroom, kitchen, plus a slender wraparound balcony with seating and hammocks from which to admire the surrounding hills. Free coffee and wi-fi too, and tubing, walks and kayaking can be arranged. Dorms $7

4

Chiriquí and Veraguas

SURFING AT SANTA CATALINA

5

Chiriquí and Veraguas

From the raging torrents of the Río Chiriquí Viejo and the verdant peaks of the Cordillera Central to the marine-rich coral, swampy mangroves and empty sands of the Golfo de Chiriquí, the diverse scenery of Chiriquí and Veraguas offers some of Panama's top natural attractions. Magnificent in their own right, they also provide the setting for a range of exhilarating outdoor adventure activities, including whitewater rafting, kayaking, diving, surfing, hiking and zip-lining. Though Veraguas is the only province in the country to border both the Atlantic and Pacific oceans, Chiriquí gets most of the headlines since – as Chiricanos will proudly remind you – the province is the *granero* (granary) or *canasta de pan* (breadbasket) of Panama. As well as growing most of the country's agricultural produce – everything from rice to strawberries – it also boasts the country's second city, David, and its best-known resort town, Boquete.

The **Tierras Altas** (Highlands) at the western end of Panama, to the north of David, attract most attention and tourists, with the cool, sunny climate and spectacular scenery of **Boquete** a magnet for North American and European retirees. The town provides a great base for exploring the surrounding cloud forests or ascending Panama's highest peak, **Volcán Barú**, which can also be approached from the less touristy settlements of **Volcán** and **Cerro Punta** on its western flanks. The latter provides a convenient springboard for the rugged, little-explored peaks of the **Parque Internacional La Amistad**.

A large area of the forested slopes of eastern Chiriquí forms part of the **Comarca Ngäbe-Buglé**, which includes some of western Veraguas on both sides of the continental divide and extends into much of Bocas del Toro province (see p.218).

South of the central cordillera lie the **Tierras Bajas** (Lowlands), home to the tranquil provincial capitals of **David** and **Santiago**, the former coming alive during its annual international agricultural fair in March (see box, p.198); the region's other main festival, celebrating flowers and coffee, takes place in Boquete every January.

South of David lies the **Golfo de Chiriquí**, a vast body of water with beautiful coastal fringes and deserted islands that stretches from the Costa Rican border to the Veraguas side of the Azuero Peninsula in the east. Surrounded by nutrient-rich waters that attract dazzling aquatic life, including humpback whales, the gulf contains the mangroves and coral of the **Parque Nacional Marino Golfo de Chiriquí** and the former penitentiary of **Isla Coiba**, which is renowned for its scuba diving and pristine rainforest. It is most easily accessed from **Santa Catalina**, a mellow fishing village and the country's top surfing venue, tucked away in the southwestern corner of Veraguas. To reach here you pass

Highlights

❶ **Coffee** Learn to tell a "buttery" from a "chocolatey" aroma on some of the world's finest gourmet coffee estates in Boquete. See p.187

❷ **Birdwatching** Seek out the resplendent quetzal and rare hummingbirds in the eerie cloud forests of the Chiriquí Highlands. **See p.187**

❸ **Whitewater rafting** Dramatic rapids set in breathtaking mountains make the Río Chiriquí Viejo an exhilarating whitewater run. See p.188

❹ **Volcán Barú** On a clear day, sunrise on Panama's highest peak affords a unique, spectacular panorama taking in both oceans. See p.191

❺ **Parque Nacional Marino Golfo de Chiriquí** Head out in a boat to explore swathes of mangrove, abundant marine life and idyllic tropical islands. **See p.203**

❻ **Santa Fé** Tranquil mountain town from which to explore the surrounding waterfalls and hills, with more strenuous hiking on offer in the nearby national park. **See p.208**

❼ **Santa Catalina** The country's capital of surf boasts first-class waves and a laidback ambience. **See p.211**

❽ **Parque Nacional Coiba** Outstanding diving, whale-watching and pristine rainforests are among the attractions of this penitentiary turned wildlife reserve. See p.213

HIGHLIGHTS ARE MARKED ON THE MAP ON PP.182–183

5

through the provincial capital, **Santiago**, a bustling commercial and agricultural centre that is also the gateway to the **Central Highlands** to the north. The standout destination here is the delightful unspoilt mountain village of **Santa Fé**, which is renowned for its orchids and waterfalls, and provides access to a little explored national park.

Brief history

The **Ngäbe** and closely related **Buglé** – both recognizable by the women's brightly coloured cotton dresses – were collectively referred to as Guaymí in colonial accounts, featuring prominently as fierce warriors. Their various tribes, alongside many others

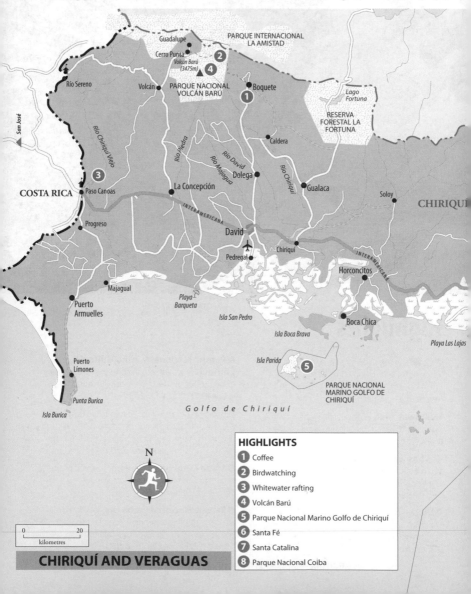

HIGHLIGHTS

1. Coffee
2. Birdwatching
3. Whitewater rafting
4. Volcán Barú
5. Parque Nacional Marino Golfo de Chiriquí
6. Santa Fé
7. Santa Catalina
8. Parque Nacional Coiba

CHIRIQUÍ AND VERAGUAS

that never survived the colonial struggle, were pushed up into the mountains by the **Spanish**, who moved into the region in the late sixteenth century. Founding major centres in Remedios (1589) and Alanje (1591), the colonizers also established numerous mission towns such as San Félix, San Lorenzo and Tolé, located just off the Interamericana. Though some Guaymí succumbed to their evangelizing efforts, others formed alliances among themselves and with passing pirates, and the towns were regularly raided and sometimes destroyed.

Following the separation from Colombia, the province of Chiriquí, which had been established in 1849, gained its own railway – though it folded around 1980 – in

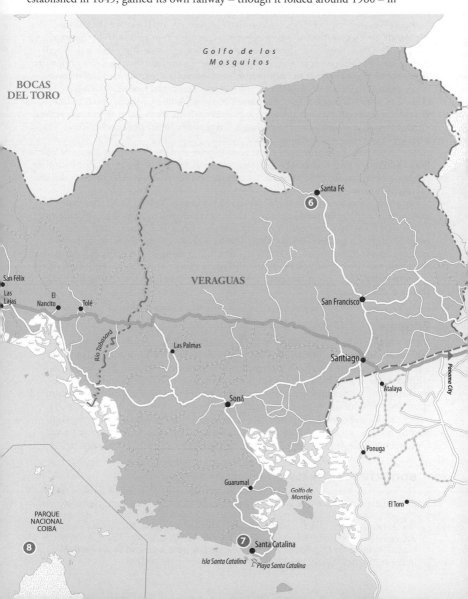

5

recognition of its agricultural importance, which further increased once the United Fruit Company began banana production round Puerto Armuelles in 1927 and coffee plantations started to thrive. It is on such plantations that the Ngäbe and Buglé now work, travelling great distances throughout the provinces of Chiriquí and Bocas del Toro – migrant wage labourers on rich lands that once belonged to their ancestors.

The Chiriquí Highlands

North of David rise the slopes of the eastern limits of the Cordillera de Talamanca, home to Volcán Barú (3475m), the country's highest point. These are the **Chiriquí Highlands**, or Tierras Altas, a region of forested peaks, fertile valleys and mountain villages. The cool, temperate climate and stark scenery give the highlands a distinctly Alpine feel, an impression reinforced by the influence of the many European migrants who have settled here since the nineteenth century. Sadly, their agricultural success poses a threat to the survival of the region's spectacular **cloud forests**, which have been cleared at a devastating rate over the past thirty years, while Chiriquí's picturesque rivers have attracted major hydroelectric projects, which are beginning to cause serious environmental damage, as well as posing a threat to the livelihoods and cultural heritage of the indigenous communities.

More positively, large tracts of forest are now protected by the **Parque Nacional Volcán Barú** and **Parque Internacional La Amistad**, whose flanks are home to wildlife including jaguars, pumas, tapirs and resplendent quetzals, and whose trails offer some of the best hiking in Panama.

Two roads wind up into the highlands on either side of Volcán Barú. The first climbs due north to **Boquete**, an idyllic coffee-growing town cradled in a picturesque valley, which has become popular among foreign retirees and tourists and is the easiest place from which to climb **Volcán Barú**. The second runs north from the town of La Concepción, 25km west of David, snaking 32km through countless dairy farms to the smaller settlement of **Volcán**, before threading its way through a steep-sided valley to **Cerro Punta**, the highest village in Panama and the best base for visiting the cloud forests and Amistad.

Boquete

Set in a scenic valley on the banks of the Río Caldera, 37km north of David and 1000m above sea level, **BOQUETE** is the largest town in the Chiriquí Highlands, with a population of over 22,000. It is to gourmet coffee what Bordeaux is to fine wine, with an array of informative tours to choose from (see p.187). It's also a popular weekend resort, offering some of the country's best hiking, birdwatching and adventure sports in a delightfully refreshing climate.

Technically, the town is separated into Alto Boquete, on the lip of the escarpment leading into the valley, and Bajo Boquete, considered by most to be Boquete proper. Dubbed the *Valle de las Flores y la Primavera Eterna* (Valley of Flowers and Eternal

---

BOQUETE'S FESTIVALS

Boquete's main festival, **Feria de Flores y Café** (⓿feriadeboquete.com), takes place midway through the coffee harvest in January. Its ten-day riot of craft stalls, flowers, stage shows and throbbing late-night music centres on the fairgrounds bordering the eastern banks of the Río Caldera. Around $20,000 is spent annually on ensuring a vibrant floral carpet – which you can still admire once the fair has ended. The fairgrounds burst into colour again for the annual **Feria de las Orquídeas** in April, while the **Boquete Jazz and Blues Festival** (⓿boquetejazzandbluesfestival.com) reels in visitors in February/March.

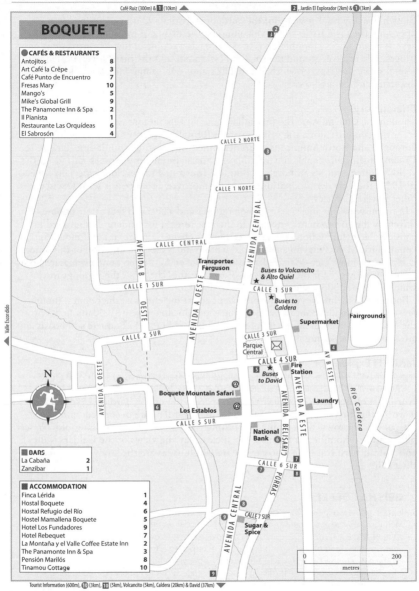

Café Ruiz (300m) & **1** (10km) ▲

2 , Jardín El Explorador (2km) & **1** (3km) ▲

BOQUETE

● CAFÉS & RESTAURANTS

Antojitos	8
Art Café la Crêpe	3
Café Punto de Encuentro	7
Fresas Mary	10
Mango's	5
Mike's Global Grill	9
The Panamonte Inn & Spa	2
Il Pianista	1
Restaurante Las Orquídeas	6
El Sabrosón	4

■ BARS

La Cabaña	2
Zanzibar	1

■ ACCOMMODATION

Finca Lérida	1
Hostal Boquete	4
Hostal Refugio del Río	6
Hostel Mamallena Boquete	5
Hotel Los Fundadores	9
Hotel Rebequet	7
La Montaña y el Valle Coffee Estate Inn	2
The Panamonte Inn & Spa	3
Pensión Marilós	8
Tinamou Cottage	10

CALLE 2 NORTE

CALLE 1 NORTE

CALLE CENTRAL

AVENIDA CENTRAL

AVENIDA B

CALLE 1 SUR

AVENIDA A OESTE

Transportes Ferguson

Buses to Volcancito & Alto Quiel

CALLE 1 SUR

Buses to Caldera

CALLE 2 SUR

AVENIDA OESTE

Supermarket

Fairgrounds

CALLE 3 SUR

Parque Central

CALLE 4 SUR

Fire Station

Buses to David

AV B ESTE

AVENIDA A ESTE

AVENIDA C OESTE

N

Boquete Mountain Safari

Los Establos

CALLE 5 SUR

Laundry

Río Caldera

National Bank

AVENIDA BELISARIO PORRAS

CALLE 6 SUR

CALLE 7 SUR

AVENIDA CENTRAL

Sugar & Spice

Valle Escondido ▲

0   200

metres

Tourist Information (600m), **10** (3km), **10** (5km), Volcancito (5km), Caldera (20km) & David (37km) ▼

Spring), the slopes surrounding the town are dotted with shady coffee plantations, lush flower gardens and orange groves, and rise to rugged peaks. The thick cloud that envelops them frequently descends on the town as a veil-like fine mist known as *bajareque*, producing spectacular rainbows when the sun emerges. Only when the sky clears, most often in the early morning, can you see the imperious peak of Volcán Barú, which dominates the town to the northwest.

Whether it's swinging across a valley in a harness, sampling gourmet coffee or chilling with a beer by the river, there's plenty to occupy visitors to Boquete for several days.

5

But while many head straight for the outdoor activities and tours described (see opposite), the town itself, spread out along the west bank of the Río Caldera and set against an impressive mountainous backdrop, has a couple of low-key attractions on its fringes. Life revolves around the small central square and the main street, dotted with several souvenir shops, of which Tucan Tile stands out, selling innovative, locally inspired hand-painted tiles.

Brief history

Though the **Guaymí** were the first inhabitants of this remote valley, seeking refuge from the conquistadors, the valley was not formally settled until 1911, when **European and North Americans migrants** joined the existing population. Drawn to Panama during the canal construction eras, these pioneering settlers started up the various coffee estates and hotels as Boquete continued to develop, especially when, in 1916, the now defunct national railway improved connections with David and other lowland centres.

In recent years, the increase in **foreign retirees** and associated **real estate boom**, driven by the government's attempts to increase foreign investment, has resulted in considerable deforestation and has forced major changes on the tranquil mountain community. Many Guaymí are only resident nowadays for the duration of the coffee harvest (sometime Oct–March, depending on the estate), when families migrate from across the province for the tiring work of picking the "cherries", the earnings from which have to support many for the rest of the year.

Boqueteños themselves remain ambivalent about the effects of the boom – though few could complain about the stunning new public library (daily 9.30am–6pm) on the main road – yet for all the unforeseen ill-effects of growth, Boquete still boasts an attractive natural setting.

Jardín El Explorador

Jaramillo Arriba • Mon–Fri 9.30am–5pm, Sat & Sun 10am–7pm (closed Mon and reduced hours in low season) • $5 • ☎ 720 1989 • Cross the bridge in Boquete and follow the road north; turn right at the fork and walk uphill to Jaramillo Arriba

Northeast of Boquete – if you've time to spare – the quirky **Jardín El Explorador** is worth the forty-minute walk uphill. Its steep gardens are decorated with tin men and scarecrows, with plants protruding from wellington boots and old TV sets, plus scattered homilies in Spanish. On a clear day the views of the Caldera Valley and Volcán Barú from the rose garden are fabulous, as are the strawberry juices at their café.

GEISHA COFFEE

In most of the world, the word "**geisha**" evokes elaborately made-up Japanese entertainers. Mention the word in Boquete and you'll be naming a deluxe beverage that took the speciality coffee world by storm in 2003, prompting ecstatic experts to exhaust their thesauruses. As with fine wine, the world of gourmet coffee-tasting or **cupping** is full of hype, jargon and poetry. Geisha has variously been characterized as spicy, honeyish, chocolatey and citrusy, with one critic likening the experience to "diving head first into a swimming pool of mixed fruits". The fuss started when the small Hacienda Esmeralda began sampling individual cups of beans from different parts of the farm – usually combined in blends – and discovered an extraordinary Abyssinian variety that had been growing neglected for some years. Having been declared the world's best coffee three times in the last decade by the prestigious Specialty Coffee Association of America, the estate's Esmeralda Especial is very much in demand, setting an auction record of $350 per pound in 2013. Since almost all the farm's slender annual hundred-bag crop is exported you have a better chance of locating it at Fortnum & Mason than anywhere in Panama. While you won't get to sample any Esmeraldas Special on a Boquete coffee tour (see opposite), you will at least learn what goes into making a great coffee.

ARRIVAL AND GETTING AROUND

BOQUETE

By bus The only way to reach Boquete by bus is from David bus terminal (every 20min, 4.50am–9.45pm, returning at similar intervals 5.45am–9.45pm; 1hr); buses drop off passengers on the west side of the main square, Parque Central, leaving just off the southeast corner of the square.

Bocas Shuttle *Hostel Mamallena* (Plaza central ☎ 720 1260) runs a daily shuttle service to Bocas del Toro,

leaving 8am ($30/person including water-taxi, $25/person for *Mamallena* guests).

On foot or by taxi Getting around the centre of Boquete is easily accomplished on foot, while a $2–3 taxi ride will get you to most places on the fringes.

By minibus Boquete minibuses head up to the surrounding hillside hamlets such as Volcancito and Alto Quiel, from various streets close to the park.

INFORMATION

Tourist information The tourist office (daily 8.30am–3.30pm; ☎ 720 4060) and adjacent café is inconveniently, if splendidly, located on the bluff overlooking the town at Alto Boquete, on the road to David. Although few speak English, the staff members are

reasonably helpful but you can get better advice from the hotels or tour operators.

ANAM office Although there is an ANAM office in Alto Boquete, all enquiries about the national parks should be made through the office in David (☎ 775 3163; see p.200).

ACTIVITIES, TOUR OPERATORS AND GUIDES

Inevitably in a tourist-boom area, everyone wants a piece of the cake, and some "**guides**" and **operators** lack the skills and equipment (eg first-aid kit for mountain guides) for the job. If in doubt, seek **advice** from someone at your accommodation. *Finca Lérida* (see below) also has good guides.

COFFEE TOURS

Coffee tours offered in English or Spanish (and Dutch in the case of Café Kotowa) range from a 45min introduction to a 3hr interactive marathon, involving a lesson on how to hone your cupping (tasting) skills and a tour of the estate and roasting facilities.

Café Kotowa Palo Alto tour reservation ☎ 720 3852, ⓦ coffeeadventures.net. The entertaining full-length tour run by Coffee Adventures (see below) of this scenic hacienda is highly recommended. The visit takes in the original century-old wooden coffee mill brought over from Scotland. Mon–Sat 2–4.30pm; 2hr 30min; $35 including hotel transfer.

Café Ruiz Av Central, 500m north of town ☎ 720 1000, ⓦ caferuiz–boquete.com. Panama's largest producer of gourmet coffee offer a nuts-and-bolts tour (Mon–Fri 8am; 45min; $9) led by multilingual Ngäbe or Buglé cuppers at the roasting facility covering the production process from plucking the cherries to packaging, distinguishing the different varieties and learning how to judge quality. It ends at their very pleasant coffee shop (Mon–Sat 7am–6pm, Sun 10am–6pm). More extensive tours focus on the tasting process (Mon–Fri 7.15am; 90min; $20), while the full works (Mon–Sat 9am–1pm; 3hr; $30) includes a visit to the plantation. The two longer tours include hotel transfer.

Finca Lérida Alto Quiel ☎ 720 2285, ⓦ fincalerida .com. Spectacular setting for a comprehensive estate tour (Most days 9.30am and 1.30pm; 2hr; book in advance; $31), which includes watching the action in the original 1922 processing plant. Take the Alto Quiel bus from Boquete or a taxi ($6) – transfers are not included.

HIKING AND BIRDING

Coffee Adventures Jaramillo Abajo ☎ 720 3852, ⓦ coffeeadventures.net. Run by a Dutch couple who offer pricey but very professional hiking and birding excursions in English, Spanish or Dutch ($60–65/half day, $160/full day, not including meals).

Feliciano González ☎ 6624 9940, ✉ felicianogonzalez 255@hotmail.com. Feliciano has taken people up and down Volcán Barú so often over the last twenty years he almost lives up there. Enthusiastic, popular and with constantly improving English and a little French, he charges modest rates that vary depending on numbers ($25–60 for two) and offers a very special four-day trip over the cordillera and down to the coast in Bocas, camping and staying in indigenous villages. If he is booked up, try Cristian (☎ 6685 9813).

RAFTING AND KAYAKING

Boquete Outdoor Adventures Plaza Los Establos ☎ 720 2284, ⓦ boqueteoutdooradventures.com. Although they can organize all types of half-day or full-day excursions ($50/90), they specialize in acclaimed whitewater kayaking and rafting trips as well as multi-day sea-kayaking in the Golfo de Chiriquí or multi-day multi-activity adventures. Family adventure holidays are also a speciality.

Boquete Safari Plaza Los Establos ☎ 6627 8829. Having taken over Panama Rafters, Boquete Mountain Safari now offers whitewater rafting day-trips ($65). Also runs a host of other tours, the pick of which are a scenic horseriding excursion to the rolling hills of Caldera, 26km southeast of Boquete ($39 including transfer), and the ever-popular ATV tours ($65).

5

HORSERIDING

Franklin Rovetto ☎6588 5054, ✉frovetto@hotmail.com. English-speaking local guide who leads a 2hr horseback excursion across the open countryside in the foothills of the cordillera round Caldera, ($35, including Boquete transfer).

CANOPY TOURS

Boquete Tree Trek Office in Plaza Los Establos, the zip line in Palo Alto ☎720 1635, ⓦboquetetreetrek.com. The impressive canopy tour ($65, including transfer from town) allows you to soar across valleys along steel cables, fastened into a harness high above Boquete (1600m) in a 3km series of adrenaline surges that scarcely give you time to admire the breathtaking scenery. After a 90min thrill you can chill at their pleasant terrace café-cum-bar-restaurant – you can even stay overnight in spacious cabins here. Departures are at 8am and 10am Mon–Sat and 10am on Sun.

MOUNTAIN BIKING

Mountain bike rental ($15/day) from a stall in the Boquete Artisans' Village on the main street – new bikes with helmets.

ROCK CLIMBING

Panama Rock Climbing ☎6764 7918, ⓦpanamarockclimbing.blogspot.com. Rock climbing and abseiling (rappelling) are relatively new to Panama – try this local outfit run by Panama's first internationally certified (bilingual) guide César Meléndez ($45/3hr). The favoured destination is the Gunko de Boquete, a fascinating lump of basalt that was spewed out of Volcán Barú when it last erupted, a 10min drive from Boquete.

SPAS

Haven Spa ☎730 9345, ⓦboquetespa.com. This highly recommended deluxe spa offers massages, facials, pedicures, manicures and the like in a tranquil spot off the main road on the way into town. Also sells day passes for $25.

Isla Verde Massage and Beauty Centre, Isla Verde, Av "B" Oeste ☎6948 6664, ⓦboquetemassage.com. Run by "a highly regarded massage therapist, acupuncturist and pain specialist", this spa's treatments include massage, facials and reflexology.

THERMAL POOLS

Almost all tour operators offer a tour to the thermal pools (*pozos termales*; $2) just outside Caldera though you can easily get there by bus from Boquete (7am, 10.45am, 1.30pm, returning from Caldera 8am, noon, 4pm; 1hr) plus a 45min hike – just ask the way; taxis $15 one way). Note that the 7am bus leaves from outside the fire station; the other buses leave as indicated on the map (see p.185). Despite the scenic location, the pools themselves are nothing special, set among the cow pats on a farm, though there's also a cold river to plunge into afterwards.

MEDICINAL PLANTS

Cloud Forest Botanicals Alto Jaramillo, north of Boquete ☎6636 8663, ⓦcloudforestbotanicals.com. Bilingual tours of cloud forest medicinal plants (Mon & Wed 9.30am; 2hr 30min; $30/person), ending with some revivifying organic herbal tea or coffee and home-made cake. Transport included.

WHITEWATER RAFTING FROM BOQUETE

Hugging the coast of Costa Rica, the tumbling waters of the 128km-long **Chiriquí Viejo** constituted one of the world's great **whitewater rafting** rivers until a controversial dam was completed a few years ago. That said, the river is still a top-class route to raft, providing an exhilarating descent with category II to IV rapids carving their way through stunning scenery. There are, however, other equally picturesque and enjoyable rivers to paddle within closer striking distance of Boquete, such as the **Chiriquí**, **Dolega**, **Gariché** and **Majagua**, with category II and III rapids. The rafting season predictably dovetails with the rains, generally June to November though the Chiriquí Viejo is navigable year-round, provided there isn't too much rain.

Although the rafting outfits (see p.187) are all located in Boquete, the entry point for the Chiriquí Viejo is a good two hours'-plus drive away (whatever the tour operators may claim) by the time you've picked up all passengers and crawled up the spectacularly sinuous road to the drop-off point. It's therefore actually better to arrange a pick-up from lodgings in **David**, or, if you're staying in Volcán, on the Interamericana at the turn-off in Concepción, which the tour operators regularly do, thus saving yourself a couple of hours' travel time. The descent ends at the Intermericana bridge close to Paso Canoas.

The two rafting companies in Boquete are professional outfits, but the sport is not without risk. Bring sun block, trainers and a change of clothes (you will get wet and possibly thrown out of the raft); don't be afraid to ask for clarification on safety issues, and know your limits – the major rapids on the Chiriquí Viejo can be truly hair-raising.

LEARNING SPANISH

As a place to hang out and **learn Spanish**, Boquete is a more relaxing venue than Panama City. Both Spanish by the River (Alto Boquete ☎720 3456, ⓦspanishatlocations.com) and Habla Ya Panama (Plaza los Establos ☎720 1294, ⓦhablayapanama.com) come recommended; the latter also has an extensive extracurricular programme and enjoys a more central location.

ACCOMMODATION

Unsurprisingly, there's a decent range of predominantly foreign-owned **accommodation**, all with hot water, in a burgeoning mid-range market. Since most places only have a handful of rooms, everywhere fills up during holiday and festival periods – when prices are hiked – so book ahead.

Finca Lérida Alto Quiel, 10km up the valley ☎720 2285, ⓦfincalerida.com. This is less about ambience and all about location: plum in the middle of a historic coffee estate, with cloud-forested slopes and birding trails above. The deluxe rooms have vast windows and private patios affording stellar views down the valley on clear days. In the evenings, snuggle up in the cosy common room. Pricier rooms with old-world charm are available in the original family home. Breakfast included. **$180**

Hostal Boquete Av "B" Este ☎720 2573, ⓦhostal -boquete.com. Great central riverside location (noisy during the festival). Nine compact rooms (mainly doubles) with a shared balcony overlooking the river at the back, and a great communal deck. **$30**

★**Hostal Refugio del Río** Av "B" Oeste ☎720 2088, ⓦrefugiodelrio.com. Lovely, spacious private house converted into a veritable Rolls-Royce of a hostel, containing several private rooms (some with shared amenities), including the more private riverside *cabañas*, and one large dorm. Set in a tropical garden beside a babbling brook, there's also a flash kitchen, TV in the lounge, free wi-fi, a gazebo with a barbecue pit and a jacuzzi. Dorms **$13**, doubles **$39**

Hostel Mamallena Boquete South side of Parque Central ☎720 1260, ⓦmamallenaboquete.com. Set right on the square in a lovely renovated wooden property, this friendly, efficient place offers small four-bunk dorms and private rooms with shared or private bathrooms, plus use of a large kitchen, TV lounge and garden and an abundance of hostel amenities. Dorms **$12**, doubles **$33**

Hotel Los Fundadores Av Central ☎720 1298. You can't miss the wacky Walt Disney castle facade as you arrive in town. This family-run enterprise makes up in friendliness what it lacks in sophistication, though rooms are clean and functional with new flat-screen TVs the only nod to modernization. The hotel's star feature is a stream that runs through its midst. **$62**

Hotel Rebequet Corner of Av "A" Este and C 6 Sur ☎720 1365, ⓦhotelerebequet.com. This long-established hotel has nine splendid rooms – spacious and generous with solid wooden furniture, including handsome beds. Good value. **$70**

★**La Montaña y el Valle Coffee Estate** Jaramillo Arriba ☎720 221, ⓦcoffeestateinn.com. A deluxe retreat in lush gardens consisting only of three bungalows, each with kitchenette, lounge, dining room and terrace affording spectacular vistas across to Volcán Barú, this intimate B&B enjoys an unparalleled reputation – advance booking is a must. Light suppers and gourmet candlelit dinners are also on offer and you get a coffee tour thrown in with your stay. The rack rates are stratospheric so look out for the promotions. **$456**

The Panamonte Inn & Spa Av 11 de Abril, off the top end of Av Central ☎720 1324, ⓦpanamonte.com. This historic hotel, founded in 1914, has hosted the likes of Roosevelt and Ingrid Bergman, and offers refined elegance in flower-filled surroundings; when the chill nights close in, huddle next to the cosy log fires while you sip your wine. Continental breakfast included. **$325**

Pensión Marilós Av "A" Este, at C 6 Sur ☎720 1380, ✉marilos66@hotmail.com. Homely place, with bags of character, knick-knacks and a talking parrot whizzing round the dining area. The good-value clean rooms (the ones at the rear are particularly light) have comfy beds and shared hot-water bathroom. **$20**

Tinamou Cottage Finca Habbus de Kwie, Jaramillo de Abajo ☎720 3852, ⓦcoffeeadventures.net. Choice retreat for birdwatching enthusiasts who don't want to be popping into town. Three snug self-catering cottages are tucked away in a small Dutch-owned hillside coffee estate a 10min drive from Boquete. Reduced rates for internet booking and long stays. You'll need 4WD access or arrange to be picked up in town. Meals can be ordered. **$112**

EATING AND DRINKING

Antojitos Av Central ☎730 9332. Pleasant and cheerfully decorated open-sided patio serving inexpensive (from US$7) Tex-Mex favourites: enchiladas, quesadillas, chilli con carne and plenty of veggie options. Daily noon–8.30pm.

★**Art Café la Crêpe** Av Central, at C 2 Norte ☎6769 6090. More Paris than Panama, this cosy US-run French café is as colourful as the art decorating the walls. Enjoy deliciously light but filling sweet and savoury crêpes (for around $9) or

5

enjoy a more conventional steak, but leave room for the crème brûlée. Tues–Sun 11am–3pm & 5–9pm.

Café Punto de Encuentro C 6 Sur off Av Central ☎ 720 2123. This pleasant terrace overlooking a garden is a popular spot for brunch, attracting Panamanians and foreigners alike, who can feast on a varied menu of eggs – with great crispy bacon, French toast, tortillas, pancakes or waffles (most around $4). Service can be slow when it's busy. Daily 7am–noon.

Fresas Mary On the Volcancito road ☎ 720 3394. Great little kiosk serving delicious *liquados* and *batidos* and fabulous bowls of strawberries with *natilla*, a particularly mouthwatering local cream concoction. 10am–7pm; sometimes closed Mon.

Mango's Isla Verde Av "B" Oeste ☎ 720 1539, ⓦ restaurantemango.com. Imaginative healthy menu including delights such as quinoa tabouleh and goat's cheese linguini, plus delicious stone-baked pizzas. Puts on Sunday brunch too (8am–2pm). Mains from around $12. Tues–Sun 11am–8pm.

Mike's Global Grill C 7 Sur, at Av Central ☎ 730 9360 ⓦ mikesglobalgrill.com. Nice location by a stream with outdoor and indoor seating, where it's more of a US sports bar with a friendly vibe. In contrast the menu is international and eclectic: from burgers to Pad Thai, falafel to tofu. Friday fried chicken night is popular with the US expats; it's also open mic then. Free wi-fi. Daily 8am–10pm.

The Panamonte Inn & Spa Av 11 de Abril ☎ 720 1327, ⓦ panamonte.com. Hands-down the most sumptuous dining in Boquete, laid on by celebrity chef Charlie Collins. Inventive gourmet dishes can either be savoured seated at candlelit damask-covered tables in the formal dining room or more casually in the fireside lounge or out on the terrace – though it's a shame about the TV. A three-course meal for two without drinks is around $70, or try a gourmet brunch weekend special (7–11am; $6–8). Mains average $14–16. Daily noon–2.30pm & 6–10pm.

Il Pianista Palo Alto road ☎ 720 2728. Intimate split-level stone restaurant a $3 taxi ride northeast of town next to a bubbling stream, illuminated at night. The Italian chef produces Boquete's best pizzas, various *bruschetti* and *antipasti* and excellent home-made pasta ($10–16). Tues–Sun noon–10pm.

★**Restaurante Las Orquídeas** Av Belisario Porras, at C 5 Sur. Small, friendly family-run restaurant in a quiet location with a few outside patio tables Good-sized portions of nicely presented and tasty home cooking. Fresh juices and *batidos* too. Mon–Sat 7.30am–6.30pm, Sun 7am–4pm.

El Sabrosón Av Central, between C 1 Sur and C Central ☎ 720 2147. Probably the most reliable of the local cafeteria restaurants – hence the long but swift-moving queues at lunchtime – hot and freshly made rice, plantain, beans, salads and a range of meat dishes plus usually some fish, all for under $4. Daily 7am–3.30pm.

NIGHTLIFE

La Cabaña Left after the bridge up past the fairground. For a loud blast of a variety of sounds and blinking plasma screens, try dancing or drinking in this joint's dark recesses. Fri & Sat 8pm–late.

Zanzibar Av Central at C 2 Norte. Bars come and go, but this unlikely African-themed watering hole has

established itself, attracting trendy young locals and travellers. Dim lighting, comfy zebra-striped cushions and mellow music provide the backdrop for sampling a vast array of excellent cocktails ($5). The place occasionally gets going on weekends when there is sometimes live jazz music. Tues–Sun 6pm–late.

Parque Nacional Volcán Barú

The two main entrances to the national park are at either end of the Sendero de los Quetzales, about 8km apart: the Alto Chiquero ANAM ranger station and refuge is at the Boquete side of the trek, whereas the El Respingo ranger station is at the Cerro Punta end of the trail. Two other small offices (no name) are at the start of the trail for climbing Volcán Barú • $5

The jade-coloured cloud forests sitting in the mist high above Boquete, many of which lie within the boundaries of the **Parque Nacional Volcán Barú**, which stretches west towards the town of Volcán, are prime birdwatching territory – and the favoured habitat of the metallic green resplendent quetzal, the Holy Grail of Boquete birding. The male in particular, with its ruby breastplate and lengthy trailing iridescent tail, which it only dons for the breeding season, is a dazzling sight. These otherwise elusive birds are at their most visible from the end of December to April, just after first light, when breeding pairs can sometimes be seen on the path.

Hiking in and around the park

Hiking trails in and around the national park range from a gentle undulating stroll round *Finca Lérida* to a four-hour-plus slog up Volcán Barú. You can undertake the shorter trails on your own, but you should only undertake the longer routes – including the popular, scenic Sendero de los Quetzales – with an experienced guide (see box, p.193), who should have a first-aid kit and emergency equipment with them. Although a number of travellers have managed to undertake these hikes without a guide in fine weather, a few have got seriously lost once bad weather has unexpectedly closed in.

Trails around Finca Lérida

Daily 7am–4.30pm • Guided birdwatching hikes cost $53/person and last about 4hr • Day visitors pay $11/person for use of the trails and are given a map

This eco-lodge (see p.189) offers good-value hikes through the 10km of trails on its estate, with a chance of seeing quetzals as well as highland hummingbirds such as the white-throated mountain gem, sulphur-winged parakeets, silver-throated tanagers and the impressive black guan. Much of the trail network actually lies within the **Parque Internacional Amistad** (see p.197 & p.241), which abuts the Barú national park. You can join a guided hiking tour, or pay for a sketch map and head off up through the coffee fields and cloud forest on your own.

Sendero Pipa de Agua

$2 • Take a bus bound for Alto Lino or Arco Iris and get them to drop you off at the trailhead (8km from Boquete) at the T-junction, on the way to the start of the quetzal trail

This modest trail follows a water pipeline up a relatively gentle incline up a dead-end valley to a waterfall and is another favourite of birdwatchers. Beware of a scam by the occasional unscrupulous taxi driver who, in order to save petrol, leaves hikers here claiming it's the start of the quetzal trail.

Sendero Il Pianista

Take a bus bound for Alto Lino or Arco Iris that can drop you off at the restaurant *Il Pianista*, by the start of the trail; alternatively take a taxi

This is a moderately strenuous hike (3hr there and back) along a well-worn route taken by Ngäbe coffee pickers, commuting for the annual harvest. Starting by *Il Pianista* restaurant (see opposite), the trail takes in fields of cows before taking you upto the continental divide, where you'll be rewarded by great views on a clear day. Don't attempt it in heavy rain as the trail becomes extremely muddy.

Sendero de los Quetzales

A far more beautiful, rugged hike than the slog up the brooding volcano it skirts, the **Sendero de los Quetzales** offers the additional thrill of a possible glimpse of a male quetzal in full regalia (Dec–April). Though formerly easily doable on your own, severe floods and landslides have made the route difficult to navigate in places, and hiring a guide will substantially enhance your chances of spotting a quetzal as well as allowing you to learn more about other flora and fauna. The 8km trail can be hiked in both directions, though conventional wisdom has it that it's easier to start from the Cerro Punta side (over 2400m) because of the drop in altitude between there and the eastern trailhead at Alto Chiquero (over 1800m). A moderately fit person soaking up the scenery and making occasional stops to spot the odd shy bird in the undergrowth should count on five to six hours to complete the trail.

Climbing Volcán Barú

The unremarkable haul up **Volcán Barú** (3474m), Panama's highest point, is rewarded at the summit, which on good day boasts a truly breathtaking panorama of the Pacific and Caribbean, both dotted with a myriad of islands. The **dry season** is the best time to attempt the ascent but even then clouds and rain can close in quickly. To maximize your chance of a clear view, you should attempt some, or all, of the climb at night – for which you'll need a **guide** (see p.187) – to arrive at dawn. Leaving at 11pm to midnight, the 13.5km ascent from the small park office takes 4–6 hours, arriving in time to enjoy a sunrise picnic before descending. No

5

rock-climbing skills are necessary, just the grit to plod up a boulder-strewn track and a little rock-scrambling. Once on top, you'll need to turn a blind eye to the radio masts and graffiti-covered rocks on one side.

If you prefer a daytime hike, but still want to enjoy sunrise on the summit, you can **camp** on the volcano's upper slopes, although there are no formal camping facilities, including no water, and nowhere particularly pleasant to pitch a tent. The police at the security post close to the summit will also allow you to sleep there for a small fee. You'll need warm, waterproof clothing, as it's cold on the summit, plenty of water and the usual hiking essentials.

Climbing Volcán Barú from the **western side** (see box opposite) is more physically demanding, and takes longer, but is more rewarding as you are taken up a path, albeit very indistinct in places, rather than a road, and across more varied terrain.

ARRIVAL AND DEPARTURE   PARQUE NACIONAL VOLCÁN BARÚ

ALTO CHIQUERO RANGER STATION
By taxi The Alto Chiquero park office, accessible by 2x4, is a steep, almost completely tarred 11km up from Boquete, reachable by taxi ($12).
By bus You can take a bus as far as the T-junction, followed by a 3km hike.

EL RESPINGO RANGER STATION
By taxi Hiring a 4WD taxi from Volcán to the park office

will cost around $20–25.
By bus You can get dropped off any Cerro Punta-bound bus from Volcán and walk the rough 5km road to the office.

THE VOLCÁN BARÚ TRAILHEAD
You'll need a 4WD taxi to take you to the trailhead ($12) and should arrange a pick-up and time, unless you walk to the main road and flag down a taxi or bus.

INFORMATION

Park information Contact the ANAM regional office in David (☎ 774 6671); ask for *Áreas Protegidas*.
Luggage transport service Backpackers wanting to hike the Sendero de los Quetzales one way but not wanting to return and who don't want to be encumbered with their rucksack should go to Transportes Ferguson

(Boquete ☎ 720 1454, Volcán ☎ 771 4566; both Mon–Fri 8am–4pm, Sat 8am–noon). They have an office in C 1 Sur at Av 1 Oeste in Boquete, and behind the petrol station in Volcán, and will charge $5–6 to courier your rucksack to the other location.

ACCOMMODATION

Bunkhouses Phone the ANAM office in David (☎ 775 3163). You can arrange to sleep in the bunkhouse at either of the ranger stations, though you'll need to take warm bedding and food, and be prepared for cold-water showers. **$15**

Camping You can camp at either of the two ranger stations, though a far nicer location is *Mirador la Roca*, a picnic spot complete with tables, though no other facilities, about halfway along the Sendero de los Quetzales. **$5**

Volcán

Spreadeagled on the lower western slopes of Volcán Barú, at an altitude of 1700m, the twelve-thousand-strong town of **VOLCÁN** (formally known as El Hato de Volcán) is little more than a glorified road junction en route to the more appealing fertile valleys of Cerro Punta and the cloud forests of the Parque International La Amistad, or the little used Costa Rica border crossing at Río Sereno. That said, it does offer the most impressive views of Volcán Barú, and as the retirement and real estate boom gradually seeps west of Boquete, tourism is beginning to take root, offering a handful of diverting excursions, not least of which is to scale the adjacent **volcano**. A couple of enjoyable days can easily be spent exploring the area, though if you're short of time push on to Cerro Punta and Guadalupe. Even if you don't overnight here, a clutch of good restaurants and relaxed ambience make Volcán a convenient pit stop and anyone set on self-catering up in the mountains should stock up on supplies (leaving the fruit and vegetables to Cerro Punta) and visit a bank.

ACTIVITIES AROUND VOLCÁN

Hiking and **birdwatching** are very much the order of the day, in particular exploring the forested slopes of the volcano within the protected boundaries of the **Parque Nacional Volcán Barú**, which lies between Volcán and Boquete. The **Sendero de los Quetzales** (see p.191) is by far the most popular destination both for hikers and birding enthusiasts, offering a wonderful twisting trail through verdant forest round the northern flanks of the volcano. Accessing the **summit** of Volcán Barú itself (see p.191) from this western side is a much more daunting though potentially satisfying prospect, clambering across overgrown lava flows and navigating round precipitous tors, where you should look out for the spectacular black and white hawk eagle soaring above. Less energetic targets include the **Pozos Termales de Tisingal**, a collection of thermal pools, or the breathtaking 80m cascade of the **Salto de Tigre**, both in a lovely setting off the Río Sereno road.

TOUR OPERATOR

Highland Adventures Cerro Punto road ☎771 4413 or ☎6685 1682, ✉ecoaizpurua@hotmail .com. Well-established company run by Gonzalo Aizpurúa (who speaks some English) from an unmissable garden shed-office. Rates include guiding service and transport and excursions include overnight treks to the summit of Volcán Barú ($170 for two), for which you'll need to bring and carry your own food and equipment, or a day-long slog ($140), which only the super-fit should attempt. Guides can also be provided for the Sendero de los Quetzales or to explore other trails in the national park or in Amistad, as well as to the Pozos Termales de Tisignal and the Salto de Tigre.

ARRIVAL AND DEPARTURE VOLCÁN

By bus Buses between David and Cerro Punto and Guadalupe pass through Volcán every 15min (5am–8pm; 1hr 20min; last return bus from Guadalupe 8pm). Buses from David also pass through Volcán en route to and from the Costa Rica border at Río Sereno (every 45min–1hr, 6.20am–6.20pm; 1hr 10min).

By taxi Taxis hover near the main junction, charging $1 for a short hop round town.

ACCOMMODATION

Cabañas Reis On the left just before Volcán ☎771 5153, ⓦcabanasreis.com. Twelve brightly painted new cement cabins (some with car porches), aimed squarely at the domestic market and accommodating two to twelve guests. There's also one slightly larger *cabaña* with a kitchen ($80). Excellent value, as rooms are clean and comfortable with decent bathrooms, and a helpful owner. $\overline{$50}$

Hostal Llano Lindo Av 2A, 1km up the Cerro Punto road off to the left ☎6514 0094, ⓦhostalllanolindo .com. Basic seven-room hostel in a friendly family atmosphere with shared kitchen-dining-TV room. Multi-day package deals also available and local tours at $75/ person. Breakfast included. Dorms $\overline{$12}$

Hotel Don Tavo Av Central, on the right ☎771 5144, ⓦhoteldontavo.com. Reliable, but slightly overpriced central hotel comprising sixteen clean en-suite rooms (for 2–5 people), though with variable mattresses, set around a courtyard garden. Service can vary. $\overline{$43}$

Las Plumas Paso Ancho, 2km north of Volcán ☎771 5541, ⓦlas-plumas.com. Excellent value for groups or families, comprising four fully equipped (laundry, satellite TV, wi-fi and phone) two- or three-bedroom modern self-catering bungalows set in manicured wooded grounds. Good long-term rates ($\overline{$250}$/week) with three-night minimum stay $\overline{$66}$

★**Volcán Lodge** 100m up the road directly opposite the bakery ☎771 4709, ⓦvolcanlodge.webs.com. Lovingly restored 1940s lodge full of wooden beams, panelling and flooring creating homely rooms and a warm atmosphere. For an extra $5 a cooked breakfast is included. The friendly Panamanian owners are bilingual (Spanish/ English) after living for many years in the US. $\overline{$50}$

EATING AND DRINKING

Burrico's Av Central, next to *Hotel Don Tavo* ☎6203 7363, ⓦburricos.net. Bright tables and cheery Mexican decorations make this an inviting place, even before you start on the food: a mix of Panamanian – superior *menu del día* with a choice of beef, chicken and pork for under $5 – and Tex-Mex faves for under $8. Tues–Sun 9am–9.30pm.

Cerro Brujo Gourmet Restaurant Brisas del Norte 500m up a dirt road signed off to the right from Av Central ☎6669 9196, ✉cerrobrujogourmet@gmail .com. The delightful, Mediterranean-style stone and tile interior is decked out with artwork and overlooks a garden. An eclectic changing menu of gourmet dishes (mains

5

$13–16) such as dorado fillet coated in sesame seeds and mushrooms does not disappoint; leave room for dessert. Regular musical or artistic evenings. Reservations preferred. Tues–Sun noon–3pm & 5–9pm.

La Maná At Volcán Lodge ☎771 4709, ⓦvolcan lodge.webs.com/restaurantemanamenu.htm. Mix of Panamanian cuisine and US comfort food, spanning the price spectrum: choose from *gallo pinto* ($5), BLTs or

burgers, to filet mignon in red wine ($13). All served in a warm wood-panelled dining room by hospitable hosts. Daily 11am–8pm.

Restaurante Mary Av Central on the left ☎6704 1237. Popular local restaurant on a breezy upstairs terrace (with inside a/c seating) serving moderately priced chicken, pork and seafood ($6–8), though try the local trout ($9), plus tasty soups and fresh juices. Daily 6am–6pm.

Around Volcán

A few kilometres west of Volcán lie several modest attractions – a couple of **lakes**, a **coffee estate** and an **archeological site** – which will appeal to enthusiasts or may be worth swinging by if you've a free couple of hours and your own transport. South of the town, the **waterfall** of Cañon Macho de Monte is a spectacular sight in season.

The Lagunas de Volcán and around

The **Lagunas de Volcán** (1300m) are Panama's highest wetlands and an important sojourn for migrating birds, and will appeal to birders, who will be keen to spot northern jacanas, masked ducks and, in the forested fringes, the rare rose-throated becard. The casual visitor is more likely to bemoan the lack of decent paths around these two shallow lakes. To the northeast of the lakes, a visit to the **coffee estate** of Finca La Torcaza (☎771 4087, ⓦestatecafe.com) is likely to be of more general appeal and can be explored on horseback.

ARRIVAL AND DEPARTURE   **LAS LAGUNAS DE VOLCÁN**

By taxi A taxi to the lakes will cost $5, or $8 for the return, plus wait time.

By car If you're driving, turn left off Av Central, by the sign to El Oasis Place, bearing right at the mini-super and

following the tarred road until you hit the disused airstrip; continue across and keep on the rutted or muddy track for another 4km (4WD needed in the wet season and high-clearance vehicle at other times).

Sitio Barriles

5km west of Volcán • Daily 7am–4pm • Guided tours in English or Spanish $5 • ☎771 4281 or ☎6575 1828 • A taxi ride to the site will cost $5

The private *finca* of the Landau family harbours one of Panama's most important archeological sites, **Sitio Barriles**, named after the barrel-shaped stones unearthed in 1947 that provided the first modern-day evidence of what is presumed to be the country's oldest pre-Columbian culture, which was prominent around 500 AD. The most interesting artefacts have been carted away to Panama City's anthropology museum (see p.64). Nevertheless, the farm possesses a couple of **petroglyphs** with the *pièce de résistance* a silky smooth slab of basalt, which when doused with water reveals yet more squiggles. There's also an unconvincing recreation of an archeological dig chamber and a small display of ceramics.

Cañon Macho de Monte

A worthwhile detour for those with their own transport, east of the Concepcíon–Volcán road, is **Cañon Macho de Monte**, a dramatic waterfall (less so in the dry season) that tumbles into a gorge. It's also a good birdwatching site, where orange-collared manakins and fiery-billed aracaris top the billing.

ARRIVAL AND EATING   **CAÑON MACHO DE MONTE**

By car From Volcán travel 13km south, turning left at the mini-super in the hamlet of Cuesta de Piedra; continue 2.5km, crossing two bridges, until you come to the

hydroelectric project. Park up on the left; across the road, a path leads to the precipice above the fall.

Mirador Alan-Her Main road, after the village of

Cuesta de Piedra. The *Mirador Alan-Her* lives up to its promised view, and is one of the best places in Chiriquí to pick up sweet delicacies, from local mozzarella and ricotta to *bienmesabe* – a slow-cooked dessert of rice, milk and *panela* – and their other Chiricano speciality, *sopa borracha* ("drunken soup"), sponge cake soaked in cinnamon-flavoured rum. Daily 6.30am–7.30pm.

East to the Costa Rican border

From Volcán, a well-paved road snakes its way 32km to the small border town of **Río Sereno**. Unless you're bound for Costa Rica, the only reason to make this glorious drive is to visit **Finca Hartmann**, a birding hotspot and charming coffee estate a 30km spectacular drive from Volcán. Heading out through open pastures scattered with dairy cattle, the journey intensifies as the road swoops round tight bends across cascading rivers and through coffee and banana plantations.

Finca Hartmann

Santa Clara • Coffee tours, in Spanish or English, last 1hr 15min ($15); trail access for day visitors $15 • ☎ 6450 1853, ⓦ fincahartmann.com

A family-run, eco-friendly coffee estate whose biodiversity acts as a magnet to birdwatchers and biologists, **Finca Hartmann** has recorded over 280 species, and is considered the best place in Panama to see the dazzling turquoise cotinga and fiery-billed aracari, as well as 62 different mammals. Birds are more easily spotted round the main farm at Palo Verde, where the coffee roasting and other operations take place. Taking a **coffee tour** (best during the harvesting season, Oct–March) also allows you to stroll the five **trails** on the estate, one of which leads up to Amistad national park.

ARRIVAL AND ACCOMMODATION   FINCA HARTMANN

By bus Take the Río Sereno bus from David via Volcán and ask to be let off at the entrance to the *finca*.

By car The *finca* is signposted right at the entry to Santa Clara, just after the petrol station, up a 1km dirt track (high-clearance 2x4, or better, required) to the farm.

★ **Ojo de Agua Cabañas** The *finca*'s two rustic cabins are tucked away in the forest. The smaller one-bedroom *cabaña* is cosier and has a kitchenette whereas the larger six-bedroom two-storey cabin with full kitchen and fireplace is more of a bunkhouse that can accommodate up to ten people. Both have hot-water showers (though neither has electricity – gas lamps and candles are used) and are regularly visited by howler and white-faced capuchin monkeys. A sturdy 4WD is necessary for access, or you can arrange transfers. One-bed *cabaña* **$90**, bunkhouse **$140**, for up to four, plus **$10**/extra person

Cerro Punta and around

Shortly after leaving Volcán, the road to Cerro Punta starts to twist and turn, threading its way up a mist-filled ravine, through which the Río Chiriquí Viejo gushes, flanked by almost vertical pine-clad slopes dotted with alpine chalets, some established by early

---

CROSSING THE BORDER AT RÍO SERENO

A 35km drive west from Volcán along a spectacular winding mountain road brings you to the somnolent frontier town of **RÍO SERENO** and the least-used border crossing with Costa Rica. It is easily reached by bus from David, via Volcán (every 45min–1hr, 5am–5pm; 2hr 30min). The last return bus to David leaves Río Sereno at 5pm, passing through Volcán after 1hr 10min. Buses leave Río Sereno from close to the T-junction at the entrance to the town. Panamanian immigration (daily 8am–5pm; ☎ 722 8054) is 400m from the bus stop, by the police station (look for the flag). The Costa Rican immigration office (same hours) is next door. Don't forget that whether entering Panama or Costa Rica you'll need to get an exit stamp from immigration in the country you are leaving and an entry stamp from immigration in the country you are entering; you will also need to show proof of onward travel and financial solvency. Should you get stranded here for the night, the town's lone accommodation, the *Posada Los Andes* (☎ 722 8112) on the main square can provide you with a rudimentary room in a fairly rickety building for $20.

5

European settlers. Roadside stalls overflow with locally produced vegetables; stop off and gorge on a heaped bowl of strawberries or blackberries and *natilla* (a local creamy custardy melange) or pick up a pot of home-made jam.

Cerro Punta

Set almost 2000m above sea level in a fertile basin-shaped valley – the scarcely recognizable crater of an extinct volcano – surrounded by densely forested, rugged mountains, **CERRO PUNTA** is the highest village in Panama. In the ninety or so years since it was formally settled, partly by Europeans, agriculture has expanded so rapidly that the area now supplies over sixty percent of all the vegetables consumed in Panama, with fields forming a tapestry of produce from lettuce, onions and carrots to commercial flowers and strawberries. This agricultural boom has come at the expense of the surrounding forests, but the village, frequently swathed in cloud, and surrounding fields are still undeniably beautiful, filled with abundant flowers and buzzing with hummingbirds. The spectacular scenery, together with the cool, crisp mountain air (temperatures drop to well below 10°C at night), makes Cerro Punta a superlative base for **hiking**, and the pristine cloud forests of La Amistad (see opposite) and Volcán Barú (see p.190) national parks are both within easy reach.

Guadalupe

Three kilometres beyond Cerro Punta, you arrive at **GUADALUPE**, an enchanting flower-filled hamlet of around four hundred inhabitants, dominated by the rustic *Los Quetzales Lodge & Spa*. From there, the road (and bus) sweeps round to the left in a wide loop, passing the turn-off to Las Nubes and Amistad to the right, then the church, before a steep climb back to the junction with the main road at the police station, where taxi drivers often hang out.

Besides hiking and admiring the scenery, there are a couple of niche-interest attractions. **Finca Dracula** (daily 8am–5pm; $5, $10 for guided tour), far from being the country retreat of a Transylvanian bloodsucker, is home to one of Latin America's premier orchid collections, boasting 2200 species, and is about five minutes' walk beyond *Los Quetzales*. It best justifies its hefty entrance fee in March and April, when more flowers are in bloom. Those interested in horses might consider **Haras Cerro Punta** (☎ 227 3371, ⓦ harascerropunta.com), which offer tours in Spanish round a stud farm that breeds racing stallions with greater lung capacity due to the altitude. The foaling season (Jan–May) is probably the most rewarding time to visit.

ARRIVAL AND DEPARTURE   **CERRO PUNTA AND AROUND**

By bus Buses from David (every 15min, 5am–8pm; 1hr 50min; last return bus at 8pm) via Volcán pull up on Cerro Punta's one main street before heading up to Guadalupe.

ACCOMMODATION

NUEVA SUIZA

★**Hostal Cielito Sur** Main road 5km south of Cerro Punta, 10km north of Volcán ☎ 771 2038, ⓦ cielitosur .com. This outstanding B&B is run by genial hosts, who provide a perfect blend of knowledgeable warm hospitality and privacy. Set amid beautiful grounds, four vast, immaculate rooms, some with kitchens, are decorated with traditional Panamanian artwork and share a homely living room. Rates include a substantial breakfast with plenty of home-made goodies. $95

CERRO PUNTA

Hotel Cerro Punta Main road ☎ 771 2020. This friendly spot comes with clean, comfortable en-suite rooms (no TV) and a reasonable restaurant serving local fare – set menus during the week ($4–5) and à la carte at weekends. $33

GUADALUPE

★**Los Quetzales Lodge and Spa** ☎ 771 2182, ⓦ losquetzales.com. Incredibly versatile place accommodating backpackers, honeymooners, Panamanian families and expats with consummate ease. Choose from superior dorms – chunky wood, quality bedding, bedside lights and really hot showers – standard rooms, suites and glorious cloud-forest cabins ($180). All guests have access to the comfy lounge and games room, full of books and sofas, warmed by a log fire, and with table tennis. Activities include spa treatments, cycling, horseriding, and walks through the surrounding cloud forest. The restaurant caters to the same range in budgets from delicious soups with home-made bread ($5), to pizza and pasta ($9), but it's worth splurging on their pricier, fancier mains, accompanied by more vegetables than you are likely to see in a month elsewhere in Panama. Restaurant daily 6.30am–8pm. Camping/tent $15/person, dorms $18, doubles $85

Parque Internacional La Amistad

Las Nubes • $5, payable at the permanently staffed park office at Las Nubes, a few hundred metres beyond the entrance

Covering four thousand square kilometres of precipitous forested mountains straddling Panama and Costa Rica, **Parque Internacional La Amistad** (International Friendship Park), often abbreviated to PILA or Amistad, forms a crucial link in the "biological corridor" of protected areas running the length of Central America. Given its varied topography, Amistad is the most ecologically diverse park in the region, including more than four hundred different **bird** species (see p.305), making it the most important protected area in Panama after the Darién. Although almost all of the Panamanian section lies in Bocas del Toro, it is far more accessible from the Pacific side of the country. There are three short **trails** with *miradores* offering excellent views of some of the highest mountains in Panama (at least before the cloud descends) and a 50m **waterfall**. A longer, steeper and less distinct trail (8km round trip) leads through virgin cloud forest to the summit of **Cerro Picacho** (2986m), but you'll need to get one of the park wardens to guide you.

ARRIVAL AND DEPARTURE   PARQUE LA AMISTAD

On foot or by taxi From Cerro Punta or Guadalupe, walk the 6km – or take a taxi ($7) – to the park entrance at Las Nubes.

ACCOMMODATION AND EATING

ANAM park refuge One of the larger, better-equipped refuges with kitchen facilities but only cold water – bring your own food and, ideally, a sleeping bag, as it gets cold at night. $15

PILA restaurant At the park entrance. Run by a local women's cooperative, the restaurant serves *comida corriente* ($3 for breakfast, $5 for lunch) such as *arroz de guandú* (rice and beans) with chicken, pork or beef, which you can enjoy on a wooden balcony. Daily 8am–5pm.

Along the La Fortuna road

Highway 4, the serpentine road that traverses the continental divide to the Caribbean coast, is Panama's most spectacular drive, with **breathtaking views** on a clear day; conversely, if you find yourself peering through thick fog to see the edge of the asphalt, it can be one of the scariest journeys you ever make. During the October and November rains, landslides are frequent, sometimes blocking the route for days. Midway across the cordillera, before descending into Bocas del Toro province, you cross the dam wall of **Lago Fortuna**, Panama's main source of hydroelectric power.

Finca La Suiza

40km north of the junction with the Interamericana on the right-hand side • Day-visitors should arrive 7–10am • $8 • ☎ 6615 3774, ⓦ fincalasuizapanama.com

At 1200m **Finca La Suiza** is both a guesthouse (see below) and a **private reserve** with a substantial network of immaculately maintained **trails** open to the public. Your entry fee will get you a map and access to the trails (3–7hr circuits) and for a serious all-day climb to Cerro Hornito (2100m) you can hire a guide ($72/group). Check before you plan a visit since at the time of writing the place was for sale.

ACCOMMODATION   ALONG THE LA FORTUNA ROAD

Finca La Suiza Km 40, La Fortuna road ☎ 6615 3774, ⓦ fincalasuizapanama.com. The *finca* offers three comfortable guest rooms with private terrace from which to soak up the views on its private reserve (see above). Take

5

the David–Changuinola bus: the *finca* entrance is on the road after approximately 40km, on the right-hand side. Two-night minimum stay. Closed Oct. $\overline{\underline{58}}$

Lost and Found Ecolodge Km 42, La Fortuna road ☎ 6581 9223, ⓦ lostandfoundlodge.com. This lodge-cum-hostel with shared kitchen or food provided is worth visiting for the views alone. Located at well over 1300m, on the edge of the Reserva Forestal La Fortuna – established

to protect the Fortuna reservoir's catchment basin – it boasts numerous trails through cloud forest and offers a range of modestly priced tours and opportunities for volunteering. To get here by bus, alight at the 42km marker, at the hamlet of Valle de la Mina, where a sign directs you up a lengthy flight of steps to the right. Camping $\overline{\underline{8}}$/ person, dorms $\overline{\underline{12}}$, doubles $\overline{\underline{33}}$

David and the Chiriquí Lowlands

In contrast to the fresh highlands – the destination for the vast majority of visitors to the province – the oppressive heat of the **Lowlands** does little to attract the punters. Nor do endless fields of maize, rice, bananas, sugar cane and cattle. Still it's hard to avoid **David**, or at least the city's vast bus terminal, since virtually all the province's public transport passes through here. What's more, Chiriquí's capital is gradually growing in appeal as a place to chill out for a couple of days and enjoy a few city comforts as its local attractions: the mangroves at **Pedregal** or the wildlife reserve at **Playa Barqueta**.

West of David, the Interamericana speeds along 47km of flattish terrain to the frontier with Costa Rica. Just before the border post, the road veers off left down the narrow **Peninsula Burica**, weaving through plantations and passing the former banana boom town of **Puerto Armuelles**, before an undulating road eventually peters out close to the southern tip, where the handful of travellers who make it this far can stroll along deserted beaches and watch the waves.

David

The only one of three Spanish settlements founded in the area in 1602 to survive repeated attacks from indigenous groups, **DAVID** developed slowly as a remote outpost of the Spanish Empire, only beginning to thrive when Chiriquí's population swelled in the nineteenth century. Today, despite being a busy commercial city of over 140,000 – the second largest in Panama – and the focus of Chiriquí's strong regional identity, it retains a sedate provincial atmosphere.

Oppressively hot and either humid or dusty, its unexceptional modern architecture spread out on a well-planned grid that derives from colonial days, David has few attractions *per se*, but its very ordinariness holds a certain appeal for a few days. It's also a good place to stock up before a trip to the highlands or break a journey between Panama City and Costa Rica or Bocas del Toro.

Parque Cervantes

David's heart is vibrant **Parque Cervantes**, where snow-cone sellers, shoe-shiners and hawkers peddling sugar cane and fresh fruit juice all vie for business, overlooked by the nondescript **Iglesia de la Sagrada Familia**. The park's curved stone seating maximizes the leafy shade, making it a prime spot for watching urban life unfold.

THE INTERNATIONAL AGRICULTURAL FAIR

David's annual highlight is its international agricultural fair, **Feria Internacional de San José de David** (ⓦ feriadedavid.com), whose ten days of festivities coincide with the patron saint day for San José on March 19. Although principally a trade show, there's plenty to entertain the public, with rodeo and lasso competitions, music and dancing, not to mention the annual *cabalgata*, a colourful horseback parade through the city streets.

5

Barrio Bolívar

A stroll three blocks southeast of Parque Cervantes down Calle "A" Norte takes you back to the city's colonial past in **Barrio Bolívar**, where the district's ever decreasing sprinkling of russet tiles, balconies and intricate wrought iron holds out against encroaching modern architecture. The historic colonial mansion on the corner with Avenida 8 Este that houses the **Museo de Historia y Arte José de Obaldía** is finally being restored after years of neglect. The building was home to successive generations of the distinguished Obaldía family – José Vicente was the president of New Granada (combined Colombia and Panama) and his son José Domingo became the second president of Panama. Just east of here, a crumbling bell tower stands over the messily restored nineteenth-century **Catedral San José de David**. See what you make of the recently renovated colonial Romanesque facade and the interior's gaudy murals.

ARRIVAL AND DEPARTURE   DAVID

BY PLANE

Airport Flights from Panama City, Bocas del Toro and San José, Costa Rica, arrive at the Aeropuerto Enrique Malek, about 5km out of town, a $4 taxi ride away. Since the airport was upgraded in 2012 there have been plans for direct flights with the US.

Flights Air Panama (☎316 9000, ⌨airpanama.com) operates three daily flights to and from Panama City ($158 one way). Air Panama also flies to San José (Mon, Wed, Fri; $192 one way).

Airline offices Air Panama has an office at the airport and in town (Mon–Fri 8am–5pm; ☎775 0812), on C 2 in Plaza Oteima.

5

BUSES TO COSTA RICA

Tracopa (☎ 775 0585, 🖥 tracopacr.com) operates two daily services to San José, Costa Rica, at 8.30am and noon (8–9hr; $21 one way). Buses leave from the main bus terminal, where the company has an office. Tickets are available in advance and should definitely be booked for peak holiday periods.

It is often quicker, though, to take one of the frequent **minibuses** from the bus terminal to the border at **Paso Canoas**, walk across, getting exit and entry stamps at Panama and Costa Rica immigration respectively, before hopping on one of the regular buses to San José. Remember that immigration for both countries are likely to ask to see proof of onward travel. Tracopa also has an office at the border (daily 7am–4pm Costa Rica time, which is 1hr behind Panama) between the two immigration offices, adjacent to the Banco de Costa Rica, with two daily departures to San José, at 8am and 4.30pm, If you miss one, take a shuttle to Ciudad Neily, the first sizeable population over the border 18km away, where there are even more connections with the capital.

BY BUS

Bus terminal The main bus terminal, which serves long-distance routes, including to Costa Rica (see box above), and local services is on Paseo Estudiante, a 15min walk from the town centre. It has good facilities, including a self-service restaurant, toilets, a left-luggage office (daily 6am–8pm) and internet café.

Buses to Panama City Terminales David-Panama, with its own a/c waiting room at the far end of the terminal is the main service provider. A newer company, Panachif (☎ 777 4217), has ten buses (7am–10.30pm) that depart from its own terminal in David on Av 1 Este between calles "E" and "F" Norte (map p.199).

Other destinations Boquete (every 30min, 6.30am–9.45pm; 50min); Caldera (10 buses, 6am–7pm; 1hr); Cerro Punta (every 15min, 5am–8pm; 1hr 50min); Las Lajas (6.45am, 2.45pm; 1hr 30min); Puerto Armuelles (via the Costa Rican border at Paso Canoas; every 15min, 5.30am–10pm; 1hr 30min); Río Sereno (every 45min–1hr, 5am–5pm; 2hr 30min); Santiago – from a terminal across the road from the main bus terminal (approximately every 1hr 30min, 5am–7.30pm; 3hr) or take one of the faster buses to Panama City; Soloy (approx every 30min when full; 7am–7pm; 1hr 30min); Volcán (every 15min, 5am–8pm; 1hr 20min).

GETTING AROUND

By taxi Taxis are plentiful and should not cost more than $2–3 for a ride in town.

By car Car rental is available at the airport with Alamo

(☎ 721 0101), Avis (☎ 774 7075), Budget (☎ 775 5597), Dollar (☎ 721 1103), Hertz (☎ 775 8471), Hilary (☎ 775 5459), National (☎ 721 0974) and Thrifty (☎ 721 2477).

INFORMATION

Tourist information The tourist office (Mon–Fri 8.30am–3.30pm; ☎ 775 2839) on C Central between avenidas 5 Este and 6 Este is friendly and courteous but thin on information.

ANAM office On the road to the airport. For the latest information on Chiriquí's several national parks, contact

the ANAM office (Mon–Fri 8.30am–3.30pm; ☎ 775 3163).

Immigration and consular services The Costa Rican consulate (Mon–Fri 8am–3pm; ☎ 774 1923) is in Torre del Banco Universal, C "B" Norte and Av Primera (Mon–Fri 9am–1pm; ☎ 774 1923); Panamanian immigration (Mon–Fri 8.30am–3.30pm; ☎ 775 4515) is on C "C" Sur at Av Central.

ACCOMMODATION

A broad range of good-value accommodation exists in David, most near the city centre and all with hot water, a/c and free wi-fi unless indicated. Note that during the Feria de David (see box, p.198) and the festival periods in Boquete (see box, p.184), it is difficult to get a room.

Bambu Hostel C Virgincita, San Mateo district ☎ 730 2961, 🖥 bambuhostel.com. Further out than most places, though within reach of amenities on C "F" Sur. A place for mellow-minded folk and those who like to party, this place offers en-suite dorm bunks, and private rooms, both with a/c and excellent mattresses, as well as cheaper beds protected by mosquito nets in a

wood-and-bamboo jungle house. The standout feature is the lush tropical garden containing a small pool with *rancho* bar and open kitchen; plus there's a table-tennis table out front. Dorms $11, doubles $34

★ **Chambres en Ville** Av 5 Este between C "A" Sur and C "B" Sur ☎ 775 7428, 🖥 chambresenville.info. A good choice for couples and mature travellers, with cosy, en-suite private rooms that are a little dark but brightened up with colourful murals. The large open-air kitchen leads to a fruit-filled garden, with hammocks and a decent-sized swimming pool – though the caged toucan might upset some visitors. French, English and Spanish spoken. Dorms $11, doubles $33

Hotel Castilla C "A" Norte between Av Cincuentenario and Av 3 Este ☎ 774 5236, ⓦ hotelcastillapanama.com. The pick of the hotels in terms of good-value comfort, and centrally located. The tiled rooms are slightly chintzy but bright and clean, and you might fancy splashing out the extra $15 for a balcony view of the main park. There's a decent, if dark, on-site restaurant. $65

Hotel Ciudad de David C "D" Norte and Av 2 Este ☎ 774 3333, ⓦ hotelciudaddedavid.com. This new sleek business hotel is the most upscale place in town, with over a hundred rooms and suites boasting contemporary furnishings and all the usual business amenities: minibars, safes and room service, as well as a sauna, pool, gym and bar-restaurant. Buffet breakfast included. $138

Hotel Gran Nacional C Central and Av 1 Este ☎ 775 2221. Before the recent arrival of the *Hotel Ciudad de David*, this was the top hotel in town with name and marble lobby to match, conveniently located a couple of blocks from the

main square. Rooms are tastefully furnished with flat-screen cable TV and other mod cons. There's also a bar, pool, casino, cinema and three restaurants. $100

Hotel Iberia C "B" Norte, between Av 1 Oeste and Av 2 Oeste ☎ 777 2002, ⓦ hoteliberia.net. Popular with business folk for its immaculately clean, functional rooms with cable TV, friendly staff and on-site restaurant offering tasty meals. $42

Hotel Toledo Av 1 Este, between C "D" Norte and C "E" Norte ☎ 774 6732. Handy for the bus terminal, this clean, comfortable hotel offers good value for money with firm beds, cable TV and friendly service. There's an on-site bar-restaurant (closed Sun). $33

The Purple House Hostel C "C" Sur at Av 6 Oeste ☎ 774 4059, ⓦ purplehousehostel.com. A David institution, this small, efficient, rule-bound, purple-clad hostel is a 15min walk from the city centre, though close to many amenities. There are two rather cramped dorms and three private rooms (shared or private bathroom) with fans (a/c $5 extra) and comfortable mattresses, plus a patio garden with a cooling sprinkler. Amenities include a kitchen and free coffee, and there's excellent tourist information. Dorms $10, doubles $29

EATING AND DRINKING

★**Cuatro** Av Obaldia and C Estudiante ☎ 730 5638, ⓦ restaurantecuatro.com. Gourmet Panamanian cuisine that oozes creativity, fusing traditional and modern flavours: try fried fish *ceviche* in passion fruit ($7) followed by mains such as *corvina* encrusted in plantain or braised pork belly with smoked cheese tamale ($13–22). Excellent quality. Daily noon–3pm, 6–10pm.

Jackelita C "E" Norte, at Av Central ☎ 774 6574. Very popular takeaway venue famous for its goat's milk yoghurt and fresh-fruit ice creams but also serving empanadas and other lite-bites. Daily 7am–11pm (from 4pm on Sat).

★**Multi-Café No. 2** C "A" Norte between Av 2 Este and Av 3 Este, next to Hotel Castilla ☎ 774 5236. Modern self-service restaurant with a/c and parking that attracts a busy weekend crowd. Vast array of local and international staples on offer, each rarely more than $5, and omelettes for breakfast. Mon–Sat 7am–8pm, Sun 7am–3pm.

Restaurante Bar El Fogón Av 2 Oeste, between C "C" Norte and C "D" Norte ☎ 775 7091. Recently expanded, spacious and airy restaurant, painted in warm colours with a friendly atmosphere. A favourite with Davideños, serving various grilled meat, poultry and seafood mains (from $6) – try the *pescado parmesano* – plus burgers and sandwiches. The quality can suffer when very busy. Mon–Sat 11am–11pm, Sun 11am–9pm.

★**Restaurante Bocachica** C "A" Sur between avenidas 4 and 5 Este ☎ 730 4057. Favoured by university students, drawn by the cheap beer, the pleasant elevated patio here is a prime spot to tuck into some tasty, good-value dishes, with seafood a speciality (mains $10–12). Daily 11.30am–10pm.

Restaurante La Típica Av 3 Este and C "F" Sur ☎ 777 1078. Busy, no-nonsense Chinese–Panamanian cafeteria serving decent food around the clock at reasonable prices. A reliable budget choice. Open 24hr.

Around David

Several pleasant **day-trips** are within striking distance of the city, all reachable on public transport, and popular with Davideños at weekends as they attempt to escape the city heat.

Playa Barqueta and the wildlife reserve

Twenty-five kilometres southwest of David, unremarkable, grainy **Playa Barqueta** is the nearest spot to dip in the sea, and has a couple of informal places to eat and enjoy a beer. A large portion of the beach lies within the boundaries of the low-key **Refugio de**

5

Vida Silvestre de Playa Barqueta Agricola (6am–3pm; $5; park warden ☎6602 5770) whose 14km stretch of sand, scrub and mangrove protects nesting sites for hawksbill, olive ridley, leatherback, loggerhead and green sea **turtles**. Arrange visits to check out the night-time nesting (May–Nov is best) with the park warden or visit the ANAM office outside David (see p.200). The reserve entrance lies east of *Las Olas Resort*, where the bus stops; alternatively the warden will come and pick you up. Visitors in their own vehicle will need a 4WD.

Balneário Barranca

A more appealing place to cool off from the sweltering heat than David's local beach is **Balneário Barranca** (daily 11am–6pm), a natural swimming pool with a *rancho* bar-restaurant and hammocks on a meander of Río Chiricagua, 20km west of David. While a festive family atmosphere prevails at weekends you can have the Tarzan swing all to yourself midweek.

Pedregal

Ten kilometres south of David, past the airport, the road fizzles out at **Pedregal**, David's small port and marina, a convenient place to contract a **boat** to explore the morass of mangroves and islands in the **Golfo de Chiriquí**, or to indulge in a tasty seafood lunch (see below). Ask around for a boatman; they usually charge around $120 per boat for a two-hour tour.

ARRIVAL AND DEPARTURE   AROUND DAVID

BY BUS

To Playa Barqueta Buses leave David at 8am & 11.20am (40min), returning at 2.30pm & 5pm, or take a bus to Guarumal and then a taxi to the beach ($6).

To Balneário Barranca Take any bus heading west to the border, Volcán or Concepción, getting off on the

Interamericana just before the Boquerón turn-off (about 20min) and walking 100m up a track to the right.

To Pedregal Buses leave from Av 2 Este between C Central and C "A" Norte (daily every 10–15min, 6am–11pm; 15min).

EATING

★**Stella's** Pedregal marina ☎721 1951. A delightful waterside restaurant serving up mouthwatering mains

such as curried jumbo shrimps in coconut cream or a rack of ribs. Mon–Sat 11am–8pm.

Peninsula Burica

Aside from a handful of die-hard surfers and fishing enthusiasts, few tourists venture down to the distant tip of the **Peninsula Burica**, resembling an upside-down skittle straddling the Costa Rican border. Here, 50km southwest of David, the remoteness is tangible and the sunsets spectacular. The gateway to the peninsula is **Puerto Armuelles**, for over seventy years Panama's thriving Pacific hub of the infamous United Fruit Company (now Chiquita Brands) until it pulled the plug in 2003 (see p.221). The rotting pier and abandoned wooden houses serve as poignant reminders of the town's former importance.

ARRIVAL AND DEPARTURE   PENINSULA BURICA

By bus Frequent minibuses run from David's main bus terminal to Puerto Armuelles (4am–10pm; 1hr 30min). A daily *chiva* (90min–2hr journey) makes the 30km trip down the peninsula from the town's waterside transport

depot to the community of Bella Vista; timing depends on the tides since much of the "road" is on the beach, only accessible at low tide – make sure you arrive before noon and bring your passport.

Paso Canoas and the Costa Rican border

It's a short hop from David along the Interamericana to Panama's main border crossing with Costa Rica at **Paso Canoas** (7am–11pm). Others are at Río Sereno, west of Volcán

> **THE BORDER WITH COSTA RICA**
>
> The **border at Paso Canoas** is by far the busiest of the three border crossings Panama shares with **Costa Rica**; in recognition of this, **immigration** is open longer hours (7am–11pm Panamanian time). Don't forget that whether entering Panama or Costa Rica you'll need to get an exit stamp from immigration in the country you are leaving and an entry stamp from immigration in the country you are entering; you will also need to show proof of onward travel and financial solvency.
>
> Paso Canoas is reached by frequent **minibuses** from David, with regular **onward transport** to San José and other destinations in Costa Rica (see box, p.200). If you are arriving from Costa Rica, you can find transport to both Panama City and David 100m down the Interamericana from the border. The Panachif (☎ 727 7054) office here sells tickets for buses to Panama City via David (7am–6.30pm; 8–9hr; $17) plus two express overnight services (9.30pm, 10.30pm; 7hr; $21). Small minibuses also scoot off down the highway to David (every 10–15min 4am–9pm; 40min), from where onward transport is easy (see p.200); after the last shuttle, you'll need a taxi ($20–25).

(see p.195) and Guabito (see p.243), over the cordillera in Bocas province. The busy frontier town exudes an edgy tackiness, with stalls, money changers and taxi drivers all competing for business.

Parque Nacional Marino Golfo de Chiriquí

The laidback fishing village of **Boca Chica**, 30km southeast of David as the vulture flies, provides the gateway to one of the province's most prized natural treasures: the **Parque Nacional Marino Golfo de Chiriquí**, a nirvana for **scuba diving**, **snorkelling** and **sport fishing** enthusiasts. Created in 1994 to protect almost 150 square kilometres of terrestrial and marine wildlife, the park comprises 25 islands – some with places to stay – and nineteen coral reefs, teeming with hundreds of fish in a rainbow of colours. The coastline to the west of Boca Chica, meanwhile, is thick with **mangroves** – which means you'll have to venture to the more distant islands to find white sand or crystalline waters. Note that when the wind drops in the rainy season, sandflies can be a nuisance, so bring repellent.

Islas Parita and Paridita

Isla Parita, by far the largest land mass, together with the much smaller **Isla Paridita**, are the only two inhabited islands on account of their fresh water sources; the rest are generally small, low-lying sedimentary outcrops that enjoy a tropical savannah climate, with beaches backed by coconut palms and manchineel trees, where the only visitors to disturb the hermit crabs and iguanas are nesting hawksbill and leatherback turtles.

Boca Brava and beyond

Across the narrow water channel in front of Boca Chica's jetty is **Boca Brava**, an island hosting two contrasting lodgings, while on the mainland a couple of upmarket fishing lodges and a small guesthouse do little to disturb the tranquillity of the place. Snorkelling trips head out into the national park, to the white-sand cove of **Isla Bolaños**, though even better snorkelling and diving is to be had round the more remote (and pricier) **Islas Secas**, **Islas Ladrones** and **Isla Montuoso**, where the marine life is breathtaking, from sea horses and starfish to giant manta and eagle rays, pods of dolphins, turtles, sharks and vast schools of fish swirling round volcanic pinnacles, with humpback whales arriving to calve from June.

5

DIVING AND KAYAKING

Snorkelling outings in the park can easily be arranged through the hotels. For **scuba diving**, contact Carlos Spragge at Boca Brava Divers (☎775 3185, ⓦscubadiving-panama.com), who offers a one-day all-inclusive dive excursion ($250, minimum 4 people; visibility is best Dec–April) and multi-day dive trips sleeping on his dive boat. The area's islands, inlets, caves and channels have also helped establish it as a nascent **sea-kayaking** destination. Boquete Outdoor Adventures (see p.187) organizes overnight and multi-day trips, though most accommodation listed have kayaks if you just want to splash about.

ARRIVAL   PARQUE NACIONAL MARINO GOLFO DE CHIRIQUÍ

TO BOCA CHICA

By bus The 1.30pm bus from David to Horconcitos, 5km south of the Interamericana connects with a new 2.30pm bus service to Boca Brava. At other times, and for a more comfortable ride, take a bus bound for Tolé or San Félix, which can drop you off at the junction, where there's usually a taxi waiting to take you to Boca Chica ($15) during daylight hours. Alternatively, you might get a miracle sighting of the tatty Boca Chica minibus, which passes the junction at around 12.30 and 4.30pm, if at all. The bus leaves Boca Chica at 9.15am and 1.30pm-ish. In the not entirely unexpected event of a no-show, you'll need to negotiate a ride.

By car Boca Chica is down a paved road, accessible in a saloon car; turn off from the Interamericana to Horconcitos, 36km east of David, and then take the middle road at the three-way fork in the village, coming to a halt at the jetty in Boca Chica 14km later. If leaving a car overnight in the village, find someone to look after it.

TO THE ISLANDS

By boat Transfer to *Hotel Boca Brava* from Boca Chica is $3. *Cala Mia*, *Isla Paridita* and the *Pacific Bay Resort* can all organize a transfer, or you can usually find someone at the dock to take you for the going rate of $60 return.

ACCOMMODATION

★ **Bocas del Mar** ☎6395 8757, ⓦbocasdelmar.com. Gaze out at the wooded landscape and glistening sea through the vast French windows in your spacious bungalow, or from your private porch, or even from the luxurious bathroom. Rooms are stylishly furnished with a contemporary feel, and include all the comforts (a/c, satellite TV, minibar) and some even have a private outdoor hot tub. The pleasant open-air restaurant is set round an infinity pool and there are a variety of inland or water-based activities to choose from. Breakfast included. High-season rack rates are pricey but promotional prices and low season offer good discounts. **$370**

Cala Mia Isla Boca Brava ☎851 0059, ⓦboutiquehotelcalamia.com. A sophisticated yet rustic retreat comprising eleven a/c bungalows, each with a gorgeous private *rancho* looking out to sea. The lovely bar-restaurant deck serves gourmet Mediterranean cuisine – the three-course dinners ($32) draw on organic garden produce. Boat rides and horseriding can be arranged and there's a small spa. Breakfast and use of kayaks included. **$195**

Hotel Boca Brava Isla Boca Brava ☎851 0017, ⓦhotelbocabrava.com. Possessing a range of accommodation from backpacker mattress and hammock space – bring a mosquito net – in a dorm to predominantly simple, tiled rooms with fans and shared or private

bathroom, this long-standing retreat offers an affordable rub with nature. The vibey cliff-top bar-restaurant (daily 7.30am–11pm) serves excellent food and lethal cocktails, attracting outsider visitors at weekends. Snorkelling trips on offer at reasonable rates; alternatively flush out the howler monkeys on the trails or chill on the modest beach. Mattress/hammock **$13**, doubles **$55**

Isla Paridita ☎6464 2510, ⓦexpeditionpanama .com. Tranquil eco-getaway on a gorgeous private island with beaches, rainforest trails and freshwater lagoons, offering simple open-sided bamboo and thatch *cabañas* (fans, solar energy) alongside communal gourmet dining. Rates include all meals, use of kayaks and snorkel gear plus one boat tour and guided hike; scuba diving and sport fishing can be arranged. Return transfer from Boca Chica $60. **$290**

Pacific Bay Resort Punta Bejuco ☎6695 1651, ⓦpacificbayresort.net. There's an unequalled panorama of the bay from the hilltop bar-dining area, though you'll earn your food (which is of variable quality) hiking there from the four well-spaced, solar-powered, wood-furnished duplex cabins. Set in an extensive forested headland with three beaches, and coves to explore by kayak, it's wonderfully relaxing. Meals are included; horseriding and moderately priced boat excursions are also on offer. Return transfer from Boca Chica $60. **$120**

Playa Las Lajas and around

The impressive broad belt of flat tan-coloured sand of **Playa Las Lajas** is by far the most popular weekend beach destination for urbanites from David (81km) and even Santiago (124km) in need of sand, sea and surf. However, since the beach, backed by wafting palms, stretches for kilometres both ways, there's plenty of space to escape the crowds. The benign waves are more suited to body surfing and playing around in than serious surfing. Many people just roll up to breathe in the sea air, tuck into some seafood and chill at the beachside bar-restaurants though there's a small, professional dive outfit (Ⓦlaslajasbeachdivers.com) that leads diving (and sometimes snorkelling) trips to the nearby **Parque Nacional Marino Golfo de Chiriquí** (see p.203) and also to Coiba (see p.213).

If you are interested in **Ngäbe** or **Buglé** culture, you should take time to visit the major communities of San Félix and Tolé north of the Interamericana; the latter, which lies east close to the border with Veraguas, is noted for its handicrafts – the versatile *kri* (string bag, or *chácara* in Spanish) made of plant fibres, or beaded *nguñunkua* (necklace, or *chaquira* in Spanish) – many sold at stalls along the Interamericana close to the turn-off. For a richer homestay experience, head for **Soloy** (see box below).

ARRIVAL AND DEPARTURE

PLAYA LAS LAJAS AND AROUND

By bus and taxi Although there are two direct buses to La Lajas village from David (6.45am & 2.45pm; 1hr 20min), most visitors to the beach take a bus from David bound for Tolé or San Félix (every 20–30min) and get off at the busy intersection, El Cruce de San Félix, 68km east of David (1hr). You are likely to find a taxi at the petrol station at the junction that can take you the 12km to the beach ($8 one way; $5–6 from the village); get a contact number for your return trip.

STAYING WITH THE NGÄBE IN SOLOY

Though the Ngäbe are Panama's most numerous indigenous citizens by far, they see considerably fewer tourists than the Guna or Emberá, and are understandably wary of outsiders given the recent history of conflict – sometimes violent – with both the Panamanian authorities and international mining corporations. Undertaking a homestay in the mountain community of Soloy (Ⓦcomarcangobebugle.com), in the southwest corner of the Comarca Ngäbe-Buglé provides a unique opportunity to begin to learn about the Ngäbe, their traditions and their present-day challenges, though you'll need some Spanish to make the most of it, and be prepared for very rudimentary lodgings and simple food. The village itself has no nucleus, but rather is strung out several kilometres along the main road and the Río Soloy. The river, and the even more powerful Río Fonseca into which it flows, are crucial to community life and are also the basis for tourist activities (most around $15/person), such as hikes to waterfalls and rafting; visitors can also go hiking (40min–6hr), horseriding and learn the processes of extracting plant fibres and mixing natural dyes to make a traditional *kri* (string bag).

ARRIVAL AND INFORMATION

Buses leave David's main bus terminal for Soloy approximately every hour when full (7am–7pm; 1hr 30min); alternatively take a bus bound for Horconcitos, get off at the turn-off south to Horconcitos from the Intermericana, where pick-up trucks heading north for Soloy leave approximately every 30min. The last bus returning to David leaves Soloy at around 4pm. Where you get off in the village depends on where you have agreed to meet your guide.

ACCOMMODATION

Homestays are currently only arranged by a handful of families as many in the community remain suspicious of tourists and tourism. Contact tourist coordinator and experienced whitewater rafting guide, Juan Carlos Bejerano (Ⓣ6638 0944, Ⓔcarlito559@hotmail.com); alternatively get in touch with Adan Bejerano (Ⓣ6468 5249). Accommodation is usually $10 per person per night with food costing $3–4 a meal.

5

ACCOMMODATION AND EATING

Casa Laguna Las Lajas lagoon – left at the beach T-junction ☎ 6896 0882, ⓦ casalagunapanama.com. Situated on the wildlife-rich lagoon, this restful B&B has three brightly painted and cheerful rooms available (fan and private bathroom), one accommodating four with private patio overlooking the garden ($110). Curl up with a book in a hammock or head for the beach. Three-night minimum stay. Simple but tasty Italian home-cooking at reasonable rates. $90

Hospedaje Ecológico Nahual At the beach T-junction ☎ 6620 6431, ⓦ nahualpanama.com. Two minutes from the sand, this very rustic backpacker retreat carries out genuine eco-practices: it recycles – including human waste; serves food from the organic garden, which is rampant (so with plenty of bugs); and is strict about allowing only biodegradable soaps and repellents and saving water and electricity – so it may not be for everyone. Dorms and triples share showers and there are shared

kitchen facilities. Healthy vegan meals served for little over $5. Dorms $10, doubles $40

Las Lajas Beach Resort Right at the beach T-junction ☎ 6790 1972, ⓦ laslajasbeachresort.com. Set back from the beach, a dozen expansive, tiled, minimally furnished rooms (one with wheelchair access) look onto the lawn through floor-to-ceiling windows. The two upstairs suites have spectacular sea views from the balcony and there's a large pool and bar-restaurant serving moderately priced American-style food. $176

La Pepita de Marañon C Principal, Las Lajas village ☎ 6225 2027, ⓦ lapepitapanama.com. Small B&B run by a young, dog-loving Italian couple. There's a quirky "glass house" double room featuring creative use of recycled bottles in the stone work and a two-storey room with two double beds that can sleep up to four ($76). Twenty minutes from the beach ($3 for transfers) the place also runs inexpensive tours to Ngäbe communities and the interior. $44

Santiago and the central highlands

The administrative, economic and cultural capital of Veraguas province, **SANTIAGO** is a bustling centre of around forty thousand inhabitants. Founded in its present location in 1637, and previously of great agricultural importance, it is now a thriving commercial hub – evidenced by the proliferation of banks and a state-of-the-art baseball stadium. Situated almost halfway between Panama City and David, Santiago is a major transit point as well as a marketing centre for the livestock, rice, maize and sugar from the surrounding farmlands. If travelling round Panama by public transport, it's highly likely that at some stage you will, at the very least, spend time in the bus terminal or stranded on the Interamericana, though there's little incentive to venture further into town unless you happen to coincide with the *patronales* around July 25, which draw in the crowds for some serious partying.

Of greater interest to the tourist is the city's status as the entry point to the undulating Pensinsula de Soná, at the tip of which lies Santa Catalina, the country's surfing capital (see pp.211–213), and as gateway to the cooler mountain slopes of the **central highlands**, which are sprinkled with tranquil farming villages and the charming hilltop village of **Santa Fé**. Closer to town, a few kilometres outside Santiago, are a couple of delightful **village churches** worth a detour, both accessible by bus.

The town centre

Most of the businesses are strung along the Interamericana and Avenida Central, which branches west off the highway heading into the town centre, coming to an abrupt halt in front of the impressive exterior of the **Catedral Santiago Apóstol**, now stunningly illuminated at night. Across the square stands the rather uninspiring – save for a few pre-Columbian ceramics – **Museo Regional de Veraguas** (Mon–Fri 9am–4pm, Sat 9am–3pm; free), housed in the former prison where three-time president Belisario Porras was incarcerated during the civil war. In the centre of the plaza, **Parque Juan Demóstenes Arosemena** takes its name from the former president, who is revered here for choosing the town as the site for Panama's first teacher-training institution. The college, **La Escuela Normal Juan Demóstenes Arosemena**, lies several blocks northeast of the square on Calle 8A Norte and is the architectural jewel of Santiago, with a majestic Baroque frontispiece.

Iglesia Atalaya

Atalaya, 8km southeast of Santiago • Buses from Santiago every 15min (30min)

From the outside, the **Iglesia Atalaya** resembles an inauspicious two-tier wedding cake; inside, its lofty vaulted ceilings covered in splendid frescoes and lovely stained-glass windows more than compensate. Tucked away in a side altar, the Cristo de Atalaya, said to date back from before 1730, is one of Panama's most venerated icons, a magnet for thousands of pilgrims every first Sunday in Lent.

Iglesia San Francisco de la Montaña

San Francisco de la Montaña, 16km north of Santiago on the Santa Fé road • Take a Santa Fé-bound bus from Santiago every 30min (20min); hop off at the fork by the police post and bear right a few hundred metres

The **Iglesia San Francisco de la Montaña** is on the road heading to the mountains of Santa Fé, north of Santiago, in a village of the same name. The simplicity of the small stone church, believed to have been built around 1727, belies the wonderfully elaborate wooden interior, with nine intricately carved Baroque altarpieces betraying both Spanish and indigenous influences. You are likely to have to ask around to get someone to open up.

ARRIVAL AND DEPARTURE   SANTIAGO

BY BUS

Panama City–David buses The more luxurious buses running between Panama City and David make their pit stops at one of two service areas, Centro Los Tucanes or the

5

more popular Centro Piramidal, at Santiago's eastern and western exits to the Interamericana respectively. If they have space, they will pick up extra passengers but at peak times – Friday afternoons and holidays you are better off taking the less luxurious services from the main terminal (see below).

Bus terminal All other transport leaves from the bus terminal on C 10A Norte, often dubbed Av Central, a 15min walk (or $1–2 taxi ride) from Los Tucanes. The terminal has a left-luggage office and public toilets.

Destinations Aguadulce (every 20min, 5am–10.45pm weekdays and until 7pm weekends); Chitré (every 30min, 5.30am–9pm; 90min); David (every 1hr 30min, 6am–7pm); Santa Fé (every 30min, 5am–7pm; 90min); and Soná (every 20min, 6am–7pm; 50min), where you change bus for Santa Catalina.

GETTING AROUND AND INFORMATION

By taxi Taxis are abundant and will ferry you to most places within town for a couple of dollars.

Tourist information The tourist office (Mon–Fri 8.30am–3.30pm; ☎ 998 3929) is on Plaza Palermo.

ANAM office The ANAM office (Mon–Fri 8.30am–3.30pm; ☎ 998 0615) is on the Interamericana.

ACCOMMODATION

Hostal de Veraguas San Martín ☎ 958 9021. A small hostel-cum-homestay house conversion in an out-of-the-way residential area behind the university. Some of the rooms are rather makeshift. Owner Lydia Jaramillo also offers Spanish lessons. Dorms $10, doubles $28

Hotel Gran David Interamericana, near Los Tucanes ☎ 998 1866. This place is popular with families on the move (so often full) and provides good value, offering nice rooms arranged around flower-filled gardens. $50

Hotel La Hacienda Interamericana, 3km west of Santiago ☎ 958 8580. A psychedelic Mexican-style ranch, with vibrant, well-appointed rooms set round two courtyards with a small pool and restaurant. $83

Residencial del Sol C 10A Norte, across from the bus terminal ☎ 993 0371. A convenient, cheap though uninspiring place to bed down, especially if you've missed the bus to Santa Fé or Santa Catalina with functional, clean, dark en-suite rooms and wi-fi. $33

EATING AND DRINKING

El Maná Av 10B Norte, opposite the bus terminal. Cosy cafeteria offering filling, inexpensive dishes featuring the usual mounds of generic noodles interspersed with more appealing fare. A place to hang out while waiting for a bus. Daily 6am–8pm.

Puerto de Perú Av Central at the Interamericana ☎ 2363 9886. This is currently Santiago's top restaurant, serving real Peruvian *ceviche* ($7) and some excellent seafood dishes, including the *cazuela de mariscos* (seafood stew; $16), albeit in a rather uninspiring a/c room. It even sells Inca Cola – Peru's favourite soft drink. Tues–Fri noon–3pm & 6–10pm, Sat noon–10pm, Sun noon–5pm.

Restaurante Tropicalísimo Av Central, at C 17 ☎ 998 3661. A range of mid-priced Cuban and Panamanian dishes (most mains under $9) can be enjoyed, such as *lechón habanero,* the house speciality, in pleasant terrace or indoor surroundings. Mon–Sat 9am–11pm.

Restaurante y Asados Alex La Placita, near the main square. A busy daytime watering hole, serving up Panamanian breakfast fry-ups and the *almuerzo del día* for under $3, plus local specialities such as *gaucho de mariscos* (seafood stew and rice). Daily 6am–3pm.

Santa Fé

A hilltop village about 60km north of Santiago, **SANTA FÉ**, is a jewel of a mountain retreat that has been a well-kept secret for years. Surrounded by a stunning necklace of verdant mountains sprinkled with sparkling cascades and serene stretches of river, with easy access to a forested swathe of national park, it is a hiker's and birdwatcher's dream. Thanks to its 500m altitude, Santa Fé (de Veraguas) enjoys a pleasant, fresh climate, and while the arrival of a real estate office may herald further development, for the moment its absence of traffic and low population density, with houses strung across the tree-dotted hillside, gives it a peaceful village feel. Santa Fé is famous for its floral abundance, boasting over three hundred species of **orchids**, which are celebrated in an annual three-day August festival, when most are in bloom, attracting aficionados from around the country (contact the tourist office in Santiago for dates).

The village

Daily activity centres on the small covered **market** area, where fresh local produce is on display alongside a smattering of predominantly Ngäbe craft stalls. Across the road stands a monument to Santa Fé's most famous resident, **Padre Héctor Gallego** (see box below), whose kidnap and murder has left the village emotionally scarred. A non-profit foundation that bears his name continues his community development work, offering support and skills training to local farmers and artisans. More visibly, the priest's legacy resides in the continued success of the cooperative he helped found; it includes a couple of supermarkets, several grocery stores, a restaurant, bus and taxi services, and the jewel in the crown, the local organic coffee mill, **Café El Tute** (☎954 0801). Tours (in Spanish) of the processing plant, where you can buy some of the delicious product, and to a nearby organic coffee farm, can be organized through the tourism cooperative (☎954 0737), which has a smart *rancho* near the centre of town.

Around Santa Fé

The area's natural beauty makes it perfect for **hiking**, **birdwatching** and **bathing** in clear streams and rivers – provided the weather holds – though the mountainous topography means there'll be steep inclines wherever you wander. A good start is to head down to the river, before the entrance to the village, below the *Hotel de Santa Fé*, or follow the road up towards Alto de Piedra

If you intend to tackle the area's loftiest peaks, Cerro Tute (930m) and Cerro Mariposa (1200m), cloaked in montane forest, or want to penetrate the wilderness areas of the park, then hiring a guide is a must (see p.209). More accessible hiking destinations include the impressive Salto Alto de Piedra and Salto El Bermejo, as well as the 30m cascade of El Salto, slightly further afield. For the hardcore, it's possible to organize a multi-day hike over the cordillera to the Caribbean coast.

Two of the most pleasurable activities in the area, given the magnificent scenery, are **horseriding** and **tubing**, floating down the nearby river for over an hour, gliding past kingfishers, herons and egrets.

ARRIVAL AND GETTING AROUND   SANTA FÉ

By bus Santa Fé is served by buses from the main terminal in Santiago (every 30min, 5am–7pm; 90min). For the return trip they leave from outside the "bus terminal" by the restaurant.

HÉCTOR GALLEGO AND THE SANTA FÉ COOPERATIVE

In the middle of the night of June 9, 1971, **Padre Héctor Gallego**, the 33-year-old priest of Santa Fé, was abducted by two uniformed men of Omar Torrijos's National Guard and was never seen again. In 2002, the Truth Commission set up by President Moscoso to examine crimes committed during Panama's two dictatorships found what they believed to be the tortured remains of the revered priest. It is generally presumed that Manuel Noriega, then head of the secret service, gave the orders, though it seems likely that Torrijos, even if unaware of events at the time, was complicit in the cover-up.

Gallego had arrived in Santa Fé from Colombia in 1967 as the town's first parish priest, and was appalled at the exploitation of the local farmers by the wealthy merchant elite, whose clout within the town and access to outside markets allowed them to buy the farmers' goods for a pittance and sell them on for a fat profit. The energetic priest soon set about educating and organizing the peasant population into becoming self-reliant, helping them to establish a cooperative so their products could be sold directly to the market, bypassing the merchants. It is not known exactly what threat Gallego was perceived to pose to the authorities, but a campaign of intimidation began, starting with insults and threats, escalating into arson and culminating in the priest's final "disappearance". "If I disappear," Gallego announced before his death, "don't look for me. Continue the struggle." His prophetic words now figure on the monument to him in the village.

5

ACTIVITIES AND GUIDES

Fundación Héctor Gallego Up the hill from the hostel (Mon–Fri 8am–8pm, Sat & Sun 8am–6pm; ☎ 954 0737). This community development organization can fix up a tour of the coffee cooperative (in Spanish) or organize a birding or hiking guide. It also offers internet access ($1/hr).

Hiking The experienced Edgar Toribio (☎ 6713 2074, ✉ edgar_toribio@yahoo.es) comes highly recommended for hiking and wildlife, and generally charges around $36/person for a full-day tour, such as to Cerro Tute – prices higher for trips if you prefer to go by car, rather than on horseback. For the fit and adventurous, enquire about the four-day trek to the Caribbean ($340) – though you'll need a tent or hammock to sleep in. Other guides charge around $15–25/person/day depending on numbers; ask your accommodation.

Horseriding Contact César Miranda ☎ 6792 0571, ⓦ aventurascesamo.blogspot.co.uk ($40 for two).

Tubing Ask your accommodation to organize or ask for directions to the house of William Abrega (☎ 6583 5944; $7/person, life jacket provided), whom it's well worth employing to show you the best line into the occasional rapids.

ACCOMMODATION

All three accommodation listings can provide home-made maps of the area for local self-guided walks to waterfalls, and can organize guides for more strenuous hikes further afield and for horseriding.

★**Coffee Mountain Inn** 500m downhill on the right-hand turn before the bus terminal ☎ 6988 0921, ⓦ coffeemountaininn.com. Set in lovely grounds this beautifully appointed lodge offers six accommodation options, ranging from a simple compact double with fan, through to more luxurious doubles with a/c and cable TV, and an apartment with kitchenette and wraparound balcony. Breakfast is included and can be served on your private terrace. Discounts for online bookings and long-term stays. $60

★**Hostal La Qhia** Just up from the bus terminal ☎ 954 0903, ⓦ panamamountainhouse.com. A relaxed yet efficient chalet-style hostel with a bohemian feel and set in a lush garden. Comprising only a small dorm with adjoining semi-open kitchen and four private rooms (three with shared hot-water bathrooms), you'll need to book. A lovely hammock-strewn balcony and *rancho* complete the tranquil scene though the cockerels will ensure an early start. Tasty breakfasts are available, as is takeaway pizza to order. Maps and guides can be arranged for excursions to local waterfalls and natural swimming pools. Dorm $12, doubles $44

Hotel Santa Fé Main road ☎ 954 0941, ⓦ hotelsantafepanama.com. Perched on the hillside 500m before town, this institution has for years attracted fleeing urbanites at weekends seeking fresh mountain air and relaxation. No-frills rooms (for 2–5 people, with cold-water showers – hot water, a/c and cable TV extra) are clean though rather uninspiring and could do with a coat of paint, but are cheap. On-site bar-restaurant and wi-fi. $28

EATING AND DRINKING

★**Anachoreo** Left after the bus station and first right down a dirt road ☎ 6911 4848. The rather unatmospheric, cavernous dining room is more than compensated for by the delicious Cambodian cuisine – stir-fried vegetables, chicken ginger and Fish Amok ($8–12) using fresh green vegetables and herbs from the garden. All dishes come with steamed rice. Wed–Sun 5–9pm.

Fonda Hermanos Pineda Just off the main road. Really friendly local restaurant serving mains for around $6. Try the plate of *picadas* – a sampler platter of deep-fried local favourites: chicken, pork, *hojaldres*, empanadas, yuca chips and *patacones* ($6). Daily 6.30am–9pm.

Restaurante El Terminal Main road ⓦ hotelsantafepanama.com. Small a/c room by the bus terminal, dishing up traditional fried Panamanian breakfasts (under $2) and filling lunches: chicken, beef or pork in tasty sauces accompanied by a mound of rice, lentils and salad – all for under $3. Daily 5am–6.30pm.

Peninsula de Soná and Isla Coiba

Dwarfed by the Azuero Peninsula to the west, the hilly **Peninsula de Soná** has recently started to open up to tourism. Small cattle farms cover the interior and fishing communities dot the rocky coastline, which protrudes into the Golfo de Chiriquí. Panama's surfing capital, mellow **Santa Catalina**, continues to expand as more people use the fishing village as the launching pad for excursions to the rainforests and coral reefs of **Isla Coiba**, which offers some of the world's finest scuba diving, snorkelling and sport fishing.

Santa Catalina

5

At the southern end of the peninsula, the sleepy fishing village of **SANTA CATALINA** reels in visitors for its internationally renowned **surf** spots and is a jumping-off point for Isla Coiba. As a result, the village has developed into a pleasantly bohemian tourist centre, with mostly foreign-owned small-scale operations scattered along the main road into the village, or spilling off the paved road that leads to the main beach, **Playa El Estero**.

ARRIVAL AND DEPARTURE
SANTA CATALINA

By minibus Only three buses a day travel the 48km from Soná to Santa Catalina (5am, noon & 4pm; returning 7am, 8am and 1.30pm), an unendearing glorified crossroads 47km from Santiago. Note that the 1.30pm bus sometimes does not run, or may only go as far as Guarumal, where there are other bus connections with Soná. There are six direct daily connections between Soná and Panama City (5hr).

By taxi Taxis, found hanging round Soná bus terminal, charge $35–40 for the trip to Santa Catalina. For the return, Chente (☎6695 5053) runs a direct shuttle service from Santa Catalina to Santiago (Centro Pyramidal on the Interamericana) in the morning, and in the afternoon too, if there's sufficient demand, for $15/person.

By car Note that there is no petrol station in Santa Catalina – fill up in Soná.

GETTING AROUND AND INFORMATION

On foot Once in Santa Catalina, you'll be on foot unless you've your own transport, but nowhere is further than a 20min hike from the bus stop.

Tourist information The village website (⊛santa catalinabeach.com) has plenty of useful information, including a map and directions for driving but does not include all accommodation options.

Money There is no bank or ATM in the village, and very few places take credit cards, so bring sufficient cash. The nearest ATM is in Soná but it often runs out of money on busy weekends.

Communications There are still no land lines apart from the two public phones (☎998 9488 or ☎998 8600) and erratic internet and mobile phone connections, so you may have to wait several days for a response when booking anything.

TOUR OPERATORS

For specialized trips you're best off going with one of the **tour operators** listed below, whose offices are spread along the 200m of main road from the junction to Playa Santa Catalina. For general snorkelling, surfing, fishing or jaunts to Isla Cébaco or Coiba you may pay less by organizing it through your accommodation or by negotiating

---

ACTIVITIES AND TOURS FROM SANTA CATALINA

The most popular day-tours from Santa Catalina are to **Parque Nacional Coiba** (see pp.213–215), and **Isla Cébaco**, noted for its sparkling clear waters and good coral; at both places you'll be sharing the sea with colourful schools of snappers, jacks, tunas, butterfly, angel and puffer fish alongside moray eels and white-tip reef sharks. At certain times of year, you're likely to have the company of even more impressive marine life such as whales, sharks and rays, especially near Coiba. Most day-trips, unless specialist dive trips, involve a look around the ANAM ranger station and the interpretive centre, a short rainforest walk and a couple of snorkelling stops.

Experienced surfers should head for Santa Catalina's most famous surf break, La Punta, which boasts an international reputation, with waves often topping 5–6m in the season (April–Aug), whereas novice surfers will be happier at Playa El Estero. *Oasis, Sol y Mar, Rolo's* and Fluid Adventures all offer beach-based lessons for beginners at varying rates ($20/hr to $35/2hr, including board rental). In addition to the above various other places rent out boards ($15/day).

While the Santa Catalina website mantra of "surf, dive, fish and chill" just about sums up what the village is about, it doesn't do justice to an array of other **activities** that includes yoga and massage (at *La Buena Vida Hotel* ⊛labuenavidahotel.com), horseriding (at *Hibiscus Garden* ⊛hibiscusgarden.com), kayaking and birdwatching.

You'll find details of **tour operators** in Santa Catalina's listings section (see p.212).

5

directly with the **fishermen** hanging out on the beach by their *pangas* (small flat-bottomed metal boats) or advertising outside their houses. Make sure you agree on exactly what the fee will cover. Expect to pay $150–200 for a boat (usually carrying up to six) for a full day of snorkelling, surfing or fishing, excluding food and drinks; budget more for the Parque Nacional Coiba ($300/boat) since it involves extra fuel. Note that park fees ($20), are not usually included in any tour price (see p.215).

Aventuras Coiba Panama By the mini-super at the junction ☎6868 1282, ⓦaventurascoibapanama.wix .com/islacoibasona. Reliable local outfit run by Victor and his brother, who know plenty of good snorkelling sites and are happy to lead tours to Coiba or closer to home.

Birding Coiba On the right, just after the junction on the road down to Playa Santa Catalina ☎654 41806, ⓦbirdingcoiba.com. Bilingual (English–Spanish) Javier Elizondo specializes in safety-conscious birding tours to Coiba and surrounding islets ($250/person for one day to $235 for three; assuming six people), including park fees, meals, snacks and lodgings. He also guides for Fluid Adventures.

Coiba Dive Center Main road between Brisas del Mar and the police station ☎6565 7200, ⓦscubadivecenter .com. This dive shop is similarly experienced and offers similar deals to Scuba Coiba.

Fluid Adventures Playa Santa Catalina ☎832 2368, ⓦfluidadventurespanama.com. Acclaimed Canadian outfit specializing in surfing and kayaking – lessons, tours and equipment rental. Kayak tours range from an easy paddle and snorkel round Isla Santa Catalina ($60), to three- or six-day kayaking and camping adventures in Coiba that offer wonderful access to wildlife ($502/$1165).

Scuba Coiba Playa Santa Catalina ☎6575 0122, ⓦscubacoiba.com. Top billing for diving goes to pioneering Austrian Herbie Sunk. Rates are $64 for two-tank trips close to Santa Catalina, $123 for Coiba national park. Multi-day trips with three-tank dives to Coiba are also available ($674 for a three-day all-inclusive tour). Gear rental ($15/day) and park fees are extra. Also does PADI certification.

ACCOMMODATION

★**La Buena Vida** Main road ☎6635 1895, ⓦlabuenavidahotel.com. Laden with original mosaic and wrought-iron work, these charming mid-range villas (with a/c, hot-water private bathrooms and patios) were designed by the artistic owners, who continue the theme on the terrace café. Yoga and massage also available. **$66**

★**Cabañas Rolo** Main road, by the beach ☎6494 3916, ⓦrolocabins.net. A Santa Catalina institution, *Rolo's*, as it's more commonly called, is one of the very few locally owned operations, and is the top choice for backpacking surfers. Its brightly painted, clean dorm rooms house 2–4 people, with comfy beds, fan and shared bathrooms. Use of kitchen, pleasant dining and social area is included. Also available is a house with neat, clean en-suite rooms with decent mattresses, pine furniture and a/c, next to *Pizzería Jamming*. Cheap kayak and board rental. Dorms **$10**, doubles **$40**

Hibiscus Garden 10min drive from Santa Catalina on the Soná road, at Lagartero, ☎6615 6095, ⓦhibiscusgarden.com. Spacious, brightly painted rooms with tasteful dark-wood furnishings and patio space in a serene beach- and riverside setting. The terrace restaurant offers a tasty varied menu (most mains $11–20), or you can self-cater in a shared kitchen, and there's no shortage of activities, on site or in Santa Catalina (shuttle service

provided): table tennis, horseriding, wakeboarding and SUP. Children under 14 free. Camping own tent **$8**/person, tent provided **$13**/person, doubles **$44**

★**Oasis Surf Camp** Playa El Estero, contact David Bortolletti (in David) ☎6588 7077, ⓦoasissurfcamp .com. Great beach location among the palms offering no-nonsense, fan-ventilated double cabins (a/c $10 extra) a couple of good-value *casonas* (large, two-storey wood-and-thatch *cabañas*) for six ($85) and camping – tents with mattresses and bedding provided if needed (only in summer). Italian dinners in the restaurant *rancho* are a highlight. Watch out for the river – you'll need to wade across at high tide. Also has some good-value beds at the new *Oasis Hostel* by the junction in the village. Camping own tent **$6**/person, tent provided **$10**/person, *cabaña* **$40**

Surfside Inn Off the beach road ☎6929 2996, ⓦsurfsidepanama.com. This recently renovated surf camp is the closest you can get to Santa Catalina's most famous surf break – La Punta – without actually being in the sea. Enjoy the view from the hammock outside the dorm and standard doubles (cold water), or from the shared terrace or balcony of the pricier more comfortable rooms (hot water, fridge & a/c) in the main house – all set round a lawn with a semi-open shared kitchen. Dorms **$17**, doubles **$50**

EATING AND DRINKING

If you are headed for Coiba and need to take **food** supplies, you should also know that the local mini-super has very limited offerings so you may prefer to bring at least some supplies from Santiago.

La Buena Vida Main road. Delightful mosaic-filled terrace that's great for a leisurely breakfast – vast fruit platters or a "Greek scramble" ($4–7) – or a light lunch of salads, tacos and sandwiches ($7–8). Also provides superior packed lunches. Daily 7am–2pm.

Dive Stop Near the beach on the main road, under *Brisa Mar*. Dark, unpromising-looking local watering hole with TV that does surprisingly decent burritos, tacos and quesadillas for around $7, or *ceviche* for just $3. Daily 10am–10pm.

★ **Pizzería Jamming** Off the beach road ☎ 6447 1373. This genuine pizzeria is the hub of the tourist-based nightlife, serving crispy, clay-oven-cooked pizzas ($7–11) under thatch or in the garden, accompanied by a steady dose of reggae. Tues–Sun 6.30–11pm; closed Oct.

Los Pibes Off the beach road. Pleasant Argentinian-run open-air bar-restaurant (with TV and pool table) dishing up empanadas, home-made burgers, fish and other meats chargrilled to perfection, complemented by fresh salads.

Mains from $7. 6.30–9.30pm; usually closed Wed.

Mama Inés Beach road just before Playa del Estero ☎ 6923 6695, ⊛ santacatalinasurfpoint.com. Perched on a bluff with a great sea view, this is an ideal location for lunch or a relaxing drink. You can tuck into some tasty tacos for $5–6 or try something more substantial such as chicken curry with coconut rice for around $10. Daily 8am–10pm.

Restaurante El Pacífico Just before the village beach on the main road. Local restaurant at local prices serving filling Panamanian favourites – fish and chicken with beans, rice and salad (around $3 for lunch), and a fry-up breakfast for much the same. Can fix up boat trips too. Daily 7am–7pm.

La Vieja Panadería Main road before the junction ☎ 6549 7464. Get here early to catch the croissants, muffins and *pain chocolats*; otherwise enjoy the great home-made bread and tasty breakfasts ($4–6). Filling packed lunches to order ($7). Tues–Sun 6.30am–4pm.

Parque Nacional Coiba

Some say "Panama" means "abundance of fish", and nowhere is this more apparent than in the crystalline waters of the **Parque Nacional de Coiba**. The 2700 square kilometres of reserve encompass Panama's largest island, **Isla Coiba**, plus eight smaller islands and forty islets, but the vast majority consists of ocean brimming with spectacular sea life, including the second-largest coral reef along the Eastern Pacific. As part of the nutrient-rich Central Pacific Marine Corridor, the park is on the migration route of humpbacks (June–Sept), orcas, pilot and sperm whales. Diving conditions are good year-round, but for land-based activities, it's better to visit the island in the **dry season** since the trails are less boggy and there's a better chance of spotting mammals.

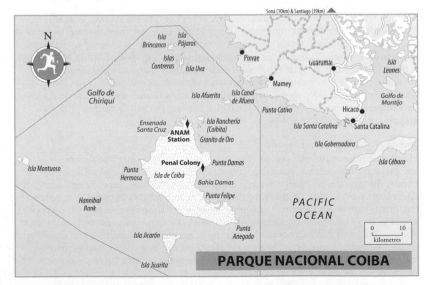

The island still possesses large tracts of **virgin forest**, most of it still unexplored, home to numerous mammal and bird species. Of the estimated 2000 different types of plant, under half have so far been formally classified. The surrounding **oceans** contain countless varieties of fish, ranging from delicate sea horses to vast manta rays, with 33 species of shark – including tiger, hammerhead and whale sharks, though most are harmless reef varieties.

For years, the island's gruesome history as a penal colony (see box opposite) helped protect its forests and waters, but the colony's animals (cattle, buffalo and dogs) are now roaming free, threatening the **ecological balance**. Incursions by large fishing vessels (limited artesanal fishing is permitted), illegal timber extraction and resort development could also damage the reserve, and ongoing negotiations between the government, environmental pressure groups and interested businesses will have a critical impact on Coiba's future.

Isla Coiba

All visitors report first to the ANAM station at Playa Gambute, on the northern tip of the island, to pay the entrance fee and sort out accommodation (for those staying on the island). You can spend a pleasant day just hanging out round the camp. There's an interpretative centre, some moderate snorkelling in the sandy cove and a couple of easy short **walks** affording pleasant views and some tranquil birdwatching. Iguanas and agoutis are frequent dawn visitors to the lawn-cum-part-time football pitch fronting the main beach, and spider monkeys are often sighted swinging through the surrounding vegetation.

A more strenuous but fascinating hike, the **Sendero de Santa Cruz**, leads from the ANAM station through primeval rainforest, crossing crocodile-infested rivers to the west coast at Santa Cruz. For this trek, you'll need to engage one of the wardens as a guide; if you have your own transport you can hike the trail one way and arrange to be ferried back to the ANAM station by boat. Indeed, access to the flora and fauna on most of the island is extremely limited without a **boat**. Many of the tourist spots are inconveniently spaced out along the lengthy eastern coastline, hence the cost of trips.

Sendero de los Monos and Granito de Oro

The first stop on a tour, only a short boat ride from the ANAM station, is usually the 1km **Sendero de los Monos**, though you'll need to be here early to encounter the elusive white-faced capuchins or the island's unique variety of howler monkey. Just across the water from the trail lies one of the most popular snorkelling spots, **Granito de Oro** ("the little grain of gold"), a speck of soft sand surrounded by translucent water, plentiful coral and prolific fish, including the occasional nurse shark and turtle. However, smaller cruise ships (Dec–April) periodically stop off here and smother the sand with deckchairs and assorted aquatic paraphernalia, causing the fish to scarper. The park rangers can advise you on timing.

South to Bahía Damas and beyond

Heading further south, you come to the main camp of the former **penal colony** (see box opposite), whose crumbling, eerie buildings are slowly being reclaimed by nature; through the iron bars you can glimpse half-opened filing cabinets and decaying documents waiting to be sorted. Continuing south across **Bahía Damas**, the aquamarine reef-filled shallows of the eastern coast provide many of the prime diving and snorkelling sites. Panama's last remaining nesting site of the spectacular scarlet macaw is at the south of the island, near **Barco Quebrado**, though these magnificent birds are more easily heard than seen in the forest canopy. Some tours take a plunge in the invigorating thermal springs at **Punta Felipe** or venture into tangled mangroves at **Boca Brava**, or at **Punta Hermosa**, on the more unexplored west coast.

THE PENAL COLONY ON COIBA

For almost eighty years Coiba was synonymous with fear and brutality, as horror stories of forced labour and torture, political assassinations and gang warfare leaked from the island. Designated as a **penal colony** in 1919, it was intended to be an open prison, staffed by civilians and aimed at reforming serious offenders – hence the inclusion at the main camp of a school, rehabilitation centre and church. But with up to three thousand prisoners on the island at one stage, scattered round sixteen different camps, most offenders were unable to access these resources, and the planned civilian custodians never materialized. Instead, prisoners worked twelve-hour shifts on farmland and forest on only one meal a day, suffering violence from gangs and guards, malnutrition, poor sanitation and scant medical care. A peek inside the decaying **high-security block** is sobering. Here ten to twenty people used to share a humid, windowless cell no more than 3m across, with nine bare concrete "beds" and a hole for a toilet, incarcerated for 24 hours a day, with no exercise, no visitors, and little chance of release. Unsurprisingly, **escape attempts** were frequent but usually resulted in failure as those who managed to get through the island's dense undergrowth, avoiding the crocodiles and snakes, generally came to grief in the shark-infested waters and strong sea currents.

Far from the public gaze, the island also gained notoriety during the **military dictatorships** of Omar Torrijos and Manuel Noriega as a prime location for "losing" political opponents, some of whose tortured bodies were unearthed in around 180 graves discovered during President Moscoso's Truth Commission investigations. The penitentiary finally closed in 2004; the only former convict still remaining on the island is "Mali-Mali", now the park's most famous ranger and much sought-after tourist guide.

ARRIVAL AND INFORMATION

BY BOAT

Day-trips from Santa Catalina Fishermen on the beaches at Santa Catalina should do the return trip for $50/person (assuming a group of six) but it'll cost more if you want them to take you round the island to some of the sights; each journey can take anything from 90min to several hours, depending on the weather conditions and the boat. Make sure you establish your itinerary and pick-up times beforehand, and check that any boat has a decent-sized engine, and preferably a roof to stop you frying. However, day-trips from Santa Catalina can be both costly and a little disappointing since the lengthy journey there plus the unavoidable *tramites* (bureaucracy) at the ranger station mean that by the time you actually venture into the rainforest any animal or bird with sense will be hiding from the heat and humidity.

PARQUE NACIONAL COIBA

Multi-day tours Because of the limitations of day-trips, it pays to spend several days on Coiba with a boat and guide willing to take you out at first light, which is why it's worth splashing out the extra for a hassle-free multi-day deal with a tour operator (see p.212).

INFORMATION

Park permits Every visitor has to buy a park permit ($20), theoretically in advance at the Santiago ANAM office (☎ 998 4271) – in practice it can be acquired on arrival at the ANAM ranger station on Coiba.

Ranger guides You can engage a ranger to accompany you on trips around the island for $15–20.

When to visit As there are no limits on visitor numbers to the national park, holiday periods and summer weekends should be avoided at all costs.

ACCOMMODATION

Coiba's accommodation is, in some ways, a great leveller – whether you're on an exclusive all-in deal or you've hitched a ride with the park wardens, everyone has to stay in the same basic huts.

ANAM cabins ANAM ranger station. Forty-odd beds spread dormitory-style around five double cabins with screening and shared bathrooms. If travelling independently, you will need to book ahead through the ANAM office in Santiago (☎ 998 4271; see p.209) in the dry season; alternatively your tour operator will make the reservation. You'll also need to bring your own food supplies from Santa Catalina, in a cool box supplied by your

boatman; for $15 (per group) the rangers let you share their kitchen (but not the fridge), though the gas occasionally runs out. The cabins have electricity and a/c after 6pm though power cuts are frequent. Other useful items to bring include mosquito coils and net (as some screens have holes), a torch, candles and plenty of insect repellent and bite cream. Limited camping spaces are available. Camping $\overline{$15}$/person, dorms $\overline{$20}$

Bocas del Toro

ISLA CARENERO

Bocas del Toro

Isolated on the Costa Rican border between the Caribbean and the forested slopes of the Cordillera de Talamanca, Bocas del Toro ("Mouths of the Bull") is one of the most beautiful areas in Panama. It's also one of the most remote – the mainland portion of the province is connected to the rest of Panama by a single spectacular road that carves its way over the continental divide, often blocked by landslides during the heaviest rains, while the island chain offshore requires a ferry ride to reach.

6

For most people, Bocas – confusingly, the abbreviation for the province, archipelago, provincial capital and even sometimes Isla Colón – means the **tropical islands**, which attract more visitors than anywhere else outside Panama City, offering opportunities for relaxing on pristine **beaches** and snorkelling and diving among **coral reefs** in a maze of tangled **mangroves** and undisturbed **rainforest**. The archipelago's unique history has made it the most ethnically diverse region in Panama outside the capital, its Afro-Caribbean, Panamanian-Chinese, *mestizo* and indigenous Ngäbe residents recently joined by North American retirees and US and European hotel owners. English is the dominant language, though Spanish is still widespread. However cosmopolitan Bocas has become, it is the languid pace of the dominant **Afro-Caribbean culture** and its distinctive vernacular wooden architecture that most clearly defines the place.

Yet the archipelago only constitutes a small percentage of the province, much of which is taken up by the Comarca Ngäbe-Buglé in the east and the inaccessible but spectacular Talamanca mountain range to the southwest, whose lofty peaks form the backbone of the vast **Parque Internacional La Amistad**, which boasts an awe-inspiring array of wildlife. The lowlands of the mainland, often dismissed as an endless stream of banana plantations, also offer a couple of notable attractions. Panama's banana capital and the province's main commercial centre, **Changuinola**, provides access to the magical **Humedales de San San Pond Sak**, the country's main refuge for the manatee and an important beach for nesting marine turtles. Inland, on the banks of the picturesque Río Teribe, a stay with the **Naso**, one of the less well-known indigenous peoples, provides a unique opportunity for intercultural exchange in a stunning natural setting.

Brief history

Archeological evidence suggests that **indigenous peoples** inhabited the islands and mainland of present-day Bocas del Toro two thousand years ago, long before an ailing Christopher Columbus limped into the bay on his final voyage in 1502 in search of a route to Asia. Later, during the colonial era, the calm waters of the archipelago provided shelter for European pirates and, by the early nineteenth century, the islands were already becoming the ethnic melting pot that characterizes them today, attracting British and US trading **merchants**, who came with their West

STRAWBERRY POISON-DART FROG

Highlights

❶ Tour an organic cocoa farm Learn how the Ngäbe make chocolate and sample the product while experiencing village life on the Bocas mainland **see p.227**

❷ Cocktails in Bocas The finishing touch to a hard day at the beach is an iced cocktail at one of Bocas Town's many waterside bars. **See p.231**

❸ Isla Bastimentos Explore the Caribbean community of Old Bank, Ngäbe villages and windswept surfing beaches while looking out for the famous red frogs. **See p.231**

❹ Cayo Crawl Snorkel among gorgeous soft corals before tucking into a seafood platter at a restaurant over the water. **See p.233**

❺ Humedales de San San Pond Sak This wetland manatee refuge also provides nesting sites for marine turtles and hosts an array of birdlife. **See p.240**

❻ Stay in a Naso village A unique opportunity to learn about Panama's only monarchy and explore the surrounding rainforest. **See p.241**

HIGHLIGHTS ARE MARKED ON THE MAP ON P.220

BOCAS DEL TORO

HIGHLIGHTS

1 Tour an organic cocoa farm
2 Cocktails in Bocas
3 Isla Bastimentos
4 Cayo Crawl
5 Humedales de San San Pond Sak
6 Stay in a Naso village

VERAGUAS

CARIBBEAN SEA

N

Golfo de
los Mosquitos

Isla Escudo
de Veraguas

Río Chucará

Río Criamola

Río Manatí

Península
Valiente

BOCAS DEL TORO

CORDILLERA CENTRAL

Archipiélago de Bocas del Toro

PARQUE NACIONAL
MARINO ISLA
BASTIMENTOS

Isla
Bastimentos

Cayos
Zapatillos

Cayo de
Agua

Isla
Popa

Laguna
de
Chiriquí

Chiriquí
Grande

Lago
Fortuna

Interamericana, David & Panama City

Swan Cay

Isla Colón

Bastimentos

Bocas
Del Toro

Isla
Solarte

Isla
Cristóbal

Silico
Creek

CORDILLERA

Canal de
Soropta

Finca 60

Almirante

BOSQUE
PROTECTOR
DE PALO SECO

Río Changuinola

Boquete

Río Majagua

David

Humedales de
San San Pond Sak

Changuinola

El Silencio

Río San San

CORDILLERA DE TALAMANCA

Cerro Punta

Río Piedra

Guabito

Sixaola

PARQUE
INTERNACIONAL
LA AMISTAD

Río Teribe

Volcán Barú
(3475m)

PARQUE NACIONAL
VOLCÁN BARÚ

Volcán

Puerto Limón

Río Sixaola

Cerro Echandi
(3163m)

Cerro Fábrega
(3336m)

Cerro Itamut
(3279m)

CORDILLERA DE TALAMANCA

CHIRIQUÍ

Río Sereno

INTERAMERICANA

Paso Canoas

COSTA
RICA

San José

kilometres

0   25

African slave workforce, founding the town of Bocas del Toro in 1826. Following construction of the **Panama Railroad** and the French canal effort, West Indian migrants continued to drift into the area.

The banana trade

For the last two centuries, the ebb and flow of the **banana trade** has most clearly defined the province. By 1895 bananas from Bocas accounted for more than half of Panama's export earnings, and Bocas Town boasted five foreign consulates and three English-language newspapers. Around 6500 were employed by the United Fruit Company in its heyday, and the company was responsible for building the now-defunct mainland railroad system and constructing canals, hospitals, telegraph networks and entire towns. But following repeated devastation by disease early in the twentieth century, the banana harvests failed, causing the archipelago's economy to languish. When the banana trade started up again in the 1950s and 1960s, Guna and Guaymí workers were also integrated into the workforce, many suffering serious ill-health from noxious pesticides. Now, the business is confined to the plantations round Changuinola, the headquarters of Bocas Fruit Company, the current incarnation of "the company" and part of Chiquita Brands International. With almost four thousand employees it is still the most important employer in the province though since the trade in "*oro verde*" (green gold) is flagging, workers now earn pitifully low wages.

Tourism and real estate

In recent years, **tourism** and **real estate** speculation have soared, generating employment and income for some residents while leaving others behind to struggle with the inevitable rise in the cost of living, increased pressure on services and the threat of being thrown off their land. Foreign investors have been allowed to purchase huge portions of the archipelago for luxury resorts and holiday homes, despite local opposition. Given the complex ecosystems involved and the lack of infrastructure on the islands due to years of government neglect, much concern exists over the sustainability of such developments.

Archipiélago de Bocas del Toro

Most tourists make a beeline for the **Archipiélago de Bocas del Toro**, scarcely setting foot on the mainland except to catch a bus or ferry. Despite the existence of several hundred atolls, islets and cays scattered across the bite-shaped gulf that shelters much of the archipelago, most tourist activity is centred on the handful of larger islands, covered in rainforest and fringed with mangroves, populated by small Ngäbe communities or, in the cases of islas Colón and Bastimentos, largely Afro-Antillean settlements.

The majority of visitors stay in the laidback provincial capital **Bocas del Toro**, which spills off a peninsula at the southeast tip of **Isla Colón**, the archipelago's largest and most developed island. During the day, launches brimming with tourists scatter outwards, heading for the reefs, beaches, mangroves and forests of the neighbouring islands of **Bastimentos**, **Solarte** and **Carenero** or the distant cays of **Zapatillas**. Other popular destinations include the **Laguna de Bocatorito**, often dubbed Dolphin Bay for the frequent sightings of dolphins, and the sea-bird colonies of **Swan Cay** off the north coast of Isla Colón. In late afternoon, the sandy streets of Bocas fill as the **waterfront bars** come to life. Dining options are plentiful and varied, reflecting the cosmopolitan population, and at weekends the energetic can usually find somewhere to dance till dawn.

Isla Colón and Bocas Town

The first port of call in the archipelago for almost all visitors – whether arriving by plane or boat – is **Isla Colón**, or, to be more precise, **Bocas Town**, the provincial capital of Bocas del Toro. Connected to the rest of the island by a slender isthmus, Bocas explodes with tourists in high season (Dec–April), and is the easiest base from which to explore the islands, beaches and reefs of the archipelago. It also offers an ever expanding choice of tours and activities, from the traditional pursuits of **surfing**, **diving** and **snorkelling** to options such as forest walks, kayaking and wildlife-viewing, as well as yoga and massage. Despite the presence of lush primary and secondary rainforest on the island, most tourist activity happens along the coastline, on the wild and relatively deserted **beaches** of the east coast or the more sheltered shallows of **Boca del Drago**, on the western point close to the mainland.

Bocas Town

Arriving in **BOCAS TOWN**, a spread of rickety wooden buildings painted in faded pastels and a laidback, mostly English-speaking, population welcome you to the island's casual melee. The town went into decline after the banana trade collapsed (see p.221), until a steady trickle of backpackers and American retirees in the 1990s, followed by a country-wide real estate boom, catapulted the town into another era. Around twenty years ago, there were only three hotels in Bocas; now there are more than seventy. Yet while Bocas Town is a fine spot for hedonistic young travellers, there are plenty of options for anyone seeking a more mellow sojourn.

The main festival is the **Feria del Mar**, held on Playa del Istmito in late September, whose endless rows of exhibition stands, craft stalls, mountainous fry-ups and late-night partying on the sands draw visitors in their thousands. There's no sightseeing

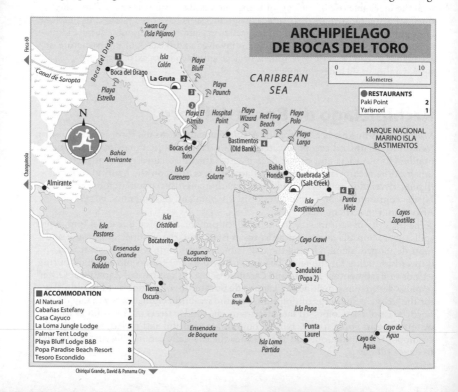

THE NGÄBE AND BUGLÉ

The province's most high-profile indigenous peoples are the **Ngäbe** and the **Buglé**. These two related peoples speak mutually unintelligible languages, and are probably the oldest surviving ethnic groups on the isthmus, descended from the great Guaymí warrior tribes, whose best-known chief, Urracá (see p.293), graces the one-cent coin. Forced into remote and mountainous lands by the Spanish, where many have remained, the majority live within the Comarca Ngäbe-Buglé, a semi-autonomous area established in 1997, covering almost seven thousand square kilometres in the eastern half of the province and pockets of Veraguas and Chiriquí. With poor access to potable water, health care and education, the *comarca* suffers Panama's highest levels of poverty.

Most Ngäbe and Buglé practise **subsistence agriculture**, supplemented by hunting, fishing and limited cash crop cultivation. Struggling to survive in an increasingly cash-based economy, some make seasonal migrations to the banana, coffee or sugar plantations, where they carry out the harshest jobs for the worst wages. A few produce traditional handicrafts – the distinctive colourful cotton dresses (*nagua*), necklaces (*nguñunkua*) and woven bags (*kri*) – to sell to tourists; others have abandoned the rural areas altogether.

Traditionally, both groups have lived in small kinship groupings – half a dozen thatched huts with dirt or wooden floors, though coastal communities prefer rectangular lodgings built on stilts – which control access to land and work in cooperation. These, and other cultural practices, such as the Ngäbe custom of polygamy (the Buglé have always espoused monogamy), have been eroded by missionary and other outside influences. One of the traditions that clings on in some places, despite attempts to outlaw it, is the **krün** (*balsería* in Spanish), a violent "sport" in which members of two teams take turns to try and knock their opponent off-balance by hurling a wooden pole at their calves. The contest is a core part of the four-day **chichería**, which involves plenty of its namesake, the potent maize-based *chicha fuerte* brew, alongside dancing and music.

6

to be done in town; experiencing Bocas is more about hanging out in the waterfront bars and restaurants, soaking up the laidback vibe, getting out on the water during the day and partying at night.

The town centre

Bocas is laid out on a simple grid system with most activity centred on **Calle 3**, the broad main street that runs north–south, spilling into Calle 1, which bulges out into the bay, where the decks of attractive wooden hotels, bars and restaurants stretch over the water on stilts. Halfway up the main drag, lined with supermarkets, souvenir shops and stalls, hotels and hostels, sits **Parque Bolívar**, the social heart of the town, shaded by coconut palms and fig trees, with a bust of the Liberator the town's sole monument.

Playa del Istmito

The nearest stretch of sand and general town beach is tatty **Playa del Istmito**, on the eastern side of the causeway that links Bocas with the rest of Isla Colón, which is a decent place for a beer, especially during September's Fería del Mar festivities (see above).

Playa Bluff and around

Three kilometres north of Bocas Town, the road divides at "La Ye"; left takes you over the hilly terrain to Boca del Drago, 12km away, while the dirt road to the right (4WD needed in the rainy season) hugs the coastline for another 5km past **surfing** hotspots **Playa Paunch** (or Punch) and **Dumpers**, until the start of the glorious 4km swathe of sand that is **Playa Bluff**. An important nesting site for leatherback and green **turtles**, it can be visited at night during the nesting season (May–Sept) by arrangement (see box, p.236). None of these beaches is suitable for swimming, with powerful waves and strong currents, but the thundering breakers on Bluff beach are a sight to behold and the golden sands provide a lengthy, scenic promenade.

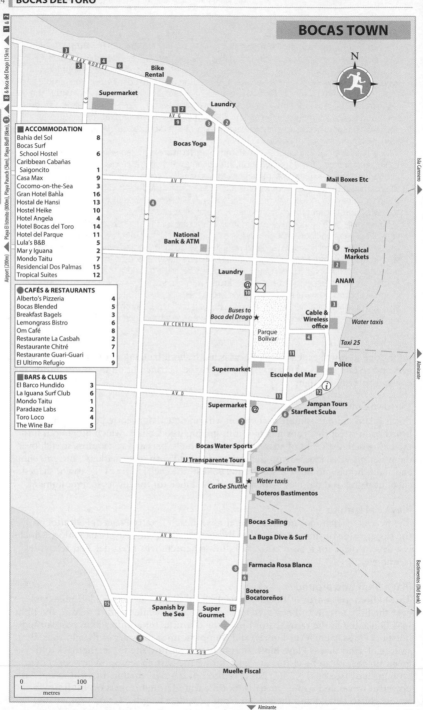

BOCAS TOWN

N

ACCOMMODATION

Bahía del Sol	8
Bocas Surf School Hostel	6
Caribbean Cabañas Saigoncito	1
Casa Max	9
Cocomo-on-the-Sea	3
Gran Hotel Bahía	16
Hostal de Hansi	13
Hostel Heike	10
Hotel Angela	4
Hotel Bocas del Toro	14
Hotel del Parque	11
Lula's B&B	5
Mar y Iguana	2
Mondo Taitu	7
Residencial Dos Palmas	15
Tropical Suites	12

CAFÉS & RESTAURANTS

Alberto's Pizzeria	4
Bocas Blended	5
Breakfast Bagels	3
Lemongrass Bistro	6
Om Café	8
Restaurante La Casbah	2
Restaurante Chitré	7
Restaurante Guari-Guari	1
El Ultimo Refugio	9

BARS & CLUBS

El Barco Hundido	3
La Iguana Surf Club	6
Mondo Taitu	1
Paradaze Labs	2
Toro Loco	4
The Wine Bar	5

Bike Rental

Supermarket

Laundry

Bocas Yoga

Mail Boxes Etc

Tropical Markets

National Bank & ATM

ANAM

Laundry

Buses to Boca del Drago

Cable & Wireless office

Water taxis

Parque Bolívar

Taxi 25

Supermarket

Escuela del Mar

Police

Supermarket

Jampan Tours
Starfleet Scuba

Bocas Water Sports

JJ Transparente Tours

Bocas Marine Tours

Caribe Shuttle

Water taxis

Boteros Bastimentos

Bocas Sailing

La Buga Dive & Surf

Farmacia Rosa Blanca

Boteros Bocatoreños

Spanish by the Sea

Super Gourmet

Muelle Fiscal

Isla Carenero

Almirante

Bastimentos (Old Bank)

Almirante

0   100
metres

AV H (AV NORTE)
AV G
AV F
AV E
AV CENTRAL
AV D
AV C
AV B
AV A
AV SUR

Airport (200m) | Playa El Istmito (800m), Playa Paunch (5km), Playa Bluff (8km) | Playa El Istmito (800m) | 8 & Boca del Drago (15km) | 1 & 2

La Gruta

On the road to Boca del Drago • No fixed hours • $2 • To get there, take the Boca del Drago bus ($1); La Gruta is signposted to the right off the main road, from where it is a short walk

Halfway across the island on the bumpy, tarred Boca del Drago road lies the small settlement of **Colonia Santeña**. The main reason to stop off here is to visit a sacred cave, often referred to simply as **La Gruta**, a place of pilgrimage on July 16 for the Festival de la Virgen del Carmen. Push the fronds of greenery aside and, depending on the time of year and the amount of rain, you'll be wading in a delightful freshwater creek or a stream of guano. The shrine to the virgin is near the entrance; flash a torch around and you'll see hundreds of bats clinging to the rock.

6

Boca del Drago

Get here on the Boca del Drago bus that leaves from the park in Bocas, or rent a bicycle; turn left at the T-junction at the top of the island

One of the most popular day-trips from Bocas Town is to take the bus to the Ngäbe community of **Boca del Drago**, at the northern end of the island. Supposedly the first place in Panama that Christopher Columbus set foot, Boca del Drago is a pleasant place to spend a relaxing day. The beach, though slight, consists of lovely white palm-fringed sand, but the real appeal is the sheltered translucent water, perfect for safe bathing and a little snorkelling while you wait for your seafood order at the beachfront restaurant (see p.231).

Playa Estrella

A fifteen-minute walk along the shoreline from Boca del Drago takes you to **Playa Estrella**, whose shallows are dotted with an amazing number of orange cushioned starfish, which should not be touched. Here the beach is backed by a string of informal seafood restaurants and bars, which are thronging at weekends and during the holiday season, though the place can be quiet midweek.

Swan Cay

One of the area's main attractions is a bird sanctuary, a fifteen-minute boat ride off the north coast, though it's accessible only when conditions are benign. **Swan Cay**, known locally as Isla Pájaros (Bird Island), is an impressive 50m stack topped with cascading vegetation. Sea birds wheel above, with star billing going to the elegant white **red-billed tropicbird**, which shares this nesting spot with a colony of brown boobies. Both Swan Cay and Boca del Drago feature on one of the popular Bocas tour routes (see box, p.228) or you can negotiate a rate with a local fisherman at Boca del Drago.

ARRIVAL AND DEPARTURE	ISLA COLÓN AND BOCAS TOWN

BY PLANE

Airport All flights arrive at, and depart from, Bocas Airport, a small building and airstrip three blocks west of the main street, C 3.

Airlines and flights Air Panama (☎ 757 9841 in Bocas; ☎ 316 9000 for general reservations) offers multiple daily flights from and to Panama City ($144 one way), which get booked up over long weekends and holiday periods. Air Panama also offers morning connections three times a week with David, via Changuinola (Tues, Thurs & Sun; $84 one way), while the Costa Rican domestic airline Nature Air (☎ 757 9390, ⊕ natureair.com) has twice-daily direct flights between Bocas and San José (Tues, Thurs, Sat & Sun; 50min; $241 one way, including carbon offsetting), as well as serving several other locations in Costa Rica. Both airlines have offices at the airport in Bocas.

Luggage allowance Air Panama flights allow 14kg of checked baggage plus hand luggage, and charge supplements for surfboards. For Nature Air the luggage allowance depends upon the fare class purchased.

BY BUS

From Costa Rica If you are arriving from the Costa Rican border at Guabito, take the bus to Changuinola (every 25min, 5.30am–7pm; 30min) or taxi (colectivo $1.25/person, private $8), and transfer to a bus bound for Almirante (see p.239).

From/to Panama City Tranceibosa runs the twice-daily bus service between Changuinola and Panama City, picking up at Almirante, at the stop on the main road at 8.30am and 7pm ($28). Tickets can be bought at the Albrook Bus Terminal in Panama City and at its office by Taxi 25 in Bocas Town (8am–noon, 1–5pm; closed Wed). Note that you will

6

DIVING, SNORKELLING AND SURFING IN BOCAS

Diving and snorkelling are the most established diversions around Bocas Town, which is no surprise as the area offers the healthiest **coral** on the Caribbean coast, covered in sponges and anemones, fed on by an array of colourful reef fish and frequented by turtles and nurse sharks, while moray eels, lobsters and crabs hide in the crevices.

The **snorkelling** highlights include the distant Cayos Zapatillas in the national marine park, though currents are strong, and, off the southern tip of Bastimentos, the magical soft coral gardens of Cayo Crawl. Closer to base, the shallows by Hospital Point off Isla Solarte are favoured by both snorkellers and divers, who can explore the impressive wall and rocky outcrop sheltering schools of fish. The main problem with snorkelling and diving in Bocas is drastically reduced visibility caused by run-off from the mainland following heavy rains, which are frequent, even in the dry season. Strong winds and rough seas limit accessibility to more remote dive sites too.

Bocas also has a reputation for **surfing**, and while it can't match Santa Catalina (see pp.211–213) for consistency of waves, it offers some excellent rides when conditions are right, generally between December and March. Numerous places rent out **boards** in various states of repair, and several places offer lessons, transfers to surf spots and even guided surf tours (see opposite). Several surf breaks lie on the east coast of Isla Colón, with other hot spots off Isla Carenero and along the northern coast of Isla Bastimentos; between the two islands, the giant waves of Silverbacks are only for expert practitioners.

need warm clothes to combat the invariably glacial a/c, especially on the overnight bus.

From/to David Buses run frequently between Changuinola and David, stopping at Almirante, on the main road ("La Ye") to pick up/drop off passengers (every 25min, 5am–7pm; 4hr). Shared taxis shuttle back and forth between here and the water-taxi terminal ($1/person).

Caribe Shuttle The Caribe Shuttle (Bocas ☎757 7048, Puerto Viejo, Costa Rica ☎2750 0626, ☜caribeshuttle.com) offers a hassle-free, door-to-door service between Puerto Viejo (4hr; $32) or San José (10hr; $69) in Costa Rica and Bocas. Departures for Bocas from Puerto Viejo are at 7.30am & noon, and from San José at 6am; departures from Bocas for

Puerto Viejo are at 8am & noon, and for San José at 8am.

BY BOAT

Water-taxis Two companies run water-taxis across the bay between Almirante and Bocas (every 30min, 6am–6.30pm; 30min; $6; see p.238); Taxi 25 has a dock by the *Barco Hundido* in Bocas, while Bocas Marine Tours operates from the main jetty, further down C 3 (see map, p.224).

Ferries The unreliable and slow car ferry leaves Almirante at 8am (Tues–Sun) but should be given a wide berth unless you're taking a bicycle ($3), or a motorbike ($10). The ferry docks at the southern end of the main street, returning to Almirante at 4pm.

GETTING AROUND

By taxi Though everything in town is within easy walking distance, taxis are readily available ($1/person). Travelling further afield, a taxi to Boca del Drago usually costs around $15–20, while a 4WD taxi to nearer Playa Bluff will set you back $8–10 depending on how far up the beach you are going, and the road condition.

By bus Transporte Boca del Drago (☎774 9065) operates the island's only bus service to and from Boca del Drago. It leaves from Parque Bolívar approximately hourly (7am–6pm; $2.50 one way) departing from outside *Restaurante Yarisnori* at similar intervals for the return trip. In high season, private minibuses leave from just south of the park when full and charge the same rates.

By water-taxi Water-taxis regularly ferry people back and forth from Bocas to Isla Carenero ($1 to the near shore) and to Old Bank on Bastimentos ($3) at fixed rates from around dawn to dusk. Taxis leave once they've gathered a few passengers, every 10–15min or so, and the rates go up at night. The main water-taxi dock for Carenero is by the *Barco Hundido* on C 1, while for Old Bank, Bastimentos, you should head for the Boteros Bastimentos' water-taxi dock, on the main street, opposite Av "C". On C 1, opposite Av "D", Jampan Tours (☎757 9619) runs a regular water-taxi service to Red Frog Beach on a fixed timetable (9am, noon, 1pm, 2pm & 5pm, returning at 9.30am, 12.30pm, 1.30pm, 2.30pm, 4pm & 5.30pm; $4 one way, $7 return).

INFORMATION

Tourist information The tourist office (Mon–Sat 8.30am–3.30pm; ☎757 9642) has toilet facilities, and may be able to provide a map but is otherwise of little help.

The website ☜bocas.com is a good resource for hotel and tour operator information and the free monthly *Bocas Breeze* (☜bocasbreeze.com) advertises local events. The sustainable tourism group, Alianza de Turismo Sostenible de Bocas del Toro, does not have an office in town but has a useful website (⊛ redtucombo.bocasdeltoro.org) and will provide further information on request.

ACTIVITIES AND TOUR OPERATORS

Bike rental Several places rent out bicycles (around $10–12/day) in varying states of repair. The main cycling destinations are Playa Bluff and Boca del Drago. Flying Pirates (☎ 6689 5050, ⊛ flyingpiratesbocas.com) also does quad-bike rental ($107/day).

Cocoa farms The communities of Silico Creek (⊛ urari .org; see p.238) and Río Oeste Arriba (⊛ oreba .bocasdeltoro.org) on the mainland offer fascinating tours of their organic cocoa farms, with plenty of tasting along the way.

Horseriding At Playa Bluff, you can arrange horseriding at Bluff Beach Retreat (☎ 6677 8867; $30 for 3hr plus tip for the guide). On Isla San Cristóbal, a highly acclaimed but more expensive operator, Panama Horseback Adventures (☎ 6915 3147, ⊛ panamahorseback.com), offers half-day ($50) and full-day tours ($75) to a Ngäbe village and, for experienced riders, an overnight trek ($200).

Kayak rental Bocas Water Sports, Flying Pirates and several lodgings rent out kayaks.

Learning Spanish Habla Ya and Spanish by the Sea are the best-known language schools, both with good reputations (weekly rates for small group classes around $200).

Massage In keeping with the boho vibe of Bocas, there's no shortage of people willing to knead your aching surfing limbs – Starfleet Scuba (see p.228) offers massage for around $50/hr; otherwise just check the hostel notice boards and posters round town.

Turtle-watching See box, p.236.

Yoga The striking lilac Bocas Yoga Centre (top end of C 4, ☎ 6658 1355, ⊛ bocasyoga.com; $5 per session, with discounts for multi-class passes) has rave reviews.

ANAM office A couple of doors down from the tourist office on C 1 (Mon–Fri 8.30am–3.30pm; ☎ 757 9244). ANAM hands out permits to camp within Parque Nacional Marino Isla Bastimentos ($10/person).

TOUR OPERATORS

There are loads of tour operators in town; below is just a small selection of the best. We give an overview of typical destinations and itineraries in our "Tours from Bocas" box (see p.228).

ANCON Expeditions At Bocas Inn Av "H", at C 3 ☎ 757 9600, ⊛ anconexpeditions.com. Excursions into the marine park and the forests on the mainland. More expensive than other operators but very organized, with good boats and experienced bilingual naturalist guides.

Bocas Sailing C3, at Av "B" ☎ 757 9710, ⊛ bocassailing .com. Offers excellent-value catamaran trips to see dolphins en route to Cayo Crawl ($45 including picnic lunch) or heads for Boca del Drago, with private charter possible (min 8 people).

Bocas Surf School Av Norte, between C 5 & C 6 ☎ 6852 5291, ⊛ bocassurfschool.com. Offers professional private lessons with qualified instructors ($60 half day, $90 full day, including board) at all levels.

Bocas Water Sports C 3, at Av "A" ☎ 757 9541, ⊛ bocaswatersports.com. Professional and well-established US-run outfit with bilingual Panamanian staff offering diving (two tanks $70), including PADI open-water certification ($250) and a taster course, plus snorkelling outings as well as kayak rental (single $3/hr, $18/day; double $5/hr, $35/day) and wakeboarding.

Boteros Bocatoreños C 3, at Av "A" ☎ 757 9760. An association of local boatmen formed to try and compete against some of the slicker foreign tour operators, offering the usual tour favourites, often at slightly lower prices, and with baqs of local tales to tell.

La Buga Dive C 3, at Av "B" ☎ 6781 0755, ⊛ labugapanama.com. Originally exclusively a dive

6

6

TOURS FROM BOCAS

Generally, you get what you pay for in a **tour**, in that the more established, pricier ones tend to use better and safer boats, take fewer people and show greater customer service and respect for the environment and the indigenous communities. Make sure you establish the itinerary and what's included in the price. Of course, it's often cheaper for a group to negotiate a deal with one of the boatmen hanging out around the dock.

The standard day-trip excursions combine snorkelling with other activities, and cater predominantly to budget travellers ($20–30/person for a minimum of 4–6 people), depending on the destination and boat quality. Most leave at around 9.30am, returning about 4–4.30pm and stopping off for a seafood meal (not included) at a local restaurant along the way, though some trips include a picnic lunch. Be aware that bad **weather** can result in a change of itinerary or cancellation and that the seas further out can get very rough. We offer a selection of the town's best **tour operators** in Bocas' listings section (see p.227).

THE ITINERARIES

There are three popular itineraries offered by most operators. The first takes you to **Laguna Bocatorito** (Dolphin Bay), where you have a good chance of seeing the rather shy **bottle-nosed dolphins** that live there year-round. This can be a hit-and-miss experience, to be boycotted in high season when the place is overrun with boats, many engaging in potentially harmful practices. The next stop is the gorgeous, rainbow-coloured soft coral of **Cayo Crawl**, where lunch is at one of the three over-the-water restaurants (from around $9–10), before returning to lounge on **Red Frog Beach** ($3 entry), sometimes with an additional spot of snorkelling nearer home.

Another similar but pricier option takes you on from Cayo Crawl to the national marine park and **Cayos Zapatillas** ($10 entry fee on top) for further snorkelling and beach lounging, stopping off at another snorkelling spot, such as **Hospital Point**, on the way back. Alternatively, boats head round Isla Colón to the easy shallows of **Boca del Drago**, with lunch at a restaurant on the beach, and to marvel at the wonderful starfish of **Playa Estrella** as well as heading out to see the sea birds at **Swan Cay** before donning the snorkel mask once more at **Punta Manglar** on the way back. Endless possibilities exist for boat excursions further afield as well: up one of the rivers into the rainforests of the mainland to visit isolated **indigenous communities** or east around the Peninsula Valiente to the remote **Isla de Escudo de Veraguas**, which aficionados consider one of the best diving spots in the whole Caribbean – *La Buga* offers overnight camping dive trips, though the seas are too rough to reach it most of the year.

centre (open-water $250), La Buga now also does surfing, snorkelling and fishing trips as well as Stand-Up-Paddle (SUP), kayak and surfboard rental.

Jampan Tours C 1, at Av "B" ☎ 757 9619. You can't miss the bright Jamaican colours of their office or boats, which run water-taxi services to Red Frog Beach and the standard day tours ($25–30), plus one that includes a visit to a Ngäbe community on Isla San Cristóbal.

Scuba 6 Diving Old Bank, Bastimentos ☎ 6722 5245, ⓦ scuba6diving.com. New dive operator offering two-tank dives ($80–110) and PADI certification (open-water $270) and taster courses for beginners ($75).

Starfleet Scuba C 1, near Av "D" ☎ 757 9630, ⓦ starfleetscuba.com. British-run company with a friendly, professional team focusing on diving (two-tank $70), including full PADI open-water diving courses ($225) but also offering massage and spa treatments. English, Spanish and German spoken.

ACCOMMODATION

There's a good range of **accommodation** in Bocas, and more hostels here than anywhere else in the country outside Panama City. Even so, rooms are scarce during high season and on holiday weekends. **Advance booking** is therefore a good idea though backpacker lodgings don't accept reservations, so try to arrive before 11am. A sprinkling of foreign-owned lodges and guesthouses are now opening up in more remote corners of Isla Colón, getting you closer to nature but more reliant on their amenities, since public transport between Bocas Town and the rest of the island is largely limited to taxis, which are expensive. Water shortages, power cuts and floods can sometimes affect these isolated islands, especially in the winter, however much you're paying.

IN BOCAS TOWN
HOTELS AND B&BS

★**Casa Max** Av "G", between C 4 & C 5 ☎757 9120, ⓦhotelcasamax.com; map p.224. A friendly, reliable choice for budget travellers not wanting a dorm, with beds decked in crisp cotton sheets and cheerful rooms (fan ventilated, or a/c for an extra $20) – some with balconies. The smart, newly renovated rooms at the back are very nice with the added bonus that you escape the noise from *Mondo Taitu* parties over the road. The wi-fi patio, which also hosts the bar-restaurant *Rum Runners*, is a pleasant spot to hang out. $44

Cocomo-on-the-Sea Av "H", at C 6 ☎757 9259, ⓦcocomoonthesea.com; map p.224. Very popular, comfortable four-room B&B in a lovely painted wooden Bocatorian house, where you'll be well looked after. Two rooms face the ocean but all have access to a waterside veranda plus free use of kayaks. Advance credit-card booking a must. Substantial breakfast included. $94

Gran Hotel Bahía C 3, at Av "A" ☎757 9626, ⓦghbahia.com; map p.224. You're definitely paying more for this 1905 hotel's history than its facilities or service (though refurbished rooms have a/c, cable TV and wi-fi) and the impressive former headquarters of the United Fruit Company is steeped in it. Hang out on the fabulous first-floor wooden veranda and splash out the extra $17 for the larger, brighter rooms upstairs. Breakfast included. $80

Hotel Angela Av "H", between C 5 & C 6 ☎757 9813, ⓦhotelangela.com; map p.224. Popular, friendly hotel offering good value in twelve clean and functional en-suite rooms, accommodating two to four people, with a/c and orthopaedic mattresses. The complimentary breakfast is a treat to be enjoyed on the waterside bar-restaurant terrace, which at other times dishes up succulent Caribbean seafood. $52

Hotel Bocas del Toro C 1, between Av "C" & Av "D" ☎757 9771, ⓦhotelbocasdeltoro.com; map p.224. Excellent, well-managed hotel in the centre of town. Attractive polished wood abounds and the eleven rooms are elegantly furnished (also with a/c, cable TV, wi-fi), some with stunning ocean-view balconies. The restaurant deck overlooks the water at the back. The hotel also organizes tours, rents out kayaks and offers massage. $142

Hotel del Parque C 2 ☎757 9008; map p.224. This warm, family-run place has a balcony overlooking the main square and a quieter hammock-hung one at the back. The cool, homely rooms (for 1–4 people) include cable TV, wi-fi, good hot-water showers and a/c (or fan) and use of a small kitchen. $50

Lula's B&B Av "H", at C 6 ☎757 9057, ⓦlulabb.com; map p.224. Professional B&B offering half a dozen spotless rooms (2 doubles, 4 triples) with private bathroom, a/c or fan, hot water and wi-fi, with a spacious communal balcony and a book exchange. The triples in particular are excellent value at $88). $66

Residencial Dos Palmas Av Sur, at C 5 ☎757 9906, ⓔresidencialdospalmas@yahoo.com; map p.224. On the quieter southern tip of town in a residential area, this locally owned lodging offers the best budget over-the-water deal, with a handful of faded but tidy rooms (a/c, cable TV and hot water) plus a terrace with hammocks and chairs from which to watch the sun set. $35

Tropical Suites C 1, at Av "D" ☎757 9081, ⓦbocastropical.com; map p.224. Aparthotel with helpful staff and sixteen well-equipped suites; particularly good value for families, these comprise a kitchen, one large double bed and pull-out double sofa bed, with a jacuzzi bath and wi-fi. Amenities include a laundry room, a good terrace restaurant and a marina complete with water slide from which to shoot into the sea. Reasonable weekly (one free night) and excellent monthly rates ($80/night), when it's worth paying the extra for the sea view. Breakfast included. $195

HOSTELS

Bocas Surf School Hostel Av Norte & C 6 ☎6852 5291, ⓦbocassurfschool.com; map p.224. Lovely converted wooden Bocatoreño house accommodating eleven travellers sharing two bathrooms, a kitchen and deck over the water at the back. Rooms are small but the bunks are ample with decent mattresses. Great for budget solo travellers who don't want a party hostel. Dorms $20

★**Hostal de Hansi** C 2, at Av "D" ☎757 9932; map p.224. Immaculately clean and tidy, catering to couples and single travellers on a budget who want to avoid the dorm party scene. Fan-ventilated singles (private or shared bathroom) and en-suite doubles have use of a communal kitchen. Singles $13, doubles $25

Hostel Heike C 3, between Av Central & Av "E" ☎757 9708, ⓦhostelheike.com; map p.224. The town's largest hostel offers packed dorms with fans (or a/c) and lockers, sharing spotless, hot-water bathrooms. The communal kitchen, balcony overlooking the main street, internet and purified water on tap make it a popular hangout. Rates include a DIY pancake breakfast. Dorms $10, doubles $22

Mar y Iguana Feria del Mar ☎6047 2413, ⓦmareiguanahostel.com; map p.224. Just across from a rather tatty beach, this mellow hostel north of Bocas Town comprises a handful of small private en-suite rooms and one dorm, all with a/c, set around a small garden – where there's room for a few tents – with a two-tier *rancho* for reading and relaxing and a good, moderately priced bar-restaurant. Camping $7/person, dorms $12, doubles $35

Mondo Taitu Av "G", between C 4 & C 5 ☎757 9425, ⓦmondotaitu.com; map p.224. Legendary, hip hostel whose daily happy hour and several themed party nights ensure the tiny cocktail bar is piled high with bodies. Not the place to stay if you want some sleep, but it is great for hooking up with other travellers. All rooms and dormitory

6

6

accommodation (fan or a/c for $2 more) share hot-water bathrooms, plus there's a communal kitchen, unlimited filtered water and free pancake breakfast. Dorms $\overline{\$11}$, doubles $\overline{\$28}$

REST OF THE ISLAND

Bahía del Sol Saigon Bay ⓦ bocasbahiadelsol.com; map p.224. Situated in a local community, a 15min walk from town, overlooking the water towards the mainland, this cosy guesthouse offers a range of rooms and prices from affordable rustic comfort (in the adjoining *Casa Rosada*) to rustic luxury. The most sought-after suite boasts an ocean veranda with open-air jacuzzi and shower. Wonderful sunsets, scrumptious breakfasts (included in the rate) and gracious hosts make this place a treat. $\overline{\$80}$

Cabañas Estefany Boca del Drago ☎ 6155 0104 ⓦ cabanasestefany.com; map p.222. On the plus side the location is lovely: by the sea amid coconut palms, a 15min walk from Playa Estrella, and has appealing, brightly painted simple *cabañas*. For the moment it's the only place to stay in Boca del Drago but since the bus stops there, you get people trekking to and from the beach at weekends. Food may be an issue too: being Italian run there's plenty of pasta on the menu (main $8–10); otherwise there's only *Yarisnori* nearby (see p.222) and a small outdoor kitchen for use. Overall, rates are high for what you get. Dorms $\overline{\$20}$, doubles $\overline{\$55}$

Caribbean Cabañas Saigoncito Saigon ☎ 6446 0787, ⓦ panamasparadise.com; map p.224. A collection of nicely renovated traditional wooden houses on stilts and balconies in lush gardens; it's in a residential area 5min from Bocas Town centre, so bike rental is included to help you get about. Some rooms can be rented separately or together as a whole cabin; others are *cabañas* with fully equipped kitchens. All are fan-ventilated, with hot water, wi-fi and cable TV. Good weekly rates. $\overline{\$55}$

Playa Bluff Lodge B&B Playa Bluff ☎ 6798 8507, ⓦ playablufflodge.com; map p.222. Set back in forest midway along the beach road, this highly recommended lodge has five spacious, cool fan-ventilated rooms with private or shared bathroom, all with terraces, in verdant surroundings brimming with wildlife, and only a stone's throw from the beach. $\overline{\$109}$

★Tesoro Escondido Playa Bluff ☎ 6749 7435, ⓦ bocastesoroescondido.com; map p.222. Delightful eco-friendly resort that generates its own wind and solar power as well as harvesting rainwater. A handful of rustic rooms, a couple of cottages and a small apartment (sleeping 2–4) are set amid lush tropical forest up on the cliff or down near the beach with plenty of terrace and porch space. Rooms and cabins are simply yet quirkily furnished with artwork from recycled items; mosquito nets are provided. You can self-cater in the communal kitchens or enjoy home cooking at reasonable rates. Good weekly or monthly discounts in low season. $\overline{\$44}$

EATING

Bocas has an excellent range of **restaurants**, with vegetarians enjoying a decent selection. Lobster, conch and other local seasonal specialities taste particularly delicious in local coconut milk and Caribbean spice preparations. **Opening hours** can be erratic, especially in low season, and service seriously soporific. **Tap water** here is not safe to drink.

BOCAS TOWN

Alberto's Pizzeria C 5, between Av "E" & Av "F" ☎ 756 9066; map p.224. This relaxing spot away from the party scene serves excellent thin-crust pizza and pasta dishes ($9–14) as well as real cappuccino or espresso. Since the place lacks ambience, order a takeaway. Mon–Sat 11am–3pm & 5–11pm.

★Bocas Blended C 1, at Av "E", by Tropical Markets; map p.224. Unmistakeable converted sky-blue bus dishing up tasty breakfasts and delectable salads and wraps filled with fresh ingredients at modest prices ($5–7), as well as smoothies. You can take away or "eat in", and take advantage of "wrappy hour" and excellent-value lunch combos. There's wi-fi too. The best table in the house is on the bus roof. 8am–10pm; closed Sat.

Breakfast Bagels La Mana, Av "G" between C 4 & 5, next to Casa Max; map p.224. This place serves decent coffee and fruit salad but the real draw is the large variety of bagels (from $4), to be enjoyed on a raised wooden deck. Service is generally slow. Mon–Sat 8am–1pm.

Lemongrass Bistro C 1, between Av "C" & Av "D" ☎ 757 9630; map p.224. More boutique than bistro, but you can't argue with the food. The creative menu of predominantly Thai cuisine, served in a delightfully airy upstairs balcony, changes daily. Often puts on live music (especially Fri). Mains $11–14. Daily 11am–10pm.

★Om Café C 3, between Av "A" & Av "B" ☎ 6624 0898; map p.224. The Canadian–Indian owner draws from traditional family recipes, dishing out excellent curries (mains $11–14), as well as juices and lassis, on a pleasant upstairs balcony. The eggs vindaloo *roti* wrap will set your day off with a blast, or choose from bagels and bowls of fruit, granola and yoghurt. 8am–noon, 6–10pm; closed Wed & Thurs.

Restaurante La Casbah Av "H", at C 4 ☎ 7547 9885; map p.224. An intimate, vibey restaurant offering freshly prepared and tasty Mediterranean cuisine though prices have been creeping up. Daily 6–10pm.

Restaurante Chitré C 3, between Av "C" & "D"; map p.224. Probably the best hot sauce and fried chicken in town: tuck into traditional staples for under $4 and watch the world go by from one of the patio tables. Mon–Sat 6am–9pm, Sun 10am–9pm.

★**Restaurante Guari-Guari** 2km from town centre along the isthmus, near the petrol station ☎6627 1825, ⓦbocasdeltoro.travel/guari-guari; map p.224. Gourmet prix-fixe, five-course meal ($23) and some of the most innovative dishes in Panama, exquisitely prepared by a Spanish chef. Served in intimate open-air surroundings, this is the place for a special night out. Reservations essential. Cash only. Daily 6–10pm.

El Último Refugio Av Sur, between C 4 & C 5 ☎6726 9851, ⓦultimorefugio.com; map p.224. West-facing waterfront venue affording the best sunset views in Bocas and an interesting, daily changing menu (mains $11–13) and fine cocktails. Mon–Fri 6–10pm.

REST OF THE ISLAND

Paki Point Playa Paunch ☎6948 6562; map p.222. Ideally situated to capture weary cyclists and tired surfers, this unashamedly touristy open-air bar-restaurant satisfies all. With decent comfort food – burgers (the jalapeño one is a favourite), *ceviche* and fresh fish – great music, vibrant artwork and a vast wooden deck strewn with sun loungers that spill onto the sand, you can watch the surfers, soak up the rays, or slide into oblivion with a cocktail. Live DJs on "Siesta Saturdays". Daily 11am–6.30pm.

Yarisnori On the beach, Boca del Drago ☎6615 5580; map p.222. This mellow open-air restaurant plum on the beach is the longest established of the casual seafood places along this stretch of coastline. Enjoy succulent snapper, mahi-mahi or grouper in garlic or creole sauce from around $10 up to $25 plus for lobster. Daily 9am–6pm.

DRINKING AND NIGHTLIFE

There are plenty of **bars** on the waterfront in Bocas, where you can relax with a chilled Balboa or cocktail and several places to dance at weekends. For more seafront partying, you can head across to Isla Carenero's *Aqua Lodge* (see p.232).

El Barco Hundido C 1, beside Cable & Wireless; map p.224. Fondly known as the "Wreck Deck" both for the illuminated shipwreck by the dancefloor and the late-night state of its clientele, this legendary hangout has DJs most nights, playing everything from Latin through reggae to pop and rock. In high season the "Barco Loco" heads out for the sunset booze cruise round 5pm. 7pm–late (gets lively after 10pm); closed Wed.

★**La Iguana Surf Club** C 1, at Av "D" ☎757 9812; map p.224. Refurbished and back in action, this popular nightspot is a mellow hangout with heavy doses of reggae (but salsa and rock too); also with live bands and DJs at weekends plus great cocktails to linger over on the waterside deck. 9pm–4am; closed Wed & Sat.

Mondo Taitu Av "G", between C 4 & 5 ☎757 9425; map p.224. Tiny bar attached to the groovy hostel bursting at the seams with exuberant backpackers, who

come for the daily happy hour (7–8pm) and lethal cocktails, plus wild, themed party nights. Daily 7pm–midnight, sometimes later.

Paradaze Labs 9 Degrees Ocean Terrace, Tropical Markets ☎6480 1757, ⓦfacebook.com/paradazelabs; map p.224. Several times a year, *Paradaze Labs* brings in big-name national and international artists for mega *electrónica* parties that pull in huge crowds. Held on an open deck over the water, it's the place to be. Tickets $5–15, with cheaper tickets for advance purchase. Events 8pm–4am.

The Wine Bar C 3, between Av "B" & Av "C" ☎6686 1736; map p.224. A mellow hangout to enjoy a selection of good wines and conversation, either lounging on comfy sofas inside under ambient lighting, or out on the veranda watching folk drift past below. The service is friendly and efficient and the lite-bites-cum-tapas hit the spot. Mon–Sat 6–11pm.

Isla Carenero

A short water-taxi ride from Bocas Town, **Isla Carenero** presents a 2km sliver of low-lying land surrounded by shallow waters and a thin necklace of beach that periodically dissolves into mud, tangled roots and, round the northeastern end, jagged rocks, where one of the archipelago's best **surf breaks** pounds the reef. Most of the four hundred occupants are squeezed onto the southwestern tip, in makeshift wooden housing on littered and boggy ground. The main reason to base yourself on Carenero, rather than in busier Old Bank or Bocas, is to stay over water you can swim in or right on the beach. That needs to be weighed against the island's vicious sandflies and the fact that there's not much to do or see; most visitors hop across for a day-trip for a drink, a bite to eat or just a change of scene.

ARRIVAL AND DEPARTURE

ISLA CARENERO

By water-taxi Isla Carenero is a 5min water-taxi ride ($1) from the dock beside *El Barco Hundido* in Bocas Town.

6

ACCOMMODATION AND EATING

Aqua Lounge Hostel Southwest side of island ⓦ bocasaqualounge.info. Friendly over-the-water party venue with its own swimming pool carved out of the deck, swings and a water trampoline. You've a choice of fan-ventilated private rooms for two, three or five people ($14/person) with shared bathrooms, cramped, hot dorms, or you can bag a hammock, though you'll need a mosquito net. Don't expect any sleep on party nights (Wed & Sat), nor any water left for a shower the next day. Dorms $12, doubles $28

Bibi's on the Beach Buccaneer Resort, southeast side of island ☏ 757 9137. Popular tourist and expat watering hole built over the water with great Caribbean views. It serves up fresh seafood – try the *ceviche* with passion fruit – and refreshing cocktails. Daily 7am–9pm.

★ **Casa Acuario** Southeast side of island ☏ 757 9565, ⓦ casaacuario.com. This delightful wooden structure built over the water, has five spacious rooms (fan, a/c and cable TV) with vast windows. The best ones at the front have their own hammock and deckchairs and there's a wraparound deck and communal kitchen-dining area, ideal for lolling about on. $88

★ **Hostal Gran Kahuna** Southeast side of island ☏ 757 9038, ⓦ grankahunabocas.com. Right on the beach, this is a solid budget option, attempting green practices, with four dorms containing lockers and surfboard storage space, and two private en-suite rooms – all with a/c at night and great mattresses. Nice garden and social area to chill in, with comfy sofas and hammocks facing the sea. Also a moderately priced bar-restaurant and kayaks and SUPs for rent. Dorms $14, doubles $55

Isla Bastimentos

The sprawling and beautiful 52 square kilometres of **ISLA BASTIMENTOS** boasts the mellow, Afro-Antillean fishing community of **Old Bank**, lush inland **forest** inhabited by strawberry poison dart frogs and marble-sand **surfing beaches**. Most visitors are day-trippers: some come independently to tuck into tasty Creole seafood in Old Bank or to hike across the island to the surfing beaches; others visit with organized tours, which generally cut across the western arm of the island to the much vaunted Red Frog Beach. If you want to escape the unashamedly tourist-oriented scene in Bocas, Bastimentos is a good place to hang out and the place where you're most likely to hear Guari-Guari, English patois embellished with Spanish and Ngäbere.

The island's two Ngäbe communities of **Bahía Honda**, in the crook of the bay of the same name on the island's south side, and **Quebrada Sal** (Salt Creek), over towards the eastern end by Punta Vieja, both welcome visitors.

Old Bank (Bastimentos Town)

Old Bank, the island's main settlement of around nine hundred, sits on the westernmost point, a quick hop by water-taxi from Bocas. An undulating, cracked concrete path acts as its main thoroughfare, snaking its way between tightly packed houses built out over the water on stilts, past reggaeton beats, discarded bikes and old men slamming down dominoes and up to a steep, green hillside dotted with some precariously built wooden homes. A jungle **path**, occasionally impassable after heavy rains, leads to several glorious beaches twenty minutes away on the other side of the island (see below).

The beaches

Renowned for riptides that claim lives every year, the sea that pounds the northern **beaches** of Bastimentos is often too dangerous to swim in, but the beaches are lovely to walk along, offering curved broad belts of creamy sand backed by palms and thick vegetation. Heading along the overland path from Old Bank (see box, p.227), you pass **Playa Wizard** (Playa Primera) after fifteen to twenty minutes, and, further east, Playa Segunda, and then **Red Frog Beach**, though you won't find its namesake waving to you from a beach towel (see box, p.233). A short hike further east brings you to **Playa Polo**, a smaller, sheltered cove protected by a reef and good for snorkelling though it can get busy. Even further east lies another surfing stretch of sand, **Playa Larga** (see p.235).

If you're planning a whole day at the beach, take enough water with you though there are a couple of restaurants on Red Frog Beach.

STRAWBERRY POISON DART FROGS

Probably Bastimentos' most famous residents, the dazzling **strawberry poison dart frogs** (*oophaga pumilio*), no larger than a thumbnail, are actually widespread along the Caribbean lowlands from Nicaragua to western Panama. But nowhere is their colouration and size – "morphs" as they are termed – as varied as here. That said, the place you're least likely to spot these amphibians, ironically, is on Red Frog Beach as local kids have captured many to impress tourists and charge for photos. Don't touch the frogs, whatever the kids may urge, both for the obvious reasons of animal welfare, but also since the poison can get into the bloodstream if you have a cut or abrasion, though it won't kill you.

The most commonly sighted poison dart frog is the smart "blue-jeans" morph, whose brilliant scarlet torso fades into cobalt blue or purple legs, though on Bastimentos these seductive amphibians span red, orange, gold, green or even white, and are often speckled with black. The "poison dart" title given to the family derived from the likes of the Colombian golden poison frog (*phyllobates terriblis*) that secretes a particularly lethal toxin – sufficient to kill up to twenty people – and which has traditionally been used by the Chocó (ancestors of the present-day Emberá) to coat darts and arrows for hunting.

While the dazzling colouration aimed at alerting would-be predators to the poison beneath their skin is what most attracts tourists to these fluorescent creatures, their behaviour is equally striking. Extremely territorial, male dart frogs can be seen locked in combat among the leaf-litter like miniature wrestlers, comically teetering on their hind legs trying to pin their opponent down in submission with the front legs. Mating occurs at any time of year and after the small clutch of eggs has been laid and fertilized, the male periodically pees on them to keep them moist. Once hatched, the female gives each tadpole a piggy-back ride, one by one, up to the canopy, depositing them in separate water-filled bromeliads. Over the next few weeks, she returns frequently to deposit unfertilized eggs in the water for the tadpoles to feed on as they mature.

Bahía Honda

Community tourism project ☎ 6726 0968 (ask for Rutilio Milton), ⓦ timorogo.org • Excursion $13 plus $4 cave entry • They can collect you from Bocas Town

The 25 or so thatched homes of the dispersed Ngäbe community of **Bahía Honda** are hidden among a dense tangle of mangroves at the eastern end of the bay of the same name, with a few across the water on Isla Solarte. In addition to a chapel and primary school, they have a restaurant, the heart of the **community tourism project** – whose star attraction is a guided excursion up the **Sendero del Peresoso** (Trail of the Sloth) to the Cueva Nivida. You'll be paddled up a nearby creek, where you can often see the trail's namesake furled round a branch and crabs and caimans in the shallows, before heading off on foot through forest that was once a cocoa plantation, to wade through a series of caves thick with stalagmites and coated with several species of Bastimentos bats. If you ring a day in advance, you can stop off at the community restaurant on the way back (see above).

Cayo Crawl

At the southern tip of Bastimentos amid a myriad of mangrove islets lies tiny **Cayo Crawl**, where three thatched restaurants do a roaring trade in seafood lunches (see p.235). After rounding the point, you come to the gorgeous soft coral fields of the same name, which feature on many day-trips.

Quebrada Sal

$22/person plus $5 community fee • $1 guide • ☎ 6155 0614, ⓦ aliatur.bocasdeltoro.org

On Bastimentos's southeast coast close to Punta Vieja, the Ngäbe community of **Quebrada Sal** (Salt Creek) is seeing an increasing number of day-trippers, generally from the lodges around that end of the island, but now offers basic accommodation in the village. The surrounding wetlands and nearby Playa Larga – part of the marine park

6

CULTURAL ECO-TOURISM IN BOCAS DEL TORO

Several **Ngäbe communities** in the province have initiated cultural **eco-tourism** projects to supplement their subsistence livelihood: Bahía Honda and Quebrada Sal (Salt Creek) on Bastimentos, Sandubidi on Isla Popa and Silico Creek and Río Oeste Arriba on the mainland are all trying to attract visitors. The less well-known and less numerous **Naso**, too, are also active in community-based tourism (see p.242). While several day tours from Bocas Town now include communities in some of their itineraries, you learn and experience much more by staying overnight (see p.227, p.233, p.237 & p.238). In addition to the obvious interest of being able to interact with the Ngäbe (or Naso) and learn about their culture, the communities often offer traditional dishes, crafts for sale and guided walks into the rainforest, with good wildlife-spotting opportunities and the chance to learn about medicinal plants. With some of the mainland communities, you can undertake more strenuous hiking.

Details of how to contact the communities directly, and therefore ensure that all your money goes directly to them, are to be found in English and Spanish on the Red de Turismo Comunitario Bocas del Toro website ⓦ redtucombo.bocasdeltoro.org.

that occupies a swathe of the island (see opposite) – can be explored via several trails during your stay, which also provides a chance to learn about medicinal plants and other aspects of Ngäbe culture.

ARRIVAL AND GETTING AROUND ISLA BASTIMENTOS

BY WATER-TAXI

To Old Bank Old Bank is a 10min ($3) ride by water-taxi with Boteros Bastimentos from their jetty on C 3 at Av "C", Bocas Town.

To Red Frog Beach Jampan Tours, C 3 at Av "B", runs a regular service at set times to a marina on the south side of Bastimentos ($4 one way, $7 return), from where it's a 10min walk (or 3min shuttle) across the island to the beach. There's a controversial $3 landing fee imposed by developers, which

ostensibly goes towards maintaining the path across the island. To avoid the fee, you can take the beach path from Old Bank though be mindful of security issues (see box, p.227).

REACHING THE NGÄBE COMMUNITIES

If you want to visit one of the Ngäbe communities and are struggling to make your own arrangements, contact the Bocas del Toro Community Tourism Network (ⓦ redtucombo .bocasdeltoro.org).

ACCOMMODATION

The handful of lodgings in Old Bank are budget-oriented and attract those wanting to experience the "real" Bocas, who need to be prepared to be lulled to sleep by ear-splitting music on occasions. They are all to be found along, or just off, the cement path that winds through the village. The all-inclusive eco-lodges elsewhere on the island (also listed) offer a more back-to-nature and luxurious experience.

OLD BANK

Caribbean View Hotel ☎ 757 9442, ⓦ hotelcaribbean view.bocas.com. Impressive two-storey structure stretching over the water containing eleven neat, compact rooms (with fan or a/c, TV and hot-water bathrooms), some with private balconies. A friendly, locally run establishment, it has a pleasant restaurant-lounge deck serving predominantly Creole seafood dishes (mains $9–14). Takes cards. **$55**

★ **Hostal Bastimentos** ☎ 757 9053. A friendly maze of a backpackers' hostel spread over the hillside behind town, offering everything from dorms to basic doubles with shared facilities ($15) and fancier en-suite bedrooms with a/c, hot water, fridge and private balcony, plus great views. Has two communal kitchens, bags of hammock space and a mellow vibe. Dorms **$8**, doubles **$20**

Pensión Tío Tom ☎ 757 9831, ⓦ tiotomsguesthouse .com. Long-standing wooden inn built over water in the thick of things (so can be noisy), with simple, clean en-suite rooms (fan and mosquito net) and a mellow over-the-water hammock deck at the back. Inexpensive food is served family style. **$32**

Rafael's House ☎ 6446 0787, ⓦ panamasparadise.com. Beautifully renovated, two-bedroom Caribbean house with fully fitted kitchen, living room and balconies front and back, one overlooking the meanderings along the main street, the other the sea. Rooms can be rented separately though the bathroom is shared. Doubles **$45**, whole house **$132**

THE REST OF THE ISLAND

★ **Al Natural** Punta Vieja ☎ 757 9004, ⓦ alnatural resort.com. Beautiful, isolated spot with half a dozen single or double-decker palm-thatched huts that open onto the sea. Decorated with hewn driftwood, and using solar-powered fans and showers (which don't always deliver), the simple bungalows have comfy beds with netting. Delicious meals are served in the bar-restaurant area, with games and reading room plus an observation deck on the upper storeys. Rates include transfer from Bocas, meals (including wine and beer), use of kayaks and snorkel gear with moderately priced excursions extra. The superior bungalows are well worth the extra $50. $239

Casa Cayuco Punta Vieja US ☎ 248 631 4112, ⓦ casacayuco.com. A three-storey lodge and five lovely raised wooden cabins (for 2–6 people) with private balconies to lounge on are tucked away in the rainforest just off the beach. Rates include transport to the lodge, communal fine dining, and use of kayaks, SUPs, boogie boards and even a sailing dinghy. $325

★ **La Loma Jungle Lodge** Bahía Honda ☎ 6619 5364, ⓦ thejunglelodge.com. On a hilltop surrounded by lush rainforest, only reachable by boat, this working cocoa farm offers four very private airy Ngäbe-style *ranchos* at incredibly modest prices. Rates include transfer, meals, a tour of the farm, trip to Red Frog Beach and use of *cayucos*, with plenty of sailing, surfing, hiking and excursions on offer for an extra fee. Gourmet cuisine, much derived from the lodge's organic garden, makes this very popular so book ahead. Some of the accommodation costs go to support the Bahía Honda community development fund. $110/person

★ **Palmar Tent Lodge** Red Frog Beach ☎ 6880 8640, ⓦ palmartentlodge.com. Simple yet delightful private safari tents and tent-cabin dorms (two-night min stay for all) set in rainforest at the back of the beach with solar-powered fans, lamps and showers plus an array of amenities, including a bar-restaurant and kayak rental. Camping (own tent) $10/person, dorms $15, doubles $50

EATING AND NIGHTLIFE

Most eating options in Bastimentos are low-key, with local flavourings at locally affordable prices. You're likely to find traditional Caribbean dishes such as *rondón*, a fish and vegetable stew in coconut milk, or *pescado "Escobich"*, a spicy marinaded fish dish.

OLD BANK AND AROUND

Alvin's Tasty, simple home cooking out over the water; choose from that ubiquitous Panamanian staple fried chicken, rice and beans to more Caribbean-style seafood dishes accompanied by coconut rice and plantains. Daily 8am–7pm.

Blue Bar Fully renovated in 2013, the island's legendary Blue Mondays hotspot has reopened delivering loud sounds, cheap booze, a chance to play pool, and plenty of vibe. If you're lucky you may catch the island's most famous musicians, the Bastimentos Beach Boys. Hours vary.

Roots A Bastimentos institution that serves up cracking fresh seafood and coconut rice dishes ($4–10). Just follow the music and you can't miss it. Noon–9.30pm; closed Tues.

Up in the Hill Signposted up the hill from Old Bank (20min walk) ☎ 6607 8962, ⓦ upinthehill.com. Well

worth the hike, this organic snack and craft shop offers fresh lemonade, delectable brownies and numerous other goodies ($3–5) on a patio surrounded by flowers. From town, follow the path near the police station and continue through the jungle, keeping watch for markers. Mon–Sat 8.30am–6pm.

THE REST OF THE ISLAND

Community restaurant Bahía Honda ☎ 6726 0968. A great place to sample some traditional cuisine, such as *morongodo*, a green plantain pancake. A plate of fish and *patacones* costs around $6. Call for hours.

Restaurante Cayo Crawl The original and still the best of the appealing wooden restaurants on stilts over the water. Catering to day-trippers to Cayo Crawl, this place serves up simple fresh fish dishes at a Caribbean pace, which you can tuck into while watching other fish swimming below. Daily 11am–5pm.

Parque Nacional Marino Isla Bastimentos

$10 entry, generally collected by a warden on Cayos Zapatillas or Playa Larga

One of the archipelago's major attractions is the **Parque Nacional Marino Bastimentos**. The 130 square kilometres of boomerang-shaped reserve sweep across a central swathe of Isla Bastimentos and include a chunk of the northern coastline, dominated by the 6km **Playa Larga**, an important nesting site for hawksbill, leatherback and green **turtles** (March–Sept). There's a park office here, and a basic refuge where you can camp; you'll need to stay overnight if you want to see the turtles lay their eggs (see box, p.236).

Cayos Zapatillas

Southeast of Isla Bastimentos, but still within the park boundary, are the **Cayos Zapatillas** (Little Shoes), so named because they resemble a pair of footprints in the sea. The two dreamy, coral-fringed islands, encircled by powdery white sand, offer snorkelling off the beach, where you'll find more and larger fish than in Cayo Crawl. The main reef is exposed to the ocean, often with strong currents and choppy water. An ANAM officer will usually find you to collect the entry fee. On the prettier northern island, camping is also possible with permission from ANAM in Bocas Town, where you can watch the stars and share the sand with nesting turtles.

ARRIVAL AND ACCOMMODATION

By tour or boat The easiest way to visit is with a tour operator (see box, p.227 & box, p.228) on a day-trip (though the park fee is always additional to the price) or by contracting a boat. If the latter, arrange for an early start to miss the tour groups at Laguna Bocatorito and Cayo Crawl.
Camping To camp ($10) at the Playa Larga refuge or

PARQUE NACIONAL ISLA BASTIMENTOS

on Cayos Zapatillas you will need permission from ANAM in Bocas Town (see p.227); if you arrive between March and July, ANAM is likely to refer you to the Endangered Wildlife Trust (see box below) since the refuge will be occupied by conservation volunteers, though you could overnight in more comfort at Quebrada Sal (see p.233).

MARINE TURTLE CONSERVATION

One of the most poignant scenes in the natural world is the laborious nesting process of the female **turtle** as she drags herself up the beach beyond the high tide mark, excavating a hole with her flippers, before depositing fifty to two hundred eggs, their sex later determined by the temperature of the sand. After around sixty days, usually under cover of darkness, the hatchlings break out from their shells en masse and scuttle down to the sea, unless they become disoriented by lights or emerge in daylight and are picked off by sea birds. Each egg has less than a one in a thousand chance of reaching maturity.

Of the five species of turtle found in the country, four are known to nest along the beaches of Bocas del Toro. Historically the **hawksbill** (*eretmochelys caretta*) and **green turtle** (*chelonian mydas*) reproduced prolifically on the province's sands but over the last fifty years, as eggs were overharvested and adults killed for their meat and shells, the populations were decimated – though significant numbers of hawksbill still nest on Islas Zapatillas (May–Sept). The 29km expanse of Playa Chiriquí, which lines the Golfo de los Mosquitos, east of the Peninsula Valiente, is the most important rookery in all Central America for gigantic **leatherbacks** (*dermochelys coricea*). Measuring around 1.5m on average and weighing half a ton, these leviathans dig seven thousand nests annually (March–June). In contrast, there are scarcely any records of **loggerheads** (*caretta caretta*) nesting in Bocas, though they can occasionally be spotted here swimming in the archipelago's shallows.

VOLUNTEERING

For the last few years, ANAM has been working together with various national and international bodies monitoring and tagging turtles and patrolling beaches. The main beaches involved are Playa Larga and Cayos Zapatillas, Playa Chiriquí in the Comarca Ngäbe-Buglé and Playa Soropta in the Humedales de San San Pond Sak. Volunteers are needed to help with the work and a week is the minimum period for volunteering (March–July); visit the Endangered Wildlife Trust next to ANAM (☎757 9962, ✉turtlevolpanama@yahoo.com).

TURTLE-WATCHING TOURS

ANABOCA (☎6553 6556, ⊛anaboca.org), a community tourism organization leads two turtle watches per evening (9pm & 10.30pm) in the breeding season (April–Sept) on Playa Bluff. The cost is $15/person for the two-hour tour, though transport from Bocas is not included. Tickets should be purchased in advance from their office in Bocas on C 2 and Av "G" (upstairs).

While watching turtles can be a captivating experience, bear in mind that female turtles can easily be spooked into not depositing their eggs. Avoid bright clothes and try to go when there is a good moon, so as not to be tempted to use a torch (unless infrared), leave your camera behind and maintain a respectful distance from the turtle.

Isla Solarte

Other islands in the archipelago are far less frequently visited and far less populated, though some of the scattered Ngäbe communities are now opening up to visitors through community-based tourism projects.

Sheltered in the leeward crook of Isla Bastimentos, thin, hilly **ISLA SOLARTE** is surrounded by tranquil waters. Its most famous feature, **Hospital Point**, at its northwestern tip, was the location of a hospital built by the United Fruit Company in 1900 during the banana boom to quarantine malaria and yellow-fever sufferers. The point is now one the most popular dive and snorkel spots, at the end of many day-trip itineraries, with a healthy reef of cauliflower and brain coral and an impressive wall full of tropical fish, shelving off a pencil-thin strip of beach.

Solarte, also known as Cayo Nancy, a corruption of "nance", the cherry-sized yellow fruit much in evidence on the island, is home to a Ngäbe village of around 250, which has a school and even a football field. Most of the villagers live from fishing and subsistence agriculture.

6

ARRIVAL AND DEPARTURE   ISLA SOLARTE

By water-taxi A 10min ride from Bocas ($5) will get you to Hospital Point on Isla Solarte.

Isla Popa

Just off the southern tip of Isla Bastimentos lies the archipelago's second-largest land mass, **Isla Popa**, home to five Ngäbe fishing communities and the only island where you can spot toucans. The northern village of **Sandubidi** (Popa 2) has a community-based tourism project that offers walks along a trail with a local guide. Nearby, on the island's northeastern tip, you'll find several thin sandy **beaches** leading off into coral-filled shallows and acres of **rainforest**.

ARRIVAL AND ACCOMMODATION   ISLA POPA

By water-taxi Isla Popa is a 1hr journey by water-taxi from Bocas Town.

Popa Paradise Beach Resort Northeastern tip of the island ☎ 6550 2505, ⓦ popaparadisebeachresort.com. The acclaimed luxury resort is spread over substantial grounds; as well as the nine *casitas* and three suites, there are five more economical lodge rooms (all things being relative) though restaurant and excursion costs remain

pricey. All meals included plus transport from Bocas for a three-night or more stay. $424

Sandubidi community project ☎ 6761 5818, ⓦ meringobe.bocasdeltoro.org. A breezy hilltop wood-and-thatch *cabaña* with a fan and a bathroom provides accommodation for overnight guests, while the restaurant serves simple dishes of fried fish, *patacones* or fried yuca with coconut rice. $20

Mainland Bocas

Mainland Bocas covers the vast majority of the province, yet its imperious jagged peaks clad in virgin forest, boggy wetlands and powerful rivers are ignored by most visitors. True, the three mainland towns of **Chiriquí Grande**, **Almirante** and **Changuinola** have little to offer the visitor, but the **Humedales de San San Pond Sak**, home to countless aquatic birds and the endangered manatee, and the spectacular wilderness **Parque Internacional La Amistad** are definitely worth the effort to reach. The two main obstacles to exploring the region – accessibility and lack of infrastructure – have helped preserve the province's natural heritage and the indigenous Bri-Bri, Naso and Bokota populations' livelihoods are now under threat from various hydroelectric projects (see box, p.242).

6

Chiriquí Grande to Almirante

From the village of Chiriquí, 14km east of David on the Interamericana, a spectacular road passes over the Fortuna hydroelectric dam, cresting the continental divide that marks the entry into Bocas del Toro before descending to the small town of **Chiriquí Grande**, the Atlantic terminus of the Trans-Panama Oil Pipeline. The road then hugs the crinkled coastline for 60km to the port of Almirante, before continuing to the main provincial town, Changuinola, a mere 17km from the Costa Rican border.

In contrast, virtually no visitors venture east of Chiriquí Grande, into the increasingly deforested **Comarca Ngäbe-Buglé**, where rivers cut through the Caribbean slopes of the Cordillera Central, flowing into the Golfo de los Mosquitos, backed by the 29km Playa Chiriquí, home to a major turtle conservation programme (see box, p.236).

Silico Creek

Km 25, Punta Peña • Community tourism ☎ 6233 8706, ⓦ urari.org

Between Chiriquí Grande and Almirante, on the border of the Comarca Ngäbe-Buglé, lies the Ngäbe community of **Silico Creek**, a dynamic village that has successfully retained traditional values while adapting to the modern economy. Though day-visits are common, you can also stay in the community's thatched *cabañas* ($15/person) or even arrange a homestay ($10/person), giving you more time to learn about the community's organic permaculture projects in coffee, plantains, banana, yuca and, most successfully, cocoa. In addition to cocoa tours ($10/person), you can hike through the rainforest to a waterfall (4–6hr; $15/person), or undertake a whole-day trek to visit an indigenous organic farm ($30/person).

Almirante

The ramshackle town of **Almirante**, its rusting tin-roofed wooden houses propped up on stilts over the Caribbean, is the departure point for **water-taxis** to the Bocas del Toro archipelago. Like Bocas, the port is a product of the banana boom, and suffered a similar decline. Unlike Bocas, there is no tourism-fuelled renaissance on the horizon. Basic services are lacking; unemployment and its associated ills are a major concern; most visitors pass through as quickly as possible.

ARRIVAL AND DEPARTURE
CHIRIQUÍ GRANDE TO ALMIRANTE

BY BUS

To Silico Creek David–Changuinola buses pass through Silico Creek (2hr 30min–3hr from David; 30–40min from Almirante; 1–1hr 30min from Changuinola).

To Almirante Through buses from Panama City, David or Changuinola will drop you at the intersection ("La Ye"), on the main road, from where it's a short, shared-taxi ride ($1/person) to the dock. Buses stopping at Almirante go to the town's small bus terminal, just after the water-taxi stop.

To David or Panama City Regular buses from Changuinola to David stop at Almirante every 25min (3.45am–7.30pm; 4–4hr 30min); there are two daily buses to Panama City (8.30am, 7.30pm; 10hr; $23).

BY MINIBUS

Minibuses career between Almirante and Changuinola (every 20–25min, 6am–10pm; 30min), where you can get connections for the border.

BY WATER-TAXI

Two companies run water-taxis to Bocas Town with little to choose between them. Bocas Marine Tours (☎ 758 4085, ⓦ bocasmarinetours.com) and Expreso Taxi 25 (☎ 758 3498) both charge $6 with boats leaving every 30min (6am–6.30pm). Find out when the next departure is from both companies before committing and watch out for touts, who will offer to carry your luggage and book your ticket for a fee, and may try to dissuade you from checking out the competition by claiming the office is closed.

BY CAR, BIKE OR MOTORBIKE

If you're coming by car to Almirante, you can leave it in a secure compound at nearby Leiza's ($3/day). Anyone wanting to take a bike or motorcycle across will need to head for the car ferry dock and get the *Palanga* (☎ 391 1754, ⓦ ferrybocas.com), which makes one very slow crossing a day (Tues–Sun 8am, returning at 4pm; $3 bicycle; $10 motorbike; $25/car plus $2/passenger).

Changuinola

Twenty-nine kilometres west of Almirante and only 17km from the Costa Rica border sits the hot, dusty town of **CHANGUINOLA**, Panama's most important banana centre. Surrounded by flat, drained wetlands, a patchwork of plantations and pastureland, this bustling, unattractive town of around fifty thousand possesses little of interest to the visitor but provides a launch pad for trips to the Humedales de San San Pond Sak or Parque International La Amistad. It is also the best place to stay if you've missed the last water-taxi to Bocas or are too late to make the Costa Rican border.

Most of the action in town occurs along the congested **Avenida 17 de Abril**, whose crowded central pavements overflowing with cheap goods soon give way to broken, potholed ground. The road runs north–south but cut through east to the parallel street and you can glimpse rusting carriages in railway sidings and disused tracks, the last vestiges of what was once an impressive rail network built by the United Fruit Company extending along the coast back to Almirante and well into Costa Rica.

6

ARRIVAL AND INFORMATION

CHANGUINOLA

BY PLANE

The airport lies just northeast of the town centre. Air Panama operates daily flights to and from Panama City (1hr; $133) and flights to David on Tues, Thurs & Sun ($84).

BY BUS

Terminal Urracá On the northern end of the main street, Av 17 de Abril, this terminal serves the long-distance buses between Panama City and David. Tranceibosa (☎758 8455) has two daily departures for Panama City, leaving at 7.30am and 6pm (11hr; $29). They fill up fast, so buy tickets as early as possible. Buses to and from David are much more frequent (every 25min, 5.30am–7pm; 4hr 30min–5hr).

SINCOTAVECOP bus terminal Set back from the main street this terminal serves all local destinations: Almirante (every 20–25min, 6am–10pm; 30min); El Silencio on the Río Teribe (every 20min, 6.30am–8pm; 25min); and Guabito (take the Las Tablas bus every 20min, 5.30am–7.30pm; 30min). The daily bus to San José, Costa Rica, operated by Transporte Bocatoreño in San José (☎2758 8511), also leaves here at 10am (6hr; $16); pay on the bus.

BY COLECTIVO OR TAXI

Colectivos and private taxis ($8) run to and from the Costa Rican border at Guabito.

INFORMATION

Immigration The immigration office (☎758 6533; Mon–Fri 8.30am–3.30pm) is on Av 17 de Abril at Calle de El Puré.

ANAM office The ANAM office (☎758 6603) is several blocks west of Av 17 de Abril (see map opposite).

Humedales de San San Pond Sak (6km), ▲ Costa Rica (Guabito) (17km) & Las Tablas

CHANGUINOLA

0   100
metres

Airport

■ ACCOMMODATION
Hotel Alhambra   2
Hotel Golden Sahara   1
Hotel Semiramis   3

● RESTAURANTS
Restaurante Cotty's   2
Restaurante Ebony   3
Restaurante La Fortuna 1

AV OMAR TORRIJOS

AV 17 DE ABRIL

Urracá
Bus Terminal

ANAM (100m)

Police

Bus
Terminal

CALLE CENTRAL

N

CALLE DE EL PURÉ

Immigration

El Silencio (8km) ▼ & Almirante (29km)

6

ACCOMMODATION

There are several functional hotels on the main street, Avenida 17 de Abril, mainly serving business travellers. All suffer periodic lapses in water and electricity supply.

Hotel Alhambra Av 17 de Abril ☎758 9819. Probably the best value in town but quality varies, though all are clean with a/c, hot water and cable TV. Those at the back overlook a graveyard and are much quieter. $25
Hotel Golden Sahara Av 17 de Abril ☎758 7478. This place has 28 reasonably modern rooms (a/c, cable TV, hot water), though some lack windows. Service is friendly. $32
Hotel Semiramis Av 17 de Abril ☎758 6006. Probably the most upmarket place to stay in town (though that's not saying much) with tiled a/c rooms, cable TV and bathrooms with decent hot-water showers. $33

EATING

Restaurante Cotty's Av 17 de Abril ☎6483 5565. Mounds of cheap noodles and rice dishes with indeterminate accompaniments in this small cafeteria, at rock-bottom rates Daily 7am–11pm.
Restaurante Ebony Av 17 de Abril ☎6547 6600. Chock-full of Bob Marley memorabilia, inflatable sharks and balsawood birds, this popular Afro–Antillean restaurant delivers when it comes to Caribbean cuisine though prices are high for Changuinola. Daily 11am–11pm.
★**Restaurante La Fortuna** Av 17 de Abril ☎758 9395. Very popular Chinese restaurant next to the *Golden Sahara* offering friendly, efficient service and good value in a/c comfort. The wide-ranging menu has several veggie options and set menus. Choose a sizzling hotplate dish with first-rate chips. Daily 11.30am–10.30pm.

Humedales de San San Pond Sak

At the bridge over the Río San San • Visit by appointment • $5 admission charge, payable to ANAM

One of the premier natural attractions of mainland Bocas is the **Humedales de San San Pond Sak** (with numerous variant spellings), which encompass over 160 square kilometres of coastal wetlands stretching from the Costa Rican border, past Changuinola, to the Bahía de Almirante. Only a small section of the reserve is accessible to visitors but its mix of seasonally flooded swampy forests, dense mangroves and peat bogs makes for a magical boat trip, especially at first light when the prolific birdlife – 160 species at the current tally – is at its most active.

As you glide along the river, keep an eye out for caimans and river otters lurking in the waters. A dawn visit will also heighten your chances of spotting the wetlands' most celebrated inhabitant, the shy, endangered **manatee** (see box below); though there are now an estimated 150–200 in the area, they remain fairly elusive except when banana

THE WEST INDIAN MANATEE

Occasionally called a "sea cow", the **West Indian manatee** (*trichechus manatus*) resembles a cross between a sea lion, a hippo and an elephant, its barrel-like greyish-brown body propelled by two flippers and a spatula tail, its large snout equipped with a prehensile upper lip that helps it feed. Adults average 3m in length though can reach 4.5m, including tail, and weigh in at 200–600 kilos; to sustain such a size, they have to spend 6–8 hours a day munching floating or submerged greenery. When not feeding, they often rest, floating like large logs on or below the surface, frequently surfacing to breathe. Moving easily between freshwater and marine environments, the shy yet playful mammals are surprisingly agile, and can exceed 25km/h for short bursts. In Panama, the vast majority of these aquatic behemoths inhabit the wetlands of Bocas del Toro, though in 1964 a small number were relocated to Lago Gatún by the Americans in a failed attempt to tackle the rampant spread of water hyacinth in the canal. Though lacking natural predators, manatees are threatened by **human activity**, experiencing collisions with motorboats and getting tangled up in fishing nets or canal locks, while suffering from loss or pollution of habitat. What's more, since they only give birth to a single calf every three to five years, it takes a long time to boost numbers.

leaves are provided at the viewing platforms when tour boats enter the reserve. The river eventually fills out into a coastal lagoon before emptying into the sea, its progress blocked by a sandbank, on which the poorly maintained **ANAM refuge** is located. Behind the hut lies a long stretch of beach, where hawksbill, leatherback and green turtles nest.

ARRIVAL AND TOURS

By bus Tours leave from the AAMVECONA office by the road bridge on the Río San San, 6km northwest of Changuinola, on the road to the Costa Rica border. Take the Guabito–Las Tablas bus (see p.239), getting off at the bridge, or take a taxi ($6).

Wetlands tours To visit the wetlands you can either go with a Bocas tour operator (see p.227) or with AAMVECONA (☎6679 7238, ⓦaamvecona.com), who manage activities here. The most popular excursion is the manatee tour ($45/person), which gives you several hours gliding through the wetlands by boat, with great birdwatching opportunities, in addition to waiting for,

HUMEDALES DE SAN SAN POND SAK

and, with luck, watching manatees feeding. Arrange to go early in the morning and be prepared to cover up well and/or douse yourself with repellent as the sandflies on the viewing platform are vicious.

Birdwatching A walking birdwatching tour is also offered ($25/person), and, in the season (March–July) evening excursions (8pm) are organized to watch leatherback turtles nesting ($10/person for a minimum of 6 people). You can stay overnight in the rudimentary and rather unappealing bunkhouse at the far end of the lagoon ($12), where turtle conservation volunteers lodge but you'd need to take all your food or arrange to have meals prepared.

Parque Internacional La Amistad

Divided equally between Panama and Costa Rica, the remote **Parque Internacional La Amistad** (International Friendship Park), often abbreviated to PILA or Amistad, covers a vast 4000 square kilometres of the rugged Talamanca massif, with a topography and biodiversity unmatched in Central America. Precipitous volcanic tors clad in prolific cloud forest, containing the greatest density of quetzals in the world, plunge into deep ravines, providing Panama's most dramatic mountain scenery.

From the treeless *páramo* of Cerro Fábrega (3336m), the park's highest peak, to the Caribbean rainforests only 40m above sea level, the park encompasses an incredible range of **flora** and **fauna**, including many endemics and endangered species. All five of Panama's resident cat species prowl the forests while the soaring canopy contains impressive specimens of ceiba, almendro and cedar, home to endangered harpy and crested eagles and great green macaws. A crucial link in the "biological corridor" of protected areas running the length of Central America, it is now under threat from agricultural incursions, illicit timber extraction and poaching, but most of all from the ill-considered hydroelectric projects under way. As well as imperilling the area's unique biodiversity, the projects are threatening numerous indigenous communities.

Given the park's remoteness and the ruggedness of the terrain, any **visit to Amistad** proper is a major undertaking, to be made with a good guide, suitable hiking and camping gear, a readiness for rain (over 5m tip down annually in places), and therefore mud, plus a spirit of adventure. Most visitors content themselves with a trip organized through one of the Naso communities dotted along the banks of the Río Teribe (see p.242), in the buffer zone of the **Reserva Forestal de Palo Seco**, a haven for colourful butterflies, dazzling birdlife, and a host of other wildlife.

The Naso villages

The **Naso**, boasting Central America's last remaining monarch, are one of the country's least numerous indigenous groups, whose recently history has been particularly troubled (see box, p.242). As well as inhabiting the park, they also live on the San San and Yorkin rivers and around Changuinola, where, seeking further schooling and employment, many have abandoned their traditional lifestyles. Those that have remained generally inhabit wooden houses built on stilts covered in thatch or

6

occasionally zinc, practising animal husbandry and subsistence agriculture supplemented by fishing and hunting. Though the spiritual heart of the Naso lies in their ancestral lands high up the headlands of the Teribe, the present-day capital is **Sieyik**, the largest Naso community, its five hundred inhabitants dispersed over a pleasant hillside overlooking the river, around ninety minutes upriver from Changuinola. In the grassy clearing at the centre of the village stand a medical centre, primary school and the unremarkable **royal palace**.

Three communities are involved in **eco-tourism** projects, which give visitors the chance to learn about medicinal plants, Naso history and culture, hike in the rainforest, make and travel on a traditional bamboo raft (balsa), and visit the capital, Seiyik. The Naso are warm and welcoming and the spectacular **river trips** set against the brooding backdrop of the Talamanca range alone make a visit worthwhile, though to do the place and the people justice you should plan at least a two-night stay. Among the many pernicious effects of the recent controversial hydroelectric dam (see box below) communities now suffer from periodic daytime noise – the grinding engines of construction trucks or buses transporting workers to and from the dam. Once on the WEKSO trail or up in Sieyik, traffic disturbance is thankfully absent, as it is at night.

COMMUNITY TOURS   THE NASO VILLAGES

General information Lodgings are basic: rudimentary wooden beds with mosquito nets, sporadic water and you'll need a torch as there's no electricity. Meals consist of simple traditional dishes made from local organic produce. The main expense for the trip is the fuel needed to power a dugout against a strong current. The communities are 45min–1hr 15min (depending on conditions) upriver by boat from El Silencio. To reach the Naso jetty (*embarcadero*) on the Río Teribe at El Silencio take the regular bus (every 20min, 6.30am–8pm; 25min)

from the main bus station in Changuinola. Contact details for all three are also on the Bocas del Toro community tourism website (w redtucombo.bocasdeltoro.org). Note also that web price details are not up to date, so enquire before you go. A national **park** fee ($5) is also generally collected for ANAM even though most excursions stay within the buffer zone.

ODESEN WEKSO ☏ 6569 2844 (Adolfo Villagra), w odesen.bocasdeltoro.org. The original Naso community organization, located at WEKSO, the former site

---

THE NASO KINGDOM

When the Spanish arrived in the region, the **Naso** (or Teribe) were both numerous and widespread, but centuries of conflict with the conquistadors and other tribes decimated their numbers, which declined further in the early twentieth century due to tuberculosis. Of the remaining 3500 Naso, around a third have been assimilated into the dominant Latin culture, living and working in Changuinola, while the rest mostly inhabit settlements along the Río San San and Río Teribe. Teribe is believed to be a corruption of "Tjër Di", meaning water of Tjër, the grandmotherly guardian spirit of the Naso, one of the more tangible traces of a sorely eroded culture. Since the Naso language is not taught at school, only an estimated twenty percent still know how to speak it, with Spanish often the preferred language even in the villages, though the Naso legends and colourful characters that populate them are still widely recited.

The more immediate threat to the Naso lies in the form of a hydroelectric dam under construction upstream on the Río Bonyik, a tributary of the Teribe, which has ripped the kingdom apart. In 2004, the reigning monarch, **Tito Santana**, approved the project without proper consultation, for which he was deposed and chased into exile. His uncle, **Valentín Santana**, who took over, garnered the support of national and international environmentalists and human rights groups in a battle to stop the dam and safeguard their ancestral lands and livelihood. However, as the Panamanian government refused to recognize his authority, the Naso were forced to elect a new king – Alexis – from the Santana dynasty in 2011. Since he too failed either to stand up to the hydroelectric company or make any progress with the Naso's long-standing petition to establish their own *comarca*, he too has now been ousted. As the dam nears completion and a second project is in the pipeline, time is running out for the Naso.

of General Manuel Noriega's Pana-Jungla training camp. Accommodation is offered in a simple new balconied wooden lodge set back from the main camp, surrounded by forest, with a communal dining area on the hilltop overlooking the river. Rates are inclusive of meals, transport from El Silencio, a trip to Seiyik and the WEKSO trail. If you're very fit and adventurous, a multi-day guided hike into the mountains to Palenque, the former royal seat of the Naso, is a possibility.

OCEN Bonyik ✆6569 3869 (Raúl Quintero), �🌐ocen .bocas.com. Splinter group from ODESEN, across the river from WEKSO, so nearer the new road. Guests are lodged in several traditional balconied wooden houses. Guided hikes range from 4–12hr; bring snacks and make sure you have a water bottle (with purification tablets advisable). Costs are à la carte (accommodation $15; three meals $13; return boat from El Silencio to Bonjik, or Bonyik to Seiyik $70; hikes $25–30).

Soposo Rainforest Adventures Soposo ✆6875 8125, 🌐soposo.com. The best advertised and most patronized project was set up by a US–Naso couple, and is well organized and very professional. They offer pleasant wooden cabins with porches, lit by solar lanterns, and have pricier rates: $90/person for a day-trip; $140 for a two-day tour, $275/person for a three-day tour, inclusive of lodging, meals, transport from Changuinola and a range of excursions. If travelling from Bocas, you can be met at Almirante provided you meet the additional transport costs.

Guabito and the Costa Rica border

From Changuinola, the road runs 17km to the border with Costa Rica at **Guabito–Sixaola**, where, on the Panamanian side, there is little more than a handful of shops. It's a short walk from **immigration** across the old railway bridge to Costa Rica (an hour behind Panama time), where you can change currency in the town of **Sixaola**.

ARRIVAL AND INFORMATION

GUABITO AND THE COSTA RICA BORDER

Getting to the border To reach the border from Changuinola, take a *colectivo* or private taxi ($8) hanging around the bus terminal, or, if you're in no hurry, the lumbering bus marked for Las Tablas (every 20min, 5.30am–7pm; 30min).

Onward travel in Costa Rica After getting an exit stamp at Panamanian immigration (8am–5.45pm; ✆759 7019), cross the border bridge to Costa Rican immigration (same hours though note the hour's time difference) in Sixaola. There you can catch a through-bus to San José (6am, 8am, 10am, 3pm) or to Puerto Viejo in southeastern Costa Rica (hourly; 90min).

Arriving from Costa Rica You will need an exit stamp from Costa Rican immigration before crossing the bridge to Panamanian immigration, where you may be asked to show proof of onward travel and the ability to support yourself financially. Once through immigration, head down the steps to wait for the bus to Changuinola, from where you can catch buses to other destinations in Panama. The bus may well have "Las Tablas" on the windscreen whichever direction it's headed, so be sure to check with the driver. Alternatively, cross back under the bridge to find a taxi. The rate for a private taxi is $8 to Changuinola or around $20 to Almirante; a shared taxi to Almirante is $5/person.

Immigration office The immigration office is located on the railway bridge (daily 8am–5.45pm; ✆759 7019).

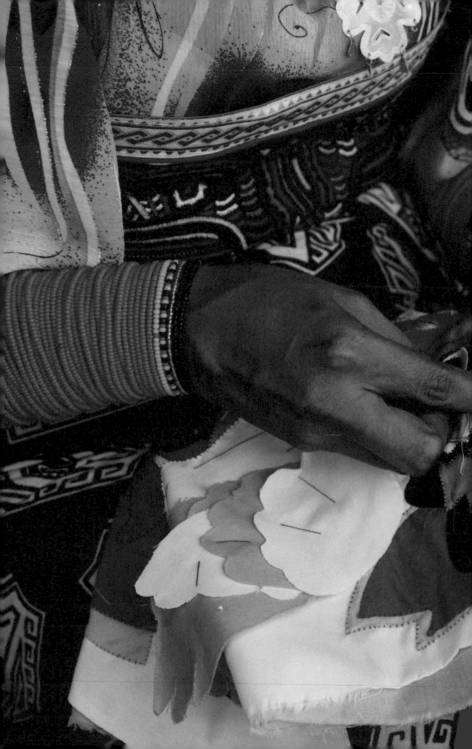

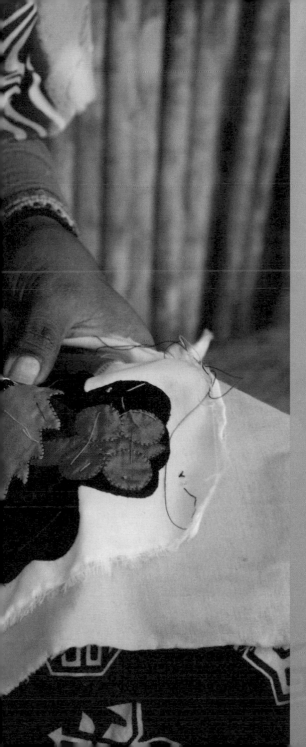

Guna Yala

MOLA MAKING, CARTI YANDUP

Guna Yala

A Guna woman in traditional attire – hair bound in a scarlet headscarf, colourful blouse tucked into a sarong-like patterned skirt, her forearms and calves bound with intricate beadwork and her nose pierced with a golden ring – is a sight that has launched a thousand travel brochures. Yet the Guna's relationship with tourism remains ambivalent, and their suspicion of outsiders (*uagmala*) and determination to ensure that tourism is conducted on their terms has been borne of bitter experience. This can make a trip to Guna Yala fairly challenging, though the benefits more than outweigh any frustrations or inconveniences. A visit is an opportunity to engage with an evolving, unique indigenous culture, to experience village life first-hand, to loll on heavenly white-sand islands and to explore the little-visited, rainforested mainland.

The Guna (pronounced "Kuna") – or the Dule (pronounced "Tule"), as they call themselves – are Panama's most high-profile indigenous people. They inhabit a vast semi-autonomous region (or **comarca**) along the eastern Caribbean coast, which stretches some 375km from the Gólfo de San Blas to Puerto Obaldía and comprises almost four hundred islands and a swathe of land whose limits extend to the peaks of the serranías de San Blas and the Darién. Around 33,000 Guna live within the Comarca de Guna Yala, with a further 47,000 predominantly spread among two smaller inland *comarcas* in eastern Panama and Panama City. For the most part the population is packed onto a chain of 36 low-lying coral outcrops close to the shore, with eleven communities established on the coast and two further inland.

The waters of the western archipelago, in particular, are sprinkled with near-deserted **cays** covered in coconut palms, surrounded by dazzling **beaches** that shelve into turquoise waters, whose coral reefs provide great opportunities for **snorkelling** (diving is prohibited across the *comarca*). Trips to the luxuriantly rainforested mainland are equally magical, whether gliding upriver in a dugout, visiting a Guna burial ground, or seeking out the spectacular birdlife. These attributes make Guna Yala a wonderfully idyllic location for a holiday, but to appreciate its unique nature, engaging with **Guna culture** in all its variations, complexities and contradictions is essential.

There are basically two types of islands of interest to the visitor. The palm-topped **deserted islands**, surrounded by white-sand beaches, are predominantly distinguished by their accommodation, ranging from simple cane *cabañas* to more comfortable rustic lodges, all owned by particular families or communities from the more densely populated **village-islands**. Chock-full of cane and thatch buildings interspersed to varying degrees with cement structures – schools, medical centres and the occasional shop – these overcrowded coral outcrops generally lack beaches. To the casual visitor, they are very much alike: jetties hold tethered dugouts and traditional over-the-water toilets, with litter often floating among the pilings, while sandy streets gravitate towards the centre, where meeting and *chicha* houses (see box, p.264) and the basketball court

ISLAND LIFE

Highlights

❶ Guna island-villages Experience a compelling mix of tradition and modernity in crowded communities such as Carti Sugdup or Ailigandi, taking in the meeting and *chicha* houses and museum. **See p.255** & **p.265**

❷ Blissful islands Camp out in a thatched *cabaña*, laze in a hammock or float in the turquoise shallows of the palm-topped white-sand islands of western Guna Yala – choose from Isla Perro, Naranjo Chico or Wailidup. **See p.257** & **p.258**

❸ Cayos Holandéses and Coco-Bandero Marvel at a marine wonderland of corals and tropical fish, the archipelago's best snorkelling. **See p.260**

❹ Río Azúcar Head upriver by dugout along one of the archipelago's loveliest rivers, cutting through plantations and forests brimming with birdlife. **See p.262**

❺ Isla Tigre Stay in the fascinating home of the Guna dance, one of the few remaining communities that still practises community-based traditions. **See p.262**

❻ Armila A very different Guna village on the forested mainland at the far southeastern end of the *comarca*, where you can explore the jungle by dugout and watch leatherback turtles nesting. **See p.268**

HIGHLIGHTS ARE MARKED ON THE MAP ON PP.248–249

stand out. Only by spending several nights in different places will you begin to appreciate the subtle differences between communities.

You've over 365 islands to choose from – one for every day of the year, as some Guna will remind you – most with two names (one in Dulegaya or Guna, one in Spanish) and a handful with the same name. However, the fact that only 36 support villages, and many are conveniently arranged in identifiable **clusters**, simplifies planning. During one visit most visitors are satisfied to explore just one.

The islands in the **western area** of the archipelago are the most popular, possessing the greatest sprinkling of tiny Robinson Crusoe-style islands and the best snorkelling,

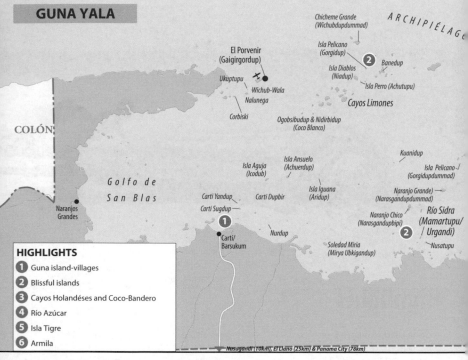

GUNA YALA

HIGHLIGHTS

1. Guna island-villages
2. Blissful islands
3. Cayos Holandéses and Coco-Bandero
4. Río Azúcar
5. Isla Tigre
6. Armila

GUNA YALA (CONTINUED)

as well as more accommodation options. Moreover, they – together with a handful of islands in the **central region** are generally more geared up for tourism. However, visitor numbers in this part of the archipelago have shot up in the last few years, putting great strain on the natural resources, and sometimes on Guna–tourist relations. This is mainly due to improvements in the only road link with the *comarca*, which makes it only a three-hour drive from Panama City. Visiting the more isolated **eastern islands**, you are likely to experience greater cultural engagement with the Guna – provided you can speak Spanish – since you may well be the only outsiders there.

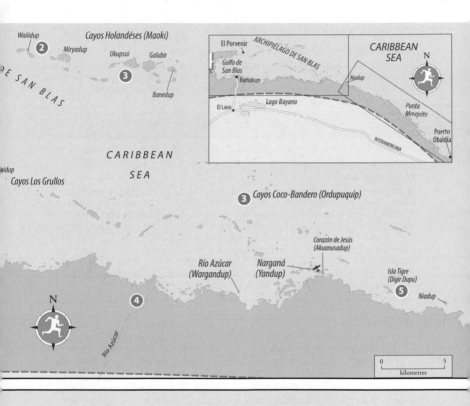

7

GUNA YALA ESSENTIALS

WHEN TO GO

Peak tourist season in Guna Yala, as elsewhere in Panama, is the **dry season** (mid-Dec to April) though for some of the period, you'll suffer from the trade winds (Dec–Feb/March), which whip up the waters, impairing snorkelling and leaving the outer islands inaccessible. Late March and April are more appealing times to visit, although water levels can be low on the mainland, restricting river trips. The **wet season** lasts from May to mid-Dec; in the early months, from May to July, the unbearable humidity from the lack of breeze is balanced by a sea that can be millpond-still – perfect for snorkelling, except during the afternoon downpours, when run-off muddies the waters. June to October spells the season for *chocosanos*, terrifying electric tempests that generate monstrous waves capable of flooding an island and dashing a ship onto a reef in an instant.

WHAT TO TAKE

A mosquito net may be a good idea, together with lashings of repellent, sun cream, a basic first-aid kit and a torch and/or candles since there is limited or no electricity on some islands. Some kind of waterproof protection, such as a plastic bin liner, is desirable to protect your gear from getting soaked in the boat, and you may want a breathable waterproof for yourself. In budget accommodation it's a good idea to take some snacks with you, as meal portions are often small. It's not advisable to drink tap water in Guna Yala. Some hotels provide purified water for guests at meals; most charge. Bottled water is on sale in most islands, but is very expensive and its disposal an environmental headache; using a water filter or purifying tablets (see p.41) is preferable.

TAXES AND MONEY

At the entrance to the *comarca* at Nusugandi, all non-Guna have to pay a **tourist tax** ($10 for foreigners), which is not included in transport costs. In addition, you will have to pay $2 at the dock. In addition, visitors generally have to pay a **community tax** ($1–14 on the island villages, $2–5 on near-deserted beach islands), even if only stopping there for half an hour – these costs are usually not included in tour packages (see box, p.252). There's only one **bank** (with ATM) in the *comarca* and it's in Narganá, so you need to take all the cash you might need with you, in small denominations. Some of the more expensive lodges accept online credit-card payments for the basic package but extras – drinks, community taxes, extra tours, snorkel hire, etc – will need to be paid in cash.

Brief history

Guna oral history traces their origins to the Sierra Nevada de Santa Marta of present-day Colombia. Fleeing from tribes such as the Emberá, they took refuge in the mountainous areas of the **Darién**, including Mount Tacarcuna – the highest peak in eastern Panama (1874m), lying just outside the *comarca* – which became a sacred place in folklore. Violent conflict ensued against the Spanish, with the Guna often forming unlikely alliances with English and French pirates, and gradually being forced towards the Caribbean. Though Guna had visited the coast for many years, colonization of the **islands** they inhabit today did not start until the mid-nineteenth century as they sought greater access to passing traders and escape from disease-carrying insects on the mainland.

Panamanian independence

Geographical isolation ensured the Guna were pretty much left alone until **Panamanian independence** in 1903, when the new state refused to recognize the **Comarca Dulenega**, which had been established by Colombia in 1870. It covered Guna territories straddling the two countries and had guaranteed a certain measure of independence.

The Revolución Dule

Tension between the **Guna Congress** and Panamanian authorities escalated as the latter granted concessions to outsiders to plunder resources in Guna territory and persistently attempted to suppress Guna culture – banning women's traditional attire or force-feeding communities with missionaries and colonial schooling. Matters came to a head in 1925, when a gathering of Guna leaders on Ailigandi resolved to declare independence and rose up in what is proudly commemorated as the **Revolución Dule** (Guna Revolution). Around forty people lost their lives, and only the intervention of the US – concerned for the safety of the canal – prevented further government reprisals. A settlement was finally reached in 1938, when the Guna agreed to recognize Panamanian sovereignty in exchange for a clearly defined *comarca* and a high degree of political autonomy.

ARRIVAL AND DEPARTURE   GUNA YALA

Most visitors, and the Guna themselves, bound for the western or even some of the central islands, now travel from Panama City by road, which connects with the western end of the *comarca*, and then transfer to a boat on arrival at the coast. The other main means of transport is by light aircraft that leave from Albrook airport. Access by boat is much more limited and unpredictable, with no scheduled services.

BY ROAD

By car It takes around three hours by road from Panama City to the dock at Cartí. Heading east out of Panama City on the Interamericana, the turn-off for Guna Yala is just east of Chepo, where the 40km El Llano–Cartí road crosses the peaks of the Serranía de San Blas to the Caribbean coast. Though now paved, the road is still treacherous as it's incredibly steep, winding, narrow and increasingly potholed, so 4WD is strongly advised. In fact, you will probably be denied entry to the *comarca* unless you are in a 4WD, and even then usually only in the summer months. Vehicle entry fee is $10; you'll then need to pay $3–5/night for parking.

Hostel/hotel transfers Hostels and hotels in Panama City can arrange a pick-up in a 4WD vehicle – $30 one way, plus taxes (see box opposite) – which usually takes four passengers, from your accommodation at around 5am. Drivers will generally stop off at a hypermarket in the outer suburbs of Panama City to allow passengers to stock up on supplies before driving on to Guna Yala.

With a private driver You can also make your own arrangements with the Guna transport organization in Panama City (C 33, Calidonia; ☎ 225 4900; or talk to "Pollo" on ☎ 6500 5376). As well as the usual pre-dawn departures for Cartí, they sometimes have vehicles that leave later in the morning. The rates are the same as those offered by the hostels and hotels.

Onward travel by motorized dugout On arrival at the Cartí or the adjacent Barsukum dock, visitors pile into a collection of waiting motorized dugouts sent by their accommodation to transport them to their island lodgings, a cost included in some deals. If travelling independently without pre-booking any package, it's worth asking the waiting boatmen about vacancies – popular backpacker islands often book up – or ask to get dropped off in Carti Sugdup ($3), a transport hub for neighbouring islands, where you can check out what other transport is leaving that day. Transfer fees vary, from around $20 return to one of the islands round Cartí and Río Sidra to $40 or more if you need to travel further afield. You may be lucky to find a community boat (carrying Guna heading for an island) that can transport you for a cheaper fare.

BY PLANE

Destinations Air Panama (☎ 316 9000, ⓦ airpanama.com) serves seven destinations within the *comarca*. Seats go quickly so book well in advance at the Air Panama office in Albrook airport or on Avenida Balboa (see p.73), especially for Puerto Obaldía. Note that flights into the *comarca* have an 11kg checked luggage allowance. There are daily flights to Achutupu, Corazón de Jesús, El Porvenir and Playón Chico and six times a week to Puerto Obaldía, as well as flights three times a week (Tues, Thur & Sun) to Mulatupo and Ogobsukum. Flights often stop off at more than one destination.

Flight times All flights depart from Albrook airport at 6am – except for the plane for Puerto Obaldía, which leaves mid-morning – though times are prone to change and delays are common so check beforehand. All flights return to Panama City the moment they've dropped off their last passengers, generally around 7–7.30am.

Fares Prices, including taxes, range from $75 (El Porvenir) to $111 (Puerto Obaldía) one way. Most of the airstrips are located on the mainland a few hundred metres from the islands themselves. When organizing return flights from the *comarca*, you can ring Air Panama and book a seat with a credit card, making the payment on arrival at Albrook airport. You can't book flights between islands.

Transfer to your hotel If you have arranged a package tour, there will be a boatman from your accommodation at the airstrip to take you to your destination. This transfer may or may not be included in the tour cost. Independent travellers may be able to catch a ride (for a fee); otherwise other boatmen are usually hanging around with whom you can negotiate a deal.

BY BOAT

The two entry points by sea are El Porvenir, in the northwest, and Puerto Obaldía in the southeastern corner,

7

where you'll almost inevitably be arriving from Colombia (see p.267). Backpackers travelling to and from Colombia by boat from Puerto Lindo or Portobelo usually spend a couple of days in Guna Yala en route (see box, p.25).

From the northwest There are no scheduled ferries, but occasional cargo boats leave Miramar in Colón Province (see p.121), arriving in El Porvenir, where you can usually find boat transport to other places within the *comarca*. Do not try to arrange passage from Coco-Solo port in Colón; though once the main, albeit extremely dangerous, sea route east, it should now be discarded in favour of safer options, though none are without risk given the unpredictability of the sea conditions.

From the southeast Smallish fibreglass motorboats (*lanchas*) head up the coast from Puerto Obaldía to Cartí ($100/person), depending on demand (see p.267), several times a week, and will drop you off at other islands en route. Note that the sea is very rough and dangerous between Puerto Obaldía and Achutupu (especially Dec–March), and the experience is likely to be extremely wet and uncomfortable. Make sure the boat has two engines and life jackets as a minimum, is robust enough to withstand the waves, and preferably has a roof.

PACKAGE STAYS IN GUNA YALA

Given the complexities of travelling independently around the archipelago, the easiest way to visit the region is to go on a **package tour**; in fact most hotels only offer package deals. This is also what the Guna prefer as it affords them greater control over tourist activities. The majority of hotels are aimed at budget travellers, and there's very little mid-range **accommodation**; the nearest luxury accommodation lies 25km west of El Porvenir (⑩corallodge.com). Panama City hostels and hotels can help organize a multi-day trip, or you can make arrangements yourself.

Most packages in the western region include return **transport** by boat from the end of the Cartí road, or the nearby airstrip at El Porvenir; three basic **meals**; rustic accommodation; and a daily **excursion**, usually to a near-deserted (there's usually someone living there to look after the place) palm-fringed island, or a cultural visit to an inhabited island or to the mainland to visit a cemetery (see box, p.259) or a waterfall. Check in advance exactly what's included. There is usually a fuel supplement to visit the Cayos Holandéses, which offer the best snorkelling in the *comarca* but are inaccessible due to rough seas for much of the peak season (Dec–Feb/early March).

On the sandy atolls, all of which are privately owned, **accommodation** is usually provided in simple white cane *cabañas*, with either a thin mattress or a hammock and perhaps somewhere to keep your belongings out of the sand. The often-basic **toilets** (which may have to be flushed with sea water from a bucket) are shared, and **electricity** is not a given; washing may be under overhead **showers**, or may involve a barrel of water and a jug or *calabash* (gourd).

Travellers looking for more **comfort** will find that several lodges in the central area fit the bill, offering cabins with private bathrooms (flush toilets, hand-basins and cold-water showers), often with private balconies, fancier cuisine and English-speaking guides.

At the budget end, **package rates** are generally $25–60 per person per night, but you'll pay $100 or more for more comfortable options. Price changes depend heavily on fuel prices.

TOUR COMPANIES

In theory only Guna-owned companies are entitled to operate within the *comarca* though several others do, including backpacker boats to and from Colombia (see box, p.25). Given the time needed to get to the islands, the three-day tours offered by some outfits are rarely worth the expense and are not listed below – short trips are better organized directly with the lodging involved. Itineraries may change depending on sea conditions.

Expediciones Tropicales (Xtrop) ☎317 1279, ⑩xtrop.com. Excellent sea-kayak tours working with trained Guna guides and communities, camping on deserted tropical islands and with plenty of snorkelling opportunities. Their three-day excursion ($900) is based on Sichirdup (where you'll be the only people staying), while the six-day package ($1,200) takes in several islands. Both trips include return transfer from Panama City by road and boat, including taxes. Two people minimum.

San Blas Sailing ☎314 1800, ⑩sanblassailing .com. Professional and pricey but providing an idyllic way to see the archipelago, offering 3–21-day sailing tours (in French, Spanish and English), generally in western Guna Yala, including kayak or dinghy forays to the mainland. Prices depend on the boat capacity and season – in high season it's cheaper to share ($175/person/day for a monohull, $225/person for a catamaran). Private charters are more expensive. Flights not included.

GETTING AROUND

WITH AN ORGANIZED TOUR

If you are on an organized tour, inter-island transport will be arranged by your hosts. Included in the package will be one or two tours per day to another beach or village-island, or to the mainland (see box opposite). Some lodgings also offer optional excursions for set prices. Generally though, if you want to visit somewhere not on the schedule you will need to pay for another boat and pilot. Cost will depend on the distance, the boat's engine size and quality (see below) and the number of people wanting to do the trip. It will also depend on whether your lodgings have two boats – not all do – although sometimes they manage to stagger timings for pick-ups and drop-offs. If you are staying in a hotel on a populated village-island such as Carti Sugdup, then you have more options for additional boat hire.

INDEPENDENT TRAVEL

Inter-island transport Since there are no fixed itineraries or schedules for boats, you need to ask around about transport heading the way you want to go. This is relatively easy in the populated western region of the *comarca*, and not too difficult if you are heading westwards in the general direction of Cartí from other parts of the region since most islands have frequent boats with Guna bound for Panama City. Transport in such cases is inevitably cheaper than hiring a boat privately. The best places to enquire are the islands' main jetties or fuel depots.

Private boat hire The further east you travel, the less frequent inter-island transport becomes and the more expensive – in part because fuel costs are higher. You are more likely to need to hire a private boat, which is fairly easy (with some Spanish) but you will probably need to cover the fuel costs for the boatman's return trip.

Cartí–Puerto Obaldía There are fairly regular speedboat services between Carti Sugdup and Puerto Obaldía, which leave when they have sufficient passengers to cover the fuel costs ($100/person). Alternatively, contact Andutu in Panama City (Av Justo Arosemena and C 34; ☎ 6060 9104, ⊛ andutu .com); they run trips between Cartí Sugdup and Capurganá in Colombia but can drop you off at Puerto Obaldía and include land transfer form Panama City in their rates.

Types of boat Always check out your boat transport before agreeing to a price since it may be a customary paddled dugout (*ulu* in Guna, *cayuco* in Spanish) for short distances or even a traditional canoe sailboat with a cotton-sheet sail attached to a rough-hewn mast and boom. More often than not, though, transport is in a (sometimes leaking) motorized dugout with a 15HP engine. If staying at one of the more expensive establishments on a package deal, you're likely to travel in a fibre-glass *panga*, or *lancha*, with a bigger engine, possibly with a roof to shade you from the sun. Otherwise, be prepared for hours of exposure to the elements and water leaking over the bow of the boat.

7

Western Guna Yala

Most visitors to Guna Yala stay at the **western end** of the *comarca*. It's more accessible by land, sea and air, with more idyllic islets enclosed in white-sand beaches, better snorkelling and more accommodation, though most is at the basic end of the scale. For independent travellers, there is also more inter-island transport available (see above) and more shops to purchase supplies, though choice is limited and prices high. The downside of greater exposure to tourism, especially in communities that have put up with more than their fair share of insensitive visitors, is that some Guna are understandably jaded with outsiders.

El Porvenir and around

The diminutive, scarcely inhabited island of **El Porvenir** (Gaigirgordup) belies its status as administrative **capital** of Guna Yala and gateway to the western isles at the northwestern extremity of the *comarca*. A sliver of bare land, it barely manages to squeeze on an airstrip. With a handful of buildings, including a police post, hotel, museum and craft shop, plus a clump of palm trees, El Porvenir is merely a transit point for most arrivals, though the water off the island's thin strip of sand is cleaner than the more heavily populated neighbouring islands.

Museo de la Nación Guna

By the airstrip • Daily 8am–5pm, though you may need to ask around to get someone to open up • $2 • ☎ 314 1293

It's worth pausing in El Porvenir to call in at the **Museo de la Nación Guna**, unless you're travelling on to Carti Sugdup, where a privately owned museum covers similar ground.

The exhibition hall displays photos of festivals and numerous ceremonial artefacts such as a necklace of pelican bones worn by the *absoguedi*'s (chanter's) assistant and a headdress decorated with macaw feathers. There's also a model Guna kitchen and a notable collection of basketry and bamboo flutes. Notices are in English, Spanish and Guna.

Wichub-Wala and Ukuptupu

Wichub-Wala is a bustling yet relaxed island that's often visited by cruise ships, hence the proliferation of arts and crafts. In addition to the usual sandy pathways and cane-and-thatch huts there are some decaying cement structures, including a former swimming pool, now full of large tropical fish. To the west, the tiny semi-submerged private coral outcrop of **Ukuptupu** was formerly home to a Smithsonian marine research station until the institute was ejected from the *comarca* in 1998. The islet, on which the accommodation is the only building, provides a mellow hideaway – there's nowhere to stretch your legs, but Wichub-Wala and Nalunega are a stone's throw away.

Nalunega

Just south of Ukuptupu lies **Nalunega**, "the house of the macaw" in Guna, since these brightly coloured birds were resident on the island when it was first colonized. A more appealing village than Wichub-Wala, with a population of around five hundred, it has broader streets dotted with shady trees populated with parrots, while traditional cane-and-thatch buildings rub shoulders with occasional aluminium-topped cement structures. At the centre lie a primary school, the meeting hall and the basketball court.

Nalunega's museum

Signposted off the basketball court • Daily 7am–6pm • $2

Nalunega's **museum** houses an unusual collection that is particularly worthwhile if you have reasonable Spanish. The curator, Teodoro Torres, offers a fascinating narrative of Guna culture illustrated through his woodcarvings and paintings from recycled materials, such as boat sails that have washed up on the beach.

GUNA NAMES AND LANGUAGE

All island communities have a **Guna name**, which often has several variant spellings, and a **Spanish name**. We have generally used the most commonly used name and given the alternative when introducing the place. Matters have been further complicated by the standardization of the Guna alphabet in 2011 in which the letters "p", "t" and "k" were removed – while other consonants were doubled – hence the relatively recent change from Kuna Yala to Guna Yala. Since this standardization has not permeated much of Guna society yet – and certainly not Air Panama's airport listings – we've kept to previous spellings of most place names, except where the community itself is now using the standardized spelling – as in Icodub – to avoid further confusion.

GUNA GLOSSARY

The most essential word to grasp in Dulegaya (Guna language) is the versatile "**nuedi**", meaning "hello", "yes" and "it's good/OK" or "welcome". "Nuegambi", meaning "thank you" is also useful. Other key cultural terms include:

saila – chief;
nele – traditional healer or shaman;
ulu – dugout canoe;
Onmaked Summakaled – Guna General Congress;
onmaked nega – meeting house;
inna nega – chicha house; *neg uan* – burial ground;
Ibeorgun – Guna prophet and religion;

Bab Dummad and *Nan Dummad* – Great Father and Mother, the creators;
Baba Nega – heavenly spirit world;
boni – evil spirits;
nuchu – carved wooden totem to ward off evil spirits;
uaga (*uagmala*) – outsider(s);
absoguedi – chanter.

Ogobsibudub and Nidirbidup

A tiny coral-sand drop in the ocean southeast of El Porvenir, **Ogobsibudub** (**Coco Blanco**) sports a small sandy beach that slides into reef-protected shallow waters. There's better swimming, however, a few hundred metres away on the neighbouring islet of **Nidirbidup** where you can also camp, being ferried over for meals on Ogobsibudub – which makes the place ridiculously crowded in peak season.

ARRIVAL AND DEPARTURE   EL PORVENIR AND AROUND

By plane Daily flights arrive at the El Porvenir airstrip from and to Panama City (25min; $75 one way).

By boat There are no scheduled boat arrivals or departures.

ACCOMMODATION AND EATING

Cabañas Ukuptupu Ukuptupu ☎ 293 8709 or ☎ 6746 5088, ⓦ ukuptupu.com. The friendly owner, Juan Garcia, who speaks good English, and his family are Ukuptupu's only inhabitants. A maze of wooden boardwalks leads between fifteen spacious but simple wooden doubles, each looking out onto the sea, with hammocks on the front deck. Good food is served under a communal central *rancho*, and traditional showers (bucket of water and soap) and toilets (a mix of traditional and flush) are shared. Prices include meals, daily tours (to both a beach and a village) and transfer from Cartí or El Porvenir. $60/person

Cabañas Coco Blanco ☎ 6700 9427 or ☎ 6058 7824, for Ligia, ⓦ cocoblancocabanas.com. Offers six superior sandy-floored cane-and-thatch *cabañas* (sleeping 2–4) with comfy beds and private bathrooms, tapped into the island's septic system. Though possessing more decorative trimmings than most and fabulously positioned on the tiny beach, the *cabañas* are tightly packed. The food is nicely prepared and usually includes lobster or other shellfish, so in the closed season (see box, p.260) the price is reduced ($85/person). Rates include meals, daily tours and transfer from Cartí or El Porvenir. $100/person

Hotel El Porvenir By the airstrip, El Porvenir ☎ 6718 2826, ⓦ hotelporvenir.com. This long-established hotel, offering the only accommodation on the island, is pleasantly situated in grassy grounds with its own veranda bar-restaurant and eleven rather gloomy concrete rooms with tin roof and private cold-water bathrooms. Rates include full board plus two daily excursions to nearby islands. Good discounted package deals available. $70/person

Kuna Niskua Lodge Wichub-Wala ☎ 259 9136 or ☎ 6709 4484. At the time of writing this popular two-storey concrete, cane-and-thatch building plum in the middle of the village was being slowly restored.

The Cartí islands and around

The dirt road connecting Panama City funnels backpackers and day-trippers into the coastal hamlet of Barsukum close to the largely disused Cartí airstrip. Only a coconut's throw away, the **Cartí group of islands**, together with the tiny uninhabited palm-covered retreats of Icodub, Ansuelo and Iguana nearby, inevitably experience the greatest number of tourists in the archipelago. The best recommendation is to stay on one of the smaller islands – Carti Yandup if you want to sample Guna village life, or Icodub for the desert-island experience – and drop by Carti Sugdup during the day to visit the excellent museum, or in the evening if some community event is on.

Carti Sugdup

Close to the mainland, densely populated **Carti Sugdup** forms the stadium-sized hub of this island group and is one of the *comarca*'s busiest communities, with around two thousand inhabitants. Motorized dugouts are constantly coming and going, so it's a good place to seek onward transport, though not a desirable place to spend the night – and the island is a favourite pit stop for cruise ship passengers.

The centre comprises a few large, functional cement buildings, such as a secondary school, medical centre, library and post office, standing amid a maze of cane and thatch. There are a couple of restaurants, and numerous stalls selling soft drinks and snacks testify to the island's popularity with tourists. The large number of people and proliferation of consumer goods has resulted in rubbish collecting in the streets and at the water's edge, and the place should be avoided at all costs when a cruise ship has dropped anchor, as Guna women selling *molas* appear from every doorway and the population almost doubles.

Museo de Cultura y Arte Guna

Centre of the island • Daily 8am–4pm • $3 • ☎ 6691 390

The main reason to visit the island is to learn more about Guna culture at the **Museo de Cultura y Arte Guna**. Stuffed full of artefacts and pictures from floor to ceiling, covering many aspects of Guna culture – *mola* making, funerary rites, traditional medicine, religious beliefs – with some bilingual signage in Spanish and English, the place really comes alive through the informative explanations of the curator, José Davies, who is happier conducting tours in Spanish but can manage some English.

Carti Yandup

A few hundred metres across the water, the pretty village – by the cramped standards of Guna Yala – of **Carti Yandup** has around four hundred inhabitants in a collection of traditional cane-built household compounds, interspersed with flowers and shrubs, with *molas* hanging out for sale.

Icodub

Community tax $5

An archetypal Caribbean picture postcard, with a wide band of sparkling white sand and translucent turquoise waters encircling a carpet of coconut palms, **Icodub** (Isla Aguja) was once the nicest place in the *comarca* to laze in a hammock. However, overdevelopment has rather spoilt the ambience – there's now a large entry gate, a tiled cafeteria-restaurant with music and a cement toilet block with mirrors. All this is aimed at satisfying high-season city day-trippers, who descend on the island in their hundreds armed with giant cool boxes and cover every speck of sand until the mid-afternoon exodus. Kept immaculately tidy despite this influx, the island still holds some appeal outside the holiday crush for its decent beach (with a volleyball court) and pleasant snorkelling.

Aridup and Achuerdup

With their slender necklaces of sand, shallow waters and ground foliage, there's little to choose between **Aridup** (Isla Iguana) and neighbouring **Achuerdup** (Isla Ansuelo), a couple of tiny tropical islets sporting banana trees interspersed among the palms.

Nurdup

Very close to the coast, four families occupy the tiny outcrop of **Nurdup**, welcoming visitors to their simple *cabañas* (see opposite). Provided your Spanish is up to the task, this intimate environment is ideal for deepening your understanding of Guna culture. Although there's no beach, daily trips are arranged to beaches.

ARRIVAL AND DEPARTURE — THE CARTÍ ISLANDS AND AROUND

By boat For independent travellers, there is always transport waiting to transfer passengers to Cartí from the dock (10–20min).

ACCOMMODATION

Cabañas Carti Yandup Carti Yandub ☎ 6537 0416, ⓦ cabanascarti.es.tl. Backpacker favourite providing a friendly environment offering a handful of rooms in and around the family compound. Traditional toilet and shower facilities are shared with the family. It's easy to arrange for some time in the village and a night or two in a hammock on Isla Diablos (see opposite), thus

experiencing both sides of Guna Yala living. $35/person **Cabañas Icodub** Icodub ☎ 6660 7908. Accommodation is in tents (mattress and pillow provided) or in a handful of cane *cabañas*, some en suite, with wind- and solar-powered electricity. Hammocks and deckchairs can be rented for the day and transport is extra, and pricey – $20 return from the mainland, and

$20–40/person for a tour. Rates include meals. Camping in rented tent $40/person, in own tent $10/person, *cabañas* $50/person

Cabañas Iguana Aridup ☎ 6807 2764 or ☎ 6151 7393. A clutch of well-maintained cane-and-thatch huts and a pleasant, small bar-restaurant on a raised wooden deck. There's a volleyball net and ball at your disposal should you tire of beachside torpor. Room rates include tours and meals; boat transfer to the mainland $20. $50/person

★**Cabañas Nurdub** Nurdub ☎ 6803 7033 (Elixto Tejada). Six immaculate cane *cabañas*, though no beach. Excursions are usually to Isla Perro for the day (see below),

or to the beautiful, deserted Piderdup, where you can also choose to camp as part of your stay. Lodgings, meals and excursions included. Boat transfer $10. $60/person

Carti Homestay Carti Sugdub ☎ 6734 3454, ⓦ cartihomestay.info. Run by Eulogio Pérez, who speaks English, this place is more of a hostel, with communal downstairs kitchen-dining area and a few upstairs dorm rooms, somewhat cramped but with comfy mattresses and large windows overlooking the village. You'll only want to stay here if you've arrived late at night or you're waiting for an early departure. Can arrange transport to Colombia. Rates include meals and a daily excursion. $50/person

Cayos Limones

Offering perfect tranquillity (provided you don't coincide with a cruise ship stopover), the gorgeous islands that comprise **Cayos Limones** are clustered east and northeast of El Porvenir. Once dedicated to harvesting coconuts, they now function primarily as prime day-trip destinations At other times, it's worth stopping overnight, allowing you to soak up the stillness by a campfire and admire the sparkling night sky.

Isla Perro and Isla Diablos

Isla Perro (Achutupu, not to be confused with a far more populated namesake further east; $3 community tax) is the most visited of the Cayos Limones, so can be overwhelmed on summer weekends and holiday periods. It offers the best snorkelling round an accessible reef and sunken cargo boat in the narrow channel separating it from adjacent **Isla Diablos** (Niadup), a favourite camping spot for backpackers.

Isla Pelicano

The idyllic, pinprick-size **Isla Pelicano** (Gorgidup) – one of several with the name – is a rewarding snorkelling spot, surrounded by a collar of soft white sand and carpeted with trimmed grass among the all-too-sparse palm trees, which sometimes struggle to provide sufficient shade for all the visitors on high season weekends. The fact that there is no toilet on the island is another reason to avoid peak periods. Hammocks can be rented for the day.

Isla Chicheme Grande

Heading towards the outer perimeter of the archipelago, the large palm-covered island of **Chicheme Grande** (Wichubdupdummad), home to a handful of families, is predominantly another day-trip location, though sailing vessels on the Puerto Lindo/Portobelo–Cartagena route often stop off here for the night. Waves thunder over the protective outlying reef, which prevents rubbish from washing up on the gorgeous beach, and the island's relative size coupled with its isolation engender a more away-from-it-all feel, though it's not really a place for snorkelling.

Wailidup

Tucked away behind a mangrove-fringed islet, **Wailidup** is arguably the nicest place to stay in the area; favoured by passing sailboats, it comprises a windward stretch of alabaster sand and an open grassy patch surrounded by willowy palms – not to mention the rare luxury of a fresh water supply.

ACCOMMODATION   **CAYOS LIMÓNES**

Alojamiento Umberto Burgos Isla Chicheme Grande ☎ 6880 4054. Basic hammock accommodation in a thatched hut, with meals. There are currently no toilet or shower facilities. Hammocks $15/person, camping $20/person

★**Cabañas Wailidup** Wailidup ☎259 9136 or ☎6709 4484, ⓦhosteltrail.com/hostels/kunaniskualodge. Run by the owner of the *Kuna Niskua Lodge* (see p.254), three superior *cabañas* are built on stilts right on the beach with sea-facing balconies, solar-powered electricity and private bathrooms ($95/person), complemented by a bar-restaurant favoured by yachties. Newer, more basic *cabañas* are also available. Room rates given include meals and trips but for $40–45/person less you can bring your own food and pay someone to cook for you. Transfer from Cartí is $40. **$35**/person

Río Sidra and around

Some 15km east of Cartí, just off the mainland, lies **Río Sidra**; formerly a key portal into the archipelago until its airport was closed a few years ago, it is still an important settlement within the *comarca*. Originally two separate islands, the communities of **Urgandi** and **Mamartupu** combined to make Río Sidra – a community of close on two thousand – by reclaiming the land in between. Each retains its own identity, maintaining separate *sailas*, meeting houses and churches – and each charge a community visitors' tax – though they share a school and basketball court, plus the two nearby public pay phones. Facing the town from the main jetty, Urgandi lies to the right, Mamartupu to the left; the main drag, a broad sandy boulevard with a number of grocery stores, bisects both, running the length of the island.

The island is convenient for visiting Nusatupu and Isla Maquina, famous for its *molas*, and is a popular village excursion for the backpacker islands of Senidup and Isla Pelicano. Other scenic diversions in the area include the lovely sandy island of **Bigirdupu** and starfish haven of **Isla Salar**, while the mainland attractions include a boat trip up the **Río Masargandi**, calling in at the cemetery at its mouth, and a trek through luxuriant rainforest to the once-sacred waterfall of Saiba ($15/group), where you can cool off in the delightful freshwater pool at its base.

Nusatupu and Isla Maquina

A small community of around four hundred just across the water from Río Sidra, the unfortunately named **Nusatupu** (Isla Ratón or "Rat Island") does not harbour any more of these rodents than anywhere else – though sandflies are a major nuisance here in winter (May–December). Diminutive nearby **Isla Maquina** (Mormarketupo), whose four-hundred-plus inhabitants are less accustomed to visitors, is known for its fine *molas*.

Isla Pelicano and Senidup

The postage-stamp-sized islands of **Isla Pelicano (Gorgidup)** and **Senidup (Isla Chiquita)**, crowned with coconut palms and fringed with strips of soft sand, are perennial favourites with backpackers at the budget end of budget since they offer the cheapest packages in the *comarca* and stays are easily organized through Panama City hostels. As a result there can often be something of a holiday-camp atmosphere on them. Of the two, Senidup is the slightly larger and better tended, though it's rather cluttered with *cabañas* and there's now an unprepossessing chainlink fence dividing the island. Possible **excursions** from both take in the village of Soledad Miria (Miria Ubigandup), which is noted for fine *molas*, or the glorious white-sand beaches of Naranjo Chico or Pidertupu.

Naranjo Chico

Belying its diminutive tag, **Naranjo Chico** (Narasgandupbipi) is the second-largest island in the area after Naranjo Grande. It is particularly lovely for its distinctive hourglass shape, gorgeous swathe of white-powder sand, off which you can snorkel, and vegetation of coconut palms, shrubs and delightful hibiscus flowers. Several families have now jumped on the tourism bandwagon, erecting cane-and-thatch dwellings, and slinging up hammocks – some cordoning off their patch. Still, with most *cabañas* set back off the sand, nestled in the undergrowth, the nicest stretch of beach remains unspoilt.

GUNA CEMETERIES

One of the most fascinating tours offered by Guna communities is to their traditional Guna **burial ground** (*neg uan*) on the mainland. From afar the cemetery resembles a miniature village, a mass of thatched rooftops, which turn out to be shelters protecting the graves from the rain. Beneath each one is an elongated mound of earth, representing the pregnant belly of Nabguana (Mother Nature) as she gives birth to the deceased in the heavenly spirit world (Baba Nega), as well as everyday utensils, clothing and food, which are left to accompany the deceased on their journey and serve as gifts for relatives who have already passed away.

Before burial the deceased is bathed in aromatic herbs and dressed in their best clothes, their cheeks painted with the natural reddish dye of *achiote*, a colour believed to ward off the evil spirits (*boni*). After villagers have paid their respects, the body is laid to rest in a deep grave in a hammock oriented towards the rising sun in the east, symbolic of the beginning of new life, which is also sometimes alluded to by laying cotton threads – representing the umbilical cord – across the corpse. A dugout tethered nearby is left to carry the deceased to their ancestors.

7

Kuanidup

Approaching the wafting coconut palms of **Kuanidup**, 10km north of Río Sidra, a row of seven smart cane-and-thatch *cabañas* at the edge of the sparkling white sand seemingly stand to attention. Though idyllically located, within striking distance of the Cayos Holandéses, the tear-drop island offers relatively little shade and the beach is small.

ARRIVAL AND GETTING AROUND

By boat Río Sidra is a 50min boat ride ($20) from Cartí. Boat transfers from Cartí to Isla Pelicano and Senidup (50min) generally cost $20. Both islands are around a

RÍO SIDRA AND AROUND

30min boat ride north of Río Sidra. Naranjo Chico is 20min north of Río Sidra by boat, 45min from Cartí, or 55min from El Porvenir.

ACCOMMODATION AND EATING

★**Cabañas Eneida** Naranjo Chico ☎6723 0436. Probably the nicest of the budget lodgings, with decent cane *cabañas*, more serviceable toilets and showers than most, good food and a pleasant beachside dining area. Campers can bring their own tent and food, or do a meal deal for an extra $15. Boat transfer $20. Camping $25/person, *cabañas* $50/person

Cabañas Kuanidup Kuanidup ☎6742 7656 (ask for Sra Petita), ⓦkuanidup.8k.com. Neat and well-kept sandy cane *cabañas* with shared toilet and shower facilities and electricity in the cabins; across the central grassy area there's a bar and a couple of open-sided restaurant areas. Rates include daily tour and transfer from Cartí. $90/person

Cabañas Narasgandup Naranjo Chico ☎6501 6033, ⓦsanblaskunayala.com. The first lodgings to be built on the island and they still have their own beach, set apart from the competition. At the back of the beach a row of traditional en-suite *cabañas* (for 2–5 people) look out to sea. A couple of pricier ones ($130/person) are over the water. Though rustic, they are nicely done, with bamboo tables and towels provided, but are still overpriced. The dining room, which serves good food, and lobster or crab once a day except in the closed season (see p.260), is superbly located on a coral landfill promontory off the

beach. All-inclusive rates include local tours and boat transfers from Cartí or El Porvenir, but trips to Isla Perro and Cayos Holandéses are extra. $80/person

Cabañas Robinson Naranjo Chico ☎6721 9885, ⓦrobinsoncabins.blogspot.co.uk. Owned by the engaging Arnulfo Robinson, who speaks English, these are probably the cheapest cane huts in the whole of western Guna Yala – so don't expect much. Shared makeshift shower and bathroom and rock-bottom-priced excursions too. Rates include accommodation and food, with transfer from Cartí $20. Dorms $25/person, *cabañas* $30/person

Cabañas Senidup Senidup ☎6945 4301, ⓔcabanas _senidub@hotmail.com. Run by a family cooperative from Soledad Miria, this place offers a handful of simple *cabañas*, plus an occasionally functioning toilet/shower, solar-powered electricity in the dining area, a shady volleyball court and a pleasant dining area. Dorms $26/person, *cabañas* $3/person

Franklin's Place Senidup ☎6156 5711 or ☎6768 4075. Officially *Cabañas Dubesenika*, this is a legendary party spot with eighteen tightly packed cane huts with sand floors, a dirt-volleyball court and dreamy views of a palm-framed Caribbean. Guests share a basic communal shower/toilet area, and luxuries such as juice, snacks, beer and cigarettes

7

> ## LOBSTER AND THE CLOSED SEASON
> If you're hoping to sample the succulent **lobster** for which Guna Yala is famous, avoid the closed season (*veda*; March–May). During this period conch, crab and octopus are also off-limits. Note that in budget accommodation there is usually a supplement if you want lobster for a meal.

---

can be bought at the English-speaking Franklin's "office". The generator runs 6–10pm, when the partying begins. Rates include (basic and sometimes small) meals. Because of the larger numbers, island-hopping boat trips and fishing excursions, though extra, are cheap. Transfer from Cartí $20. Dorms $20/person, *cabañas* $35/person

Hotel Guna Yala Nusatupu ☎ 6887 1400 (Alejandro López), ✉ hotelkunayala@gmail.com. Housed in a two-storey cement structure with a canteen producing tasty meals on the ground floor and a handful of breezy rooms upstairs, each with two windows, ensuring good views. Rooms are basic with beds of varying quality and minimal, if any, other furniture, plus a shared flush toilet and shower. Make sure you get up onto the rooftop, which affords a splendid panorama. Rates include meals and a daily tour and transfer from Cartí. $80/person

Restaurante Petita By the main jetty, Río Sidra. Serves home-baked fresh bread and coffee for breakfast, as well as a decent main meal with dessert and coffee for around $6 at other times of the day. Daily 7am–8pm.

Cayos Holandéses and around

Three groups of predominantly **uninhabited cays** forming an equilateral triangle provide the archipelago's most spectacular underwater scenery. At the top of the triangle, marking the outer limit of the *comarca* 30km from shore, **Cayos Holandéses (Maoki)** are the most remote, yet most visited of the three. Effectively out of bounds during the fierce winds and high waves of December to the end of February, at other times this chain of around twenty densely forested islands acts as a magnet for yachts drawn to the sheltered anchorage and shallow, translucent waters. The protection is afforded by the outlying **Wreck Reef**, which has ensnared Spanish galleons and the odd drug-smuggling vessel, parts of which still protrude through the pounding surf. The resulting bays form clear natural swimming pools displaying a stunning array of sponges and soft and hard corals – fire, elkhorn, brain, fan – that attract rays, reef sharks, moray eels, starfish and a plethora of polychromatic fish.

Cayos Los Grullos and Coco-Bandero

Strung out along the 30km expanse of sea between Río Sidra and Narganá and Corazón de Jesús, **Cayos Los Grullos** and **Cayos Coco-Bandero (Ordupuquip)** – two clusters of around a dozen or so cays – comprise thin powdery beaches peppered with driftwood encircling densely forested isles and coral-filled shallows. Popular with cruising yachts, they attract Guna dugouts selling *molas* and fresh produce to the visitors.

ARRIVAL AND DEPARTURE   CAYOS HOLANDÉSES AND AROUND

By boat For budget travellers staying on the inner isles near Cartí or Río Sidra, an excursion to Cayos Holandéses usually requires a $30 fuel supplement, and will entail a couple of hours in a boat.

Central Guna Yala

The main appeal of the **central isles** lies in **Isla Tigre**, which sustains many traditional Guna practices, and **Río Azúcar**, one of the most beautiful rivers in the *comarca* – both accessible by **plane** via the twin-island hub of **Corazón de Jesús** and **Narganá**. Forty kilometres further east, sprawling **Playón Chico** presents an interesting combination of modernity and tradition but is generally only visited by guests at two of the *comarca*'s more comfortable lodgings, which lie close by and make sound bases for exploring the area. The region possesses a handful of delightful sand-fringed coconut isles on which to idle, but its beaches don't match the breathtaking beauty of many in the western end of the archipelago, though the mainland excursions into primeval **rainforest** more than compensate.

Narganá and Corazón de Jesús

A quick glance round either **Narganá** (Yandub) or **Corazón de Jesús** (Akuanusadup) and it's easy to forget you're in Guna Yala. The paved squares are dotted with benches, lampposts flank wide sandy streets, evening sound systems blast out reggaeton and bachata, and traditionally clad women are conspicuously absent. Some Guna see the twin islands as a warning of the fate of the *comarca* if the spread of *uaga burba* – the spirit of outsiders – proceeds unchecked. On the plus side, however, the location of the two islands is enchanting, nestled in a bay, fringed with mangroves fronting forest-clad hills. Moreover, if you've been travelling around the *comarca*, you might find Narganá's Western-style, air-conditioned hotel a welcome relief.

Corazón de Jesús, in keeping with its name, has a statue of Christ in its central plaza, which is illuminated at night. Other than that, the island's main features are its airstrip, a handful of government buildings and a church; there's a small cemetery at the northern tip. Most of the action occurs down at the wharf and at its opposite number across the dividing channel of water in Narganá: boats load up with supplies and drop off passengers, and yachts bob at anchor.

Across the bridge, the gleaming golden statue of Carlos Inaediguine Robinson, educator and major player in the 1925 Guna Revolution, stands as if in defiance at the centre of **Narganá**'s main plaza, where spacious sandy streets lead off in grid formation, in stark contrast to most Guna communities' cramped, labyrinthine layouts. Cement houses, occasionally surrounded by a hedge or garden, alternate with traditional cane-and-thatch dwellings, sometimes sprouting satellite dishes. Given that the first missionaries to the *comarca* settled in Narganá, it's no wonder the place has four churches.

7

ETIQUETTE WHEN VISITING GUNA YALA

In Guna Yala, particularly in the more remote areas, it is important to remember that you are a guest of the Guna, irrespective of how much you have paid for the privilege, and should abide by their laws. On islands less frequented by visitors it is customary to ask **permission** from the local *saila* when you visit a particular community or wish to stay on an island, as indeed the Guna themselves do. **Photography** is another contentious area: on some islands it is forbidden, on others it is governed by strict regulations. Never photograph anyone without asking. Traditional beliefs still held by some of the older generation maintain that a photograph takes away a part of the soul, which is why you should resist the temptation to surreptitiously snap away. Generally $1 is charged to take a single photograph, more for group shots, whereas video cameras, if permitted, can cost around $15. Women selling *molas* – the distinctive brightly coloured embroidered cloth panels – will usually allow you to photograph them if you purchase an item, but do not presume that the cost includes the photo charge.

While lazing in a hammock on one of the coconut islands, beachwear is fine, but you should **dress** more modestly in villages – no bikini tops or bare chests; villagers may not say anything, but it doesn't mean you haven't caused offence. The Guna are particularly sensitive about the *onmaked nega* (meeting house) and the cemeteries on the mainland – never enter or photograph these without permission. **Alcohol** too is a thorny issue. Traditionally large clay pots of *chicha* are prepared for the whole village for ceremonies; once the jars are exhausted, the drinking spree is over. Nowadays, communities vary in their regulations on alcohol: in some places drinking is unregulated, but people are fined if found drunk; some allow seco and beer to supplement the *chicha* at celebrations but not at other times; some have licensing hours; and others ban alcohol completely, though may allow its sale to tourists. Always enquire first, and drink discreetly if alcohol is available to tourists but not to villagers.

7

ARRIVAL AND DEPARTURE

By plane There are daily flights from Panama City to Corazón de Jesús ($78). The Air Panama office in Corazón de Jesús is by the wharf, though is generally only open early morning (5–7am) at flight time. For the return flight, you need to check in there around 5.30am before they transfer you by boat to the landing strip on a nearby outcrop.

ACCOMMODATION AND EATING

Café Noris Behind the primary school, Narganá. Informal café frequented by yachties, where you can tuck into tasty roast chicken and chips ($7 for half) or a toasted sandwich, washed down with a beer. Fri–Sun 6am–10pm.

Hotel Noris Two blocks from the main square, Narganá ☎ 6039 6842. Seven rooms with a/c or fan. Tiled bathrooms are shared and in good condition, but

NARGANÁ AND CORAZÓN DE JESÚS

By boat Although there are no fixed schedules, there are frequent early-morning departures for Cartí. Enquire at the wharf in Corazón de Jesús; in Narganá a good source of information is Paco, the owner of *Hotel Noris*, who runs the island's fuel depot by his home at the back of the primary school.

the rooms are in need of attention and the mattresses are variable. $15

Restaurante Tentene Express Narganá main square ☎ 6132 8927. Small bamboo restaurant with a few plastic tables and chairs offering fried or stewed chicken and beef in addition to the usual seafood options: octopus, conch, fish and lobster. Most mains $6–10. Daily 6.30am–10pm.

Río Azúcar

Five kilometres west of Narganá, the distinctive faded blue tower of the Catholic church and a large water tower herald your arrival at the crowded, vibrant village of **Río Azúcar** (Wargandup), where Westernization has left its mark. Yos Aranda (see below) can organize a **river trip** – either as a day-trip or overnight stay – up the beautiful Río Azúcar (Guebdidiwar), where you can awake to the sound of howler monkeys in the morning and the birdlife is truly spectacular. This trip is highly recommended, especially when the water level is high enough for you to penetrate further upriver by dugout.

ARRIVAL AND ACCOMMODATION

By boat Río Azúcar is a 15min boat ride from Corazón de Jesús, the nearest airstrip.

Village accommodation Yos Aranda (public phones ☎ 299 9069 or ☎ 299 9013), one of the community's many

RÍO AZÚCAR

sailas, is in charge of tourism and can sort out a family homestay or river trip. Overnight river trips are possible (with extremely basic hammock accommodation).

Isla Tigre

Populous yet spacious, elongated **Isla Tigre (Digir Dupu)** has the rare luxury of a couple of slender beaches. It is a community which is managing better than most to sustain Guna mores while opening up to tourism, partly due to partitioning off the village from the grassy community-run tourist areas, where you can loll in a hammock, enjoy a beer at the community restaurant, or sit on the sliver of **beach** in your swimwear – provided you cover up to go into the village. Possible **excursions** for modest fees ($25–30) include to the mainland cemetery, a three-hour hike to waterfalls or snorkelling round one of the nearby islands, where coconuts are harvested.

FESTIVALS IN GUNA YALA

The main party to catch in the *comarca* is the celebration of the **Guna Revolution**, which takes place February 23–25 (February 19–21 in Ailigandi) in various forms around the archipelago. Skirmishes between Panamanian forces and Guna are re-enacted on land and sea, accompanied by storytelling, parades and drinking. Arriving in October, however, would allow you to catch the **Feria de Isla Tigre** (see above).

Many aspects of **traditional living** are still practised: the conch is sounded to call men to plant or harvest the crops, and families rotate to harvest coconuts. The community has its own NGO and is actively involved in lobster protection and recycling practices. The Guna dance – involving men playing panpipes and women shaking maracas – originated here and during the mid-October **Feria de Isla Tigre** dance troupes from across the *comarca* compete for prizes. You can catch them practising at weekends.

ARRIVAL AND DEPARTURE   ISLA TIGRE

By boat Isla Tigre is a 30min boat ride ($5) from Corazón de Jesús, the nearest airstrip.

ACCOMMODATION AND EATING

Cabañas Digir ☏6099 2738, or ☏6023 9224 (Leonardo Serrano, tourist coordinator). Cheap dorm-style beachside *cabañas* (likely to be redone soon), with cement floors, squidgy mattresses and electricity, share toilet and shower facilities. Alongside, three newer and nicer private *cabañas* on stilts have private bathrooms. Dorms $10/person, *cabañas* $15/person

★ **Restaurante Digir Dupu** ☏6099 2738. Across from the *cabañas*, this open-sided bar-restaurant offers some of the best cuisine in the *comarca*; $6–7 will get you succulent lobster and crab in a delicious sauce with decent sides. Attracting Guna from other islands for the quality of the food and the relaxed atmosphere, it's a good place for some cross-cultural conversation. Daily 6am–10pm.

Playón Chico

Two cemeteries atop hills on the mainland announce your arrival at the sprawling administrative hub of **Playón Chico (Ukupseni)**, home to around three thousand. A large flat coral-filled pancake packed with cane-and-thatch dwellings, interspersed with functional concrete buildings, the island is wrestling to balance traditional customs with modern developments, but is a vibrant and welcoming place for all that.

The wharf opens out onto the main square-cum-basketball-court, and a stage painted in the Guna colours of red and yellow. A concrete pedestrian bridge leads to the **mainland**, where a football pitch, airstrip and several government buildings, including a secondary school, are located. In the early morning, men armed with machetes stride up the path leading to the cultivated lands (*nainumar*). Westernizing influence is evident in the numerous churches scattered round the island, and in the presence of electricity, which allows for a weekend film night at the community hall by the basketball court, and results in the sound of competing TVs penetrating the paper-thin walls as you try to sleep.

Attractive **excursions** include hikes into pristine rainforest taking in the cascading waterfall of Saibar Maid, birdwatching up Río Grande and some lazy sun-lounging, moderate snorkelling and fishing off nearby coconut isles.

ARRIVAL AND INFORMATION   PLAYÓN CHICO

By plane There are daily flights from Albrook airport in Panama City ($84 one way).
Community tax Visitors to Playón Chico need to sign in at the police station at the wharf and pay a hefty community tax ($10).

ACCOMMODATION AND EATING

There is limited accommodation on Playón Chico, with most tourists ferried out to the relatively swish lodgings situated on tiny private islands a 5min boat ride from Playón Chico.

★ **Yandup Island Lodge** Yandup ☏394 1408, ⓦ yandupisland.com. Five lovely octagonal *cabañas* with private balcony and bathroom sit over the water, while three slightly cheaper rooms are set further back. The tiny island, with a small beach and nearby reef, has a breezy waterside *rancho*-restaurant with full bar, which serves excellent seafood-based cuisine, and service is friendly and attentive. Costs include two daily excursions with an English-speaking guide, but not the community fee ($10). Credit cards accepted. $134/person
Sapibenega "The Kuna Lodge" Iskardup ☏215 1406 (Panama City), ⓦ sapibenega.com. The most luxurious

accommodation in the *comarca*, though overpriced, consisting of a handful of spacious bamboo twin cabins (for 2–4 people) decorated with Guna art, built over the water and set round a grassy interior covering the entire coral outcrop of Iskardup.

Each room has a private balcony, hammock and tiled bathroom. A well-stocked bar-lounge area complements the top-notch over-the-water restaurant-gazebo. Discounts for three-night stays or more. $155/person

---

THE TRADITIONAL GUNA WAY OF LIFE

Historically the Guna have lived collectively and worked cooperatively. Though some hunting was practised, **fishing** and **subsistence agriculture** – yuca, plantain, rice, maize, sugar cane, cocoa, fruit trees and coconuts – were the mainstay of the economy for many years. In the late 1960s, **coconuts** accounted for seventy percent of the *comarca*'s revenue, bartered for dry goods, such as fuel, clothing and cooking oil, sold by the brightly painted Colombian trading vessels that you still see tethered to the main jetty at communities across the region. Over three million coconuts are still harvested annually.

Guna society is traditionally both matrilocal (when a man marries he moves into his in-laws' compound and works for them) and matrilineal (property is inherited down the female line). But these practices are slipping, and while women's views are respected, men play a larger role, as chiefs, healers and interpreters in community meetings. Men undertake most of the agricultural labour, and the entire Guna Congress is male.

Families traditionally live in compounds of cane-and-thatch dwellings, the living quarters crammed with hammocks and the rafters laden with clothing, buckets and utensils. Villages without aqueducts bring fresh water by canoe from the mainland. Seafood accompanied by plantain, rice and coconut are staples, and *tule masi* – a fish stew containing boiled green plantains, coconut and vegetables – is effectively the Guna national dish.

At the heart of community life stands **onmaked nega** (the meeting house), where villagers, including children, congregate most evenings. The **saila** – usually recognizable by his hat – is the leader in all village matters, though some communities now have several *sailas* to fulfil particular functions. A mixture of songs, chants, stories and talk filter through the walls, as Guna history, mythology and religion are as much a part of the reunions as information-giving, public debate and conflict resolution. Another key community building is the **inna nega**, where the *chicha brava* (*inna* in Guna), the potent mind-numbing sugar-cane-based homebrew, is left to ferment in large clay urns for major celebrations such as a young girl's puberty ritual (see box, p.267).

CHANGES TO GUNA SOCIETY

As in any society, Guna life is evolving: numerous communities now have piped fresh water from the mainland; electricity (albeit limited) is available on many village-islands; cement block buildings are increasingly common; shops stock canned food, sweets and biscuits, whose wrappers often litter the streets; mobile phones are mushrooming; and the iconic Guna traditional dress is declining among women. That said, *molas* – the colourful, embroidered, multi-layered panels that make up the most distinctive part of their traditional blouses – are now a major source of income for the Guna.

Christian churches have taken root on some islands, on the understanding that they respect traditional **religion**. Despite the Guna authorities' success in insisting on intercultural bilingual **education**, schooling is primarily about preparing young people for a modern industrialized society. In this respect, many Guna hope that tourism, if managed carefully, may help ensure that changes in lifestyle can coexist with more established mores.

Already, tourism has played a pivotal role in the Guna's reluctant but inevitable metamorphosis from a collective barter economy – the word for "money" does not exist in Guna – to a more individualistic cash economy. The resulting **economic inequalities** have put a strain on communities that are already struggling to deal with major social upheavals due to increasing contact with outsiders (*uagmala*) and returning urbanized Guna who are no longer prepared to live as their ancestors did. **Environmental damage** by outsiders and the Guna themselves constitutes a further challenge, often exacerbated by tourism. Issues include overfishing, particularly of lobster, reef degradation, the deforestation of the mainland, and waste disposal.

San Ignacio de Tupile

Ten kilometres southeast of Playón Chico, midway along the *comarca*, lies the well-organized community of **San Ignacio de Tupile** (**Dad Nagued Dupir**, which translates as "where the sun rises"). As you step out of a boat at the community pier, you are greeted by a statue of the Virgin Mary – an indication of the island's fairly widespread evangelization – who is often surrounded by an assortment of goods awaiting shipment from the adjacent warehouse of one of the *comarca*'s main distributors. Soft drinks, dry foodstuffs, fuel and vegetables such as onions, potatoes and garlic, all pass through, and shops here are consequently better supplied than on many islands, so it's a good place to stock up. Though tourists rarely visit, the vibe among the 1500 inhabitants is relaxed and welcoming, particularly if your visit coincides with the patron saint festivities (July 28–31), when you can join in the celebrations marked by rowing races and various competitions.

Beyond the statue stands the primary school, where a wide main boulevard peels off left. The streets are kept spick-and-span, as community regulations mean families are held responsible for disposing of rubbish on the mainland. Rules are equally strict about getting a permit to leave the island, aimed at curbing what elders see to be the moral decline among some of the younger members of the community. Squeezed between two public phone boxes, the strangely whitened face of General Inatikuña, the community's first *saila* when the settlement relocated from the mainland to the island in 1903, stares out across the street.

Excursions are available to the unremarkable nearby beach on Ilestup ("Isle of the Englishman", after a gent who lived there in the 1700s) and to the Río Yuandup Gandi, where alligators laze on sandbanks and a rainbow of birds flit in and out of the foliage.

ARRIVAL AND DEPARTURE   **SAN IGNACIO DE TUPILE**

By boat San Ignacio is a 40min boat ride from Playón Chico, the nearest airstrip.

ACCOMMODATION AND EATING

Community restaurant By the wharf. The community's only restaurant is up the stairs to the right by the wharf, and serves a decent plate of fried fish with rice and plantain. Daily 6am–7pm.

Obued Nega At the far end of the island behind the church, close to the generator ☎ 333 2001/2/3/4 (public phones). This place has basic cement and wood rooms with reasonable mattresses and private or shared bathroom; the better upstairs rooms have a balcony and hammocks. Meals served at a waterside *rancho*. The room price is fine but the all-inclusive package is on the high side. Doubles **$25**, packages with meals and tours **$60**/person

The eastern isles

What might loosely be described as the **eastern isles** stretches over the whole of the eastern half of the *comarca*, which, outside the sprinkling of lodges near Achutupu and Mamitupu, sees precious few outsiders beyond the odd yacht and Colombian trading vessel. Here, lacking the protection of an offshore reef, the seas are rough and transport between communities sparse. After storms, rubbish jettisoned from boats will wash up on the shore in places.

Ailigandi

Westernmost of the eastern islands, overlooking coastal mangroves (*ailan* means mangrove), **Ailigandi** has its spot firmly cemented in Guna history as the first place of organized resistance in the Guna Revolution of 1925, symbolized in the Guna swastika flag (representing an octopus) fluttering proudly above the rooftops. It's therefore a good place to witness the annual revolution celebrations (see box, p.262). A pivotal figure in the rebellion was Chief Olokindibipilelel (Simral Colman), whose **statue** – incongruously clad in suit and bowler hat – claims a central position on the densely populated island of around 1200, next to the obligatory basketball court. A warren of pathways weaves through tightly packed thatched dwellings, in the midst of which is squeezed the tiny **Museo Olonigli** (no fixed hours; donations welcome). As with other museums in the *comarca*, it's a single room stuffed with artefacts whose significance only becomes clear through the explanations (in Spanish) of the owner-curator, Roy Cortéz Olonigli. He elaborates on traditional culture drawing on his own woodcarvings, which depict Guna symbols and rituals.

ARRIVAL AND DEPARTURE   AILIGANDI

By boat Ailigandi is a 10min boat ride from Achutupu airport.

ACCOMMODATION

7

Dad Ibe Lodge Dad Ibe island, 5min boat ride west of Ailigandi ☎ 6112 5448, ⓦ dadibelodge.net. There's no accommodation on Ailigandi, but the private island of Dad Ibe, to the west, is home to an appealing lodge of three brightly painted wooden waterside cabins with plenty of hammock space to curl up with a book. Rates include meals, one daily excursion, use of *cayucos* – including to Ailigandi – and airport transfer. A strenuous all-day hike to a waterfall, or river exploration by dugout, is worth the additional cost. $106/person

Achutupu and Mamitupu

Five kilometres east of Ailigandi, the unusual crescent-shaped island of **Achutupu** has a deceptively spacious feel, dotted with banana trees and coconut palms. There's a strip of sand that might optimistically be called a beach, though swimming is inadvisable due to the usual pollution. The village has a primary school, health centre and restaurant by the pier, alongside a basketball court. There's nowhere to stay on Achutupu itself, but a couple of higher-end accommodation options are close at hand.

Only a few hundred metres east of Achutupu, **Mamitupu** has ten *sailas* governing a traditional village of about 1200. Photography is forbidden here, though it is permitted on excursions to the mainland.

ARRIVAL AND DEPARTURE   ACHUTUPU AND MAMITUPU

By plane The airstrip, 200m across from Achutupu on the mainland, receives daily Air Panama flights ($85 one way). Motorized dugouts greet the plane and will ferry you to Achutupu, or Mamitupu (a 5min boat ride away), for a few dollars.

ACCOMMODATION

Akwadup Lodge West of Achutupu ☎ 396 4805 or ☎ 6137 7668, ⓦ akwaduplodge.com. Located a 5min boat ride west of Achutupu, this exclusive lodge offers comfort and seclusion in a row of seven comfortable (two double beds in each) over-the-water wooden bungalows – rather close together but nicely decorated – with solar-powered ceiling fans and hot water. Rates, which are on the high side, include meals, lodgings and airport transfer, but snorkel rental ($10) and community taxes ($14) are extra. $149/person

Cabañas Mamitupu Mamitupu ☎ 7030 5846 (Pablo Nuñez, who speaks English); or contact Agostín Silva at Hotel Costa Azul in Panama City (☎ 225 4703). Set apart from the main village in a palm-shaded grassy end of the island stand four simple sandy-floor cane huts, with decent mattresses protected by mosquito nets, a good-size table, private washing area (for bucket and water ablutions) and solar-powered electricity. Flush toilets (using a septic tank) are shared, as is the pleasant *rancho* dining area. $75/person

Dolphin Lodge (Uaguinega) Uagitupo ☎ 836 5333, ⓦ dolphinlodgepanama.com. A stone's throw across the water from Achutupu, on a tiny islet, this easy-going place has simple wood-and-cane *cabañas* facing the water. Palm trees are sprinkled over a grassy area with a central *bohío* and a pleasant and breezy restaurant, where you can tuck into delicious seafood while gazing out to sea. Also offers satellite internet access. Community tax ($14) extra. $124/person

Ogobsukum and Ustupu

Beyond Mamitupu, completing the remaining 75km to Puerto Obaldía, you pass the densely matted thatch rooftops of the *comarca*'s most populous communities: the four-thousand-strong twin settlements of **Ogobsukum** and **Ustupu**, renowned for their gold craftwork. The next notable community is the pine-clad **Isla Pino (Dupak)**, which unlike any other island in the *comarca* has a large hill; though only just over a square kilometre in size, it boasts a couple of forest trails and a picturesque waterside thatched village.

Travellers rarely venture this far east to these more traditional communities, where you will need to check in with the police and ask **permission** of the *saila* to visit or stay on an island (make sure you are appropriately clad). It is usually possible to negotiate with a family for a hammock or bed and engage the services of someone to explore some of the rivers and rainforest on the mainland. The seas along this stretch of coastline are particularly rough here and should only be navigated in a decent boat – not the shallow leaking dugout favoured by many.

ARRIVAL AND DEPARTURE   OGOBSUKUM AND USTUPU

By air Air Panama flights three times a week (Tues, Thurs & Sun) to Ogobsukum ($85) from Albrook airport   in Panama City (see p.251).

Puerto Obaldía

Puerto Obaldía is the last major "town" before the Colombian border. Despite a tidy park, a decent playing field, clean streets and a scenic seaside location, it is an unendearing encampment, where the frontier police in combat gear guard against drug runners, Colombian guerrillas and smugglers. Though technically within the *comarca*, the community has a mixed population of Guna, Colombian refugees and non-Guna Panamanians. You could end up with a more intimate knowledge of the town than you would like unless you've booked an air ticket to Panama City in advance, since seats are often oversubscribed.

ARRIVAL AND INFORMATION   PUERTO OBALDÍA

BY PLANE
Air Panama (☎316 9000, ⌨airpanama.com) operates mid-morning flights to Puerto Obaldía from Panama City

every day except Saturday, with almost immediate return flights to the capital (1hr; $78). The airstrip is a two-minute walk from the "town centre".

PUBERTY RITUALS

Whereas adolescent boys pass into adulthood unheralded, a **young girl** undergoes two important ceremonies. The first, **innamutiki**, at her first menstruation, prompts several days of confinement in a small ceremonial enclosure cloaked in banana leaves (*surba*) within the house, where she is purified in herbal baths and finally painted from top to toe in the indigo jagua dye before being allowed to join the festivities outside. The second celebration, **innasuit**, involving the whole village, entails the young woman being officially named and receiving a ceremonial haircut, a protracted affair signifying that she is now available for marriage. Food is shared, pipes are passed and *chicha* abounds, though the presence of cigarettes and seco in some communities reflects the changing times.

Ironically the young woman at the heart of the festivities misses out on most of the fun, remaining in seclusion until the actual hair-cutting. In an increasing fog of rituals, chants, cocoa-bean incense, tobacco and alcohol, the celebrations, aimed partly at affirming the coexistence of the material and spiritual worlds, continue for several days, until the *chicha* has run out, by which time several people have usually passed out.

7

BY BOAT

To Guna Yala There are regular though unscheduled boats that head west up the *comarca* to Cartí (6hr; $100/person) from Puerto Obaldía, usually departing before 9am; ask around. You should also be able to negotiate a price if you want to be dropped off at another community along the way. Seas can be particularly rough and dangerous over the first three hours (especially Dec–Feb), even when conditions are considered "safe". It is imperative that you check the condition of the boat beforehand (see p.252).

To Colombia Visitors travelling on to Colombia from Puerto Obaldía (see p.24) take a launch (1hr; $15) to the resort town of Capurganá, from where a further ferry to Turbo and onward bus to Medellín are possible.

IMMIGRATION

Before crossing the Colombian border, or arriving from Colombia, you'll need to visit immigration (daily 8am–4pm; $20/person charge to attend at other times), just off the park, for an entry or exit stamp. You may also be asked for proof of onward travel out of the country and evidence of the means to support yourself financially. You then need to swing by the police post, to register and have your belongings searched (see p.25).

ACCOMMODATION AND EATING

Pensión Condé Half a block from the park. Currently the only place to stay, with friendly owners. Accommodation is rudimentary, comprising a mix of dark wooden or cement rooms; bathrooms are private or shared, though water is sporadic, and fan ventilation is from 6pm. $12

Las Tres 'L' Corner of the park. Friendly restaurant with a pleasant patio where you can get a decent breakfast and lunch, though options will be limited. Get there early for lunch since food often runs out when visitor numbers are high. Daily 6.30am–4pm.

Armila

Highly recommended is a detour to the welcoming Guna community of **Armila**, which is idyllically located at the base of a forest-cloaked hill where two rivers empty into the sea. Atypically spacious, and run by five *sailas*, the village boasts an intriguing mix of traditional cane *cabañas* and more substantial Afro-Antillean-style wood-and-thatch houses, sometimes painted, or on stilts. Beyond, over 4km of cream-coloured windswept beach extends along the coast. This is one of the world's most important nesting sites for **leatherback turtles**, consisting of several thousand nests protected by the community. The visitor community fee ($6) goes towards the conservation and monitoring project. Nesting occurs between February and August, peaking between late April/May to July, and a major **turtle festival** is hosted annually the third week in May, involving traditional music and dancing. Turtle-watching is one of several tourist activities; others include jungle walks, river trips by dugout and swimming in the local freshwater lagoon. Provided the sea is calm, beach and snorkelling trips can be organized to the lovely Playa Blanca at La Miel, by the Colombian border.

ARRIVAL AND DEPARTURE ARMILA

By boat Although only a 20min boat ride up the coast from Puerto Obaldía, landing on the beach (there is no jetty) is frequently impossible due to rough waves (especially Dec–Feb and sometimes July–Aug), or water spilling out of the river mouths following torrential rain.

On foot When conditions are too rough to travel by boat, you will need to make a moderately strenuous uphill hike (1hr 30min–2hr) to reach Armila from Puerto Obaldía, accompanied by a guide.

SECURITY IN THE FRONTIER ZONE

The **security situation** in the frontier zone is liable to change at a moment's notice so make sure you check out the latest information on the ground before you head into this area. In addition to the relatively safe boat-hopping route (see p.24), some travellers take the unofficial overland route from Puerto Obaldía via La Miel, hike across the border to Sapzurro in Colombia, and then on to Capurganá. However, this is not advisable; although numerous people make the journey without a hitch, a few never arrive.

ACCOMMODATION

★**Cabañas Ibedi** ☎ 6093 7802, ⓦ ibedialnatural.net. Run by Ignacio Crespo, known as "Nacho", an engaging trained biologist and conservationist. Simple, tidy raised cabins of varying sizes with private porches among trees and a lovely hibiscus garden. Basic toilet/shower facilities are shared and there's solar-powered electricity at night. Food is tasty and activities and transfers from Puerto Obaldía are included. Cheaper deals can sometimes be negotiated for budget travellers. 4-day all-inclusive package for two sharing: $255/person

Village accommodation ☎ 333 2060 (public phone). Inexpensive community lodgings were due to be built at the time of writing.

7

The Darién and eastern Panama

DAWN IN THE DARIÉN

The Darién and eastern Panama

Mention of the Darién conjures up a host of images, some alluring, others less so; some true, others vastly exaggerated. What is not in dispute is the region's status as one of the last true tropical wildernesses – though even this is under threat – encompassing swathes of mountainous forest containing an astounding array of wildlife, most notably in the Parque Nacional Darién, which provides unparalleled opportunities for serious hiking and birdwatching.

The largest of Panama's nine provinces, the **Darién** abuts Colombia and covers a sparsely populated rugged expanse that sprawls across almost twelve thousand square kilometres, reaching its highest point at Cerro Tacarcuna (1875m) by the border, but including numerous peaks over a thousand metres. The province also boasts Panama's longest river, the **Río Tuira**, which empties into the Golfo de San Miguel, a vast mangrove-lined body of water that opens out into the Pacific Ocean. Yet travellers are increasingly drawn to the Darién as much by its people as by its compelling scenery. The main indigenous groups, the closely related **Emberá** and **Wounaan**, are gradually opening up their communities to tourists; in the **Comarca Emberá–Wounaan** or in communities outside such as **La Marea** and **Mogué**, you can stay overnight in a village and learn the intricacies of basketry or woodcarving, for which they are world-renowned, or hike through steaming rainforest to spot harpy eagles – the area boasts the greatest concentration of these raptors in the world. **Guna** communities are also present, mainly in eastern Panama province, historically considered part of the Darién. Their two small *comarcas* stretch along the shores of **Lago Bayano**, a vast reservoir 100km east of Panama City, which enjoys a picturesque setting in an increasingly deforested landscape, and has an impressive network of caves.

Brief history

The Darién bore witness to some of the bloodiest confrontations between the invading conquistadors, greedy for gold and power, and the indigenous groups desperate to defend their territories, most notably at **Santa María La Antigua del Darién**, the first successful Spanish settlement on the mainland since the time of Columbus (over the border in present-day Colombia). Balboa took Santa María in 1510, and later intercepted an attempt to reclaim the city, led by Cacique **Cémaco**, a pivotal figure in the indigenous resistance; he captured all the alliance's chiefs, bar Cémaco, and had them hanged as an example. It is perhaps only fitting that Balboa, who first espied the Pacific from the Darién, also met his end here – beheaded by Pedrerías Dávila in the coastal town of Acla (in present-day Guna Yala) – while Santa María was eventually abandoned by the Spanish in favour of Panama City, and was razed to the ground by indigenous forces in 1524.

The region's population

The indigenous peoples most in evidence today are the **Emberá** and **Wounaan**. Both groups may have migrated from the Chocó regions of Colombia (which is why they are

Highlights

❶ Lago Bayano Take a boat ride in search of caiman lurking in the lake's muddy fringes, and venture into the bat-infested Cuevas de Majé. See p.277

❷ Parque Nacional Darién On the banks of a picturesque river, the ANAM refuge of Rancho Frío provides the best access to the natural wonders of the Parque Nacional Darién. See p.282

❸ Staying with the Emberá Spend a few nights in the villages of Mogué, La Marea or La Chunga, where you can learn about Emberá culture and the surrounding rainforest. See p.284

❹ Harpy eagle nest Stake out the nest of the world's most powerful raptor and wait for a parent to swoop into view and deliver a monkey to their needy chick. See p.286 & p.287

❺ Río Sambú A gloriously sinuous river, lined with mangroves and rainforest, and populated with ibis, herons and kingfishers. See p.288

HIGHLIGHTS ARE MARKED ON THE MAP ON P.274

often referred to collectively as Chocós). **Guna** presence is still recalled in some of the place names, notably the snaking Río Tuira, and though most Guna moved to the Caribbean coast, pockets remain in the more recently formed *comarcas* of Madugandi and Wargandi, and in isolated communities in Panama and Darién provinces. The other substantial population, dominant in the regional capital of La Palma and in settlements lining the Golfo de San Miguel, are the **Afro-Darienites**, descendants on the whole of the *cimarrones* – escaped slaves brought over by the Spanish, who fled and waged warfare from their own strongholds (*palenques*) in the rainforest, forming strategic alliances with pirates and indigenous tribes. Some of their communities are now mixed with Emberá and Wounaan, and in some parts with **Afro-Colombian refugees**, escaping the civil conflict across the border. The completion of the Interamericana to Yaviza in 1979 opened the floodgates to **colonos** (the name often given to migrating *mestizo* cattle ranchers and farmers predominantly from the Azuero Peninsula), who have now cleared vast tracts of land along the highway for pasture, and constitute around fifty percent of the total population of Darién province.

Local conflicts

Though the joint Comarca Emberá–Wounaan was established in 1983, covering around 25 percent of Darién province, there have been increasingly violent clashes with

THE EMBERÁ AND WOUNAAN

Two separate but related ethnic groups speaking mutually unintelligible languages, the majority of Panama's **Emberá** (warriors famed for their poisonous blow-darts) and **Wounaan** (more noted for their artistry) inhabit wood-and-thatch huts along the Darién's numerous rivers – though the increasing presence of zinc roofs and cement buildings is indicative of encroaching modernization. As former semi-nomadic hunter-gatherers, it is only relatively recently that their communities started to live in fixed villages, a government-encouraged project primarily to facilitate schooling and access to modern health care; before, family homes, though still sprinkled along the rivers as they are today, formed temporary bases from which to hunt and practise limited slash-and-burn agriculture before moving on, allowing the forest to recover.

The groups' wooden **houses** are built on stilts, to protect them from wild animals and unwelcome intruders, as well as rising floodwaters. Semi-open sides allow cooling breezes to enter while preserving a degree of privacy. The platform, accessed by a tree trunk, with notches carved out as steps, constitutes a living space with a fire pit for cooking; crucially, the heat prevents the thatched roof from rotting during the rainy season. Traditionally, the largest building in the community is the *bujia* or *casa comunal*, a splendid circular construction with a soaring conical ceiling, where meetings are held, guests are received and ceremonies take place. Missionaries have been chipping away at traditional **beliefs** since the time of the conquistadors, and while shamanism persists, villagers are more likely today to head for the government medical centre than put their trust in traditional medicine.

For an up-close experience of life in an Emberá or Wounaan village, consider **staying the night** (see box, p.284).

8

mestizo settlers encroaching on their lands, while overlap with the national park, whose regulations restrict traditional hunting and agricultural practices, fuel frictions between indigenous communities and government.

ARRIVAL AND GETTING AROUND — THE DARIÉN

Most tourists visit the Darién on a **tour** but it is entirely possible, and becoming more common, to visit **independently** – though you need to be flexible and have sufficient time, Spanish and, more often than not, funds.

INDEPENDENT TRAVEL

BY PLANE

To Jaqué Air Panama (☎ 316 9000, ⌨ flyairpanama.com) operates mid-morning flights from Albrook airport to Jaqué via Bahía Piña (Mon & Fri; 1hr 15min; $95 one way), with almost immediate return flights to the capital.

To Garachiné or Sambú Air Panama flies to Garachiné ($85 one way) and Sambú ($87 one way), in two hops mid-morning (Wed & Sat; 1hr), with almost immediate return flights to the capital.

BY BUS AND BOAT

To Yaviza and Metetí Direct services from Albrook bus terminal leave before dawn (every 40min, 3.15–11.30am; 6–7hr) bound for Yaviza, via Santa Fé and Metetí. After the last bus to Yaviza, you can take a later bus to Metetí (every 40min 3.15am–4.40pm; 5–6hr) and transfer to a local minibus to Yaviza (see p.280). There is also a more expensive express bus to Yaviza ($14) that leaves Panama City at midnight.

To La Palma To reach La Palma and other destinations in the Golfo de San Miguel take the bus to Metetí, then transfer to the minibus shuttle to nearby Puerto Quimba (every 30min, 6am–5pm; 20min), from where you can catch a water-taxi to La Palma (every 30min, 5am–6pm; 40min).

GETTING AROUND

Once in the Darién proper, transport is by boat, generally in a motorized dugout (*piragua*), and it entails a fair amount of waiting around as many communities are on tidal rivers, only accessible at high tide, especially in the dry season. It's also infinitely cheaper, though far less comfortable, to travel on a community boat already heading to your destination, than hiring a boat privately, where you will have to cover the cost of the fuel (often for the return trip, even if you're only travelling one way), the captain and probably a poleman; find out fuel costs and the likely amount required for your journey from another source before you start negotiating prices, and note that if hiring someone's services for an overnight stay in a village, you may need to pay for *their* lodging and meals, too.

LOCAL GUIDES

Most villages have local guides who will probably only

SAFETY IN THE DARIÉN

For many years the general rule of thumb for **safety** in the Darién has been to draw an imaginary line from by the Caribbean Colombian border, through Yaviza, to Bahía Piñas, on the Pacific coast, beyond which you should not travel. Rancho Frío excepted this still holds; however, due to the occasional flare-up in violence, and drug-trafficking related incidents in other areas of the Darién in recent years (see p.24), the Panamanian frontier police, SENAFRONT, has now placed draconian restrictions on independent foreign travellers.

At the time of writing, foreigners were only allowed to travel as far as Metetí, La Palma, Yaviza and El Real (but not to the national park) without a permit. If you are travelling on an organized tour (see below) or with a registered Panamanian guide, they will organize the paperwork for you. Independent foreign travellers are required to obtain a (free) **permit** from the main office of SENAFRONT– who are based in Corozal (see map, p.54), close to the Panama Railroad terminal in Panama City (Mon–Fri 8.30am–3.30pm; ☎ 527 1000), and are likely only to understand Spanish. You need to take your passport and a written letter, preferably in Spanish, detailing where you are intending to go and when, and naming your guide, if you have one. The whole process is supposed to take three days.

Many of those who know the Darién well, including community leaders, believe these current travel restrictions are overly strict, overstating the level of danger on the ground, and are unnecessarily bureaucratic. That said, the security situation in the Darién is changeable, so you should always seek local advice both before and during your travels.

speak Spanish (and their indigenous language) and will have varying levels of knowledge about the rainforest and its wildlife. Guiding services generally cost $10–20/day.

ORGANIZED TOURS

Though customized itineraries can also be arranged, all-inclusive tours generally leave Panama City, the majority from December to the end of April, and include transport to and around the Darién as advertised, as well as accommodation, meals and non-alcoholic drinks, activities and bilingual guiding services in Spanish and English. Prices given here are per person.

ANCON Expeditions ☎ 269 9415, ⓦ anconexpeditions .com. The Rolls-Royce of tour operators, with top-notch bilingual naturalist guides, offering four-day tours to its comfortable lodge in the Punta Patiño Reserve, with prices to match ($803 assuming two sharing). A visit to Mogué is included and one of the nights can be spent there, rather than in the lodge, for an extra $48. Minimum of four people required.

Canopy Camp Border of Reserva de Filo de Tallo, beyond Metetí, off the Interamericana ☎ 264 5720, ⓦ canopytower.com. Part of the Canopy "family", this award-winning camp comprises eight luxurious African safari tents (with electricity and fans) on raised platforms that extend to provide private observation decks. There's plenty of storage space made from locally sourced teak, also prominent in the main social and dining areas. Though aimed primarily at birders, the eight-day package contains excursions of interest to the general nature-lover too. Eight-day tour $3150.

Ecocircuitos ☎ 315 1305, ⓦ ecocircuitos.com. Among their vast array of tours is a four-day Darién Ethnic Expedition ($1040), which combines visits to Emberá communities with a two-night stay at ANAM's ranger station at Rancho Frío in the national park. Minimum of four people required.

Jungle Treks ☎ 6438 3130, ⓦ jungletreks.com. Former ANCON Expeditions guide Rick Morales now runs his own trekking outfit with local guides. The Deep Darién Adventure is just that, involving two days' travel and six days of backpacking and camping – plenty of sleeping in hammocks and eating dehydrated food – from Sambú across the Serranía del Sapo before following the Río Piña down to the Pacific coast. Requires a minimum of four people. Between $2500–2900.

Panama Exotic Adventures ☎ 6673 5381, ⓦ panamaexoticadventures.com. Experienced French-run organization offering the greatest variety of multi-day trips to the Darién (and Guna Yala), often involving more camping and hiking. A five-day trip to the Golfo de San Miguel includes a stay in their own lodge at the Reserva de Filo de Tallo near Metetí, a visit to the Wounaan community of Puerto Lara, and camping on an island near La Palma ($1250). An eight-day expedition takes in the Sambú area, with plenty of hiking in the rainforest and visits to the Emberá villages of Villa Queresia and Pavarandó, before trekking over the Serranía del Sapo to Playa de Muerto ($1750). Minimum of four people required.

Panama Orgánica ☎ 6079 6825, ⓦ panamaorganica .com. Small, reliable outfit offering customized budget tours to hard-to-access areas such as the Darién and Guna Yala, working with local communities and independent operators. Can also help arrange transport to Colombia and day-trips from Panama City.

Panama province

Aside from the Altos de Cerro Azul, **Panama province** east of the canal is known more for the continuing urban spread out towards Chepo and rampant deforestation than for any sightseeing charms. That said, **Lago Bayano**, some 90km east of Panama City and voted one of the country's top ten attractions in a nationwide tourist-board poll, is worth at least a day's sojourn, while the indigenous communities just off the Interamericana at **Ipetí** provide the other main reason to stop en route to the Darién proper, though the relatively barren location lacks the rainforest charm of other villages in Darién province.

Chepo and around

It's hard to imagine the agro-commercial town of **Chepo**, which looks set to be swallowed up in Panama City's greedy expansion eastwards, as the gateway to the Darién Gap only forty-odd years ago, where the Pan-American Highway ended and rainforest began, so devastating has been the pace of deforestation.

Though the town itself holds little to detain you, nearby **Puerto Coquira** on the Río Chepo (also known as Río Bayano) is the jumping-off point for boats (from $40 return) to the delightful island of **Isla Chepillo**, 4km from the mangrove-filled river mouth. A popular weekend day-trip from Panama City, the tiny island supports a pretty fishing village, plus a beach pounded by good **surfing** waves, and served by a **surf camp** (⌨chepillosurfcamp.0catch.com/1.html).

ACCOMMODATION   **CHEPO AND AROUND**   **8**

Burbayar Lodge Llano-Cartí Road, Km14 ☎ 236 6061 or ☎ 6949 5700, ⌨burbayar.net. The slightly cooler climate is just one of the many plus points of this delightful rustic eco-lodge that attracts serious birders – with a list of around three hundred species – as well as casual nature-lovers. All-inclusive rates include lodging and meals, as well as pick-up in Panama City (book in advance). After the first night the rate is reduced. Popular day-trips from the lodge include Lago Bayano, and an exhausting trek down to the coast in Guna Yala (6–8hr). $200/person

Lago Bayano

Though now earmarked for "development", **LAGO BAYANO** remains a picturesque location, perfect for boat rides and picnics, and with a fascinating cave network at its southeastern tip. Its apparent charm and tranquillity, however, belie the anger of indigenous communities – displaced when the reservoir was formed in 1976 and still awaiting full compensation from the government – and the acres of forest that were submerged when the Río Chepo (or Río Bayano) was dammed to supply Panama City with more hydro-power; dead tree trunks protruding eerily from the water act as poignant reminders. The economic mainstay of the sixteen lakeside communities – including those of the Guna **Comarca de Madugandi**, as well as Emberá, Wounaan and Ladino settlements – is the commercial fishing of tilapia.

Named after Bayano, a charismatic leader of a major settlement of *cimarrones* (see box, p.278), the 350-square-kilometre reservoir is a popular day-trip destination from Panama City; at weekends, families spill out of vehicles at the impressive **Puente Bayano**, which fords the lake's narrowest point, and pile into motor **launches** for island picnics, fishing trips or tours of the lake, on the lookout for caimans, crocodiles and otters slithering around the muddy banks.

Cuevas de Majé
Southeastern tip of Lago Bayano • $2

Lago Bayano's most fascinating destination is the **Cuevas de Majé**, comprising a 1km-long system of limestone caverns, replete with colonies of bats clinging to calcitic formations. Towards the end of the dry season, it's possible to wade your way (up to

EL "REY NEGRO BAYANO"

While his origins and death remain enveloped in a fog of conjecture, it is unequivocal that El "**Rey Negro Bayano**" (also known as Ballano or Vaino) was the most successful leader of the *cimarrones* and the undisputed king, referred to as such even by the Spanish. Commanding the loyalty of between 400 and 1200 followers, he constructed an impenetrable hilltop fortress from where he repeatedly attacked Spanish forces and plundered mule trains on the Camino Real. Despite conducting three major campaigns against him (1553–56), the Governor of Panama failed to quell the resistance, prompting the Viceroy of Peru to charge a certain Captain Pedro de Ursúa with the specific task of crushing the *cimarrones* rebellion. Realizing it would be impossible to take Bayano's mountain stronghold by force, Ursuá used deceit. Pretending to offer a peaceful settlement in which the land would be divided equally between the Spanish and Bayano and his followers, the conquistador arranged a celebratory feast. He then ordered poison to be mixed with the wine to stun Bayano and his men. The plan worked: feeling the worse for wear from the potent cocktail, they were easily taken, thus ending six years of triumphant revolt against the Spanish Crown.

your chest) through the entire system, emerging in a steep-sided verdant gully, dripping with mosses and ferns. At other times, the raised water level means you'll need to go partway in a boat before stepping into the water, and may not be able to make it through on foot. In either case, you'll need a headlamp, footwear with a good grip and a minimum amount of clothing that you're happy to get soaked. Make sure your tour also takes in the impressive **rock walls** that enclose the entrance to the nearby Río Tigre.

Comarca de Madugandi
Entry fee $2

The indigenous community of **Akua Guna** (or Loma de Piedra) at the western end of the Puente Bayano marks the entry to the Guna **Comarca de Madugandi**, established in 1996, which includes eighty percent of the reservoir's surface area and extends from the forested northern shores of the lake up the mountainous backdrop of the Serranía de San Blas. Well over three thousand Guna inhabit the *comarca*, dispersed among fourteen communities, some of which, such as **Icanti**, **Pintupu** and **Tabardi**, are beginning to open up to tourists. Enquire at Akua Guna if you wish to visit.

ARRIVAL AND TOURS   LAGO BAYANO

By bus Buses depart from Albrook bus terminal for Puente Bayano (daily every 40min, 4am–4.40pm; 2hr), which hosts the first of several police checkpoints.

Boat tours It's worth reserving your launch in advance (especially at weekends) as organizing a boat and guide on the spot (from $60/boat) may take time: for lake tours,

contact Noy Ortega (☎6959 6833, prefers 24hr notice), who also runs the small bar by the bridge, or Mateo Cortéz (☎297 0157). Increasingly, tour companies are also offering excursions here from the capital (around $150), but it's far cheaper and not too difficult to organize a visit yourself.

ACCOMMODATION

Guna community hostel Akua Guna. You can stay on a camp bed at the basic community hostel by the bridge (there's an equally basic *fonda* over the road), a single large

room with a TV/DVD player the centrepiece, where some Hollywood action film is likely to be drawing a crowd even as you try to sleep. Dorm $\overline{$10}$/person

Ipetí

Guna and Emberá communities exist either side of the highway at **IPETÍ**. South of the road by the bus stop, a dirt road leads a kilometre down to what was formerly a single community – relocated after their lands were flooded by Lago Bayano – which has split in two, situated on the very picturesque banks of the Río Ipetí. The first and larger settlement announces itself as **Ipetí-Emberá**; it's more set up for tourists, offering a range of **activities**, including horseriding and birdwatching ($10). The smaller splinter community of **Bahu Pono** is even more delightful than Ipetí-Emberá, in a cleaner, quieter (lacking the noisy generators – and electricity), shadier spot, and offers body painting in jagua dye, purchase of *artesanía* and the opportunity for intercultural interaction. Both make an ideal weekend excursion from Panama City, at under three hours from the capital, but with more time it's worth pushing on much deeper into the Darién proper, especially in the dry season, when the river here is too low to swim in and the countryside too denuded to enjoy.

ARRIVAL AND DEPARTURE   IPETÍ

By bus Any eastbound bus from Panama City heading for Metetí or Yaviza, or westbound bus returning to Panama City, will drop you off at the entrance to Ipetí. From here it is a 20min walk down a dirt road.

ACCOMMODATION AND EATING

Village accommodation Accommodation is provided in the *casa comunal* of both communities in a hammock or tent with mattress. Contact Secairo Dojirama (☎6014 6161) for Ipeti-Embera and Esther Caisano (☎6374 3281) for Bahu Pono. Basic meals are available ($3–4/person). $10/person

The Interamericana to Yaviza

Agua Fría No. 1, a place easily missed were it not for the police checkpoint, marks the entry into Darién province. From here, traffic tends to speed along the remaining 110km of virtually straight (predominantly tarred) road past pastureland, the odd settlement and occasional teak plantation to the end of the tarmac at Yaviza, spelling the end of the Interamericana.

8

Puerto Lara

Five kilometres downriver from the important agricultural community of **Santa Fé** lies **Puerto Lara**. One of the few communities to receive plenty of technical support and funding, this Wounaan village of around six hundred people has a functioning fishing association and a computer centre, and produces high-quality crafts (see ⓦpuertolara .com). Though both Emberá and Wounaan are renowned for their **basketry** and **carving**, it is the Wounaan who historically have been artists and have the greater reputation; many pieces from Puerto Lara are sent straight to Panama City for sale, but some can still be perused in the village, where workshops in *artesanía* are also held. Tagua carving and basketry are the main crafts practised. Beyond the village, **boat trips** to various destinations, **guided hikes** (within a small patch of forest of modest appeal), fishing and traditional dances can all be arranged by contacting the president of the tourism committee (see p.280).

ARRIVAL AND DEPARTURE   PUERTO LARA

TO/FROM METETÍ OR PANAMA CITY
By bus and boat Buses between Metetí and Panama City stop at Santa Fé (every 30min; 40min from Metetí and roughly 4hr 30min from Panama City). From Santa Fé, take a bus or *colectivo* taxi a few kilometres to Puerto La Cantera. You will need to have contacted the tourist coordinator in advance to arrange for a *piragua* ($10) to meet you. Boats can only land at La Cantera when the tide is high. From Puerto La Cantera it is a 10–15min boat ride to Puerto Lara.
By bus and 4WD Buses between Metetí and Panama City can drop you at the turn-off to Puerto Lara on the

Interamericana. Enquire at the house at the junction for a 4WD taxi, which costs around $12 for the 11km dirt road to Puerto Lara, which is in appalling condition. Occasional *colectivos* leave the village ($2) for the Interamericana, from where you can catch a bus. In the rainy season (May–Dec) the road is sometimes impassable.

TO/FROM PUERTO QUIMBA
By boat Occasional boats leave for Puerto Quimba ($10/person). Boat hire for a special trip is around $60–80 for the boat.

ACCOMMODATION AND EATING

Village accommodation Contact the president of the tourist committee, Dionisio Negria (☎6765 3086). A plain open-sided wooden "lodge" overlooking the main street offers several partitioned rooms with mattresses (and one pricier, relatively deluxe room with private bathroom) and shared toilet and shower round the back. For meals visitors are charged for the food bought to be cooked and there is a $10 daily fee each for the tourist coordinator and cook assigned to each group. Doubles $25

Metetí

A police security checkpoint that looks set for a siege heralds your impending arrival in **METETÍ**, a long, strung-out settlement that is an increasingly important commercial and administrative hub. It's hardly an endearing place, but if you're travelling around much in the Darién, you're likely to pass through more than once, since it offers good links with both Yaviza – from where it a shortish hop to El Real, the main gateway to the national park – and **Puerto Quimba**, which provides a water-taxi link to La Palma, capital of the Darién and access point for many of the surrounding Emberá and Wounaan communities.

The village's de facto centre lies across the bridge at the turn-off to Puerto Quimba, where there's a taxi rank, a handful of warehouse-like shops and a bus stop. Most of the village lies up the turn-off to the right.

ARRIVAL AND DEPARTURE   METETÍ

By bus The bus station is 1.5km up the Puerto Quimba road from the main junction. Buses to Yaviza (every 30min, 5.30am–6pm; 1hr) leave from the bus station but also pick up passengers at the junction with the Interamericana. There are direct services to Panama City (every 40min, 3am–5 or 5.30pm; 5–6hr), or you can flag down one of the buses coming from Yaviza at the junction with the Interamericana. Buses also run to Puerto Quimba (every 30min, 6am–5pm; 20min), to meet the water-taxi to and from La Palma (every 30min, 5am–6pm; 40min).

ACCOMMODATION AND EATING

Hotel Felicidad Interamericana, 300m before the junction ☎299 6544. The only half-decent place to stay offers thirty clean, compact rooms with private bathroom, a/c, cable TV and secure parking, though like most places in Metetí, it suffers from water shortages. $27
Restaurante Bellagio Signposted off the Puerto Quimba road to the right ☎6521 8753. The best place to eat in town, and in air-conditioned comfort. Dishes, including rabbit and peccary, are roasted or grilled, a rare pleasure in the Darién (mains from $6). It's due to open accommodation too. Daily 11am–10pm.
Restaurante Paso a Paso Interamericana, 200m up from the junction. The cosy patio is a pleasant enough spot to tuck into a tasty breakfast fry-up for a couple of dollars. Inexpensive *almuerzos* and *cenas* ($3–4) with pork, chicken or beef are also served. Daily 6am–10pm.

Yaviza

The gently rolling final 50km of the Interamericana to **YAVIZA** – now predominantly tarred, though gaining potholes – is mercifully more tree-lined than the stretch between Chepo and Metetí. Even so, pastureland still prevails until the highway comes to an abrupt halt at the banks of the Río Chucunaque, hidden behind a new, high chainlink fence and reams of barbed wire, signs of recent moves to strengthen security.

Marking the official start of the infamous **Darién Gap** (*Tapón del Darién* – Darién cork or plug), the highway hiatus between Central and South America, Yaviza simultaneously exudes a lethargic end-of-the-road torpor and an edgy frontier-town feel – the mixed population of around three thousand (Afro-Darienite, Emberá, Wounaan and *mestizo*) eyes outsiders warily, while pairs of gun-toting frontier police officers routinely patrol the town at night togged up in full camouflage combat gear.

The town's only interest to visitors is as a stepping stone to El Real, the gateway to the Parque Nacional Darién, or to the Distrito Cémaco, the northern segment of the Comarca Emberá–Wounaan (currently out of bounds on account of the presumed security situation).

During the day, most of the action occurs at the **wharf**, where the buses pull in: supplies are loaded onto a flotilla of motorized *piraguas* headed for communities upriver, while mounds of plantain and yuca bound for the city are heaved onto trucks, and the surrounding makeshift *fondas* and restaurants do a thriving trade.

ARRIVAL AND INFORMATION

YAVIZA

By bus Buses leave from Albrook bus terminal in Panama City (every 40min–1hr, 3.15–11.30am; 6–7hr) via Santa Fé and Metetí. After the last direct bus to Yaviza, you can take a bus to Metetí and transfer to a local minibus to Yaviza (see opposite). For the return journey, buses leave Yaviza for Panama City (every 40min–1hr, 3.15am–1pm; 6–7hr) and for Metetí (every 30min, 6am–6pm; 1hr).

Police registration On arrival, the heavily fortified frontier

police station (take the left-hand pavement from the bus stop) should be your first port of call, provided you have your SENAFRONT permit from Panama City (see box, p.276).

ANAM office The regional ANAM office (Mon–Fri 8am–4pm; ☎ 299 4495), where you need to pay the $10 national park entry fee, lies 100m beyond the SENAFRONT barracks. They can also advise on hiring a guide if you have not done so in advance.

SCOTLAND'S DOOMED DARIÉN VENTURE

In one of Panama's lesser-known historical footnotes in the late 1600s, the Scots gambled their country's future on a **trading colony in the Darién** in the hopes of transforming **Scotland** into an imperial power to rival England. The undertaking was the brainchild of **William Paterson**, one of the founders of the Bank of England, who, having failed to convince the English government of the plan's viability, managed to rouse the nationalist pride of the Scots, forming the Company of Scotland in May 1695 and persuading rich and poor alike to pour their often meagre savings into the scheme. In the excitement that accompanied preparations, the fact that Paterson had never set foot in Panama and was wholly ignorant of conditions there passed unnoticed. Soon, a sizeable chunk of the kingdom's wealth resided with the company.

A fleet of five ships and 1200 Scots, including Paterson and his family, set sail from Leith in July 1698, their hulls laden with the most unlikely collection of personal possessions and trading goods, including 4000 wigs, 25,000 pairs of shoes and 1500 Bibles. Within days, many of the ships' supplies – including meat, butter and cheese – had spoiled and rations were cut, quickly demoralizing the crews. After four months at sea, the fleet finally anchored in Caledonia Bay, and for five months the settlers worked hard to build **New Edinburgh** (in modern-day mainland Guna Yala), despite disease, low rations, drunken infighting – 5000 gallons of brandy had been transported along with copious amounts of claret and rum – and the tropical environment constantly conspiring against them. To make matters worse, the English king, who was keen not to upset the Spanish, had forbidden any of the Caribbean colonies to assist, despite the fact that the Scots were also his subjects. Only **the Guna** were prepared to help – the Scots seemed infinitely preferable to the Spanish – though they were as uninterested as everyone else in trading with any of the colonists' bizarre wares. When the promised supply ships failed to materialize, and the onset of the rainy season brought another wave of disease, morale slumped further. After ten months, and news that a Spanish fleet was on its way, the colony's council called it a day and decided to weigh anchor. Only one ship made it back to Scotland, carrying a quarter of the original population, including Paterson, though his family had died in Panama.

When rumour of the colony's abandonment reached the ears of the company directors, it was roundly dismissed; refusing to believe that the men they had sent forth "could be guilty of so much groundless cowardice, folly and treachery", the directors sanctioned a second fleet of four ships and 1300 would-be settlers, no better equipped than the first. Arriving to find a deserted colony, the second expedition soon encountered the same problems that had ruined the first and, worse, their renewed presence further riled the Spanish along the coast in Portobelo. Small **battles** soon broke out between the Scots, aided by the Guna, and the Spanish, and six months after arriving in April 1700, the Scots finally surrendered. Thanks to the respect bestowed on them by the Spanish governor, they were all allowed to leave, though none of the ships made it home and only a handful of folk survived.

The venture crippled Scotland financially, leaving the country at the mercy of rival England, which in 1707 eventually agreed to compensate all investors as part of the deal for Scotland conceding to the creation of the United Kingdom of Great Britain.

8

ACCOMMODATION AND EATING

Travellers heading to the Parque Nacional Darién should note that Yaviza is a better place to stock up with **supplies** than El Real. After 7.30pm, you'll be unlikely to unearth anywhere serving food.

Hotel Yadarien 50m along the pavement from the wharf ☎ 6757 6186. This is the town's best accommodation, but basic; its grubby twenty rooms contain beds in varying states of repair, with fan or a/c and cable TV ($9 extra) and private bathrooms. A small first-floor balcony affords a prime view of happenings in the street below. $15

Restaurante Oderay 40m along the pavement from the wharf. This reasonable eating option dishes up a decent plate of fried chicken or fish (and has a good toilet). Daily 7am–7pm.

Parque Nacional Darién

Outranking all of Panama's national parks in both size and reputation, the **PARQUE NACIONAL DARIÉN** is nevertheless one of the least visited protected areas in the country – reaching the refuge at Rancho Frío requires considerable organization – yet the awe-inspiring greenery, laced with rivers and waterfalls, all rich in wildlife, is well worth the time and money, providing a truly magical experience.

Created in 1972 and, at 5790 square kilometres, the most expansive protected area in Central America, the park hugs the Colombian border, a forested carpet rising from the mangroves, coastal lagoons and deserted beaches of the Pacific, rippling over the volcanic ranges of the Serranía del Sapo and Cordillera de Jungurudó northeast to the park's highest point of Cerro Tacarcuna (1875m) on the continental divide of the Serranía del Darién, and stopping just short of the Caribbean coast. Numerous important rivers scythe their way through the green mantle, including the Tuira, Sambú and Balsas.

Now that hiking the Darién Gap has been consigned to history, **visiting the national park** these days means going on a guided tour (see opposite & p.276) and staying at the only permanent camp: ANAM's refuge at Rancho Frío, reached via El Real (see opposite).

8

WILDLIFE IN THE PARQUE NACIONAL DARIÉN

The biodiversity present in the **Parque Nacional Darién** is staggering even as it is shrinking. Over 450 **bird species** have been recorded, including an array of vibrantly coloured macaws and parrots and strange-named rarities such as the beautiful treerunner, scale-crested pygmy tyrant and Chuck-will's-widow. Mammal species top 168, with numerous endemics and endangered animals lurking in the lush vegetation; the park offers the best chance, albeit slender, of glimpsing any of the big-five cats, or a Baird's **tapir** – though spotting their footprints in the early morning mud is more likely – and even the occasional **spectacled bear** has been sighted. Yet the arboreal richness of the **rainforest** in the Darién demands just as much attention, with tracts of primary and secondary growth and a towering canopy of barrigón, spiny cedar and graceful platypodium. A visit in March or April is rewarded with the golden crown of the guayacán, heralding the start of the rains, and the russet bloom of the silvery cuipo trees looking down on the already lofty forest canopy, favourite nesting site of the world's largest concentration of **harpy eagles** (see box, p.286). Most of this can only truly be appreciated from the air, or from breaks in the tree line when ascending the region's peaks. On the forest floor, the scene is very different: dark and dank, and dominated by gnarled tree trunks entwined with vines or studded with vicious spines, vast buttress roots, dangling lianas, ferns and rotting leaf litter.

Declared a UNESCO World Heritage Site in 1981 and a Biosphere Reserve in 1983, the **protection** offered the park in practice is worth little more than the paper it's written on, as illegal hunting, logging, extraction of rare plants and animals, and slash-and-burn agriculture continue unchecked. Ironically, the long list of undesirables that have taken refuge in the rainforest – FARC guerrillas, right-wing paramilitaries, drug traffickers, smugglers and bandits – have acted as unwitting conservationists by frightening off most settlers and major developments, though the fighting over the border in Colombia has also resulted in an influx of refugees, who themselves are clearing land to cultivate.

PARQUE NACIONAL DARIÉN ESSENTIALS

Fees The park entry fee ($10) is payable at the ANAM office in Yaviza (see p.281). Even if you are on an organized tour from Panama City, the park fee may not be included in the package but your guide may collect the fee on behalf of ANAM.

Guides To visit the ANAM refuge at Rancho Frío – currently the only place to stay in the park – you need to hire a guide. ANAM-recommended guides are Isaac Pizarro (☏6242 5220, ✉ipizarro.3003@hotmail.com) and Luis Pacheco (☏67041486). Pizarro charges $50/day per person plus

transport costs. However, it is much cheaper to ask ANAM to contact one of the park wardens (*guardaparque*) to meet you in El Real and guide you up to the refuge.

Permits If you're travelling independently, you'll need to obtain a permit from SENAFRONT in Panama City (see box, p.276) to access the Parque Nacional Darién, although the guides can sort out the permits on your behalf if you contact them in advance of arrival in the Darien. Provide them with your passport details.

El Real

The deceptively fast-flowing waters of the Río Chucunaque snake down 6km from Yaviza through variegated walls of water chestnuts, banana plantations, expansive trees and pastureland to the low-key grassy bank "jetty" of **EL REAL** on the Río Tuira. From the jetty, it's a sweltering fifteen-minute walk into the town proper – another one-time fortified colonial settlement, now a pleasant if somnolent collection of houses constructed from various combinations of wood, zinc and concrete, and a couple of churches, interwoven with a network of cement pathways. The vibe in El Real is far more relaxed than in Yaviza, though, as with Yaviza, it's only likely to serve as a jumping-off point to somewhere else, either a boat trip down the sweeping meanders of the Río Tuira, or, more likely, a hike to the ANAM refuge at Rancho Frío.

ARRIVAL AND INFORMATION   EL REAL

By boat *Piraguas* regularly make the 45min journey from Yaviza to El Real, unless delayed by a major downpour;

colectivo rates are generally $7/person.

ACCOMMODATION AND EATING

Fonda Caña Blanca If you're just after a drink, head for this traditional thatch-and-cane *cantina*. Daily 7am–7pm.

Hotel El Nazareño ☏ 228 3673. Housed in a dilapidated wooden two-storey building which looks on the verge of

collapse, with intermittently functioning plumbing and a DIY shower. $15

★**Restaurante Doña Lola** Near the church. This friendly place serves very tasty food – plantain, lentils and fried chicken. Daily 7am–8pm.

Rancho Frío

The only ANAM refuge still in operation within the park, **Rancho Frío**, sometimes called Pirre Station, is scenically situated on the shady banks of the Río Perescenico, with several **trails** leading off from the camp, including the serious overnight trek to the cloud forest of **Cerro Pirre** (1200m), which requires lugging tent, sleeping bag and provisions up the mountain; it can be chilly at night, so pack something warm. The **Sendero de las Antennas** provides a stiff all-day alternative that culminates in a hilltop police post, affording sweeping views of La Palma and the Golfo de San Miguel, with the Pacific as backdrop. Less strenuous walks can be had closer to camp, but still require a guide – the most popular is the two-hour circular **Sendero Rancho Frío**, which takes in a waterfall and natural *piscina*. During the wet months, the rivers and waterfalls are truly spectacular, though the refuge and mountain trails are often swathed in mist and the quantity of mud to wade through can scarcely be imagined, making even the shortest hike a major physical achievement. In the dry season, paths are easier to hike, views more frequently glimpsed and your chances of spotting mammal life – driven to the river to drink – is greatly enhanced.

ARRIVAL AND INFORMATION

By 4WD In the dry season, the easiest access from El Real is to arrange transport by 4WD as far as the village of Pirre Uno, 12km upriver ($15), from where it is a gentle 1hr 30min walk to the refuge. Or you can arrange for a horse to take you ($15).

By boat In the rainy season, you can sometimes get further upriver from El Real to Pijebaisal (around $30 for the *piragua* from El Real, plus the cost of three gallons of diesel each way), an hour's hike away.

ACCOMMODATION

★ **Rancho Frío** The refuge has recently been renovated and now has limited electricity. All provisions need to be brought with you, including enough for the park warden and/or guide; be sure to pack bottled water or, better still, a water filter or purifying tablets. Camping $5/person; dorms $15

Around the Golfo de San Miguel

Stacked up on a hilly peninsula, the ramshackle collection of wooden buildings that constitute the lively provincial capital of **La Palma** jut out into the widening expanse of the Río Tuira as it empties into the **Golfo de San Miguel**, a large bite-shaped body of

---

VISITING AN EMBERÁ OR WOUNAAN VILLAGE

Staying the night (or preferably several nights) in an **Emberá or Wounaan village** is a great way to interact with villagers, and learn about their day-to-day activities, as well as venturing into the rainforest. Communities used to tour parties tend to have slightly better **facilities** (showers, flush toilets and maybe even mattresses and mosquito nets), whereas others may provide little more than a wooden floor for you to sleep on, possibly with a family, a fire to cook your own food, and a bucket of water for washing.

The location of many settlements on tidal rivers only accessible at high tide often entails a lot of hanging around by jetties waiting for the water level to rise – generally, you need to be flexible yet more organized, taking **food supplies** with you where possible, since many communities expect you to provide the food to cook and village shops are thinly stocked. While **bottled water** – or the means of purifying it – is both necessary and scarce, beer is more widely available, though check on the village etiquette before indulging and be discreet in your drinking, except when the whole village is having a party.

Most visitors head for villages round the **Golfo de San Miguel** or in the **Distrito Sambú** section of the **Comarca Emberá–Wounaan**, where you first need to report to the *comarca* office in Puerto Indio (see p.289) and pay the $10 entry fee. Mobile-phone signals are fickle, so it is sometimes better to ring the village public phone and ask to speak to the *coordinador de turismo* – you may need to ring back again while the person who answers the phone goes to fetch them. The tourist coordinator (or president) is also the person to ask for on arrival. They can tell you the prices and whether money needs to be paid to them (to be disbursed later to the relevant people) or directly to anyone who provides a service. They will also allocate you a personal tourist coordinator (usually $10/group/day), who will organize all aspects of your stay. Accommodation will either be in a traditional communal house (raised, thatched, open-sided structure) or with a family. Families usually take turns in hosting visitors to ensure that wealth is distributed across the community, but it is essential to sort out what's to be paid to whom from the outset to prevent misunderstanding. **Costs** are generally charged per person and itemized separately – village community fee (usually $5–10), accommodation ($8–10/night), meals ($3–4), services of a cook ($10), guided hikes or fishing trips ($10), jagua dye body painting ($5) and dance performances ($40/group) – so assuming one excursion and three meals a day, you should budget around $40–50 per person per day, plus **transport** ($15–25/person, depending on the distance and the number of people, if you manage to catch a *colectivo piragua*; $80–150 if you hire a boat privately).

Sales of **handicrafts** are also an important aspect of village visits, displayed in a small shop or by the artisans themselves, and at set prices (usually from $20) that are inevitably lower than in Panama City. If you don't intend to buy anything, alert the tourist coordinator to avoid embarrassment; otherwise, try to spread your purchases round several artisans.

water penetrating into Panama's southeastern Pacific coastline. Just across the water from La Palma, Isla El Encanto (or Boca Chica) hosts the scarcely visible crumbling remains of the overgrown **Fuerte de San Carlos de Boca Chica**; though little more than a watchtower, it was a crucial link in a chain of defences that safeguarded the gold mines at Cana. Sprinkled along the coastline amid the mangroves are several predominantly Afro-Darienite communities such as **Garachiné** – comprising a collection of fairly dilapidated buildings and negligible services. The rivers that flow into the Golfo de San Miguel are the means of access to the **Comarca Emberá–Wounaan** and to the villages of **La Marea**, **Mogué**, **La Chunga** and, of course, **Sambú** itself.

La Palma

Resembling no other town in Panama, **LA PALMA**, a predominantly Afro-Darienite settlement of around six thousand, is the regional administrative and commercial hub, where motorized dugouts from the coastal and riverine communities jostle for position at the narrow and non-too-salubrious main jetty. The town's one sultry street is chock-full of hole-in-the-wall restaurants, bars and hotels, and shops selling welcome piles of fresh produce and other goods that are regularly shipped in from Panama City. Most visitors gravitate to La Palma to connect with transport to Emberá communities such as La Marea and Mogué, or those further afield up the Río Sambu, and you'd be well advised to stock up with supplies while here – the (pricier) village stores are unlikely to provide much beyond tinned fish, rice and biscuits. If you don't have the means to purify water, make sure you pick up a flagon or two of the bottled variety.

8

ARRIVAL AND DEPARTURE
LA PALMA

By water-taxi Water-taxis to La Palma run from Puerto Quimba (every 30min, 5am–5.30pm; 40min; $4). The last return water-taxi to Puerto Quimba leaves around 5.30pm.

ACCOMMODATION AND EATING

★ **Hotel Biaquirú Bagará** C Principal ☎ 299 6224. If you need to spend the night in La Palma, this family-run hotel is the place to head for, with a dozen neat wood-panelled rooms, some with fan and shared bathroom, others en suite with a/c, and a couple even have a balcony. $30

Hotel Tuira C Principal ☎ 299 6316. For the budget traveller who fancies being in the thick of the noisy action, this friendly hotel provides rooms with fan or a/c ($10 extra) and communal balconies overlooking the estuary. $15

Restaurante Nayelis C Principal. No phone. Serves inexpensive Panamanian and Dominican dishes, but like most places in La Palma it can close early and suffer from a lack of provisions and desultory service. Daily 5am–9pm.

La Marea

Forty minutes' boat ride southeast from La Palma up the sinuous tree-lined Río La Marea, the small, welcoming community of **LA MAREA** provides a perfect introduction to the Emberá way of life. The "*marea*" (tide) is crucial to village logistics since the place is only reachable at high tide, and even then, at the backend of the dry season, the *piragua* scrapes along the riverbed. Traditional open-sided wooden-and-thatch dwellings are dotted across a sloping expanse of neatly trimmed grass ending at the riverbank, where a small *rancho* is used for dance performances and craft displays; opposite this, a tiny shop sells beer and a few tinned essentials.

An infectious tranquillity pervades the settlement – aside from the two hours in the evening when the generator is on – and for most of the night it is illuminated by starlight and kerosene lamps. Unlike in some communities, many of the 160 villagers choose to go about their business clad in traditional attire, except when heading into town. The surrounding forest abounds in **wildlife**, worth exploring with a guide following a trail leading to a waterfall or a lake, or embarking on a substantial hike, or a shorter horseride, to a **harpy eagle nest**, where a willingness to stake the place out for several hours can often be rewarded by a truly special sighting. Otherwise, the days can happily slip by interacting with villagers, getting your body painted in jagua dye and cooling off in the river.

ARRIVAL AND ACTIVITIES   LA MAREA

To reach the community, contact the chief, Gabriel Mengisana (☎ 6736 4368) – who can also organize visits to the less-frequented community of Aldea, another hour upriver and accessible via the La Palma–Chepigana road in the dry season.

By boat Ask around at La Palma on a weekday and you may be able to catch a *colectivo piragua* ($15).

Hiking The village trail goes straight into the rainforest ($10); guiding services are $15/group.

ACCOMMODATION AND EATING

Community accommodation A traditional house is set aside for visitor accommodation, with space to hang your hammock or spread a sleeping bag, and a family allocated either to cook food (which they prefer you to provide; $10–20/group) or lend you their fire pit and some pans to prepare your own meals. $8/person

Mogué

There's a *Heart of Darkness* feel about entering the **Río Mogué**, enclosed by forbidding walls of mangroves, flecked with perching white ibis, which eventually clear at a scenic mooring, ten minutes' walk from the village of **MOGUÉ**. The name derives from Mogadé, a mythical Emberá creature that lived in the mountains and ate people – though Panama City would seem to have devoured more of the dwindling village population as they leave in search of employment. Besides a little tourism, agriculture – plantain, yuca and a variety of other fruits and vegetables – constitutes the economic mainstay of the community, though a minority still fish or hunt iguanas, agoutis and other small animals with traditional arrows or a gun. Another important source of income is basketry – especially masks – for which Mogué is justifiably renowned.

SAVING THE HARPY EAGLE

Instantly recognizable for its splendid slate-grey back, brilliant white chest and distinctive crest, the **harpy eagle** (*águila harpía*) is the largest eagle in the Neotropics and one of the most powerful worldwide, with talons the size of a grizzly bear's claws. The larger female can weigh up to 9kg and measure over 1m long, yet despite a vast wingspan of over 2m, it can reach speeds of up to 80kph while accelerating through trees to stab its prey.

Formerly widespread across the lowland primary forests of the Darién and Bocas del Toro, the harpy eagle has suffered years of decline due to loss of habitat and hunting. However, recent concerted **conservation efforts** are beginning to pay dividends. An increasingly successful breed-and-release programme run by the Peregrine Fund (Ⓦ peregrinefund.org) has caused numbers to swell to over two hundred pairs, resulting in Panama now having the greatest concentration of harpy eagles in Mesoamerica. It will be a long recovery process, though, as harpy eagles are lethargic breeders, laying two eggs once every three years; worse still, once the first egg has hatched, the second is discarded as the pair focus on nurturing the single chick in the nest for another six months, and taking care of it for a further two years.

Working with local communities and conducting educational campaigns in schools, the conservation project has succeeded in heightening public awareness and interest in the harpy eagle. Fittingly, it was legally recognized as the **national bird** in 2002, and since 2006 must by law top the national coat of arms. Additionally, the raptor now even enjoys its own **national day**, on April 10. All this publicity, it is hoped, will help ensure the harpy eagle's continued survival.

For more on the efforts to save the harpy eagle, see Fondo Peregrino-Panamá (Ⓦ peregrinefund.org) and Patronato Amigos del Águila Harpía (Ⓦ aguilaharpia.org).

The focus of community life is the new zinc-roofed **casa comunal**, where on Saturdays or Sundays the leaders preside over the weekly village gathering. The tri-weekly Evangelical services are also a draw for a large number of the community, while late afternoon the football pitch provides an important social focus for both the men's and women's teams, and visitors are welcome to join in.

ARRIVAL AND ACTIVITIES   MOGUÉ

By boat Transport to the village makes the journey expensive unless you catch a village boat ($15 one way from La Palma). Enquire at the main jetty as boats leave with the rising tide most days, but especially Monday and Friday. Otherwise, ring the *presidente de turismo*, Alberto Rito (❶ 6653 3379), to arrange a boat pick-up in La Palma; ask for the cool box to be brought along, which you can fill with fish, chicken or shrimps from the market for meals; otherwise your diet will be very limited.

Hiking and birdwatching It takes 15min to reach the more luxuriant rainforest from Mogué, and a further 1hr 30min along a well-trodden trail to an active harpy eagle nest, though there are numerous less-frequented paths to explore with a guide ($10, plus $10/group for the guide, $20 to visit the harpy eagle) populated with toucans, sloths and monkeys.

Horseriding and fishing These activities can be organized for $10.

ACCOMMODATION AND EATING

Casa comunal Accommodation is on a mattress in a small tent or in a hammock in the *casa comunal*, whose breezy raised platform affords a prime spot to eavesdrop on village life. Food is served at a table there ($10/day for the cook's services/group, plus $3–4/meal). Mattress or hammock **$10**/person

Reserva Punta Patiño   8

Established in the early 1990s, **RESERVA PUNTA PATIÑO** is Panama's first and, at 300 square kilometres, largest private reserve, occupying the entire headland at the tip of the choppy Golfo de San Miguel, just beyond the lively Afro-Darienite fishing village of **Punta Alegre**.

While the landscape is nowhere near as dramatic as the jungle-carpeted peaks of the interior, the regenerating hinterland forest – once devastated by cattle ranching, timber extraction and coconut plantations – is filling up with native hardwoods, though it's an hour's hike to primary forest. The area also covers a stretch of charcoal **beach**, an important expanse of **mangroves**, and mud and **salt flats** that attract an abundance of resident and migratory sea birds.

Managed by the environmental organization **ANCON**, the reserve is not without its critics, not least the Emberá, who feel the land should be theirs. Moreover, the area can only be visited by splashing out on an all-inclusive four-day tour through ANCON Expeditions (see p.75), which includes a day or overnight excursion to Mogué. Still, there's no denying that this is a magical spot to soak up glorious sunsets, aerial displays by diving pelicans, and occasional sightings of bottle-nosed dolphins and humpback whales. On land, mammals to look out for include the weasel-like tayra, grey foxes and the extraordinary-looking capybara, the world's largest rodent, which resembles a giant guinea pig and weighs in at 55kg. Needless to say, the location necessitates lashings of insect repellent to ward off the prolific uninvited guests.

ARRIVAL AND ACCOMMODATION   RESERVA PUNTA PATIÑO

By bus and boat Included in the Ancon Expeditions package, you travel from Panama City to Puerto Quimba, and back, by minibus (4–5hr), then take a boat (1hr 30min) to the reserve.

Punta Patiño Lodge The lodge accommodation is comfortable, comprising ten *cabañas* with single beds, a/c, private cold-water bathrooms and balconies. Perched on a bluff overlooking the bay, the main lodge offers great views, best appreciated from a hammock on its wraparound balcony. Package prices include full board, transport from and to Panama City, and bilingual naturalist guide. It's an extra $96 to overnight in Mogué. **$1606**/person

Garachiné

Set against the imposing backdrop of Cerro Sapo (Toad Hill), the small, neglected fishing community of **GARACHINÉ** surprisingly boasts an airstrip and a road (leading to Sambú before looping back to the coastal Wounaan community of Taimatí), making it another entry point into the rainforest – though time your visit for low tide and you'll be wading knee-deep across alluvial mud flats to the shore.

ARRIVAL AND GETTING AROUND
GARACHINÉ

By plane Air Panama operates twice-weekly flights from Panama City (Wed & Sat; 45min; $85 one way).

By boat Regular connections (Mon, Wed & sometimes Fri)

from La Palma ($25) and Puerto Quimba ($30).

Police registration There is a police checkpoint on the beach, where the boats pull up.

ACCOMMODATION AND EATING

Fonda Carlos Alberto C Principal. Head here for a plate of rice and fried chicken or fish, washed down with a beer from the rather grim local *cantina*. Daily 7am–8pm.

Hospedaje San Antonio C Principal ☎299 6428

(public phone), or ☎6042 8504 (Efrain de Olmedo). The only accommodation is housed in a two-storey wooden building. Basic facilities but a good place to enquire about transport to Sambú or further afield. $12

Río Sambú and the Comarca Emberá-Wounaan

Portal to the twelve communities of the **Distrito Sambú** of the **Comarca Emberá-Wounaan**, 12km up the serpentine **Río Sambú**, the twin settlements of **Sambú** and **Puerto Indio** are generally only reached by river at high tide. The boat trip, sweeping round the river's tortuous bends, causing flocks of white ibis to fly off in unison, is highly atmospheric. As the Río Sambú's waters swell during the rainy season, *piraguas* can penetrate as far upstream as the tiny village of Pavarandó; more easily accessible downriver is the fairly dispersed community of **La Chunga**, which lies a few minutes' paddle up a quiet tributary.

Sambú and Puerto Indio

Outside the waiting room at the airstrip, a hyperbolic wooden sign announces the "Sendero del Paraíso Sambú!". While **SAMBÚ** and its counterpart **PUERTO INDIO**, connected by a footbridge, are pleasant enough places, they serve more as a gateway to what might more aptly merit the description: swathes of primeval **forest** and a serpentine waterway leading to **Emberá** and **Wounaan communities** further upriver.

The contrast in mood and architecture between the two villages is striking: in bustling Sambú – where all accommodation and eating options are located – cement pathways wind between tightly packed houses of various architectural styles, accommodating a mixed population of Emberá, Wounaan, *mestizos* and Afro-Darienites; across the river, quieter Puerto Indio, at the western limit of the Distrito Sambú, of which it is the capital, comprises an indigenous population living in traditional wooden housing raised on stilts, where afternoon social activity centres round the basketball court or football pitch.

TOURS FROM SAMBÚ AND PUERTO INDIO

In **Puerto Indio**, the tourism committee, based in the Oficina del Congreso, offers a range of day **excursions to the Distrito Sambú** (for which you'll need to provide your own food and water), including a guided walk round the village taking in a nearby lake, a half-day excursion to a waterfall involving a 45-minute boat ride and a modest rainforest walk, and lengthier ventures to the communities of La Chunga or Pavarandó. In all cases, **overnight stays** can easily be arranged, either in the *casa comunal* or in someone's house. Arquinio Dogirama (☎emberaguia @yahoo.es) and Domicilio Cardena (La Chunga public phone ☎333 2516) are **guides** authorized by the *comarca*'s tourism committee, though each village has its own guide.

    Sambú guides are not allowed to guide within the *comarca*, but can offer excursions to rainforest and Emberá communities that lie outside the *comarca* boundaries.

ARRIVAL AND INFORMATION

By plane Air Panama operates two flights a week from Panama City via Garachiné (Wed & Sat; 1hr; $87 one way).
By boat Most commercial traffic to Sambú and Puerto Indio ($22 from La Palma, $25 from Puerto Quimba) occurs on Mondays and Fridays.
By boat and 4WD If there isn't a boat going directly to Sambú, in the dry season (Jan–April) you could go to

SAMBÚ AND PUERTO INDIO

Garachiné (see opposite), where you can usually hitch a ride to Sambú along the dirt road ($5–6/person for a *colectivo*, $40 in total if a special trip is necessary).
Police registration The police checkpoint is halfway down the airstrip in Sambú.
Fees The $10 entry fee to the *comarca* should be paid at the Oficina del Congreso in Puerto Indio.

ACCOMMODATION AND EATING

Aqui me Quedo By the airstrip. Housed in a sturdy cane building behind the shop, Benedicta prepares good breakfasts and solid lunches for around $4. Evening meals are a case of what's left over. Daily 7am–8pm.
Mi Sueño By the airstrip ☎ 333 2512 (public phone). Eleven small, wooden-fan-ventilated rooms with shared bathroom, and a large communal balcony affording a pleasant view of the surrounding hillside. The occasionally

functioning restaurant offers cheap meals. Tours to the Emberá village of Villa Queresia can also be arranged. **$12**
★ **Villa Fiesta** By the airstrip ☎ 333 2512 (public phone) or ☎ 6687 2271. Three bright, good-value rooms (a/c & fan) with excellent beds, private bathroom and fridge; meals can also be arranged. Former Emberá *cacique* Ricardo Cabrera, the genial owner and proprietor of the downstairs shop, is fluent in English and a mine of local knowledge. **$25**

La Chunga

Closer to the mouth of the Río Sambú, a small tributary navigable only at high tide leads to the hamlet of **LA CHUNGA**, named after the ubiquitous palm used for basketry. At other times, you land at a pontoon on the main river, from where it's a twenty-minute walk along a boardwalk through mosquito-infested swamp to the village.

An avenue of cedar trees marks the entrance, opening out onto an overgrown basketball court surrounded by a handful of traditional homes. **Basketry** is still widely practised by the women.

While you're here, a village guide can take you **birdwatching** upriver, or you can make a six-hour round trip to a **harpy eagle nest**. Make sure you check out the village **stocks** (*sepo*); miscreants who commit an offence and are unable to pay the fine are placed there for a couple of hours, an experience made particularly painful by being made to sit on a pile of cooked rice, which attracts vicious ants that tuck in to the penitent's buttocks.

ARRIVAL AND ACCOMMODATION

By boat Although La Chunga has its own motorized transport that occasionally travels to and from La Palma ($20) on weekdays, you can also catch a ride in the Sambú/ Puerto Indio boats, which will drop you at the La Chunga pontoon on the Río Sambú, from where it is a 20min walk.

LA CHUNGA

Village accommodation ☎ 333 2516 (public phone). Overnight guests are made comfortable in someone's home on mattresses with mosquito nets and even sheets and pillows. Bathrooms are shared and rudimentary. You pay $12 to someone to do your cooking. **$10**/person

The southeastern Pacific Coast

The Darién's **Pacific coast** is as remote and unexplored as the jungle-filled interior: to the northwest of the Golfo de San Miguel, the coastline is dominated by mangroves, but to the southeast it comprises miles of deserted beaches interspersed with rocky outcrops, cliffs and expanses of pristine forest, with the brooding serranías del Sapo and Jungurudó a dramatic backdrop. Three places of interest stand out here: the Emberá village of **Playa de Muerto**, which receives more visitors than you might think in their community *cabañas* (☎ 299 6428, public phone), and is visited by a couple of tour companies (see p.276); the sport fishing magnet of **Bahía Piñas** (see ⓦ tropicstar.com); and **Jaqué**, the last sizeable community before Colombia, from where it is possible to catch the occasional cargo boat heading across the border to Bahía Solano.

GOLD PLAQUE, COCLÉ PROVINCE

Contexts

History

Though the Republic of Panama is only over a century old, humans have lived on the isthmus for thousands of years. Its location as a slender bridge between two vast land masses has been as crucial to its development as its eventual link between two expanses of ocean.

Pre-Columbian society

Panama's scarce archeological remains give little clue to the societies that inhabited the region, in part because many early excavations were poorly executed and finds were damaged or looted. Lacking the huge structures and sophisticated carvings that epitomize the Mayan, Aztec and Toltec civilizations of Mesoamerica, the trading societies of Central America have always taken an historical back seat. Yet central Panama boasts the earliest traces of **pottery-making** in the Americas with ceramics from Monagrillo, in the northern Azuero Peninsula, carbon dated to 2500–1200 BC. A nearby fishing village in Sarigua is considered to be the isthmus' **oldest settlement**, from around 11,000 BC.

The most sophisticated societies inhabited central Panama, with the richest archeological finds in the **necropolis** of Sitio Conté, outside Penonomé. Excavations by American academics in the 1930s opened up around a hundred **tombs** to reveal thousands of intricate **gold pieces of jewellery** alongside sophisticated **polychrome ceramics** and other artefacts dating back to the first century, most of which were shipped off to the States.

Just down the road at El Caño, near Natá, lies a **ceremonial site** believed to have become a cemetery dating from 500 to 1200 AD, though its original function and significance is left to conjecture, not helped by the fact that a US adventurer decapitated the heads of over a hundred basalt **standing stones**. In the Western Highlands, outside Volcán, another important site indicates the existence of what has been termed the **Barriles culture**, at its apogee around 500 to 800 AD, whose curious **stone statues** of a figure wearing a conical hat carrying another on his shoulders are on display at the anthropological museum in Panama City. A large **ceremonial grinding stone**, or *metate*, adorned with human heads – also in the museum – has led to speculation about human sacrifice. Sprinkled round Sitio Barriles and elsewhere in western and central Panama on moss-covered boulders are numerous **petroglyphs**; the largest example is La Piedra Pintada outside El Valle.

Arrival of the Spanish

The first European credited with setting foot on the isthmus was the Spanish aristocratic notary **Rodrigo Galván de Bastidas**, who in 1501 made a low-key arrival, trading his way peacefully up the Caribbean coast as far as present-day Colón. In contrast, **Christopher Columbus** (Cristóbal Colón), who arrived a year later on his fourth and final voyage to

11,000 BC	2500–1200 BC	1501–02
The first settlement is established on the isthmus, a fishing village, in the Azuero Peninsula.	The earliest traces of pottery-making in the Americas are also found in the Azuero Peninsula.	Spanish explorers Rodrigo de Bastidas and Christopher Columbus visit modern-day Panama.

the "New World", headed for the western and central Caribbean coast, keen to lay his hands on the legendary gold. He attempted to establish the first European settlement on the isthmus, prompting violent conflicts with indigenous populations. Though relations between Columbus and the local chief or *cacique*, **Quibián**, known as "El Señor de la Tierra", were initially friendly, the mood changed once it was clear the Spanish intended to stay. When Columbus left his garrison at Santa María de Belén (in present-day Veraguas) to seek reinforcements, Quibián rallied local leaders to destroy the settlement but was captured by Columbus's brother Bartolomé, who had been left in charge. While being transported as a prisoner downriver to Belén, the chief dived out of the dugout and was presumed drowned. He survived, however, and went on to lead an assault against the invaders, eventually forcing them to flee.

The respite was short-lived. In 1505 the King of Spain, Ferdinand II, intent on expanding and consolidating his empire, dispatched two men to take charge of what had been named "*Tierre Firme*" (extending from present-day Venezuela to Panama): **Alonso de Ojeda** was to govern the land between Cabo de la Vela in present-day Colombia through to the Golfo de Urabá, known as Nueva Andalusia, while **Diego de Nicuesa** was to oversee the west from the gulf to Gracias a Dios on what is now the border between Honduras and Nicaragua (and was known as Castilla de Oro, after its supposed riches). Both campaigns ended in disaster; indeed, of Nicuesa's eight hundred men only a hundred survived.

Though estimates of the indigenous population at the time of the Spanish conquest vary from two hundred thousand to two million, what is not in dispute is the speed at which the local communities were decimated, as much by **disease** brought by the conquistadors as through **massacre** and **enslavement**. The remainder retreated to inhospitable remote mountain areas, where they either lay low or continued their resistance against the invaders. The Spanish instituted a feudal-style system of **encomiendas**, theoretically entrusting "free" indigenous peoples to the stewardship of colonizers for their well-being and instruction in the Catholic faith in return for labour; in practice, workers were more often treated like slaves. Though the system was eventually abolished in 1720, it did not spell the end of intense hardships for many of the rural population.

Balboa and the Mar del Sur

There's little in **Vasco Núñez de Balboa**'s inauspicious early life to suggest he would rise to prominence. After setting foot on the isthmus as a member of Bastidas's expedition, he settled on Hispaniola, where, failing as a pig-farmer, he fled his creditors by stowing away on a boat bound for the mainland. Upon discovery, he was saved from being thrown off the ship thanks to his knowledge of the isthmus. As the incipient Spanish settlements struggled to survive, including the new regional centre **San Sebastián de Urabá** founded by Ojeda, Balboa recommended relocating across the gulf. **Santa María de la Antigua del Darién** (located just on the other side of the current Panama–Colombia border) was thus established on a site that had been seized from followers of Cacique **Cémaco**, a pivotal figure in the indigenous resistance. It was the first successful Spanish settlement on the isthmus, eventually becoming the capital of **Castilla de Oro** until the seat transferred to Panama City in 1524.

1505	1510	1513
The Spanish conquest intensifies; indigenous populations are massacred or enslaved, though some resist.	Conquistador Diego de Nicuesa establishes Nombre de Dios, one of the earliest Spanish settlements in the New World.	Vasco Núñez de Balboa crosses Panama, becoming the first European to see the Pacific Ocean.

CACIQUE URRACÁ

The mighty indigenous chief **Urracá** was the most famous of three Guaymí heads in western Panama (the others being Natá and Parita, after whom the Spanish named settlements) who provided the colonizers' fiercest resistance. He managed to unite tribe leaders who were traditional enemies and conducted guerrilla-type raids from his mountain stronghold above Santa Fé de Veraguas. The Spanish repeatedly failed to defeat Urracá, so resorted to deception, luring him down to Natá under the pretence of negotiating a peace settlement. Here he was immediately seized and taken in chains to Nombre de Dios, from where he was to be deported to Spain. Managing to escape, he returned to his people, vowing to fight the invaders to the death. By this stage the Spanish were reportedly so afraid of his warriors that they avoided conflict with them whenever possible, while the chief continued his nine-year campaign of resistance until he died in 1531.

In the meantime Balboa continued his acquisition of power by subjugating, negotiating and making peace with local tribes; popular with his men and brutal with the local population, he was, nevertheless, more just than his cruel, murderous successors. Hearing from the locals about another sea to the south and land dripping in gold and pearls, Balboa found a route through the forests of the Darién to become the first European to look out onto the **Pacific Ocean** on September 25, 1513. Several days later, in true imperialist fashion, Balboa waded into the water in full body armour, sword in one hand, statue of the Virgin Mary in the other, and claimed possession of the "Mar del Sur" in the name of the King of Spain. Yet he received scant reward for his "discovery" – in 1519 his jealous superior **Pedro Arias de Ávila**, known as Pedrarias the Cruel or *Furor Domini* (Wrath of God), the first governor of Castilla de Oro, had him beheaded despite having given him one of his daughters in marriage.

Panama City and the Camino Real

In the face of appalling losses from disease, Pedrarias moved his base from the Caribbean side to the slightly more salubrious Pacific coast, where he **founded Panama City** (Panamá La Vieja) in 1519. The new settlement became the jumping-off point for further Spanish inroads north and south along the coast, and, after the conquest of Peru in 1533, it began to flourish as the transit point for the fabulous riches of the **Incas** on their way to fill the coffers of the Spanish Crown. From Panama City, cargo was transported across the isthmus on mules along the paved **Camino Real** to the ports of Nombre de Dios and later Portobelo, on the Caribbean coast. A second route, the **Camino de Cruces**, was used to transport heavier cargo to the highest navigable point on the Río Chagres, where it was transferred to dugout canoes to be carried downriver to the coast.

The flow of wealth attracted the attention of Spain's enemies, and the Caribbean coast was under constant threat from European **pirates**, the first of whom, the Englishman **Francis Drake**, successfully raided Nombre de Dios. He received support from the **cimarrones**, communities of escaped African slaves that lived in the jungle and often collaborated with pirates in ambushing mule trains and attacking their former masters.

1519	1533	1595–1739
Panama City is founded on August 15 by conquistador Pedro Arias de Ávila (known as Pedrarias).	The Camino Real flourishes as the main transit route for plundered riches from South America bound for Spain.	The Spanish are constantly threatened by European pirates and privateers; Henry Morgan sacks Panamá Viejo in 1671.

In the most daring assault, in 1671, Welshman **Henry Morgan** and his men sailed up the Río Chagres, having destroyed the fortress at San Lorenzo at the river mouth en route, and crossed the isthmus to ransack Panama City. Though Morgan is generally blamed for the fire that then engulfed the place, it was more likely due to the detonation of the city's gunpowder supplies ordered by the defeated Spanish governor.

The city was rebuilt in 1673 on today's Casco Viejo behind defences so formidable that it was never taken again, but the raiding of the Caribbean coast continued, until finally in 1746 Spain rerouted the treasure fleet around Cape Horn. With the route across the isthmus all but abandoned, Panama slipped into decline.

Independence from Spain

Independence movements in South America, headed by **Simón Bolívar** and **José de San Martín**, were gathering pace by the turn of the nineteenth century. Though the isthmus initially remained fairly detached from the process, it was not devoid of nationalist sentiment. On November 10, 1821, the tiny town of La Villa de Los Santos unilaterally declared that it would no longer be governed by Spain, in what was known as the *Primer Grito de Independencia* (First Cry for Independence); the rest of the country soon followed suit, declaring **independence** on November 30. It retained the name of Panama, as a department of what historians have subsequently termed "Gran Colombia"; with the secession of Ecuador and Venezuela it quickly became Nueva Granada. Almost immediately conflicts emerged between the merchants of Panama City, eager to trade freely with the world, and the distant, protectionist governments in Bogotá, leading to numerous, if half-hearted, attempts at separation. As the century wore on, US influence asserted itself, most notably in the 1846 **Mallarino-Bidlack Treaty**, which granted the US government rights to build a railroad across the isthmus and, significantly, accorded them power to intervene militarily to suppress any secessionist uprisings against the New Granadan government – a theoretically mutually beneficial accord that was to seriously backfire on Bogotá.

The **discovery of gold** in California in 1849 sparked an explosion in traffic across the isthmus. Travel from the US east coast to California via Panama – by boat, overland on foot, and then by boat again – was far less arduous than the trek across North America, and thousands of "Forty-niners" passed through on their way to the goldfields. In 1850 a US company began the construction of a **railway** across Panama. Carving a route through the inhospitable swamps and rainforests proved immensely difficult – thousands of the mostly Chinese and West Indian migrant workers died in the process – but when the railway was completed in 1855, the Panama Railroad Company proved an instant financial success, earning $7 million in profit in the first six years, despite having cost $8 million to construct. The railway also marked the beginning of a new era in foreign control: within a year, the first **US military intervention** in Panama had taken place (see box opposite).

The French canal venture

In 1869 the opening of the first transcontinental railway in the US reduced traffic through Panama, but the completion of the **Suez Canal** that same year made the

1746	1821	1830
Spain re-routes the treasure fleet around Cape Horn, resulting in economic decline.	Panama declares independence from Spain, and joins the confederacy of Gran Colombia (Bolivia, Peru, Ecuador, Venezuela, Colombia and Panama).	Panama becomes a province of Colombia after the dissolution of Gran Colombia.

THE WATERMELON WAR

The completion of the railroad left many Panamanian labourers, including the new immigrant workforce, unemployed and resentful of their well-paid US counterparts, some of whom showed scant respect for their hosts or local customs. On April 15, 1856, tensions spilled over. An intoxicated (white) American named Jack Oliver, who had been killing time in the bars waiting for the boat, grabbed a slice of **watermelon** from a local (black) stall holder and refused to pay. When the trader drew a knife, Oliver's mate tossed a dime at him, further enraging the merchant, and as he advanced on Oliver, the latter drew a gun. An attempt to disarm the American resulted in a bystander getting shot, prompting a full-scale anti-US **riot**. Many Americans holed up in the railway depot and gunfire was exchanged with the crowd, which was attempting to batter down the door. Rather than control the situation, the **police** joined in the affray, which continued until a trainload of the vigilante **Isthmus Guard** arrived to disperse the mob. While the number of casualties in the so-called "Watermelon War" – 17 dead and 29 wounded, predominantly American – was not disputed, blame for the violence was. Amid claims and counter-claims of racism, the US government dispatched two warships to Panama and occupied the railway station – though only for three days – but their demand for total control of the railroad was refused.

long-standing dream of a canal across the isthmus a realistic possibility. Well aware of the strategic advantages such a waterway would offer, Britain, France and the US all sent expeditions to seek a suitable route. The French took the initiative, buying a concession to **build a canal**, as well as purchasing the Panama Railroad, from the New Granadan government. In 1881, led by ex-diplomat **Ferdinand de Lesseps**, the driving force responsible for the Suez Canal, the Compagnie Universelle du Canal Interocéanique began excavations.

Despite de Lesseps' vision and determination, the "venture of the century" proved to be a disaster, not least because of his technical ignorance and arrogance. In the face of impassable terrain – forests, swamps and the shifting shales of the continental divide – the proposed sea-level canal proved unfeasible, while yellow fever, malaria and a host of other unpleasant diseases ravaged the workforce. In 1889 the Compagnie collapsed; $287 million had evaporated as a result of financial mismanagement and corruption, implicating the highest levels of French society in what an official described as "the greatest fraud of modern times". Hundreds of thousands of ordinary French investors lost everything.

The War of the Thousand Days

At the end of the nineteenth century the simmering feud between the Conservative and Liberal parties erupted into a bloody three-year **civil war** referred to as the **War of the Thousand Days** (*Guerra de los Mil Días*). Though there were distinct ideological differences – ruling elite **Conservatives** supported a strong central government, limited voting rights and close bonds between church and state whereas the merchant class and educated **Liberals** wanted more decentralized, federal government, universal voting rights and a greater division between church and state – there were also many factions within each party. The violence was triggered by alleged election fraud by the landed Conservatives in their bid to remain in power, but by the time the bloody conflict had

1850–55	1881	1902
The California gold rush prompts construction of the Panama Railroad across the isthmus.	French architect Ferdinand de Lesseps begins excavations for the Panama Canal. Some 20,000 workers die before the venture is abandoned in 1889.	End of three-year civil war – La Guerra de los Mil Días – which claimed 100,000 lives.

PEDRO PRESTÁN AND THE FIRE OF COLÓN

Another ugly episode between Liberals and Conservatives and a further example of US intervention resulted in the public hanging of **Pedro Prestán**, a Liberal revolutionary who took advantage of the absence of Colombian troops in Colón – they had headed over to Panama City to quell an attempted coup – to seize control of the city. After looting businesses to raise money, he and his band of rebels purchased arms from the US, which arrived on a steamship that anchored in the bay. When the steamship agent refused to unload the arms, Prestán took the agent, US consul and several other Americans **hostage**, threatening to kill them if the US naval vessel stationed nearby landed troops and if the arms were not handed over. Though the weapons were promised and the hostages released, the Americans reneged on the deal. Fleeing to Monkey Hill outside the city, Prestán and his poorly armed combatants fought with the Colombian troops now back from Panama City. The rebels were routed and the **city caught fire**; built entirely of wood, it was totally engulfed in flames, killing eighteen and leaving thousands homeless. Prestán, who had fled by boat to his native Cartagena, became the scapegoat. Many of his men were rounded up and **executed** while Prestán himself was captured, tried and convicted by a partisan jury, and left to hang above the railway tracks in Colón.

ended in 1902, claiming around a hundred thousand lives, it was hard to pinpoint what much of the fighting had actually been about. It's also unclear whether key Liberal protagonists were motivated more by the desire for separation or greater democracy and social justice; regardless, most Liberals were subsequently elevated to the status of nationalist heroes.

In Panama the initial Liberal revolt was led by **Belisario Porras**, the popular exiled lawyer, who later won three periods of office as president of Panama. With the support of the presidents of Nicaragua and Ecuador, Porras entered western Panama on March 31, 1900, with an invasion force commanded by Colombian **Emiliano Herrera**, at the insistence of President Zelaya of Nicaragua. Their antagonism was a major factor in the ultimate Liberal failure. Moving towards Panama City, they gathered numerous supporters, but slow progress allowed reinforcements to arrive from Colombia. On arrival outside the capital, Herrera rejected Porras's attack plan and led a botched single-pronged assault on the city that resulted in a thousand dead. Though the Conservatives reasserted their authority, small bands of Liberal sympathizers ran riot in the interior, especially in the central rural areas under the leadership of **Victoriano Lorenzo**, a local official of mixed race from Coclé and a champion of the indigenous population.

In 1901, a second Nicaraguan-backed Liberal force managed to take Colón and effectively immobilize the railway, forcing the Colombian government to ask the US to broker an armistice. The Liberals, fearing intervention by the US government, agreed to the peace conditions but Lorenzo refused to accept the terms. In a sordid collusion between both Conservative and Liberal social elites, Lorenzo was tricked into capture. In disregard of the amnesty detailed in the accord, he was summarily tried and executed by firing squad on May 15, 1903, in the Plaza de Armas (today's Plaza de Francia) of Panama City. Six months later Panama separated from Colombia.

1903	1914	1924
Backed by the US, Panama declares separation from Colombia but essentially hands the US control of the future Canal Zone "in perpetuity".	The canal is completed. Around 56,000 people from 97 countries have a hand in its construction.	President Belisario Porras completes his third term in office, having established Panama's transport, health, education and legal systems.

Separation from Colombia

Despite the French canal debacle, the dream of an interoceanic waterway remained as strong as ever. The US government took up the challenge; President **Theodore Roosevelt**, in particular, felt that the construction of a canal across Central America was an essential step to becoming a major sea power. At first the favoured route was through Nicaragua, but the persuasive lobbying of Philippe **Bunau-Varilla**, former acting director and major shareholder in the French company, swung the Senate vote in Panama's favour. His masterstroke was to buy ninety Nicaraguan stamps that showed an erupting volcano – a major argument against the Nicaragua route – and send one to each senator just three days before the vote. In 1903 a **treaty** allowing the US to build the canal was negotiated with the Colombian government, whose senate refused to ratify it, understandably wary that the US would not respect their sovereignty. Outraged that "the Bogotá lot of jackrabbits should be allowed to bar one of the future highways of civilization", Roosevelt gave unofficial backing to Panamanian secessionists.

In the event, the **separation** was a swift almost bloodless affair with only one casualty. The small Colombian garrison in Panama City was bribed to switch sides and a second force that had landed at Colón agreed to return to Colombia without a fight after its officers had been tricked into captivity by the rebels. On November 3, 1903, the **Republic of Panama** was declared and immediately recognized by the US, whose gunship standing offshore prevented Colombian reinforcements from landing to crush the rebellion.

The canal

A new **canal treaty** was quickly negotiated and signed on Panama's behalf by the slippery Bunau-Varilla, who had managed to get himself appointed a special envoy, theoretically only with negotiating powers. The Hay-Bunau-Varilla Treaty gave the US "all the rights, power and authority…which [it] would possess and exercise as if it were the sovereign", in perpetuity over an area of territory – the **Canal Zone** – extending five miles (8km) either side of the canal. In return, the new Panamanian government received a one-off payment of $10 million and a further $250,000 a year. (Of particular interest to Bunau-Varilla was the $40 million the French canal company received for all its equipment and infrastructure.) Even American Secretary of State John Hay admitted the treaty conditions were "vastly advantageous to the US and we must confess…not so advantageous to Panama". Panama's newly formed national assembly found the terms outrageous, but when told by Bunau-Varilla that US support would be withdrawn were they to reject it – a claim he invented on the spot – they ratified the treaty, and work on the canal began.

It took ten years, 56,000 workers from 97 countries and some $352 million to complete the task, an unprecedented triumph of organization, perseverance, engineering and, just as crucially, sanitation, during which time chief medical officer Colonel **William Gorgas** established a programme that **eliminated yellow fever** from the isthmus and brought malaria under control. As a result the **death toll**, though still some 5600 workers predominantly of West Indian descent, was substantially lower than it would otherwise have been. Meanwhile the two men in charge, **John Stevens**, a brilliant railway engineer, and his successor **George Goethals**, a former army engineer, managed to solve the problems that had stymied the French. The idea of a sea-level canal was

1925	1936	1940
The Dule Revolution results in the establishment of the semi-autonomous Comarca Guna Yala.	Despite a treaty limiting US rights, tensions continue to build between Panama and the US territory of the Canal Zone.	Fascist president Arnulfo Arias Madrid sets about disenfranchising Afro-Antillean and Chinese Panamanians while pursuing racist immigration policies.

quickly abandoned in favour of constructing a **series of locks** to raise ships up to a huge artificial lake formed by damming the mighty Río Chagres. Stevens was responsible for maximizing the potential of the railway, devising an ingenious pulley system that enabled them to excavate over 170 million cubic metres of earth and rock, three times the amount removed at Suez. The 13km **Gaillard Cut**, which ran through the continental divide, required a mind-boggling 27,000 tonnes of dynamite. The end result, overseen by Goethals, was the largest concrete structure, earth dam and artificial lake that the world had ever seen, accomplished with pioneering technology that set new standards for engineering. On August 15, 1914, the SS *Ancón* became the first ship to officially transit the canal, which was completed six months ahead of schedule.

An enormous **migrant workforce**, at times outnumbering the combined populations of Panama City and Colón, was imported to work on the canal's construction, and many of these workers – Indians, Europeans, Chinese and above all West Indians – stayed on after its completion, indelibly transforming the racial and cultural make-up of Panama. Work was carried out under an apartheid labour system, where white Americans were paid in gold and the rest – the vast majority of whom were black – in silver. Employees were "**gold roll**" or "**silver roll**", a categorization that permeated every aspect of life. The gold roll employees and their families enjoyed higher wages, superior accommodation, better nutrition, health care and schooling; even toilets and drinking fountains were set aside for the exclusive use of one group or the other. Unsurprisingly, the mortality rate among black workers was four times higher than among whites.

The New Republic

Though their economy boomed during the canal's construction, it was soon apparent to Panamanians that they had exchanged control by Bogotá for dominance by the US. The government, largely controlled by a ruling **oligarchy** known as the "twenty families", was independent in name only; the US controlled everything – trade, communications, water and security. Moreover, the de facto sovereignty and legal jurisdiction that the US enjoyed within the Canal Zone made it a strip of US territory in which Panamanians were denied the commercial and employment opportunities enjoyed by the US "**Zonians**", a situation that lasted well beyond the completion of the canal. The US agreement to guarantee Panamanian independence came at the price of intervention whenever the US considered it necessary to "maintain order", a right they exercised on several occasions.

One such action followed the Dule or **Guna Revolution** in 1925, an eventual result of the Panamanian government refusing to recognize the relative autonomy granted by the Colombian authorities in 1870 through the Comarca Tulenega. Pressure mounted when outside groups were given concessions to plunder Guna resources and persistent attempts made to suppress Guna culture. Following an **armed revolt** led by Sailas (chiefs) Nele Kantule and Olokindibipilele (Simral Colman), which resulted in around twenty fatalities on each side, the Guna declared independence. Forestalling government retaliation, the US stepped in and mediated a **peace agreement** that granted the Guna the semi-autonomous status they still retain.

The Republic of Panama's first president, the respected Conservative **Manuel Amador Guerrero**, was actually from Colombia, though he had been heavily involved in the

1964	1968	1977
"Martyrs' Day" flag riots, precipitated by a student protest, leave 21 Panamanians dead and over 500 injured in the Canal Zone.	Charismatic Omar Torrijos, Chief of the National Guard, overthrows president Arnulfo Arias and imposes a military dictatorship.	Torrijos secures a new canal treaty with US President Jimmy Carter, who agrees to transfer the canal to Panamanian control in 1999.

separatist movement, and more important, was well known to the Americans as the former medical officer for the Panama Railroad. But the first Panamanian president of real impact was **Belisario Porras**, elected to office in 1912 for the first of three terms (1912–16, 1918–20, 1920–24). A trained lawyer and prominent Liberal leader from the War of a Thousand Days, he is largely credited for establishing the basic infrastructure necessary for a newly independent state – roads, bridges, hospitals, schools, libraries, a legal system, communication networks, even the cherished national lottery.

The rise of nationalism

Despite a **new treaty** limiting the US right of intervention in 1936, resentment of American control became the dominant theme of Panamanian politics and the basis of an emerging sense of national identity. **Arnulfo Arias Madrid**, a fascist and Nazi-sympathizer – earning him the nickname "Führer Criollo" – exploited this while going on to become one of the country's most popular leaders. Of middle-class farming stock from Coclé, he was the first Panamanian graduate of Harvard Medical School but abandoned medicine in favour of politics on his return to Panama. He founded Acción Communal, the political precursor to the Partido Nacional Revolucionario and present-day **Partido Panameñista** (PP), which espoused his nationalistic and initially racist doctrine of **Panameñismo**. After assisting his older brother Harmodio Arias Madrid to the presidency in 1932, he won office himself in 1940, for the first of three periods (1940–41, 1949–51 and 1968).

During his first term he set about disenfranchising Afro-Antillean and Chinese Panamanians and pursuing **racist** immigration policies. On the positive side he instigated the social security system, improved many workers' rights (a policy strand abandoned in his later term), modernized banking and gave the vote to women. Crucially, he was adamant about pushing for a better deal with a US government intent on expanding its military defences outside the Canal Zone. But the US-backed Panamanian Policía Nacional (National Police) and its successor, the Guardia Nacional (National Guard), made sure that no president who challenged the status quo lasted long in office and Arias was ousted by military coup each time, the last after only two weeks.

Nevertheless, **anti-US riots** erupted periodically over the next thirty years. The ten-thousand-strong protest in 1947 against the US attempt to extend the lease on World War II-era bases outside the Canal Zone helped persuade the deputies not to ratify the proposal. By 1948, the US military had withdrawn from outside the Zone. The most infamous disturbances, however, were the so-called **flag riots** of 1964. The flying of flags was a trivial but symbolic battleground for Panamanian–US antagonism. To ease tensions, the US government agreed to the Panamanian flag being flown beside the Stars and Stripes in selected places in the Zone. When in Balboa High School the US flag was flown on its own for two days in succession, two hundred Panamanian students arrived at the school to raise a Panamanian flag. A skirmish broke out during which the Panamanian flag was torn, prompting full-scale mob violence. The 21 Panamanians who died in the fracas were later elevated to the status of **national martyrs**, commemorated annually on January 9, Día de los Mártires (Martyrs' Day). A diplomatic protest about US aggression ensued, going all the way to the UN and resulting in President Lyndon Johnson's promise of a new canal treaty.

1983	1988	1989
Colonel Manuel Noriega becomes de facto military ruler. He is initially supported by the US, but also cultivates drug-cartel connections.	US charges Noriega with rigging elections, drug smuggling and murder; Noriega declares state of emergency, dodging a coup and repressing opposition.	US troops invade Panama and oust Noriega, but also kill and leave homeless thousands of civilians.

Omar Torrijos and the new canal treaty

After a brief power struggle following the coup to oust Arnulfo Arias in 1968, Lieutenant Colonel **Omar Torrijos** of the National Guard established himself as leader of the new military government. Fracturing the political dominance of the white merchant oligarchy (known disparagingly as the *rabiblancos*, or "white tails") in his pursuit of a pragmatic middle way between socialism and capitalism, he was a charismatic, populist leader. Over twelve years he introduced a wide range of reforms – a new constitution and labour code, nationalization of the electricity and communications sectors, expanded public health and education services – while simultaneously maintaining good relations with the business sector, establishing Colón's **Zona Libra** and initiating the banking secrecy laws necessary for Panama's emergence as an international financial centre. On the debit side, he was extremely intolerant of political opposition and his critics were often imprisoned or simply "disappeared"; several **mass graves** from the period were unearthed during a Truth Commission instigated by President Moscoso, though there was no evidence of Torrijos' direct involvement in the atrocities.

Central to Torrijos' popular appeal was his insistence on gaining Panamanian control over the canal. After lethargic negotiations with the Nixon and Ford administrations, Torrijos signed a new canal treaty with US President Jimmy Carter on September 7, 1977. Under its terms the US agreed to a gradual withdrawal, passing complete control of the canal to Panama on December 31, 1999; in the meantime it was to be administered by the **Panama Canal Commission**, composed of five US and four Panamanian citizens. Even so, the US retained the right to intervene militarily if the canal's neutrality was threatened. Under pressure from Washington to democratize, Torrijos formed a political party, the **Partido Revolucionario Democrático** (PRD), and began moving Panama towards free democratic elections. In 1981, however, he died in a plane crash in the mountains of Coclé Province. Many Panamanians believe that there was some involvement by the **CIA** or by Colonel **Manuel Noriega**, Torrijos's former military intelligence chief.

Manuel Noriega and the US invasion

After a period of political uncertainty, Noriega took over as head of the National Guard, which he restructured as a personal power base and renamed the Fuerzas de Defensa de Panamá (**Panama Defence Forces** or PDF), becoming the de facto military ruler in 1983. Although the 1984 elections gave Panama its first directly elected leader in nearly two decades, Nicolás Ardito Barletta, the real power lay in the hands of Noriega, backed by the US government.

A career soldier, Panama's new military strongman had been on the US Army's payroll as early as the 1950s and the CIA's from the late 1960s. After training at the notorious School of the Americas, he was made chief of intelligence for the National Guard in 1970. In the early 1980s, Noriega assisted the US by supporting its interests elsewhere in Central America, especially Nicaragua. Whereas Torrijos had supported the leftist Sandinistas in Nicaragua's civil war, Noriega allegedly became an important figure in covert US military support for the Contras, helping to funnel money and weapons to the guerrilla force – a charge he denies. Noriega was also busy building his relations

1992	1999	2003
US court finds Noriega guilty of drug charges, sentencing him to forty years in prison.	Mireya Moscoso, widow of Arnulfo Arias, becomes the country's first female president, and presides over the handover of the canal to Panama in December.	A countrywide strike over mismanagement of the nation's social-security fund shuts down public services and turns violent.

with the Colombian cocaine cartels in Medellín. Although this extracurricular activity was ignored by the US for years, in 1986 the **Iran-Contra Affair** – in which the US government sold weapons illicitly to Iran and used the proceeds to fund the Contras – brought an unwelcome glare of publicity on the cosy arrangement between Noriega and the CIA. Deciding it was politically expedient to drive Noriega from power, the US government began economic sanctions in 1987, followed by Noriega's indictment on drug charges in the US in February 1988.

On December 20, 1989, US President George H.W. Bush launched the ironically named "**Operation Just Cause**", and 27,000 US troops invaded Panama. They quickly overcame the minimal organized resistance offered by the PDF. Bombers, helicopter gunships and even untested stealth aircraft were used against an enemy with no air defences, and hundreds of explosions were recorded in the first twelve hours. The poor Panama City barrio of El Chorrillo was heavily bombed and burned to the ground, leaving some 15,000 homeless; indeed, a Human Rights Watch report noted that civilian deaths were over four times higher than military casualties among the PDF. Noriega himself evaded capture and took refuge in the papal nunciature, before being forced to surrender on January 5 after a round-the-clock diet of ear-splitting heavy metal and rock music blasted from the car park. He was taken to the US, **convicted of drug trafficking** and sentenced to forty years in a Miami jail before being extradited to France to face trial on money-laundering charges.

Estimates of the number of Panamanians killed during the invasion vary from several hundred to as many as ten thousand. That the invasion was **illegal**, however, was clear: it was condemned as a violation of international law by the United Nations and the Organisation of American States, both of which demanded the immediate withdrawal of US forces. Despite most Panamanians being relieved to see the back of Noriega, they were outraged at the excessive use of force and America's blatant disregard for Panamanian sovereignty.

The twenty-first century

In an interesting twist, the presidential elections of 1999 were contested between Martín Torrijos, illegitimate son of the former military ruler, and the widow of Arnulfo Arias (the man Torrijos ousted in 1968), **Mireya Moscoso**, who became Panama's first female leader. On December 31 she presided over the seamless **handover of the canal**, which is now efficiently managed by the independent Autoridad del Canal de Panamá. The US withdrawal was a mixed blessing for Panama's economy: many jobs disappeared with the closure of the bases, but the valuable real estate and infrastructure Panama inherited created investment opportunities. Still, a number of the former US buildings lie abandoned, and relations with the US remain complex.

Moscoso's term in office got off to a rocky start when, before the first budget vote, she gave Cartier watches and jewellery as "Christmas presents" to the 72 members of the legislative assembly. It set the tenor for the presidency, which was scarred with accusations of corruption and incompetence. Her term ended in similarly controversial fashion as she tried to push through construction of a tarred road linking Boquete and Cerro Punta through the national park of Volcán Barú. Opposition to the outrageous plan successfully united numerous national and international environmental groups

2004	2006
Martín Torrijos, son of former dictator Omar Torrijos, is elected president and the canal earns record revenues of one billion US dollars.	Referendum on a $5.3-billion plan to expand the Panama Canal is passed by an overwhelming majority. Panama and the US sign a free-trade agreement.

THE BILLION-DOLLAR GAMBLE: EXPANDING THE PANAMA CANAL

The ongoing **canal expansion** programme aims to accommodate most post-Panamax vessels (ships that don't currently fit in the canal) through a larger set of locks and improve the canal's efficiency by widening the Gaillard Cut. Initially budgeted at $5.3 billion, with a completion date of 2014, the project may not be finished until 2016 and its costs have soared. Many regard the two-week strike by workers in early 2014 over who should pay for the $1.6 billion in cost overruns – ironically just as the canal was celebrating its centenary – as an ominous sign of further troubles to come. As it is, some modern ships are too large even to fit through the new lock gates, and once again there are plans to construct a rival canal across Nicaragua, this time backed by the Chinese.

and became a major election issue allowing **Martín Torrijos**, heading the PRD, to become president.

Though Torrijos junior was elected on a platform of "zero corruption" it did not take long before scandals started to emerge; nor was his administration's record on the environment particularly memorable, approving countless hydroelectric projects in Chiriquí and Bocas del Toro Provinces with scant environmental assessment studies and little negotiation with the indigenous populations most affected. One of his major challenges was to reform the Social Security Fund, which was on the verge of financial collapse, but unpopular proposals to increase workers' contributions and raise the retirement age provoked angry street protests, forcing the government to back down and pass a watered-down bill. He did, however, help to tighten measures against drug-trafficking and money-laundering. And in his biggest gamble, he green-lighted the **canal expansion** project (see box above).

The elections in May 2009 broke the political stranglehold that the PRD and PP had enjoyed for the previous seventy years as conservative multimillionaire supermarket magnate **Ricardo Martinelli** swept to power. Head of the new **Cambio Democrático** (Democratic Change) party, he immediately launched popular initiatives: increasing the minimum wage; establishing pensions; and ensuring free books and uniforms for school children. The country enjoyed sustained economic growth – though the gap between the "haves" and "have-nots" continued to increase – and the government spent a staggering $20 billion on roads, schools and bridges across the country, as well as packing the capital with countless more skyscrapers, the new Metrobus and Metro systems and the extension of the Cinta Costera, in the form of a highly controversial ring-road round Casco Viejo.

However, as with Martinelli's predecessors, corruption scandals flourished, and his increasingly autocratic ruling style – alleged phone-tapping of political opponents, curtailment of the press and overuse of police force, especially against indigenous communities – provoked much criticism at home and internationally. In the 2014 elections, Martinelli's estranged vice-president, **Juan Carlos Varela**, who had fallen out with his former ally after being dismissed as foreign minister, won a surprising victory for the Partido Panameñista. His family owns the country's biggest distillery, and he is a member of Opus Dei, but it remains to be seen what is on his political agenda.

2009

Right-wing supermarket magnate Ricardo Martinelli is elected president in a landslide victory, breaking the 70-year-old electoral stranglehold of Panama's two main parties.

2011

Noriega is extradited back to Panama, after prison terms in the US and France, to serve another twenty years for murder and money laundering.

PANAMA'S INDIGENOUS POPULATION

While Panama's national economy enjoys one of the highest growth rates in Latin America, the distribution of wealth remains highly skewed, the poorest twenty percent living below the poverty line, receiving less than 1.5 percent of the earnings. This includes most of Panama's 415,000 **indigenous citizens**, who comprise around thirteen percent of the total population according to the 2010 census. Some have been assimilated to varying degrees into urban life; most, though, inhabit the rural regions, with around half living in the various *comarcas* – semi-autonomous areas demarcated by the state over the last sixty years – many without access to clean water, health care, electricity, decent schooling or paid employment.

Panama has eight indigenous groups, the most numerous by far being the **Ngäbe** (180,000), who share a vast *comarca* in western Panama, spanning Bocas del Toro, Chiriquí and Veraguas, with the less numerous **Buglé** (10,000). The groups are culturally similar but speak mutually unintelligible languages. The first *comarca* established was Guna Yala in 1953, the result of a revolution by the **Tule** (or **Guna**) people (62,000) in 1925, which stretches out along the coastal strip of eastern Panama to the Colombian border, incorporating over four hundred tiny islands. Much later, the smaller inland *comarcas* of Wargandi and Madugandi were added. The **Emberá** (23,000) and **Wounaan** (7000) inhabit the forests of the Darién, though some have now migrated to the Chagres river basin nearer Panama City. Around 35 percent remain in the two *comarcas*; many others are scattered among around forty riverside communities across the province. At the other end of the isthmus in Bocas del Toro Province, the **Naso**, also known as the Teribe, number just over three thousand and live around Changuinola and along the rivers heading up into the mountains. A few kilometres north, on the banks of the Río Sixaola, live the **Bri-Bri** (2500). The oft-forgotten **Bokota** number less than a thousand and are often mistakenly considered Buglé since they speak Buglere; they live around the Bocas–Veraguas provincial boundary in the Comarca Ngäbe-Buglé.

Suffering the highest levels of poverty, some Ngäbe and Buglé migrate for seasonal jobs on banana, coffee and sugar plantations to earn cash to sustain them the rest of the year. Guna, Emberá and Wounaan women, in particular, earn an income from their fine craftwork – though villages in remote areas more or less compete with each other for the small percentage of visitors that venture past Panama City and the canal.

Although the *comarcas* cover a fifth of Panama's land, these territories as well as those of indigenous communities residing outside their boundaries are under constant **threat**. Some lands lie within national parks and reserves, which has enabled government, generally through ANAM, to apply restrictions on traditional lifestyles in the name of conservation, while simultaneously allowing mining or hydroelectric projects to go ahead often with minimal or no consultation with indigenous authorities and no compensation to those forced to move. Government and big business are not the only threats: poor cattle farmers, *colonos*, desperate for fresh grazing land, have been encroaching on indigenous lands for years, particularly in eastern Panama.

By far the most organized politically are the Guna, who have had the greatest success in defending their rights against the state and possess three representatives at government level. The other main indigenous groups have tended to follow the Guna model, electing a **General Congress** consisting of a *cacique* and community representatives. Leaders from the various indigenous parties have begun working together to tackle attempts to marginalize them or incorporate them into models of development they do not espouse. In 2008, a petition listing indigenous peoples' grievances against the state was presented to the American Commission on Human Rights. The resulting landmark victory for the Ngäbe living along the Río Changiunola, who secured an injunction to halt the dam threatening their village, gives reason for some optimism.

2012	**2014**
Countrywide protests by the Ngäbe and Buglé over mining and hydroelectric concessions on their land ends in police violence leaving thousands wounded and three dead.	The canal expansion programme falters with spiralling costs, strikes and delays as Juan Carlos Varela is voted in as new president.

Wildlife

One of Panama's major attractions is its varied and abundant wildlife. For its diminutive size – slightly larger than the Republic of Ireland, smaller than the US state of South Carolina – Panama's biodiversity and level of endemism is astounding. Located at the barely touching fingertips of two continents, the country hosts fauna from both land masses: deer and coyotes more readily associated with temperate North America as well as jaguars and capybaras from the tropical South, and a cornucopia of astounding marine life. The flora is equally diverse: an estimated ten thousand vascular plant species grow on the isthmus, predominantly in the country's luxuriant tropical rainforests, which cover an estimated 45 percent of the land.

Flora

Panama's **tropical wet forests**, or **rainforests**, which by definition receive an annual rainfall of more than 2m and can receive up to three times that amount on some of the Caribbean slopes, are what most excite nature-lovers. **Primary** rainforests – original, undisturbed growth – are highly prized for their greater biodiversity, comprising seventy percent of the country's forested area. In these complex ecosystems most animal and plant activity occurs in the forest "roof" or **canopy** and the **sub-canopy**, where dangling vines and lianas provide vital transport links. Poking out of the canopy, which filters out over ninety percent of the sunlight, are a sprinkling of robust **emergent trees**, generally around 60–70m tall, able to withstand being buffeted by storms and scorched by sunlight. Most easily recognized, and visible from a great distance, is the ringed silvery grey trunk of the **cuipo** (*cavanillesia platanifolia*), which exhibits a bare umbrella-like crown during the dry season; particularly abundant in the Darién, it is a favourite nesting site of the harpy eagle. Equally distinctive from above is the lofty **guayacán** (*tabebuia guayacan*), whose brilliant golden crown stands out against the dense green canopy carpet, blooming a month in advance of the first rains. Not atypically, both species drop their leaves in the dry season to reduce water loss through evaporation. From the forest floor, the vast buttress roots of the **ceiba** (silk-cotton or kapok tree; *ceiba petandra*), or thinner versions on the **Panama tree** (*sterculia apetela*), are more striking; so, too, the vicious protective spines on the **spiny cedar** (*pachira quinata*), or the swollen midsection of the aptly named **barrigón** (*pseudobombax septenatum*) – "*barriga*" meaning "pot belly" in Spanish – which can double its waist size to store water and whose pretty pompom flowers open for evening pollination.

Dominated by vines, ferns, saplings and shrubs typically 10–25m tall, the forest **understorey** and **forest floor** below are relatively sparsely populated in the cathedral-like primary forest, in contrast to the dense and tangled vegetation of **secondary** forest. It's in these lower layers that you'll come across the pinkish hues of **heliconias**, such as the vividly named "**lobster's claw**" (*heliconia rostrata*), edged with yellow, and the more solid "**beefsteak**" (*heliconia mariae*), a "medium-rare" dark pink, or the pouting scarlet bracts of the Warholian "**hotlips**" (*psychotria poeppigiana*), which lure butterflies and hummingbirds to the almost invisible central flowers.

Topping the higher mountainous ridges, especially in western Panama, and almost permanently enveloped in mist, are dense patches of eerie fern-filled **cloud forest**, characterized by shorter, stockier trees covered in **lichen** and dripping with **mosses**. Boughs here are more heavily laden with **epiphytes**, including many of Panama's thousand-plus species of delicate **orchid** and **bromeliads**, whose leaves trap moisture, providing water for numerous tree-dwelling organisms. Back down on the coast, some 1700 square kilometres of mostly **red, white** and **black** mangroves constitute a vital buffer zone, serving both terrestrial and marine ecologies.

Fauna
Though most visitors yearn to catch sight of a jaguar or tapir, you'll likely have to settle for smaller mammals and the less elusive members of the avian and amphibian populations, which can be just as fascinating.

Birds
Panama lays claim to 978 recorded species of **bird**, more than Canada and North America combined, and greater than any Central American state. The 17km Pipeline Road in the former Canal Zone alone boasts a species list of over four hundred. Even Panama City harbours egrets to elaenias, parakeets to pelicans: avian-rich locations within the greater city boundaries include the Metropolitan and other parks, Panamá Viejo, the Amador Causeway and round Cerro Ancón and Balboa.

Acting as a continental funnel, Panama sees many **migrants**, with numbers peaking in September and October and returning in more dispersed fashion from March to May. During this period, over a million shore birds carpet the Pacific coastal mud flats, though it is the **raptor migration** that captures the imagination: hundreds of thousands of **turkey vultures**, interspersed with **Swainson's** and **broad-winged hawks**, ride the thermals, wheeling their way along the isthmus (late Oct to Nov), a spectacular sight best appreciated from the summit of Cerro Ancón or one of Gamboa's several canopy lookouts.

While twitchers may get excited locating a dull-coloured rare endemic in the undergrowth, average nature-lovers will be more impressed by the visually dazzling birds. The cloud forests of Chiriquí afford an unparalleled opportunity to spot the iridescent emerald-and-crimson **resplendent quetzal** – especially visible and striking during spring courtship displays – while the Darién jungle maintains a similar reputation for the **harpy eagle**, Panama's gigantic national bird and arguably the world's most powerful raptor, with its distinctive tousled crest and ferocious giant talons (see box, p.286). Other glamour birds include the country's multicoloured, raucous **parrots** (loros), including five species of endangered **macaw** (*guacamaya*); sadly depleted through the pet trade, loss of habitat and hunting – their flashy tail feathers make a customary adornment for some traditional costumes and dances – they have been forced into more remote areas, with the **scarlet macaw** making its last stand on the island of Coiba. Panama's seven varieties of **toucan** (*tucán*), including toucanets and aracaris, are another psychedelic feature of the landscape; their oversized rainbow-coloured bills help pluck hard-to-reach berries and regulate body temperature. Abundant in the canal area and round Cerro Ancón, they are most easily spotted croaking in the canopy early morning or late afternoon. Panama's 55 types of **hummingbird** (*colibrí*) are spellbinding as they hover round flowers and feeders as if suspended in air, or whizz past your ear at some 50km/h. Lustrous **tanagers**, smart **trogans** and the distinctive racquet-tailed **motmots** will also turn heads.

Some birds are more notable for their behaviour: **jacanas**, whose vast, spindly feet enable them to stride across floating vegetation, are nicknamed "lilly-trotters"; minute fluffy **manakins** conduct manic acrobatic courtship displays in their communal mating arenas known as *leks*; and the prehistoric-looking **potoo** is a nocturnal insectivore that camouflages itself on the end of a tree stump during the day, invisible to would-be predators. Spend enough time in the western highlands, especially in the breeding season (March–Sept), and you're likely to hear the distinctly unbell-like metallic "boing" of the strange-looking **three-wattled bellbird** complete with what look like strands of liquorice hanging from its beak; audible from almost a kilometre away, it is considered one of the loudest bird songs on earth. Mention should also be made of the ubiquitous **oropéndola** (gold pendulum); these large, generally russet-toned birds with outsize pointed beaks and golden tails, are renowned for their colonies of skillfully woven hanging nests, which dangle from tall trees like Christmas decorations.

Terrestrial mammals

Spotting any of Panama's 230-plus mammal species – half of which are small **bats** – requires luck and persistence and is nigh on impossible when it comes to Panama's "big-five" wild cats, which in descending size order are the **jaguar**, **puma**, **jaguarundi**, **ocelot** and **margay**. Nocturnal and shy at the best of times, from years of human predation, they are most numerous in the country's two remaining wilderness areas at either end of the isthmus: the Darién and Amistad.

Spotting tracks in the morning mud is the closest you're likely to get to a jaguar in the wild. Referred to as a "*tigre*" (tiger) by indigenous populations and revered as a symbol of power and strength, the jaguar is the world's third largest feline after the lion and tiger, weighing in at around 60–90kg, and with leopard-like markings. It's more probable you'll encounter its dinner, be it **deer** (*venado*), the raccoon-like **coati** (*gato solo*), or large rodents such as the **agouti** (*ñeque*) or the nocturnal **paca** (*conejo pintado*, literally "painted rabbit" on account of its white spots). Panama also harbours the world's largest rodent, the **capybara**, which can tip the scales at 65kg; resembling a giant guinea pig, it wallows in the shallows round Gamboa and grazes at Punta Patiño, in the Darién. A more ambitious feature of the jaguar's diet is the **peccary**, a kind of wild boar. Two barely distinguishable species forage through the rainforest undergrowth in Panama: the more frequently seen **collared** peccary (*saíno*), which lives in small herds, and the elusive, aggressive **white-lipped** peccary (*puerco de monte*), which can travel in battalions of several hundred and be dangerous when threatened.

One of the largest, most extraordinary-looking mammals in the Neotropics is **Baird's tapir** (*macho de monte*). Another endangered nocturnal creature, it resembles an overgrown pig with a sawn-off elephant's trunk stuck on its face, which is actually a stubby prehensile nose and upper lip used to grip branches and eat off the leaves and fruit. Though the adults are dull brown, baby tapirs have spotted and striped coats for camouflage. More commonly espied are **sloths** (*perezosos*) and **anteaters** (*hormigueros*), both of which arrived on the planet shortly after the demise of dinosaurs. Panama's **two-toed** and **three-toed** sloths spend much of their time literally hanging around treetops, either curled round a branch camouflaged as an ants' nest, or gripping with their long curved claws, doing everything in slow motion to conserve energy. Inexplicably, they make a near-suicidal descent to ground level once a week to defecate. In contrast, the **northern tamandua**, a type of anteater, moves nimbly along the branches, hoovering up ants and termites. Not an uncommon sight in the Metropolitan Park, even though mainly nocturnal, they are widespread across the country, whereas the wholly terrestrial **giant anteater** is verging on extinction nationally, as is the **spectacled bear**, named after the cream-coloured markings around its eyes.

Monkeys are an almost guaranteed sighting in Panama, which hosts all seven Central American species. A distinctive feature of the tropical landscape, the large, shaggy **mantled howler monkey** (*aullador negro*) is more likely to be heard before being seen; the ape's stentorian cries travel for kilometres, with large troops announcing dawn and dusk and even the onset of heavy rain. The other two more widespread species are the cherub-like **Geoffroy's tamarin** (*mono tití*), found in central and eastern Panama, and the larger, highly intelligent **white-throated capuchin** (*mono cariblanco*). Named for their physical resemblance to brown-robed Capuchin friars, though also somewhat misleadingly dubbed "white-headed" or "white-faced", the monkey's pink anthropomorphic face makes it a popular pet. Catching sight of a troop of **black-headed spider monkeys** (*mono araña negro*) – one of several types of endangered Panamanian spider monkey – elegantly gliding through the canopies of eastern

Panama is a magical experience. At the other end of the isthmus, the **owl** or **night monkeys** (*mono de noche*), with their saucer-like eyes, are restricted to the Caribbean lowlands of Bocas, while over on the Pacific side, the delicate **squirrel monkey** (*mono ardilla*) is occasionally sighted in the Burica Peninsula in southwestern Chiriquí.

Reptiles

Mention the fact that you intend to hike in the jungle, and someone is bound to alert you to the dangers of **snakes**, though a relatively small percentage are venomous and snakebites are rare – most serpents are as wary of humans as humans are of them. The most feared, accounting for almost all fatal snakebites in Panama, is the **fer-de-lance** pit viper, which inhabits a variety of lowland habitats. Commonly dubbed *"equis"* ("X") for the markings on its well-camouflaged brown, cream and black skin, it often exceeds 2m. The female gives birth to fifty to eighty live young, which incredibly are already 30cm, not to mention venomous, when born. Initially arboreal, feeding on frogs and lizards, they become terrestrial with age. The world's largest pit viper, the dangerous **bushmaster**, can reach 3m, but fortunately is only encountered in remote forests and like most pit vipers is nocturnal. In contrast, Panama's various species of **coral snake**, both venomous and benign, all possess striking black, red and yellow-banded markings; since it's difficult to differentiate among them, it's best to assume danger. Positively mellow in comparison – though packing a powerful bite if provoked – the giant **boa constrictor** is Panama's only endangered snake, hunted for its prized skin.

Similarly threatened is the **green iguana**, which ranges from lime-green to dusty brown in colour and is pursued for its eggs and tasty meat, earning it the nickname *"gallina de palo"*. Despite its dragon-like appearance, it is a docile forest-living herbivore that likes to be near water; the large flaps of skin under its chin (dewflaps) are used to regulate body temperature and for courtship and territorial displays. The tetchier, charcoal-grey **spiny-tailed** or **black iguana** is most commonly found on the Azuero Peninsula. The world's fastest lizard, it escapes predators by hitting speeds of up to 35kph; the miniature version, a 30cm **basilisk**, takes flight across water on its hind legs and partially webbed feet, earning it the nickname **"Jesus Christ" lizard**.

In Panama's mangrove-filled estuaries and mud-lined waterways, including around Lago Gatún and Lago Bayano, **crocs** and **caimans** lurk. The endangered, aggressive **American crocodile** has actually increased its numbers here, as has the smaller, more docile **spectacled caiman**.

Amphibians

Of all amphibians, **frogs** are the most compelling. The country's emblematic and revered **golden frog** (see box, p.136) is, sadly, under grave threat due in part to the **chytrid fungus**, which has been decimating amphibians worldwide; this has prompted an Amphibian Ark rescue mission (Ⓦamphibianrescue.org) to seek out healthy specimens to breed in captivity (see p.137). The brilliantly coloured miniature **poison-dart frogs**, with markings as varied as wallpaper, are relatively easy to see, especially in Bocas del Toro (see box, p.233), as they hop around the leaf litter under trees by day. But the rainforests harbour other equally extraordinary specimens, less visible since they're primarily nocturnal: the tiny lime-green **glass frog**, whose inexplicably transparent belly affords you the dubious pleasure of observing its viscera and digestive processes; the **flying frog** with giant webbed feet that help parachute it through the air; and the **milk frog** – so named after the toxic mucous it secretes when threatened – which possesses two giant vocal sacs either side of the head that also act as buoyancy aids in water.

Insects and arachnids

Although **insects** don't generally set the pulse racing, **butterflies** are the exception. With sixteen thousand species, Panama hosts approximately ten percent of the world's Lepidoptera, from the enormous **owl butterfly**, so-called after the large "eyes" on its mottled brown wings, to the tiny delicate **glasswing**, whose translucent wings are reminiscent of a stained-glass window. Most magnificent of all, is the iridescent **blue morpho**, whose drunken zigzagged flight makes it particularly hard to photograph.

Ants can be found in abundance; tiny Isla Barro Colorado alone has 225 species. Most distinctive are the packed highways of industrious **leafcutter** ants bearing enormous segments of leaf to their vast underground complex, where they are pulped to cultivate a "fungus garden", which in turn feeds the ants. Also easy to spot is the enormous black **bullet ant**; the size of a large grape and prevalent in low-lying forests, it holds the dubious distinction of causing the world's most painful insect sting.

Panama also possesses over a thousand species of **spider**, a fair proportion of which are poisonous though rarely lethal to humans. One such is the innocuous-sounding **wandering spider** – until you realize its scientific name derives from the Greek for "murderous" (*phoneutes*) – which is a hairy arachnid that stalks the forest floor at night rather than ambushing prey in a web or lair. It is often mistaken for the stockier, hairier and relatively harmless **black tarantula**; also a night-time predator, it can be seen poking out of its lair, in a hollowed-out log or semi-submerged under leaf litter, during the day. Worth avoiding is the female **black widow spider**; recognizable by the glossy black abdomen and red hourglass mark on the underbelly, she has a potent venom with which to inject her prey. The **golden silk orb-weaving spider** makes the largest web; a magical sight on a sunlit morning in the rainforest, it really does glisten like gold thread.

Marine life

With coastlines on two oceans, Panama's **marine biodiversity** is impressive, especially where warm ocean currents and upwellings of cool nutrient-rich waters converge along the Pacific's Golfo de Chiriquí. **Humpback whales** calve in this area (July–Oct) and can also be sighted off the Pearl Islands and the tip of the Azuero Peninsula. These 15m giants are exciting to behold though **whale-watching** in Panama is in its infancy. Earlier in the year (Feb–July), you may be lucky enough to catch sight of the gargantuan but placid **whale shark**, the world's largest fish, as it moves submarine-like through the waters round Coiba. **Hammerhead** and **tiger** sharks are occasionally spotted though **white-tipped reef** sharks are more common. The distinctive black and white **killer whales**, or **orcas** – actually the world's largest dolphin – prey on younger and weaker marine mammals, but aren't as widespread as **bottle-nosed** dolphins. From October to December schools of diamond-shaped **golden rays** glide like floating autumn leaves, occasionally leaping 2m into the air, as well as more solitary **manta** rays; boasting a colossal 6m wingspan, one weighs as much as a small car.

In general the Pacific coast boasts a greater number of large fish – **blue** and **black marlin**, **amberjack**, **wahoo**, **dorado** and **tuna**, to name a few – while the **coral reefs** on the Caribbean side, particularly around the archipelago of Bocas del Toro and parts of Guna Yala, are populated with a greater variety of soft and hard corals. These feed and shelter aquatic life from sinuous **moray eels** and spiky **sea urchins** to delicate **sea horses** and a rainbow of dazzling fish. Iridescent **parrot fish** (30–50cm) are among the most distinctive, named less for their technicolour coats than for their serrated parrot-like "beaks" that gnaw algae and coral polyps off the reef. The ground coral is digested and excreted as sand – up to an estimated 90kg per fish annually – a major factor in the formation of Panama's glorious **white-sand beaches**. The Caribbean's other mammalian draw is the **manatee**, or sea cow, an amiable elephantine herbivore with a paddle-like rudder and flabby fleshy snout, found in the Humedales de San-San Pond Sak in Bocas del Toro.

Five species of **marine turtle** lay their eggs on both Atlantic and Pacific shores, roughly between March and October/November (timings depend on species and location; see box, p.236). In the Caribbean, Bocas del Toro is the easiest place to visit **hawksbill**, **leatherback** and, to a lesser extent, **green** turtle nesting sites while **loggerheads** frequent the shallows. On the Pacific side, Isla de Cañas, off the Azuero Peninsula, is renowned for the mass **olive ridley** nesting (May–Nov), though the other species also deposit their eggs there in smaller numbers.

Environmental issues

As elsewhere in the tropics, the rainforests of Panama are disappearing at an alarming rate, threatening the country's wildlife and, ultimately, human survival. While 45 percent of the country is still covered in forest, and deforestation rates have slowed substantially since the millennium, the country is losing around one percent of its species-rich primary growth a year. A third of the land lies in national parks and reserves, but many of these are "paper parks" since the perennially underfunded ANAM – the government's environmental department – is short of money and, in some cases, political will to enforce the regulations.

Deforestation

Drive along the newly tarred road in eastern Panama and you'll frequently pass enormous trailers carrying vast trunks of mahogany, cedar or purpleheart destined for European and North American markets. The timber industry inevitably is a major contributor to **deforestation** but in recent years has been more stringently controlled even if illegal logging, and more insidiously, selective thinning continues.

By far the main driver of deforestation is **colonization**, clearing the land for cattle ranching and subsistence agriculture. Having already denuded the entire Azuero Peninsula and most of the Pacific slopes of central and western Panama, *colonos*, or "colonists", have been moving into eastern Panama in recent years along the Darién highway and Caribbean coast. Despite the richness of tropical forests, the layer of nutritious topsoil is particularly thin so that once cleared it soon becomes worthless, forcing farmers to move on to fell new areas. Some indigenous communities are also contributing to deforestation thanks to population increases and forced changes in lifestyle. In some cash-strapped communities they are even leasing land to farmers for cattle grazing or colluding with illegal timber extraction. Panama's coastal mangrove forests – considered to be the most extensive, healthiest and most diverse in all Central America – are critically threatened, from agricultural expansion and coastal development on the mainland and water pollution, overfishing and sedimentation on the islands and marine areas.

Small-scale initiatives have begun across the country aiming to improve **environmental awareness**, ranging from assistance for micro-enterprises such as plant nurseries, production of organic fertilizers and agroforestry projects to tree-planting and recycling, often backed by NGOs and international environmental organizations. One such programme is supported through Fundación Nacional Parque Chagres, the result of a "debt-for-nature" swap whereby $10 million of debt to the US government is eradicated as long as Panamanian government banks spend $700,000 annually over fourteen years on green-oriented projects and education. Of course it's no coincidence that this is taking place in the Chagres river basin, which is vital to the functioning of the Panama Canal, the lifeblood of Panama's economy and not insignificant to the US.

As well, **reforestation programmes** in Panama have become more common in the last few years. Initially they were all teak plantations, which arguably further degrade the soil, do nothing to sustain biodiversity and being a monoculture are more susceptible to disease; however, there has been a positive recent move towards more sustainable mixed plantations of native species. The Azuero Earth Project (wazueroearthproject .org), another Panama–US collaboration, is attempting to establish a biological corridor in the Azuero Peninsula, working with local landowners to regenerate tropical dry forest, as well as carry out community outreach and education programmes.

Mining and hydroelectric projects

Another area of environmental concern is the **mining industry**. After the hiatus in mineral exploitation during the 1990s due to its unprofitability, prices have risen again and the threat looms once more. In 2008 a sobering revelation was made by a new Panamanian environmental watchdog, CIAM (Centro de Incidencia Ambiental), namely that the amount of land involved in mining concessions that have either already been granted or are awaiting consideration totals three times the country's surface area. The Petaquilla open-cast gold mine has restarted operations despite still owing $2 million in fines and damages for environmental negligence and trampling on local people's rights. Cerro Colorado, potentially one of the world's largest copper mines, smack in the middle of the Comarca Ngäbe-Buglé is the current battleground. Tensions have escalated between the government and Ngäbe and Buglé protesters who managed to bring the country's economy to a standstill in 2012 by blocking the Interamericana for six days, a protest, which ended in violence as the police were sent in, leaving three dead and many wounded.

Protests also continue against the displacement of communities for the many **micro-hydroelectric projects** underway or planned for western Panama – around seventy in Chiriquí at the last count – one of which has already resulted in intervention by the Interamerican Human Rights Commission. Environmentalists are particularly concerned about projects that lie within the Amistad National Park or its buffer zone of Palo Seco.

Tourism and environmental impact

In the midst of this ecological gloom stands the difficult balance between promoting tourism, which has been on the rise, and limiting the environmental and social impact.

Indigenous communities above all are being encouraged to engage in **cultural eco-tourism**, inviting visitors to learn about their traditional ways of life and selling their handicrafts. With little financial support from the government, some groups have benefited from assistance from NGOs or local Peace Corps workers. Emberá communities along the Chagres, in particular, have gained valuable income from cruise ship tours and day-trip groups from travel agencies in Panama City because of their proximity to the capital. But the long-term effect when large groups swamp small villages in high season, eroding the land of the village and tramping en masse down the same rainforest trail, is more difficult to gauge. Moreover, the impact on the marine environment of the cruise ship industry – the area of tourism in which the government has invested most heavily – is a further unknown.

By and large, visitor numbers are small in most indigenous communities that engage with tourism, the exception being in the western end of Guna Yala. This is partly due to the completion of a road across the cordillera from the Panamerican Highway, which has allowed faster, cheaper access. Day-tripping Panamanians and beach-loving backpackers make up the bulk of the visitors: for small, overpopulated islands with inadequate sanitation and often ad hoc waste disposal, there's untold pressure on the natural resources.

The beautiful islands of Bocas del Toro, the most visited area outside the capital, suffer from similar problems as water and electricity systems struggle to cope with the high visitor numbers and without proper sewage and water treatment works, the current situation is unsustainable. On the positive side, turtle watching is taking off here, and in other areas of Panama, which as an income-generating project might eventually help protect their nesting sites. However, in Bocas, as elsewhere in Panama, visitor numbers are not regulated, which puts untold pressure on natural resources.

Books

Bookshops are far from plentiful in Panama, with most located in Panama City (see p.85), generally stocking a small, pricey selection in English. The colossus of contemporary Panamanian literature is Enrique Jaramillo Levi – internationally acclaimed short-story writer, poet, essayist, editor and critic, who, despite such accolades, has had relatively few works translated into English.

THE CANAL

William Friar *Portrait of the Panama Canal: From Construction to the Twenty-first Century.* Very readable account by a former Zonian and *New York Times* journalist. This paperback coffee-table offering contains a few wonderful historical photos as well as some more mundane contemporary glossies of the canal and Panama.

★**Julie Greene** *The Canal Builders: Making America's Empire at the Panama Canal.* The builders of the title are the workforce, the men and women who in dreadful conditions and facing all sorts of discrimination worked to achieve the realization of America's grandiose dream of empire. You also meet the big players whose ambition ignored the human cost.

Ulrich Keller *The Building of the Canal in Historic Photographs.* A clear case of pictures speaking louder than words, as 164 detailed black-and-white photos evoke the lives of both rich and poor engaged in the monumental struggle to build the canal.

★ **David McCullough** *The Path Between the Seas: The Creation of the Panama Canal, 1870–1914.* Though a detailed scholarly work of nigh on seven hundred pages, it is the plot-twisting narrative and larger-than-life characters that sweep the reader along, together with a consistent emphasis on understanding the underlying causes of events.

★**Matthew Parker** *Hell's Gorge: The Battle to Build the Panama Canal* (also published as *Panama Fever*). A gripping account of the struggle with jungle, disease, engineering impossibilities and disastrous ignorance, which is a meticulously researched yet wide-ranging narrative that focuses on the oft-neglected labour force that lived and died digging the Big Ditch.

OTHER HISTORY AND POLITICS

Kevin Buckley *Panama.* Written by a former *Newsweek* correspondent, this book provides what many consider to be the most reliable account of events leading up to the US invasion of Panama in 1989. Buckley vividly brings the complex web of corruption and political intrigue to life.

Peter Earle *The Sack of Panama: Captain Morgan and the Battle for the Caribbean.* A swashbuckling account of the real-life pirates of the Caribbean and the efforts of the Spaniards to defeat them, focusing on the Welsh privateer Henry Morgan and his exploits along the Caribbean coast, and culminating in the sack of Panama in 1671.

John Esquemeling *The Pirates of Panama: True Account of the Famous Adventures and Daring Deeds of Sir Henry Morgan and other Notorious Freebooters.* Based on a lively firsthand account originally written in Dutch, the first English edition was published in 1684. The author was barber surgeon to Henry Morgan and accompanied him on his notorious expedition against Panama City.

Aims McGuinness *Path of Empire: Panama and the Californian Gold Rush.* A look at the key role played by the isthmus during the Gold Rush in the mid-1800s as the fastest link between New York and San Francisco, the consequences of building the Panama Railroad and the first of many military interventions by the US.

Andrew Parkin *Flames of Panama: The True Story of a Forgotten Hero, Pedro Prestán.* A dramatized true story of a man of mixed race from Cartagena who rose to eminence in Colón as a lawyer and became a Member of the Assembly only to be hanged as a leader of the rebel forces, falsely accused of burning Colón to the ground in 1885. A poignant tale that would have worked better as a factual account.

John Lindsay Poland *Emperors in the Jungle: The Hidden History of the US in Panama.* A human rights campaigner and investigative journalist explores the role of the US military in Panama and the dubious uses to which it put the land it acquired.

John Prebble *The Darien Disaster.* Highly detailed and often turgid exploration of the doomed attempt by the Scots to colonize the Darién. The minutiae, such as the numbers of cases of rum loaded onto the ships, obscure the depth of the tragedy that bankrupted Scotland.

John Week and Phil Gunson *Panama: Made in the USA.* Written in 1991, this much-praised analysis of the 1989 American invasion of Panama and its historical background deals with the legal implications and political consequences, while shining a light on the part Noriega played leading up to the attack.

ART AND CULTURE

James Howe *Chiefs, Scribes and Ethnographers: Kuna Culture from Inside and Out.* Written by a professor of anthropology who has spent considerable time among the Guna over a 35-year period, this recent book deals with accounts that the Guna chiefs themselves have given of their life and culture. Like his previous books – *A People Who Would not Kneel; Panama, the United States and the San Blas Kuna* and *The Kuna Gathering; Contemporary Village Politics in Panama* – it's a serious but rewarding read.

★ **Salvador Mary Lyn (ed.)** *The Art of Being Kuna: Layers of Meaning among the Kuna of Panama.* Glossy coffee-table book full of fascinating photos and scholarly insights on the interweaving of Guna art, culture and environment.

Michael Perrin *Magnificent Molas.* Lavishly illustrated, this book explores the *molas* or fabric "paintings" of the Guna women, tracing the links between the patterns used and traditions and rituals in the lives of the women.

Anton Rajer *Paris in Panama/Paris en Panama: Robert Lewis and the History of His Restored Art Works in the National Theatre of Panama.* Intriguing bilingual book tracing the history and restoration of Panamanian-born Roberto Lewis's (1874–1949) masterpieces painted in Paris but installed in the National Theatre of Panama (see p.59).

Joel Sherzer *Stories, Myths, Chants and Songs of the Kuna Indians.* The author, a linguistic anthropologist, lived among the Kuna people photographing and recording their oral tradition of songs and ritual performances. He reveals their close association with plants and animals and their belief in myths and magic.

Jorge Ventocilla, Heraclio Herrera and Valerio Nuñez *Plants and Animals in the Life of the Kuna.* Written by two Guna biologists and a Panamanian colleague, this book is aimed at the Guna reader as well as outsiders, providing fascinating insights into the Guna perspective on ecology and cosmology as they relate to environmental issues.

FICTION

Iain Banks *Canal Dreams.* More nightmare than dream in which an unloveable famous Japanese cellist is trapped on a ship in the Panama Canal that is captured by guerrillas. The violence she and her lover suffer at their hands leads her to an equally violent revenge.

Jane Bowles *Two Serious Ladies.* An avant-garde classic of 1943, this story follows two ladies seeking freedom from the confines of social convention. On holiday in Panama, one falls in love with a young prostitute and leaves her husband to live in the brothel in Colón. Offering a glimpse of the city's red-light district, it also includes a scene in the historic *Washington Hotel.*

Douglas Galbraith *The Rising Sun.* A detailed, somewhat rambling historical novel about the Scottish expedition to the Darién, fuelled by human greed but leading to unbelievable hardship and the eventual bankruptcy of Scotland. It is difficult to warm to the main character who tells the story, but the horror comes across.

James Stanley Gilbert *Panama Patchwork Poems.* A fascinating collection, published between 1901 and 1937, by a one-time employee of the Panama Railroad Company. Though "Poet Laureate of the Isthmus" may be a tad exaggerated, his accessible verse provides a powerful evocation of pre-canal hardships for settlers in Colón.

★ **John Le Carré** *The Tailor of Panama.* With an explicit nod to Graham Greene's *Our Man in Havana,* this satirical spy thriller is a classic. Set just before the US handover of the Canal, a young unscrupulous British agent embarks on an elaborate fiction of intrigue. While both American and British intelligence services are lampooned as much as Panamanian high society, the novel, nevertheless, caused some upset in Panama on its publication.

Enrique Jaramillo Levi *The Shadow: Thirteen Stories in Opposition.* Short stories by Panama's pre-eminent (post) modern writer, though some tales are scarcely more than vignettes. You'll either be seduced by the originality of his imagination and fluid prose or left baffled and irritated as meaning slips through your grasp. More accessible is his edited collection of short stories by Costa Rican and Panamanian women, *When New Flowers Bloomed,* tackling a range of subjects from gender relations to political events.

William Penn *The Panama Conspiracy.* A thriller which manages improbably to link all the US enemies, from Fidel Castro through Red China to Osama Bin Laden, in a complex plot culminating in a plan to blockade the Panama Canal.

★ **Eric Zencey** *Panama.* All but the first chapter is actually set in Paris with a deftly drawn cast of real and imagined characters woven into a historically intriguing murder mystery that centres on the financial scandal surrounding the Panama Canal debacle.

BIOGRAPHY AND MEMOIRS

Darrin Du Ford *Is There a Hole in my Boat? Tales of Travel in Panama Without a Car.* The author sets out to explore Panama using public transport or hitching a lift, by dugout or on foot, aiming to get closer to the life and culture of the people than the average tourist; he never seems to turn down a new experience.

Christian Giudice *Hands of Stone: The Life and Legend of Roberto Durán.* Meticulously researched biography of Panama's most famous boxer and one of the sport's all-time greats, drawing on plenty of fascinating, original interview material. A warts-and-all rags to riches tale that tracks his rise to fame from the slums of Panama City, giving a view of his contradictory character inside and outside the ring.

Graham Greene *Getting to Know the General: The Story of an Involvement*. Greene provides a personal slant on Omar Torrijos, the country's most charismatic leader, whom the author befriended during his time in troubled late 1970s and early 1980s Panama.

Malcolm Henderson *Don't Kill the Cow Too Quick: An Englishman's Adventures Homesteading in Panama*. Entertaining and informative, especially for expats thinking of following a dream, this book follows a couple's retirement in Bocas in the late 1990s, where they eventually established an organic farm.

Leo Mahon *Fire under my Feet: A Memoir of God's Power in Panama*. The moving story of a compassionate Roman Catholic priest sent in 1963 to a poverty-stricken town in Panama to found a church.

Martin Mitchinson *The Darien Gap: Travels in the Rainforest of Panama*. An entertaining account of eighteen months spent in the trackless jungle trying to retrace the route to the Pacific made by the first European, Balboa, in 1513. It's a successful blend of personal experience, history and local lore.

Manuel Noriega and Peter Eisner *America's Prisoner: The Memoirs of Manuel Noriega*. The other side of the story of a leader who was vilified, arrested and put on trial by America. A controversial book, it is worth reading for its revelations about the American attitude to Panama and Latin America.

WILDLIFE

George Angehr, Dodge Engleman and Lorna Engleman *A Bird-finding Guide to Panama*. You need to read the title carefully – this excellent, detailed guide tells you where to find the birds and how to get there by car, but is not a bird identification manual. Details updated on the web at ⓦ audubonpanama.org.

Juan Carlos Q. Navarro *Panama National Parks* (Ediciones Balboa). Bilingual Spanish/English guide to Panama's national parks accompanied by gorgeous glossy photos that will make you want to pack your rucksack and head for the hills immediately. The information is also on the ANAM website.

★**Rainforest Publications** *Panama Field Guides* (numerous titles). This company has produced an excellent series of illustrated laminated concertina-style pocket field guide pamphlets on Panama's flora and fauna, giving scientific, Spanish and English names. Available in Panama or online (ⓦ rainforestpublications.com).

Robert Ridgely and John Gwynne *A Guide to the Birds of Panama*. This weighty tome is *the* birding bible for Panama although it's in desperate need of updating.

★**Jorge Ventocilla and Dana Gardner** *A Guide to the Common Birds of Panama City* (Smithsonian Tropical Research Institute & Panama Audubon Society). Excellent, beautifully illustrated pocket book aimed at the average nature-lover – perfect for anyone basing their stay in the capital and wanting to identify the city's surprisingly abundant birdlife.

Language

Spanish is the national and official language of Panama and the first language of more than two million of the population. A recorded thirteen other first languages are spoken across the country, including English, which is used by many black Afro-Antilleans (see p.44) – though outside Panama City and the touristy areas of Bocas del Toro and Boquete, it's not widely spoken. Learning at least the basics of Spanish will make your travels considerably easier and reap countless rewards in terms of reception and understanding of people and places.

Pronunciation and word stress

In Spanish, each word is **pronounced** as written according to the following guide:

A somewhere between the "A" sound of "back" and that of "father"

E as in "get"

I as in "police"

O as in "hot"

U as in "rule"

C is soft before E and I, otherwise hard; *cerca* is pronounced "SERka".

G works the same way – a guttural "H" sound (like the "ch" in "loch") before E or I, a hard G elsewhere; *gigante* is pronounced "HiGANte".

H is always silent.

J is the same sound as a guttural "G"; *jamón* is pronounced "ham ON".

LL sounds like an English Y; *tortilla* is pronounced "torTIya".

N is as in English, unless there is a "~" over it, when it becomes like the N in "onion"; *mañana* is pronounced "maNYAna".

QU is pronounced like an English "K" as in "kick".

R is rolled, **RR** doubly so.

V sounds like a cross between B and V, *vino* almost becoming "beano".

X is a soft "SH", so that *Xela* becomes "SHEla"; between vowels it has an "H" sound – *México* is pronounced "ME-hi-ko".

Z is the same as a soft C; *cerveza* is pronounced "serVEsa".

Getting the **word stress** right makes a big difference: *PAgo* means "I pay", *paGÓ* she/he paid. The rule is simple: if a word ends in a vowel, "s" or "n", the stress is on the syllable before last. If it ends in any other consonant, the stress is on the last syllable. Exceptions are marked with an accent on the vowel of the stressed syllable.

Latin American Spanish lacks the lisp common in Spain, where *cerveza* is often pronounced "therVEtha". One feature of the speech of many Panamanians which makes understanding more difficult is the aspiration of the "S" sound at the end of a syllable or word, such that the word *cascada* is pronounced more like "cahcada". Also, words containing a "ch" such as *muchacho* may sound more like "mushasho". Generally the Spanish of indigenous Panamanians is easiest to understand.

Formal and informal address

For English speakers one of the most difficult things to get to grips with is the distinction between formal and informal address. Generally speaking, the third-person **usted** indicates respect and is used in business, for people you don't know and for those older than you. Second-person **tú** is for children, friends and contemporaries in less formal settings. (Remember also that in Latin America the second-person plural – *vosotros* – is never used, so "you" plural will always be *ustedes*.)

Verbal courtesy is an integral part of speech in Spanish and one that – once you're accustomed to the pace and flow of life in Panama, especially out of the city – should become instinctive. Saying *Buenos días/Buenas tardes/Buenas noches*, or the abbreviated *buenos* or *buenas*, and waiting for the appropriate response is usual when asking for something at a shop or ticket office, for example, as is adding *señor* or *señora* (in this instance similar to the US "sir" or "ma'am").

On meeting, or being introduced to someone, people are likely to say *con mucho gusto*, "it's a pleasure", and you should do the same. On departure you will more often than not be told *¡Que le vaya bien!* – literally meaning "May all go well with you", it often translates better as "Take care" or "Travel safely".

BASIC WORDS

a lot	mucho	more	más
afternoon	tarde	morning	mañana
and	y	night	noche
bad	mal(o)/a	no	no
big	gran(de)	now	ahora
boy	chico	open	abierto/a
closed	cerrado/a	or	o
cold	frío/a	please	por favor
day	día	she	ella
entrance	entrada	sir/mister	señor
exit	salida	small	pequeño/a
girl	chica	thank you	gracias
good	bien/buen(o)/a	that	eso/a
he	él	their	suyo/de ellos
her	ella	there	allí
here	aquí	they	ellos
his	suyo	this	este/a
hot	calor/caliente	today	hoy
how much	cuánto	tomorrow	mañana
if	si	what	qué
later	más tarde/después	when	cuando/cuándo
less	menos	where	dónde
ma'am/missus	señora	with	con
man	señor/hombre	without	sin
maybe	talvez	yes	sí
miss	señorita	yesterday	ayer

BASIC PHRASES

Hello	¡Hola!	Do you speak English?	¿Habla (usted) inglés?
Goodbye	Adiós		
See you later	Hasta luego	I (don't) speak Spanish	(No) Hablo español/castellano
Good morning	Buenos días		
Good afternoon	Buenas tardes	What (did you say)?	¿Mande?/¿Cómo?
Good evening/night	Buenas noches	Could you... please?	¿Podría... por favor?
Sorry	Lo siento/Discúlpeme	...repeat that	...repetirlo
Excuse me	Con permiso/perdón	What's your name?	¿Cómo se llama usted?
How are you?	¿Cómo está (usted)?/ ¿Qué tal?	My name is...	Me llamo...
		Where are you from?	¿De dónde es usted?
Nice to meet you	Mucho gusto	I'm from...	Soy de...
Not at all/ You're welcome	De nada/para servirle	How old are you?	¿Cuántos años tiene? (usted)
I (don't) understand	(No) Entiendo	I am...years old	Tengo...años.

I don't know	No sé	in Spanish?	español/castellano?
Do you know…?	¿Sabe…?	There is (is there)?	Hay (?)
I want/I'd like	Quiero/Quisiera	Do you have…?	¿Tiene…?
What's that?	¿Qué es eso?	What time is it?	¿Qué hora es?
How much is it?	¿Cúanto es/cuesta?	May I take a photograph?	¿Puedo sacar una foto?
What is this called	¿Cómo se llama este en	It's hot/cold	Hace calor/frío

BASIC NEEDS, SERVICES AND PLACES

ATM	cajero automático	market	mercado
bank	banco	money	dinero/plata
bathroom/toilet	baño/sanitario	museum	museo
beach	playa	pharmacy	farmacia
border crossing	frontera	post office	el correo
church	iglesia	restaurant	restaurante
internet café	cibercafé	supermarket	supermercado
laundry	lavandería/lavamático	telephone	teléfono
map	mapa	tourist office	oficina de turismo

NUMBERS (NÚMEROS), MONTHS (MESES) AND DAYS (DÍAS)

1	un/uno/una	second	segundo/a
2	dos	third	tercero/a
3	tres		
4	cuatro	January	enero
5	cinco	February	febrero
6	seis	March	marzo
7	siete	April	abril
8	ocho	May	mayo
9	nueve	June	junio
10	diez	July	julio
20	veinte	August	agosto
21	veintiuno	September	septiembre
22	veintidos	October	octubre
30	treinta	November	noviembre
40	cuarenta	December	diciembre
50	cincuenta		
60	sesenta	Monday	lunes
70	setenta	Tuesday	martes
80	ochenta	Wednesday	miércoles
90	noventa	Thursday	jueves
100	cien	Friday	viernes
1000	mil	Saturday	sábado
		Sunday	domingo
first	primero/a		

GETTING AROUND

bus	autobús	car	carro/auto(móvil)
minibus	buseta/colectivo	engine	motor
bus station	terminal de autobuses	4WD/4X4	doble tracción/
bus stop	parada de autobús		cuatro por cuatro
boat	barco/lancha/panga	taxi	taxi
dugout canoe	cayuco/piragua	lorry/truck	camión
dock/pier	muelle	pick-up	camioneta
airplane	avión	bicycle	bicicleta
airport	aeropuerto	motorcycle	moto

petrol/diesel/gas	gasolina	I would like to rent a...	Me gustaría alquilar
ticket	billete pasaje		un/una...
ticket office	taquilla/ventanilla	Where does... to...	¿De dónde sale
I'd like a ticket to...	(Necesito) un billete	leave from?	...para...?
	(pasaje) para...	What time does the	¿A qué hora sale
...one way	...sólo ida	...leave for...?	...para...?
...return/round trip	...ida y vuelta	What time does the	¿A qué hora llega...
		...arrive in...?	en...?

DIRECTIONS

Where is...?	¿Dónde está...?	south	sur
How do I get to...?	¿Por dónde se va	east	este
	a...?	west	oeste
I'm lost	Estoy perdido/a	street	calle
Is it far?	¿Está lejos?	avenue	avenida
left/right	izquierda/derecha	block	cuadra
straight ahead	derecho/recto	corner	esquina
north	norte	(main) road	carretera

ACCOMMODATION

Is there (a)...nearby?	¿Hay...aquí cerca?	...one person	...una persona
...hotel	...un hotel	...two people	...dos personas
...cheap, small hotel	...una pensión/	...for one night	...una noche
	un hospedaje	...one week	...una semana
...hostel	...un hostal	Does it have...	¿Tiene...?
Do you have...?	¿Tiene...?	...a shared bath	...baño compartido
...a room	...un cuarto	...a private bath	...baño privado
...with two beds	...con dos camas	...hot water	...agua caliente
...a double bed	...con cama	...air conditioning	...aire-acondicionado
	matrimonial	...a mosquito net	...mosquitero
...a dorm room	...cuarto colectivo/	May I see a room?	¿Puedo ver un cuarto?
	dormitorio	May I see another	¿Puedo ver otro
...a cabin	...una cabaña	room?	cuarto?
It's for	Es para	Yes, It's fine	Sí, está bien

FOOD AND DRINK

BASIC DINING VOCABULARY

almuerzo	lunch	vaso	glass
cafetería	self-service	Soy vegetariano/a	I'm a vegetarian
	restaurant	Tengo hambre/sed	I'm hungry/thirsty
carta (la)	menu		
cena	dinner	### BASIC FOOD VOCABULARY	
comedor	basic restaurant	aceite	oil
comida corriente	cheap set menu,	ajo	garlic
	usually lunch	arroz	rice
comida típica	traditional cuisine	azúcar	sugar
cuenta	bill	chile	chilli
desayuno	breakfast	galletas	biscuits/crackers
fonda	inexpensive, informal	hielo	ice
	local restaurant	huevos	eggs
mesa	table	mantequilla	butter
plato fuerte	main course	mermelada	jam
plato vegetariano	vegetarian dish	miel	honey
silla	chair	natilla	sour cream
		pan (integral)	bread (wholemeal)

pimienta	pepper
queso	cheese
sal	salt
salsa de tomate	tomato sauce

FRUTAS (FRUIT)

aceitunas	olives
chirimoya	custard apple
coco	coconut
fresa	strawberry
guanábana	soursop
guayaba	guava
guineo	banana
limón	lemon
manzana	apple
maracuyá	passionfruit
marañon	cashew
melón	melon
mora (zarzamora)	blackberry
naranja	orange
papaya	papaya
piña	pineapple
plátano	plantain
sandía	watermelon
uva	grapes

LEGUMBRES/VERDURAS (VEGETABLES)

aguacate	avocado
cebolla	onion
champiñón (hongo)	mushroom
ensalada	salad
espinaca	spinach
frijoles	beans
gallo pinto	mixed rice and beans
lechuga	lettuce
lentejas	lentils
maíz	sweet corn/maize
menestra	bean/lentil stew
papa	potato
papas fritas	chips/French fries
tomate	tomato
zanahoria	carrot

CARNE (MEAT), AVES (POULTRY) AND MENUDO (OFFAL)

bistec/lomo	steak
carne	beef
cerdo	pork
chuleta	pork chop
jamón	ham
mondongo	tripe and chorizo stew
patas	trotters
pollo	chicken
res	beef

ropa vieja	shredded spicy beef and rice

MARISCOS (SEAFOOD) AND PESCADO (FISH)

almejas	clams
anchoa	anchovy
atún	tuna
calamares	squid
camarón	shrimp
cangrejo	crab
ceviche	raw seafood marinated in lime juice with onions
concha	conch
corvina	sea bass
langosta	lobster/crayfish
langostina	king prawn
mejillónes	mussels
mero	grouper
pargo rojo	red snapper
pulpo	octopus
trucha	trout

BOCADOS OR BOCADITOS (SNACKS)

carimañola	mashed boiled yuca stuffed with beef
churro	ribbed, tubular doughnut-cum-waffle
empanada	cheese/meat-filled pastry
emparedado	sandwich
hamburguesa	hamburger
hojaldre	deep fried doughy pancake
patacones	fried green plantains
salchichas	sausages
tortilla	thick fried maize patty
tortilla de huevos	omelette
tostada	toast

BEBIDAS (DRINKS)

agua mineral	mineral water
...con gas	...sparkling
...sin gas	...still
agua potable	drinking water
aromática	herbal tea
batido	fresh fruit milk shake
café	coffee
cerveza	beer
chicha	maize drink
chicha fuerte	fermented maize drink
jugo	juice
leche	milk
licuado	fresh fruit shake
pipa	fresh coconut juice

raspados	flavoured ice shavings	a la plancha	grilled
refresco/soda	(cold) soft drink	apanado	breaded
ron	rum	asado	roast
té	tea/coffee	encocado	in coconut sauce
vino blanco/tinto	white/red wine	frito	fried
		picante	spicy hot
COOKING TERMS		puré	mashed
a la parrilla	barbecued	revuelto	scrambled

Glossary and acronyms

ACP Autoridad del Canal de Panamá (Panama Canal Authority)

Afro-Antillano Panamanian of African heritage from the West Indies

Afro-Colonial Panamanian of African heritage from the Spanish colonial era

ANAM Autoridad Nacional del Ambiente (Department for the Environment)

ANCON Asociación Nacional para la Conservación de la Naturaleza – Panama's most prominent environmental NGO

artesanías traditional handicrafts

ATP Autoridad de Turismo Panamá

barrio neighbourhood; suburb

bohío see rancho

bomba pump at a petrol station, often shorthand for the petrol station itself

cacique chief (originally a colonial term, now used for elected leaders/figureheads of indigenous comarcas)

campesino peasant farmer

cantina local, hard-drinking bar, usually men-only

chiva rural bus, which may be a converted pick-up

colectivo shared taxi/minibus, usually following fixed route (can also be applied to a boat – lancha colectiva)

colono generally a mestizo farming settler who originated from the Azuero Peninsula and central areas and moved to colonize other parts of the country

comarca semi-autonomous area demarcated for the major indigenous peoples

cordillera mountain range

diablo rojo colourful painted buses of Panama City

feria fair (market); also a town fête

finca ranch, farm or plantation

gringo/gringa any light-skinned foreigner, particularly a North American

guardaparque park warden

huaca pre-Columbian gold treasure buried with the dead in a tomb

INAC Instituto Nacional de Arte y Cultura (government department in charge of museums and preservation of cultural heritage)

indígeno/a an indigenous person (also used adjectivally)

ladino a vague term – applied to people it means Spanish-influenced as opposed to indigenous, and at its most specific defines someone of mixed Spanish and indigenous blood

mestizo person of mixed indigenous and Spanish blood, though like the term ladino it has more cultural than racial significance

metate pre-Columbian stone table used for grinding corn

mochilero backpacker

montuno traditional male costume consisting of a loose cotton shirt and knee-length trousers

(fiestas) patronales patron saint festivals enjoyed by every town or village

pollera embroidered dress with full skirt considered to be the national costume of Panama

quincha adobe

rancho open-sided (wooden) structure with palm-thatched roof (see bohío)

sancocho thick meat or chicken soup with root vegetables

STRI Smithsonian Tropical Research Institute

Small print and index

A ROUGH GUIDE TO ROUGH GUIDES

Published in 1982, the first Rough Guide – to Greece – was a student scheme that became a publishing phenomenon. Mark Ellingham, a recent graduate in English from Bristol University, had been travelling in Greece the previous summer and couldn't find the right guidebook. With a small group of friends he wrote his own guide, combining a highly contemporary, journalistic style with a thoroughly practical approach to travellers' needs.

The immediate success of the book spawned a series that rapidly covered dozens of destinations. And, in addition to impecunious backpackers, Rough Guides soon acquired a much broader readership that relished the guides' wit and inquisitiveness as much as their enthusiastic, critical approach and value-for-money ethos.

These days, Rough Guides include recommendations from budget to luxury and cover more than 120 destinations around the globe, as well as producing an ever-growing range of eBooks.

Visit **roughguides.com** to find all our latest books, read articles, get inspired and share travel tips with the Rough Guides community.

Rough Guide credits

Editors: Natasha Foges, Ann-Marie Shaw
Layout: Jessica Subramanian
Cartography: Rajesh Chhibber
Picture editors: Marta Bescos, Michelle Bhatia
Proofreader: Karen Parker
Managing editor: Mani Ramaswamy
Assistant editor: Prema Dutta
Production: Charlotte Cade

Cover design: Nicole Newman, Marta Bescos, Jessica Subramanian
Photographer: James Brunker
Editorial assistant: Rebecca Hallett
Senior pre-press designer: Dan May
Programme manager: Helen Blount
Publisher: Joanna Kirby
Publishing director: Georgina Dee

Publishing information

This second edition published November 2014 by
Rough Guides Ltd,
80 Strand, London WC2R 0RL
11, Community Centre, Panchsheel Park,
New Delhi 110017, India
Distributed by Penguin Random House
Penguin Books Ltd,
80 Strand, London WC2R 0RL
Penguin Group (USA)
345 Hudson Street, NY 10014, USA
Penguin Group (Australia)
250 Camberwell Road, Camberwell,
Victoria 3124, Australia
Penguin Group (NZ)
67 Apollo Drive, Mairangi Bay, Auckland 1310,
New Zealand
Penguin Group (South Africa)
Block D, Rosebank Office Park, 181 Jan Smuts Avenue,
Parktown North, Gauteng, South Africa 2193
Rough Guides is represented in Canada by Tourmaline
Editions Inc. 662 King Street West, Suite 304, Toronto,
Ontario M5V 1M7
Printed in Singapore by Toppan Security Printing Pte. Ltd.

© Sara Humphreys, 2014
Maps © Rough Guides
No part of this book may be reproduced in any form
without permission from the publisher except for the
quotation of brief passages in reviews.
328pp includes index
A catalogue record for this book is available from the
British Library
ISBN: 978-1-40935-343-0
The publishers and authors have done their best to ensure
the accuracy and currency of all the information in **The
Rough Guide to Panama**, however, they can accept
no responsibility for any loss, injury, or inconvenience
sustained by any traveller as a result of information or
advice contained in the guide.
1 3 5 7 9 8 6 4 2

MIX
Paper from
responsible sources
FSC
www.fsc.org FSC™ C018179

Help us update

We've gone to a lot of effort to ensure that the second edition of **The Rough Guide to Panama** is accurate and up-to-date. However, things change – places get "discovered", opening hours are notoriously fickle, restaurants and rooms raise prices or lower standards. If you feel we've got it wrong or left something out, we'd like to know, and if you can remember the address, the price, the hours, the phone number, so much the better.

Please send your comments with the subject line "**Rough Guide Panama Update**" to @mail@uk. roughguides.com. We'll credit all contributions and send a copy of the next edition (or any other Rough Guide if you prefer) for the very best emails.

Find more travel information, connect with fellow travellers and plan your trip on ⑩roughguides.com

ABOUT THE AUTHOR

Sara Humphreys A freelance researcher, writer and educator, Sara's main claim to journalistic fame is that she simultaneously worked for *The Sun* and *The Guardian*, albeit in Botswana. Otherwise, she has toiled, travelled and tarried in various countries in Latin America, Africa and Europe and, when not energetically bailing out a dugout in Panama, can be found swinging in a hammock in Barbados.

Acknowledgements

In addition to the many Panamanians and foreign travellers encountered along the way who offered assistance, information and advice, Sara Humphreys would like to thank: Helen Wormald for countless long bus and boat journeys – from Coiba to Boquete and to Bocas – and some serious cocktail sampling; Raffa Calvo for rapid recces of the central Caribbean coast and the Azuero, plus forays into the Darién and island-hopping in Guna Yala; not forgetting the Mogue women's football team for helping resuscitate the author's goalkeeping skills. Thanks also to Val for doing a trawl of new books on Panama and to Micah Smith, Russell Vinegar and Thea Winnips for their various suggestions; also to Ricardo Garcés for tips on the hot nightspots of Panama City.

Back in the office, appreciation is due to Natasha and Annie for some sympathetic editing, to Melissa Graham for some constructive "deconning", and to Michelle Bhatia and Marta Bescos for persevering with the pics. Also to Mani for letting the author loose in Panama once again.

Photo credits

All photos © Rough Guides except the following:
(Key: a-above; b-below/bottom; c-centre; f-far; l-left; r-right; t-top)

p.5 Danita Delimont Stock/AWL Images
p.9 Connie Coleman/Getty Images (t); Leila Cutler/Alamy (bl); Christian Heeb/AWL Images (br)
p.11 Ben Lascelles/naturepl.com (t); Alfredo Maiquez/Lonely Planet Images/Getty Images (c); Schickert/Bildagentur-online/Alamy (b)
p.13 Aurora Photos/Alamy (t)
p.14 Ken Welsh/Robert Harding Picture Library
p.15 SuperStock (c)
p.16 Peter Schickert/Robert Harding Picture Library (t); Wayne Lynch/Corbis (c); SuperStock (b)
p.17 Alfredo Maiquez/Robert Harding Picture Library (t); Alfredo Maiquez/Alamy (bl); M. Timothy O'Keefe/Alamy (br)
p.18 Christian Ziegler/Corbis (t); Jon Arnold Images Ltd/Alamy (c); Richard Wareham Vervoer/Alamy (b)
p.19 Guillermo Johnson/Corbis (bl); Christian Heeb/Corbis (br)

p.20 Jane Sweeney/AWL Images (tl); Tobias Friedrich/SuperStock (tr)
pp.50–51 Alvaro Leiva/SuperStock
pp.90–91 Massimo Ripani/4Corners
pp.126–127 JJM Stock Photography/Alamy
p.129 Oyvind Martinsen/Alamy
pp.150–151 Alejandro Bolivar/Corbis
pp.216–217 Jane Sweeney/AWL Images
p.219 Thomas Marent/Visuals Unlimited/Corbis
pp.270–271 Oyvind Martinsen/Alamy
p.273 Andoni Canela/Robert Harding Picture Library
p.290 Peter Horree/Alamy

Front cover Starfish beach © Tobias Friedrich/SuperStock
Back cover Hammocks in a beach hut © Panoramic Images/Getty Images (t); Mamardup village, Guna Yala © Bruno Morandi/Hemis/Corbis (l); Casco Viejo, Panama City © Photoshot (r)

Index

Maps are marked in grey

Map symbols

The symbols below are used on maps throughout the book

✈	Airport	E	Embassy	⌣	Bridge	▭	Market
✕	Airstrip	♦	Place of interest	▲	Mountain peak	▬	Building
★	Transport stop	∴	Ruin	☀	Viewpoint	⇥	Church
Ⓜ	Metro station	⊤	Gardens	◠	Cave	◯	Stadium
@	Internet café/access	🏠	Ranger station	♟	Museum	▢	Beach
ⓘ	Information office	⛽	Fuel station	⌐	Beach	▨	Park
✚	Hospital	↑	Border crossing	✟	Cemetery	⊞	Cemetery
⊠	Post office	⋙	Swamp				

Listings key

■	Accommodation
●	Café/restaurant
■	Bar/club